The Garland Handbook
of African Music

The Garland Handbook of African Music

edited by Ruth M. Stone

GARLAND PUBLISHING, INC.
A MEMBER OF THE TAYLOR & FRANCIS GROUP
New York and London   2000

Published by Garland Publishing, Inc.
A member of the Taylor & Francis Group
19 Union Square West
New York, NY 10003

10 9 8 7 6 5 4 3 2 1

Library of Congress Cataloging-in-Publication Data

The Garland handbook of African music / edited by Ruth M. Stone.
      p.   cm. — (Garland reference library of the humanities ; vol. 1170)
    Articles originally published in: The Garland encyclopedia of world music, v. 1, Africa. 1998.
    Filmography: p. ****
    Discography: p. ****
    Includes bibliographical references (p. ****) and index.
    ISBN 0-8153-3473-7 (alk. paper)
    1. Music—Africa—History and criticism.   I. Stone, Ruth M.
II. Garland encyclopedia of world music. 1. Africa.   III. Series.
ML350.G54   1999
780'.96—dc21
                                         99-40652
                                         CIP

The Garland Handbook of African Music is an abridged paperback edition of *Africa,* volume 1 of *The Garland Encyclopedia of World Music,* with the addition of one new article, "Exploring African Music." Unless otherwise noted, all interior illustrations were provided by the authors of articles and sections in this Handbook.

Printed on acid-free, 250-year-life paper
Manufactured in the United States of America

Contents

Audio Examples

The following examples are included on the accompanying audio compact disc packaged with this volume. Track numbers are also indicated on the pages listed below for easy reference to text discussions. Complete descriptions of each example may be found on pages 379–381.

Track page reference

Contributing Authors

Peter Cooke
West Midlands, England

David B. Coplan
University of Witwatersrand
Johannesburg, South Africa

Jacqueline Cogdell DjeDje
University of California
Los Angeles, California, U.S.A.

Angela Impey
University of Natal
Durban, South Africa

John E. Kaemmer
Seattle, Washington, U.S.A.

Andrew L. Kaye
Albright College
Reading, Pennsylvania, U.S.A.

Michelle Kisliuk
University of Virginia
Charlottesville, Virginia, U.S.A.

Gerhard Kubik
University of Vienna and University of Mainz
Vienna, Austria and Mainz, Germany

Patience A. Kwakwa
University of Ghana
Legon, Ghana

Stephen H. Martin
Portland State University
Portland, Oregon, U.S.A.

Lester P. Monts
University of Michigan
Ann Arbor, Michigan, U.S.A.

Kazadi wa Mukuna
Kent State University
Kent, Ohio, U.S.A.

Cynthia Schmidt
University of Washington
Seattle, Washington, U.S.A.

Kay Kaufman Shelemay
Harvard University
Cambridge, Massachusetts, U.S.A.

Ruth M. Stone
Indiana University
Bloomington, Indiana, U.S.A.

Christopher Waterman
University of California
Los Angeles, California, U.S.A.

Caroline Card Wendt
Indianapolis, Indiana, U.S.A.

Preface
Ruth M. Stone

In this handbook, we are pleased to present a selection of articles from *Africa,* volume 1 of the *Garland Encyclopedia of World Music.* We have chosen articles that are particularly accessible and appropriate as an introduction to the world of African music. Thus the handbook is suitable for use as a text for an introductory course in African music.

This handbook covers the making of African music, its performers and audience, theories of musical conception, and the exchange of music among peoples on the continent and beyond. It presents a view of the music of Africa from the perspectives of those who have studied it and those who make it.

The authors whose articles are gathered here come from Africa, Europe, and the United States. They have all conducted fieldwork in Africa, experiencing firsthand the artistry about which they write. Together, their articles reflect the current state of scholarship about music in Africa.

All these authors have met frequently at international conferences around the globe. Their ideas have developed in dialogues with musicians, ritual specialists, and audiences. In some cases, direct quotes convey the performers' voices. The compact disc brings an even more immediate experience of their creativity. Scholars and performers speak and make music with multiple voices, which at some points converge in consensus and at others diverge into contrast. Without unfairly promising to be an exhaustive representation of the universe of performance in Africa, this volume celebrates the explosion of ideas that recent scholarship has generated. As a written document, it sketches outlines that continue to unfold, and for which our knowledge must be considered emergent.

In this handbook, we emphasize thematic issues and processes. As experience has taught us, musical practices often transcend political boundaries, many of whose lines were drawn during the colonial period, dividing ethnic groups. Political divisions have influenced many things—like roads, which tend, particularly in West Africa, to lead from the coast inward, not across national boundaries. Some political divisions are under challenge by armed struggles. Therefore, the potential choice of a political entity (like a country) as a descriptive unit would reinforce, even if implicitly, a geographic containment that echoes the colonial period. Themes that have emerged from research on music become the focus of organization. These themes transcend regional boundaries. Though such issues are anchored in specific examples and interpretation of local practice, their relevance is often not limited to a single political region.

This work, then, deliberately highlights concepts of intra- and intercontinental movement. Beyond this, the goal is to emphasize Africans as individuals and groups who have initiated travel and action, and have not—as many colonial accounts imply or state—simply waited for outside forces to act upon them. By beginning with such assumptions, we seek to counteract the idea that only Westerners or outsiders were, or are, active travelers on the continent. About one hundred years before the oldest extant written report of a European voyage of discovery, the Egyptian pharaoh Necho hired Phoenicians to circumnavigate the continent, which they did in three years. The first Greek settlement on the continent, Cyrene, was founded about 631 B.C., on land that is now in Libya. Even today, Egypt remains a center of active intellectual life and architectural monuments of the Islamic world.

Among the significant streams of exchange were the contacts of Arabs with Africans as caravans moved across the Sahara Desert, bringing musical instruments and ideas about musical performance with their salt, gold, and ivory. Along Africa's eastern coast, Arabs came in ships, carried by seasonal winds; the Omanis in particular set up city-states along the coast. Many Africans went to Arabia, some of them as slaves, where they performed music whose styles continue to influence local practices.

Europeans—the Portuguese and later the British, the French, the Germans, the Dutch, and others—moved to colonize Africa, and social connections between Europe and Africa still accent musical life in Africa. The Americas became the home of many West and Central Africans brought as slaves into the New World, where the impact of slavery continues. Long before Europeans "discovered" Africa, interchange with the Indian subcontinent, the Malay and Indonesian worlds, and the Far East also moved along the ocean highways.

HOW THIS HANDBOOK IS ORGANIZED

Issues and processes

Encompassing broad geographical spans and multifarious musical practices, the volume treats a selection of the artistic riches that African cultures cherish. Part 1 profiles Africa and the arts as a whole. The articles in the first section of Part 2 focus on themes and issues that, crosscutting local practices and sensibilities, integrate the performance of music and other arts. Among these themes are notation and oral tradition (Shelemay) and dance and human movement (Kwakwa). The articles in the second section of Part 2 focus on themes that have emerged from the movement of peoples within and beyond Africa: Islam and its effects on music in West Africa (Monts), the guitar and its music (Kaye), the Kru mariners of Liberia (Schmidt), and responses to Latin American music in Zaïre (Mukuna). Part 2 concludes with a survey of African popular music (Impey).

Selected regional case studies

Part 3 presents five overview articles on regional musical practices in Africa: West (DjeDje), North (Wendt), East (Cooke), Central (Kubik), and Southern (Kaemmer). Each of these articles gives a bird's-eye view of music in social context. Case studies (Waterman, Wendt, Martin, Kisliuk, and Coplan) then offer in-depth accounts of musical practices in local settings.

Studies of Africa have sometimes separated the continent into the area north of the Sahara Desert and the area south of it. By statement or implication, the sub-Saharan area has been considered the more characteristically African. This volume, however, takes Africa as a whole, with the assumption that travel across the desert has carried musical practices with it; even farther afield, sub-Saharan musical practices survive and prosper in the eastern coastal region of Arabia. The Sahara is not a neat dividing line of musical styles, and our choice of the continental borders as boundaries for this volume is more arbitrary than indicative of actual practice. The article on the Tuareg (Wendt) shows how the same group of people occupies two separate countries—Algeria and Niger—on the edge of the desert.

Influences between Africa and other parts of the world can be studied in articles that treat music and maritime activity on the West African coast (Schmidt), the effect of Islam on musical practice (Monts), and the influence of Latin American musical practice on central African performance (Mukuna). Thematic connections also link the articles. Popular music, for example, is the focus of five articles that can be read together (Kaye, Mukuna, Impey, Waterman, and Coplan).

Research tools

Readers will find research aids throughout the handbook. Maps help locate the places and peoples mentioned in the text; references at the end of each article specify further readings and recordings to consult. Cross-references to articles in this handbook are indicated within brackets. For readers seeking a general bibliographic guide to African music, John Gray's compilation *African Music: A Bibliographic Guide* (1991) is the most comprehensive recent source [see GUIDE TO PUBLICATIONS]. The handbook provides a wealth of other illustrations, including photographs, drawings, and graphs.

Musical examples

Throughout the handbook, musical examples supplement the verbal representations of musical sound. In most cases, these appear as staff notation or some variation of it. One article (Shelemay) addresses the concept of notation in the study of African music. It explores indigenous and foreign notations, written and aural—notations that have been applied to African music, including a music-notation system traditionally employed in Ethiopia.

Writing music, like writing in general (many would say or think), marks a high level of knowledge and sophistication. Yet most African peoples perpetuate their musical traditions through aural forms of notation (Shelemay). The value of the written is largely the researcher's value. Because most notations ignore indigenous concepts, we may fail to see in them the intricacies of indigenous aural notations.

Glossary

A glossary of over seven hundred entries provides definition or identification for ethnic groups and musical concepts, instruments, and genres. Readers will find selected terms and their glosses reproduced on the top of many pages.

Discography

The discography provides reference to commercially produced sound recordings. These reflect the late-twentieth-century proliferation of tapes, compact discs, and other recordings of African music. Many more recordings exist in archives around the world.

Compact disc

A selection of recorded examples is available on the compact disc that accompanies this handbook. These examples are intended to illustrate and supplement the discussions found in the articles. Our goal has been to seek recordings that are commercially unavailable. In the margins of the text, a number specifies the track of the recorded example illustrating a particular discussion. A booklet of notes on the recordings is packaged with the compact disc and duplicated in the back of the handbook, preceding the index.

ACKNOWLEDGMENTS

More than most academic enterprises, a handbook is a team effort. I have been aided by a host of people who helped shape and complete this project. Since 1989, I have worked with several editorial assistants: Mary Dart, Susan Oehler, and Nicole Kousaleos. Frank Gunderson, Nina Fales, and Cathy Brigham helped with final details. Daniel Reed produced and Aeter Alyea engineered the sound recordings. An ever-present companion in the editing process has been Jacob Love, who has served as copy editor and brought an eagle eye to the manuscript. Colleagues at the Archives of Traditional Music who provided reference research included Mary Bucknum, Marilyn Graf, Karen Metelnick, and Suzanne Mudge.

The shape of the larger project developed in a series of meetings in 1988 and 1989, when the founding editors, James Porter and Timothy Rice, facilitated discussions among interested scholars. Africanist ethnomusicologists who attended and contributed included J. H. Kwabena Nketia and Jacqueline Cogdell DjeDje. I am grateful to Gerhard Kubik, who spent several weeks in Bloomington in 1991 working on his contribution and making suggestions about the shape of this work.

I must thank Leo Balk, Richard Wallis, and Soo Mee Kwon, who represented Garland Publishing. Each in his or her own way provided a strong commitment to this project and gave sound advice at crucial moments.

Finally, my family—Verlon, my husband, and Angela, my daughter—have long supported this project and the time I have devoted to it, and this support I value beyond measure. In the end, I take responsibility for the manuscript.

ORTHOGRAPHY

ɛ or ẹ   = "eh" as in **bet**

ɔ or ọ   = "aw" as in **awful**

ŋ or ṇ   = "ng" as in **sing**

γ or yg = "ch" as in German **ach**

ʃ or ṣ   = "sh" as in **shout**

ɓ   = implosive "b"

ɗ   = implosive "d"

!   = click sound

´   = high tone

`   = low tone

^   = high-low tone

~   = nasalized sound

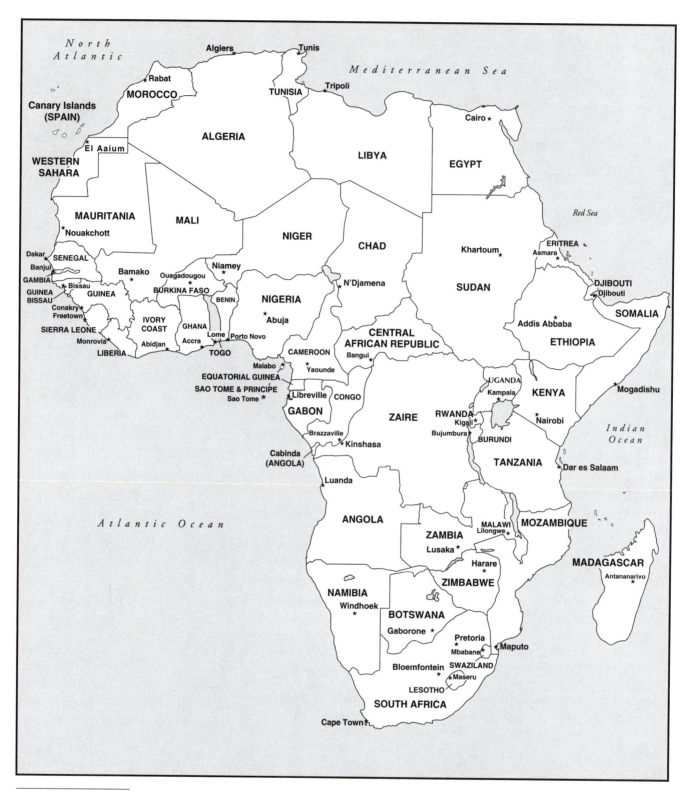

In 1997, a new government in Zaïre changed the name of the nation to "Democratic Republic of the Congo."

Part 1
Introduction to African Music

Africa astounds with its geographic expanse and its regional diversities. Because of its rich cultural heritage, we see today an extraordinary vitality in the performing arts. We begin with an introduction to African artistic expression and a survey of the history of our knowledge about African music.

Profile of Africa
Ruth M. Stone

Peoples and Languages
Subsistence and Industry
Transport and Trade
Social and Political Formations
Religious Beliefs and Practices

The African continent first impresses by its size: the second-largest of the continents of the world, it encloses more than 28 million square kilometers, spanning 8,000 kilometers from north to south and 7,400 kilometers from east to west. Islands dot the coasts, with Madagascar in the southeast being the largest.

Bisected by the equator, lying predominantly within the tropical region where thick rainforests grow, the continent consists of a plateau that rises from rather narrow coastal plains. Vast expanses of grassland also characterize its inland regions. The Sahara Desert dominates northern Africa, and the Kalahari Desert southern Africa. Vast mineral resources (of iron, gold, diamonds, oil) and deep tropical forests enrich the continent.

PEOPLES AND LANGUAGES

The population of the continent constitutes only one-tenth of the world's people, though many urban areas and countries (like Nigeria) have a high density, counterbalancing vast regions of sparse population. Large urban areas have sprung up in nearly every country of Africa, with high-rise office buildings and computers part of the milieu. People cluster into nearly three thousand ethnic groups, each of which shares aspects of social identity. The most widely known reference work that classifies these groups is George Peter Murdock's *Africa: Its People and Their Culture History* (1959).

About one thousand distinct indigenous languages are spoken throughout Africa. Joseph Greenberg (1970) classifies them into four major divisions: Niger-Kordofanian, Nilo-Saharan, Hamito-Semitic, and Khoisan. The Niger-Kordofanian is the largest and most widespread of these, extending from West Africa to the southern tip of Africa; its geographical distribution points to the rapid movement of people from West Africa eastward and southward beginning about 2000 B.C. and extending into the 1600s of the common era.

Swahili, an East African trade language (with a Bantu grammar and much Arabic vocabulary), reflects the movements of peoples both within Africa and to and from Arabia. Bambara and Hausa, other trade languages (spoken across wide areas of

FIGURE 1   Playing technique of the *nkangala* mouth bow in Malawi. Photo by Gerhard Kubik.

West Africa), are but a few of the languages that show Arabic influence. In addition, the Austronesian family is represented by Malagasy, spoken on the island of Madagascar, and the Indo-European family by Afrikaans, spoken by descendants of seventeenth-century Dutch settlers in South Africa.

Following colonial rule in many countries, English, French, and Portuguese still serve as languages of commerce and education in the former colonies. Several languages of the Indian subcontinent are spoken by members of Asian communities that have arisen in many African countries, and numerous Lebanese traders throughout Africa speak a dialect of Arabic.

From the 1500s to the 1800s, trade in slaves produced a great outward movement of perhaps 10 million people from West and Central Africa to the Americas, and from East Africa to Arabia. A token return of ex-slaves and their descendants to Liberia during the 1800s represented a further disruption, as African-American settlers displaced portions of local populations. The long-term effects of this loss of manpower, and the attendant suffering it produced, have yet to be adequately understood. The movement of peoples, however, contributed to the formation of languages, such as the Krio of Sierra Leone and Liberian English of Liberia—hybrids of indigenous and foreign tongues.

Though indigenous systems of writing were not widespread in Africa, some peoples invented their own scripts. These peoples included some of the Tuareg and Berber groups in the Sahara and more than fifteen groups in West Africa, including the Vai and the Kpelle of Liberia, whose music is studied in this volume.

SUBSISTENCE AND INDUSTRY

A majority of Africans engage in farming for their employment. In many areas, farmers use shifting cultivation, in which they plant a portion of land for a time and leave it to regenerate, moving to another plot. This form of agriculture is characteristically tied to a complex system of communal ownership. Increasingly, however, people and corporations, by acquiring exclusive ownership of large areas of arable land, are changing African land-use patterns.

International commerce has resulted in a shift from subsistence to cash crops: cocoa, coffee, palm oil, rubber, sugarcane, tea, tobacco. The wage laborers who work

Typical of early African kingdoms were large retinues of royal musicians, who enhanced state occasions and provided musical commentary on events.

with the crops migrate from their home villages, settling permanently or temporarily on large farms. Grassland areas throughout the continent support flocks of camels, cattle, goats, and sheep, and people there are predominantly herders, who frequently live as nomads to find the best grazing for their animals.

In many areas of Africa, rich natural resources—coal, copper, diamonds, gold, iron, oil, uranium—contribute to employment for notable sectors of the population. Processing these materials provides wages for workers and exports for the resource-rich nations.

TRANSPORT AND TRADE

For trade and travel, people have long moved across African deserts and savannas, and through African forests, but the intensity and speed of their movement increased with the building of roads, railways, and airports, particularly since the 1950s in many parts of the continent.

Suddenly, perishable fruits and vegetables could be shipped from interior farms to coastal urban areas. Taxis and buses built a lively trade shuttling people and goods up and down roads, from local markets to urban areas and back again. Manufactured goods were more readily available from petty traders and shopkeepers alike, and foods like frozen fish became part of the daily diet.

Among all that activity, cassettes of the latest popular music of the local country and the world became part of the goods available for purchase. Feature films of East Asian karate, Indian loveplots, or American black heroes became available, first from itinerant film projectionists, and by the 1980s from video clubs. On a weekly and sometimes daily basis, maritime shipping was now supplemented with air travel to Europe and the rest of the world.

SOCIAL AND POLITICAL FORMATIONS

Several African kingdoms with large centralized governments emerged in the Middle Ages. Among these were Ghana in the West African grasslands area around the Niger River (A.D. 700–1200); Mali, which succeeded Ghana and became larger (1200–1500); and Songhai (1350–1600), which took over the territory of ancient Mali. Kanem-Bornu flourished further east in the interior (800–1800). In the forest region, Benin developed in parts of present-day Nigeria (1300–1800); Ashanti, in the area of contemporary Ghana (1700–1900); Kongo, along the Congo River (1400–1650); Luba-Lunda, in the Congo-Angola-Zambia grasslands (1400–1700); Zimbabwe, in southern Africa (1400–1800); and Buganda, in the area of present-day Uganda (1700–1900) (Davidson 1966:184–185).

Archaeological evidence is only now providing information about the full extent of indigenous African empires, fueled by long-distance trade in gold, ivory, salt, and other commodities. Typical of these kingdoms were large retinues of royal musicians, who enhanced state occasions and provided musical commentary on events. Benin bronze plaques, preserving visual images of some of these musicians, are in museums around the world.

Alongside large-scale political formations have been much smaller political units, known as stateless societies. Operating in smaller territories, inhabited by smaller numbers of people, these societies may have several levels in a hierarchy of chiefs, who in turn owe allegiance to a national government. At the lowest level in these societies, government is consensual in nature; at the upper levels, chiefs, in consultation with elders and ordinary citizens, make decisions.

West Africa supports Poro and Sande (called secret societies by Westerners), organizations to which adults belong, and through which they are enculturated about social mores and customs. Children of various ages leave the village and live apart in the forest, in enclosures known as Poro (for men) and Sande (for women). There, they learn dances and songs that they will perform upon emergence at the closing ceremonies. Required parts of their education, these songs and dances are displayed for community appreciation at the end of the educational period. It is during this seclusion that promising young soloists in dance and drumming may be identified and specially tutored.

Kinship, though long studied by anthropologists in Africa, has proved complex and often hard to interpret. Ancestors are noted in formal lineages, which may be recited in praise singing and often reinterpreted according to the occasion and its requirements. Residence may be patrilocal or matrilocal, depending on local customs. And the extended families that are ubiquitous in Africa become distanced through urban relocation and labor migration, even if formal ties continue.

Settlements may take the form of nomadic camps (moving with the season and pasture), cities, towns, or dispersed homesteads along motor roads. They may also develop around mines, rubber plantations, and other work sites. Camps for workers who periodically travel home may become permanent settlements, where families also reside.

RELIGIOUS BELIEFS AND PRACTICES

Though indigenous religious beliefs and practices exhibit many varieties of practice, they share some common themes. A high, supreme, and often distant creator god rules. Intermediate deities become the focus of worship, divination, and sacrificial offerings. Spirits live in water, trees, rocks, and other places, and these become the beings through whose mediation people maintain contact with the creator god.

Indigenous religious practices in Africa have been influenced and overlaid by Christian and Islamic practices, among other world religions. New religious movements, such as *aladura* groups have skillfully linked Christian religious practices with indigenous ones.

Elsewhere, Islam penetrated the forest region and brought changes to local practices, even as it, too, underwent change [ISLAM IN LIBERIA]. The observance of Ramadan, the month of fasting, was introduced, certain musical practices were banned, and altered indigenous practices remained as compromises.

REFERENCES

Davidson, Basil. 1966. *African Kingdoms.* New York: Time-Life Books.

Greenberg, Joseph H. 1970. *The Languages of Africa.* Bloomington, Ind.: Research Center for the Language Sciences.

Murdock, George P. 1959. *Africa: Its People and Their Culture History.* New York: McGraw-Hill.

African Music in a Constellation of Arts
Ruth M. Stone

Concepts of Music
Concepts of Performance
Historic Preservation of African Music

African performance is a tightly wrapped bundle of arts that are sometimes difficult to separate, even for analysis. Singing, playing instruments, dancing, masquerading, and dramatizing are part of a conceptual package that many Africans think of as one and the same. The Kpelle people of Liberia use a single word, *sang*, to describe a well-danced movement, a well-sung phrase, or especially fine drumming. For them, the expressive acts that gives rise to these media are related and interlinked. The visual arts, the musical arts, the dramatic arts—all work together in the same domain and are conceptually treated as intertwined. To describe the execution of a sequence of dances, a Kpelle drummer might say, "The dance she spoke."

CONCEPTS OF MUSIC

Honest observers are hard pressed to find a single indigenous group in Africa that has a term congruent with the usual Western notion of "music." There are terms for more specific acts like singing, playing instruments, and more broadly performing (dance, games, music); but the isolation of musical sound from other arts proves a Western abstraction, of which we should be aware when we approach the study of performance in Africa.

The arts maintain a close link to the rest of social and political life. In performance, they both reflect upon that life and create it. Highlife songs are famous for having been employed in political campaigns in Ghana, poetry in Somalia has influenced political history, and work is both coordinated and enhanced as bush clearers follow the accompaniment of an instrumental ensemble. The arts are not an extra or separate expression to be enjoyed apart from the social and political ebb and flow. They emerge centrally in the course of life, vital to normal conduct.

While musical specialists in the West have often used notions of "folk," "popular," and "art" to categorize music, these concepts prove problematic in African settings. They often indicate more of the social formations associated with music than of musical sound. "Folk" is often equated with "traditional," or music performed in rural areas, "popular" is commonly associated with mass audiences and urban areas, and "art" is associated with elite, upper-class, written notation. These terms also imply a prejudicial tilt toward things written and reserved for a few, but in African

Instruments are more than material objects: they frequently take on human features and qualities. Certain solo instruments may have personal names, be kept in special houses, receive special sacrificial food or other offerings, and be regarded as quasi-human.

FIGURE 1   Mpumpu, king of the masks among the Mbwela and Nkhangala of Southeastern Angola, 1965. Photo by Gerhard Kubik.

settings, aural traditions are highly developed and practiced forms of transmission, no less competent or effective in artistic creation.

A further complication is that African practices often mingle musics from apparently disparate idioms. African and Western elements may be codominant, as Akin Euba asserts (1992:308) is the case for J. H. Kwabena Nketia's composition *Volta Fantasy.* Djimo Kouyate, performer on the twenty-one-stringed harp-lute (*kora*) of Senegal, performs with Mamaya African Jazz, an eight-member ensemble, which performs a fusion of African music and worldbeat, the latter a form of international popular music (Brown 1994). The West African superstar Baaba Maal recorded an album, *Firin' in Fouta,* in three phases, each reflecting a different kind of music. He began by returning to his ancestral village (Podor, northern Senegal), where he recorded instruments and songs of everyday life. In Dakar, the capital, his band, Dande Lenol, transformed these sounds into rhythm tracks. Finally, he took those tracks to England, where he added vocals, synthesizers, and Celtic instruments. The resultant album draws on local African music to inform high-tech Western dance music (Himes 1995).

Some scholars have delineated musical style areas within Africa. Perhaps the most commented upon, and the most criticized, is that of Alan Lomax, who, using musical traits as discerned by Western listeners, divided Africa into fifteen regions: North Africa, Sahara, Western Sudan, Moslem Sudan, Eastern Sudan, Ethiopia, Guinea Coast, Equatorial Bantu, Upper Nile, Northeast Bantu, Central Bantu, African Hunters, South African Bantu, Madagascar, and Afro-American (Lomax 1968:91–95). But the limitations of such mapping derive from the interpretations of Western listeners, who may or may not know much about the conception of that sound.

CONCEPTS OF PERFORMANCE

Some generalizations can be drawn about performance in Africa, emphasizing the perspectives of the performers and their ideas about creating that performance. However, we must bear in mind that great variation exists, even about fundamental ideas.

Performers

To some extent, most people in African communities are expected to perform music and dance at a basic level. Performing is considered as normal as speaking. In many areas, social puberty is marked by singing and dancing, as young people display their accomplishments in token of their maturation. Solo performers may be trained to excel because they have shown aptitude for an instrument, or they may be selected because they come from a family whose occupation is to be musicians, as is frequently the case among the *griots* of West Africa.

Soloists develop their skills most often with the aid of a tutelary spirit or some form of supernatural assistance. At musical performances, spirits are sometimes present, forming an elusive audience, which certain human participants will sense. The elusive teacher can make a singer's voice particularly fine. The tutelary spirit makes high demands, however, and fame does not come easily. For aiding the singer, the spirit may exact much, even the singer's life.

The tragedy of Pona-wɛni

Such a relationship, always treacherous, can end in tragedy. My own fieldwork shows such a case. In 1970, I recorded Pona-wɛni, a fine female singer, as she performed with Wokpɛɛ, a male soloist. They sang "*Giing*," the favorite song of the year in central Bong County, Liberia; in 1972, it was included on a Folkways recording. In 1975, on my return, I gave the singer a copy of it.

On a market day in late 1988, I returned to Totota, where I met musicians from the town of Gbeyilataa, performers I had worked with at various times over the last eighteen years. As we sat under a tree and conversed about various people from their town, they talked easily of who was around and performing, and who had moved elsewhere. Of Pona-wɛni, they said nothing.

Eventually, I inquired if the musicians would like to hear some of the music some of them had performed in 1970. With eagerness, they responded that they would. By chance, I selected "*Giing*" to be played. Immediately on hearing its beginning, several people looked astonished, and one woman burst into tears. As I stopped the tape, the story of Pona-wɛni poured out.

During my absence, Pona-wɛni had excelled, become famous for her talent. But some villagers murmured that she had exceeded herself. One day, as she was crossing a log bridge over a swollen creek, a tutelary spirit pulled her down into the torrent, from which she never emerged. The special power that had helped her succeed and be admired had been responsible for balancing benefits with misfortune.

Performance as an engine of national policy

While ensembles of performers are formed and perform within a local region, often traveling to neighboring towns, some ensembles have been formed to represent contemporary nation-states. The ensembles may meld performers from various locations and teach them to adapt their performances to meet the requirements of the Western stage.

Some African countries have set up national training centers where musicians and dancers work together to create ensembles. These performers are often paid by the national government. They travel around the country or tour the world, representing a blend of musics from the particular region, adapted to outsiders' expectations for performance.

Musical instruments as human extensions

The people of Africa make and use a vast array of musical instruments. Beyond an expected variety of drums, musicians play harps, harp-lutes, lutes, lyres, and zithers, to name but a few of the stringed instruments found across the continent.

Within African contexts, instruments are more than material objects: they frequently take on human features and qualities. Certain solo instruments may have personal names, be kept in special houses, receive special sacrificial food or other offerings, and be regarded as quasi-human. To the musician playing them, these instruments provide power and sometimes special aid. A close, humanlike partnership sometimes develops between musician and instrument.

While ethnomusicologists categorize instruments as aerophones (bullroarers, flutes, horns, oboes), chordophones (harps, lutes, zithers), membranophones

Myths, legends, epics, oral histories, and life histories were only a few of the genres that embodied memories of performances.

(drums), and idiophones (rattles, lamellophones, xylophones), African peoples frequently employ other ways of grouping instruments. Among the Kpelle of Liberia, instruments are either blown (*fɛɛ*) or struck (*ngale*); all aerophones fit into the former category, and all other instruments fit into the latter. All Kpelle stringed instruments are plucked, and so the finger, from a Kpelle conception, "strikes" the string (Stone 1982:55–57).

Exchange among voices

Ethnomusicologists describe musical sounds according to pitches (labeled with numbers or letters of the alphabet), but peoples in Africa often conceive of these sounds as voices. People, instruments, and birds all employ voices, which, in performance, musicians imitate. Performers conceive of one voice singing a part and another voice responding, in a call-and-response kind of dialogue.

In the idea of call and response, the conversational metaphor captures many exchanges that are the fabric of the performance. Kpelle choral singing always has a counterpart to the solo or the first part. A master drummer may create the first part, and a vocal soloist may become the counterpart to the drum. But then, when the chorus members come in as a response to the soloist, the vocalist and master drummer function as a pair, to which the chorus answers. A web of balances is created, and interchanges abound at many levels. The voices that create these exchanges are frequently described in terms like *large* or *small*, implying certain aspects of pitch, timbre, and dynamics.

Some peoples stress the primacy of the transaction between paired performing parts (Stone 1985:139–148). Two players of the *mangwilo*, a xylophone of southeast Africa, sit at the same instrument facing one another. One is called the starting one (*opachera*) and the other the responding one (*wakulela*) (Kubik 1965:36). Similarly, among the Shona of Zimbabwe, a solo mbira player designates one part he or she plays as *kushaura* 'to lead the piece, to take the solo part' and the second as *kutsinhira* 'to exchange parts of a song, to interweave a second interlocking part' (Berliner 1978:73).

Motoric patterns in performance

In the early twentieth century, Erich M. von Hornbostel called for the study of patterns of human movement to aid our understanding of African rhythm (1928:30–62). Though many scholars have found fault with his conclusions, some, taking leads from his work, have explored issues of bodily movement.

Gerhard Kubik has underscored the importance of the acoustic, motoric, and visual elements of rhythm (1972:28–39; 1977:253–274). Moses Serwadda and Hewitt Pantaleoni have shown how drumming and dancing link: "A drummer will indicate the dance motions sometimes as a way of explaining and teaching a [drum] pattern" (1968:52).

In multipart textures, individual parts often interweave or interlock in short, repetitive motives (ostinatos), which become layered in complex ways. Certain of these motives are invariant; others subtly transform in variation as the performance develops. A sense of multiple layering emerges as the density increases, ideally with contrasting timbres among parts.

HISTORICAL PRESERVATION OF AFRICAN MUSIC

Documentation of African performances predates the arrival of the Europeans or sound recordings. Oral traditions served to preserve in dynamic ways the aspects of performance that people wanted to remember. Myths, legends, epics, oral histories, and life histories were only a few of the genres that embodied memories of performances.

Almost a thousand years before the phonograph was invented, Arab travelers wrote about their impressions of African music. Perhaps the most famous, Mohammed ibn Abdullah ibn Battuta, vividly described court music scenes in the kingdom of Mali in the 1100s (Gibb 1929). When first the Portuguese, and then other Europeans, arrived in Africa, Arabs had long been active in exploring the continent. We should beware of assuming that the "dark continent" (as Europeans unsubtly dubbed it) suddenly came to life with the arrival of the Europeans. African contacts with the outside world—especially with West, South, and Southeast Asia—were lively long before Europeans "discovered" the continent.

As Europeans began to study Africa, and in particular its music, their interpretations emphasized a music of rather monotonous stasis and inaction, discovered by ever-adventurous Europeans, who, conversely, associated themselves with music of change and development. Such interpretations are especially curious when we note that motion and action are central to the aesthetic principles of many African groups. The most charitable assessment is that European misperceptions came from a lack of appreciation of African musical subtleties, including the language of performance. Especially after the publication of Charles Darwin's *Origin of Species* (1859), theories of musical evolutionism, which ascribed a more limited development to Africans than to Europeans, fueled the outsiders' mistaken notions.

Before the twentieth century, African music was preserved for Western posterity in verbal descriptions and musical notation. These forms of writing froze and isolated moving sounds into static forms. As wax cylinders were etched with sound (beginning in Africa in the early 1900s), they opened up new horizons while fixing sound images, though perhaps not to the same extent (or in the same way) as written musical transcription.

Western adventurers collected examples of African sounds in much the same manner as they collected samples of African flora and fauna. These examples were transported back to archives and museums to be sorted, duplicated, and catalogued (Stone and Gillis 1976). Africans, in contrast, have over the years been more concerned with continuing their live performance traditions, and have paid less attention to acquiring and preserving samples of sounds.

REFERENCES

Berliner, Paul. 1978. *The Soul of Mbira*. Berkeley: University of California Press.

Brown, Joe. 1994. "Djimo Kouyate." *Washington Post,* 28 January.

Darwin, Charles. 1859. *Origin of Species.* London: British Museum.

Euba, Akin. 1992. "Creating Authentic Forms of New African Art Music." International Conference on African Music and Dance: Problems and Prospects. Working documents. Bellagio Study and Conference Center, Bellagio, Italy, 12–16 October.

Gibb, Hamilton A. R. 1929. *Ibn Battuta, Travels in Asia and Africa.* London: Darf.

Gray, John. 1991. *African Music: A Bibliographical Guide to the Traditional, Popular, Arts, and Liturgical Musics of Sub-Saharan Africa.* New York and Westport, Conn.: Greenwood Press.

Greenberg, Joseph. 1970. *The Languages of Africa,* 3rd ed. Bloomington and The Hague: Indiana University and Mouton.

Himes, Geoffrey. 1995. "Maal's African Dance Mix." *Washington Post,* 20 January.

Hornbostel, Erich M. von. 1928. "African Negro Music." *Africa* 1:30–62.

Kubik, Gerhard. 1965. "Transcription of Mangwilo Xylophone Music from Film Strips." *African Music* 3(4):35–41.

———. 1972. "Transcription of African Music from Silent Film: Theory and Methods." *African Music* 5(1):28–39.

———. 1977. "Patterns of Body Movement in the Music of Boys' Initiation in South-East Angola." In *The Anthropology of the Body,* ed. John Blacking, 253–274. London: Academic Press.

Serwadda, Moses, and Hewitt Pantaleoni. 1968. "A Possible Notation for African Dance Drumming." *African Music* 4(2):45–52.

Stone, Ruth M. 1982. *Let the Inside Be Sweet: The Interpretation of Music Event among the Kpelle of Liberia.* Bloomington: Indiana University Press.

———. 1985. "In Search of Time in African Music." *Music Theory Spectrum* 7:139–158.

Stone, Ruth M., and Frank J. Gillis. 1976. *African Music and Oral Data: A Catalog of Field Recordings, 1902–1975.* Bloomington and London: Indiana University Press.

Exploring African Music
Ruth M. Stone

Early Accounts of African Music
Shaping Sound
Timing in Sound
Feeling in Sound
People Who Perform
Instruments as Extensions of Performers

Music permeates the daily life of people in Africa. An ivory horn ensemble precedes a chief as he travels with his entourage. Highlife singers promote candidates for political office. Professional praise singers convey messages to and for their patrons. For ordinary citizens on the streets of Monrovia, Liberia, the sounds of Bob Marley and reggae come from the "money bus": to the rhythm of the music, the driver's assistant jogs alongside the vehicle, supervising its passengers. At local markets, cassette sellers promote recordings by local bands and international music artists.

In all these settings, music tightly interweaves with dance, words, drama, and visual art to create a complex event. As the former director of the Ghana Dance Ensemble, A. M. Ipoku, expressed it, dance and music should be so closely connected that one "can see the music and hear the dance." A Kpelle audience member from Liberia described "the dance she spoke." African terms that are the equivalent of "performance" or "event," whether the Kpelle *pele* or the Basotho *lipapali,* refer not only to music making, but also to children's games and sports. In many places in Africa, choruses and drum ensembles energize fans at soccer games, providing a backdrop for the playing of the match.

Events incorporate and intermingle multifarious forms from streams of influence coming from within and without Africa. The Bundu Boys of Zimbabwe may take a Shona story-song from a rural tradition and give it a popularized performance in an urban nightclub, using electric guitars to replace the *mbira,* a plucked idiophone. The East African *beni* and West African highlife draw upon brass-band music. The Congolese *soukous* echoes soul and disco music. The South African *makwaya* joins European vocal harmonies and American ragtime elements with Xhosa rhythms. The album *Graceland,* including performances by Paul Simon and the South African group Ladysmith Black Mambazo, "represents a global soundscape in which the boundaries between the symbols, perspectives, and interpretations of culturally distinct spheres have become almost seamlessly enmeshed with each other" (Erlmann 1996:312).

The Shona of Zimbabwe describe individual keys: "mad person, put-in-a-stable position, lion, swaying of a person going into trance, to stir up, big drum," and "mortar," to show how the keys function in the music.

EARLY ACCOUNTS OF AFRICAN MUSIC

Some of the earliest accounts of African music were recorded by Arab travelers. In the year 1067, Al Bekri of Grenada, Spain, wrote about music making in the royal court in the kingdom of Ghana: "The beginning of the royal audience is announced by the beating of a kind of drum which they called *deba*, made of a long piece of hollowed wood. The people gather when they hear this sound" (Davidson 1964:72). In 1352, Mohammed ibn Abdullah ibn Battuta, who traveled widely in East as well as West Africa, sensitively captured court music scenes in Mali:

> The sultan was preceded by his musicians, who carry gold and silver *gumbris* [two-stringed guitars], and behind him come three hundred armed slaves. He walks in a leisurely fashion, affecting a very slow movement, and even stops from time to time. On reaching the *pempi* he stops and looks round the assembly, then ascends it in the sedate manner of a preacher ascending a mosque-pulpit. As he takes his seat, the drums, trumpets and bugles are sounded. (Gibb 1929:326)

As Europeans explored Africa, starting at the coasts and pushing inward, they followed Arabs who had begun traversing the continent hundreds of years earlier. Mungo Park, traveling in 1860, richly detailed the interactive aspects of the arriving traveler and his subsequent engagement with music performers:

> This happened to be a feast day at Dalli, and the people were dancing before the Dooty's house. But when they were informed that a white man was come into town, they left off dancing, and came to the place where I lodged, walking in regular order, two and two, with music before them. . . . They continued to dance and sing until midnight, during which time I was surrounded by so great a crowd as made it necessary for me to satisfy their curiosity by sitting still. (Park 1860:104–105)

Park became part of an ongoing scene of action, and as the performers adjusted their music making to his appearance, he was obliged to sit and act the part of an audience member. This is a rare account in which we learn of responses—both from him and the performers—to his arrival and the disruption of the ongoing event.

The writings of these explorers have allowed readers to imagine the music making that occurred in early African history. After the invention of the cylinder phonograph by Thomas Alva Edison, in 1877, Westerners were actually able to *hear* the music making, most notably from the famous Berlin Phonogramm-Archiv Demonstration sampling of early recordings made between 1900 and 1913 in distant parts of the globe, including Africa, and locations in Europe and America where Africans traveled.

SHAPING SOUND

Sound is a favored sense for experience in many African communities. People notice, shape, and admire it. Truck drivers blow horns that play complex tunes to announce their arrival. Postal workers cancel stamps with a deliberate rhythm while they whistle familiar songs. Oral traditions document such admiration. The Kpelle people, for example, say the inspiration for transverse horns came from *tuu-tuu* birds. Several women, so the story goes, were fishing in a creek. When they came back to town, they asked the chief how they might capture the wonderful sound of the birds they had heard:

> "What can we do to record the sound?" The chief kept sitting, he kept sitting. He said, "Go into town and quickly kill two cows." They then returned to where the *tuu-tuu* were responding. When the *tuu-tuu* sang, they imitated them [on the cow horns]. (Stone 1976)

And so it was that sounds of nature were transformed into music, captured for music making. The Vai of Liberia tell of a king who was defeated and shown how to travel to the underwater world, where he and his entourage settled and lived a good life. Their celebrations can be heard on a quiet night, but when humans hear them, their sounds are a sign of an upcoming death.

Sounds in much of Africa are voices—not only of humans, but also of instruments. Since instruments possess human attributes, the low-pitched string of a frame-zither may serve as a mother's voice, and a higher-pitched string as a child's voice. Two closely pitched strings may be called brother and sister. The Lugbara of Uganda name the five strings of the lyre with status terms for women. The Shona of Zimbabwe name the manuals of the *mbira* "the old men's voices" for the lowest register, "the young men's voices" for the middle register, and "the women's voices" for the highest register. They go further to describe individual keys: "mad person, put-in-a-stable position, lion, swaying of a person going into trance, to stir up, big drum," and "mortar," with the names showing something about how the keys function in the music.

Africans favor complex timbres or tone colors, which musicians often create by adding rattles to drums, zithers, and *mbira*s. Singers disguise their voices to multiply the tone colors. Players add a buzzing to the sound of xylophones by attaching pieces of spiders' egg sacs to the resonators.

Africans combine pitches in a wide variety of scales or pitch inventories, ranging from the pentatonic (five tones to the octave) to the heptatonic (seven tones to the octave). The distance between tones is highly variable—a trait that permits a great assortment of contrasting tonal inventories.

African musicians learn sound patterns through oral, rather than written, notation. Mnemonic phrases guide their playing. Some of these phrases may create what is called a timeline, a rhythmic pattern that continually repeats throughout a composition. In West Africa, a well-known timeline may be verbalized as *kong kong ko-lo, kong kolo.* The syllables as performed convey rhythm and tone color. If notated, this pattern might look as follows, assuming that *x* represents the striking of an instrument and a period (.) implies silence or the continuation of a sustained sound.

```
12   x   .   x   .   x   x   .   x   .   x   x   .
 8   kong   kong   ko- lo      kong      ko- lo
```

The timeline is often played by a struck clapperless double bell. Each other instrument in the ensemble plays its own pattern, verbalized in phrases such as *ku-gu, ku-*

Young people may receive training with their peers during periods of seclusion in a secret society or while attending Western schools. Emerging from the secret society into the public event that marks their graduation, they display their new knowledge by performing elaborate dances wearing fine costumes.

gu and *i-za-pa-ni-pa-ti.* Even the master drummer, who varies and changes his line, frequently identifies his sounds by verbal patterns. The vowels indicate something of the tone color, for /u/ and /o/ indicate timbres of "dark" sounds on low pitches, while /i/ and /a/ are "brighter" sounds on higher pitches. Thus, a palette of timbres and rhythms can be spoken in syllables.

When ethnomusicologist George Herzog made cylinder phonograph recordings in the 1930s, he discovered that the Jabo of Liberia labeled musical sounds as large and small, meaning that the largest sounds are in the lowest register of pitch, while the smallest sounds are in the highest register. These terms refer to birds that live near each other and respond to one another's call. The Kpelle also refer to large and small voices and include tone color as an attribute of these sounds. A large voice is resonant and hollow ("voice swallowed"), while a small voice is more penetrating and less resonant ("voice coming out").

TIMING IN SOUND

The placement of sounds in time shows delight in the clashing of parts, and draws from distinctive patterns of ordering. Observers have long admired African rhythmic complexity, which has been the focus of considerable scholarly attention (figure 1). If we think of a West African ensemble with the various instruments playing different patterns, the simpler patterns are those of supporting parts, and the more complex

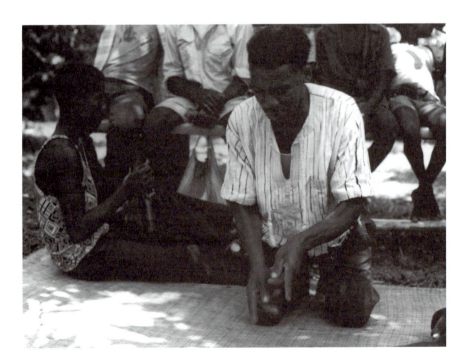

FIGURE 1   A bottle-player provides rhythmic background to an epic performance in the Central Kpelle area in Bong County, Liberia.

and varying patterns are those of the master drummer. Yet as these parts blend, each fits with the others in precisely prescribed ways. If a timeline is being played, all other parts will have an individual and specific entry point within that pattern. In southeast Africa, two xylophonists sit opposite one another to play the same instrument: one takes responsibility for starting the performance, and the other responds. Analogously, an *mbira* player of Zimbabwe designates one part he plays as *kushaura* 'to lead' and the other as *kutsinhira* 'to exchange parts of a song'. The Kpelle say a solo singer "raises the song" and the chorus "agrees underneath."

This relationship of parts is transactional in its call-and-response construction, but musical transactions can be structured in other ways. Singers may create a texture known as hocket, in which each voice performs only intermittent notes, but the combination of the notes through time creates the appearance of a single melody. Workers performing bush-clearing songs may use their voices to create such an effect. Pygmies combine yodeling with hocketing to create complex and distinctive textures. Instrumentalists also perform in hocket: each instrument may have a one- or two-note motif, but as many as six flutes or horns may fit these motifs into a larger unit. The Shona of Zimbabwe interlock panpipe sounds with vocal syllables. Sound is here segmented and fragmented only to be combined in fascinating ways. Kpelle musicians and audiences find the fracturing and recombining of sound to be the highest form of music making.

FEELING IN SOUND

Emotion powerfully informs music and influences how music touches its makers and listeners. Music in Africa may stir people to dance if they hear drums, or to become calm if they are grieving. Ge-weli-wula, a blacksmith and ritual specialist from Liberia, told me of the transformative power of music:

> What I know about song, it came from sadness. . . . Even if you cry, you do everything, you must perform. . . . The man is performing, the inside of his heart has cooled. If your heart hurts, you can't sit quietly again. But before you sit quietly, you must sing.

Sometimes a particularly fine performance will move someone to offer the singer a valuable gift. This response may be particularly apt at certain points in a performance. Among the Kpelle, a singer alerts the audience to such upcoming moments in her singing: "Put your ear to my singing song: as I am singing it, I am opening its net." Emotion may be embedded in nonverbal patterns played by a drummer. Kao, a master drummer of Gbeyilataa, described how he achieved the special quality of proverbs (*sang*) in his playing: "The *sang* are in your stomach. When it becomes your wisdom, and it rises into all your fingers, and they know it, then you play all those *sang* with them."

PEOPLE WHO PERFORM

As young people mature in many parts of Africa, they learn to perform music. They are socialized through learning to dance and sing together. They may immerse themselves in a rich sonic environment that includes samples from the global world in which they live. They may receive training with their peers during periods of seclusion in a secret society or while attending Western schools. Emerging from the secret society into the public event that marks their graduation, they display their new knowledge by performing elaborate dances wearing fine costumes. Young people with special talent will take up an apprenticeship with a master drummer, singer, or other professional, from whose instruction they seek advanced competence.

Carved humanoid features adorn many instruments: the head and face of a woman at the end of a Mangbetu harp, the waist rings and feet of a woman at the base of a goblet drum, an *mbira* built on the belly of a carved wooden figure of a person with arms uplifted.

The makers of music include singers, dancers, storytellers, actors, and instrumentalists. As receivers of the performance, members of the audience judge the presentation and in turn help shape it. Kpelle audiences offer praise, in the form of token gifts or speeches, and they criticize what they have heard, in words with finely honed allusions. On one occasion, the town chief of Gbeyilataa offered the following words as he stepped into the performing circle and stopped the sound so that he might speak:

> All of you, thank you, thank you.
> My name is Taa-tii.
> I come from Bonotaa.
> My mother is Goma, my father's name is Leepolu.
> I bring some water to soak the drumhead.

By identifying his hometown and family, he provided a way for the audience to relate to him and evaluate his words. People laughed at his reference to "water" (fermented cane-juice), because they knew that the musicians to whom he was handing it would use it to wet their tongues, rather than their drums.

Ancestors and tutelary spirits may join the living participants. Though their presence may be acknowledged and known to only a few select insiders, they influence and often enhance the music. A player sang "Gbono kpate-wee!" as he invited the spirit of a deceased great player to enter the arena. When people heard the player call *oo!* in a high-pitched voice, they knew this spirit had arrived. Virtuoso performers attach themselves to tutelary spirits in a private and dangerous relationship. For making a performance extraordinary, a spirit may exact a great deal from the musician—sometimes even the musician's life.

INSTRUMENTS AS EXTENSIONS OF PERFORMERS

Musical instruments carry human attributes and can become more or less human, depending on their roles within the music they produce. Carved humanoid features adorn many instruments: the head and face of a woman at the end of a Mangbetu harp, the waist rings and feet of a woman at the base of a goblet drum, an *mbira* built on the belly of a carved wooden figure of a person with arms uplifted. Musicians may designate parts of their instruments by the names of human body parts, such as the waist, the foot, and the ear. Kao, the master drummer of Gbeyilataa, called his goblet drum Gomaa ('Share-with-Me'), a woman's name suggesting physical beauty and personal vitality. Other musicians offered food sacrifices to their instruments to protect the bond between the human world and the spirit world. Thus, for many musicians, these material objects possess human and spiritual attributes and serve to connect the various worlds that people inhabit.

African peoples categorize instruments in ways that differ somewhat from the Western orchestral categories of string, woodwind, brass, and percussion sections. African groupings also differ from the ethnomusicological classes of aerophone, chordophone, membranophone, and idiophone. Much more research is needed to understand classification systematically across the continent, but we know some interesting things already. The Kpelle, the Vai, and the Dan of the Guinea Coast see all instruments as either struck (including percussion and string) or blown (including brass and woodwind). The Kpelle use the term *ngale* for 'struck', meaning literally 'to break', as a millet stalk breaks. Plucking a string is considered to be a kind of breaking.

African musicians draw upon many kinds of instruments. Drums are best known to the outside world, and they come in many shapes: goblet, hourglass, conical, barrel, cylindrical, and frame (tambourine). These drums range from small hand-held instruments to those that need large stands to support them or several men to carry them in procession. They produce a broad spectrum of "voices" or timbres. Famous ensembles include the tuned drum ensembles (*entenga*) of the kings of Uganda and the processional drums played on horseback in northern Nigeria. The hourglass drum of West Africa glides from pitch to pitch as the player deftly presses thongs to tighten and loosen the heads. The skillful use of hands and stick produces myriad pitches and tone colors.

J. H. Kwabena Nketia describes the visual-display aspect of the *durbar* in Ghana, making the climax of the forty-day ritual cycle honoring the ancestor-kings. On this occasion, the paramount chief exhibits the regalia of his court in a splendid procession. Gold and silver ornaments abound, worn by the king and members of his entourage. Of the music, Nketia says,

> The drumming, singing and dancing during the procession keeps [*sic*] the procession alive. Different drum ensembles may be played simultaneously at different points within the procession. . . . As the music goes on, individuals may take turns at dancing in the open ring and the chief himself may grace the occasion by dancing to the music of the royal *fontomfrom* drums. (1973:82)

Other percussion instruments are known ethnomusicologically as idiophones, instruments whose own materials, without having previously been stretched (like strings and skins), create sounds. In this grouping are rattles of all kinds, both container and those with a bead network on the outside. Struck clapperless bells often set timelines within ensembles. Hollowed-out logs are played alone or in ensemble, and often reproduce the relative pitches of speech in tonal languages to communicate specific messages. The variety of struck, plucked, and shaken instruments is broad. Many instruments of the other categories, such as membranophones, sport attached idiophones in the form of rattles, which enrich the sound. Among idiophones is the *mbira* or sansa, with its plucked metal tongues. When it is played at a healing event for the Shona, the crowd waits for the mediums to become possessed. The *mbira* is central to creating the ambience of the event.

The Benin bronzes of Nigeria, cast from about A.D. 1550 to 1650, display scenes of a hollowed log, a struck single bell, a double bell, a clapper bell, a pellet bell, a calabash rattle, a rattle staff, and other instruments. These and other archaeologically discovered artifacts indicate the long-standing richness of African idiophones.

Chordophones, or stringed instruments, are sometimes the "hidden" instruments of Africa, no less remarkable than the percussion instruments, but often unheard outside individual cultures. The kora, a harp-lute, is the personal extension of the West African griot, the itinerant praise singer, genealogist, and social commen-

One musical group I recorded in a village some distance from a motor road was delighted when an audience member, in offering a token of appreciation, pretended to write a check, showing awareness of the modern economy and how banks transfer money in urban areas.

tator of the Mali and Sengal area of Mande West Africa. Multiple bow-lutes, frame zithers, musical bows, harps, lyres, and lutes of many kinds contribute to musical performance across the continent. The haunting vocal illusion of the "whispered song" of East Africa is hard to forget. The performer plucks a trough zither (*inanga*) to make low, resonant sounds while he whispers nonpitched syllables. The listener mentally attaches the zither's pitches to the performer's whispers, and imagines that the performer is really singing them.

Spirits often speak through blown or wind instruments, such as flutes, whistles, bullroarers, and horns. The spirit of the Kpelle Poro secret men's society, for example, speaks and sings through globular pottery flutes. Transverse horns, made of wood, cow horn, elephant tusk, or metal and played in ensembles, have often been associated with kings and chiefs. They accompany rulers and may play exclusively for royal courts. A Kpelle paramount chief sent his ensemble of six ivory trumpets trimmed in leopard skin to honor President William Tolbert on his 1976 inauguration. In the Asante area of Ghana, local chiefs historically kept short horns, while paramount chiefs maintained long horn ensembles. The Ba-Benzele of the Central African forest play a flute that rapidly leaps from low to high registers. Ba-Benzele performers may alternate between the voice and the flute, singing and playing in similar tone colors.

Evidence shows that African music has always changed, even if some forms have changed more rapidly than others. With increasing travel and mass media, the pace of change has quickened, and contexts for performance are shifting. Christian church groups in Liberia send representatives to the United States each year to learn the latest African-American gospel styles for incorporation into their singing. Even villagers living in the far interior sport hair styles and dress patterns of international popular music stars. One musical group I recorded in a village some distance from a motor road was delighted when an audience member, in offering a token of appreciation, pretended to write a check, showing awareness of the modern economy and how banks transfer money in urban areas.

Numerous countries today support troupes that select local dances and songs for presentation on local or international stages, adjusting their performance to suit the expectations of audiences. Peter Adegboyega Badegjo's opera *Asa Ibile Yoruba* ('The Ways of the Land of the Yoruba') premiered before an enthusiastic audience in Schoenberg Hall on the campus of the University of California at Los Angeles. When the National Dance Troupe of Guinea performed at the Brooklyn Academy of Music in New York, they included a modified Poro ceremony, transforming the setting in radical ways.

Many schools in Africa have invited performers to teach children local styles, even in Western educational contexts. At school graduations, student troupes show off their newly acquired skills of dancing and choral singing. Competitions in southern Africa evoke lively interest, as choirs compete for prizes.

Music in Africa today accompanies a wide variety of events, involving dazzling arrays of instruments, costumes, movements, and forms, and sometimes juxtaposing the old and the new: a carved goblet drum may be played alongside a synthesizer or an electric guitar. The international world, in which performers oscillate between the global and the local, is very much in evidence. The Internet, MTV, and international popular music flavor and color local performances, as people incorporate many influences, shaping them in ingenious ways and presenting results that surprise and delight audiences.

REFERENCES

Davidson, Basil. 1964. *The African Past: Chronicles from Antiquity to Modern Times*. New York: Grosset and Dunlop.

Erlmann, Veit. 1996. *Nightsong: Performance, Power, and Practice in South Africa*. Chicago: University of Chicago Press.

Gibb, H. A. R. 1929. *Ibn Battuta, Travels in Africa and Asia*. London: Darf.

Nketia, J. H. Kwabena. 1973. "The Musician in Akan Society." In *The Traditional Artists in African Societies*, ed. Warren L. d'Azevedo, 79–100. Bloomington: Indiana University Press.

Park, Mungo. 1860. *Travels in the Interior of Africa*. Edinburgh: Adam and Charles Black.

Stone, Ruth M. 1976. "Field journal for 1975–76." Unpublished.

———. 1982. *Let the Inside Be Sweet: The Interpretation of Music Event among the Kpelle of Liberia*. Bloomington: Indiana University Press.

———. 1985. "In Search of Time in African Music." *Music Theory Spectrum* 7:139–148.

Part 2
Issues and Processes in African Music

Music in Africa is part of a tightly connected bundle of arts that also include dance, drama, and folklore. A study of these performing traditions reveals the importance of such topics as sound, technology, time, religion, and the migration of populations both within and beyond the continent. By observing the ways in which these processes affect musical expression, we gain an understanding of how music in Africa is firmly embedded in its many societies.

The *kwela* embouchure demonstrated by
Donald Kachamba. Photo by Gerhard Kubik.

Notation and Oral Tradition
Kay Kaufman Shelemay

Indigenous Musical Notations
Musical Transcripton in Africa
African Use of Western Notation

African music presents a notational paradox. Africans transmitted most of their musics orally, without indigenous forms of written representation, but their musical traditions stand among those most frequently sampled for transcription in foreign notational systems. Scholarly discussion of African musical styles has usually relied on systems of music writing to capture aural phenomena otherwise resistant to analysis, whether or not the discussion has explicitly acknowledged the centrality of the process of transcription. Any notational discussion of African musical traditions must therefore consider two distinct, yet related, subjects: the indigenous technologies Africans employed to transmit and convey their own musics, and the ways African musics have been transmitted and notated, primarily by outsiders, both within Africa, and to a broader world.

The word *notation*, derived from the Latin *notare* 'to mark', is conventionally defined as "the use of a system of signs or symbols," while a single unit of the same, the *note*, is defined as "a mark or token by which a thing may be known" (Webster 1978:1224). In practice, Western presumptions of literacy constrain these definitions, and locate considerations of representations primarily within written (or printed) technologies. As a study of the relationship between dance motion and artistic icon has proved (Thompson 1974), full consideration of indigenous African representations of music requires a broader framework, which may include other forms of the symbolic representation of music in, and as, performance. Additionally, through electronic notation of music on tape, video, and film, twentieth-century technologies of recording have provided new forms of representation within Africa, and have been integrated into the process of transcription as a source of, or model for, various written notations.

A second issue is the geographical boundaries of an inquiry into African notation. Any discussion of African music is incomplete, because of the size of the continent, the diversity of its musical traditions, and the massive body of scholarship these materials have generated. To limit its range and complexity, this discussion will exclude North Africa, which contrasts with most of the rest of the continent, in having generated an extensive corpus of indigenous written sources, some of which contain forms of musical representation. Developed largely within an Islamic cultural framework, and nourished by cultural trends from regions of West and Central Asia, North African musical sources have for decades received close attention from scholars, and are more properly treated elsewhere (Farmer 1957:453–454; Wright 1978:216–244).

INDIGENOUS MUSICAL NOTATIONS

Discussion is compounded by insufficient historical study of written African sources. Until the fifteenth century, such sources were evidently rare: except for indigenous Ethiopian manuscripts in Ge'ez (the liturgical language of the Christian church in Ethiopia), writings of foreign travelers and geographers in classical languages and Arabic predominated (Djait 1981). After that century, autochthonous African literatures developed, first in Arabic and then in indigenous languages; scribes wrote the earliest contributions in Arabic script, but later contributions used the Latin alphabet.

The earliest West African texts in indigenous script were produced by the Vai in 1833. The beginning of the twentieth century saw the invention of a special script in Cameroon (Hrbek 1981:135–136). However, no forms of written musical representation emerged from these West African societies, nor has music writing been documented among other peoples of Central, Southern, or East Africa.

Music writing in Ethiopia

The most exceptional example of a written form of musical representation in Africa is an indigenous notational system in Ethiopia, a modern nation-state in the Eastern Horn, with historical roots of nearly two millenia in the Aksumite Empire. After the conversion of its emperor (A.D. 332), Ethiopia became a Christian country, and by the sixth century had its own literature and script in Ge'ez. Though it maintained close ties with the Coptic Church of Egypt (which until 1950 appointed the Ethiopian patriarch), its church was otherwise independent, and developed a distinctive liturgy, associated with a complex musical system.

History

The writing of Ethiopian liturgical texts in parchment manuscripts dates back to the earliest periods of Ge'ez literary activity, but the Ethiopian Christian musical tradition (*zēmā* 'chant') was for many centuries transmitted orally. A change occurred when a cataclysmic invasion by Muslim forces between 1529 and 1541 destroyed most churches and monasteries, and devastated much of Ethiopia's literary heritage. In what must have been a response to the near destruction of their musical and liturgical traditions, and an attempt to ensure transmission in the future, Ethiopian clerics in the mid-sixteenth century invented *melekket* 'signs', a system of musical notation. According to a manuscript of that period, "at the time of King Galawdewos [1549–1559], there appeared Azzaj Gera and Azzaj Ragu'el, priests trained in *zēmā*. And they began to make rules for the *melekket* of the *Deggwā* [hymnary] and taught the priests of Tadbaba Maryam, which this prince had built" (Basset 1881:336). Other sources mentioning Gera's and Ragu'el's contributions imply that the notation may have derived in part from earlier indigenous models, of which all evidence disappeared during the invasion. Whatever the precedents for the sixteenth-century innovations in music writing (and they do not seem to be widespread, or to predate the fifteenth century), the earliest surviving manuscript with musical notation dates from the sixteenth century.

The church has maintained the *melekket*: in handwriting on parchment, using medieval scribal techniques, Ethiopian students, as part of their training, still copy notated manuscripts. The continuity in the manuscript tradition, and its perpetua-

FIGURE 1   Ethiopian church notation for the
Day of Saint John (*Masehafa Deggwa* 1959:1).

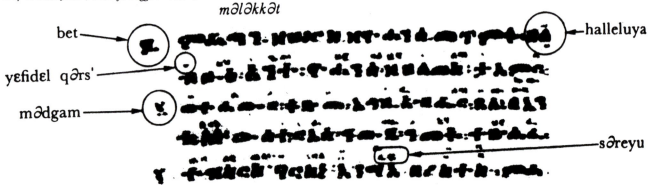

tion in performance, have made possible the combination of ethnographic research
with traditional source-and-text critical studies, permitting an understanding of this
African musical notation as transmitted and performed (Shelemay and Jeffery 1993).

Structure

The Ethiopian notational system primarily consists of some 650 signs, the *melekket*.
Each sign consists of one or more characters from the Ge'ez syllabary. Deriving from,
and serving as an abbreviation for, a word or phrase from the text of a well-known
liturgical piece (known within the tradition as a portion), each sign cues the particular melody associated with that source text. Each sign cues a short melody, not an
individual pitch. When a *melekket* occurs above a word of another text from the liturgy, it indicates that the singer should chant that text to the melody associated with
the abbreviated word or phrase. Figure 1 is an example of Ethiopian church notation,
annotated to show the types of signs discussed below.

Slightly more than one hundred *melekket* make up a special class of signs, the *bɛt*
'house', abbreviations that identify the melodic group or family of which some liturgical portions are members. Unlike the interlinear *melekket*, a sign of a *bɛt* occurs in
the margin beside a text of a chant, signaling the text's relationship to other texts of
the same genre; each sign derives from the textual incipit of a particularly important
chant, which serves as the "model" for an entire "house."

In addition to the signs derived from the syllabary, the notation employs three
other types. The *yafidal qers* 'shape of the signs' prescribe aspects of articulation, continuity, placement of melismas, motion, and vocal style (figure 2). Interlinear, often
modifying a particular *melekket*, these signs are *yezat* 'sustain', *ch'erat* 'accent', *darat*
'in the throat', *hedat* 'speed up', *rekrek* 'slide', *qenāt* 'melisma', *defāt* 'bend the voice',
ders 'cadence', *qerts* 'abrupt cutoff', *anber* 'cadence'.

In liturgical performance, many portions follow the word *halleluya*, sung from
one to ten times. Just before the beginning of each chant, the Ge'ez word glossed

FIGURE 2   The *yafidal quers'* in Ethiopian chant (Makonnen n.d.:7).

italicized term	definition	italicized term	definition
yezat	sustain	*ch'erat*	accent
darat	in the throat	*hedat*	speed up
rekrek	slide	*qenāt*	melisma
defāt	bend the voice	*ders*	cadence
qert'	abrupt cutoff	*anber*	cadence

"in," and a red numeral placed afterward, specify the number of repetitions: "in 1," "in 2," and so on. The halleluyas are sung to melodies derived from the bet.

A final type of sign is the *medgem*, a number placed in the margin alongside a portion, to specify how many times in liturgical performance it repeats.

Modal categories

The Ethiopian *melekket* divide into three categories, reflecting their correlation with one of the three classes of melody in the Ethiopian Christian musical system. Thus, knowledge of the notational signs both derives from and reinforces broader notions of musical organization. But while the notational system carries considerable information about the melodic and liturgical organization of the Ethiopian Christian liturgy, it does not provide a guide to specific pitches: it represents and cues phrases that have a substantially fixed textual and melodic identity; it leaves room for individual singers to reshape the basic musical materials according to contemporary, local, and personal norms.

Oral transmission

To read the notation, a singer must know all the notational signs, plus the melodies of the portions from which they derive. In practice, however, the *melekket* serve primarily as a mnemonic aid during training or study. During the day, musicians in training learn skills in reading and writing; at night, they practice the chants strictly from memory. During liturgical performances, most musicians sing from memory, without referring to notated manuscripts.

The Ethiopian Christian notational system does more than cue the melodic content of liturgical portions. It fuses word and melody, the smallest segments within the musical system, and revisits the learning process. In oral study, outside the context of a complete liturgical performance, the teacher often chants liturgical portions phrase by phrase; students repeat, in units that approximate the length of individual *melekket*. The notational system therefore emanates from, and refers to, the processes of oral acquisition.

Ethiopian musical notation is not a guide for the uninitiated: without prior knowledge of the oral tradition, it is indecipherable. It also does not provide a complete map for the Ethiopian musician, but encapsulates enough information to guide someone already immersed in the liturgical and musical materials. In contrast to the linearity of Western staff notation, the *melekket* symbolize a multidimensional, referential system. They intersect with the whole tradition at the microlevel of melodic segments, at a midlevel of portion type, and at a macrolevel of liturgical occasion. Notation implicitly encodes a broader world of practice. It draws on both the knowledge received from teachers, and the singer's personal experience. Furthermore, the notational system is in flux: each notated manuscript represents an open window on the processes of transmission: it merges tradition with individual innovation.

The notational system does not convey important aspects of the musical system and performance practice. Most strikingly, beyond subtle cues for tempo change associated with one of the *yafidal qers'*, the *melekket* give few hints about rhythmic

tusona   Graphic configuration of dots circumscribed by lines of the Luchazi culture of Angola and Zambia

beni ng'oma   A synthesis of dance and competitive modes, influenced by colonial brass-band music in East Africa

Orchestra Ethiopia   Ethiopian ensemble founded in 1963 for a modern presentation of traditional music

organization. The lack of notated rhythmic detail is a potentially important omission, for on holidays, the Ethiopian liturgy is accompanied by elaborate drumming, which demands years of special study. Yet other than occasional signs for choral entries, no written cues for the drumming exist. However, musicians name fixed rhythmic patterns, traced in the air during liturgical performance through motions of the prayer staff and sistrum, and danced during rituals (Shelemay 1989:184–190). Therefore, rhythmic aspects of the Ethiopian chant tradition may be notated kinesthetically, not tied to written guides, but traced in space by the musicians in the act of performing.

Other indigenous systems

To achieve a fuller understanding of what may be other indigenous representations of African music, scholars may need to move away from Western concepts of notation as music writing. Scholars have done little substantive research on this subject; yet the literature contains provocative references, such as the observation that Ewe call drumstrokes by "spoken syllables (vocables), which, in effect, constitute an oral notation" (Locke 1982:245). Because of the chance that scholars working within a framework shaped by literacy have overlooked alternative forms of musical representation in Africa, such suggestions merit discussion.

Angolan sand ideographs

In a study of space time concepts in Luchazi culture (of Eastern Angola and Northwestern Zambia), Gerhard Kubik discusses Angolan sand ideographs, *tusona* (sing. *kasona*), graphic configurations of dots circumscribed by lines, usually drawn with the fingers on a plane of white sand, on house walls, or more rarely, on objects (1987a:57). *Tusona* provide visual symbols of deep structures in the cultural heritage of the Ngangela-speaking cultures of Angola. Artists, who draw them to convey ideas about existing institutions, to stimulate fantasy, to abstract logical thinking, and to aid meditation, can give verbal explanations of the ideographs, some of which have long narratives and function as mnemonic aids.

While acknowledging that Angolan musicians do not derive musical connotations from the ideographs, and that he cannot find parallels between ideographic construction principles and music of the area of Angola where the ideographs occur, Kubik argues for relationships between the ideographs and music in more distant regions (notably among the Kiganda and in Cameroon). Space and time, he suggests, universally give rise to synesthetic experiences, because distance can be spatial or temporal; therefore, spatial distance can symbolize temporal distance. This hypothesis raises methodological problems in postulating a historical connection between Bantu traditions across different perceptual realms and remote geographical regions, but its exposition on the synesthetic experience of space and time challenges future scholarship. The documentation of "path images" of performances of tayil traced on the ground by Mapuche women in southwestern Argentina (Robertson 1979) confirms that such forms of musical notation exist elsewhere.

Composite systems

In urban Africa of the 1990s, multiple changes have led to several composite forms of expression, such as the *beni ng'oma*, a synthesis of indigenous dance and competitive modes, influenced by colonial brass-band music (Ranger 1975). A similar confluence of internal precedents and outside notational influences led to the invention of a system of music writing by Orchestra Ethiopia, an Ethiopian folklore ensemble. Founded in 1963 at the Creative Arts Centre of the then Haile Selassie (now Addis Ababa) University, it began as a forum for "modern presentation of orchestral songs through the traditional musical modes and instruments of Ethiopia" (Shelemay 1983:572). From disparate provinces, it recruited solo musicians, who together played a pan-Ethiopian repertory, performed in concert and on television. Its leaders quickly faced difficulties in getting the group to "play in symphony" and "adhere to set tunes and melodies" (p. 572). That the notational system they designed draws on concepts from both Ethiopian church notation and Western notation is not surprising: at the national music school (in Addis Ababa), all had seen both kinds of notation, and one had studied music in the United States.

Subsumed under the indigenous designation *melekket*, the orchestra's notational system uses four classes of signs (figure 3): alphabetic, diagrammatic, pictographic, numerical. Additional numerical signs specify strings or instrumental fingerings. If Ethiopian church notation is the clear inspiration for signs 1–15, many of the diagrammatic signs have precedents in Western rhythmic and percussive notation. In contrast, the pictographic signs are probably an innovation, independent of Ethiopian and Western models.

In Dakar, Senegal, at the École des Arts, *kora* player Mamadou Kouyaté developed a composite notational system (Knight 1972:29). To meet similar challenges of musical performance and pedagogy, additional composite systems may exist in other African urban centers.

MUSICAL TRANSCRIPTION IN AFRICA

From early dates, outsiders' systems of music writing have entered the discussion of African music. Long before 1885 (when musical scholarship formally emerged), travelers who encountered African music in live performance tried to notate it. Many of the earliest transcribers provided contextual information. They described or drew musical instruments, and related whatever details they could about musical content. Among the earliest such examples is a rendering by William Burchell (figure 4),which incorporates a drawing of a named musician playing the *goura* (musical bow), with a musical transcription in staff notation. After detailing the exertion necessary for the musician to produce the sound, Burchell describes his process:

> I was . . . obliged to exercise two faculties at the same time, one to listen to and learn the notes he was playing, so as to enable me to write them down correctly, the other to draw his figure and portrait. The accompanying plate presents a likeness of him and is a copy of the drawing made on the spot. Beneath are added the notes expressed in the manner in which they were played, or at least as they sounded to my ear. . . . The whole piece played once through occupied just seventy seconds,

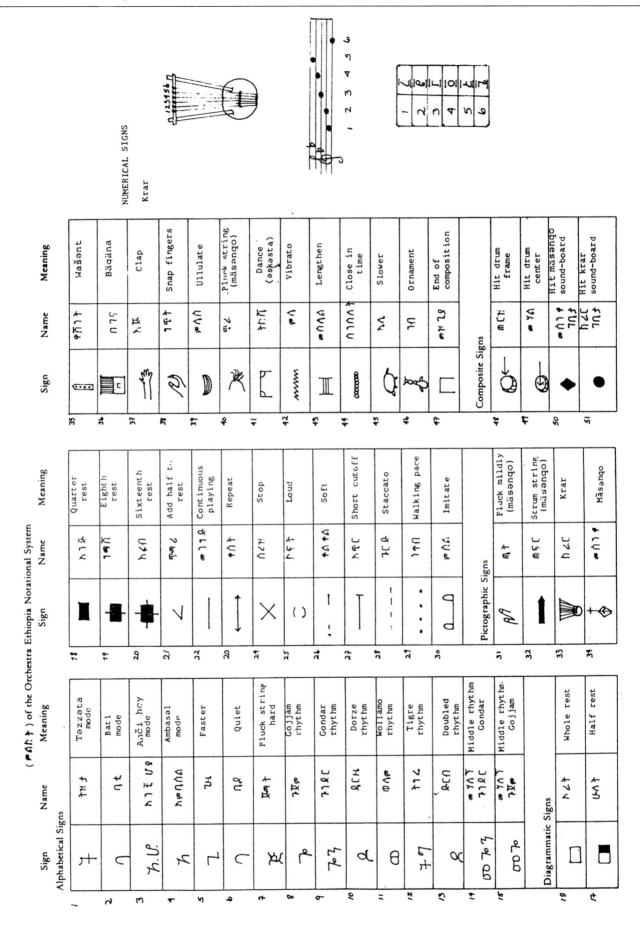

NUMERICAL SIGNS

Krar

(ምልክት) of the Orchestra Ethiopia Notational System

Alphabetical Signs

No.	Meaning
1	Tazzeta mode
2	Bati mode
3	Anči hčy mode
4	Ambasel mode
5	Faster
6	Quiet
7	Pluck string hard
8	Gojjam rhythm
9	Gondar rhythm
10	Dorze rhythm
11	Wollamo rhythm
12	Tigre rhythm
13	Doubled rhythm
14	Middle rhythm Gondar
15	Middle rhythm Gojjam

Diagrammatic Signs

No.	Meaning
16	Whole rest
17	Half rest
18	Quarter rest
19	Eighth rest
20	Sixteenth rest
21	Add half to rest
22	Continuous playing
23	Repeat
24	Stop
25	Loud
26	Soft
27	Short cutoff
28	Staccato
29	Walking pace
30	Imitate

Pictographic Signs

No.	Meaning
31	Pluck mildly (mäsänqo)
32	Scrum string (mäsänqo)
33	Krar
34	Mäsänqo
35	Wašent
36	Bäqäna
37	Clap
38	Snap fingers
39	Ullulate
40	Pluck string (mäsänqo)
41	Dance (askasta)
42	Vibrato
43	Lengthen
44	Close in time
45	Slower
46	Ornament
47	End of composition

Composite Signs

No.	Meaning
48	Hit drum frame
49	Hit drum center
50	Hit mäsänqo sound-board
51	Hit krar sound-board

FIGURE 4 "Bubi of Fernando Po Playing upon the Musical Bow" (Burchell 1810–1812, cited in Balfour, 1902).

FIGURE 3 (*opposite*) Four classes of notational signs used by Orchestra Ethiopia.

and was repeated without variations. (Burchell 1810–1812:458, cited in Balfour 1902:162)

Edward Bowdich, who sought to transcribe from memory in Western notation the West African musical styles he encountered, published another early transcription (figure 5). Bowdich comments on the problem of producing a descriptive transcription that does not distort the music of another culture: "To have attempted anything like arrangement, beyond what the annexed airs naturally possess, would have altered them, and destroyed the intention of making them known in their original character. I have not even dared to insert a flat or a sharp" (Bowdich 1824:197).

In addition to reflections on the processes and problems of representing in Western notation an unfamiliar music, some early transcriptions contain what has been verified to be extraordinarily accurate musical data. Visiting Zimbabwe, the German traveler and geologist Carl Mauch encountered the *mbira dzavadzimu*, and recorded in his journals of 1869–1872 the earliest sketch of that instrument, with a chart of its tuning, plus three transcriptions of instrumental patterns for three songs. Comparison of Mauch's tunings with those from transcriptions Andrew Tracey made some eighty-eight years later proved the two to be identical (Kubik 1971).

Other transcribers were less concerned with method and precise description than with the production of prescriptive notation. They harmonized African songs, and suggested that "some of these airs seem capable of ready adaptation to bugle or band marches"; this effort, they thought, extended "a nice compliment to the nations whose melodies have interested so many" (Moloney 1889:297).

As transcription became a standard part of the practice of comparative musicology, a few general theoretical discussions treated the subject cross-culturally (Abraham and von Hornbostel 1909–1910). In the study of African music, musical scholars came to use transcription almost universally; but during the first half of the twentieth century, with a few exceptions, explicit comments about the process of transcription are absent from their writings.

Only after 1950, with the emergence of technologies that both reshaped the conventional process of transcription and provided electronic aids, a new phase of theoretical discourse about transcription began (C. Seeger 1958). Ethnomusicological discussion tended to center on the reliability of conventional methods of transcription versus notations prepared with or by mechanical devices, but Africanists' interest in transcription focused more on other concerns: first, problems in notating multipart African music in a manner that made it amenable to analysis (Arom 1976:483); and second, a debate about whether such systems of representation, and

FIGURE 5 "The Oldest Ashantee and Warsaw Air," transcribed by T. Edward Bowdich (1824 [1819]:197).

prescriptive transcriptions　Notation that indicates to performers how to create particular musical sounds

direct transcription　Writing down music notations during live performances or from memory

inherent rhythms　Rhythms that may be heard by the listener, but are not played as such by any of the performers

the analyses stemming from them, could, or should, reflect indigenous perspectives on the music (Berliner 1978:53).

Concepts behind transcription

A recurrent issue in notating African music is the question of what percentage of a musical event or recording ought to be transcribed. Within discussions, many scholars incorporate brief transcriptions, which one source terms "specimens of tunes" (Kirby 1965:115). A. M. Jones argued forcefully against this practice. He recommended the transcription of full scores with "complete" performances of African music and dance (Jones 1959:7). Part of his argument was that these transcriptions were the necessary first step in achieving musical understanding, as well as the "accurate and definitive statement of facts" (Jones 1958:14). Virtually all transcriptions of African music have been thought by their preparers to be objective, and, at least in part, to serve purposes of description. Simha Arom, who intends his transcriptions to impart the germane aspects of pitch, duration, and form, thereby to provide "a satisfactory picture of . . . structural principles" (1991:170–171), endorses this argument. Some African musical studies have consisted entirely of descriptive transcriptions of recorded music, analyzed by the transcriber according to conventional (Western) notions such as melodic type, rhythm, and form (Brandel 1961; Günther 1964).

Whether or not transcriptions of African music were classed by their realizers as either descriptive or prescriptive (Seeger 1958), staff notation with metric markings and bar lines widely served both purposes; within the work of a single scholar, the same notation can serve both to describe, for analysis, one West African style of drumming (Locke 1982), and "to function like a score, guiding the instrumentalist toward adequate performance" (Locke 1987:4). The most important examples of prescriptive transcriptions (Jones 1957) are in Western notation, so they will be accessible to the audience for which they were produced.

The practice and discussion of musical transcription also provide a setting in which major theoretical assumptions about African music have resonated. The debate over the nature of time reckoning in African music, in particular the concepts of timeline and downbeat (Merriam 1981; Stone 1986) have provided a background for all attempts to notate African music. Yet how Western notation represents African rhythm is often markedly similar, whether the author's intent is to identify and notate aspects of African rhythm according to non-African notions such as "hemiola" (Brandel 1959), or to link concepts of African rhythm with indigenous ideas of the people who perform the music (Chernoff 1979). Through transcription, scholars have tested basic assumptions about aspects of African rhythm. They have explored musical-analytical issues (Agawu 1986), the relations between drum rhythm and language (Locke and Agbeli 1980; Agawu 1987), fixed improvisations (Rycroft 1958; Erlmann 1985; Agawu 1990), and connected motoric and acoustic images (Kubik 1962).

Sources for musical transcriptions

To evaluate systems of musical notation, one must scrutinize the transcription process. For transcriptions of African music, scholars have used varied sources: live performances, sound recordings, and films.

Live performances

Before the age of recordings, transcribers necessarily worked during live performances or from memory; but long after sound recording had become a standard tool, some Africanists continued to undertake "direct transcription." This undertaking became an explicit tenet of the philosophy of several leaders of musical research in Africa. For the researcher,

> nothing can take the place of the discipline entailed in the hard grind of direct transcription. . . . It brings us face to face with the fundamental problems involved and develops that detached critical attitude which takes nothing for granted and seeks for subtle checks within the score to prove whether the transcription is valid or not. (Jones 1958:12)

The need for observing different voices or instruments when transcribing multipart music likely contributed to the continuing emphasis on "direct transcription" in African ethnomusicology, long after new technologies had made it unnecessary.

Sound recordings

The recording industry entered southern Africa early in the first decade of the twentieth century (Coplan 1979:143), but regular recording on a large scale did not begin in sub-Saharan areas until the late 1940s (Gronow 1981:253). With the beginning of LP technology (just before 1950), scholars began to participate actively in recording for archival and commercial purposes. Hugh Tracey, viewing the LP as a tool to save endangered musical traditions on the continent, made sound recording his primary activity (Shelemay 1991:283). His recorded materials played an important role in the study of African music, and made possible historical perspectives of a substantial time depth on an array of African repertories from diverse geographical locales. Recordings also enabled scholars to transcribe and analyze African music without having undertaken fieldwork on the continent. An example of the latter phenomenon is Brandel's 1961 work, which contains fifty-two transcriptions, all prepared from field and commercial recordings made after 1930, some drawn from disks released by Hugh Tracey (Brandel 1961:107). Brandel fully transcribed the recordings, and measured pitch in cents. She usually included text underlay, but the roughly phonetic transliterations, made without knowledge of the languages involved, are problematic. For descriptive and comparative analysis, Sue Carole DeVale used field recordings made by Klaus Wachsmann and Hugh Tracey (DeVale 1985:286).

Africanists' resistance to transcription from recorded sources alone is manifest in a review of Brandel's book, which deplores the idea that the lack of firsthand "experience of the originals" is no bar to "an adequate method" of conducting research on them (Kubik 1962b:116). In Africanist scholarship, the strong censure of transcription solely from recorded sources emerges primarily from sensitivity to a perceptual quirk that occurs when listening to multipart music. Termed the "problem of inherent rhythms," it involves rhythms that "may appear to be heard by the listener but are not played as such by any of the performers" (Kubik 1962b:117). Thus, in African instrumental music, the "image as it is heard and the image as it is played are often different from each other" (Kubik 1962a:33).

While concern about perceptual issues has not prevented Africanists from using

Musical transcription is a complex and multifaceted process, but it generates a visual product, which, to permit analytical examination, can be fixed in time.

sound recordings in the process of transcription (usually alongside careful observation of performance in the field), it has both informed their use of these technologies, and encouraged innovation. Recognizing the problems inherent in "composite recordings" of complex African rhythms, Jones proposed making "analytical records," on which each contributor would play separately (1958:11–12). Arom (1976) described a detailed methodology for preparing analytical recordings that could serve the purposes of transcription. Paul Berliner (1977:1) published an analytical recording of the sort Jones proposed.

Films

In addition to the problem of distinguishing between what the musician plays and what the ear perceives, Gerhard Kubik suggested (1962a:40) that African drumming sets up inaudible cross-rhythms between the movements of a musician's hands (the motoric image) and the pattern actually emerging in sound (the acoustic image). Kubik's proposal relates closely to the Africanist music scholars' long-standing concern with kinetic concepts of rhythm (Blacking 1955).

Seeking better to understand the interrelationships of motoric and acoustic images, Kubik proposed a methodology to transcribe multipart Mangwilo xylophone music from filmstrips (1965, 1971, 1987b). He also used sound recordings (1965:3). Though the aim of his method is primarily analysis, the method has a potentially prescriptive quality: "the final transcription is a kind of score"; from it, performers can reproduce the music (1971:32).

FIGURE 6   Notation for vocal and instrumental phrasing in a Zulu song for musical bow (after Rycroft 1975:63).

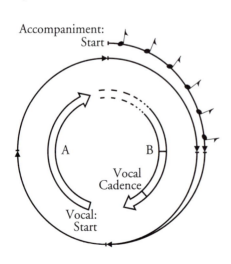

Visual representation

Musical transcription is a complex and multifaceted process, but it generates a visual product, which, to permit analytical examination, can be fixed in time. Scholars in African music have used many kinds of representations. The variables that shape the notational process in turn help determine the final form of a transcription. These include the nature of the musical tradition, the sources of the sounds, the problem under consideration, and (not infrequently) the intended audience.

Following the standard bias of staff notation, most transcriptions by non-Africans have sought to capture specific pitches and rhythms, even when using an alternative system of representation. However, some transcriptions incorporate elements beyond pitch and rhythm. Some individuals have sought to transcribe speech tones, often in relation to melodic contour, using diagrammatic notations or graphs (Carrington 1943; Blacking 1967:199; Simon 1989:198–199). Occasionally, novel diagrams have represented the structures and forms of phrases. Figure 6 reproduces a notation that diagrammatically shows how Zulu vocal and instrumental phrases interrelate.

Conventional staff notation

Nearly all published transcriptions of African music use conventional staff notation (Gray 1991). It often serves by default, and most frequently appears in sources where no rationale for the system of transcription occurs. Scholars often select it because of its ubiquity and easy readability. Occasionally, it "translates" another notational system. Kubik says, though "the graphic notation shows much more clearly than conventional notation what happens in this music, I have nevertheless transferred the graphic scores into staff to help the reader who might not be accustomed to the graphic notation" (Kubik 1965:37).

The drawbacks of using Western symbolic-linear notation for representing music outside the Western cultural orbit (Seeger 1958:169–171) apply to African music. There further exists the chance that the major theoretical issues in African musical studies, in particular the debate over aspects of rhythm, derive in part from the inability of staff notation to represent the complexities of multipart musics, and its tendency to force African music into a rigid, binary time continuum. Staff notation subtly embodies Western musical traits, and tends to transmit them to the music transcribed (Koetting 1970:125). For these reasons, African musical scholarship has seen an unusual amount of activity in designing new systems of musical representation.

Modified staff notation

The most straightforward manner by which scholars have tried to adjust staff notation to the exigencies of transcription followed widespread ethnomusicological precedent: scholars modified it with special signs. In the Africanist literature, many examples of modified staff notation exist; they serve both descriptive and prescriptive purposes. Rose Brandel's transcriptions (1961) employ it, modified by signs for raised or lowered pitch, glissando, and vocal register. To mark the occurrence of spoken interjections, she includes "clarifying phrases" (p. 120), which describe aspects of vocal style: "breathy-explosive" (p. 118), dancers' inhalations (p. 150), and the possible presence of harmonics (p. 169).

Jones (1959) uses conventional Western symbols, but tells readers to interpret them specially: at the right of the clef, he brackets sharps and flats, not to define a tonality, but to sharpen or flatten the notes "right through the piece unless accidentals occur"; they show "the special tuning of the drum for the particular dance." Though he used staff notation, he prepared his transcriptions from recordings enhanced with a mechanical aid: a drummer tapped on metal plates, which printed patterns on paper strips. He converted the patterns into staff notation.

Graphs

Primarily for transcribing the music of membranophones and idiophones, scholars of African music have developed graphic notations. The most widely discussed may be TUBS, the Time Unit Box System, developed at University of California at Los Angeles in 1962, for didactic purposes in West African drumming (Koetting 1970:125–126). TUBS uses boxes of equal length, put in horizontal sequence (figure 7). Within a piece of music, each box represents one instance of the fastest pulse. If no sound occurs in a time unit, its box remains empty. The box receives symbols for pitch, loudness, tone quality, and carrying power (p. 127).

For the xylophone, Gerhard Kubik designed a graphic notation that he characterized as a "kind of tablature" (Kubik 1972:31). Like a graph, the notation uses separate strips of five-line graph paper, but each line is equivalent to one of the five keys of the xylophone, with the respective hand identified by empty or black circles. The notation thus reads like a tablature. These transcriptions are of particular interest

FIGURE 7   Transcription of one of three ensemble pieces performed by Ashanti master drummer Kwasi Badu. The transcription shows the relationship of the *dawuro* 'gong pattern' and the *kete* 'master drum' (Koetting 1970:136).

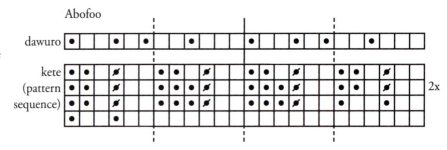

because Kubik made them from silent films, without reference to sound; marking off equal boxes, the vertical lines represent a single frame of film, not rhythmic values. The graphic notation of frames is rewritten to present basic rhythmic pulses; a third and final transcription is a "type of score," which shows the number of repetitions of each structure; from it, an instrumentalist can perform (p. 32).

Of particular concern to many Africanists has been the limited ability of conventional staff notation to convey aspects of musical sound such as texture. For the notation of texture in Ugandan music, Sue Carole DeVale developed a graphic system, applied to recorded sound of harp and voice. It employs a square time frame. Within each frame, the vertical placement of symbols shows the density of sounds, their intensity, and their volume (figure 8). Scholars have also used graphs to compare master drum rhythms with speech tone patterns, showing their close correspondence (Locke and Agbeli 1980:48–49).

Tablature

Tablature places numbers or letters on a diagram that resembles the strings or keys of an instrument; it specifies the location of the fingers on keys or strings (Read 1969:21). Like its historical use in Renaissance Europe, where it widely served for the lute, tablature has been employed in African music to notate music of chordophones, such as the *kora*. Because standard staff notation cannot adequately convey the playing technique of the *kora*, Roderic Knight designed a tablature (figure 9) that shows the interaction and coordination of the right and left hands (1972:30).

Other notational systems

Other scholars have innovated systems of visual representation idiosyncratic to a particular musical tradition or a specific analytic goal. For Ghanaian drumming, Moses Serwadda and Hewitt Pantaleoni designed a system of transcription, modeled after Labanotation (Serwadda and Pantaleoni 1968). For descriptive and analytical purposes, this notation represents the movements that produce sound, rather than the sound itself. Figure 10 reproduces one sign from the system. Reading from the bot-

FIGURE 8   Textural notation for harp and voice (DeVale 1985).

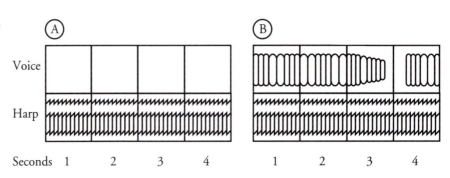

FIGURE 9   Four-column tablature for the strings of the *kora* (Knight 1971:31).

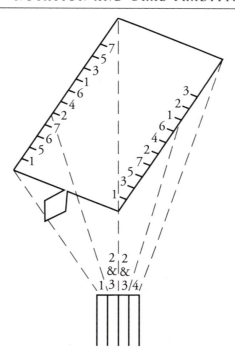

FIGURE 10   Notation for the slapstroke in Ghanaian drumming (Pantaleoni 1972:6).

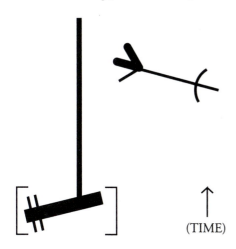

(TIME)

tom to the top, the action of the left hand occurs first; the vertical line drawn upward from the left hand extends its pressing action through the moment when the right hand contacts the skin of the drum (Pantaleoni 1972:6).

Scholars have developed notational systems for special purposes, including convenience of representation. Hugh Tracey's analytical system for Chopi orchestral music conveys information in symbols that any typewriter can make (Tracey 1970:161). Knight has produced transcriptions of Mandinka *balafon* music in a numeric notational system (Jessup n.d.:78).

Occasionally, scholars use multiple forms of representation. Alongside graph notation, Artur Simon displays conventional staff notation and Western percussion notation (1989:216–217). Figure 11 illustrates Kubik's use of staff notation to translate xylophone graph notation.

A study of Ethiopian Christian chant contains multiple representations, including reproductions of indigenous Ethiopian notation, transcriptions in conventional staff notation, and electronically produced graphs (Shelemay and Jeffery 1993). The 650 indigenous Ethiopian notational signs (*melekket*) are further represented by alphanumeric designations (like "G1" for the first *melekket* in the Ge'ez mode, cued to a "dictionary of signs" in the publication). The alphanumeric symbols are subsequently used in charts comparing notation from a cross-section of dated manuscripts and are superimposed on staff transcriptions to show the relationship between the sign as notated in manuscripts and as actually sung.

AFRICAN USE OF WESTERN NOTATION

As a result of the European missionary and colonial presence on the continent, staff notation was introduced to Africa and used by Africans. In an acknowledgment at the end of a late nineteenth-century article on West African music, the author thanks "two native gentlemen of considerable musical promise, Mr. A. C. Willoughby and Mr. O. E. Macaulay, of Lagos, whose English education has enabled them to commit to music the Yoruba, Dahomey, and Houssa melodies" (Moloney 1889:297). Some of the transcriptions included in that article therefore may be among the first published by African musicians in Western notation. For transcription and analysis of oral traditions, twentieth-century African scholars have preferred to use staff notation

FIGURE II   Xylophone graph notation, translated into staff notation (Kubik 1989:38).

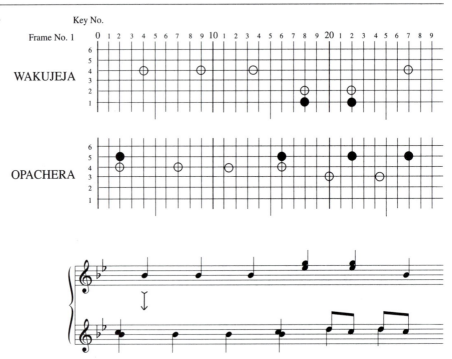

rather than alternative systems (Kyagambiddwa 1955; Nketia 1963; Ekwueme 1975–1976; Agawu 1987, 1990).

By the late twentieth century, Western musical notation, taught formally at schools of music in urban centers throughout the continent, had dispersed throughout Africa. Notated collections of African church music have circulated widely (Kaufman n.d.). In part a heritage from the colonial past, Western musical notation became domesticated and indigenized.

Tonic Sol-fa

Throughout Kenya and Tanzania, Tonic Sol-fa, introduced to East Africa by British music educator J. Curwen (1816–1888), widely serves in the transmission of Christian hymns (Gunderson 1991:44). It is placed above a staff: the vertical lines function as bars; the periods and dashes are rests (figure 12).

Transcription and the nature of scholarship

Attention to transcription in African musical studies has consistently characterized the work of scholars resident in Africa, and has often been published in the *Journal of the Society of African Music*, but there exists a broader international network of individuals engaged with transcription of oral tradition and an ongoing discourse about the subject of representation. Publications reflect much interaction between these

MANENO YOTE YA INJILI

1. Maneno yote ya Injili mitume, } (x2)
tangazeni pote duniani.

Haya sasa fungueni masikio, (x2)
Maneno ya Injili yaenezwe.

2. Yesu aliwaambia mitume: } (x2)
tangazeni pote duniani.

FIGURE 12 Tonic Sol-fa and staff notation in an East African hymnal (*Tumshangalie Bwana* 1988: 158–159).

scholars. Innovations in transcription have often entailed borrowing from a preexisting system. Knight's tablature for the kora draws on several different precedents: he borrows the rhythmic element of TUBS, while suggesting, "to maintain consistency with the examples of Labanotation and the Pantaleoni method, it should be read up" (Knight 1972:31).

In contrast to the decline of transcription in late-twentieth-century ethnomusicology, many scholars remain committed to musical transcription as an integral part of research in African music. Of particular interest is the response of Africanists to armchair ethnomusicologists, who transcribe music without studying it *in situ*. General ethnomusicology has criticized transcription based on sound recordings alone, because it separates music from the context of performance, and from broader fields of signification within the culture. In contrast, Africanist ethnomusicologists have largely rejected such efforts on perceptual grounds, believing that without the ability to see and hear music performed by live musicians, the scholar risks misinterpreting and misrepresenting the musical materials themselves. Scholarship on music in Africa has largely remained "music-centric," even as theoretical concerns of the discipline have elsewhere shifted to emphasize the humanistic and social aspects of music making.

REFERENCES

Abraham, Otto, and Erich M. von Hornbostel. 1909–1910. "Vorschläge für die Transkription exotischer Melodien." *Sammelbände der Internationalen Musikgesellschaft* 11:1–25.

Agawu, Kofi. 1986. "'Gi Dunu,' 'Nyekpadudo,' and the Study of West African Rhythm." *Ethnomusicology* 30(1):64–83.

———. 1987. "The Rhythmic Structure of West African Music." *Journal of Musicology* 5(3):400–418.

———. 1990. "Variation Procedures in Northern Ewe Song." *Ethnomusicology* 34(2):221–243.

Arom, Simha. 1976. "The Use of Play-Back Techniques in the Study of Oral Polyphonies." *Ethnomusicology* 20(3):483–519.

———. 1991. *African Polyphony and Polyrhythm,* trans. Martin Thom et al. Cambridge and Paris: Cambridge University Press and Editions de la Maison Des Sciences de L'Homme.

Balfour, Henry. 1902. "The *Goura,* A Stringed-Wind Musical Instrumental of the Bushmen and Hottentots." *Journal of the Anthropological Institute* 32:156–176, plus appendices.

Basset, M. René. 1881. "Etudes sur l'histoire d'Ethiopie." *Journal Asiatique,* 7th ser., 17:315–434.

Berliner, Paul F. 1977. *Africa: Shona Mbira Music.* New York: Nonesuch Records. LP disk.

———. 1978. *The Soul of Mbira.* Berkeley, Los Angeles, London: University of California Press.

Blacking, John. 1955. "Some Notes on a Theory of African Rhythm Advanced by Erich von Hornbostel." *African Music* 1(2):12–20.

———. 1967. *Venda Children's Songs.* Johannesburg: Witwatersrand University Press.

Bowdich, T. Edward. 1824 [1819]. "On the Music of the Ashantees," extracted in *The Harmonicon* 2:195–198.

Brandel, Rose. 1959. "The African Hemiola Style." *Ethnomusicology* 3(3):106–116.

———. 1961. *The Music of Central Africa: An Ethnomusicological Study.* The Hague: Martinus Nijhoff.

Carrington, John F. 1943. "The Tonal Structure of Kele (Lokele)." In *African Studies,* vol. 2, ed. J. D. Rheinallt Jones and C. M. Doke. Johannesburg: Witwatersrand University Press.

Chernoff, John Miller. 1979. *African Rhythm and African Sensibility.* Chicago: University of Chicago Press.

Coplan, David. 1979. "The African Musician and the Development of the Johannesburg Entertainment Industry, 1900-1960." *Journal of Southern African Studies* 5(2):135–164.

DeVale, Sue Carole. 1985. "Prolegomena to a Study of Harp and Voice Sounds in Uganda: A Graphic System for the Notation of Texture." *Selected Reports in Ethnomusicology,* vol. 5, ed. J. H. Kwabena Nketia and Jacqueline Cogdell DjeDje, 284–315. Los Angeles: University of California.

Djait, Hichem. 1981. "Written Sources before the Fifteenth Century." *General History of Africa,* 1, 87–113. Paris, London, Berkeley: Heinemann, California, UNESCO.

Ekwueme, Lazarun E. N. 1975–1976. "Structural Levels of Rhythm and Form in African Music." *African Music* 5(4):27–35.

Erlmann, Veit. 1985. "Model, Variation and Performance: Ful'be Praise-Song in Northern Cameroon." *Yearbook for Traditional Music* 17:88–112.

Farmer, Henry George. 1957. "The Music of Islam." In *The New Oxford History of Music,* vol. 1 (Ancient and Oriental Music), ed. Egon Wellesz, 421–477. Oxford: Oxford University Press.

Gray, John. 1991. *African Music: A Bibliographical Guide to the Traditional, Popular, Art, and Liturgical Musics of Sub-Saharan Africa.* Westport, Conn.: Greenwood Press.

Gronow, Pekka. 1981. "The Record Industry Comes to the Orient." *Ethnomusicology* 25(2):251–286.

Gunderson, Frank. 1991. "The History and Practice of Christian Gospel Hymnody in Swahili-Speaking East Africa." M.A. thesis, Wesleyan University.

Günther, Robert. 1964. *Musik in Rwanda. Ein Beitrag zur Musikethnologie Zentralafrikas.* Tervuren, Belgium: Musée Royal de L'Afrique Centrale.

Hrbek, Ivan. 1981. "Written Sources from the Fifteenth Century Onwards," *General History of Africa,* 1, 114–142. Paris, London, Berkeley: Heinemann, California, UNESCO.

Jessup, Lynne. N.d. *The Mandinka Balafon: An Introduction with Notation for Teaching.* N.p.: no publisher.

Jones, Arthur M. 1957. *Studies in African Music,* vol 2. London: Oxford University Press.

———. 1958. "On Transcribing African Music." *African Music* 2(1):11–14.

———. 1959. *Studies in African Music,* vol. 1. London: Oxford University Press.

Kaufman, Robert, ed. N.d. *African Church Music; Hymns from Many Countries.* Umtali, Rhodesia: All African Church Music Association.

Kirby, Percival R. 1965. *The Musical Instruments of the Native Races of South Africa.* Johannesburg: Witwatersrand University Press.

Knight, Roderic. 1972. "Towards a Notation and Tablature for the Kora." *African Music* 1(5):23–35.

Koetting, James. 1970. "Analysis and Notation of West African Drum Ensemble Music." *Selected Reports in Ethnomusicology,* vol. 1, no. 3. Los Angeles: University of California.

Kyagambiddwa, Joseph. 1955. *African Music from the Source of the Nile.* New York: Frederick Praeger.

Kubik, Gerhard. 1962a. "The Phenomenon of Inherent Rhythms in East and Central African Instrumental Music." *African Music* 1:33–42.

———. 1962b. Review of *The Music of Central Africa: An Ethnomusicological Study*, by Rose Brandel. *African Music* 1:116–118.

———. 1965. "Transcription of Mangwilo Xylophone Music from Film Strips." *African Music* 3(4):3–50.

———. 1971. "Carl Mauch's Mbira Musical Transcriptions of 1872." *Review of Ethnology* 3(10):73–80.

———. 1972. "Transcription of African Music from Silent Film: Theory and Methods." *African Music* 5(2):28–39.

———. 1987a. "Space/Time Concepts and Tusona Ideographs in Luchazi Culture." *Journal of International Library of African Music* 6(4):53–89.

———. 1987b. *Malawian Music: A Framework for Analysis.* Zomba: University of Malawi.

Locke, David. 1982. "Principles of Offbeat Timing and Cross-Rhythm in Southern E*ʋ*e Dance Drumming." *Ethnomusicology* 26(2):217–246.

———. 1987. *Drum Gahu.* Crown Point, Indiana: White-Cliffs Media.

Locke, David, and Godwin K. Agbeli. 1980. "A Study of the Drum Language in Adzogbo." *African Music* 6(1):32–51.

Makonnen, Berhanu, ed. N.d. "Selaqeddus Yared Tarik [Concerning the History of St. Yared]." Mimeographed typescript in Amharic.

Masehafa Deggwa. 1959. Addis Ababa: Berhananenna Selam.

McKechnie, Jean L., ed. 1978. *Webster's New Twentieth Century Dictionary.* Unabridged 2nd ed.

Merriam, Alan P. 1981. "African Musical Rhythm and Concepts of Time-Reckoning." In *Music East and West: Essays in Honor of Walter Kaufmann,* ed. Thomas Noblitt, 123–142. New York: Pendragon Press.

Moloney, C. A. 1889. "Of the Melodies of the Volof, Mandingo, Ewe, Yoruba, and Houssa Peoples of West Africa." *Journal of the Manchester Geographical Society* 5:7–9, 278–298.

Nketia, J. H. Kwabena. 1963. *Drumming in Akan Communites of Ghana.* Toronto: Thomas Nelson and Sons.

Pantaleoni, Hewitt. 1972. "Toward Understanding the Play of *SOGO* in *ATSIA.*" *Ethnomusicology* 16(1):1–27.

Ranger, T. O. 1975. *Dance and Society in Eastern Africa.* Berkeley and Los Angeles: University of California Press.

Read, Gardner. 1969. *Music Notation,* 2nd ed. Boston: Crescendo Publishers.

Robertson, Carol E. 1979. "'Pulling the Ancestors': Performance Practice and Praxis in Mapuche Ordering." *Ethnomusicology* 23(3):409–410.

Rycroft, David. 1958. "The Guitar Improvisations of Mwenda Jean Bosco." *African Music* 2(1):81–98.

———. 1975. "The Zulu Bow Songs of Princess Magogo." *African Music* 5(6):41–97.

Seeger, Charles. 1958. "Prescriptive and Descriptive Music Writing." *Musical Quarterly* 44(2):184–195.

Serwadda, Moses, and Hewitt Pantaleoni. 1968. "A Possible Notation for African Dance Drumming." *African Music* 4(2):47–52.

Shelemay, Kay Kaufman. 1983. "A New System of Musical Notation in Ethiopia." In *Ethiopian Studies Dedicated to Wolf Leslau,* ed. Stanislav Segert and Andras J. E. Bodrogligeti, 571–582. Wiesbaden: Otto Harrassowitz.

———. [1986] 1989. *Music, Ritual, and Falasha History.* East Lansing: Michigan State University Press.

———. 1991. "Recording Technology, the Record Industry, and Ethnomusicological Scholarship." In *Comparative Musicology and the Anthropology of Music,* ed. Bruno Nettl and Philip V. Bohlman, 277–292. Chicago: University of Chicago Press.

Shelemay, Kay Kaufman, and Peter Jeffery. 1993. *Ethiopian Christian Liturgical Chant: An Anthology,* 3 vols. Madison: A-R Editions.

Simon, Artur. 1989. "Trumpet and Flute Ensembles of the Berta People." In *African Musicology: Current Trends,* vol. 1, ed. Jacqueline Cogdell DjeDje and William G. Carter, 113–125. Los Angeles: University of California at Los Angeles.

Stone, Ruth M. 1986. "The Shape of Time in African Music." In *Time, Science, and Society in China and the West,* ed. J. T. Fraser et al. , 113–125. Amherst: University of Massachusetts Press.

Thompson, Robert Farris. 1974. *African Art in Motion.* Berkeley and Los Angeles: University of California Press.

Tracey, Hugh. 1970. *Chopi Musicians.* London: Oxford University Press.

Tumshangalie Bwana; Kitabu cha Nyimbo. 1988. Nairobi: St. Benedict's Monastery.

Wright, Owen. 1978. *The Modal System of Arab and Persian Music: A.D. 1250– 1300.* London: Oxford University Press.

Dance in Communal Life

Patience A. Kwakwa

Functionality of Dancing
Dance as an Integrated Art
Dancers and Types of Dancing
Dancers' Training
Role of Drummers, Singers, and Praise Singers
Interdependence of Dancers and Musicians
Dancers and Musicians in Communal Life

Many people who watch African dancing enjoy the sight of the dance formations and body movements, and the sound of the music. Technically, however, other factors help give an event its aesthetic vigor and vitality. These factors are the unifying and sustaining dynamics of the interactions between dancers and musicians, and between dancers and local audiences.

Academic treatments of these concepts appear in scholarly publications by social anthropologists, students of African traditional religion, and writers on African art. The greater portion of the literature on African dance, however, is cursory. It consists of descriptions of specific dances and their contexts, and of captions to photographs of dancing. Such brief notices do not offer much insight into the tempers and complexities of African dances.

Of the literature in English, studies of African dances treat Zambia (Brelsford 1949), the *masabe* of the Tonga (Colson 1969), the *shetani* of the Segegu (Gray 1969), the Kalabari of Nigeria (Horton 1960, 1973), sub-Saharan Africa (Huet 1978), the medicinal dance of the !Kung (Marshall 1969), the Akan and the Gã (Nketia 1952), and vodoun of the Fon of the Republic of Benin (Herskovits 1967).

African Arts, a quarterly magazine published since 1960 by the University of California at Los Angeles, has featured studies of African dances (Rood 1969; Wemba-Rashid 1971; Monts 1984). These studies give detailed accounts of specific African dances—both as art forms and as social events.

At the University of Ghana, dance has been an academic subject since 1962, and the university has accepted several theses on indigenous dances of African countries (Sackeyfio 1968; Yamoah 1971; Serwaddah 1971; Awuku 1991; Affour 1992; Adu-Asare 1992). At the School of Performing Arts, final-year students in dance, each investigating a dance practiced by his or her own ethnic group, have uncovered deeper meanings (often symbolic or otherwise hidden) in the dances, and have provided information on how their respective communities maintain their traditional dances.

Traditional African dances do not occur in isolation. They often have a specific role within an event or a complex of events organized for a specific occasion. Many have value as entertainment, but entertainment is not their most important function: dancers perform for sociocultural, historical, political, and religious purposes. Thus,

chisungu Nubility rite for a Bemba girl where scenes of maize grinding and potato collecting are enacted

fontomfrom Slow dance that an Asante chief performs on installation. He portrays his predecessors to assert status

abofoo Dance performed by Akan hunters that cleanses the hunter who killed the animal

sasa-ture Dance for a chaotic social situation from the former Bauchi state, Nigeria

khomba A turning dance to make Tsonga women fertile

the traditional dances of Africa differ from the artistic and contemporary dances of Africa, and from classical ballet and modern dance, performed in America and Europe for the entertainment of paying audiences.

FUNCTIONALITY OF DANCING

In many African communities, many occasions—the birth of a child, the initiation of boys and girls into adult status, the installation of chiefs, a marriage—present opportunities to express joy. In some instances, the rituals and ceremonies associated with them require elaborate preparations. These rituals and ceremonies take different forms. In general, there is feasting, drinking, and merrymaking. Within these contexts, dances serve as mediums for honoring, welcoming, and ushering individuals, and for incorporating them into the community at large as new members—as adults, chiefs, or married couples. In the *nsogwe*, danced by the Nsenga and the Southern Chewa, after the birth of a woman's first child,

> the women, entirely nude, assume a squatting posture, raising and lowering their bodies on the heels, accompanying the motion with quivering of their belly muscles. . . . The dance is a kind of lustration to cleanse the mother after a period of taboo. (Brelsford 1949)

Most of the dances performed during the *chisungu* (a nubility rite for a Bemba girl) enact scenes like maize grinding and potato collecting. The ceremony, called "dancing the girl," teaches nubile women the duties of womanhood.

On installation, an Asante chief performs the *fontomfrom*. To portray his predecessors (whose valor he has inherited), he employs symbolic gestures. His using these gestures asserts his status as a peerless leader, for others who take turns in the dance ring (a circular space, defined by the placement of audience and dancers) may not use a chief's gestures.

Dances performed at death ceremonies may be mediums for honoring the dead or placating ancestral spirits (Brelsford 1949), or, in Lugbara society, for signaling the destruction of the territory by the death of the elder (Middleton 1960). After killing a big animal, Akan hunters may perform the *abofoo,* a dance that cleanses the hunter who killed the animal, and protects him from its soul. Dances may also celebrate the long and prosperous life led by a deceased elder.

In worship and ritual healing, dances serve as mediums for characterizing and impersonating communal spirits, enabling them to converse with living persons. When the spirits come, they may cure illnesses they or others have caused, and may join in merrymaking as people give thanks for blessings the spirits have sent (Kwakwa 1974).

Specific occasions call for the performance of dances, and these serve clearly defined goals. In Ture communities (in former Bauchi State, Nigeria), what people consider a chaotic social situation might occasion the performance of *sasa-ture*, a dance that draws attention to interpersonal conflicts, and advises people to live peacefully. Approval for its performance can come only from elders of the community. The chief can command a performance, but must slaughter a fowl before it starts. Onlookers may not take part in it.

African dances may provide a socially sanctioned medium for behavior that under normal circumstances would be unacceptable. Performance of the *saransara* (a dance feast of the Maguzawa of Kaduna State, northern Nigeria) licenses people to express dissatisfaction with their chief. They put their sentiments into the texts of songs for dancing. During the *apoo* and the *aboakyere* (festivals of the Brong and Effutu of Ghana), any local resident may speak freely about the chief and get away with it. During festivals, the dance may serve as a background for other activities, or as a concluding event, in which, for blessings bestowed throughout the year, an entire community may express joy and thanks to God, lesser deities, and ancestors.

DANCE AS AN INTEGRATED ART

African dance is an integrated art, which can combine movement, music, mime, costume, ritual, ceremonial objects, official insignia and regalia, and makeup. In Zambia, *malaila* (from a Bantu word, *kulaila* 'to take leave of or say goodbye'), a dance performed amid praise singing by colleagues of a man slain in war, once used spears and sticks "to underline the prowess of the deceased" (Brelsford 1949).

Secret songs associated with Tsonga initiation for girls have connotations of fertility. The *khomba*—a turning dance, combining mime, dance, and music—"exhibits an extraordinary amount of functional complementarity, the purpose of which is to make women fertile" (Johnston 1974). In it, charms attached to leather belts strengthen the dancers, so they keep their balance. For guidance, masked dancers of the Bété of Côte d'Ivoire attach medicinal substances to their ankles and feet (Rood 1969).

DANCERS AND TYPES OF DANCING

As in music, African dances differ in importance and complexity, and in the extent of participation they offer. Some dances are open to everyone, but participation in others requires special knowledge and skills, and still others may be open only to members of particular social groups or associations. Those who interact in a dance event do so as both performers and members of a social group.

In a dance event, two groups of participants may be discernible: those who play specifically assigned roles (the dancers and the musicians), and those who have no specially marked status (the observers). These groups are often distinct, but in some informal and recreational situations, performers and observers may interact, at various levels of complexity. Temporarily, an onlooker may spontaneously step into a dance ring. Such a person may be a performer who lacks a role assigned for the occasion, a novice who wishes to test his or her skills, or a visitor from a neighboring community. A performer might step out of the ring to relax for a while—to instruct an inadequate performer, to appraise the event, or to make room for others to perform. Specific roles in the dance may be open only to a particular group of people within the community. Selection may depend on age, sex, occupation, sociopolitical status, affiliation with (or membership in) a religious group or cult, the context and function of the dance, and the distinctive feature, character, or nature of the dance. As a result, though people representing a cross-section of a community may perform many dances, some dances have exclusive associations with specific groups: youths, *dayirigaba*   Dance of youths among the Nyamalthu or Terawa of the former Bauchi State in Nigeria

take   Praise-name performance among the Nyamalthu of the former Bauchi State in Nigeria

gagra   Dance that tests men's bravery among the Higi of northern Nigeria

wasan maharba   Hunters reenact personal experiences of going on hunts in this dance

adult males or females, girls, newly initiated men, newly married women, bachelors, mothers, farmers, warriors, blacksmiths, hunters, royalty, cultists.

Among the Nyamalthu or Terawa of Akko and Gombe local government areas in former Bauchi State of Nigeria, *dayirigaba* is a dance of youths. On the day of a marriage, while people are taking the bride to the groom's or the groom's father's house, young men and women perform it. It also serves purposes of courtship, for some men choose their brides during a performance.

The same people consider *ngorda*—full of pomp and majesty—the dance of the nobility. Only the *kuji* (chief of the Nyamalthu), the seven *basarake* (titled men), and their wives, may dance it. Traditionally, people performed it on four occasions: when the guinea corn flowers, during the harvest of millet and guinea corn, at the installation of a *kuji* or *basarake*, and at the funeral of a *kuji* or *basarake*. The Nyamalthu say it is a gift from their supreme deity, whom it enables them to thank while entertaining themselves. Its movements consist of elegant walks and turns. Drummers help the dancers move. To call each dancer, they play a special praise (*take*). A dancer whom a drummer singles out must answer by kinetically interpreting the rhythms of the drums.

The Nyamalthu consider the *dan* the dance of the brave. One person, usually a man on whom the community has bestowed the title *jarumi* 'brave one', performs it, on the occasion when he receives the honor. In the days of interethnic warfare, drummers incited warriors by playing music for the *dan*.

In some Higi communities, young men between the ages of seventeen and twenty who passed through the *zhita* (a boy's initiation ritual) performed the *zhita* dance. Until quite recently, newly initiated youths had to dance at a ceremony organized to mark the successful completion of their initiation. A youth who had not gone through the *zhita* could not marry. One important social function of the *zhita* was that youths who had gone through it together saw themselves as age mates. They remained friends for life, and accorded each other certain privileges, such as not having to remove one's sandals in the house of another. *Zhita* was also the means by which the youths showed the members of their communities, particularly their parents and young women, that they had come of age. *Zhita* occurred once a year, at planting time. It involved an entire community. As the youths danced, members of their clans gave them gifts. The organizers of the ceremony whipped any uninitiated boys who tried to join in.

Gagra is a Higi dance that tests men's *mazakuta* 'bravery and magical power'. It forms part of the activities organized by hunters' and warriors' guilds in honor of renowned ones among them. Custom bars women and male weaklings from performances. The Higi also associate the dance *gula-gula* with bravery. Only married men between the ages of twenty-five and thirty dance it. The occasion relates to ceremonies associated with the ripening and harvesting of a variety of guinea corn. The Higi say a man who participates in *gula-gula* is mature and trustworthy. If a man's first child dies, or his wife is barren, people attribute his misfortune to nonparticipation in the dance.

In courtship, Higi youths perform *garba* 'look for a wife', a dance organized when millet and other crops are ripe. The occasion, like that of the *dayirigaba*, creates a forum for young unmarried men to secure their wives. Hence, married men, who lead settled lives, do not show much interest in its performance. Youths believe if they do not perform *garba*, they will neither meet girls nor get married.

In northern Nigeria, many communities ascribe dance forms to specific groups of local residents. Similar observations are true for the Jarawa, the Bankalawa, the Galambawa, the Ham (Jaba), the Margi, and many other groups in northern Nigeria.

Sometimes the physical nature of a dance may be a factor in restricting a dance to one group of people. Team dances are dances of youths. These include *takkai*, performed by youths from Jamji; *gatzal* of the Bankalawa of Bajar; *kode* of the Kagoro; *sarewa* of the Jarawa; *saransara*, *rambada*, and *tabaje*, of the Maguzawa (in Malumfashi, Funtua, and Dustin-Ma); *ishedi-ishurwa* of the Piti; *woza* of the Kurama of Woba; *gaja* of the Chawai in Nigeria; *bawa* of the Dagari; and *agbekor* of the Anlo Ewe in Ghana. These dances employ energetic, intricate steps and movements, which require strength, versatility, and agility. To the Bankalawa, a vigorous display symbolizes youthfulness, while whipping proves courage and manliness. The physical demands of these dances make them difficult for elderly persons, who support performances only as onlookers.

Men actively participate in dances organized and performed in association with men's occupations. Women follow, singing or ululating; they execute simple steps or movements. Some men's dances are further restricted to men engaged in a specific occupation, or to those who belong to a specific association or guild. During public appearances, nonmembers (boys, and even adult males) may not perform with members. Dances of professional hunters, warriors, farmers, and blacksmiths, fall within this category. Nigerian examples include the *shappal*, the Jahunawa Fulani war dance; the *gagra*, the hunters' and warriors' dance of the Higi of Michika; the *ngangara*, the professional hunters' dance of the people of Guguba in Jega state; the *wasan maharba,* hunters' dance of the Ham (Jaba) of Kwoi; the *wasan noma,* farmers' dance; the *wasan garma* 'hoe play', and the *wasan makera* 'blacksmith play' of the Hausa in Kaduna state. The movements dancers execute in each of these dances resemble the movements the men employ in their respective occupations. The men may mime, or give stylized or exaggerated versions of the routine movements. War dances, while reenacting warriors' deeds through mime and movements, exhibit manly strength and power. To praise singing accompanied by the *molo* (a plucked lute), hunters in the *wasan maharba* reenact personal experiences of going on hunts. To fixed musical rhythms, farmers in the *wasan noma* stylize the movements of their labor in the fields. The goal of some performances is to impress onlookers into giving gifts.

Among the Bankalawa and the Galambawa, women do not usually take active roles in dances that involve the *dodo*, a masked dancer. (*Dodo* is a Hausa word that means 'anything frightful'; in this context, it refers to a masked dancer.) Some communities bar women from attending such performances, even as bystanders, for it is taboo for them to see a masked individual. Since communities punish culprits, women and children run and hide as the *dodo* approaches them. Galambawa women who see the *dodo* have to remove their head ties, and keep them off until the *dodo* has disappeared. But the *dodo* to the Bankalawa is also a medium for correcting social ills—a duty usually assigned to the men of a community.

Because of participation by one *dodo,* the *mijin dare* 'night male', Nomana women do not take part in the *wasan gora*, a dance performed in association with postharvest rituals. After dancing it in the bush, men return home at night, when

Interested individuals learn to execute the accepted steps and movements—by watching and imitating the experts in the dance ring, at home, and during recreational periods.

women will be out of sight. People consider any man who does not take part in the dance a weakling or a woman.

Dances organized and performed in association with what the people regard as female occupations are largely the prerogative of female members of a community. The *bala* (danced by married Kanuri women), the *dunu* (a suite of dances performed by women in the Kwayam and Bodiwe areas of former Borno state in Nigeria, and the *shila* (originally a Shuwa Arab dance) are examples. In Hausa communities, young girls dance the *kalangu* on moonlit nights during the dry season. In Ghana, to express values and ideals associated with female nubility, women and young girls dance the *otofo*, the *dipo*, the *nde*, or the *bragoro*.

Cult dances may be open only to members of the cult. Both male and female members may participate in them. The Maguzawa *wasan bòorii,* the spirit-possession dance that occurs in many Hausa communities, is an example. Male and female members perform it, mounted by their spiritual horses, so they become the media of the possessor spirits. Through the execution of dance movements and the use of costume, ritual paraphernalia, and speech, they exhibit the spirits' idiosyncracies. They dance the *bòorii* to cure illnesses caused by malevolent spirits (*iskoki*). By contrast, at the early stage of performance, observers of the *akem* (a dance performed by the Akan in Ghana) may take turns in the dance ring; as soon as possessed priests and priestesses begin to enter the ring, they leave it.

DANCERS' TRAINING

Whatever the criteria for selecting dances are, dancers must go through some form of training to gain the technical skills necessary for executing the required movements and steps. Dancers must have a disciplined body, good musical sense, and a regard for decorum. They must have the intuitional tools for expressing feelings and ideas, the enactment of historical traditions, and the dramatization of beliefs and values. In some dances, a dancer takes a particular role because of an ability to follow precisely the rhythms of the drum and the nuances of the texts. In some dances, selection depends on the ability to shake the body well (Harper 1970).

The contexts provided for dances create informal opportunities for interested individuals to learn to execute the accepted steps and movements—by watching and imitating the experts in the dance ring, at home, and during recreational periods.

Some would-be dancers undertake formal and intensive training, which may occur in an initiation camp (as with *zhita* and *rawan dodo*), or in an occupational guild (as with *wasan makera*). The training inculcates technical skills and enables dancers to understand what they are doing, so they may do it well.

ROLES OF DRUMMERS, SINGERS, AND PRAISE SINGERS

The men of a community usually undertake its drumming. They are selected primarily on the basis of their ability to play the drum and other musical instruments.

Except within the context of a cult, considerations such as age and membership in a group may be unimportant.

Highly talented musicians receive training through a system of apprenticeship. Often, they learn their skills from a father or other man of the extended family, and some families have renown for the ability to drum and interpret rhythms. Hausa drummers are quick to say "*Mun gada* 'We inherited it'"; many claim descent from renowned drummers. Often, training begins at an early age. A few drummers claim they gained their skills by watching and imitating master drummers during performances, or in a recreational situation. Some musicians are excellent dancers. The Higi say the best dancers in the *shila* are horn players, for they can interpret the language of the drums.

During organized performances, drummers do not step into the dance ring. By playing rhythms that correspond to the dancers' steps and movements, they help dancers perform correctly. *Ngorda* dancers say the drummers help them move majestically.

In many Hausa dances, the role of the praise singer (*maroka*) is highly important. In young girls' dances and dances associated with royalty, hunting, farming, and marriages, he showers praises on individuals. In some dances, he is also the master drummer, or plays the only accompanying musical instrument. As he praises a married couple in the Kanuri *bala* or the Nyamalthu *dayirigaba*, he reminds them of their communal responsibilities. This is clear in a song for the *kuru*, the Maguzawa farmers' dance.

> Let us go back to the bush and farm, which is why we live.
> Whatever we get in this world, we get it from the farm.
> Young men, let us leave home to go to the farm.
> Those who do not make it in the educational system
> Will find their way back to school—their farms.

In the *turu* (the dance of Daura royalty), praise singers praise the dancer's parents and grandparents, in descending order, from the first chief to the present emir. Dancers say a praise singer makes them feel proud. They sense that their ancestors are watching them.

INTERDEPENDENCE OF DANCERS AND MUSICIANS

The reciprocal relationship between music and dance inevitably creates a similar type of interdependence between dancers and musicians. They ensure that their parts continue in the manner the community expects to see, and that through appropriate variations and signals (or the subtleties of expressions) they interact or respond spontaneously to each other during the performance.

Whether or not a performance reaches standards acceptable in a community may depend on the degree of seriousness with which local musicians and dancers regard their efforts. Music and dance go hand in hand. In various ways, dancers and musicians influence the animation of the performance.

DANCERS AND MUSICIANS IN COMMUNAL LIFE

Though dancers and musicians take important roles in communal life, they do not usually enjoy special treatment or privileges. Nevertheless, to suggest that other members of a community look down on dancers and drummers would be wrong. The degree of respect accorded them reflects the role dance itself plays within a community. If dance functions primarily as entertainment, and participants are people whom a

The Bankalawa equate dancing to going to school: it informs every aspect of their lives.

community considers inferior, dancers will get little or no recognition from the community.

The Kanuri believe musicians and dancers occupy a low position. Though much depends on how a performer comports himself, some praise singers have enjoyed patronage, and have even become wealthy, but are still not likely to move up the social ladder.

Higi, Bankalawa, Nyamalthu, and Longuda communities do not look down on dancers and musicians. The Higi may attribute certain types of ill fortune and weakness in men to lack of participation in a particular dance. In many communities like those of the Higi, dance provides a medium through which social relationships develop. Such communities, being more likely than others to appreciate the contributions made by dancers, praise singers, and drummers, accord them respect. The Bankalawa equate dancing to going to school: it informs every aspect of their lives. The Chawai say they like dancers and musicians because they make people proud of their group inheritance.

REFERENCES

Adu-Asare, Michael. 1992. "Extinct Akan Dance from the Akuapem Traditional Area." Diploma thesis, University of Ghana, Legon.

Affour, E. A. 1992. "The Role of Dance in the Daa Festival of the People of the Tongo." Diploma thesis, University of Ghana, Legon.

Awuku, Robert S. 1991. "Agbekor Dance of Anlo Afiadenyigba." Diploma thesis, University of Ghana, Legon.

Brelsford, W. V. 1949. *African Dances of Northern Rhodesia.* Livingstone, Zambia: The Livingstone Museum.

Colson, Elizabeth. 1969. "Spirit-Possession among the Tonga of Zambia." In *Spirit Mediumship in Society in Africa,* ed. John Beattie and John Middleton, 69–103. London: Routledge and Kegan Paul.

Gray, R. F. 1969. "The Shetani Cult among the Segeju of Tanzania." In *Spirit Mediumship in Society in Africa,* ed. John Beattie and John Middleton, 171–187. London: Routledge and Kegan Paul.

Harper, Peggy. 1970. "A Festival of Nigerian Dances." *African Arts* 3(2):48–53.

Herskovits, Melville J. 1967. *Dahomey: An Ancient West African Kingdom,* vol. 2. Evanston, Ill.: Northwestern University Press.

Horton, Robin. 1960. "The Gods as Guests." *Nigerian Magazine.* Special edition.

———. 1973. "The Kalabari Ekine Society: A Borderland of Religion and Art." In *Peoples and Cultures of Africa,* ed. Elliot P. Skinner. New York: Doubleday.

Huet, Michael. 1978. *The Dance, Art and Ritual of Africa.* New York: Pantheon Books.

Johnston, Thomas F. 1974. "A Tsonga Initiation." *African Arts* 7(4).

Kwakwa, Patience A. 1974. "Dance and Drama of the Gods." Master's thesis, Institute of African Studies, Legon.

Marshall, Lorna. 1969. "The Medicine Dance of the !Kung Bushmen." *Africa* 39(4):347–381.

Middleton, John. 1960. *Lugbara Religion.* London: Oxford University Press.

Monts, Lester. 1984. "Dance in the Vai Sande Society." *African Arts* 7(4):53–59, 94.

Nketia, J. H. K. 1952. *African Music in Ghana.* Evanston, Ill.: Northwestern University Press.

Rood, Armistead P. 1969. "Bete Masked Dance." *African Arts* 2(3):36–43, 76.

Sackeyfio, Godfrey. 1968. "Music and Dance of Otu Gods of Gã Mashi." Diploma thesis, University of Ghana.

Serwaddah, Moses. 1971. "Ndongo, a Wedding-Dance of the Baganda of Uganda." Diploma thesis, University of Ghana.

Wemba-Rashid, J. A. R. 1971. "Isinyago and Midimu: Masked Dancers of Tanzania and Mozambique." *African Arts* 6(2):38–44.

Yamoah, Felix. 1971. "Installation Ceremony of An Ashanti Chief." Diploma thesis, University of Ghana, Legon.

Islam in Liberia
Lester P. Monts

Since the 1750s, Islam has influenced the coastal forest region of present-day Liberia and Sierra Leone (Owen 1930:57). The assimilation of Islamic ideology into African life brought changes in the local world view. Muslim influence was variable and uneven: some ethnic groups staunchly resisted it; others blended it with traditional practice, after a syncretic model like that of other regions in West Africa. For the Vai ethnic group, however, it formed a unique relationship, and began a process that culminated in a move toward orthodoxy.

In northwest Liberia, over a twelve-year period (1977–1988), people in the town of Bulumi restructured the basic aspects of their lives, and conceptually reordered their musical system. Studying the impact of the new religious orientation on Vai artistic expression provides a tool for understanding Islamic development in West Africa, where changes in art reveal the profound effects a new ideology can have on aesthetic values.

ISLAMIZATION AND MUSIC IN VAI

West Africans, most of whom call themselves Muslims, know two general types of Islam: "normative" and "popular" (Levtzion 1979:215). The former type, the more orthodox and conservative, derives all social and moral codes from strict Islamic law, as perceived by local Muslims. The latter, the more marginal, tolerates variant practices: "For most people . . . acceptance of Islam meant no more than memorising a few Arabic formulae and using talismen sold by Muslim doctors. Of the five 'pillars' of Islam—confession of faith, ritual prayer, fasting, almsgiving, and (as an ideal goal) pilgrimage—it is unlikely that many people observed any of the last three" (Jones 1981:176). Echoing this notion, Lewis (1980:59) suggests that the requirements for a person to be considered a Muslim, especially during the early phases of Islamization, were to "acknowledge the fundamental doctrine—there is no god but Allah, and Muhammad is his Prophet—and a handful of related injunctions and prescriptions."

From the beginning, Islamic philosophy questioned Vai perceptions of social and religious order. Its entry into Vai life began a long-term dispute between two antagonists—tradition and modernity—and the contradiction between them was

Bulumi Vai town in northwest Liberia, Tombe chiefdom, on the Liberia–Sierra Leone highway

Poro Generic term for men's secret society in West Africa

ɓɛli Vai term for the men's secret society, Poro

everywhere apparent, especially in the conflict between initiation societies and Islamic dogma. Until the late 1900s, the alternate factions were willing to compromise: "It is the compromising attitude—the symbiosis of Islam and the African traditional religion—which was typical of Islam in West Africa before the eighteenth century" (Levtzion 1979:208). By the 1970s, a stricter, more conservative Muslim religious order began to prevail. After 1977, several Vai towns experienced a striking shift from marginal Islam to a conservative orthodoxy, which affected the role of music in ritual, ceremony, and other celebratory occasions. Between the extremes arose a third type, transitional Islam. Changes during the period 1977–1988 document the dynamics affecting both musical and religious life.

The acceptance of a new ideology radically affects music, because music mirrors the cultural variables of traditional social and religious institutions. As a form of expressive culture, music is a pawn, an element over which conflict can develop. It is a battleground, where factions can test the strength of their cultural and spiritual values. A decline in the performance of a representative type of music can signal the demise of a religious ideology.

BULUMI IN 1977–1978

With a population of about three hundred fifty, Bulumi (often written "Bomi" or "Bumi") is the largest town in the Tombe chiefdom. It stands on a peninsula between the Atlantic Ocean and Lake Piso, along a road that connects the Liberia–Sierra Leone highway with Robertsport. Like most towns along this route, Bulumi lies within the sphere of influence of the urban areas of Monrovia and Robertsport. It receives radio broadcasts from Monrovia and from Freetown, Sierra Leone. Several townspeople have relatives in Robertsport and Monrovia, and many commute regularly to those areas. As the largest and most progressive town in the Tombe chiefdom, Bulumi takes the lead in social reform. Accordingly, Muslims seek to introduce their beliefs there (Levtzion 1979:1–20).

Secret societies and music

In the 1970s, two secret societies—Poro for men, Sande for women—dominated local life. (*Poro* is a generic term used throughout the region; the Vai refer to the institution as *ɓɛli*.) They formed the crux of the crisis between Islam and traditional practice. People considered the societies at Bulumi among the best run in the region. The societies supported the practice of ancestor veneration. The sacred groves of the Poro conveniently grew near the graves of lineage leaders, where people frequently made sacrifices to ancestors.

For many Vai, participation in secret societies reinforced the search for metaphysical meaning. Basic to that search was the supposition of a reality beyond the realm of mortal perception, a powerful supernatural reality, which manifested itself in ancestral and nature spirits, and in a supreme being. To understand that reality, and to live in accord with it, the Vai relied on the powers of spiritual leaders or guardians. The secret society component first combined men and women as corporate units, and through the traditional belief system allied them with the forces in the spirit world. Unseen spirits, in their roles as guardians of values, represented the core of the Vai world view, which played itself out in ritual and ceremony.

Poro and Sande molded intermediary relationships with their authoritative entities of the spirit world. In Sande, a Zooba masked dancer impersonated a male ancestral water spirit; in the Poro, the *dadɛwɛ* (not impersonated by a mask) was a "bush spirit." Though a nature divinity, the *dadɛwɛ* was more powerful than the ancestral spirits impersonated by Zooba: Poro assumed a higher authoritative role than Sande.

The ancestors were intermediaries between the living and the supreme being, but their powers covered only the aspects of life they experienced. Human existence and well-being also depended on the environment, whose forces flowed from a pantheon of spirits—natural divinities, which, sometimes with ancestral spirits, lodged in cotton trees, in the depths of lakes and rivers, and on mountaintops (Johnson 1954:16). People regularly held sacrifices at those locations. The lore and mythology surrounding the secret societies tells of the powers of natural divinities and ancestor spirits.

Because of the multidimensionality of their roles, and the fine line that distinguished the sacred and the secular, the secret societies operated in alternate realms. On the sacred side, they instilled initiates with the basic elements of the belief system, including respect for the power of the supreme being, which manifests itself through the ancestors and the cultic spirits *dadɛwɛ* and Zooba. The basic belief was that an extraordinary force allowed people in the Poro and Sande to speak with "one voice," and to share in a set of behaviors and moral values that promote social continuity.

Socially, both Poro and Sande played central roles in the life cycle activities of its members. Membership established a lifelong fraternal or sororal bond, and initiates referred to one another as "brother" or "sister." The collective consciousness of the societies affected the funerary ceremonies of their members, especially chiefs and high-ranking officials. It was in part through the auspices of the societies that the doctors, morticians, musicians, gravediggers, and other specialists and ritual leaders, developed their skills.

Major occasions associated with the secret societies and other communal activities called for the services of music specialists. Bulumi was the home of several professional musicians, and of eight masqueraders. The male masqueraders included Bowu (figure 1), Nafali, Kɔlɔpɔɔ, Joobai, and Yavi. Male musicians performed on a conical drum (*saŋgba*); a wooden slit drum (*keleŋ*); a box-shaped lamellophone (*koŋgoma*); and a set of basket rattles (*jeke*). The Sande society sponsored two Zooba spirit impersonators, and female instrumentalists were the exclusive players of the *sasaa* (gourd rattle). Two of the chiefdom's most celebrated performers lived at Bulumi: Varni Tawe, a *saŋgba* player; and Kuna Kiatamba, the oldest and highest-ranking female musician in the coastal region (figure 2). Both of them played prominent roles in secret society activities. Several musicians of lesser skill stayed at Bulumi as students of Varni Tawe, and accompanied him at out-of-town performances. The local paramount chief and the county superintendent (based at Robertsport) frequently called for the services of drummers and masqueraders from Bulumi to entertain visiting dignitaries, or to accompany them to traditional and governmental occasions.

Because of the stature and skill of its musicians and dancers, Bulumi gained a reputation throughout the region as a dance town; it was the place to go for a good feast or holiday celebration. In 1977–1978, it hosted more feasts and holiday celebrations than any other town in the chiefdom. Such occasions were not the only reasons

imam   Islamic teacher, doctor, scribe, song leader, and interpreter of the Qur'ān

hadj   Pilgrimage to Mecca that devout Muslims are encouraged to make

d'aabo kulɛ   'Arabic voice', Vai stylistic designation for recitation of the Qur'ān

Ramadan   Month of fasting that faithful Muslims observe

FIGURE 1   The masked dancer Bowu. Bulumi, 1977.

FIGURE 2   Kuna Kiatamba, the celebrated *kengai* of Bulumi, performs on the gourd rattle (*sasaa*). Bulumi, 1977.

to celebrate. At the end of rice harvest season (October), communal dances occurred nightly there. When the rice harvest was bountiful, musicians and dancers from neighboring towns often joined in. On national and Christian holidays, Bulumi occasionally sponsored "cultural shows," which featured visiting masqueraders and musicians from as far away as Gola and Mende country.

Institutional Islam

Like all Vai towns, Bulumi had an imam (*aimaami*) and a mosque (*misii*), and though nearly everyone professed a commitment to Islam, a few men stood out as devout Muslims. Other than the imam (figure 3), no one in the town could read Arabic. Hence, the imam was the Islamic teacher, doctor, scribe, song leader, and interpreter of the Qur'ān. Several of the devout Muslims wanted to go on pilgrimage (*hadj*) to Mecca, but none had the money to do so; several, however, considered pilgrimage a lifelong goal.

During the day, people worked their farms, and did not regularly attend prayers in the mosque. Congregational prayer was not a common practice. The most devout Muslims kept prayer mats in huts on their farms, where they prayed daily. Even in the evening, attendance in the mosque was sparse. Many people, including most women, preferred to pray at home.

In 1978, the imam had seven boys in his school. Every night, they sat by an open fire near the imam's house, and recited the Qur'ān from inscriptions written on wooden boards (*wala*). In exchange for Qur'ānic training, three of the boys had come

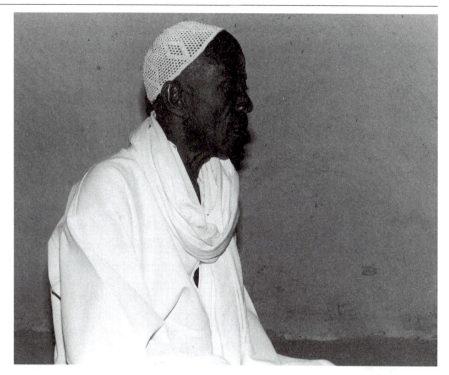

to Bulumi to live with the imam, and to work on his farm. After successfully completing the first stage of training, the sons of clerics, with other boys who showed an interest in the religion, went away to regional Islamic centers for advanced studies. By the fire, the boys learned to chant the Qur'ān in a standard, rudimentary style. Further training would enable them to recite in a style called *ɗaabo kulɛ* 'Arabic voice'. While that is the Vai stylistic designation, the recitation of men who were said to have this technique was not stylistically similar to that of Arabic-speaking Qur'ān-reciters. The *ɗaabo kulɛ* was merely a more precise pronunciation of the Arabic text.

During the late 1970s, people seldom observed the major holidays of the Islamic calendar; and during Ramadan (*tɔŋ kalo*), only a few kept their fast. The Vai recognized and celebrated three major Islamic holidays: Milaji (Miraj), Mahodi (Mawlid), and Bɔtɔndɔ (Id al-Fitr). Excepting Bɔtɔndɔ, the town sponsored no major Islamic celebrations in 1977–1978. The other events, celebrated by a small group of people, were confined to the quarter where the imam lived. Bɔtɔndɔ was a celebratory occasion, and because drummers and masked dancers participated in the ceremonies, local and out-of-town guests participated freely. Though it was a sacred occasion, many less devout participants (which included most) drank alcoholic beverages, and engaged in other behavior Muslims considered unbecoming. Most people considered Bɔtɔndɔ a purely social occasion, and paid little attention to its underlying religious purpose.

During the 1970s, no local Friday prayer service took place at Bulumi, but the imam and a few men occasionally traveled to the town of Misila to pray. As a weekly obligation, Friday prayer was not a widespread practice among the rural Vai: only four towns in all of Vai country (Makbɔuma, Misila, Sinni, Zogboja) held it; immigrant Koniaka Muslims had founded all but one of these towns. Because of the conservatism of their religious principles, the Vai called them *Mɔli sanja* 'Muslim towns'. Only a few older people spoke the Koniaka language; and beyond allegiance to Islam, people in these towns considered themselves to be Vai, and accepted other aspects of Vai culture. In the late 1970s, influence from these towns, and from large Mandingo and Fula mosques in Monrovia, impressed on the rural communities that Friday prayer was an important part of their devotional commitment.

When people announced that the musicians had arrived and were about to begin a procession through the town, all other activities ceased.

Most of the people at Bulumi considered themselves Muslims. They measured their commitment, not by what they omitted from their lives, but by what they included. Compared with their immediate neighbors, the Vai had a clear commitment to Islam. Several elements of local culture were clues about the degree to which the people had appropriated Islamic elements. Funerary rites were one of the first traditional practices to absorb Muslim traits.

The fortieth-day death feast

The fortieth-day death feast (ɗaa) is the most elaborate and frequent of Vai social occasions. By Islamic tradition, ɗaa is the last of three celebratory feasts; the others occur on the third and seventh days after death. In the distant past, ɗaa often lasted as long as one month; but in 1977–1978, because of employment, and the distances family and friends had to travel to attend, the feasts held at Bulumi lasted only three days, Friday through Sunday. The size of ɗaa depended on two major factors: the social or political status of the deceased, and the fund-raising ability of the host family.

In 1978, a fortieth-day feast for a former paramount chief at Bulumi began on Friday, when out-of-town friends and relatives arrived and offered their condolences, with gifts of money and foodstuffs. At dusk, two micromusical events involving Islamic and traditional practices took place. To summon men to the mosque, the Muslim prayer caller (wandai) performed the call to prayer (azan). In a style adopted from Koniaka immigrants, his call was heightened speech (figure 4). The evening prayer consecrated the memory of the deceased, whom the imam eulogized.

In another part of town, women were pounding rice in a mortar to prepare their guests' evening meal; they accompanied their work with Islamic songs (figure 5). Throughout the night, small groups of people participated in processions, singing praise songs in honor of the deceased chief and his family; each group included a male representative, with singers and a rattle player. At the house of the deceased, a prominent male in the group made an oration to the family. (By custom, this person was one who had known the deceased and the history of his clan.) He recounted the deceased's exploits—as warrior, political leader, husband of many wives, and father of many children. Taking a section from the speech, singers accompanying the group extemporized a song of praise.

> Woja nyi o o.
> Woja nyi, woja bɛɛ bɛlɛ nyi, o mba o o.
> O yaa. Woja nyi, woja bɛɛ bɛlɛ nyi.
>
> To have a family is good.
> To have a fine family is good, oh mother.
> Oh yes. To have a fine family is good.

FIGURE 4 Excerpt from the call to prayer (*azan*), a kind of heightened speech. Bulumi, 1978.

By Saturday afternoon, most out-of-town participants had arrived, and the town was teeming with excitement. Everyone eagerly awaited the arrival of invited musicians and dancers: Seku Gbɔnda and his professional troupe. Without such participation, no major musical events could occur. When people announced that the musicians had arrived and were about to begin a procession through the town, all other activities ceased. To greet the musicians, crowds—including a senator, a member of the national legislature, and a county superintendent—lined the procession route. Afterward, to discuss accommodations and pay, the musicians met with the sponsors.

Just before sunset, the musicians began a procession to the center of town, where the masqueraders would perform. En route, for encouragement, persons in the crowd gave the musicians money. Six male masqueraders—Nafali, two Bowunu (the Vai suffix -*nu* marks the plural of nouns), Yavi, two Zooba—joined the musicians. On arrival at the dance arena, the musicians encouraged bystanders to participate in singing dance songs. As participants reacted to the competitive spirit and skill of the musicians and dancers, tension rose. After about two hours of masked dancing, the musicians began another procession through the town; throughout the night, it repeatedly visited the house of the deceased, to offer songs of praise and monetary gifts. Other processions also formed, and filled the town with music.

Early Sunday morning, men gathered in the mosque for the *fidao*, a ceremony of redemption held for the deceased. To perform the ceremony, men simultaneously read or recite from memory sections of the Qur'ān. After the *fidao*, in front of the mosque, local butchers slaughtered a cow and several sheep, and distributed the meat

FIGURE 5 A rice-pounding song as performed in Bulumi, 1978. Fragments of the text recall the original Arabic *La ilaha ila' Allah* 'There is no god but God'.

Vai text: ai lai lai hu lai lai hu lai la la hu lai ai
Text fragments of the original Arabic: La ilaha ila' Allah
There is no god but God (Allah)

Traditional music and dance, and Islamic songs,
recitations, and prayers, were cultural resources that
supported a cohesive celebratory structure.

FIGURE 6   At the fortieth-day death feast (d'aa),
the master musician Seku Gbɔnda performs on
the basket rattles (jeke); instrumentalists accompany him on the box-shaped lamellophone
koŋgoma. Bulumi, 1978.

to cook stations in each quarter of the town. Meanwhile, women began to prepare a
special rice product called dɛɛ, for use in the final sacrifice. As they beat the rice with
pestles in the mortar, they sang Islamic songs. After the midday meal, male relatives
and participants met in the mosque for the final sacrifice. Male representatives from
neighboring towns, or relatives living in Monrovia or Robertsport, individually
offered the bereaved family condolences: words of praise, and money. People offered
a sacrifice of money, kola nuts, and rice flour. The imam asked everyone to stand;
with hands extended, he led them in a recitation of the *al fatiha*, the opening section
of the Qur'ān. As the final formality, the *tɔmbɔ jala-mæ* (the appointed event leader)
proclaimed the feast a success, and acknowledged the donors of time and money. He
made a special point of mentioning the musicians. The meeting adjourned with
applause for Seku Gbɔnda and his troupe (figure 6).

This feast interwove Islamic and traditional practices. The participants did not
consciously rate its traditional and Islamic contents. For them, those elements were
alternative parts of a long, complex tradition. Traditional music and dance, and
Islamic songs, recitations, and prayers, were cultural resources that supported a cohesive celebratory structure.

SACRIFICES AT ZÓNTORI

Remnants of another traditional religious practice continued surreptitiously in
1977–1978. Sacrifices to ancestors and natural divinities were essential in the prac-

tice of traditional Vai religion. To ensure peace and prosperity, people propitiated spirits by ritual sacrifice, which Muslim leaders considered blasphemous: they objected, not to the practice itself, but to the entities to whom the people directed it. They tried to impress on participants in those activities that a higher authority could grant benefits that far outweighed those of the ancestors, and that, with proper behavior and devotion, people could easily reap these benefits. Such proclamations had some effect, but did not stop the sacrifices.

One region where such rites continued was around Tombe: people thought mighty spirits inhabited the top of Cape Mount and the swamp areas near the coast. Legends extol the virtues of these spirits, and cite the benefits they have provided. Near the town of Latia,

> there is a piece of water "Zóntori," and the reason why it bears that name is as follows:—At the time of the conquest, when Zong, the king of the place, had lost his warriors in the battle, he fled into the forest with Tóri, his queen: there they met a benign being of the other world, who showed them a way down into the regions under the water, the happy abode of the departed. Thither all the warriors followed them, and the rest of their subjects. There they now enjoy an existence free from care and full of pleasure, and the sound of their songs, or the noise of their feasts and frolics, are sometimes heard by the living during the silence of the night. (Koelle 1854:iv–v)

Islam notwithstanding, people in the late 1970s made several sacrifices at these locations, under a dark veil of secrecy.

In traditional society, the success of these events depended on the participation of a strong specialist. During the late 1970s, two elderly women in the chiefdom reportedly had a special relationship with the spirits; each bore the title of *siekɛ-mɔɔ* 'offering bringer'. Authoritative figures in the local Zooba Sande, they resisted encouragement to pray as Muslims. For their traditional beliefs, people called them *kaffi* (from Arabic *kāfir* 'infidel'). Despite Muslim taunts, the women enjoyed an aura of fear and respect, because of the special relationship they had with the spirits that reigned supreme in Vai lore. People attributed to these women several miraculous acts, which caused some to fear and respect their power. During a sacrifice, when the spirits did not respond to the normal procedures, these women reportedly dived into the depths of the water, and conversed with the spirits for up to 45 minutes.

Unlike in the distant past, when the local *siekɛ-mɔɔ* (or *jakɛ-mɔɔ*) had considered ritual practices part of his or her contribution to society, the necessary special arrangements and extreme costs more recently associated with these practices made them unmanageable for most individuals. By 1978, a small group or an entire town would pool resources for single sacrifices. In addition to the $100 fee charged by the *siekɛ-mɔɔ*, patrons had to provide a 100-pound (45-kilogram) bag of rice, a white sheep, 3 gallons of palm oil, and several kola nuts. In 1977–1978, people reportedly sponsored three sacrifices: for a man seeking the office of paramount chief, for a Monrovia-based football team hoping to maintain a winning record, and for a person who simply wanted to be a "big man."

People traditionally held sacrifices to bring greater prosperity to the chiefdom, especially when they planned a new road, and when they believed rumors that construction of a port would occur at Robertsport. They consulted ancestors on actions to take to bring these prospects to fruition. They believed that despite Islam's fervor, only traditional means could resolve certain issues.

People considered ancestors music-loving spirits, and during the rituals, they

Music was an important element in these rituals; without it, the act would not have been valid.

sang old songs, dating from the ancestors' lifetimes. At the start of the sacrifice, the *siekɛ-mɔɔ* told the people the spirits wanted them to sing a particular song, while she was carrying out one of two procedures. One version required the *siekɛ-mɔɔ* to put a basin of sacrificial food on her head, and diving into the water, to serve it to the spirits; afterward, she would return, to report the spirits' advice. Another version says the *siekɛ-mɔɔ* cut the throat of the sheep, and allowed the blood to flow into the water: if it flowed in a straight line to the center of the pool, the ancestors had accepted the sacrifice, and would grant the people's request; much rejoicing and feasting would then occur, and the spirits sometimes participated. People believed they could hear singing from beneath the water, and thought several Zooba spirit impersonators had emerged from beneath the water to dance on the opposite bank. In still another version, the *siekɛ-mɔɔ* used a canoe to carry a metal basin containing sacrificial food to the center of the water: the basin floated on the surface; but after a few minutes, the water became turbulent, and the basin sank. People in the towns of Latia and Fali claim to have heard rejoicing from the waters throughout the night. The next day, if they found the basin on the shore and clean, they knew the ancestors had accepted the sacrifice.

Music was an important element in these rituals; without it, the act would not have been valid. Like the clandestine activities it accompanied, it was not performed openly. People were unwilling to sing out of context the songs associated with the sacrifices, and to allow their recording.

Unlike Vai funerary activities, these rituals did not include Muslim practices, ritual or musical. Some Vai viewed these activities as a serious challenge to Muslim teachings, while others justified them as a way to call upon powers that serve purposes outside the purview of Islam. This tension created turmoil between Muslim and traditional factions. The Muslim profession of faith—*Lai, lai, i lai, lai, lai, Muhammadu la sura lai* 'There is one god, and Muhammad is his prophet'—articulated the dispute. The practice of spirit veneration through sacrifice or idols (such as Zooba) conflicted with the central Muslim tenet.

In 1982, when the ideological crisis escalated in Bulumi, proponents of the secret societies emphasized the importance of coexistence. For more than one hundred fifty years in Vai country, Islam and the societies had operated side by side. Many people who in 1982 denounced the societies had formerly championed them. People at Bulumi began to discuss ritual sacrifices: discussion afforded catharsis for staunch Muslims who wished to allay the guilt surrounding their past participation. Eventually, the Muslim opponents of traditional ritual practices made a claim that impressed many townspeople: God could tolerate violations of Islamic doctrine only so long; for blasphemous acts associated with the societies, he had cursed Bulumi, and was holding back modern development and prosperity. The assertion persuaded many who had experienced hardship; others, however, kept the old ways. A wary tolerance between Islam and traditional religious practices continued.

THE END OF PORO, CHANGES IN SANDE

In 1984, two closely related events extensively remodeled religious life at Bulumi: the setting up of a Friday mosque, and the abolition of the traditional versions of the secret societies. In that year, the imams, with pressure from occasional itinerant Muslim missionaries, imposed a ban on all Poro activities in the Tombe chiefdom. Local Muslim leaders petitioned the regional Islamic Council to institute a Friday mosque (*jami*). The Council responded favorably, on condition that Bulumi ban all Poro activities. In a highly emotional sermon (*kabande*), the Makbɔuma Imam Momo Nyei, an outspoken opponent of the secret societies, brought the issue before the townspeople. Musa Deke, the head of Poro activities (*dazoo*) at Bulumi, was so moved, he stood up and repented, renouncing his past involvement in Poro, and calling for its end.

As the men moved to abolish Poro, pressure mounted to adopt the Muslim version of Sande. Without fanfare, Bulumi voluntarily transformed its Sande into an acceptable Muslim version called *mɔli* Sande; other towns followed suit. By the 1990s, most Vai towns in the coastal region had adopted the Muslim version of Sande, which does not have the Zooba. At Bulumi in 1977, a *zoo kɛŋ* 'ritual specialist's house', where people kept the Sande spirit impersonator costumes and other ritual paraphernalia, stood prominently in the center of town. The events of 1984 resulted in the razing of the *zoo* house, and its replacement with a civic meeting hall.

The decree to ban the traditional versions of Poro and Sande was a victory for the conservative Muslim faction, and a defeat for those who preferred coexistence between the secret societies and Islam. Many felt the town had relinquished to an alien force its ties to the past, and had succumbed to fanatical persecution. The secret societies had been arbiters of culture, patrons of the arts, preservers of tradition, and transmitters of social skills. Its carvers provided masks for dancers; its weavers and seamstresses designed and made costumes for initiate dancers and masqueraders in Sande and Poro; its master teachers had trained instrumentalists and dancers; and the events of the Poro-Sande cycles had afforded much communal entertainment, and had helped maintain the social order.

The abolition of Poro at Bulumi was not a fluke. By the late 1970s, Vai Poro was already on the decline. In the neighboring Gawula chiefdom, the Manobala clan had banned the institution about forty years before, and its men had ceased sending their sons for Poro training (Ofri 1972:6). Many men did not feel much impact, since they had other opportunities for employment, education, and camaraderie. The change, however, was particularly devastating to women, who had operated Sande lodges throughout the Tombe chiefdom. Women were left to ponder their social responsibilities, their mortality, and their musical roles in society. They no longer had a systematic way to develop their musical skills.

In traditional society, Sande songs had served a variety of purposes, ranging from instructional songs (to teach initiates personal hygiene) to highly esoteric ones. Sande songs—which included songs in the Mende, Gola, Dei, and Vai languages—represented the largest corpus of songs in the Vai music repertory. Outside of Sande, women used these songs as lullabies, to accompany work, or simply for pleasure. The banning of Sande halted the rituals and ceremonies that transmitted these songs from one generation to another. Many songs will live as part of Mende, Gola, and Dei Sande, since those ethnic groups shared the repertory; but for all practical purposes among the Vai, the songs will die with the last generation of women initiated into a traditional version of Sande. The Muslim version of Sande offers little hope of preserving traditional songs, since that repertory consists primarily of Islamic songs in Arabic.

The change to the Muslim version of Sande ended several feasts that contributed

Zooba   Masked dancer in the Sande society who impersonates a male ancestor water spirit

kengai   Vai women who supervise all Sande musical activities; expert dancers and singers

tɔmbɔ kɛ bɔɔnie-nu   Dance troupe for young initiates of the Sande society among the Vai people

to social life. Mɔli Sande retains many of the occasions, but the absence of the traditional music and dance components deprives them of fervor and excitement. A conservative Islamic approach to Mɔli Sande bans dancing and playing the gourd rattle (*sasaa*), though Bulumi does not subscribe to that outlook. Such is the case in the "Muslim towns," where Mɔli Sande started; Sande there provides the models from which other Mɔli Sande derive.

The fate of Zooba

The demise of once-important elements in Sande ritual and ceremony had a big impact on the traditional version of the Sande—and by extension, on most traditional music performed by women. Zooba, the central figure in this controversy, the Sande masked spirit impersonator, requires special discussion, since Muslims targeted it as one of the main violations of Islamic doctrine.

Tolerance for the male masqueraders was notably different from that accorded Zooba. Early in the 1900s, Yavi, Bɔwu, Nafali, Joobai, and Kɔlɔkpɔ, came from Mende and Gola areas. Among the Vai, they had no spiritual importance, and no connection with the Poro society. Little (1951:246–247) calls them Poro Spirits. Among the Vai, however, individual wealthy men or groups of men sponsored them in quasi-secret societies (*gbonji-nu*). Past observers' connecting them with Poro derives from the fact that formerly a man had to be a member of Poro in order to wear a mask. Masked dancing was like any manly endeavor: Poro membership was prerequisite to participation. Even in the late 1980s (well after the demise of Zooba at Bulumi), the male masqueraders continued to play an important role at celebratory occasions. But they were merely professional entertainers, members of an itinerant troupe who performed for pay. The Vai called them *tɔmbɔ kɛ feŋ-nu* 'playthings'. Since their activities did not challenge Muslim views on idolatry and spirit representation, their support was far different from that of Zooba.

In towns favoring marginal Islam, both Zooba and the male masqueraders continued, while the towns that adhered to a conservative Islam did not allow masked dancing. They may still have allowed dancing by the male masqueraders, but as Islam gained a greater hold, it too faced an unhappy fate. The continued presence of the male masked dancers, and the absence of Zooba, are key factors in characterizing Islam at Bulumi as transitional.

Zooba was more than an entertainer. Having been a part of the Vai Sande society for more than one hundred fifty years, it was part of a notable number of institutionalized ritual practices. Recognition of a masked spirit impersonator in Vai Sande first appears in Koelle (1854:203), under the designation "Nou"; later, Büttikofer (1890:255, 307–310), Johnston (1906:1032–56), and Ellis (1914:54, 71) mention the dancer, providing pictorial documentation.

Practically every Sande jurisdiction had one or more Zooba. As an important part of Sande, Zooba's participation had to occur at no less than five major esoteric Sande rituals, and possibly at others that took place in secret.

In traditional society, Zooba personified supernatural power. As the impersonator of a founding male ancestor, Zooba commanded the respect of its followers. Myth and lore register the origin of the Sande spirit guardian. Asked where the Zooba came from, Vai women say they found it near the river, or that it came from the water. The Mende and the Gola share that belief. For a fuller account of the Sande spirit impersonator among the Mende, see Phillips (1978) and Boone (1986); and among the Gola, see d'Azevedo (1973).

Muslims oppose the Zooba on legalistic grounds: as a spirit impersonator, it violates Islamic laws against idolatry. However, the psychological reasons go deeper. Zooba served as an agent of social control, and as the bearer of strong Sande medicines, for which men had no antidote. The mask bearer's identity was secret; and men were always curious as to whose wife was behind the mask. The Zooba mask may be the only mask women wear in Africa, though Vai women do not know that. Because of its controlling powers, Zooba was a major stabilizing force in conflicts between men and women. In the past, Sande women, bolstered by the power of Zooba, could levy heavy fines on men (or even uninitiated women) who violated laws protecting the Sande and women in general. In addition to fines, other Sande reprisals could result in a man's illness, including scrotal elephantiasis, a dreaded disease. Hence, it was in part men's fear of Zooba's underlying power that enforced traditional law. In the presence of Zooba, further restrictions limited men's freedom. Men could not lawfully approach within ten feet of the dancer. Without proper settlement, an accidental bump could result in a fine or a Zooba-induced sickness. Men often complained that their wives pledged greater allegiance to the Sande and Zooba than to them.

Musically, Zooba Sande provided opportunities for female musicians and dancers. Months or years of training preceded the artisans' taking part in public rituals. Women bearing the title *kengai* supervised all Sande musical activities. Well versed in Sande music, the *kengai* was the person most knowledgeable about the repertory. She was an expert dancer, singer, and *sasaa* player. Having received musical training in Sande herself, she had the responsibility of teaching to novice Zooba dancers, and to girls in the initiate dance troupe (*tɔmbɔ kɛ bɔɔmiɛ-nu*), the intricate style of dance and its *sasaa* rhythms. Her musical responsibility extended to the general Sande membership. It was her job to teach the songs associated with all phases of Sande ritual and ceremony. For talented female dancers, instrumentalists, and singers, the traditional version of Sande was a pathway toward participation in local musical life.

Zooba Sande reaffirmed the solidarity of women, and served as a symbol of female values and beliefs. It was the mechanism women employed to identify themselves as a corporate unit, and to maintain boundaries between themselves and men. As a sign of both self-identity and group affiliation, Sande prescribed and asserted traditional social values.

Islamic Sande

In the mid 1980s, Zooba was no longer a subject for open debate, but some people at Bulumi still expressed opposing views on the new musical and social orientation for Sande. Many believed the advent of Mɔli Sande and its associative songs in Arabic deprived women of the intracultural communicative function of song. The songs of Mɔli Sande appeal to God and praise Muhammad, in affirmation of Islamic values. Unlike the songs of the traditional Sande, they are not the codified, denotative forms of expression that communicate direct and immediate meaning through a commonly

Zooba Sande reaffirmed the solidarity of women, and served as a symbol of female values and beliefs.

understood language. Traditional Sande provided women a power base from which to set up boundaries; each three-year session was a revalidation of women's aesthetic, sacred, and social values. Many people who otherwise opposed the new orientation believed it unlikely that Mɔli Sande would instill such a strong social consciousness among women. Because its sessions were short (three weeks), failure to provide substantive musical training, and inability to instill and strengthen a lifelong bond left many women unfulfilled, knowing their experience differed from that of their mothers and grandmothers.

The proponents of Mɔli Sande expressed different opinions about its role and purpose in contemporary society. Some said the training purportedly provided by Zooba Sande in the past was no longer needed. Girls' mothers could teach them about sexual behavior, childrearing, and other duties of wife and mother. By participating in the everyday life of women, girls could learn about fishing, rice farming, and their other occupational duties. Modern feminist philosophy was not foreign to this debate. Many women felt the longer session common to Zooba Sande deprived girls of opportunities to get a Western-style education, live in an urban area, and pursue a professional career.

Economic elements also entered the objection to Zooba Sande. Men, especially, decried the exorbitant amount of money needed to keep a girl in Sande for a three-year period. Beyond the religious challenge, many saw Sande as a moneymaking scheme. One man said it cost him five bags of rice and over one hundred dollars to keep an older daughter in Zooba Sande for three years; but his younger daughter spent only three weeks in Mɔli Sande, at a cost of only $25. Others said it cost less to send a girl through government school than to put her through Zooba Sande. They added that Mɔli Sande advanced the peace and prosperity of a community: it does not operate by secrecy and fear. Men could enter the secluded area, which formerly they never could have done. Muslim belief opposed fear-instilling elements, and there was no Zooba to scare people.

Mɔli Sande culled out the most offensive aspects of Zooba Sande, and retained those elements acceptable to his interpretation of Islam, including clitoridectomy. While the musical repertory was much smaller, the corpus of Mɔli Sande songs had a unique richness. The "Muslim towns" rejected traditional songs and *sasaa* playing; but from traditional versions, Bulumi retained instrumental performance, plus many of the song types in the Vai, Mende, and Gola languages. These included praise songs for new graduates, *ziawa* dance songs, and processional songs. Even songs that once served to praise the Zooba gained a new function, and often served to greet and praise the head of the Sande, known as *maazo*. Keeping in mind the religious intent of this version of Sande, the girls received the opportunity for formal religious training; and in the confines of secluded areas, male clerics gave them instruction. Most importantly, unlike Zooba Sande, Mɔli Sande had divine approval.

Overall, despite the absence of Zooba and the mysteries that formerly surround-

FIGURE 7   New graduates of the *Zooba Sande*
society in traditional dress. Bulumi, 1977.

FIGURE 7   New graduates of the *Zooba Sande* society in traditional dress. Bulumi, 1977.

ed the institution of Zooba, and despite the singing of Islamic songs, the public face of Sande at Bulumi changed very little. The women did, in fact, try to maintain the female-bonding role and other essential attributes of Mɔli Sande. From the traditional version, they retained the sororal element, the aesthetic principles associated with femininity, the showering of gifts, and the special treatment and privileges accorded new graduates several weeks after graduation (figure 7). Islam's impact on the celebration affected only spirit impersonation and the rituals done in the bush—elements women would not discuss for the record.

BULUMI IN 1987–1988

By 1987, more changes had occurred. The scope of these developments provides an interesting contrast with the state of Muslim affairs in the period ten years earlier. At the individual level, changes had taken place in the occupational roles of religious leaders, musicians, and ordinary worshippers. On another level, changes in the secret societies and Muslim sectarian groups had occurred. Several classes of music had disappeared from the repertory, and Islamic classes had joined it. Social occasions that had required traditional musical resources now required Islamic interpretations. Bulumi had indeed changed, and much of the difference came from Islam. A look at some of the major developments can show the variety of the changes.

With the newfound commitment to Islam, Muslims sought to solidify their control over religious life. They had ended the secret societies, and people began to pursue the wider Islamic world. Local entrepreneurs sought to acquaint the citizenry with universal Islam. From Monrovia, they brought foreign-produced cassettes that contained recordings of prayers, call to prayer (*azan*), and koranic cantillation, educating local people on the eloquence of Islamic vocalizing. Books on Muslim formalities, ranging in scope from the role of women or bathing the dead to praise poetry for holiday ceremonies or picture posters of Muhammad, found their way into households. The new generation of young Muslims took a more conservative approach to the religion; the conflict that in previous years had erupted between Islamic and traditional factions did not distract them.

The musical life of the town also changed. Many of the younger schoolchildren

Some young men at Bulumi memorized the styles of Qur'ānic chant on audio cassettes purchased from sidewalk merchants.

were less familiar with the musical repertory of the secret societies than children of the same age ten years earlier. Their knowledge of Islamic songs, however, far exceeded that of their older peers. The demise of the traditional versions of the secret societies, the importation of Islamic material items from urban centers, and changing concepts of the role and performance of Islamic music, placed Bulumi on the path toward a conservative Islamic environment.

Bulumi gained greater contact with the wider Islamic world when two young townsmen returned from study in Guinea and Iran. In 1985, the town appointed Varni Kamara an assistant imam, and in 1986 it hired Muhammad Manobala as the Arabic teacher at the Mohammed Kamara English-Arabic School. In 1987–1988, in addition to memorizing passages in the Qur'ān, several boys and girls were learning to read and write Arabic. Music became an important part of the curriculum. Students accompanied with song the morning flag-raising ceremony, and marched between classes singing popular Muslim anthems.

Not all Vai people noticed the cultural achievements of Islamic societies. Young scholars, through travel and education, in the Middle East and other parts of Africa, were the main conduits for local people to learn about a world with a deeply intellectual, artistic, religious, and historical background. The influence of these young scholars became a key impetus for further change in religious life at Bulumi. Among the many innovations their influence spawned were fresh interpretations of the Qur'ān and Muslim law, local libraries of contemporary books on the life and sayings of Muhammad, and new approaches to the performance of music.

After four years of study in West Asia, Muhammad Manobala put his newly acquired knowledge to use as the town's *suku-ba* (professional Qur'ānic reciter and cantor). He had not received formal training in Arabic music theory or composition, but his travels had exposed him to new concepts about the performance of music in Islamic contexts. At prayer time, people often gathered around the mosque to hear his call to prayer. His talent earned him a special distinction among townsfolk. He was the one with the fine voice (*nyia kulɛ*). He was equally adept at reciting the Qur'ān in genuine Arabic style. His talent earned him a reputation as the most professional music maker in town, and he often served as a celebrant for Muslim occasions in distant towns. In the past, before it replaced the call-to-prayer drum (*tabula*), the *azan* resembled heightened speech; but with the new awareness of Islamic practices brought from Iran by Muhammad Manobala, it became routine to hear a call to prayer containing melodic elements common to music in that region (figure 8). Similar innovations occurred in ceremonies of prayer, and in Qur'ānic chant.

By 1988, young men at Bulumi began to strive to recite the Qur'ān in *d'aabo kulɛ* 'Arabic voice'. Many of them traveled to study with expatriate Lebanese and Syrian Muslims in Monrovia, while others memorized the styles of Qur'ānic chant on audio cassettes purchased from sidewalk merchants. Many achieved exceptional results, learning by rote the diction, timbre, embellishments, and melodic structures

FIGURE 8 Excerpt from a new
azan. Bulumi, 1988.

Al la hu Ak bar Al la hu Ak bar Al la hu

Ak bar Al la

hu. Ak bar Ash ha du an la î la ha

ill' Al lah Ash ha du an la

îl la ha ill' Al lah

Ash ha du an na muham ma du ra soo lu 'llah

common to Middle Eastern recitation. Most young scholars supported themselves as Arabic teachers; hence, they passed their musical tendencies on to their students.

Change was manifest everywhere. People integrated Muslim practices into their daily lives. Because they were away at work on their farms, few participated in day-time prayers at Bulumi, but they attended evening prayers in large numbers. In the 1970s, the town had no Friday service; but a decade later, it teemed with people from throughout the chiefdom, who made the weekly journey to pray. Theoretically, Islam recognizes no institutionalized clergy; yet local, regional, and national Muslim clerics functioned within a hierarchy. Musa Kamara, the town imam, became head Muslim celebrant in all of Tombe; for all practical purposes, he was the region's main spokesman on religious matters.

In the past, Musa Kamara and other imams had been hesitant to raise in public the issue of the secret societies and spirit worship. In 1977, many were openly apologetic to audiences about disparaging statements others had attributed to them. By 1988, the conservative faction asserted itself obtrusively. Imams publicized their opposition to secret societies, while spreading Islam's message of life, knowledge, and gratitude. People often accused the imams of practicing witchcraft, and of using the power of the Qur'ān in despicable ways, such as making poisonous potions, or empowering dangerous animals to attack opponents. People recognized, however, that the good works these men did in their communities (as doctors, advisers, clerics) offset such allegations. In addition to the power local clerics wielded in the religious arena, they also advised paramount and town chiefs on major political and social issues.

By the late 1980s, the people of Bulumi no longer participated in the activities at Zontori, or conducted sacrifices to local ancestors. Officials brought before the town court anyone accused of such acts. The songs associated with these practices were no longer a part of the repertory. People now frowned on activities involving secular forms of singing and dancing, and devout adherents were quick to point out blasphemous behavior, either directly to individuals, or through sermons in the mosque.

FIGURE 9   Portion of
dhikr. Bulumi, 1988.

ilai   ilai   i lai lai hu lai   ilai   i lai lai hu lai   ilai   i lai lai hu lai   ilai   i lai lai

SUFISM AT BULUMI

After the transformation of Sande and the abolition of Poro, the men of Bulumi were
without a comparable sodality. There was an attempt to revive the age-old circumcision institution known as Bili; but like Poro, it did not meet Islamic standards. Men
who desired a stronger relationship with the new religion, and who hoped to instill
the sense of male camaraderie lost with the Poro, looked to the Islamic brotherhoods.

The two brotherhoods found among the Vai—Qaddiriyya and Tijaniyya—trace
their roots to the Sufi sects of North Africa and West Asia. They do not, however,
maintain the mysticism of the parent groups. Qaddiriyya, the first sect to enter Vai
country, came with the Koniaka immigrants during the 1800s, and persisted in the
region till the 1930s. In the early 1990s, it had only a few adherents, in Zogboja and
Makbɔuma. Tijaniyya is widespread throughout Vai country, and is the only sect represented at Bulumi. It came first to Misila, introduced to Liberia in the mid 1930s,
by the marabout Al-Hajj Mohammed Ahmad Tunis. After coming to Liberia (from
southern Sierra Leone), he, through several miraculous acts, influenced the beginnings of the Tijaniyya in Vai country. (For an account of his influence, see Goody et
al. 1977:289–304). His most influential student was Braimah Nyei, a resident of
Misila, whose followers were instrumental in spreading Tijaniyya to Bulumi. People
credit Tunis with bringing several new Islamic songs to Liberia, and his role as leader
of the Tijaniyya sect inspired his followers to compose others.

Chief Elder Senesee Kroma and Imam Musa Kamara underwent training in
Tijaniyya at Misila, and in turn became leaders of the sect at Bulumi. Musa Kamara
became the local sect leader (*muqaddam*). Because of the required commitments and
rigorous training, only six older men at Bulumi are Tijaniyya adherents. Only one of
the young scholars mentioned earlier has attained the necessary status to begin the
training for membership. Adherents to Tijaniyya represent the strongest of the faithful: they refrain from drinking alcohol, smoking tobacco, and other proscribed recre-
ations, such as adultery and gambling. For them, becoming a member of the
Tijaniyya means achieving a higher religious status, one that places them closer to the
deity.

On Thursday nights, members of the Bulumi Tijaniyya gather in the mosque for
the weekly *dhikr.* (A degree of secrecy surrounds the Tijaniyya; and while nonmembers are permitted to watch the *dhikr* and other activities, its adherents are reluctant
to speak openly about its inner workings.) People discharge in private the other
obligatory functions of the sect, or make them part of daily prayers. For *dhikr*, men
dress in long gowns, spread a white cloth on the floor, sprinkle perfume about, and
proceed to recite key Muslim phrases, only occasionally moving to a tonally elevated
vocal production (figure 9). With the *tasabia*, a string of prayer beads, they tell the
repetitions. During the ritual, they appear to move into a state of ecstasy, though the
phenomenon of altered states of consciousness associated with some forms of Sufism
is uncommon.

These men have no money for the pilgrimage to Mecca. Therefore, they forgo the external journey, and rely on the power of their faith as expressed in the *dhikr* for a purely inner voyage, a voyage to the birthplace of the faith. As Sufis, they seek within themselves the meaning behind the teachings of the Qur'ān. Through the ritual procedure of the *dhikr*, they hope to achieve the state of consciousness that made the advent of Muhammad possible. Meditation, reflection, and commitment to the faith, are the means of achieving the inner *hadj*. People reported that a Tijaniyya adherent in a nearby town had achieved such a close relationship with the deity, he miraculously traveled to Mecca each night to pray. Such reports, and the belief that such events actually occur, intensify faith in the power of the sect.

THE EVOLVED FORTIETH-DAY DEATH FEAST

Few traditional social occasions match the magnitude of the fortieth-day death feast (*ɗaa*). These funerary celebrations now use music in novel ways. While crowds continue to attend such occasions, musical activities involving masquerades and itinerant professional musicians are less common. People disparage these activities, especially when a family that has accepted a more conservative approach to Islam sponsors the feast. People also understand that the Mahodi Kɔŋpiŋ will not contribute to the cost of hiring musicians or dancers. The Mahodi Kɔŋpiŋ is a voluntary association, originally set up to oversee the celebration of the prophet's birth, but it claims the added responsibility of financing the funerary activities of its members.

The main features of the fortieth-day death feasts in 1988 were the preparation of the rice powder (*dɛɛ*), which involved the singing of Islamic songs; the processions and speeches at the home of the deceased, which involved a mixture of Islamic and traditional praise songs; the collective reading of the Qur'ān (*fidao*); and the final sacrifice, involving Muslim prayers, songs, and eulogies. Thus, the Muslim elements that formerly mixed with traditional celebration of *ɗaa* now stand alone, as the main features of contemporary Muslim feasts. People at Bulumi say there is no prohibition against the incorporation of traditional practices into *ɗaa*. The consensus is that conservative Muslims reserve the right not to contribute to, or participate in, those portions that infringe on their religious principles.

CELEBRATION OF MUHAMMAD'S BIRTH

Large-scale celebrations of Islamic holidays are recent additions to Islamic life at Bulumi. Because of the cost associated with large social occasions, Bulumi and the nearby town of Tɛɛ jointly host the yearly celebrations of Milaji (Miraj, Muhammad's birth) and Mahodi (Mawlid). Besides Ramadan, people consider Mahodi the most important Muslim occasion. At Bulumi, the *Mahodi manja* 'Mahodi chief', leader of the Mahodi Kɔŋpiŋ, is responsible for inviting the celebrants, collecting contributions from townspeople, and coordinating with people of Tɛɛ the annual celebration. As with other holidays, the structure of Mahodi spread to Bulumi from the town of Misila, which celebrated its first Mahodi in 1937. Celebrations of Muhammad's birth had occurred (under the name *al nabi sota*) in previous years at Makbɔuma, another "Muslim town."

As in other parts of the Islamic world, Mahodi at Bulumi occurs on the twelfth day of the third month of the Islamic calendar (*rabi al-'awwal*). Its structure matches that elsewhere: retelling events from Muhammad's life, and offering praises of him (al Faruqi 1986:79). The Bulumi version lasts twelve hours. It occurs in the town's meeting hall, which has enough space and ventilation.

As an aesthetic form, Mahodi brings together many artistic elements the Vai rec-

The people of Bulumi think Muhammad, though physically absent, is in spiritual contact with them, and their celebrations provide the opportunity to exhibit commitment to his teachings.

ognize: the art of reading Islamic praise poetry, literature, and the Qur'ān; the elegant accoutrements of Islam, joyous singing, and dance. Celebrants come from the learned classes, those who have an exceptional knowledge of Islam and its teaching. They divide into three groups: readers (reciters), interpreters, and song leaders. Readers recite from the Arabic text in a style similar to that of Qur'ānic chant. In a normal voice, the interpreter speaks a phrase-by-phrase interpretation of the Arabic. Thus, both the readers and interpreters must be fluent in Arabic; during the event, they often exchange roles. The *suku-ba* is the song leader who interjects songs, which may derive from several sources, taking many forms—musical interpretation of a particularly profound statement in the text, a cantillation based on poetic verse that appears in the text, a set of improvised sections of the Qur'ān, or a famous Muslim anthem sung responsorially with the audience. The texts come from a variety of sources. At Bulumi, people call them simply Mahodi books. Publishers in the Sudan and Egypt ship them for sale in Islamic bookstores in Monrovia.

In 1987–1988, the *suku-ba* at the Bulumi celebration was also fluent in Arabic, and thus had the ability to improvise on the text. He cued the audience to provide a simple response, over which he improvised. When inspired, an audience member could begin a song, which all would join. In such musical interludes, people often sang commonly known panegyric anthems, in the basic responsorial style.

The people of Bulumi add a dramatic touch to the celebration of Mahodi. In general, the texts emphasize the moral state of the world before Muhammad's birth—the period leading up to the his birth; his mother's anguish in childbirth; discussions between God, Adam, and Gabriel about him; and his life on earth. During the episode leading to his birth (often the last segment of the event), three women dressed in white come forward and sit before the celebrants. One of the women takes the role of Muhammad's pregnant mother; the others take the role of midwives. The reading becomes impassioned, and the audience stands and joins in song with the celebrants. The celebrants hold a white sheet over the women's heads, and slowly lower it over them and the main celebrant. As the *suku-ba* leads the audience in song, people dance about, clapping and rejoicing. Underneath the sheet, moans and groans associated with childbirth sound. When members of the audience lift the sheet, the main celebrant appears, drinking milk from a glass. The climactic ending symbolizes the birth of Muhammad and the taking of his first nourishment from his mother. It inspires more intense singing and dancing, which spills outside the meeting hall. The celebrants and audience members conclude the event in an hour-long procession of singing and dancing around the town.

Like other major events, Mahodi is an auspicious, joyous occasion. The people of Bulumi experience a passion that moves them to dance, rejoice, and weep. They think Muhammad, though physically absent, is in spiritual contact with them, and their celebrations provide them the opportunity to exhibit commitment to his teachings.

CHANGING CONCEPTS ABOUT MUSIC

In addition to the changing role of music in solidly embedded traditions, or its role in newly introduced Muslim occasions, a deeply Islamic philosophical underpinning has changed Vai concepts about music. Islam's roots draw sustenance from a philosophy that challenges music itself. This philosophy commonly finds expression in the language used by the Vai to distinguish song for traditional purposes from song used for Islamic or Islam-sanctioned occasions.

The Vai language has no generic term for the Western concept of music, though there are words for 'dance' (tɔmbɔ), 'song' (dɔŋ), and 'instrumental performance' (seŋ feŋ). People do not use the term dɔŋ in association with Islamic music. They refer the form of sound perceived as 'song' to suku, from Arabic shukran 'give thanks'. This tendency has far-reaching implications for sung performances, in all their sacred and secular contexts.

Throughout the Islamic world, scholars make attempts to distinguish secular music from the systems of sound associated with Islam. They do not consider koranic chant, with its myriad melodic interpretations, song or music. Lois al-Faruqi makes an analogy that has widespread application in the Islamic world: in an Islamic context, musiqa, the Arabic term for music, does not apply. Hence, al Faruqi refers to "music" in Islam, not as musiqa, but as handasah al sawt 'the art of sound'. The implication is that Islam has no music, and people should avoid such a designation. The scholars at Bulumi recognized this concept: asked to translate the Arabic term musiqa into Vai, they overwhelmingly responded with the Vai word dɔŋ.

Al-Faruqi's distinction between musiqa and handasah al sawt is similar to the Vai's distinction between dɔŋ and suku, but still another factor is germane: that of textual language. Ideally, all suku should have an Arabic text; otherwise, the performer is not using the deity's words. The Vai believe Arabic to be sacred; the ability to read, write, and sing in it is a special gift. In a religious setting, this linguistic element transcends its customary use; and nowhere is the practice clearer than in the manufacture of amulets, medicines, and other magical items. The Vai tell countless stories of people with "special gifts" to influence malevolent and benevolent forces by reading sections from the Qur'ān. Muslims believe written Arabic words have power, which they can capture in inscribed talismans, or in holy-water medicine (made by washing Arabic texts from slates). The Vai believe power flows from the text of the Qur'ān. The musical extension of this belief is that the chanting of Arabic through Qur'ānic verses or prayers, and the singing of suku, are also assets of Islam. In any socioreligious context, the performance of suku is an act to invoke divine favor, and a step toward holiness.

The Vai believe suku has the power to enunciate a set of spiritual principles for all to espouse. Further research may record and illuminate the purposes suku serves, and the forms it takes. Its melodies and structures are nearly as variable as words in the texts; but beneath the apparent variety, it shares a common intent with ritual prayer and koranic chant—to communicate with unseen omnipotence.

THE ISLAMIC MUSICAL REPERTORY

Islam has no hierarchy of songs. The Vai do not consider koranic chant suku; and though they hold people in high esteem for reciting it in a sweet voice (nyia kulɛ) or an Arabic voice (dʼaabo kulɛ), they recognize no professional class or style of recitation. They believe everyone—regardless of status, gender, or ethnicity—is free to recite the Qur'ān, in direct communication with God.

Stylistically, Vai Islamic music has few similarities with that found in parts of the Islamic world outside of West Africa. Vai Islamic music is entirely vocal. The Arabic-inspired instruments and instrumental genres of Nigeria, Ghana, and regions of the

The profession of faith in song may serve aptly in a funeral, or at a chief's installation.

Western Sudan, have not penetrated the coastal plain. For an account of Arabic and Islamic musical influences in the Western Sudan, see Farmer (1924, 1939), Nketia (1971, 1974), and Hause (1948). Other than a few new approaches to the call to prayer or Qur'ānic chant, brought by people returning from lengthy visits to other Islamic regions (styles the people have not widely adopted), the traits of Vai Islamic music are similar to those commonly associated with West African music. Most of the repertory came with the Koniaka immigrants. It does not differ markedly from that found in other Islamized areas of Liberia, southern Sierra Leone, or southern Guinea, where Koniaka traders settled and spread the faith.

The structures of Vai Islamic music typically use responsorial patterns, choral unison, and sporadic harmony in organum at the fourth—features commonplace in traditional Vai music. The more sophisticated styles are two-part songs with repeated refrains and an improvised solo line, most commonly performed at holiday celebrations by a *suku-ba* with audience accompaniment.

The Vai do not recognize a hierarchy for pieces in the Islamic musical repertory; nor, though they designate some items as funeral songs, school songs, dance songs, and songs specifically for the Mɔli Sande, do they try to fit songs into neatly organized classes. Over several years, for the enactment of Mahodi, people at Misila composed a group of songs; but they also performed those songs as anthems at political meetings and funerals. Thus, many songs were transferable to different social and religious contexts. The profession of faith in song may serve aptly in a funeral, or at a chief's installation.

What role, if any, does original composition play in Vai Islamic music? The question is difficult, since the Vai do not approach composition formally. The Islamic repertory expands by incorporating precomposed songs, brought to Bulumi by itinerant clerics and learned from radio and commercially produced audiotapes. These songs serve as anthems and panegyric hymns.

From fragments of Qur'ānic verses or Muslim sayings or anecdotes, people compose other songs locally, and soon forget them; other songs last longer, to become permanent parts of the repertory. The texts of these songs are often mixtures of several languages (Vai, Koniaka, Arabic) and vocables. A textual analysis reveals little semantic coding. Texts have an implied meaning, however, which people cannot precisely explicate, because of their lack of command of the language; but as Nketia has noted, songs with unintelligible texts can have an "intensity value" outsiders may fail to appreciate:

> The obscurity of meaning resulting from the use of unintelligible texts and mixed languages or the use of a language foreign to worshippers does not detract from the intensity value of the songs as corporate utterances of worship. Worshippers may sing them with as much zest and religious emotion as they sing songs in familiar languages, for the intensity value of religious songs comes first and foremost from

awareness of their ritual value, that is, their value as avenues for establishing contact with the unseen. (1988:58–59)

The composition of Islamic song types follows constructive processes similar to those of the composition of traditional song types. In certain Islamic and traditional contexts, a successful occasion depends on the compositional inventiveness of the performers. Both Vai and Islamic traditions prize invention and creativity: the mutual ideal is to work with a standard set of conventions and formulas that townspeople learn as part of the normal enculturative process. What counts is the inventiveness and manipulation of these concepts—the ability to use them to exploit extemporaneously the excitement of an occasion.

REFERENCES

al Faruqi, Lois I. 1986. "Handashah al Sawt or the Art of Sound." In *The Cultural Atlas of Islam*, ed. Isma'il al Faruqi and Lois Lamya' al Faruqi, 441– 479. New York: Macmillan.

———. 1986. "The Mawlid." *The World of Music* 28(3):79–89.

Boone, Sylvia A. 1986. *Radiance from the Waters: Ideals of Feminine Beauty in Mende Art*. New Haven, Conn.: Yale University Press.

Büttikofer, Johann. 1890. *Reisebilder aus Liberia*. 2 vols. Leiden: Brill.

d'Azevedo, Warren L. 1962. "Some Historical Problems in the Delineation of a Central West Atlantic Region." *Annals of the New York Academy of Sciences* 96(2):512– 538.

———. 1973. "Mask Makers and Myth in Western Liberia." In *Primitive Art and Society*, ed. Anthony Forge, 126–150. London: Oxford University Press.

Ellis, George W. 1914. *Negro Culture in West Africa*. New York: Neale. Repr. New York: Johnson Reprint Corporation, 1970.

Farmer, Henry George. 1924. "The Arab Influence on Music of the Western Soudan." *Musical Standard* 24:158–159.

———. 1939. "Early References to Music in the Western Sūdān." *Journal of the Royal Asiatic Society of Great Britain and Ireland,* part IV (October):569–579.

Goody, Jack, et. al. 1977. "Writing and Formal Operations: A Case Study among the Vai." *Africa* 47(3):289–304.

Hause, Helen. 1948. "Terms for Musical Instruments in the Sudanic Languages." *Journal of the American Oriental Society* 68(1). Supplement 7.

Johnson, S. Jangaba. 1954. *Traditional History, Customary Laws, Mores, Folkways, and Legends of the Vai Tribe*. Monrovia: Department of the Interior.

Johnston, Harry. 1906. *Liberia*. 2 vols. London: Hutchinson.

Jones, Adam. 1981. "Who Were the Vai?" *Journal of African History* 22:159–78.

Koelle, S. W. 1854. *Outlines of a Grammar of the Vei Language*. London: Church Missionary House.

Levtzion, Nehemia, ed. 1979. *Conversion to Islam*. New York: Holmes and Meier.

Lewis, I. M., ed. 1980. *Islam in Tropical Africa*, 2nd ed. Bloomington: Indiana University Press.

Little, Kenneth. 1951. *The Mende of Sierra Leone: A West African People in Transition*. London: Routledge and Kegan Paul.

Nketia, J. H. Kwabena. 1971. "History and Organization of Music in West Africa." In *Essays on Music and History in Africa*, ed. Klaus P. Wachsmann, 3–25. Evanston, Ill.: Northwestern University Press.

———. 1974. *The Music of Africa*. New York: Norton.

———. 1988. "The Intensity Factor in African Music." In *Performance in Contemporary African Arts*, ed. Ruth M. Stone, 53-86. Bloomington, Ind.: Folklore Institute.

Ofri, Dorith. 1972. "Sowolo 1969: An Ethnomusicological Case Study of the Vai People in Liberia." Paper presented at the Conference on Manding Studies. School of Oriental and African Studies, University of London.

Owen, Nicholas. 1930. *Journal of a Slave-Dealer: "A View of Some Remarkable Axcedents in the Life of Nicholas Owen on the Coast of Africa and America from the Year 1746 to the Year 1757,"* ed. Eveline Martin. London: Routledge.

Phillips, Ruth B. 1978. "Masking in Mande Sande Society Initiation Rituals." *Africa* 48:265–277.

The Guitar in Africa

Andrew L. Kaye

Late Nineteenth and Early Twentieth Centuries
The 1920s and 1930s
The 1940s to 1960
The 1960s to the 1990s

In Africa as abroad, the guitar commonly has two types: acoustic and electric. These types accommodate many structural variations, which embrace distinctive sonic qualities, depending on the number and types of strings, the kinds of wood for the sound box, and—in electric guitars—the number and placement of pickups, the use of distortion, and other electrical or electroacoustic elements, such as solid body or hollowbody (semiacoustic) design. The Spanish or classical guitar, with a fretted neck and six strings (tuned E–a–d–g–b–e′), is a structural prototype for many varieties. There are several tablature notations for the guitar. Staff notation normally puts guitar music in the treble clef, to sound an octave lower than shown.

The system of von Hornbostel and Sachs (1961) classifies the guitar as a composite, lute-type chordophone. The earliest development of this group began in West Asian civilizations of the third and second millennia B.C. An Akkadian cylinder seal dated about the twenty-fourth century B.C. has the earliest known iconographic representation of the lute type, or more precisely, the "long-necked lute." Similar instruments appear in Egyptian iconographic sources of the New Kingdom, dated about the sixteenth to the thirteenth centuries B.C. (Anderson 1980:74).

The short or short-necked lute, the subtype to which Harvey Turnbull ascribes the guitar, probably developed in the first millennium B.C. (1984:89). From approximately the first century B.C., sculptures at Gandhara, in northwestern India, depict short-necked lutes. From the same period, a frieze at Airtam, Uzbekistan, shows an instrument with an in-curved waist, similar to the shape of a guitar (Turnbull 1984:89, fig. 2).

During Europe's Middle Ages, lutes evolved in a multiplicity of forms and directions. The term *guitar*, from Greek *kithara* (possibly via Arabic *qitara*), appears in European texts from about the thirteenth century (Marcuse 1975:218). Scholars, however, have difficulty sorting out the types and names of lutes that appear in iconographic and literary sources during the later medieval period, and confusion over medieval typologies—guitar, gittern, mandola, citole, viola—remains (Tyler 1980:xii, 15–17).

Despite persistent problems of overlapping terms and typologies, scholars agree that by the later 1400s, the guitar had appeared in Europe as a recognizably distinct instrument. It had at least two major subtypes, one with four courses, and one with five. Both subtypes usually had double courses of silk strings, wound with gut and wire. These instruments share the general outline of the modern guitar (which dates to the 1800s), but had smaller dimensions, though the specifics of size and structure varied notably (Evans and Evans 1977; Tyler 1980).

Possibly at that point, the guitar (as it was coming to be defined) entered into the African musical heritage. It may have been introduced into Africa by the Portuguese in the course of their exploration and trading along the West African coast, beginning in the early 1400s. Confirming evidence for this, however, is unavailable, and we cannot prove the European guitar was present in Africa until the end of the 1800s.

We find references to guitars or guitarlike instruments in missionaries' reports and travelers' accounts. Such references, however, must be understood to have been impositions of the European term onto a diversity of African stringed instruments, as a means of describing the instruments for European readers. One such reference, published in a late-seventeenth-century account of Guinea coast travels, cites "a sort of guitar" with six strings (Villault 1669 [1670]:208). This note, however, undoubtedly signifies the harp-lute, called by Bowdich (1819 [1966]) the *sanku*, and now known in the region as the *seperewa*, rather than the guitar.

There is also the curious case of the *ramkie*, a plucked lute with three or four strings, which southern Africans in the Cape Town area may have played as early as the 1730s, but whose origins are unclear (Kirby 1965:249–250; Rycroft 1977:241). The spread of this and other lutelike instruments along the East African coast and in Madagascar may well reflect Arab or Islamic influence and the Indian Ocean trade, as do certain other East African plucked lutes, such as the Swahili *udi* (*'ud*) and the Malagasy *kabosy* (in the Comoro Islands, *gabusi*). However, we know little about the process of diffusion of stringed instruments in Africa before 1800, whether via European or Islamic trade routes.

LATE NINETEENTH AND EARLY TWENTIETH CENTURIES

Toward the end of the 1800s, the development of the colonial system, and the encroachment of urban, commercial, and administrative centers, spreading inland from the coast, brought to Africa many European musical instruments; and surely the guitar was one of them. During the 1800s, the six-string guitar achieved its modern form, after the work of Antonio de Torres Jurado (1817–1892), a Spanish maker. The Spanish guitar may have entered Nigeria with Brazilian and Cuban immigrants in the late 1800s (Omibiyi 1981:162; Waterman 1990:31–32); it may have come to the west coast of Africa with Caribbean and black American immigrants to Liberia and Sierra Leone, and with sailors, soldiers, missionaries, and workers, coming from Europe or the Americas (Darkwa 1974:26).

Other possible sources for the nineteenth-century introduction of the guitar include black American minstrel troupes, which toured South Africa as early as 1887 (Coplan 1985:39). The guitar was well known in Cape Town by the late 1800s, and Cape musicians helped introduce a style of guitar playing like *tickey draai* to towns and mining compounds in the interior (1985:14).

An early twentieth-century photograph shows a racially mixed group of men posing with two guitars, a banjo, a flute, possibly a rattle, and a man holding a book. One of the men has draped over his knees what looks like an American flag. The guitars are of the six-string variety, comparable to flat-top acoustic guitars produced in Europe or America in the late 1800s and early 1900s, such as the American companies Martin, Bruno, and Washburn. The neck of the one on the left is capoed at the third fret. For acoustic guitar music, the use of a *capotasto* is common in Africa,

It is not surprising that the emergence of a circle of guitarists in and around Mombasa dates to the mid- to late 1920s.

FIGURE I "Band on Primrose Mine" (Kallaway and Pearson 1986:22–23).

because it allows the musician to play in higher keys while using first-position fingerings (Kubik 1965).

In 1918, a serialized short story mentions Africans' use of the guitar (Sekyi 1918). The account describes the festivities at Christmastide in Cape Coast.

> The town is gay, giddy, and unsafe for unhardened youths. Men are merry, and some roam the town in rowdy parties, singing songs and playing guitars, accordions, concertinas, tambourines, etc. Music and revelry and noise are abroad. (Sekyi 1918:378)

This account shows the guitar was a familiar instrument in Cape Coast, as it was in Lagos by the period of the Great War, 1914–1917 (Waterman 1990:45). Still, few authors cite the guitar in Africa up to that point, and we must assume the instrument was rare, even among Europeans—for whom brass bands, the organ, and the piano had greater cultural significance.

The passage of the guitar from a position as a limited instrument to one of cultural impact beyond the confines of European communities seems to have taken place in the mid-1920s and in the 1930s. This transition parallels a simultaneous change in interest in the guitar in the West (Danner 1986:296). The classical guitar revival largely associated with Andrés Segovia was one of several factors favoring the instrument in the 1920s. From that time, it had an increasingly prominent role in several American musical genres heard on records and radio, including the blues, country and cowboy music, Hawaiian guitar music, and jazz. Manufacturers developed and marketed diverse types or designs of guitars: the Hawaiian guitar, the Dobro resonator guitar, the twelve-string guitar, the arch-top and flat-top steel-strung guitars, the four-string tenor guitar. In the early 1920s, Lloyd Loar, working for the Gibson company (Kalamazoo, Michigan), experimented with electric pickups for guitars.

It is thus not surprising that the emergence of a circle of guitarists in and around Mombasa dates to the mid- to late 1920s (Kavyu 1978). Rao Rebman, a worker for the East African Railways and Harbours, was then supposedly one of the main guitar teachers. He may have learned to play from one "Jonathan Gitaa" (Kavyu 1978:113). He played with a band formed at the Nyika Club in Rabai in 1926; it included two guitars, banjo, violin, mandolin, double bass, saxophone, and clarinet (Kavyu 1978:117).

Afọlábí Alájá-Browne (1985) and Christopher Waterman (1990) similarly attribute to the 1920s and 1930s the emergence of Yoruba syncretic musical styles using guitars. Waterman suggests that by the 1920s, styles performed on the guitar in Lagos included Spanish, *maringa*, ragtime, European waltzes, and foxtrots (1990:46), plus "a two-fingered style of playing reputedly spread by Kru sailors from Liberia . . . and known by Lagos musicians as *Krusbass*" (1990:47). Several common guitar fingering patterns were associated with Kru styles: mainline, *dagomba*, and fireman (Collins 1989:222). Other patterns used in Nigeria were "Johnny Walker," *yaponsa* (from the Ghanaian song "*Yaa Amponsah*"), and "C-Natural" (Waterman 1990:46–48). These may have comprised the nascent coastal West African genre Collins calls palm wine guitar or palm wine highlife (1989:222); Waterman calls it "the urban West African palm wine guitar tradition" (1990:55). Collins further suggests that, while styles such as mainline should be associated with guitar-playing idioms in the larger towns and ports of the coastal regions, related styles, practiced in hinterland villages, resembled in many ways older traditional idioms. These were known under a host of other names: *ohugua, opim, odonso*, "native blues" (Collins 1987:180, 1989:222; Alájá-Browne 1985:14).

The contexts for guitar playing, as the multiplicity of prevalent styles implies, were variable. They included informal amateur playing and singing among friends, playing at palm wine drinking bars and urban nightclubs, playing for dancing, and performing at traditional or community occasions (weddings, "outdoorings," funerals). The use of Christian lyrics in some guitar songs from the 1920s suggests a possible church use for the guitar.

In the two-finger styles, scholars often assume influence from playing techniques of traditional African plucked stringed instruments. On the guitar, this technique involves the use of the thumb and index finger of the plucking hand (usually the right hand). The thumb picks out a bass figure on the lower three strings, while the index picks out an interlocking rhythmic pattern on the treble strings. Many variations occur, however: the thumb and index finger may work in strict alternation, play a variety of arpeggiated figures, or strike the strings simultaneously, with the index finger strumming a chordal figure over several strings (Kubik 1965; Low 1982b; Rycroft 1961, 1962).

A hint of this playing technique appears in a photo of an ensemble John Collins identifies as the Kumasi Trio (figure 2). He believes it was taken in London in 1928, on the group's recording tour for Zonophone (Collins, personal communication, 1988). The leader of this group, known as "Sam," was one of the pioneers of guitar

Early in 1932, [*The Gold Coast Spectator*] reported
that Augustus Williams, "actor, tap dancer, guitarist
and singer of comic songs," was the first stage
entertainer "to accompany himself on the guitar."

FIGURE 2   Kumasi Trio, ca. 1928. Photo courtesy John Collins.

playing in Ghana (Collins 1985:13). Two of the musicians in the photo pose with
guitars that resemble the guitar on the left in figure 1. As in that picture, the necks of
the guitars are capoed at about the third fret, here with what looks like a pencil, held
in place by a rubber band. The guitarist on the right holds the thumb and index finger of his right hand in playing position. The guitarist on the left appears to finger a
C-major chord, or possibly C-dominant-seventh chord—two of the chordal configurations common in this music. This chord position is comparable to those in photos
of American guitarists from the period (Oliver 1984:32, 50).

In figure 2, further signs are difficult to decipher. The strings were likely of steel,
as they commonly were by the 1920s, though they may have been of gut. Judging by
the fingering-position noted above, we may postulate the instrument uses the standard tuning for the six-string guitar. This, however, is by no means certain, since
alternate guitar tunings abounded in Africa. Waterman reports that musicians in
Lagos used tuning schemes such as Spanish (possibly influenced by American blues
guitar tunings), and tunings similar to Hawaiian slack-key guitar tunings (for example, the open tuning consisting of the intervals fourth-fifth-fourth-major third-minor
third) (1990:46–48).

It is not possible to determine the absolute tuning of the strings, but guitars in
Africa do not usually vary much from the norm of tuning from E on the sixth string.
They may be tuned slightly higher than E, but tend to be tuned slightly lower, to
reduce tension on the strings, and thus to prolong their life (Kubik 1976:168).

THE 1920S AND 1930S

In the 1920s and 1930s, probably the strongest indicator of the coming importance of the guitar in Africa was the issuing of the first extended series of commercial recordings of African music that feature the guitar. Among more than four hundred gramophone records listed in a catalogue of West African records (*Catalogue of Zonophone West African Records* 1929), fifty-seven include the guitar. They include one instrumental trio featuring concertina, guitar, and drum; one guitar solo with vocal refrain; and sixty-two other songs with guitar accompaniment, or the accompaniment of a consort of instruments, including some combination of guitar, banjo, concertina, tambourine, castanets, and drum. The guitar is represented on performances by six of forty-three performers listed in the catalogue. Five of the performers—Daniel Acquaah, George Williams Aingo, Nicholas de Heer, Ben Simmons, and Harry Eben Quashie—were likely Ghanaians, since the catalog lists them as singing in Akan languages (Fanti, Ashanti, Twi). One, Domingo Justus, was evidently a Yoruba speaker from Nigeria. Though they may have made these recordings in Accra or Lagos, they may have made some of them in London (Collins 1985:13).

One of the Zonophone recordings available for analysis, held in the collection of the National Sound Archives (London), is George Williams Aingo's "*Na Mapa Nu Kyew*," called on the record label a "Song in Fanti with guitar and castanets" (Aingo n.d.:B). His commercial recordings of African songs with guitar accompaniment, dating to about 1925, are perhaps the first of their kind (Collins 1985:149–150). He may have recorded them in Accra, but more probably did so in London.

This song suggests an incipient form of the syncretic highlife idiom, which emerged during this period. If the tuning was standard, the guitar was likely capoed on the third fret, and played as if in the key of C in the first position (the actual key is about a minor third higher). Probably using the thumb and index finger, the guitarist picks out the bass line on the lower strings, arpeggiates and strums chords, and occasionally plays the vocal melody in parallel sixths. The song, which concerns a marital dispute (Kwabena N. Bame, personal communication, 1989), consists of a strophic repetition of a Western-type four-bar melody in 4/4 time, in these harmonies:

$$ I--- \mid I^{b7} - IV^6 - \mid IV - I^6_4 - \mid V^7 - I - $$

This pattern, which includes a dominant seventh on the tonic degree in transition to the subdominant chord with the added sixth, is common in guitar music of the Guinea Coast, and is familiar in the guitar music of some other African regions (Low 1982b:106).

Nineteen gramophone records by the Kumasi Trio appear in a later Zonophone catalogue, dating to about 1930. These include thirty-eight songs with guitars and castanets or guitars and drum. Four of them are "sacred songs," of which two have titles that name Jesus and David.

In addition to gramophone recordings, references to the guitar in *The Gold Coast Spectator*, a weekly journal published in Accra from the late 1920s, also suggest a growing presence for the guitar. Early in 1932, the paper reported that Augustus Williams, "actor, tap dancer, guitarist and singer of comic songs," was the first stage entertainer "to accompany himself on the guitar" ("Augustus Williams" 1932:207). Later, encouraging readers to study the instrument seriously, it singles out the guitar as "the most abused instrument," because players are "contented to manipulate one or two popular songs on the instrument without making any effort at improvement" (Danso 1932:432).

In 1934, Percival Kirby suggested the guitar was becoming more common in

FIGURE 3   A phrase from "*Na Mapa Nu Kyew*," a song by George Williams, ca. 1925 (Aingo n.d.:B).

South Africa, where it was available for purchase at cheap prices in trading stores. He noted that it and certain other European instruments "tend, in some cases, to supplant the natives' own" instruments (1965:257). He reported that popular guitar playing consisted of the "rhythmic strumming of two, or perhaps three, of the 'primary' chords" (1965:257).

In the mid-1930s, the British label His Master's Voice (after 1931, part of the EMI conglomerate) issued recordings in which the guitar figures even more prominently than in the Zonophone catalogue of 1929 (Collins 1985:150; Waterman 1986:201–202). This is especially so in the Twi and Fanti (Ghanaian) songs with guitar accompaniment. A later edition of the West Africa catalogue (ca. 1952) lists 118 such songs, by ten performers or groups, with guitar accompaniment. They were presumably recorded in Accra, between 1929 and 1939. Possibly excepting Sam, believed to have recorded with the Kumasi Trio, the performers probably differ from those who appear on the earlier Zonophone recordings. They include Kwamin, Kwesi Pepera, Mireku, Kwabena Mensa, Kwesi Menu, Kofi Mabireh, Piasah, Appianing, and Kamkam.

The typical ensemble for these Twi and Fanti guitar songs was a trio or a quartet. It included a lead vocal part provided by a solo male singer of the tenor range, supporting vocals provided by one or several other men's voices, one or two guitars, and simple percussion provided by a struck idiophone such as an iron bell, a bottle, a cigarette tin, or a wooden box (*adakem*), such as appears in figure 2. Occasionally a drum is indicated. A large lamellophone with three or four metal tongues, known under a variety of names in West Africa (*kongoma, prempresiwa, agidigbo*), sometimes appears.

Mainly by harmonic criteria, the songs group in two classes: (1) songs based on Western diatonic harmony, and (2) songs based on indigenous harmonies. Songs of the first type use cyclic harmonic patterns (sometimes called short forms), over which a human voice spins out a melody. The harmonic patterns are typically of a functional, tonic-subdominant-dominant-tonic nature. Songs of the second type use Western guitar chords, but in ways dictated by indigenous styles. (This distinction may match the stylistic division noted by Collins between coastal and hinterland styles, though these classes do not stand as real geographic divisions, since both styles occurred in both regions.) The use of the guitar in these styles also suggests the guitar was supplanting older, indigenous, stringed instruments (such as the *seperewa* harp-lute), which may previously have served for these idioms (Coplan 1978:101–102).

"*Ampa Afful*" (Sam n.d.), dated to about 1930, exemplifies the first type. It recalls the song of figure 3, but with much more complexity. The artist is again identified as Sam. The ensemble includes two guitars, a tapped idiophone, and a solo vocal part, sung in a high tenor register, with a forceful head voice. At the end of the song, the singers supply a cadential chorus. The song rhythmically develops an off-the-beat timeline pattern in common time (4/4), tapped out on the idiophone. This

FIGURE 4 "*Ampa Afful,*" by Sam. Excerpt transcribed from the instrumental introduction (Sam n.d.). Original key is A-flat. Guitar 1 is capoed at the eighth fret.

Guitar 1 is capoed at the eight fret.
Actual key is A-flat.
Guitar 2 sounds major 10th lower than notated.

guitar 2 repeats last two measures
as a basso ostinato figure

pattern appears in highlife and related genres (figure 4). Its chord progression is similar to that of figure 3. It has a repetitive two-measure pattern, in a subdominant-dominant-tonic relationship.

By playing arpeggiated chords and dyads in sixths, the first-guitar part supports the singer during the verse. In the instrumental introduction, and between the verses, it fills in with a kind of *ritornello* figure, consisting of scalar runs and alternating thirds in a high register, played above the eighth fret. In a lower register, the second guitar provides an ostinatolike figure.

The vocal melody is structured over the eight-pulse cyclic rhythmic and harmonic pattern. It is sung in a recitativelike style, with rather short phrases that often follow a descending contour. The lyrics, sung in Fanti, are topical, with elements of praise song. The singer recounts how some Europeans with a recording machine got interested in recording their music (lyrics translated by Daniel Amponsah and James Osei, personal communication, 1989).

Figure 5 illustrates a song of the second type, "*Agyanka Odede,*" by Kwesi Menu

FIGURE 5 "*Agyanka Odede,*" by Kwesi Menu. Excerpt transcribed from the instrumental introduction (Menu n.d.). Original key is A minor. The guitar is capoed at the fifth fret.

(Capoed at fifth fret; actual key carrier is on A)

In 1947, Bobby Benson, "the father of Nigerian highlife," introduced the first electric guitar in Lagos.

(n.d.), dating about 1939. In Twi, the title roughly translates as "The Orphan's Inquietude"; the lyrics express the complaints of a rejected soul (trans. Daniel Amponsah, personal communication, 1989). The timeline is a 12/8 pattern, common in traditional genres of the region, and widespread in African music.

The song uses a heptatonic scale, also common in traditional genres, and comparable to the mode beginning on the third degree of the diatonic scale (the Phrygian or E mode). The song is in verse-refrain form, with the verse sung by the leader, and a refrain sung by the supporting singers, with resultant tertial harmonies, also common in Akan vocal styles (Nketia 1974:161).

The guitar was likely capoed on the fifth fret, and played as if in the first position key of E minor (the original tonal center is a fourth above, on A). The guitar arpeggiates and strums two alternating chords, on the first and second scale degrees, and plays melodic passages of parallel thirds in the instrumental introduction and between the verses. In the middle part of the song, over a sustained, arpeggiated harmony (played on the guitar), the lead singer sings an extended passage in recitative style.

By the 1930s, the guitar was becoming a well-tuned addition to African ensembles, both for performance, and for original work. The Kumasi Trio and the groups represented in the His Master's Voice JZ series are prototypical for the guitar band (as it became known in Ghana), a commonly established ensemble type by the later 1930s and 1940s, at least along the Guinea Coast. The guitar band used several regional styles, including palm wine, native blues, and *jùjú* in Nigeria, *maringa* in Sierra Leone, and highlife in Ghana. In Ghana, guitar bands became associated with dramatic troupes, which toured towns and villages presenting "concerts" or "comic opera"; they thus reached a wide audience (Collins 1985:21–22).

As an ensemble typology, the guitar band contrasted with the dance band, another type of ensemble, which developed in the early decades of the twentieth century, contemporaneously with or slightly earlier than the guitar bands. Dance bands were distinguishable by instrumentation, repertory, and context. Instrumentation typically featured wind instruments (clarinet, trumpet, saxophones, trombone), stringed instruments (violins, double bass, guitar), and percussion. Repertories included European-international ballroom music (waltzes, tangos, foxtrots), American ragtime, and West African highlife. Urban contexts typically included formal ballrooms and dance halls (Collins 1986:3; Waterman 1990:42–44).

THE 1940S TO 1960

In the period after 1945, the story of the guitar in Africa grew more complex, as the acoustic guitar began to spread rapidly around the continent, while amplification and the electric guitar progressively entered the urban African musical scene. Other guitar varieties, such as the Hawaiian guitar, also found occasional usage in Africa. The Rhino Band, for example, formed by Joseph Sheila of Rabai (Kenya) in the early

1940s, featured one "Hawaii guitar," in addition to three guitars, mandolin, accordion, and drums (Kavyu 1978:117). African participation in the Allied armies, 1939–1945, was important for the expanding influence of Western music and its popular instrumentation in Africa (Kubik 1981:92).

No one knows when the first electric guitars arrived in Africa, but the instruments were probably not there before 1945. Several American companies (Rickenbacher, National, Gibson) first marketed them in the United States in the early 1930s. By the later 1940s, in both their semiacoustic and solid body varieties, they had secured increased importance in popular musical genres (jazz, country and western, rhythm and blues). In 1947, Bobby Benson, "the father of Nigerian highlife," introduced the first electric guitar in Lagos; and in 1949, amplified guitar was a standard part of the *jùjú* ensemble of Ayinde Bakare, a leading musician there (Waterman 1990:83–84). The Zaïrean guitarist Wendo first played an electric guitar in the Ngoma recording studio in Kinshasa in 1949 (Stapleton and May 1990:144).

The acoustic guitar, however, was still the predominant instrument; and by the late 1940s, we have references to its popular use in many corners of sub-Saharan Africa. Anglophone regions of Africa know the acoustic instrument as the box guitar and the dry guitar; Francophone regions, as the *guitare sèche*. In 1949, in Kissidougou (eastern Guinea), Arthur Alberts recorded a *jaliya*-type ensemble that featured singers identified as "Sudanese minstrels," accompanied by a *kora* and "two imported guitars" (Alberts 1950:18).

In field reports for 1948 and 1949, Hugh Tracey documented the use of guitars in South Africa, Zambia, Zimbabwe, and Malawi. In those countries, he found a mixture of influences on guitar-playing styles, including local zither-playing techniques (1950b:36) and music heard on Afrikaans recordings (possibly the guitar-accompanied style of the well-known South African folk singers Marais and Miranda). In "cowboy films" in Salisbury (Harare), he saw musicians, wearing four-gallon hats, "strum their guitars with monotonous loyalty to one key" (1948:11). In that period, American "singing cowboy guitarists" had influence in South Africa (Coplan 1985:187). Tracey also noted that guitar music influenced performances on African stringed instruments (1950b:37). Recalling the trend cited by Kirby in 1934, Richard Waterman observed that the guitar, at least in West Africa, had by 1950 "become in most respects a native instrument" (1950:10).

In 1952, the African Music Society awarded first prize of the Osborn Awards for "best African music of the year" to the guitar song "*Masanga*," by Mwenda-Jean Bosco, a guitarist from Zaïre, who would become widely known in Africa through his recordings and tours. In 1949 in Jadotville, Belgian Congo (now Likasi, Zaïre), Tracey had first recorded him (1953a:65–67; Rycroft 1961:81). Acknowledgment of Mwenda's song as "best African music" was a sign of the guitar's growing importance in African music.

Mwenda's songs have interested several ethnomusicologists. David Rycroft, who transcribed several of his guitar songs (1961, 1962), determined the music consisted of short cyclic sequences of "chords or broken chords," lasting from two to four measures in duple or compound meter, with 16-beat timeline patterns as rhythmic accompaniment, and often in modes similar to Western diatonic modes beginning on C or G (1962:87–100). Rycroft emphasized the complexities of Mwenda's accentuation and rhythmic play, and compared these traits to traditional African ones (1961:82–83, 1962:100–101). Collins proposed that "*Masanga*," as transcribed by Rycroft (1961:87–98), involved the "West African 'mainline' style played in the G position" (1987:192).

John Low, who, with Mwenda and others (particularly Losta Abelo and Edouard Masengo), did fieldwork in the Shaba region, southern Zaïre, has added detail to the

FIGURE 6   Cyclical pattern in
"*Antoinette muKolwezi*," by
Ilunga Patrice and Misomba
Victor (Tracey 1957a:B6).
Original key is A. Guitar 1 is
capoed at the fifth fret.

(Capoed at fifth fret; actual key center is on   A)

analysis of what he calls the Katanga guitar styles, which he dates to the 1940s and 1950s (1982b). He emphasizes the use of thumb and index-finger picking, including the alternating-bass style, where the thumb plays low notes on strong beats, and the index finger provides offbeat interest. This technique is allegedly similar to country blues and ragtime styles of the United States (1982b:19). He also identifies the use of the pull-off and hammer-on techniques (1982b:115), and the widespread use of certain common chords, notably the subdominant chord with added major sixth (F^6), which he suggests bears the influence of church music (1982b:106).

Low also identifies several common guitar tunings used by these musicians, and those in the neighboring region: Zambian guitarists call the tuning D–a–d–f♯–a–c♯′ *Espagnol*; Masengo guitarists call it *Hawaiienne* (1982b:95). Other common tunings include G–a–d–g–b–e′, F–a–d–g–b–e′, and F–a–d–g–c–e′ (1982b:107). He suggests that some of the tunings and nomenclature of tuning, with certain techniques of playing, show African-American influence (1982b:109–111). He finds the common alternation between high and low notes resembles techniques used for playing African lamellophones, but the musicians he worked with did not acknowledge "inspiration from a local traditional instrument" (1982b:103).

In the 1950s, Hugh Tracey issued several records, including one on the London label, with the title *The Guitars of Africa* (Tracey 1953b). These included guitar songs by Mwenda and several dozen others, recorded over a wide region in Central, Southern, and Eastern Africa, in field trips beginning in 1948 (Tracey 1973). A variety of guitar-playing styles appears in his recordings—from simple strumming to the thumb-and-index-finger technique. The general musical characteristics of these pieces resemble those of Mwenda's style; in many ways, they remind us of Twi and Fanti recordings of guitar-accompanied songs from the 1930s and 1940s.

Figure 6 transcribes an excerpt from the song "*Antoinette muKolwezi*," performed by "Ilunga Patrice and Misomba Victor, and friends" (identified by Tracey as Luba-Hemba speakers), recorded in 1957, at the Kolwezi copper mine, Katanga (Shaba) Province, Zaïre (Tracey 1957a:B6). This song uses a diatonic major harmonic system, and a timeline in 12/8 meter. In the treble register, the first guitar plays a cyclic melody, which ornaments the vocal part. The second guitar plays an ostinato bass. Other songs in Tracey's collection, such as "*Iuwale-o-iuwale*" (Tracey 1957b:A3) from Zambia, show the guitar's usage in stylistically traditional idioms.

Between about 1956 and 1960, the electric guitar began to take on an increasingly dominant role in African music—not entirely displacing the acoustic guitar, but matching it, in its appeal to African youth and the radio-listening and record-buying public (Manuel 1988:98). We can note a particularly prominent role for electric guitars in the emerging Congolese urban pop of this period, centered in Kinshasa (then Léopoldville) and Brazzaville.

Between 1956 and 1959, O. K. Jazz, a Kinshasa-based band, which would soon become popular across sub-Saharan Africa, made recordings that featured two electric guitars (one playing "rhythm"; the other, "solo" or "lead"), two or three male vocalists, jazz and African-Latin percussion, muted trumpet, clarinet, tenor saxophone, and double bass. This group's instrumentation, urban setting, and repertory (songs based on Latin-American dance rhythms, but usually sung in local languages), suggest we should view it as a dance band, rather than a guitar band, though the distinction is fluid.

Judging from photographs of other urban African dance bands in the 1950s, we can probably assume the guitars used in these recordings are of the semiacoustic electric type, favored in American jazz and country of the period. A 1952 photograph of the Tempos Band, a prominent Ghanaian highlife group led by E. T. Mensah, shows two archtop semiacoustic guitars with f-holes—the type of electric guitars commonly used in this period in American jazz, and in country music (Collins 1986:25; similar photo in Coplan 1981:448). Dating to about 1956, a photograph of African Jazz, a leading Congolese dance band formed in Kinshasa in 1953, shows two similar instruments.

Latin American dance music strongly influences the recordings by O. K. Jazz. This influence comes in part from the popularity of a series of Cuban dance music issued by His Master's Voice, starting in the late 1920s or early 1930s, and circulating afterward in Africa (Low 1982a:23; Waterman 1986:131–132). During the 1930s and 1940s, Latin American dance music was likely heard over the radio in many African urban centers. Ngoma Records, one of the major record companies of Kinshasa in the 1950s, had a studio band, which from available records copied Latin styles of dancing, and reproduced them on disk. They sing in Spanish the lyrics of some of the songs (Kubik 1965:13). Jazz guitar styles performed in Kinshasa by resident European musicians influenced Congolese electric guitar technique; one of these musicians, Bill Alexander, a Belgian, bore the influence of Django Rheinhardt (Ewens 1986:13).

These early songs by O. K. Jazz follow basic Latin or African-Caribbean dance music structures, and it is also not surprising to hear elements of other styles of pop. Of the sixteen songs on the RetroAfric reedition of O. K. Jazz's early recordings, eleven are listed as rumba, two as "biguine," two as bolero, one as merengue, and one as "tcha tcha tcha." Most of the texts of these songs are in Lingala, a lingua franca of the western Congo region. The text of at least one, "*La Fiesta*," is in Spanish.

In this music, the rhythm guitar strums chords, while the lead guitar plays melodic lines, sometimes in parallel thirds, in single lines accompanying melodies played on the trumpet or clarinet at the third, and sometimes in counterpoint to the vocal and wind parts. The lead guitar often plays in a high register of the guitar, past the twelfth fret on the first two (highest) strings. The sound of the guitar is "open," with a touch of reverberation, for a ringing, bell-like quality.

In the eponymous song "*On Entre O. K., On Sort K. O.,*" composed by Franco (Luambo Makiadi), guitarist and later leader and star of the group, the electric guitar harmonizes in thirds with a muted trumpet in the instrumental refrains, while the double bass provides a rumba rhythm. During the verses sung in Lingala, to punctuate the vocal phrases, the guitar interjects a figure in thirds. In "*Ejoni Banganga,*" recorded between 1956 and 1959 (Franco 1987:B4), the guitar provides decorative counterpoint, complete with chromatic passages, scalar figures, and repeated notes high on the fretboard, which would become a staple in modern African electric guitar styles. In "*Passi Ya Boloko,*" from the same period, also a rumba (Franco 1987:A3), an electric guitar solo recalls the blues-tinged guitar solos heard in bluegrass and rockabilly music of the 1950s, with its characteristic insistence on the opposition of the major-third and minor-third degrees of the scale (figure 7). In essential harmonic and melodic elements, "*Ejoni Banganga*" is almost identical to "*Pini Ochama,*" a song

recorded in 1950 by Luo musicians in Kenya (Tracey 1950a:B7). This reminds us of the increasing interconnectedness of the African musical regions after 1945. From at least the 1950s, many of the nightclub musicians in East African cities came from the Congolese regions.

THE 1960S TO THE 1990S

In 1959, A. M. Jones observed "the guitar bought from a European music shop" had been claimed by "the young African of today . . . as his own," and that "it is every-where" (Jones 1959:257). The last statement was an exaggeration, but Jones's comments nonetheless suggest the guitar was coming to have a large impact in Africa, especially in the major towns and urban centers. In 1961, the Arts Council of Ghana sponsored a national guitar band competition, and bestowed on the winner, Kwabena Onyina, the title "King of Guitar." At about the same time, Franco gained fame in the Congo region (and later in many other parts of Africa), and became known by the sobriquet "*sorcier de la guitare*" (Ewens 1986:14). These trends reflect rising popularity in the guitar in the West during the period, and its prominent part in rock and roll, emulated by African bands in the early 1960s (Collins 1977:56).

In 1965, Kubik asserted the guitar was a "key instrument," located at the "mid-dlepoint" of modern African musical developments (Kubik 1965:1–7). He argued that in urban Africa, the guitar, as a nontribal instrument, had become symbolic of modernity and opposition to rigid traditionalism (1965:16). An advertisement in *Drum* magazine (Ghana edition, February 1966) makes this kind of association explicit: above the caption "Progressive people bank with B·W·A" (Bank of West Africa) is a drawing of a television studio, showing a female worker taking notes, and a camera crew recording a male African musician performing on the electric guitar. A more potent and radical kind of symbolism, which the guitar has sometimes taken on in Africa, informs a political cartoon published in the same magazine a year later ("Guitar Boy" 1967). It depicts the "Guitar Boy," the nickname given to a young officer who led an abortive coup. The cartoon shows him firing a guitar as if were a rifle (figure 8).

The guitar's transition from a peripheral to a central position in African musical culture in the period between about 1920 and 1965, reflects broader, international trends in the instrument's history. In the United States, popular interest in the guitar, and guitar sales, increased dramatically between 1955 and 1965 (Fleming 1966:40–41; American Music Conference 1987:5). The extent of the guitar's musical usage in the urbanizing parts of Africa, and the fluidity of its symbolic usage, however, imply the processes of indigenization of the guitar in Africa seen by earlier writers were effectively completed by the mid-1960s.

A Zaïrean guitarist who had a wide influence on the playing of electric guitars in Africa during the 1960s was Nicolas Kasanda Wa Mikalayi, popularly known as "Docteur Nico." In 1953, he helped found the Congolese music ensemble African

FIGURE 8   Political cartoon depicting the "Guitar Boy" ("Guitar Boy" 1967).

Jazz. During the 1960s, as leader and lead guitarist of several groups (including African-Fiesta and African-Fiesta Sukisa) he was influential in expanding electric guitar sonorities and playing techniques for contemporary African popular music, and in the development of *soukous*, a Congolese style (Stewart 1989b:19).

A photograph published on the cover of a reedition of some of his material from the 1960s shows him playing a Fender-type solid-body electric guitar with three pickups and a "tremolo arm"; between his thumb and forefinger, he holds a plectrum. The Africa Fiesta recordings of the mid-1960s highlight his playing. His solos often combine contrasting timbres. He uses different pickup settings (as in "*Yaka Toya Mbana*," Nico 1985b:A3), echo, sustain, "choked" notes, and Hawaiian-guitar glissandos (as in "*Mambo Hawaïenne*," Nico 1985a:A7).

Alan Merriam singled out Francis Bebey as an exemplar of the "African art music guitarist" (1967:4). A performer on, and composer for, the classical guitar, Bebey added an extra dimension to the repertory of African guitar music. He was born in Douala, Cameroon, in 1929; at the age of 25, he moved to Paris, where he studied at the Sorbonne, and became influenced by Segovia's guitar playing. His first compositions for the guitar date to 1963, and he released his first album, *Pièces pour Guitare Seule*, in 1966. In the late 1960s and 1970s, he became known through his recordings and concert performances on the classical guitar. He played a mixed repertory, of arrangements of Western classical music, Brazilian and Latin American guitar music, and original compositions. In the use of folk material and dance rhythms, his pieces for guitar bear the influence of Spanish and Latin American styles; and his harmonic language sometimes reflects the influence of French Impressionist composers.

Bebey's compositions include "*Accra se mit à danser autour de Noël*" (Bebey 1978:B2), a fantasy, based on the Ghanaian folk song "*Yaa Amponsah*." His "*Ndesse*" (Bebey 1978:A2) provides guitar accompaniment to a recited poem by Léopold Senghor. To convey a sense of African rhythmic vitality on the guitar (Roberts 1979), he has applied special percussive playing techniques, including the tapping of the soundbox, as in "*Danse des Criquets Pèlerins*" (Bebey 1966:B6).

Most guitar playing in Africa since the 1960s has been associated with the popular urban bands (which play contemporary Western or African-American and African-Caribbean popular music), plus emergent African popular musical idioms. In Kenya, Roberts noted urban bands greatly indulged styles of pop: twist, *kwela*, "Congo-influenced" styles, and "urban electric-guitarred Kenyan pop song" (1968:53).

For other urban centers of Africa by the late 1960s, a similar picture emerges. Local rock bands modeled themselves after Western groups. They featured singers, electric guitars, electric bass, and trap drum set, and performed a mix of pop music styles. Naomi Hooker, who did fieldwork in Freetown, Sierra Leone, in 1969, reported (1970:12) that bands there performed "Congolese," soul, West Indian "rock steady" and "blue beat," and "mixed Latin" (meringue, cha-cha, pachanga, rumba). In Ghana, using the guitar, several bands arose in the 1960s and 1970s. They played pop music styles: reggae, soul, Afro-Beat. The Psychedelic Aliens, formed in 1968, "released records in 1971 combining the Jimmy Hendrix guitar technique with African drum rhythms" (Collins 1977:58).

Ethnomusicologists writing in the 1970s and 1980s continue to report on the growing importance of the guitar, and its tendency to replace older indigenous African instruments. Writing of Ghana, Esi Sylvia Kinney states, "the guitar has practically replaced the indigenous stringed instruments . . . and many guitars are made and redesigned locally" (1970:6–7). Robert Kauffman (1972) notes that in urban areas of Zimbabwe, the solo acoustic guitar mimicked the mbira, in both social function and musical relationship (1972:52). Similarly, Rycroft (1977) writes, "the most

soukous   Popular form of music from Kinshasa, featuring three guitar parts and solo singer

chimurenga   Liberation-movement music in Zimbabwe with dry, percussive guitar sound

mbaqanga   Popular music style of South Africa in which a clean lead-guitar sound is preferred

popular instrument among young Zulu men who come to town from the country, as temporary manual workers, is the common Western guitar. It has adopted almost exactly the functional role previously fulfilled by the *umakhweyana* gourd bow (1977:228–229). He also notes teenage boys commonly make their own instruments (1977:241). Writing of Zambia, Moya Aliya Malamusi notes, "the young generation is almost exclusively tuned to electric guitar based popular music" (1984:189).

In the 1980s, in the West, and to a certain degree in Japan and elsewhere, attention increasingly focused on African popular music and African styles of playing the guitar (Duncan 1989; Goodwin and Gore 1990). In 1982, Island, a British-American company, signed Nigerian *jùjú* star guitarist King Sunny Ade, who then began releasing records and going on international tours. In 1986 and 1987, Paul Simon released his *Graceland* album, and staged its world tour.

The role of the guitar in Ade's *jùjú* music was a central point of interest for his audiences. Nigerians knew him as *Alujonu Onigita* 'Wizard of the Guitar' (Waterman 1990:133). In February 1984, *Guitar Player* magazine devoted a feature article to him, with a separate article devoted to Demola Adepoju, the steel guitar player in his band (Kaiser 1984a, 1984b). Ade's nineteen-piece group, the African Beats, included four electric guitarists, a pedal-steel guitar, and an electric bass (Kaiser 1984a:32).

Describing the interrelationship of the guitar parts in contemporary *jùjú* ensembles, Waterman cites the use of ostinato "interlocking support patterns . . . frequently harmonized in thirds," played by the tenor guitars, which function in a similar way to "conga-type" drums (Waterman 1990:183–184). The guitar-playing of the "band captain" consists of "percussively struck triads" and "short distinctive motifs," often played in a high register; they signal new sections in the song. Solos may be played by a lead guitarist, who may employ a variety of effects, including echo, fuzz, and the sound of the wa-wa pedal. The Hawaiian or pedal steel guitar adds "sustained chords and swooping melodic figures," and sometimes extended solos (Waterman 1990:183).

In African popular music of the 1980s, produced for both African and Western audiences, the guitar prevailed, not only in sound, but in image. The symbolic placement of an African musician holding an electric guitar as the central figure on the cover of an issue of *West Africa* (17 December 1984) puts into visual form Kubik's suggestion that the guitar figured as the "middlepoint" of the new African music (Cover illustration 1984). In this drawing, the guitarist not only commands the center, but overshadows in scale the other musicians, including a *kora* player and a *balafon* player. For a much broader, indeed international audience, a similar symbolic conjoining of the electric guitar and African music came from the organizers of the Live Aid concerts, which took place in London and Philadelphia in 1985, and were televised internationally to a potential audience in the hundreds of millions. The logo for this event dramatically merged the shapes of the electric guitar and the continent of Africa (Gladwell 1986).

FIGURE 9 Excerpt from a Choc Stars *seben*. Transcription by Banning Eyre and Joe Gore (Eyre 1988:82).

Between 1985 and 1990, an increasing number of popular and scholarly books and articles, plus records and compact discs, highlighted the role of the guitar in African music. Congolese styles, Kenyan *benga*, and South African *mbaqanga*, prefer a "clean," "Fender-type" lead guitar sound, with few distortion effects (Mandelson 1985:10). "The major recording centre for modern Congolese music is now Paris," where a small pool of guitarists reproduces a "distinctive sound," which reappears in recordings by many different bands (Mandelson 1985:10; Stewart 1989a). In Zimbabwean *chimurenga* 'liberation' music, guitarists such as those in Thomas Mapfumo's band may "play double notes in fourths while deadening the strings at the bridge with the flesh of the palm" (Mandelson 1985:10). To imitate the sounds of traditional instruments (*balafon*, *kora*), groups from Mali, Senegal, Guinea, and Gambia, use special timbral effects: sustain, delays, fuzztone, chorus. These groups include Bembeya Jazz National of Guinea, led by guitarist Sékou Diabaté; Les Ambassadeurs of Mali, with guitarist Kante Manfila; and Youssou N'Dour's Super Étoile, a Senegalese group that specializes in *mbalax*, a dynamic popular musical style.

In a discussion of modern Afropop forms—mainly *soukous*, *chimurenga*, *mbaqanga*—Banning Eyre examines the role of the electric guitar (1988). *Soukous*, a popular form coming from Kinshasa but influential throughout central and eastern Africa, and in other parts of Africa, ideally has three guitar parts (solo, mi-solo, accompaniment or rhythm) and bass guitar. The solo guitarist plays a repeated figure in a high register, usually above the twelfth fret. In the densely textured *seben* section of the song, the mi-solo plays a contrastive rhythmic and melodic pattern (figure 9). The rhythm guitarist plays "an arpeggio figure or a steady bass line set off by a series of double stops on the middle strings" (Eyre 1988:82). Varying the use of plectra and finger picking achieves contrasting timbres. Despite the importance of the electric guitars in *soukous*, the singers take precedence as stars, and as musical centers of focus for the public in Zaïre, for whom lyrical and vocal qualities appear to provide primary values (Eyre 1988:82).

By combining two electric guitars and a bass, *chimurenga* replicates the structural relationships of mbira music (Eyre 1988:87). *Chimurenga* guitarists prefer a dry, percussive tone, which they achieve by using plectra and playing with repeated downstrokes, while damping the strings as described above. Figure 10 shows the interaction between the electric guitars and bass in such a passage. South African styles of playing include strumming, and, as in *soukous*, plectrum playing in a high register; to enable this "high-on-the-fretboard guitar work," Marks Mankwane uses a twenty-four-fret Ibanez Artist (Eyre 1988:85). The Zulu-guitar style featured in the playing of Johnny Clegg and others, emphasizes finger-picking styles, the use of open-string drones, a "regular pulse provided by the thumb," and "slides, hammer-ons, and pull-offs," executed in lower positions, below the fifth fret (Eyre 1988:86).

The period after about 1982 also saw a revival of interest in African acoustic guitar music, particularly among folk-musical audiences in the West. An increasing

FIGURE 10 Basic phrases from "*Gwindingwe Rine Shumba*," by Thomas Mapfumo. Transcription by Banning Eyre and Joe Gore (Eyre 1988:87).

number of records issued on labels based in London, Paris, and New York, focused on this music (Richardson 1990). In 1982, the "comeback" of Mwenda-Jean Bosco was reported when he made a modest tour of Europe ("Mwenda Jean Bosco's Comeback" 1982). *Repercussions*, a British television documentary aired in 1984, included "Africa Come Back," a program on African popular music, directed by Dennis Marks. It featured the "palm wine guitar music" of the Ghanaian musician Koo Nimo. In 1988, in England, S. E. Rogie also made a comeback—as "the palm wine music man" (During 1988:670); he was a Sierra Leonean guitarist, singer, and songwriter, who in the 1960s had made some popular recordings, notably the song "My Lovely Elizabeth" (reissued on Rogie 1986:B1). The musical style of Koo Nimo and Rogie represents a development of the two-finger idioms of the Guinea Coast region, dating to the 1920s and 1930s, now called palm wine guitar (Fosu-Mensah 1990; Rogie 1989; Topouzis 1988).

A contrastive idiom of African acoustic guitar music finds expression in the music of Malian guitarists Ali Farka Toure and Boubacar Traoré, plus guitarists from the western Sudan region of Mali, Guinea, and Senegambia. The style of some of these musicians resembles that of American blues guitarists like John Lee Hooker; and Toure, for one, has acknowledged this influence (Richardson 1990:39).

On the album *Ali Farka Toure* (Toure 1987), Toure sings both original and traditional songs, in several regional languages (Malinke, Bambara, Songhai, Fula), to the accompaniment of a steel-strung acoustic guitar, calabash, and bongos. The guitar part in the song "Timbarma" (A1) features hammer-on trills, ornamental slides, and melodic runs on an anhemitonic pentatonic scale. These traits may recall the blues, but probably relate more closely to musical styles performed on the internal-spike lutes that may accompany the same repertory in the region. Traoré's style combines the musical idiom of Khassonke, his native region, with traits drawn from the blues and European folk song (Duran 1990).

The acoustic guitar finds other notable usage in western Sudan, where it entered several modern *jaliya*-type ensembles, either replacing the *kora* and *ngoni*- or *xalam*-type internal-spike lute, or, as in recordings issued in the 1980s by Amy Koita (1986), Tata Bambo Kouyate (1989), and others, playing side by side with the traditional stringed instruments. The guitar also finds at least occasional usage in village contexts. Pascal Diatta, a guitarist of the Casamance region of southern Senegal, performs the guitar at traditional events, like weddings and circumcisions (Anderson 1989:33).

Despite the diversity in the guitar's use, and its prominence as a pop music instrument, it remains limited in its distribution in Africa, because it is essentially an expensive import, beyond the purchasing power of most people (Eyre 1988:80). Even strings for guitars are often hard to find and buy. Professional musicians in Africa must sometimes rent their guitars, which may be in poor condition; to buy a satisfactory instrument, they often depend on finding work abroad. As musical centers outside Africa have become major centers for African guitarists, and for the recording and dissemination of African guitar music, this situation may have important repercussions for the future development of African styles of playing (Stewart 1989a).

In some regions in Africa, the guitar still has little use. As a performative and compositional instrument, it is a predominantly urban phenomenon (Kubik 1964:42). In parts of Ghana, "the guitar has practically replaced the indigenous stringed instruments" (Kinney 1970:14). In southern Ghana, it has replaced the *seperewa* 'harp-lute'; and at funerals and other traditional occasions, rural guitarists perform traditional idioms on it (Kwabena Nketia, personal communication, 1990). In rural northern Ghana, however, the indigenous *kologo* 'internal-spike lute' is far more common than the guitar.

In rural regions, even where the guitar does not enjoy local use, people know it as a cultural model almost exclusively through performances by groups touring from cities, plus through radio, cassette, and (less frequently) television, video, and cinema; and some local individual often plays it. In Madagascar, the *kabosy*, derived from West Asian pear-shaped lutes, and diffused along Islamic trade routes, commonly takes on the formal appearance of a miniature acoustic guitar. In towns in Cameroon, and undoubtedly elsewhere in Africa, children build nonfunctional copies of electric guitars and use them as "air guitars," playing imaginary roles as stars (Alec Leonhardt, personal communication, 1990).

By the 1990s, the guitar in Africa was thus a critical element in diverse musical styles, particularly popular ones, which dominate contemporary urban music, and are increasingly familiar in the countryside.

REFERENCES

Advertisement for the Bank of West Africa. 1966. *Drum* (Ghana edition), February.

Aingo, George Williams. n.d. *Na Mapa Nu Kyew.* Hayes, Middlesex: Zonophone EZ9, B. 78-rpm disk.

Alájá-Browne, Afọlábi. 1985. "Jùjú Music: A Study of Its Social History and Style." Ph.D. dissertation, University of Pittsburgh.

Alberts, Arthur. 1950. "Descriptive Notes." In *Tribal, Folk, and Cafe Music of West Africa,* 16–19. New York: Field Recordings.

American Music Conference. 1987. "Music USA 87." Chicago.

Anderson, Ian. 1989. "A Guitar Man." *Folk Roots* 70:28-33.

Anderson, Robert. 1980. "Egypt: Ancient Music." *The New Grove Dictionary of Music and Musicians,* ed. Stanley Sadie. London: Macmillan.

"Augustus Williams." 1932. *The Gold Coast Spectator,* 13 February, 207.

Bebey, Francis. 1966. *Pièces pour guitare seule.* Paris: OCORA. LP disk.

———. 1978. *Francis Bebey: ballades africaines: guitare.* Paris: Ozileka 3306. LP disk.

Bowdich, Thomas. 1819 [1966]. *Mission from Cape Coast Castle to Ashantee,* 3rd ed., ed. W. E. F. Ward. London: Frank Cass.

Catalogue of Zonophone West African Records by Native Artists. 1929. Hayes, Middlesex: British Zonophone Company.

Collins, E. John. 1977. "Post-War Popular Band Music in West Africa." *African Arts* 10(3):53–60.

———. 1985. *Musicmakers of West Africa.* Washington: Three Continents.

———. 1986. *E. T. Mensah, King of Highlife.* London: Off the Record Press.

———. 1987. "Jazz Feedback to Africa." *American Music* 5(2):176–193.

———. 1989. "The early history of West African Highlife Music." *Popular Music* 8:221– 230.

Coplan, David. 1978. "Go to my Town, Cape Coast! The Social History of Ghanaian Highlife." In *Eight Urban Musical Cultures,* ed. Bruno Nettl, 96–114. Urbana: University of Illinois Press.

———. 1981. "Popular Music." In *The Cambridge Encyclopedia of Africa,* ed. Roland Oliver and Michael Crowder. Cambridge: Cambridge University Press.

———. 1985. *In Township Tonight! South Africa's Black City Music and Theatre.* London: Longman.

Cover illustration. 1984. *West Africa,* 17 December.

Danner, Peter. 1986. "Guitar." *The New Grove Dictionary of Music and Musicians,* ed. Stanley Sadie. London: Macmillan.

Danso, Robert O. 1932. "Mistakes in Practical Music." *The Gold Coast Spectator,* 9 April, 432.

Darkwa, Asante. 1974. "The New Musical Traditions in Ghana." Ph.D. dissertation, Wesleyan University.

Duncan, Amy. 1989. "Ambassadors of Afropop." *World Monitor*, October, 74–77.

Duran, Lucy. 1990. Liner notes to *Boubacar Traoré: Mariama*. London: Stern's Africa 1032. LP disk.

During, Ola. 1988. "The Palm Wine Music Man." *West Africa*, 11 April: 670.

Evans, Tom, and Mary Anne Evans. 1977. *Guitars: From the Renaissance to Rock*. New York: Facts on File.

Ewens, Graeme. 1986. *Luambo Franco and Thirty Years of O. K. Jazz*. London: Off the Record Press.

Eyre, Banning. 1988. "Soukous, Chimurenga, Mbaqanga, and More: New Sounds from Africa." *Guitar Player* 22(10):80–88.

Fleming, Shirley. 1966. "The Guitar on the Go." *Hi-Fidelity*, July: 40–45.

Fosu-Mensah, Kwabena. 1990. *Koo Nimo: Osabarima*. Liner notes. Adasa Records, ADR 102.

Franco (Luambo Makiadi). 1987. *Franco et le T.P.O.K. Jazz: originalité—The original 1956 recordings of O.K. Jazz*. London: RetroAfric 2. LP disk.

Gladwell, Malcolm. 1986. "Fact, Fancy, and the Mystique of Africa." *Insight* (*The Washington Times*), 26 May: 8–11.

Goodwin, Andrew, and Joe Gore. 1990. "World Beat and the Cultural Imperialism Debate." *Socialist Review* 90(3):63–80.

Graham, Ronnie. 1988. *The Da Capo Guide to Contemporary African Music*. New York: Da Capo.

Grunfeld, Frederic. 1974. *The Art and Times of the Guitar: An Illustrated History*. New York: Da Capo.

"Guitar Boy" (cartoon). 1967. *Drum* (Ghana edition), August.

Hommage au Grand Kalle. 1984. African LP 360 142.

Hooker, Naomi. 1970. "Popular musicians in Freetown." *African Urban Notes* 5(4):11– 18.

Hornbostel Erich Moritz von, and Curt Sachs. 1961. "Classification of Musical Instruments," trans. Anthony Baines and Klaus P. Wachsmann. *Galpin Society Journal* 14(March):3–29.

Jones, A. M. 1959. *Studies in African Music*. London: Oxford University Press, 1959.

Kaiser, Henry. 1984a. "King Sunny Ade: Nigeria's Jùjú Superstar." *Guitar Player* 18(2):32–42.

———. 1984b. "Demola Adepoju." *Guitar Player* 18(2):35–36.

Kallaway, Peter, and Patrick Pearson. 1986. *Johannesburg: Images and Continuities*. Braamfontein: Ravan Press.

Kauffman, Robert. 1972. "Shona Urban Music and the Problem of Acculturation." *IFMC Yearbook* 4:47–56.

———. 1979–1980. "Tradition and Innovation in the Urban Music of Zimbabwe." *African Urban Studies* 6:41–48.

Kavyu, Paul. 1978. "The Development of Guitar Music in Kenya." *Jazzforschung* 10:111– 119.

Kinney, Esi Sylvia. 1970. "Urban West African Music and Dance." *African Urban Notes* 5(4):3–10.

Kirby, Percival. 1965. *The Musical Instruments of the Native Races of South Africa*, 2nd ed. Johannesburg: Witwatersrand University Press.

Koita, Amy. 1986. *Amy Koita*. Paris: Espérance ESP 7517. LP disk.

Kouyate, Tata Bambo. 1989. *Tata Bambo Kouyate*. London: Globestyle ORB 042. LP disk.

Kubik, Gerhard. 1964. "Harp Music of the Azande and Related Peoples in the Central African Republic." *African Music* 3(3):37–76.

———. 1965. "Neue Musikformen in Schwarzafrika." *Afrika Heute* 4:1–15.

———. 1976. "Daniel Kachamba's Solo Guitar Music." *Jazzforschung* 8:159–195.

———. 1981. "Popular Music in East Africa since 1945." *Popular Music* 1:83–104.

Low, John. 1982a. "A History of Kenyan Guitar Music: 1945–1980." *African Music* 6(2):17–36.

———. 1982b. *Shaba Diary: A Trip to Rediscover the 'Katanga' Guitar Styles and Songs of the 1950's and '60's*. Vienna: Fohrenau. Acta Ethnologica et Linguistica, 54.

Malamusi, Moya Aliya. 1984. "The Zambian Popular Music Scene." *Jazzforschung* 16:189–195.

Mandelson, Ben. 1985. "African Guitar Styles." In *Talking Book*, vol. 2, *An Introduction to Africa*, ed. Phoebe Beedell et al. (Bristol: WOMAD Foundation).

Manuel, Peter. 1988. *Popular Musics of the Non-Western World*. New York: Oxford University Press.

Marcuse, Sibyl. 1975. *Musical Instruments: A Comprehensive Dictionary*. New York: Norton.

McKinnon, James W., and Robert Anderson. 1984. "Lute, 2: Ancient Lutes." *The New Grove Dictionary of Musical Instruments*, ed. Stanley Sadie (London: Macmillan), 2:551–553.

Menu, Kwesi. n.d. *Agyanka odede*. Hayes, Middlesex: His Master's Voice JZ 5002. 78-rpm disk.

Merriam, Alan P. 1967. "Music." *Africa Report* 12(1):4.

"Mwenda Jean Bosco's Comeback." 1982. *African Music* 6(2):132–134.

Nico, Docteur (Nicolas Kasanda Wa Mikalayi). 1985a. *Merveilles du Passé: Éternel Docteur Nico, 1963–65: Orchestra African Fiesta*. Paris: African 360152. LP disk.

———. 1985b. *Merveilles du Passé: Éternel Docteur Nico, 1967: Orchestra African Fiesta*. Paris: African 360159. LP disk.

Nketia, J. H. Kwabena. 1974. *The Music of Africa*. New York: Norton.

Oliver, Paul. 1984. *Songsters and Saints*. Cambridge: Cambridge University Press.

Omibiyi, M. A. 1981. "Popular Music in Nigeria." *Jazzforschung* 13:151–168.

Richardson, Derk. 1990. "African Voices." *Acoustic Guitar* 1(2):38–41.

Roberts, J. S. 1968. "Popular Music in Kenya." *African Music* 4(2):53–55.

————. 1975. "Africa: the Guitar's Role." *Guitar Player* 9:22-23.

Rogie, Sooliman E. 1986. *The 60s' Sounds of S. E. Rogie,* vol. 1. Berkeley, California: Rogiphone R2. LP disk.

————. 1989. *The Palm Wine Sounds of S. E. Rogie: The King of Palm Wine Guitar Music.* Workers Playtime PLAYLP9. LP disk.

————. 1979. "Francis Bebey: African Third Stream," *Village Voice,* 19 Feb.

Rycroft, David. 1961. "The Guitar Improvisations of Mwenda Jean Bosco." *African Music* 2(4):81–98.

————. 1962. "The Guitar Improvisations of Mwenda Jean Bosco (Part II)." *African Music* 3(1):86–102.

————. 1977. "Evidence of Stylistic Continuity in Zulu 'Town' Music." In *Essays for a Humanist,* 216–260. New York: Town House Press.

Sam. n.d. *Ampa Afful.* His Master's Voice JZ 97. 78-rpm disk.

Sekyi, Kobina. 1918. "The Anglo-Fanti, Part I: Boyhood Festivals." *West Africa,* 6 July: 378.

Stapleton, Chris, and Chris May. 1990. *African Rock: The Pop Music of a Continent.* New York: Dutton.

Stewart, Gary. 1989a. "The Session Men." *The Beat* 8(6):28–29.

————. 1989b. "Soukous, Birth of the Beat." *The Beat* 8(6):18–21.

Topouzis, Daphne. 1988. "The Kings of Jùjú and Palm Wine Guitar." *Africa Report,* November-December:67–69.

Toure, Ali Farka. 1987. *Ali Farka Toure.* Mango MLPS 9826. LP disk.

Tracey, Hugh. 1948. "Recording Journey from the Union into the Rhodesias." *African Music Society Newsletter* 1(1):9–12.

————. 1950a. "Pini ochama." In *Sound of Africa,* B7. Roodeport, Transvaal: International Library of African Music, AMA TR-168. LP disk.

————. 1950b. "Recording Tour 1949." *African Music Society Newsletter* 1(3):33–37.

————. 1953a. "The Osborn Awards: The Best African Musicians of the Year." *African Music Society Newsletter* 1(6):65–67.

————. 1953b. *The Guitars of Africa.* London LB-829. Music of Africa, 5. LP disk.

————. 1957a. "Antoinette MuKolwezi." In *Sound of Africa,* B6. Roodeport, Transvaal: International Library of African Music, AMA TR-25. LP disk.

————. 1957b. "Iuwale-o-iuwale." In *Sound of Africa,* A3. Roodeport, Transvaal: International Library of African Music, AMA TR-19). LP disk.

————. 1973. *The Sound of Africa* Series. Catalogue. Roodepoort, Transvaal: International Library of African Music.

Turnbull, Harvey. 1984. "Guitar: Origins." In *The New Grove Dictionary of Musical Instruments,* ed. Stanley Sadie, 2:87–90. London: Macmillan.

Tyler, James. 1980. *The Early Guitar.* London: Oxford University Press.

Villault, Nicolas Le Sieur. 1669 [1670]. *Relation of the Coasts of Africk Called Guinee.* London: John Starkey.

Waterman, Christopher. 1986. "Jùjú: The Historical Development, Socioeconomic Organization, and Communicative Functions of a West African Popular Music." Ph.D. dissertation, University of Illinois, Urbana.

————. 1990. *Jùjú: A Social History and Ethnography of an African Popular Music.* Chicago: University of Chicago Press.

Waterman, Richard. 1950. "Laboratory Notes." In *Tribal, Folk, and Cafe Music of West Africa,* ed. Arthur Alberts, 5–11. New York: Field Recordings.

Kru Mariners and Migrants of the West African Coast

Cynthia Schmidt

Historical Background
Music of the Kru
Late Twentieth-Century Transitions

In the early twentieth century, the intermingling of cultures in African coastal towns and industrial centers led to the development of new musical genres. This process was most striking along the western seaboard, where the protagonists were mariners and migrant laborers.

At the forefront of these peoples was an ethnic group of workers, the Kru, originally from Liberia. Traditionally mobile and seagoing, the Kru have for several centuries traveled around the coast of Africa, and even to the Caribbean and England. They have spent much of their lives working away from home, often relocating permanently to ports, where they have interacted with people of other nations, regions, and ethnicities.

The Kru influenced many of the cultures they contacted. Scholars have credited Kru mariners as the disseminators of an important idiom of pidgin English (Tonkin 1971; Dalby 1970), but in contemporary musical expression their influence is more sweeping. Throughout West Africa, they diffused guitar-playing traditions, particularly in palm wine guitar style (Collins 1985, 1989).

Excepting random mentions of creative achievements and scanty information in scattered sources, the role of the Kru as composers and musicians has been inadequately described. This essay shows that they composed music and introduced instrumental styles that contributed to the emergence of popular music consciousness and repertory in the west and central African coastal region from the 1920s to the 1950s.

Music produced by members of an emergent African working class, and the cultural processes that surround migration, have been a focus of attention of several excellent studies (Coplan 1985; Erlmann 1991). The most effective mechanism of African cultural dynamics has been interethnic cultural contact through the migration of laborers (Erlmann 1991). An increase in the number of musicians, with other demographic, social, economic, and political factors of migration, precipitated important musical changes.

This essay draws on the notion of *musical confluence*, suggested by Barbara Hampton (1980) as a useful concept in studying the Kru experience. Various authors have pointed out the inadequacies of a more widely used term, *syncretism* (Collins and Richards 1982:37). Musical confluence refers to the merging of different streams of music, in which old and new elements combine to articulate an interethnic experience.

HISTORICAL BACKGROUND

Nearly every account of West African history since 1820 mentions the Kru; they were the African mariners most widely employed on land and sea in the nineteenth and twentieth centuries. Vessels engaged in legitimate trade on the Windward Coast sporadically hired Kru from the end of the 1600s, and hiring became regular during the 1780s. Kru involvement in European maritime activities was probably motivated by economics. Uneven economic development along the coast encouraged the migration of Kru labor. As a Kru seaman stated, "When times get hard, we travel."

Since Krumen had a long tradition of this type of work and were considered most adept, shipping companies preferred them. They were praised as "born sailors," as "industrious" and "robust" people, commanding special skills (such as swimming and language abilities), and having a reputation for "dependability" (Brooks 1972:3). Consequently, those attached to European traders enjoyed considerable personal freedom.

Some of the Kru were boiler cleaners, woodcutters, and stokers for wood-burning steamers. Some worked as deckhands on merchant and military ships plying the coast. Some were stewards, some loaded palm oil, and some relayed messages for the African Telegraph Company. Some moved between dock labor and stevedoring. The stevedores traveled down the coast, loading and unloading at various ports of call. American, German, and British shipping lines, knowing the advantages of working continuously with the same men, employed "shore headmen" and "ship headmen," who selected and controlled their gangs. Embarking at Freetown or Monrovia, they traveled down the coast to Douala or Congo-Matadi and back. Occasionally the headmen took on separate gangs at each port. The trips lasted a month or six weeks, or even longer. Between trips, the stevedores worked intermittently or "rested," finding time for leisure and music. Some stayed away from home for months or years, returning when they had gained property or money for their families.

Written nineteenth-century references and oral reports from older seamen tell how the work was "relieved by song." These men speak of "heavy-lift songs." When they did a difficult job, they sang "*Tobogee-o, Nyanwule* 'We will do this thing, Nyanwule [the name of a strong man]'." (As Ol' Man Thompson told me in 1987, Tobogee also referred to the older traditional war dances of the Kru.) The headman led the chorus:

> It is their custom to sing; and, as the music goes on, they seem to become invigorated, applying their strength cheerfully, and with limbs as unwearied as their voices. One of the number leads in recitative, and the whole company responds in chorus. The subject of the song is a recital of the exploits of the men, their employments, their intended movements, of the news of the coast and the character of their employers. (Bridge 1853:16–17)

An "Old Coaster" advocated being informed by their communications: "By singing extemporaneous songs, when at work, they communicate intelligence of any transaction on board, which is echoed from the nearest ship to the next, so that hardly a circumstance regarding trade, or any other matter, can transpire, but all become acquainted with it" (Smith 1851:105).

The mariners were given nicknames—such as "Shilling," "Bottle of Beer," "Flying Jib"—to which they answered through life. Their heroic deeds were sung and recited to crowds at parties in Kru country (Brooks 1972:28). Scholars have studied the contribution of the Kru to the spread of Kru pidgin English in West Africa in the

The Kru homeland is the southeastern Atlantic
coastal area of Liberia.

late 1800s (Brooks 1970; Davis 1976; Tonkin 1971). The Kru were early known as
interpreters, or talk men—sometimes called proper talk men by traders—and thus
they became the chief agents for disseminating pidgin English along the West Coast
and Indian assistants to the British for expediting commerce (Brooks 1972:19).

The Kru in Liberia

The Kru homeland is the southeastern Atlantic coastal area of Liberia. The Kru came
from disparate communities there—small, dispersed settlements, often hostile to
each other—whose autonomy may have prevented individuals from recognizing the
common elements of the life they shared. These complexities are important because
the Kru expounded varied attachments and localisms when working down the coast.

In the 1800s, there was some ambiguity in the term *Kru*. Mariners called
Krumen (or Kroomen) and Kruboys (or Krooboys) represented different peoples of
eastern Liberia—Kru, Grebo, later the Sabo and Gola—and of Ivory Coast.
Wherever their homes, these men found security in identifying with other Liberians
and feeling that they belonged to a wider community (Martin 1982:2). They were
predominantly Liberian speakers of Kru or Krao, a language Joseph Greenberg tenta-
tively classified as belonging to the Kwa group, though later linguists classified it as a
separate branch within the Niger-Congo family.

Kru mariners were first recruited from five towns: Settra Kru, Nana Kru, Little
Kru, Krobah, and King William's Town. Other types of migrant workers, however,
seem to have come from other areas, such as Grand Cess and Sasstown. An individual's strongest affiliations were with the members of his or her *dako,* a communal
unit, with a territorial and social identity and a specific dialect. The bulk of the Kru
who manned ships sailing from Monrovia were from the Jloh and Gbeta *dako.*
Certain *dako* came to be associated with particular Kru settlements in the diaspora.
People originating from the five towns were associated with Freetown, and later with
London and Liverpool; the Grand Cess people went to Accra and Lagos.

By 1900, nearly every town on the Liberian coast had sent laborers aboard ships.
New Kru expatriate communities began to dot the coast, contributing to the expansion of the Kru-coast concept noted by historians: "The system of labor migration
was patterned, continuous, integrated with life at home, and considered an important part of a mature man's development and the community's life" (Martin 1982:2).
Kru who had never worked on ships were called bushboys, for the Kru believed that
growing up required travel down the coast (Martin 1982:2).

The Kru have long lived in established communities in Monrovia, where they
are one of the largest ethnic groups. Reports in 1879 described Monrovia as being
made up of two sections, one being Krutown (at the northern base of the lagoon),
which by 1900 had a population of about one thousand, with most of the men working on coastal ships (Büttikofer 1890). In 1945, for the building of a new port, the
evacuation of Krutown led to a division of Monrovia along class lines. From the

1930s to the 1950s, Kru dock workers and stevedores were the largest locally concentrated work force in Monrovia (Fraenkel 1964:40). Most lived in newer Kru communities, formed on Bushrod Island, near the port; the largest are New Krutown, Claratown, and Westpoint. This series of communities and neighborhoods, isolated from some of the residential areas and from Monrovia's social and economic center of activities, remain ethnically the most homogeneous areas, excepting Bassa and Grebo seamen. The Kru population there increased during the 1950s, when immigrants from Freetown, Accra, and other West African ports arrived in Monrovia (Fraenkel 1964:74).

In 1959, the Kru governor in Monrovia organized a demonstration of Kru loyalty to President Tubman. In it, Kru representatives from settlements abroad—Ghana, Nigeria, Freetown—participated. The songs of solidarity sung during this celebration are still performed in Kru communities of Lagos and Freetown. Participation in the common occupation was the basis of strength of Kru urban organization. Since there was traditionally no mechanism for cooperation between the *dako,* the degree of implied ethnic solidarity was unusual (Fraenkel 1964:83).

The Kru in Freetown

The third-largest natural harbor in the world, Freetown was the first major objective of Kru traffic in the late 1700s. The first Kru laborers who traveled abroad reportedly arrived in Sierra Leone in 1793 as crewmen on British naval and trading vessels. They were attracted by the Sierra Leone Company, which, to reestablish the colony, had instituted standard wages for African laborers—an unprecedented practice for this part of West Africa. By 1800, the colony was employing fifty Krumen, and in the early 1800s the number increased. Recorded estimates of the number of Kru living in Freetown between 1800 and 1850 vary widely, and an estimated five hundred were living there in 1819 (Fyfe 1962:45).

In the following years, the number of Kru migrating to Sierra Leone, attracted by greater possibilities of employment aboard merchant vessels, continued to grow. By the 1850s, Freetown had the largest Krutown, exceeding that of Monrovia (Schuler 1986:185). Colonial authorities encouraged them to settle in Freetown, and in 1816 a special enactment allocated a section of Freetown as a Kru reservation. Kroo Town, overlooking the harbor and Kroo Bay, was the land set aside for exclusive use by the Kru for Kru migrant labor, the only separate neighborhood for a single ethnic group in Freetown. In the 1830s, five streets were cut through with names based on the Kru origins—Settra Kroo, Little Kroo, Nana Kroo, King Williams, and Grand Cess. The Kru migrants cohabited with liberated African and indigenous women until 1880, when Kru women began to settle in the area (Banton 1957).

Thomas Ludlam, governor of the colony for fourteen years (1797–1811), remarked on Kru adaptability to various tasks. Their chief diversion, he said, was dancing. Though he added few details on Kru dance and music, he mentioned shipboard dancing and a boat dance on an American man-of-war. He also noted how the Kru hoarded their earnings to invest in European goods to carry home: pursuing the "white man's fashion," they expected to take home clothes, hats, and other articles of the best attire, which, while they paraded through the streets at the end of their trip, they wore as symbols of their new life-style (Ludlam 1812:87).

The Kru constituted a single, oftentimes special, population; in some centers of the diaspora, local Africans preferred not to have contact with them. Their culturally distinctive unity—evident away from home, but not necessarily at home—resulted from intensified social interactions among them, and from competitive economic interaction with Africans of other ethnic origins who, like them, were seeking economic or political advantage in port city society (McEvoy 1977:68).

"down the coast"   The area south and east of
Liberia, including Fernando Po and other
West African countries

tuku   Single-headed, wooden goblet drum
that accompanied music of the Kru living
in Liberia

During the Great War (1914–1918), increased shipping and port activity offered
more work for the laborers, whom it attracted in droves. Freetown became a port of
assembly for merchant ships awaiting convoy. Because of Britain's special historic
relationship with Sierra Leone, Freetown became the British base for Elder
Dempster's line, and the Kru population increased from about 1,200 in 1891 to
4,744 in 1921 (Banton 1957:225).

The Freetown Kru community, as in other West African ports, divided into
small groups with decentralized authority. The Freetown Kru remained isolated from
the rest of the population—and were Christians, rather than Muslims. Cultural institutions that kept their vitality abroad were voluntary associations. While in Monrovia
and Lagos these were primarily women's associations, which functioned as mutual aid
groups; in Freetown, the Kru also organized "friendly societies," which were not gender specific. In the 1950s, forty-seven of these societies were registered, three of them
Seamen's Clubs, modeled on officers' organizations on ships where the Kru worked
(Banton 1957). Since the men were away from home for long periods, the women's
societies were especially powerful. They pooled their resources to provide for their
members' wakes and burials. They served both a cultural and an economic function,
providing some basis for economic stability.

The Kru "down the coast"

By the 1830s, Kru migration had extended "down the coast" to cocoa plantations in
"Nanny Po" (Fernando Po, formerly occupied by the Spanish); by 1848, some Kru
were working as far south as Calabar, Nigeria. As their reputation grew, demands for
their labor increased. In Lagos, both Nigerians and Europeans hired them. The bulk
of their labor, concentrated in the Lagos and Oil rivers up to the time of the Great
War, gradually shifted up the coast to Ghana, where they found employment in gold-
mines (Martin 1982:3). Later they worked in Accra, Sekondi, and Kumasi. They also
worked in the Congo, present-day Angola, Namibia, and South Africa. They emigrated as migrant laborers to the Guianas, Jamaica, Trinidad, and Martinique
(Schuler 1986:156). Some assisted in building the Suez and Panama canals. Many
who in 1914 went to Liverpool, primarily from Freetown, never returned to live in
Africa.

Most Kru remained versatile, working in many different jobs. The men always
stressed that their work down the coast was temporary, even when they began to stay
abroad for long periods of time. Englishmen frequently labeled Kru the Irishmen or
Scotsmen of West Africa, because they sought their fortunes away from home.
Though down the coast they took on a proletarian status, readily selling their labor,
they worked to improve their lives back home.

Between 1900 and 1920, new types of work and patterns of living developed
among the downcoast Kru. Both men and women traveled to Nigeria, and their links
with the Nigerian communities increased, though they did not intend to take up per-

manent residence (Martin 1982:8). As they had done in Takoradi and Abidjan, they helped construct the port of Lagos and the railroad running north from Lagos.

The largest permanent downcoast Kru community emerged on Lagos Island behind Tinubu Square, where a majority of Krumen had gone since the 1870s (Martin 1982:9). By 1897, the acting governor estimated the "floating" Kru population to be 1,200, a number that by 1911 had more than doubled, surpassing the Kru population in Freetown. The census of 1921 shows that there were 13,000 Liberians in Ghana—most of them no doubt Kru, while in southern Nigeria 2,635 Liberians were counted.

MUSIC OF THE KRU

Kru music from the homeland in eastern Liberia is predominantly vocal music, accompanied by a single-headed, wooden goblet drum (*tuku*) and other percussive instruments. Aside from warrior songs, the oldest genre of Kru music is that sung by women's associations for wakes, funerals, and social gatherings (figure 1). These songs, called *si-o-lele,* are sung in a chorus-refrain style, with the chorus beginning with the nonlexical syllables that comprise the title. The export and exchange of these songs spread the repertory to Ghana and Sierra Leone. Two of them, recorded with contemporary orchestration in Freetown, have achieved wide popularity (Ajua and Victoria Dollah, personal communication, 1990).

The acquisition of new instruments

During their travels, the Kru acquired wealth and new ideas from other parts of Africa and the West. Among the new products from Europe on the African market were musical instruments. Consequently, the number of musicians increased rapidly, and these musicians began to link innovative musical developments with the introduction of novel instruments (Alájá-Browne 1989:234).

Of particular fascination to the Kru was the acoustic guitar. According to older seamen interviewed in the 1980s, guitars were sometimes available in shops in Ghana or Nigeria in the 1920s. The mandolin, also a popular instrument, could be purchased in Europe or places like Fernando Po. Stringed instruments were not unfamiliar to Kru musicians, who, back in their homeland, had played a plucked lute, a calabash with a carved stick for a neck, fastened with rattan and supporting five or six

FIGURE 1   A Kru women's group performs a *si-o-lele* song.

Kru musicians' trademark was a two-finger style of
picking, in which all right-hand passages were played
with the right thumb and index finger.

strings (personal communication, Jacob Musa, 1989). Accordions, banjos, concertinas, harmonicas, and tambourines were among the instruments available for those
who could afford them.

The Kru along the coast in Liberia played a cane flute. Down the coast in urban
areas, pennywhistles (and later, European flutes and piccolos) were among the instruments on which the Kru excelled. A famous pair, Sunday Davis and Friday Peters,
developed a virtuosic style of flute playing that boosted Kru musicians' popularity
and marketability in Nigeria.

In the late 1930s, brass bands became popular on the Kru Coast in Liberia.
Though Grebo seamen were probably the first to bring them from Ghana, the Kru
also participated for a while. Sibo, a man from Grand Kru County who had learned
to play instruments in Ghana, established a band of brass instruments (*ba*), including
trumpet, trombone, bass, sousaphone, and bass drum (personal communication Ol'
Man Thompson, 1988, Monrovia). The bands played both European and African
tunes, and for many years provided the music in Liberia for dances such as quadrilles,
in which large numbers of people participated. To the accompaniment of palm wine
guitar music or other Western instruments, one of the dancers called the figures,
which the couples executed.

Palm wine guitar styles

Kru sailors had a reputation for being among the most innovative of African musicians. This reputation was partly based on their life-style, for leisure time in the ports
gave them opportunities to relax, relate anecdotes of travel, and exchange musical
ideas. But it was also based on their facility in playing palm wine guitar music, a style
they introduced in ports from Freetown to Fernando Po.

According to Sylvester Thomas, a well-known musician in Monrovia, the sound
of a ship's horn would bring local musicians down to the harbor to meet the seamen,
hoping to find musicians on board. Thomas explained (personal communication,
1988):

> When the ship came in, they always brought something new. We went aboard the
> ship carrying drinks and tobacco, and as we spoke and drank, we played music.
> Sometimes we sat under a large palmtree where we'd always meet. I watched their
> fingers [on the guitar], and that's where I got the training. For any unusual situation
> in town, we made lyrics to fit. Eventually there was a kind of social demand, partic-
> ularly among the young people.

Palm wine guitar music swept the West African coast, and its popularity reached as
far east as Zaïre. In the ports, a guitarist would join with local percussionists, who
would tap out the rhythms on a bottle or kerosene can (*chegbe*), mesmerizing the
audiences who gathered to dance and drink the local toddy.

Kru musicians' trademark was a two-finger style of picking, in which all right-hand passages were played with the right thumb and index finger. As seagoers, the Kru helped spread this style, which proliferated from the 1930s to the 1950s. Rather than imitating Western manners of playing, palm wine guitar musicians invented and developed a style of playing based on complex African patterns.

In Nigeria, the style based on the two-finger technique was called Krusbass (Alájá-Browne 1985:17). Kru gathered every weekend for merrymaking in the Elegbata (Olowogbowo) area of Lagos, where many resided (Alájá-Browne 1985:24). This style influenced early jùjú artists in Lagos, such as Tunde King, who also employed a Kru phrase to signal the end of his performances (Waterman 1990:72).

During the 1930s in Monrovia, from the name of a guitar-rhythm pattern in the song "Dagomba Waye Tangebu 'Dagomba [a ship] wired Tangebu [a seaman]'," Kru guitarists were called dagomba boys (Boy Davis, personal communication, 1990). Palm wine music in Monrovia was also called sea breeze music; it was played with a guitar and a bottle or a bamboo slit-drum (kono) (personal communication, Sylvester Thomas, 1988, Monrovia). A later variant of this style, developed by the descendants of African-American settlers, emphasized the strumming more than the picking.

Early highlife music in Ghana was rooted in palm wine guitar style. The Kru or Liberian style that most influenced early highlife in Ghana was also called dagomba style. However, dagomba was but one of three acoustic guitar styles that became popular in Ghana; the other two were "mainline" and "fireman" styles (Collins 1985:110). As early as 1928, Kwame Asare, a Ghanaian, recorded guitar music of this milieu. In the mid-1990s, Koo Nimo, a renowned Ghanaian guitarist, internationally performs palm wine guitar music and other styles. In the hinterlands of Ghana, where the seperewa (a harp-lute with six to twelve strings) is traditionally played, acoustic guitar continues to be a vital tradition in palm wine bars, perhaps because seperewa players have an affinity for interlocking African patterns, and for playing on unamplified stringed instruments.

In Sierra Leone, a popular meeting place during the 1930s and 1940s in Freetown was the club Prapade; located at Adelaide Street Junction, it drew a wide audience for palm wine guitar music. The Kru met there to play music with fellow seamen, most often with Krio musicians, who, despite antagonistic social relations based on Freetown class structure, enjoyed performing the same types of urban music. Kru guitarists of that era included Taiwo Toby, Ekun Daio, Anthony Forde—and Chris Walker, who wrote one of Freetown's favorite songs, "Well, na de now 'Well, the time has come'."

Another variant of palm wine guitar style was maringa, played by the Krios of Freetown. It made more use of strumming, and incorporated West Indian rhythms, predominantly a calypso beat, brought to the region by the West Indian Frontier Force, which in the mid-1800s came to stay in Freetown. Maringa was popularized by Ebenezer Calendar, a celebrity with his own program on radio (Bender 1991). In the mid-1990s, to audiences in London, S. E. Rogie, another accomplished guitarist from Freetown, regularly plays elegant and simple palm wine guitar songs from the 1940s and 1950s, such as "My Lovely Elizabeth."

Styles of guitar playing developed their distinctiveness in various parts of West Africa, depending on different musical influences. Superficial resemblances to West African music employing two-finger techniques could also be heard in Congo and Zaïre, where Zaïrian guitarist Wendo stated that sailors introduced the style in Matadi in the 1930s (Gerhard Kubik, personal communication).

Two-finger picking

The Kru adapted two-finger styles of picking to traditional melodies and patterns in complex and sophisticated ways. While repeating rhythms and varying them slightly,

A form of music that rivaled local musics in Freetown and Lagos was Liberian highlife.

the guitarist picked the strings with the thumb and index finger. Often a second guitar played the melodic phrases with an ostinatolike pattern continuing throughout. The style was strongly rhythmic, with interest added through cross-rhythms.

Figure 2 shows a typical Kru guitar song in *dagomba* style. Its text refers to Havana, Cuba, an active city at the time, particularly known to Kru musicians of the 1940s and 1950s, who were attracted to Latin rhythms and dances. It alludes to the reputed excesses of life in Havana—a life whose overindulgences can kill. A popular song, it was known from Freetown to Port Harcourt, Nigeria. It was sung in a form of pidgin English spoken in Nigeria similar to Sierra Leonean Krio. According to Packard Okie, who recorded this song in 1947 in Liberia, the guitarist and singer Mr. Freeman, as a ship's mechanic had learned it from a Kru seaman (personal communication, 1994).

The music of this song artfully mixes two basic patterns: L, patterns for solo guitar and instrumental variation between passages, which alternate with R, patterns in which the guitar supports the voice. Cross-rhythms can be heard in the larger four-beat phrase (R_1 or R_2). The second R-pattern seems to answer the first in a responsorial or conversational style. In an excerpt (figure 2), the R_1-pattern has the bass C–G–G–G, answered by the R_2-bass C–D–E–G. The guitar chords move from tonic

FIGURE 2   "*Abana kili mi, dai-o* 'Havana kills me, I die, oh'," a Kru song in *dagomba* style, transcribed by Steve Elster from a recording made in Bromley, Liberia (Okie 1955:B:4).

FIGURE 3   Two-finger picking patterns in "*Abana kili mi, dai-o*": *a*, R₁, a guitar rhythmic pattern, supporting the voice; *b*, R₂, a variant pattern, answering R₁ in responsorial style; *c*, L, a melodic pattern of the solo guitar.

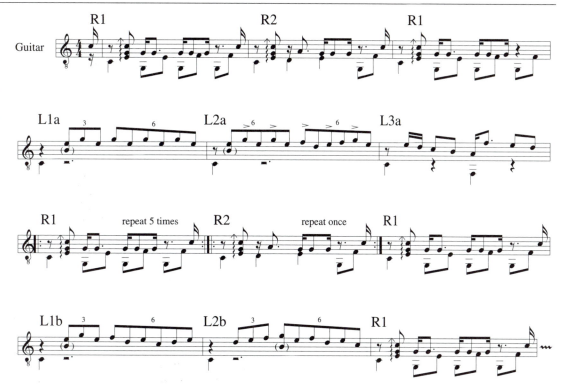

to dominant, shifting between the two repeated rhythmic patterns, and creating a contrast with the solo melodic passages (L₁ and L₂). A clear rhythmic pattern is presented, then varied, treating the guitar almost as if it were a drum. Each time the lead pattern returns, it receives subtle variation, displaying the artist's skill. The combination and sequence of patterns is variable.

Figure 3 shows the interplay of parts between the thumb and index fingers: the first two excerpts (R₁ and R₂) are guitar rhythmic patterns, and the third (L₁) is the melodic pattern. The transcriber, Steven Elster, an accomplished guitarist, notes that by using just thumb and index fingers, the player creates a close interlock between upper and lower voices, particularly in the dotted figures (R₁ and R₂), which, to be effective when played in two-finger picking style, require rhythmic precision. An additional feature of this example is an upstrum preceding the down-strum at the beginning of each phrase, adding a unique rhythmic feature that lends to the complexity and subtlety of the style.

Multiethnic mix: the 1940s and 1950s

The maritime industry declined in the early twentieth century, but Kru migrant laborers continued to travel to Sierra Leone, Nigeria, and Ghana, where they intermingled with other Africans, Caribbeans, and African-Americans. From the early 1940s to the late 1950s, multiethnic forms of musical expression emerged in the seaports and urban areas.

A form of music that rivaled local musics in Freetown and Lagos was Liberian highlife. Though guitar based, it employed a new type of orchestration, distinctively involving wind instruments such as pennywhistles and flutes. There was a craze for this type of music, particularly in Nigeria, where Kru musician Sunday Davis (also known as Sunday Harbour Giant) had introduced an improvisatory style of playing a penny whistle. He played a highly embellished melody or virtuosic phrases while interacting musically with other instruments. According to a Lagosian musician, other artists sought him out, wanting to imitate his style; he experimented with musical instruments such as the flute, the mandolin, and the organ (Alájá-Browne 1985:43).

Performing for radio broadcasting and recording became a means of generating income and fame.

Sunday Davis was a Kru seaman who went from Freetown to Lagos and became a truck driver. For nearly two decades, he remained well known in Lagosian musical life. He played with the Jolly Orchestra, comprised of Yoruba, Ashanti, and Kru musicians—such as BlueBlue, Motajo, Abiodun Oke, and Bobodi on guitar; Ambrose Adekoya Campbell on *jùjú* drum; and Sunday Harbour Giant on penny whistle. Their hit "*Àtàrí Àjànàkú*" was based on a Yoruba proverb: *Àtàrí Àjànàkú, kìí serú omodé* 'An elephant's head is not a load for a child'. This song, like others of the Jolly Orchestra, reflected the multiethnicity of performers in a blend of phrases sung in Yoruba, Kru, Pidgin English, and various Ghanaian languages heard along the marina in Lagos (Waterman 1990:49).

Music emphasizing flutes was played and recorded by the Kroo Young Stars Rhythm Group. Since this band consisted of Krio and Kru musicians, its music employed Krio and Kru lyrics. Its performances impacted Freetown and indigenous communities of Sierra Leone. Its rhythms closely resembled calypso rhythms and Cuban *charanga*, with long, flowing, improvisatory lines played on flutes. Its popularity paralleled the period of *tango ya ba Wendo* in Zaïre, when Latin American musical traits were introduced to Zaïre—a period when West African and Zaïrian musicians were intensively sharing ideas (Mukuna 1992:72–84).

The Kroo Young Stars transformed Kru music by adding new orchestration to older Kru songs. They expanded their audience by recording one of the *si-o-lele* songs sung by women's associations in Freetown. Though the song was never a big hit, the Kru appreciated the gesture because it opened up opportunities for Kru women to be recorded, and it introduced the *si-o-lele* repertory to the public. Subsequently, in the late 1950s, Ebenezer Calendar, a Krio musician in Freetown, also recorded a *si-o-lele* song in his trademark *maringa* style on a 78-rpm commercial record.

According to Kru musicians in Freetown and Monrovia, the tune of "*Àtàrí Àjànàkú*" (played by Sunday Davis's band) was based on "*O gio te bo* 'She has come for it again'," an older traditional Kru song, sung by the Freetown Kru. 'O.G.T.B.' as it was called in a version popularized by Kroo Young Stars, was a favorite among the Freetown Kru during the 1920s and 1930s, when it was sung at social gatherings and wakes. The Kru strongly identified with it, and it became a signature tune across West Africa among Kru musicians in various ports, and even in Liverpool. As one Kru guitarist in Liverpool said, "That song was grand. Everybody loved that tune, and a lot of songs came from it—different, different versions of 'O.G.T.B.' It was the main song for the Kru" (personal communication Danny Morris, Liverpool, 1990).

In many popular songs of the late 1940s and 1950s, renditions of "O.G.T.B." could be heard either in the melodic line, or in the improvisations of an accompanying instrument. The harmonic sequence and the interplay of phrases provided a musical formula or a model for many other songs which the Kru recognized as based on "O.G.T.B."

The advent of radio made syncretic adaptation possible on a new level, and regional styles became widely popular. Performing for radio broadcasting and recording became a means of generating income and fame. In the late 1940s, music could be heard on rediffusion boxes in homes in Lagos. According to one musician, the Nigerian Broadcasting Service brought musicians to its studio and paid them two pounds sterling, while paying singers 7 shillings each in 1953, to perform "O.G.T.B." for the music to be played on radio broadcasts.

European record companies sent representatives to scout West Africa for talent. In the early 1950s, British Decca Records of London even had a mobile studio unit in Freetown and other cities to record musicians such as the Kroo Young Stars. They drove this unit into the provinces, where they paid musicians a flat fee for full rights to their songs. The Kroo Young Stars, featuring Kun Peters on flute, recorded "O.G.T.B." on Decca Records in Freetown in 1953. Chris Walker, one of the most accomplished Kru seamen-guitarists, was lead singer and mandolinist for Kroo Young Stars. He had traveled frequently to Nigeria from the 1930s to the 1950s, and was recruited for the United African Company Band, where he learned to read music and play a variety of styles. Later, Ebenezer Calendar gained popularity in playing the guitar-based *maringa* music, with more of a vamping style; he recorded a rendition of "O.G.T.B." sung in Krio and Limba.

About the same time, another version of "O.G.T.B." was recorded in Ghana. It was frequently played at Sugar Baby, a Fanti club. Many Kru, stranded by the decline of the seafaring business, stayed on to live in Ghana.

LATE TWENTIETH-CENTURY TRANSITIONS

After the 1950s, the decline of the maritime industry was devastating to the Kru, and Kru music went into oblivion. With electronic amplification of instruments, the acoustic guitar played a reduced role in commercialized settings. Independence in African countries limited the musical, social, and economic role of Kru migrants.

The nationalistic tendencies of the period after African countries achieved independence brought changes in culture and the arts. Radio stations at the time were government subsidized. With liberation, West African governments revamped their cultural policies. Sources for musical material changed, often now linked to national issues.

Despite the potential to adapt and modernize, the Kru were linked to a minority group seen as marginal. Kru musicians talk of how Nigerians called for more indigenized music, and as one seaman states, "Before that, any nation could sing [in Lagos]." Kru musicians in the newly independent nations became, in a sense, marginalized. Their cultural and musical role did not transfer to a more political role that could easily survive the changing political climate in other parts of West Africa. Kru music was never promoted into the mainstream of African popular musics. Only several decades earlier could the Kru, in moving from place to place, create a broad audience and to some degree negotiate cultural differences through music.

The Kru experience represents an important stream of influence in the development of contemporary West African forms of expression. As the dissemination of the European-African lingua franca of pidgin English set patterns of communication in West Africa, so the propagation of African styles of guitar playing and the music of Kru mariners and migrant workers affected the development of music along the West African coast.

Relaxed social gatherings, palm wine bars, and music ensembles served as points of orientation for Kru migrant musicians, providing intersections between each worker and a network of musical interaction. The Kru were as adept at intermingling as they were at being musical adventurers and innovators.

Out of these settings, musical confluence emerged; the old and new forms combined with a multiethnic mix of expressive forms. The period was followed by an era of independence and nationalism, which created many difficult challenges for the Kru living away from their homeland. Their mobility ended, leaving few effects of a cosmopolitan life-style, but their musical legacy endures in ongoing forms of musical expression through Africa and the diaspora.

REFERENCES

Alájá-Browne, Afọlábi. 1985. *Jùjú Music: A Study of Its Social History and Style.* Ph.D. dissertation, University of Pittsburgh.

———. 1989. "A Diachronic Study of Change in Jùjú Music." *Popular Music* 8(3):231– 242.

Banton, Michael. 1957. *West African City: A Study of Tribal Life in Freetown.* London: Oxford University Press, for International African Institute.

Bender, Wolfgang. 1991. *Sweet Mother.* Chicago: University of Chicago Press.

Bridge, Horatio. 1853. *Journal of an African Cruiser,* ed. Nathaniel Hawthorne. New York: George P. Putnam.

Büttikofer, Johann. 1890. *Reisebilder aus Liberia.* Leiden: E. J. Brill.

Brooks, George. 1970. *Yankee Traders, Old Coasters and African Middlemen: A History of American Legitimate Trade with West Africa in the Nineteenth Century.* Brookline, Mass.: Boston University Press.

———. 1972. *The Kru Mariner in the Nineteenth Century.* Newark, Del.: Liberian Studies Association Monograph.

Collins, John. 1985. *African Pop Roots.* London: W. Foulsham.

———. 1989. "The Early History of West African Highlife Music." *Popular Music* 8(3):221–230.

Collins, John, and Paul Richards. 1982. "Popular Music in West Africa." In *Popular Music Perspectives,* ed. David Horn and Philip Tagg, 111–141. Goteborg, Exeter: International Association for the Study of Popular Music.

Coplan, David. 1985. *In Township Tonight! South Africa's Black City Music and Theatre.* London and New York: Longman; Johannesburg: Ravan Press.

Dalby, David. 1970. "Black through White: Patterns of Communication." Bloomington: Indiana University African Studies Program.

Davis, Ronald. 1976. *Ethnohistorical Studies on the Kru Coast.* Liberian Studies Monograph Series No. 5. Newark: University of Delaware.

Erlmann, Veit. 1991. *African Stars.* Chicago: University of Chicago Press.

Fraenkel, Merran. 1964. *Tribe and Class in Monrovia.* London: Oxford University Press.

Fyfe, Christopher. 1962. *A Short History of Sierra Leone.* London: Oxford University Press.

Hampton, Barbara. 1980. "A Revised Analytical Approach to Musical Processes in Urban Africa." *African Urban Studies* 6:1–16.

Kroo Young Stars Rhythm Group. 1953. *O Gi Te Bi.* Decca DKWA 1335. LP disk.

Ludlam, Thomas. 1812. "The Account of a Tribe of People Called Kroomen on the Coast of Africa." *The African Repository and Colonial Journal* 1:43–55.

Martin, Jane. 1982. *Krumen 'Down the Coast': Liberian Migrants on the West African Coast in the 19th Century.* Boston: African Studies Center, Boston University. Working Papers, 64.

McEvoy, Frederick. 1977. "Understanding Ethnic Realities Among the Grebo and Kru Peoples of West Africa." *Africa* 47(1):62–80.

Mukuna, Kazadi wa. 1992. "The Genesis of Urban Music." *African Music* 7(2):72–74.

Okie, Packard, ed. 1955. *Folk Music of Liberia.* New York: Folkways Records, FE 4465.

Schuler, Monica. 1986. "Kru Emigration to British and French Guiana." In *Africans in Bonda*ge: *Studies in Slavery and the Slave Trade,* ed. Paul E. Lovejoy, 155–201. Madison: University of Wisconsin Press.

Smith, J. 1851. *Trade and Travels in the Gulph of Guinea.* London: Simkin, Marshall.

Tonkin, Elizabeth. 1971. "Some Coastal Pidgins of West Africa." In *Social Anthropology and Language,* ed. Edwin Ardener, 239–255. London: Tavistock.

Waterman, Christopher. 1990. *Jùjú: A Social History and Ethnography of an African Popular Music.* Chicago: University of Chicago Press.

Latin American Musical Influences in Zaïre

Kazadi wa Mukuna

The Role of Radio
The Role of Recordings
The Role of Concerts

Until the late twentieth century, the scrutiny of cultural exchange between Africa and the Americas was a one-way concern. Scholars focused their attention only on the flow of African cultural elements into the New World. In addition to identifying those elements in the cultural fabrics of the Americas, scholars theorized on the processes by which those elements became transformed. Published studies of African influences on cultural expressions in the New World abound in anthropology, sociology, linguistics, religion, and history. In ethnomusicology, methodological guidelines like one proposed by the Grupo de Trabajo outline approaches that consider not only inferences drawn from the humanities and social sciences, but also the effects of cultural renewal, an effort by people to refresh their cultural knowledge.

In Africa in the 1970s, a new trend in scholarship, supported by studies in urban musicology, began. Scholars realized that urban musical expressions are legitimate sources of information about social change. African musical processes reflect the convergence of musical material from within and without the continent, summarize the world views of their societies, and record events that affect the lives of their makers and audiences. The rise of urban musical expressions in Africa warrants the analysis of their musical styles. The influence of Latin American music did not affect the parts of the continent equally, but the development of urban musical expressions in Africa may have resulted from the impact of a combination of similar phenomena and events, such as the installation of foreign companies, leading to the formation of detribalized centers, marked by the introduction of foreign musical instruments and musical forms.

The rise of Latin American societies and cultures has received attention from humanists and social scientists (Dealy 1992; Lang 1993; Zavala 1992). The convergence of three racial groups (African, European, Amerindian) in the New World tested several processes of acculturation and assimilation. These groups did not interact in similar ways or degrees. European masters had more opportunities to interact with their African slaves than with Indians, whose souls their church requested they save. The result was a new cultural expression, embodying elements from Europe and Africa.

Assimilation is an advanced stage in the process of cultural exchange. It follows

In 1997, a new government in Zaïre changed the name of the nation to "Democratic Republic of the Congo."

Of countless Latin tunes broadcast and sold on records, none was more appealing and influential than "*El Manisero* 'The Peanut Vendor'."

phases during which people accept or reject cultural elements as compatible or incompatible with their needs. These phases include

- the listing of cultural materials, when people with different origins in an emerging society discover what they share, and define common denominators that might become features of their new culture;
- the evaluation of common denominators according to new sets of norms and values;
- the reinterpretation of compatible common denominators in the light of the new context, the stage at which, as they reach the point of assimilation, they change and receive new functions.

Cultural elements are either retained or rejected. Further examination of the process of the emergence of a new cultural context brings to light three major levels of consideration that operate in concert, though not in a particular order: (a) the survival of a context of which a cultural element is part; (b) the resilience of a cultural element in the new society; and (c) the functionality of a cultural element for the needs of the ruling class. Each of the racial groups that converged in the New World had a cultural background that people cherished and protected. To ensure survival in the emerging society, each group made itself receptive to a new set of norms and rules. The continuity of a cultural element is an assertion of its persistence and assimilation. Resilience of cultural elements to the new set of norms and rules made this process possible.

African slaves brought to Latin America the knowledge of certain musical instruments and concepts of organizing certain musical elements. In the New World, these elements survived within cultural manifestations that had surrounded them in Africa. As a way of insuring their survival, African slaves began to recreate cultural details that gave meaning to their lives. In certain areas, the European ruling class, by encouraging the formation of social brotherhoods of slaves (such as those known in Brazil as nations, and in Cuba as *cabildos*), fostered this process. Though Europeans' primary intent was to control the slave population by keeping a firm hand on its leaders (who had to answer for the misbehavior of their brothers), the brotherhoods provided opportunities for slaves to recreate and perpetuate portions of their cultural calendar. They were the basis for promoting observances of African social and religious festivals and rituals (Mason 1992:9).

The encounter of Spanish and African concepts of musical organization in the New World resulted in the creation of new musical forms, including the *cumbia* in Puerto Rico; the rumba, the *columbia*, the mambo, and the *guaguancó* in Cuba; the samba in Brazil; the tango in Argentina; and the merengue in the Dominican Republic. These styles displayed a distinct rhythmic tapestry, a product of the fusion of rhythmic concepts from both worlds. Where there were not similarities (such as in harmonic implication, melodic structure, style of vocal production, and melodic musical instrumentation), ruling-class adaptation to the new style was inevitable. By being compatible with existing local forms, most of these forms served as models for urban music and dances in African countries. In Zaïre, the impact of Latin music on urban musical expression was more momentous than elsewhere in Africa.

The date these forms initially became known in Africa is unknown, but musical contacts between Latin America and Africa began to flourish in the 1930s and 1940s, and continued until the 1960s. These contacts took three forms: radio broadcasts, recordings, and concerts (Rondón 1980:3–37; Mukuna 1993:65–71).

THE ROLE OF RADIO

The first two radio stations to operate in Kinshasa were the Jesuit-owned Radio-Léo, which began broadcasting in January 1937, and Radio Congolia (owned and operated by Joseph Hourdebise, assisted by his wife, Madeleine Demont), which began broadcasting on 4 September 1939. Radio-Léo's goals—bringing Roman Catholic culture to the European population in Zaïre and converting the local population—remained for the duration of its existence, which ended on 15 July 1967. Those of Radio Congolia, aimed primarily at bringing news and commercial advertisements to the black population, continued until 28 February 1948. Elsewhere in the country, five privately operated stations came into existence during that time, but Radio Congolia was "the first in Congo to broadcast programs for the black population" (Pauwels-Boon 1979:182).

The first government-controlled station, Radio Congo Belge (RCB), began operating in Kinshasa on 1 October 1940. Its primary goal was to inform the colonial population about developments of the war in Europe. In 1948, the central government took over the broadcasts of Radio Congolia, which it renamed Radio Congo Belge pour les Indigènes (RCBI). The new station operated for eleven years (1949–1960), and then became Radio Nationale Congolaise (RNC). Through programming, RCBI and Radio Congolia exposed the population of Kinshasa—and cities as far away as Accra, Dakar, and Lagos—to the musical styles of the Americas, and promoted Zaïrean urban music. Their broadcasts featured Congolese dance music with Latin American rhythms (Pauwels-Boon 1979:182). To diversify its programming, Radio Congolia aired live studio broadcasts of performances by bands that had achieved success in Léopoldville (Pauwels-Boon 1979:180). These broadcasts, coupled with the influence of traveling Latin bands, stimulated the creation of "jazz bands"—street ensembles that, despite their name, played music bearing little resemblance to American jazz.

THE ROLE OF RECORDINGS

Before 1948, when Ngoma (a Greek-owned studio in Kinshasa) began operations, 78-rpm recordings of Afro-Cuban music and American jazz were popular in Zaïre and other parts of the continent. These recordings became a source of musical materials that local bands learned by rote and performed in bars, which numbered about 100 in Kinshasa in 1945. The most successful recordings sold in Kinshasa that year were of dance music. To popular melodies, local composers sometimes added words in Lingala (a local language) or Spanish words (Comhaire-Sylvain 1968:36–39).

The proliferation of studios in Kinshasa, and the increase in air time of music from Latin America and the United States, reinforced this popularity. Of countless Latin tunes broadcast and sold on records (released on labels such as His Master's Voice, Vaya Records, and Fania Records), none was more appealing and influential than "*El Manisero* 'The Peanut Vendor'," in which the Cuban composer Moises Simon experimented with combining the rhythm of the *son* with that of the *pregón*.

musique Zaïroise moderne   'Modern Zaïrean music', a new style of guitar music in the 1960s

maringa   Intertribal social dance, popular on the west coast of Africa from Sierra Leone to Zaïre

kwasa-kwasa   Popular music in Zaïre from 1986, based on a variant of the rumba

zekete-zekete   Popular music from 1977 to 1987 in Kinshasa, based on a variant of the rumba

madiaba   Popular music in Kinshasa from 1988, based on a variant of the rumba

The popularity of this and other Latin tunes reached an apogee in the 1950s, and remained a fixed part of local bands' repertories until the late 1960s. By the mid-1960s, however, most Latin tunes had become obsolete. A new style of music for guitar, *musique Zaïroise moderne* 'modern Zaïrean music', taking traditional ethnic music as its inspiration, supplanted them. In the 1990s, Europeans were still miscalling this style by the name of its 1966 variation, *soukous*.

The studios played a role equally important in the dissemination, establishment, and promotion of Latin American music in Zaïre. A variety of profitable music-related activities—an increase in the number of musicians and musical ensembles in the country, and the adoption of the term *rumba* over *maringa* (an intertribal social dance, popular on the west coast of Africa, from Sierra Leone to Zaïre)—proves the strength of this role. For more than a decade (1948–1960), studios provided promising young Zaïrean musicians with European and Latin American musical instruments, of which congas, bongos, guitars, flutes, clarinets, saxophones, claves, and maracas were the most common. The studios hired European virtuosos to give lessons. The studios set up a pool of local musicians capable of accompanying traditional and Latin dance music on the new instrumentation. The result was an increase in the number of freelance studio musicians, who remained at the service of the studio that had trained them. Several important musicians started their career in this fashion, playing in occasional ensembles composed of musicians from one studio. Eventually, through recordings and performances in bars, some of the ensembles gained celebrity. Two of the most prominent of the 1950s were African Jazz and O.K. Jazz. The former, founded in 1953 by musicians from Opika studio, included Joseph "Le Grand Kalle" Kabasele, Charles "Dechaud" Mwamba, and André "Damoiseau" Kambite. The latter, founded in 1956 by musicians from Loningisa studio, included Luambo "Franco" Makiadi, Victor "Vicky" Longomba, Daniel "De-la-Lune" Lubelo, and Edward "Edo" Nbanga.

The marketing of Zaïrean popular music, both in the country and throughout Africa, was a deciding factor in the adoption of the name of the Cuban dance rumba in Zaïre. Examination of Cuban rumbas and Zaïrean variants reveals that what occurred in Zaïre was not the adaptation or assimilation of Cuban dance forms, but the reinterpretation of the name. The music returned to the style of the *maringa,* whose associated movements (comparable to those of the Cuban rumba) consist of shifting body weight from one leg to the other; but the studios maintained the name "rumba," since they found it had more commercial appeal. After the novelty of Latin influences had worn off, musicians looked back to *maringa,* which they could easily interpret on the new instrumentation, and fit to traditional musical patterns and dances. The new instruments added a dimension to *maringa* music that traditional musical instruments lacked. They brought new harmonic possibilities and new timbres, though their functions were at first limited to roles fulfilled by the traditional instruments they were replacing. (The guitar, for example, replaced melodic instruments such as the *mbira* and the *madimba*, a local xylophone.) With the new instrumentation, the Zaïrean rumba became adaptable to the structure of traditional music and dance. Traditional tunes could find their way into the rumba without modifying or giving up the principles of their rhythmic organization. Zaïrean rumba and its variants—*soukous* (1966), *zekete-zekete* (1977–1987), *kwasa-kwasa* (1986), *madiaba* (1988)— became a source of influences for rising urban musical expressions throughout Africa, including *makossa* in Cameroon, *jùjú* in Nigeria, *marabi* in South Africa, and *kwela* in Malawi.

THE ROLE OF CONCERTS

In 1912, foreign companies in Zaïre introduced a policy that allowed migrant workers to sign extended contracts, instead of the three-month contracts then in force. (The short-term contracts had forced workers to move repeatedly from one company to another.) The imposition of the new policy helped crystallize the foundation of detribalized centers, composed of people of different nationalities and ethnic backgrounds (Cornevin 1966:210; Alexandre-Pyre 1969:143). In Kinshasa, these companies mainly hired West Africans to work in offices (Comhaire-Sylvain 1968:49–55). The resulting concentration of West Africans brought changes to social and musical activities in the city. The brass tradition, introduced by West Africans with such bands as the Coastmen and Excelsior, provided a model that led to the creation of brass bands by Zaïrean musicians throughout Kinshasa, with such names as "L'Harmonie Kinoise" and "Odéon Kinois," both in 1940.

By the mid-1960s, the dissemination of Latin American musical sounds led to the local demise of the brass-band tradition. Surviving bands, such as L'Harmonie Kinoise, adapted their instrumentation to those of Latin *charangas* and *orquestas típicas*, which frequently toured the country. These musical formations had a profound impact, not only on the musical style of the country, but also on stage presentation, clothing, and even the artists' names—so an Edward became Edo, a François became Franco, a Nicolas became Nico, and a Baloji became Baroza. Latinized names served as musicians' stage names. The orchestration of rising new ensembles included stringed instruments (guitars: lead, rhythm, bass), woodwinds (clarinets, flutes, saxophones), and an array of percussive instruments (conga drums, maracas, güiros, claves, rhythm sticks).

Urban musical ensembles reached Kinshasa with the introduction of Latin American dance forms (cha-cha, *charanga*, bolero, mambo, merengue, rumba, *pachanga*), all of which had first gained popularity in New York, promoted there by Latin ensembles. (Some of the earliest preserved examples of *maringa* music were those recorded by Pepper 1942 and Tracey 1956.) One such ensemble was Machito and his Afrocubans, founded in New York in 1941 by Mario Bauza and Frank "Machito" Grillo. It included Latin American and Caribbean musicians, who performed regularly in such dance halls as the Palladium and the Blen Blen Club. Possibly the most influential of the traveling Latin bands was that led by the Dominican flutist Johnny Pacheco, whose name became associated in Kinshasa with the Latin sound. His influence was so strong, promoters invited him to perform at events associated with the championship fight between boxers Mohammed Ali and George Foreman (Kinshasa, 1974).

Latin musical genres provided expressions that served only for specific circumstances. Lyrics, imitating Latin ensembles, often took the form of broken Spanish (Comhaire-Sylvain 1968:36–37). For songs of humor and joy, audiences preferred the cha-cha, the merengue, and the *pachanga*; for lamentations and elegies, they preferred the slow tempo of the bolero.

By 1965, most forms of Latin music and dance had become obsolete in Zaïre.

However, the compatibility of the rumba and the *maringa* helped the adaptation and assimilation of the rumba into the musical expression of urban centers. Questions continue to arise about the African authenticity of the *maringa,* whose popularity had spread along the west coast of Africa from Sierra Leone to Zaïre well before 1970.

REFERENCES

Acosta, Léonardo. 1991. "The Rumba, the Guaguancó, and Tío Tom." In *Essays on Cuban Music: North American and Cuban Perspectives.* ed. Peter Manuel, 49–73. New York: University Press of America.

Alexandre-Pyre, S. 1969. "L'origine de la population du centre urbain de Lubumbashi." *Publications de l'Université Officielle du Congo à Lubumbashi* 19:141–150.

Bergman, Billy, et al. 1985. *Hot Sauces: Latin and Caribbean Pop.* New York: Quill.

Carpentier, Alejo. 1979. *La Música en Cuba.* Habana: Editorial Letras Cubanas.

Collins, John. 1985. *African Pop Roots: The Inside Rhythms of Africa.* London: W. Foulsham.

Comhaire-Sylvain, Suzanne. 1968. *Femmes de Kinshasa hier et aujourd'hui.* Paris: Mouton.

Cornevin, Robert. 1966. *Histoire du Congo Léopoldville-Kinshasa: dès origines préhistoriques à la République Démocratique du Congo.* Paris: Berger-Levrault.

Dealy, Glen Caudill. 1992. *The Latin Americans: Spirit and Ethos.* Boulder, Colo.: Westview Press.

Díaz Ayala, Cristobal. 1981. *Música Cubana del Areyto a la Nueva Trova.* San Juan: Editorial Cubanacan.

Lang, James. 1993. "Sociology and Development." *International Journal of Contemporary Sociology* 30(1):5–19.

Léon, Argeliers. 1991. "Notes toward a Panorama of Popular and Folk Music." In *Essays on Cuban Music: North American and Cuban Perspectives,* ed. Peter Manuel, 1–23. New York: University Press of America.

Mason, John. 1992. *Orin Orisa: Songs for Selected Heads.* New York: Yoruba Theological Archministry.

Mukuna, Kazadi wa. 1992. "The Genesis of Urban Music in Zaïre." *African Music* 7(2):72–84.

———. 1993. "L'évolution de la musique urbaine au Zaïre pendant les dix premières années de la Seconde République." *Aquarium* 11/12 (Printemps 1993):65–71.

———. 1990–1991. "The Study of African Musical Contributions to Latin America and the Caribbean: A Methodological Guideline." *Bulletin of the International Committee on Urgent Anthropological Research* 32–33:47–49.

Pauwels-Boon, Greta. 1979. *L'Origine, l'évolution et le functionnement de la radiodiffusion au Zaïre de 1937 à 1960.* Tervuren: Musée Royal de l'Afrique Centrale.

Pepper, Herbert. 1942. *Anthologie de la vie africaine.* AST 6001–03. 3 LP disks.

Rondón, César Miguel. 1980. *El Libro de la Salsa: Crónica de la Música del Caribe Urbano.* Caracas: Editorial Arte.

Roberts, John Storm. 1992. "The Roots." In *Salsiology: Afro-Cuban Music and the Evolution of Salsa in New York City,* ed. Vernon W. Boggs, 5–22. New York: Greenwood Press.

Schuler, Monica. 1986. "Kru Emigration to British and French Guiana, 1841–1857." In *Africans in Bondage: Studies in Slavery and the Slave Trade,* ed. Paul E. Lovejoy, 155–201. Madison: University of Wisconsin Press.

Tracey, Hugh. 1956. International Library of African Music. Roodepoort, Transvaal.

———. 1972. *The Music of Africa: Musical Instruments 6.* [The *maringa* music in Tracey 1956.] Kaleidophone KMA 6.

Zavala, Iris M. 1992. *Colonialism and Culture: Hispanic Modernisms and the Social Imaginary.* Bloomington: Indiana University Press.

Popular Music in Africa
Angela Impey

The Commercialization of African Music
African Popular Music and the International Market
Trends in the Major Regions of Africa
Intra-African Connections

Africa is an extraordinary and powerful continent. Almost three times the size of the continental United States, it consists of fifty-three countries, inhabited by some 700 million people. It has vast savannas, expanding deserts, tropical forests, lofty mountains, riverine valleys, palm-fringed coastlines, and spice-producing islands. Its people are differentiated from one another by ethnic identity and cultural practices, by religion, language, class, and urban and rural identification (Martin and O'Meara 1995:4).

Most African people still live in rural areas, but the continuous flow of people between town and country is a significant characteristic of the continent—a trait that remains basic to emerging expressive forms. The renowned Cameroonian saxophonist Manu Dibango has said that in Africa,

> you have a two-way traffic between town and village, village and town. You have a sound that arrives in the town and returns to the village, changed. The echo which comes back is not the original. When a note arrives in town from the village, the town returns it with electronic delay, with reverb, limiter and all the studio technology, but it is the same note that came from the village. (Ewens 1991:7)

Thus, modern-day national boundaries do not necessarily reflect differences between people, nor do they always carry meaning in relation to cultural and musical developments. The movement and interchange between artists from different countries who play similar kinds of music tend rather to reflect related languages, religions, and cultural practices. For instance, Manding *griot* music is played across West Africa, Congo-Zaïre rumba is prevalent throughout the Central and Eastern regions, *taarab* is performed by most coastal Swahili peoples, and elements of South African township music can be identified in the popular music of most southern African countries (Ewens 1991:24).

All the countries of Africa, with the exception of Ethiopia and Liberia, have undergone a period of foreign domination. Colonial governments, which occupied African territories between the 1880s and the second half of the twentieth century, brought with them trappings of a foreign culture, affecting, to varying degrees, the

Instruments such as guitars, violins, accordions, concertinas, and pedal organs were introduced into Africa by European traders, then reinvented to suit indigenous systems of tuning and styles of performance.

economic, political, and cultural infrastructures of the societies they controlled. These systems had a profound impact on the composition and distribution of popular cultures in Africa. For one, the adoption of European languages by colonized societies differentiated francophone West and Central Africa from the anglophone South and East and the lusophone states of Angola, Mozambique, and Guinea-Bissau. For another, colonial governments employed different strategies of cultural development, influencing the nature of the imaging, production, and distribution of popular music, both within their respective colonies and abroad.

The following survey of popular African music concentrates on the sub-Saharan region. On the basis of religion, North Africa is generally separated from countries south of the Sahara Desert, the north having been more influenced by Islam (Martin and O'Meara 1995:5). Though the discursive division of the continent is overemphasized (since much of sub-Saharan Africa is also Muslim), for the purpose of expediency I exclude the Maghrib [see NORTH AFRICA]. Further, I focus on musical genres that have circulated intracontinentally and internationally, and hence on the countries where those genres originated.

THE COMMERCIALIZATION OF AFRICAN MUSIC

This article discusses music mediated by a complex corporate network comprising companies that record, manage, advertise, publish, and broadcast mass-produced music. This network first reached into Africa around 1900, when entrepreneurs in the West began to recognize the potential for marketing musical instruments, gramophones, and records there. Since then, styles and peoples have circulated extensively between African centers and countries abroad. This circulation has included African influences on the music of the diaspora extending back through the slave trade, a circulation that is as much about commonalities of style as it is about ideologies of blackness. Influences also spread through the movement of artists between African countries and centers of production in Europe (mainly Paris and London), where technologically sophisticated studios and established performance circuits have long attracted professional African musicians.

Instruments such as guitars, violins, accordions, concertinas, and pedal organs were introduced into Africa by European traders. These instruments were reinvented to suit indigenous systems of tuning and styles of performance. The spread of acoustic guitars, and later electric guitars, was one of the most important developments in African popular music, both as topical acoustic music performed solo or in small groups, and as amplified music for dancing (figure 1).

The introduction of gramophone records (from 1907) presented African musicians with a new spectrum of imported styles. Among these were African-American jazz, Dominican merengue, Cuban salsa and *son*, Anglo-American rock and country, African-American soul, and Jamaican reggae. Radio was established in most parts of the continent by the 1920s, initially for a European listenership. During World War

FIGURE 1   In an informal setting in
Chitungwiza, Zimbabwe, a youth plays a homemade guitar. Photo by Bror Karlsson.

II, the airwaves were used to broadcast to African audiences in the attempt to enlist
material and moral support for the war effort. Shortly thereafter, in response to the
demand for broadcast music, recording studios were established. These institutions
became critical to the development of popular music, with competition between
multinational companies and emerging local ones being a recurrent theme. By the
1930s, HMV, Odeon, Columbia, and Pathé-Marconi were distributing their products across Africa. Most foreign companies established subsidiaries in Africa, and the
most advanced infrastructures were developed in Nigeria, Côte d'Ivoire, South
Africa, Tanzania, Kenya, and Zimbabwe (Manuel 1988:89).

Most African music industries in the 1990s are extremely vulnerable to economic and political instability, and countries such as Nigeria and Tanzania, which once
boasted thriving industries, are no longer significant producers of recorded music.
Most industries are thwarted by the lack of vital resources, such as musical instruments, public-address systems, recording equipment, and capital to finance music
production. Ineffective policing of copyright infringements and the rampant pirating
of cassettes rob local industries of substantial income.

Local production of popular music formerly took the form of 45- and 78-RPM
records. Albums were often released as compilations of national hits, and were produced in smaller numbers so as to be affordable to local buyers. The 1980s marked
more or less the end of vinyl. Most local companies have invested in the high-speed
C-60 cassette market, and cassettes now outsell records five to one. There is little evidence that the compact disc market will succeed in Africa apart from South Africa,
since CD equipment is expensive, and CD technology is not yet considered hardy
enough to withstand local conditions.

South Africa stands apart from the rest of the continent in that it boasts state-of-
the-art recording technology with the potential to become the new center of production for African music. Started in 1914, when the Brothers MacKay, agents of His
Master's Voice Company (based in London), began selling records from the back of
ox-drawn wagons, the South African industry has developed into a multimillion-dol-

By the mid-1900s, gombay had gained mass appeal, and it had spread into other West African countries, where it became the basis for localized permutations, such as Ghanaian highlife.

lar industry, with transnational companies such as BMG and Sony operating out of Johannesburg alongside major local companies.

AFRICAN POPULAR MUSIC AND THE INTERNATIONAL MARKET

All African pop embodies creative interaction between foreign values and local styles. Popular music is therefore a site for adaptation, assimilation, eclecticism, appropriation, and experimentation. In light of the intensity of global communications (which have accelerated during the last century), stimulated by capital, conquest, migration, and technology, African pop has become a global phenomenon.

African pop is consumed internationally under the marketing tag of world music. World music is one of the largest growth areas in record stores in the UK and Europe. The term was coined about 1987 by small, independent, British labels (Hannibal, Sterns, World Circuit, and others) in response to growing interest in popular African and other non-European music and the lack of provision of dedicated space for such musics in record stores. The gap in the market was made more obvious with crossover ventures like Paul Simon's *Graceland* album, whose award-winning collaboration with South African musicians opened the way for major international labels to sign up groups such as Ladysmith Black Mambazo (Howard 1996:2).

The world-music movement has been fueled by an increasing interest in African music in the European, Asian, and American festival circuits. Perhaps the most important platform for launching popular African musicians has been the World of Music Arts and Dance (WOMAD) festival, conceived by the British rock musician Peter Gabriel in 1980. Now staged worldwide, these festivals aim to stimulate broad interest in the potential of global multiculturalism through concerts, workshops, and educational resources, and through the affiliated record label, Real World.

The term *world music* lacks definition. On the one hand, it may refer to musical diversity of the world, originating from all the world's regions and cultures. On the other hand, as a commercial label, it broadly refers to non-Western music, since mainstream rock and metal do not fall into its purview. In the context of world music, African pop is packaged as *traditional, authentic, roots* music, albeit a blend of local and international sources.

Images of tradition are partly created by the market to appeal to local tastes. For instance, some pop styles have been consciously traditionalized within African markets to reflect nationalist movements and symbolize cultural unity. Other African pop styles have deliberately maintained an indigenous sound through the use of traditional instruments (in an otherwise contemporary instrumental lineup) to appeal to Western audiences whose need for roots reflects their own sense of communal loss. The growing demand for "authentic" African music by the world-music market has profoundly affected the nature of the production of music, whose construction involves a complex trade in opportunity and exploitation, fantasy and imagination, style and recollection, appropriation, assimilation, and dispossession.

TRENDS IN THE MAJOR REGIONS OF AFRICA

The African popular-music market may be fraught with contradictions, but what remains uncontested is the energy and diversity of musical creativity in the continent. The following review is therefore only the tip of this iceberg, and further research remains to be done.

West Africa

West Africa hosts an immeasurable range of popular music. A comprehensive overview of the range of styles, with each one's own blend of local and external influences and fascinating social histories, regional permutations, and influences on diasporic musics, would require dedicated volumes. I feature those countries better known for their musical exports and therefore more likely to be accessible to foreign students. Since the major genres of certain countries (such as Nigeria) have been explored in detail in other articles in this volume, they are discussed only in passing.

Modern political boundaries in West Africa do not systematically reflect ethnic or linguistic groups. The *griot*, for instance, the itinerant poet-musician who remains the custodian of historical and cultural knowledge, dominates the making of music in Mali, Senegambia, Côte d'Ivoire, and Guinea Bissau. Today, the music, instrumentation, and vocal styles of the *griot* tradition provide the basis of much contemporary music from these countries, and are best illustrated in the music of Youssou N'Dour (Senegal), Salif Keita (Mali), Baaba Maal (Senegal), and Mory Kante (Guinea).

The fusion of musical influences occurred in West Africa long before the twentieth century. Coastal cultures experienced a long history of assimilation because of intercontinental trade. The prevalent pattern of West African popular styles is typically a blend of traditional sources with predominantly Cuban, African-American, and Congo-Zaïrean styles.

The first popular music of West Africa is believed to have developed in Freetown, Sierra Leone. Its style became known as *gome* or *gombay*, and is believed to have derived from the *gumbay*, a frame drum brought to Freetown by freed Jamaican slaves in the early 1900s. By the mid-1900s, this style had gained mass appeal, and it had spread into other West African countries, where it became the basis for localized permutations, such as Ghanaian highlife. Effectively, it represented the closing of a cycle of a musical idiom that emanated from Africa, developed in the New World, and returned to Africa (Collins 1989:221). Transatlantic feedback of this sort constitutes the substance of most African popular music, inspired by musical and political identification.

Côte d'Ivoire

Culturally, Côte d'Ivoire is a melting pot that has experienced significant domination by imported musics. Despite an attempt to establish an indigenous Ivorian popular style during the mid-1960s, the country has remained open to outside influences, such as Zaïrean *soukous*, Ghanaian highlife, and American soul. In addition, its music industry has attracted musicians from the entire west coast, establishing the city of Abidjan as a center for musical exchange (Wentz 1994:284).

Abidjan hosts an important biannual music industry trade fair, MASA (Marche des Arts et Spectacles Africains), and the sophistication of the city's industry is rivaled only by that of Johannesburg, in South Africa. Until 1995, MASA had been exclusively a marketplace and showcase for francophone African music, but its success has encouraged participation by other African countries. This fair has become an impor-

Salif Keita is undoubtedly one of the most talented and innovative musicians in the African pop world. Because he was a descendant of a noble family, his decision to become a professional musician was deeply scorned.

tant meeting ground for entertainment-oriented executives from all over the world, producing new possibilities for the growth of networks of performance and distribution, which until the mid-1990s reflected the colonial East-West continental divide.

Mali

Mali has a long regal history, associated with the ancient Mali kingdom of Mansa Musa. An ancient culture layered with influences of Islam and French colonialism, Mali boasts a rich cultural diversity. Though it has several ethnic groups marked by mutually unintelligible languages (Dogon, Peul, Manding, Songhai), the Mande-speaking peoples remain dominant. Manding culture retains the tradition of craft groups (castes) that have ritual responsibilities and professional obligations. Prominent among these is the caste of musicians, known locally as *jalolu* (sing. *jali*) and known abroad as *griots*.

When modern electric instruments were introduced in Mali, popular music developed in two directions: *jalis* provide the main source of inspiration to a cool, meditative genre of popular music, for which the gourd-resonated xylophone (*balafon*) remains the instrumental foundation. Second, guitar-based bands flourished in the capital, Bamako, and large groups such as the Rail Band and Les Ambassadeurs embraced a combination of modern urban pop with the harp-lute (*kora*), the gourd-resonated xylophone, and soaring Islamic vocals.

The women of Wassoulou

Mali stands apart from other West African countries in that a large proportion of Malian popular artists are women. Women play a particularly important role in the traditional making of music in the south, an area known as Wassoulou. Women of this area are nonhereditary musicians (unlike the *jalolu*), and their concerns focus on love, hunting, and the exploration of human goodness.

Wassoulou music is based on a pentatonic scale, and is characteristically accompanied by a six-stringed harp (*kamele ngoni*), a goblet-shaped drum (*djembe*), modern keyboards, and a double bass. Though some women of Wassoulou have been recording for more than a decade and have long been recognized in Mali (testimony to the vitality of the local cassette-recording industry), certain newcomers to the commercial scene, namely Oumou Sangare and Sali Sidibi, have become major attractions on the international performance circuit.

Salif Keita

Known as the golden voice of Africa, Salif Keita (b. 1949) is undoubtedly one of the most talented and innovative musicians in the African pop world (figure 2). His were not easy beginnings, however. He is a descendant of the most revered Malian ancestor, Soundiate Keita, founder of the Mandinka Empire in 1240. However, born an

FIGURE 2   Salif Keita on the Mansa of Mali tour in Johannesburg, South Africa. Photo by Peter McKenzie, 1994.

albino, he was never fully accepted by his people. As a young adult, he sought solace in Islam and the soothing sounds of muezzins' calls to prayer, which awoke in him an intense interest in music. Because he was a descendant of a noble family, his decision to become a professional musician was deeply scorned. Though the traditional griot has an acquired status (albeit a low one), any band musician of the 1970s, despite the social importance of his or her function, was regarded as a vagabond and a drunkard. Undeterred, Keita moved to Bamako, the capital of Mali, where he joined the Rail Band, a state-sponsored big band, which performed a repertory that blended Cuban and Mandinka sounds.

Keita soon began to make a name for himself with his piercing, emotional vocals, which derived from a combination of muezzins' calls, Mandinka *griots'* vocals, and James Brown's style of singing. In 1973, Keita established his own group, Les Ambassadeurs, a twelve-piece band, with which he performed for five years before it moved to the capital of Côte d'Ivoire, where it became known as Les Ambassadeurs Internationaux. His move to Paris, in 1984, led him to a recording contract with Island Records' Mango label—-a deal that launched his international career on a monumental scale.

Senegal

Senegal is situated on the farthest point of West Africa, bordered by Mauritania to the north, Mali to the east, and Guinea and Guinea-Bissau to the south. Its capital, Dakar, has served as the center of francophone Africa for most of the twentieth century. The main languages spoken in Senegal are Wolof, Bambara, Tukulor, and Mandingo; most of them are also spoken in neighboring countries.

Precolonial music in Senegal, like that of Mali, was dominated by *griots*, whose mystical oratory and vocal styles provide the basis for contemporary Senegalese music known as *mbalax*, a Wolof word referring to percussion-based music. This genre highlights a combination of Cuban rhythms and *kora*-based traditional melodies, sung in high-pitched style. So influential was Cuban music in Senegal that only with independence from French colonial rule (in the 1970s) did local musicians begin to substitute traditional melodies and vernacular lyrics for Cuban covers sung in Spanish. To indigenize the music further, they reintroduced into the lineup the *kora*

The music of Congo-Zaïre has had the most widespread and lasting impact on commercial music in sub-Saharan Africa, and Kinshasa-Brazzaville, the twin capitals on the Congo River, have been the undisputed musical trendsetters.

and the gourd-resonated xylophone, and they added two drums, the *tama* (a small, "talking" drum) and the *sabar* (a congalike, upright drum).

It is undoubtedly the superstar Youssou N'Dour (b. 1959) who has placed *mbalax* on the international map. Though his initial performances were heavily influenced by Cuban styles and he began his career singing in Spanish, he was the first major Senegalese musician to draw on local styles, to sing in vernacular languages, and to reintroduce the *tama* into his rhythm section. His music is widely popular throughout West Africa, as shown in a review of a performance by N'Dour in Brikama, The Gambia:

> The place was packed. Couples danced the *pachanga*, the Cuban dance that Aragon and Johnny Pacheco made famous in Africa, and you could hear hundreds of feet shuffling across the cement floor as if one. Then, the *tama*, the little laced drum that 'talks', would play a short burst in counter rhythm, and something magical happened to the audience—-circles formed, people clapped to the rhythm, and dancers, abandoning their shoes and partners, stepped into the centre to do the Wolof dance the Gambians called *ndaga*; lots of swinging, suggestive hip, bottom, and leg movement. (Duran 1989:276)

Benin

Benin lies at a musical crossroads between West, Central, and North Africa, its soundscape colored by Cameroonian *makossa*, Congo-Zaïrean rumba, and North African Arabic *rai*. Formerly the Kingdom of Dahomey, and colonized by the French at the end of the 1800s, Benin is situated between Nigeria and Togo. Like most other African countries, it embraces a great many languages, cultures, and artistic traditions (Graham 1988:154). Dominated by the more commanding commercial musics of Ghana, Nigeria, and Senegal, it has not made much of an impact on the regional popular-music scene, but one Beninoise musician—Angelique Kidjo, the "queen of African crossover pop"—has won international acclaim.

Kidjo (b. 1960) grew up as an aficionado of the music of Earth, Wind, and Fire, Santana, *makossa*, rumba, and *rai*. It therefore comes as no surprise that the music she creates is highly eclectic. She made her musical debut as a jazz singer. Based in Paris since 1983, she has worked on many collaborations, such as Archie Shepp's 1988 *Mama Rosa* album. Her powerful voice and innovative compositions have moved through afrodisco to a style more closely linked to the sounds and sentiments of her home country. Her dynamism and vocal force often equate her with such divas as Grace Jones, Chaka Khan, and Tina Turner (Barlow and Eyre 1995:51).

Ghana

Ghana, the colonial "Gold Coast," is home to more than a hundred languages and countless musical styles. Rural music continues to play a central role in Ghanaians' lives, and it remains a rich source for urban electronic music. Ghana is best known for highlife, the British-derived entertainment style of dressing up and dancing—living the "high life," to which the local elite aspired. The term was coined in Ghanaian coastal towns in the early 1920s. The genre, considered the national music, is regarded one of Africa's most popular, enduring, and potent forms of popular music (Graham 1994:288).

Highlife became popular primarily in anglophone West Africa (Sierra Leone, Liberia, Nigeria), and has evolved out of indigenous and Western influences. Over the decades, three distinct styles have emerged: dance-band highlife, developed by ballroom bands for the coastal Christian elite; *adaha* highlife, which grew out of colonial military-band music; and palm-wine highlife, a guitar-based style, associated with palm-wine bars frequented by "low-class" audiences. Highlife thrived from the 1930s through the 1960s, and records of it were distributed throughout the West African market. In Ghana in the 1970s, however, Nigerian Yoruba-based *jùjú* gained popularity [see YORUBA POPULAR MUSIC], as did the hundreds of disco bands in Ghana, and highlife experienced a decline in popularity. With the translocation of many of the prominent highlife artists to the recording centers of Europe and the subsequent development of the world-music market, the genre has experienced an international revival, regaining its position as one of West Africa's most influential popular styles.

Central and East Africa

While certain aspects of Congo-Zaïre rumba may be closely associated with West African highlife, the overwhelming influence of Zaïrean music on East African pop is irrefutable. The flow of ideas from Central Africa into the east was eased in Kenya by a thriving recording industry, which attracted artists from less fortunate countries and stimulated record sales throughout the region. In addition, a proliferation of Congo-Zaïre rumba bands in Kinshasa-Brazzaville forced artists to search for professional opportunities in neighboring states, particularly Kenya, Tanzania, and Uganda.

Central and East Africa are musically interconnected by the guitar, which Portuguese traders imported into Zaïre in the 1800s. During the early years of the twentieth century, the guitar made its way into Shaba, the southeastern mining district, where the Katanga style, best exemplified by Mwenda-Jean Bosco (b. 1930), was created. This style was characterized by a thumb-and-forefinger technique of plucking, to which was added a rhythmic timeline pattern struck by the blade of a knife on a bottle. For fuller effect, the mbira (*likembe, sanza*) and the accordion (*lindanda*) would occasionally be added. The style rapidly spread into Northern Rhodesia (Zambia), Southern Rhodesia (Zimbabwe), Nyasaland (Malawi), Tanganyika (Tanzania), Uganda, and Kenya, laying the foundation for much subsequent East African pop.

Congo-Zaïre and rumba

The music of Congo-Zaïre has had the most widespread and lasting impact on commercial music in sub-Saharan Africa, and Kinshasa-Brazzaville, the twin capitals on the Congo River, have been the undisputed musical trendsetters. Known variously as *soukous, kirikiri,* and *kwasakwasa,* the Zaïrean style is most widely known as rumba. It is lyrical and passionate, and comprises a simple musical formula that has inspired artists across the continent since the 1960s. It is slick, high-fashioned, and sophisticated, characterized by a flowing interplay of rhythm, guitar solo, and melodic structure, and accompanied by soft lyrics, sung in French and Lingala. Its most defining trait is its multilayered guitar riffs, which roll relentlessly above a strict bass-drum rhythm section. In essence, rumba is the quintessential mass-marketed music in Africa, aimed to appeal to the broadest public possible by transcending differences of language, class, gender, and age (Ewens 1991:126).

In the 1970s, a new generation of rumba musicians appeared on the scene with a bold and streamlined rendering known as *soukous*.

With the introduction of the gramophone in the 1920s, African-American and Caribbean music—mainly the Dominican merengue and the Cuban salsa and *son*—found their way into local styles. Significant influences also came from Christian hymnody, with its characteristic harmonic constructions based on parallel thirds, and from military bands, which stimulated an interest in brass and winds (Ewens 1991:130). However, the real origins of rumba are disputed, and composers do not consider African rumba a derivative of Latin music. On the contrary, they believe that Cuban popular music was developed by African slaves sent to Cuba, and conclude that rumba is profoundly African:

> Many people think they hear a Latin sound in our music. Maybe they are thinking of the horns. Yet the horns are only playing vocal parts in our singing style. The melody follows the tonality of Lingala, the guitar parts are African and so is the rumba rhythm. (Luambo Mikiadi Franco, quoted in Ewens 1991:131)

During World War II, Radio Congo Belge was established, providing an important promotional outlet for local music. After the war, recording studios were established in Kinshasa by Greek settlers who recognized the commercial potential of local music. This period marked the *belle époque* of rumba. The first commercial bands to become publicly acclaimed (in the 1950s and 1960s) were brass-heavy big bands: OK Success, African Jazz, African Fiesta, Les Bantous, and Congo Success. OK Success later moved to Zimbabwe, where for years it remained a resident performing group.

The singer-composer Joseph "Le Grand Kalle" Kabasele (d. 1983) is considered the founding father of Congo-Zaïre rumba. He and his definitive band, African Jazz, attracted a following beyond the borders of Congo-Zaïre. He was succeeded by guitar genius Luambo Makiadi Franco (1938–1989) and his T. P. O. K. Jazz. Franco, one of the most widely known and loved postwar artists, was called the grand master of rumba, the Balzac of Zaïrean music, and the godfather of African music. He was such a prolific composer that at the time of his death, he claimed to have recorded more than a thousand songs, spanning a period of forty years and ranging in technology from 78-RPM recordings to digitally recorded compact discs (Ewens 1994:37).

In the 1970s, a new generation of rumba musicians appeared on the scene with a bold and streamlined rendering known as *soukous*. Led by the intrepid group, Zaiko Langa Langa, this music mingled indigenous sounds with the forceful pop attitudes of the 1960s. Perhaps the most favored among those who emerged on the new international scene was Papa Wemba. What distinguished him from many hundreds of other groups was his ability to merge slick Western production techniques with traditional expression. Wemba also became a high-profile leader of *sapeur* fashion, a scene that has become inextricably linked with Zaïrean music. *Sapeurs* (the Society of Ambienceurs and Persons of Elegance) characteristically dress in a style reminiscent of 1950s Paris fashion and eighteenth-century dandyism: pleated pants, slick jackets buttoned to the neck, pointed shoes, and carefully coiffed hair. Wemba established

his own fashion trend based on three-quarter-length trousers, colonial pith helmets, leather suits, and eight stylish ways of walking (Ewens 1991:148) (figure 3).

The women of rumba

Though the role of women in popular music in Congo-Zaïre has been limited, the establishment of recording studios in Kinshasa afforded women the opportunity to record from as early as the 1950s. More often than not, however, women were recruited simply to adorn male orchestras.

In the 1970s Abeti Masikini became the first female artist to lead her own band, Les Redoutables. One of her protégés, Mbilia Bel, began her career as a dancer with this band. She was subsequently recruited by Tabu Ley Rochereau (b. 1940), a popular rumba artist who had once featured in Franco's T. P. O. K. Success, and with whom she performed in the only male-female duo on the continent at the time. In the 1990s, she separated from Ley, and subsequently achieved the status of first female superstar of Zaïre. She was closely followed by the much admired M'pongo Love (1956–1990), who became known as *la voix la plus limpide du Zaïre* 'the clearest voice of Zaïre'. Love achieved international renown in the early 1980s, when she moved to Paris and recorded with some of the best West African musicians of the time. She was a role model for young female artists, most notably Tshala Mwana and the post-punk-styled Deyess Mukangi. While Mbilia Bel, M'pongo Love, Tshala Mwana, and Deyess Mukangi are somewhat out of the mainstream of Zaïrean rumba (which has always been dominated by male artists), their marginality has enabled them to experiment more freely with new ideas, and thus to contribute toward the development of the genre.

Though Lingala and French are the dominant languages of Congo-Zaïre, Kiswahili (spoken in eastern Zaïre) links the central region and Kenya, the Indian Ocean Islands, Tanzania, Uganda, Malawi, Zambia, southern Sudan, and northern Mozambique. Kiswahili is a lingua franca that identifies several different cultural groups and constitutes possibly the most widely established surviving culture in Africa (Ewens 1991:158). Swahili is an extremely old culture, which owes much to its

One of Tanzania's most enduring musicians is Remmy Ongala. With his newly formed group, Orchestra Super Matimila, he has become Tanzania's most important musical export.

roots in Arabic and Indian Ocean cultures. It is largely Islamic, though not all Kiswahili-speakers are Muslims. The historical capital of Swahili culture is the tiny island of Lamu, off the Kenyan coast, but Dar-es-Salaam and Zanzibar (in modern-day Tanzania) and Mombasa (in Kenya) have also served as historically important centers.

The manufacture and distribution of music

In East Africa, the manufacture and distribution of music has a long history. Nairobi has always been the hub of the East African music industry (Paterson 1994:337). The first recordings in Kenya were made in 1902, shortly after the establishment of British colonial rule. Much trade in East Africa was conducted by Asian merchants, and by the 1920s, 78-RPM recordings served to attract consumers into their shops. The market potential for African music was soon recognized, and by 1928, musicians were being sent to Bombay to record for the Indian Branch of the British HMV label. The first genre of music recorded was *taarab*, the music of Zanzibar, and records of performances of *taarab* were distributed throughout Kenya, Tanzania, Zaïre, and Uganda. By the 1940s, non-Islamic popular music began to flourish, and styles generically called *dansi* began to be performed in all dialects. One of the first interethnic styles to emerge was *beni*, associated with British marching bands from the Great War (1914–1918). Brass instruments were imitated on calabash kazoos, played to intricately designed processional choreographies. The genre spread to Tanzania (where it became known as *mganda*), Malawi (*malipenga*), and Zambia (*kalela*) (Ranger 1975:x). Today, beni continues to be performed in modified forms in Malawi, northern Mozambique, and Zimbabwe.

World War II was a definitive period in the evolution of popular music in East Africa. Many Africans were recruited into the British forces, serving in Ethiopia, India, and Burma. Some coastal musicians were drafted into the Entertainment Corps, where they collaborated with musicians from other East African countries. At the end of the war (1945), the Entertainment Corps continued to operate commercially as the Rhino Band. During the war, the establishment of the East African Broadcasting Corporation enhanced the subsequent distribution of Kenyan pop, and in response to the demand for radio music, recording studios proliferated in Nairobi in the 1950s.

Kenya

The ex-guitarist for the Rhino Band, Fundi Konde, emerged during the 1950s as a leader of a "new generation" of guitarists, further developing the style of plucking originated by guitarists from Katanga, Zaïre. Most Kenyan guitarists formed duos or small guitar-based bands. They sang in two-part harmonies to simple percussion accompaniment on maracas, woodblocks, a tambourine, and a struck bottle. In the 1960s, the simple acoustic-guitar style began to lose ground to more complex electric-guitar music, which incorporated newly introduced genres, like South African *kwela* and Congo-Zaïre rumba.

The 1970s were a period of transition in Kenyan music. While many dance bands preoccupied themselves with Congo-Zaïre covers, African-American soul, and international pop, a new style, called *benga*, began to emerge. Developed in the western regions among the Luo people, *benga* has come to be seen as the definitive Kenyan pop, played by most musicians regardless of language or regional identification. Probably the best exponent of the genre is D. O. Misiani (b. 1940) and his Shirati Jazz, whose style is characterized by soft, flowing two-part harmonies and a hard, pulsating rhythm section.

Tanzania

Much of Kenya's Swahili pop is rooted in the Tanzanian styles of the 1970s. Dar-es-Salaam has always been alive with music and competition between groups is fierce (Graebner 1989:247). The success of a band depends largely on the topicality of the lyrics of its songs and the force of its *mtindo*, the dance-and-fashion trademark it devises to attract a following.

One of Tanzania's most enduring musicians is Remmy Ongala. Born into a musical family in eastern Zaïre, he moved to Dar-es-Salaam in 1964 to join his uncle's band, Orchestra Makassy. In 1981, when Makassy disbanded, he joined Orchestra Matimila. His outgoing personality and challenging lyrics developed mass appeal, and with his newly formed group, Orchestra Super Matimila, he has become Tanzania's most important musical export.

Zanzibar and taarab

Off the Tanzanian coast, the "spice island" of Zanzibar has for millennia served as a focus of trade. In 1832, it came under the formal control of the Sultan of Oman; in 1890, it became a British protectorate; and in 1963, British rule was overthrown in a revolution conducted by socialists from the mainland. In 1964, Zanzibar joined Tanganyika to form the Republic of Tanzania. The island is a dynamic multicultural mix of African, Asian, and Arab influences, and the music that best expresses local people's identity is *taarab*.

Taarab originated on the island of Lamu, the ancient capital of Swahili culture. The genre is culturally linked to the Arabian Gulf and Asia, and is closely related to the Egyptian *firqah* orchestra, the precursor of modern Egyptian film music, prominent in the 1930s and 1940s. Latter-day *taarab* is strongly influenced by Indian film music. *Taarab* dances derive from Arabic styles and exhibit strong aspects of inland African dances and *ngoma* rhythms (see below).

Taarab (an Arabic word meaning 'joy, pleasure, delight') is an inextricable part of everyday life of the coastal Swahili peoples. *Taarab* is lyric poetry sung in Swahili and performed most notably at lavish weddings. The most famous of all Swahili musicians was the *taarab* singer Siti bint Saad, the first East African to be recorded in the Bombay HMV studios, in 1928.

In the 1950s, full-sized *taarab* orchestras were common in Stonetown, the capital of Zanzibar, and a typical orchestra would comprise ten singers, a short-necked plucked lute (*oud*), a tambourine (*rika*), an obliquely blown flute (*nai*), an Arabic goblet drum (*dumbah*, also called *dumbak*), an electric guitar, an organ (keyboard), an accordion, a cello, a double bass, and a variety of percussion instruments and drums. Today, violas, violins, and cellos occasionally join the lineup.

The emergence of women's *taarab* clubs is significant. Since it is women who organize weddings (the main context for *taarab*), women play an important part in determining the nature of musical performance. Poetry, music, and aesthetics from

Instruments were reinvented to suit new systems
of tuning and arrangements of sound required by
the emerging styles of South African popular
music, which were rough and experimental and
accompanied by vibrant dances.

other exclusively female African performative styles were incorporated into *taarab*,
and women's groups became harshly competitive. While instrumental performance
and musical composition remain the creative sphere of men, lyrics have become the
expressive domain of women. Less concerned with issues of love and happiness
(which dominated earlier *taarab* wedding songs), women's poetry today can be hard-
hitting, addressing topical arguments and moral concerns. In a society governed by
strict Islamic codes of gender separation, *taarab* has become a powerful medium of
expression for women (Topp-Fargion 1993:133).

Southern Africa

Southern Africa comprises twelve countries, connected regionally by a cooperative
forum known as the Southern African Development Community (SADC). Though
historically interdependent, the region is characterized by vast economic disparities
and cultural differences. The Republic of South Africa has the most advanced economy of the entire continent; Mozambique, however, is by some measures the poorest
country in the world. SADC tries to formalize alliances between countries and to
manage the regional distribution of resources. Regional cooperation has extended
into the area of culture, and the first SADC Music Festival was held in October
1995:

ZIMBABWEANS SOON TO RELISH IN REGIONAL RHYTHMS!

Zimbabweans, prepare yourselves for a spectacular musical feast! The first-ever
SADC Music Festival, which will be held between September 29–October 8, is an
invitation to all those wishing to dance their way into summer, to do so to the sweet
beats of the African sub-continent.

  *Marrabenta, taarab, kalindula, zamrap, maskanda, langarm, chimurenga, afro-
ma* and *afrojazz* are but a sample of the musical smorgasbord which will be dished
up by musicians from the 11 participating SADC states. From the Harare Sheraton
Conference Centre, the Seven Arts auditorium, Rufaro stadium and three day-time
stages at the Harare Gardens, there will permeate diverse musical flavours: some
spicey and specific, some stirred, blended and remixed.

  The festival will be a musical voyage of discovery through the SADC region.
Beginning at the southern-most tip of South Africa with the Malay and Khoisan-
inspired Cape jazz sounds of master flute and saxman, Robbie Jansen, we then
meander through South Africa to the sounds of Zulu guitars and concertinas and
the pan-African melodies of the internationally acclaimed group, Bayete. We hear
the gourd-bows, accordions and powerful vocal ensembles resounding from the
mountain kingdoms of Swaziland and Lesotho. We travel northwest into Namibia
to discover the Afrikaans-based *langarm* dance music of Peter Joseph !Augab and
cross the desert into Angola to the beat of Brazilian-inspired tropical dance band,
Os Zimbos. We move east into Botswana to the heavenly voices of the 60-strong
Kgalemang Tumediso Motsete choir, and into Zambia to rave to *zamrap* with

Daddy Zemus, and rumba to *kalindula*, the urban guitar music of the northwestern provinces. In Malawi we discover, amongst others, the Makazi Band, a lakeside jazz band whose instruments are entirely made from tins, bottles and animal skins.

Violins, accordions and the sweet sounds of *dumbak, tabla* and *rika* percussion drift our way, *taarab*-style, from the Islamic Swahili spice island of Zanzibar. We hear the earthy call of gourd-heavy *timbila* xylophones emanating from the northern regions of Mozambique and pass through the vibrant *marrabenta* rhythms of Ghorwane in late-night Maputo. We finally arrive home to the ancestral call of *mbira dzavadzimu* performed by a mixed ensemble of master musicians, and settle into the *jit* and *jive* of Zimbabwe's very own Simon Chimbetu and Orchestra Dendera. (South African Development Community 1995)

This section reviews the popular music of South Africa, Zimbabwe, Angola, and Mozambique. Though a member of SADC, Tanzania is more closely affiliated with East Africa with regard to cultural, linguistic and religious practices, and is therefore featured under the Central and East African subsection.

The SADC region has a long history of interregional trade, which has inspired mass migration and has influenced linguistic and cultural interaction. Since the beginning of the twentieth century, however, the movement of people has been largely the result of domination by British, Dutch, Portuguese, and German interests, and of the development of a system of migrant labor in South Africa, Zimbabwe, and Zambia. The gathering of diverse people has resulted in new forms of cultural blending. Semiurban and urban styles of music have emerged out of a creative fusion of traditional musical structures and rhythms, and have fused with elements from Western trends.

South Africa

South Africa has the oldest and most sophisticated music industry in southern Africa [see POPULAR MUSIC IN SOUTH AFRICA]. Because of the magnitude of its infrastructure (which includes external networks for broadcasting, promotion, and distribution), South African music has had the farthest-reaching stylistic impact on regional pop. The economic backbone of South Africa rests on the mass migration of laborers to the mines, around which most of the present-day cities have sprung up. The music and culture that emerged from the ferment of colonial occupation, dispossession, and industrialization count among the most resilient examples of African urban expressive culture (Erlmann 1991:1).

One of the earliest urban settlements in Johannesburg was Sophiatown, which from the 1920s to the 1940s was inhabited by people of all racial, religious, and cultural backgrounds. It was overpopulated and squalid, known for its dangerous gangs, illegal bars (shebeens), and cultural energy. Shebeens were established in slum-dwellers' backyards. They were typically run by women, whose only source of income was the sale of home-brewed beer and prostitution. Enterprising "shebeen queens" would attract clients by providing live music. The entertainers who provided this music came from different musical backgrounds, reflecting the ethnic and regional diversity of the community. They came from various parts of South Africa, and from as far afield as Malawi, Zimbabwe, Mozambique, and Zambia.

Music was performed on an assortment of Western instruments: pedal organs, guitars, banjos, concertinas, pennywhistles, and violins (imported by German traders during the early 1900s). These instruments joined traditional African gourd-resonated bows, hand-held rattles, and drums homemade from paraffin tins, animal hide, and pieces of scrap metal. Instruments were reinvented to suit new systems of tuning and arrangements of sound required by the emerging styles, which were rough and experimental and accompanied by vibrant dances.

The album *Graceland* initially provoked
international outrage. However, the record-breaking
success of the album worked in favor of South
African musicians, and helped to return them to the
international limelight.

Fundamental to much of the musical mix was the influence of African-American jazz, introduced into South Africa by transnational record-distribution networks in the 1920s. Most South African jazz musicians could not read scores, so they developed their own jazz flavor, mixing American swing with African melodies. The dynamic blend of African-American structure and African style became the basis for early South African township jazz, known as *marabi*.

Most of the musical forms that emerged in the ghettos survived only through live performance, since it was not until the 1940s that the state-controlled radio and local white-owned record companies began to recognize their marketability. For instance, *kwela* (pennywhistle jive) was a genre performed in the 1950s by young boys on street corners. When local record companies recognized its commercial potential, recordings rapidly led performers such as Spokes Mashiyane off the streets and to the top of the charts. However, when Mashiyane transferred to saxophone, pennywhistle *kwela* was rapidly thereafter transformed into an urbane, brassy sound. This jive idiom became the most popular recorded black genre of its day, and was called by the newly coined term *mbaqanga* (Allingham 1994:378).

Mbaqanga thrived in the 1960s with the introduction of the electric guitar, and a new female vocal style, based on close five-part harmonies, was conceived. Occasionally, the women, called *simanjemanje*, would be fronted by a male "groaner," whose deep vocal style would contrast with that of a soft female chorus. Simon "Mahlathini" Nkabinde is an acclaimed groaner, and his accompanying *simanjemanje* group, the Mahotella Queens, have become one of the most internationally celebrated South African bands of the 1990s (Allingham 1994:380) (figure 4).

Bars and clubs became gathering places for black professionals in the 1950s. These were the spaces where jazz, and the culture of jazz, became linked with the struggle against apartheid. It was the era when many of the great South African jazz musicians—Miriam Makeba, Hugh Masekela, Abdullah Ibrahim—made their debuts. Increasingly repressive race laws of the 1950s and 1960s led many jazz musicians into exile with the political activists of the day, and the music, like the political movement with which it was associated, effectively went underground. It was not until the late 1980s that South African jazz began to experience a revival, which once again was associated with mass political action. Following the country's first fully democratic elections (in 1994), many exiled jazz musicians have returned to South Africa.

The mid-1980s witnessed two landmark musical collaborations that assisted in the relaunching of South African music on the international scene after long years of cultural isolation. Johnny Clegg (b. 1953), a white South African, joined forces with Sipho Mchunu, master of Zulu guitar-based music (*maskanda*), to form the innovative duo called Juluka. The traditional Zulu structure of their compositions, their inclusion of instruments associated with traditional and neotraditional Zulu music (including the mouth-resonated bow, *nqangala*, and the concertina), combined with

FIGURE 4   Mahlathini and the Mahotella
Queens at the Johannesburg International Arts
Alive Festival. Photo by Motlhalefi Mahlabe,
1993.

the integration of lyrics in English and Zulu, presented South African audiences with
a dynamic new collaborative musical concept. In 1985, the duo disbanded, and
Clegg formed a second group, Savuka, which has developed broad international
appeal.

In 1986, Warner Brothers released the LP album *Graceland*, a musical collaboration between Paul Simon and various South African artists. This release initially provoked international outrage, and Simon was accused of appropriating South African
music to serve his own musical and commercial ends; however, the record-breaking
success of the album worked in favor of South African musicians, and helped to
return them to the international limelight. After years of isolation, the recognition
accorded to groups such as the male a cappella group Ladysmith Black Mambazo
gave a major boost to South African music, which subsequently became valued
worldwide (Meintjes 1990:40).

In the 1980s, a slick, highly produced, synthesized dance music known as bubblegum was popularized, principally by Yvonne Chaka Chaka and Brenda Fassie (b.
1964). Bubblegum has short melodic phrases sung in call-and-response patterns, pro-
grammed electronic drumming propelled by a disco beat, and mass youth appeal.
While Chaka Chaka's popularity throughout the African continent is based on well-
crafted melodies and socially responsible lyrics, Fassie's allure is her outrageously bad-
girl image, not unlike that of Madonna. Brenda, dubbed South Africa's first lady of
pop, has been grappling with excesses of her untamed spirit, and has recently turned
to gospel, a genre that enjoys a major following throughout the country.

The South African cultural calendar is marked by several festivals involving
music. The Standard Bank Grahamstown Arts Festival, held in July, is the largest and
most securely established festival in the country. Vast and various, its program profiles the best performances and exhibitions selected from the previous year. Its off-
shoot, a fringe festival unfunded by the main festival, highlights more experimental,
street-oriented, cutting-edge explorations from less mainstream creative quarters. The
Johannesburg International Arts Alive Festival, established in 1992 and staged annually in September, encourages experimental interchanges between international and
local artists, and nurtures an interest in the arts of the African continent and the diaspora. In the mid-1990s, the Karoo Festival, a cutting-edge Afrikaans-language festival, gained mass public appeal.

Thomas Mapfumo, the dreadlocked "Lion of Zimbabwe" and Zimbabwe's most famous musician, is credited with bringing the electric *mbira* to its maturation.

Zimbabwe

Zimbabwe has a small, though tenacious, music industry. Its recording infrastructure has long attracted musicians from Malawi, Zambia, Zaïre, Mozambique, Botswana, and even Namibia, and many of them have settled in its capital, Harare, to perform on the club circuit there.

As in South Africa, Zimbabwean music reflects its political past in dramatic ways. Colonized by the British in 1890, Zimbabwe fell under the authoritarian charge of British colonial rule with its program of Christian nationalism and separate development. Christian choirs and traditional music were first recorded in the 1930s by a one-track mobile recording facility of the government-controlled broadcasting station. Commercial music production followed in the 1950s with the establishment of white-owned record companies that operated as subsidiaries to South African companies, and on whose marketing decisions they depended entirely. The record companies were responsible for the distribution of recorded Anglo-American and South African music in Zimbabwe and for establishing a touring circuit of South African artists throughout the region.

Imported music inspired Zimbabwean musicians to form their own groups, which, until the mid-1970s, were largely preoccupied with performing covers of pieces in the repertories of jazz, soul, blues, rock, and *mbaqanga*. Zaïrean rumba also made a notable impact on Zimbabwean music. A major transition in the popular music of Zimbabwe took place during the war of liberation (1967–1980), when folk songs were used to politicize rural people. These songs, known as *chimurenga* 'songs of liberation' were based on ancient melodies and instrumental structures derived from the music of the *mbira dzavadzimu* [see MUSIC OF THE SHONA OF ZIMBABWE]. In the mid-1970s to appeal to the tastes of urban nightclubs and bars, popular musicians began to adapt *mbira* melodies to a lineup of an electric bass, two guitars (lead and rhythm), and drums. Electronic *chimurenga* rapidly became the most popular musical genre of Zimbabwe, and it was equated with a new Zimbabwean cultural identity.

Thomas Mapfumo (b. 1945), the dreadlocked "Lion of Zimbabwe" and Zimbabwe's most famous musician, is credited with bringing the electric *mbira* to its maturation. Initially venturing into a combination of traditional rhythms, characteristic Shona yodeling (*mahonyera*), and non- Zimbabwean features like reggae, he has subsequently reincorporated *mbira* and hand-held rattles (*hosho*) into his lineup, establishing a rootsier, more traditional, sound.

Mapfumo is by no means the only important *chimurenga* musician in Zimbabwe. Oliver M'tukudzi (b. 1952) is well loved for his *chimurenga*-rumba-*mbaqanga* music and for his morally charged lyrics. Comrade Chinx, one of the leading conductors of exiled *chimurenga* choirs during the war years, has subsequently moved into synthesizer *chimurenga* with messages of love and reconciliation. In addition, Robson Banda, Simon Chimbetu, Leonard Dembo, Jonah Moyo, and Devera

Ngwenya combine elements of *chimurenga* with high-energy, rippling Zimbabwean rumba, as did the late James Chimombe (d. 1990).

Women set the ball of jazz rolling

Women have played a significant role in the Zimbabwean music industry; however, unlike South African women (whose careers in music have been inspired by role models such as Miriam Makeba), Zimbabwean women still battle to overcome prejudices regarding their place on the stage. Despite these prejudices, women have been actively engaged in Zimbabwean commercial music since the 1930s, either as backing singers or, as in the case of the Gay Gaieties and the Yellow Blues, as members of all-female groups. During the early years of the production of commercial music in Zimbabwe, women enjoyed public acclaim, as is expressed in this review of Lina Mattaka, reputed to be the first woman of the Zimbabwean stage:

> The era of Makwaya [choirs] came to an end and Lina was again to be seen pioneering in Tap-dance. For half a decade, tap-dance was chic, it really dominated the musical strata just to be replaced by Jazz in the late forties and who was to seen at the forefront? None other than Lina Mattaka and those other women who had followed in her footsteps. To this day, and more than any other woman alive, Lina tramped the thorny African musical Hi-Way. She toured and brought the message of stage emancipation of the African woman. (*African Daily News*, 1 February 1958, quoted in Impey 1992:82)

New trends

In the 1960s, a new trend, *simanjemanje,* emerged in South Africa. This was a term used to describe a style, something new. The music associated with *simanjemanje* was electric guitar-based *mbaqanga*, and was characterized by a male singer who fronted a troupe of women. Its rapid rhythms and synchronized styles of dancing stimulated the formation of similar female troupes throughout southern Africa. Many Zimbabwean women imitated these raunchy groups, such as the Mahotella Queens, provoking moral condemnation of women in popular music—a sentiment that continues.

Though *mbira dzavadzimu* is usually considered a men's instrument, some highly skilled women play it. Best known in Europe is Stella Chiweshe (b. 1946), the so-called queen of mbira, who combines sacred and commercial music while retaining the mystique of her instrument. Beauler Dyoko (b. 1945) of Zimbabwe (figure 5), originally from Mozambique, is another mbira player whose inspired compositions have come to be recognized in recent years. As she reveals in a brief autobiography, she received from the spirit of her father the metaphysical guarantee that enabled her to play the instrument:

> The time started about this mbira music, I started getting sick. I went to the doctors, to the hospital. They said, "I can't see anything wrong." But I was fainting, fainting for nothing! I went to the hospital and they say, "She is not sick." They said, "It is for the Africans. She must go to a herbalist."
>
> My mother, she was confused again. "I don't want to go to the *n'angas*!" She didn't want to hear about the herbalist or *n'angas*. She didn't want. She is a Catholic. Now she says that if you go to *n'angas*, they tell lies!
>
> Now it was sore, my body, my stomach, my legs, my head, my chest, all over, here. And then I said, "Mummy, well let me go then."
>
> I went with them [to the *n'angas*]. We were told, "Your child, she's got *mudzimu* [ancestral calling]."
>
> Now she [mother] says, "she's got *mudzimu*?" To her, these people [women], they don't possessed. "The brothers are here, why don't they go to the brothers? The *n'angas*, they just told me that she's sick about ancestors."

Like many African popular genres that have adopted strong Caribbean or African-American qualities, Angolan popular music has a strong Latin presence, largely because of a long history of transatlantic cultural exchange.

FIGURE 5   Beauler Dyoko in Chitungwiza, Zimbabwe. Photo by Bror Karlsson.

Now it started worrying me now, dreaming playing mbira, singing, dancing, dancing mbira. In the morning, I get up. "Mummy, I dream singing, playing mbira."

She says, "Playing mbira? Your father [who died when Beauler was an infant], he was playing mbira music. But how can it come to you?"

I say, "I don't know! But the music, it was so nice! I wasn't feeling sore in my body the time I was dreaming this thing."

She says, "Ah, I don't believe it, these things."

We stayed again. I was getting more sick, getting thin. The ancestors, they were punishing me! They were punishing me that I must agree. I mustn't refuse them. My mother says, "Okay, what must I do? I can do what the *n'anga* told me. They say that if you refuse, she'll die." That's the thing she didn't want to hear to the *n'angas*.

And then she brewed beer and had a *bira* [ceremony for the ancestors]. You feel funny, like a person whose getting mad, if you possessed [with the spirit of an ancestor]. My father, he says that time, "I'm here. I came for my job. She must play mbira, what I was doing. She must do what I was doing."

You know, when that spirit it will come to you, then you speak how he was speaking. Now he [father's spirit] was speaking Chichikunda from Mozambique. Now this mbira also in Mozambique, they play, but different made. They call it *njari*. Now from here they say, "I can't give those from Mozambique. People in Zimbabwe, the MaShonas, I must teach *dzavadzimu*."

So my mother, she went, go and buy mbira. It was only five dollars. They were so cheap that time! I took that mbira. I put it under my bed, near to my head, that side. I started playing song, "*Nhemamusasa*." I get up in the morning. I told mummy that I dreamed playing this song. She says, "You joking! Playing these big wires? Do you think this is for you? It is for the man. They say if womens plays this, they don't cook good food!" You don't cook good food because you keep on thinking about playing mbira.

And I say, "It's not my fault, mummy. It's worrying me!"

I start again: "Let me try." I went, go and sit under the peach tree near the shed; put my mat there, sit down. Started just doing like that. Find it's same, the song I was singing in that dream. It was so nice! Even mummy, she wanted also that song. (Impey 1992)

Angola and Mozambique

Documentation of popular music from Angola and Mozambique is limited because of extreme poverty and widespread warfare, shortage of media facilities and recording infrastructures, and, under Portuguese rule, decades of political and cultural subversion and isolation.

Angola

The Angolan war of liberation from Portuguese rule occurred from 1960 to 1975. The achievement of national political independence soon led to an internecine civil war, which kept Angolans from forming a local recording industry; however, this is not to say that Angolan popular music has not developed and thrived.

Like many African popular genres that have adopted strong Caribbean or African-American qualities, Angolan popular music has a strong Latin presence, largely because of a long history of transatlantic cultural exchange. Angola provided a rich recruiting ground for the deportation of slaves to Brazil and Cuba in the 1600s and 1700s, and with the expatriation of substantial numbers of people, musical knowledge crossed the ocean. One particular Angolan instrument, a gourd-resonated bow (*mbulumbumba*) is recognized in Brazil today as the *berimbau* (Kubik 1975–1976:98).

Angolan music embraces a range of musical cultures. Before 1900, to quell internal rebellions, Portuguese colonizers used Brazilian soldiers, who brought to Angola the steamy percussive sounds that had originated in Africa. More recently, Angola hosted several thousand Cuban soldiers, whose tastes permeated modern Angolan music. Further, Angola shares a long-standing affinity with Zaïre, its neighbor to the east, exhibiting strong rumba roots.

Angola is too poor to support a competitive recording industry. Most local musicians cannot afford instruments, and few venues are adequately equipped to host major performers. Since 1975, the Ministry of Culture has monopolized most of the production of commercial music in the country. To revive the music industry, it has sponsored folklore-oriented groups and urban dance bands. It founded a national orchestra, Semba Tropical, to showcase some of the country's top artists, including the singer Kuenda Bonga. Likewise, Sensacional Maringa da Angola (a fifteen-piece merengue band) and Os Zimbos (who frequently join forces with a folklore-oriented group, Kituxe e os Acompanhantes) perform a powerful combination of merengue, rumba, and rural Angolan styles.

Mozambique

Like Angola, Mozambique is still suffering the devastation of war. Independent from Portuguese rule since 1975, Mozambique subsequently suffered a debilitating civil war, from which it has barely begun to recover. As in Angola, widespread poverty and trauma of the war did little to impede the quality, passion, and potency of Mozambican popular music (figure 6).

FIGURE 6   The lead dancer of the Mozambican national dance company addresses Mozambican refugees in Zimbabwe. Photo by Angela Impey, 1992.

Musicians, music companies, and governments in Africa are beginning to challenge the dominance of Europe and the United States in producing and promoting African pop.

Mozambique is a large, elongated country, which embraces many different languages. Each of several areas displays a unique tradition of music and dance. Possibly the best known Mozambican music is that of the BaChopi xylophone orchestra (*timbila*) [see SOUTHERN AFRICA]. Mozambican music is profoundly influenced by its history of coastal trade with Arabs from the Indian Ocean and the Portuguese—trade that dates back to the 1500s. In addition, its proximity to South Africa and the inclusion of many thousands of Mozambican men as migrant laborers in its mines and cities have resulted in the infiltration of South African urban styles into much Mozambican pop.

The popular style best known in Mozambique is *marrabenta*, best described as topical music. It developed in the 1950s in the suburban slums of Maputo (the city known as Lorenço Marques under Portuguese rule), where it communicated issues of the day and provided a revolutionary voice for oppressed people. It was performed on three guitars made from olive-oil tins or petrol canisters, and danced in a sexually suggestive style, modeled on rock of the 1950s and 1960s. Its basis is an indigenous rhythm known as *majika*, modified to incorporate new influences: ska, soul, rumba, reggae and Brazilian percussion.

Two Mozambican bands that became popular in the world-music market in the 1980s are Ghorwane, a large and highly impressive group (which uses a lineup of the usual three guitars, trumpet, sax, and percussion), and Eyuphoro, a spicy group from Ilha de Mozambique, a Swahili-speaking island off the northeast coast of Mozambique.

INTRA-AFRICAN CONNECTIONS

Much of this article has been concerned with the translocation of styles and influences, both intercontinentally and within Africa. The flow of styles between subregions has reflected trade, colonial commercial and broadcasting networks, and the migration of labor. Many of these exchanges have been determined by exogenous relationships of power, money, media, and ideology; however, since the late 1980s, a more concerted strategy to develop a viable internal live music and distributional circuit has begun to take root.

The existence of developed arts circuits and associated funding of the arts in the West has eased live performance of African music, and small recording labels and studios have stimulated the generation of musical products, but few benefits from the Western production and promotional infrastructure for African music extend to the continent itself. Though a market for cassettes thrives within Africa, most of these products do not appear in markets outside the continent. Music from Zambia, for instance, whose cassette culture produces a sizeable annual turnover of *zamrap*, *kalindula*, and *zamrock*, is little known outside of the country because of a severely underresourced industrial infrastructure. A style such as *afroma*, pop music from Malawi, has emerged despite a severe shortage of resources, to the extent that much Malawian

FIGURE 7   South African musician Pops Mahommed plays a kora obtained from master Senegambian players during their tour in southern Africa. Photo by Peter McKenzie.

pop is performed on homemade instruments. However, musicians, music companies, and governments in Africa are beginning to challenge the dominance of Europe and the United States in producing and promoting African pop.

The importance of festivals

Music festivals in Africa have become important sites for the promotion and exchange of local musics. The SADC Music Festival (Zimbabwe) and MASA (Côte d'Ivoire) formalize more recent attempts to facilitate intra-African exchanges. In South Africa, Steve Gordon of Making Music Productions (Cape Town), through his Reconnection Project, is engaged in forging musical links within the continent by promoting performances by major West and Central African artists.

Highly acclaimed musicians such as Youssou N'Dour are testing the dominance of European production centers by building state-of-the-art recording studios in their home countries, thus assisting in the development of an infrastructure of local production and stimulating local talent. Similarly, musicians from various African regions are increasingly utilizing the sophisticated recording technology in South Africa, thus supporting emerging African centers of production over the established monopolies of Paris and London.

In the late 1990s, West African megastars such as Salif Keita have performed in South Africa, Botswana, Namibia, and Zimbabwe, forging links for the first time with the southern region of the continent. Their successes have encouraged southern African musicians to blend West African musical elements into new and experimental pan-African idioms. Important intra-African crossovers also include the intercultural exchange of musical instruments (figure 7).

REFERENCES

Allingham, Robert. 1994. *Township Jive: From Pennywhistle to Bubblegum: The Music of South Africa.* N.p.

Barlow, Sean, and Banning Eyre. 1995. *Afropop! An Illustrated Guide to Contemporary African Music.* Edison, N.J.: Chartwell Books.

Broughton, Simon, Mark Ellingham, David Muddyman, and Richard Trillo, eds. 1994. *World Music: The Rough Guide.* London: Rough Guides.

Collins, John. 1989. "The Early History of West African Highlife Music." *Popular Music* 8(3):221–230.

Duran, Lucy. 1989. "Key to N'Dour: Roots of the Senegalese Star." *Popular Music* 8(3):275–284.

Erlmann, Veit. 1991. *African Stars: Studies in Black South African Performance.* Chicago: University of Chicago Press.

Ewens, Graeme. 1991. *Africa Oye! A Celebration of African Music.* London: Sango Publications.

———. 1994. "Franco File." *Folk Roots* 136 (October):36–37.

Graebner, Werner. 1989. "Whose Music? The Songs of Remmy Ongala and Orchestra Super Matimila." *Popular Music* 8(3):243–258.

Graham, Ronnie. 1988. *The Da Capo Guide to Contemporary African Music.* New York: Da Capo Press.

———. 1994. "Gold Coast: Highlife and Roots Rhythms of Ghana." In *World Music: The Rough Guide*, ed. Simon Broughton, Mark Ellingham, David Muddyman, and Richard Trillo, 287–293. London: Rough Guides.

Howard, Keith. 1996. "Cultural Fusion." *Gramophone: World Music Supplement.* April:2.

Impey, Angela. 1992. "They Want Us with Salt and Onions: Women in the Zimbabwean Music Industry." Ph.D. dissertation, Indiana University.

Kubik, Gerhard. 1975–1976. "Musical Bows in South-Western Angola 1965." *African Music* 5(4):98–104.

Manuel, Peter. 1988. *Popular Musics in the Non-Western World.* London and New York: Oxford University Press.

Martin, Phyllis, and Patrick O'Meara, eds. 1995. *Africa*, 3rd ed. Bloomington: Indiana University Press.

Meintjes, Louise. 1990. "Paul Simon's Graceland, South Africa, and the Mediation of Musical Meaning." *Ethnomusicology* 34(1):37–73.

Paterson, Doug. 1994. "Until Morning: The Life and Times of Kenyan Pop." In *World Music: The Rough Guide*, ed. Simon Broughton, Mark Ellingham, David Muddyman, and Richard Trillo, 337–348. London: Rough Guides.

Ranger, Terence O. 1975. *Dance and Society in Eastern Africa 1890–1970: The Beni Ngoma.* Berkeley: University of California Press.

South African Development Community (SADC). 1995. Press release for first SADC Music Festival (October).

Topp-Fargion, Janet. 1993. "The Role of Women in Taarab in Zanzibar: An Historical Examination of a Process of 'Africanisation.'" *Proceedings from the Eleventh Symposium on Ethnomusicology, Durban, South Africa,* 130–134. Grahamstown, South Africa: International Library of African Music.

Wentz, Brooke. 1994. "Ivory Towers: The Abidjan Recording Industry." In *World Music: The Rough Guide*, ed. Simon Broughton, Mark Ellingham, David Muddyman, and Richard Trillo, 284–286. London: Rough Guides.

WOMAD International Tour Book. 1991. Corsham, Wilts.: WOMAD Communications.

Part 3
Regional Case Studies

The regions of Africa—north, west, central, east, and south—reflect the great diversity that is a hallmark of the continent's cultural traditions. Representative studies of each region's musics give us insights into the factors that contribute to such variety. At the same time, we see those elements and processes that cross regional boundaries and create a distinctly "African" musical flavor.

Ngombi (eight-stringed harp) of the Faŋ played by André Mvome, priest of the Aŋgɔm-Ibɔγa religious group at Oyem, Gabon, 1970. Photo by Gerhard Kubik.

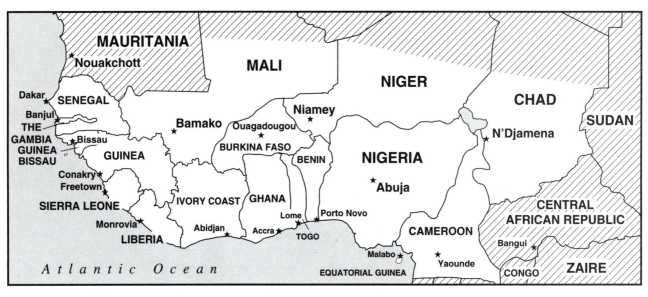

West Africa

West Africa

West Africa most clearly exhibits the polyrhythmic, multiple layered aspects of music in Africa. With a wide variety of musical instruments, performances here reflect the heritage of cultural interchange with North African traditions, especially in the savannas and deserts. It is in the west also that several of the early kingdoms and nation-states of Africa developed.

West Africa: An Introduction
Jacqueline Cogdell DjeDje

The Savanna
The Forest

The music of West Africa includes musical traditions from many different societies, but scholars regard this area as a homogeneous unit. To emphasize the point, they represent it with the music of a specific ethnic group, or a stylistic feature unique to one society. Their generalizations sometimes overshadow distinctions that may exist between different groups. Unity exists, particularly within certain regions, but there is much diversity.

Of the general studies of West African music, the most numerous are overviews and investigations of instruments and styles, primarily focusing on rhythm. Other studied topics are performers, the impact of African culture on the music of African Americans, the impact of Western music on African music, the development of contemporary genres, and relationships between Arab and African music (for sources on these subjects, see Gray 1991:61–67, 249–250). In the treatment of the material, overviews have used a similar approach. Themes or topics central to the musical culture of the area usually serve as the basis for discussion (as in Eno Belinga 1972 and Nketia 1971). Excepting a few publications (like Alberts 1950), scholarly works rarely include enough ethnographic and music material to give readers a thorough understanding of the area as a whole.

The geographical area of West Africa extends roughly from 5 degrees to 17 degrees north latitude, and from 17 degrees west to 15 degrees east longitude. It includes all or portions of Senegal, The Gambia, Guinea, Guinea Bissau, Mali, Burkina Faso, Niger, Nigeria, Benin, Togo, Ghana, Côte d'Ivoire (Ivory Coast), Liberia, and Sierra Leone.

The environment, which varies from forest in the south to grasslands and desert in the north, has dramatically affected history and culture in the area. The Sahel savanna (a region of low rainfall and short grasses, located directly south of the desert and north of the Guinea savanna) has been an area of significant population movement and political development. The invention of agriculture in Africa occurred among the Manding people, who live in the western part of the savanna belt of West Africa, around the headwaters of the Niger River (Murdock 1959:64–65). Much of the Guinea savanna (an area directly north of the forest) is sparsely populated, but some of the most densely settled areas are in the forest belt, which migrant groups settled from the north, displacing or absorbing indigenous peoples (Mabogunje 1976:5).

The languages of peoples that inhabit West Africa belong to three families: Niger-Congo, Songhai, and Chad (Greenberg 1970). As a result of differences in environment and culture, West Africa divides into two geographical regions: savanna and forest.

THE SAVANNA

Several groups in the savanna have played a large role in the history of West Africa, for some have established empires and nation-states. Most have felt influence from North Africa, and have to some degree adopted Islam. Many are agriculturalists, and several participate in cattle herding and trade. A few exploit industries in textiles and leatherworks. The social organization of many West African societies follows a stratified system, similar to that of the Wolof, which includes "a landed aristocracy, a hereditary military class, members of craft guilds, free peasants, hereditary house servants, and slaves" (Mabogunje 1976:19).

The musical culture of societies in the savanna displays much uniformity, particularly in social organization, role and status of musicians, types of instruments, and styles of performance. Despite the history of interaction, important differences among groups require a regional division into three clusters: the Western Sudanic, the Central Sudanic, and the Voltaic.

The Western Sudanic cluster

This region is the setting for many ethnic groups that have influenced the cultures of West Africa. Several of them (Soninke, Mandinka, Bambara) speak languages of the Mande subfamily of the Niger-Congo family. By the eleventh century, the Mandinka (Manding, Malinke, Mandingo, Maninka) had organized a small state, Mali. In the 1200s, the Mali Empire dominated most of West Africa—from the edge of the tropical forest in the south, to Senegal in the northwest and Aïr in the northeast. It went into decline in the 1400s, and by the late 1900s, Manding speakers had dispersed widely—into Mali, Guinea, Guinea Bissau, Senegal, The Gambia, and parts of Burkina Faso, Côte d'Ivoire, Sierra Leone, and Liberia.

To the west of the Mandinka are the Tukulor, the Fulɓe (also Fulo, Fula, Foulah, Fulɓé, Foulbe, Peul, Pullo, Pulo, Fulani, Fellani, Filani, Fellata), the Wolof, the Serer, and the Jola (Diola), collectively called Senegambians. Their language belongs to the West Atlantic subfamily of the Niger-Congo family. They live in Senegal, The Gambia, Guinea, Guinea Bissau, and Mali; and related peoples have migrated to Sierra Leone and Liberia.

Throughout the savanna region of West Africa from Senegal to Cameroon, the Fulɓe are in the minority. They live among more populous groups, such as the Soninke, the Mandinka, the Bambara, the Hausa, and the Mossi. They came from the middle Senegal area, and are the product of an intermixture between the Tukulor and Berbers. Beginning in the 1100s and continuing into the 1800s, they spread eastward and southward across the savanna. Few accepted Islam, and most who were Muslims tolerated other religious beliefs. Their sedentary kinsmen—better educated, more sophisticated in political matters, less tolerant of non-Muslims—turned to military aggression in the form of a jihad to attain political dominance (Mabogunje 1976:26–27).

Because of migrations throughout West Africa, terms for the Fulɓe are varied. Among groups in the Western Sudanic cluster, they are often called Fulɓe (a Mande term); in the Central Sudanic and Voltaic clusters, they are called Fulɓeni (a Hausa term). Other groups in West Africa call them as follows: Fellata, by the Karuri and

dyeli   Also *griot*, in French; a professional musician among the Manding of Mali who usually belongs to a specific caste

kora   Harp-lute of the Manding with nineteen or twenty-one strings; accompanies singing of praise or historical songs

xalam   Also *halam* or *khalam*; five-stringed plucked lute of the Wolof

konting   Mandinka five-stringed plucked lute found in The Gambia

bolon   Large, arched harp, with three or four strings, of the Manding and Ful6e; has historical associations with war

nyanyuru   One-stringed bowed lute of the Ful6e and Tukulor

diassare   Five-stringed plucked lute in Senegal

others in the Chad Basin; Peul (a Wolof term), by the French; Ful6e, by the Germans; and Fellah by Arabs of the West Sudanic cluster. Many refer to themselves as Ful6e (sing. Pullo), and their language is Fulfulde (Stenning 1960:140, 1965:323).

The Wolof are a fusion of elements of diverse origins (Serer, Mande, Ful6e). Their ancestors occupied the southern area of current Mauritania, where they cohabited with the Ful6e. In the 1300s, the Wolof developed their Jolof states. By 1450, fiefs of their kingdom extended from the Senegal River to the Gambia River (Boulegue and Suret-Canale 1985:503–505).

The social organization of musicians within this cluster is similar. In each ethnic group, professional musicians or full-time specialists bear specific titles. Among the Manding of Mali, a professional musician is a *dyeli*, and among the Maninka of Guinea and the Mandinka of The Gambia, such a person is a *jali* (pl. *jalolu*). Originally, there was one Manding family (the Kuyate) of musicians; but over time, other families (such as Jobaté, Suso, Kanute, Sacko) have chosen the profession (Duran et al. 1987:235). The Wolof and Ful6e of The Gambia and Senegal call a musician *gewel* and *gawlo* (pl. *awlu'be*), respectively. Because members of the various cultures regard them as socially and ethnically distinct, they usually belong to a specific caste. Most craftsmen and artisans among the Ful6e are not pure Ful6e (*rim'be*, plural of *dimo*), but belong to one of the castes, generalized as *nyeeny(u)'be* (sing. *nyeenyo*). Three of these groups are musicians: *maabu'be* (sing. *maabo*), also weavers; *wammbaa'be* (sing. *bammbaa'do*); and *awlu'be*. The *wammbaa'be* have the longest and closest association with the Ful6e, and the others are of Sarakolle (Soninke), Mandinka, or Wolof origin. In the Ful6e context, the French term *griot* denotes singers in any of these categories (Arnott 1980:24).

Professional musicians' patterns of marriage vary, and this variance affects recruitment, training, function, and patronage. Those who belong to an endogamous family are born into the profession, and at a young age receive training from their kin. One generation teaches the repertory orally to the next. A musician's family adheres to a specific patron (a royal person, an important official, a particular occupational group). People expect musicians to know details about the history and genealogy of their patrons, sing praises in their honor, serve as custodians of the repertory, and act as advisers and confidants. Women are known primarily as singers, particularly among the Manding, where they excel as performers of historical songs and praise songs. Freelance musicians not attached to a patron or institution receive training through apprenticeship with an established musician. There is no specific age or time for a freelance musician's schooling; it begins when an individual expresses the desire to gain the skills necessary for that profession (DjeDje 1982).

In precolonial times, musicians relied on patrons for their livelihood, their housing, and their status. With the breakdown in the social structure of traditional society during the colonial period, both the role of the professional musician and the patronage system changed. No longer do musicians depend on the patronage of certain individuals. To some degree, political leaders provide subsistence because of the services that professional musicians can provide them, but most musicians must hunt for patrons. Begging is far more common. Since it interferes with listeners' appreciation for the music, people avoid musicians, and disdain their profession (Duran et al. 1987:235).

Nonprofessional musicians stand in the shadow of professionals, from whom their social role differs little. Manding drumming requires much training and skill. Musicians study with established artists before they feel capable of performing at activities. Those who perform for hunters enjoy similar patronage.

Musical instruments

Similarities in the Western Sudanic cluster are most apparent in material culture. Noteworthy is the variety of stringed instruments. Bowed and plucked lutes follow North African models, but harp-lutes and arched harps are indigenous to the region. The one-string bowed lute or fiddle (*nyanyuru, nyaanyooru, nyanyaur, gnagnour*) is associated primarily with Ful6e and Tukulor cultures. As a result of Ful6e interaction and migration throughout West Africa, other groups have adopted or referred to the instrument. Terms for the bowed lute usually derive from a word that describes the action of rubbing one string across another—in Senegal and The Gambia, Wolof *riti*, Ful6e *nyanyuru*, and Mandinka *susaa*; in Sierra Leone, Temne *gbulu*, Limba *kuliktu*, and Mandingo *kalani*. The distinguishing feature of all fiddles within this cluster is the placement of the resonating hole on the gourd or body of the instrument, rather than on the membrane.

The plucked lute is common to most groups in the cluster. Excepting the *molo* of Senegal (constructed with one string), lutes have three to five strings. The shape (oval, circular, hourglass) and type of material (gourd or wood) used for the resonator vary. The Mandinka plucked lute—*konting* or *kontingo* (with five strings) in The Gambia, and *koni* (four strings) among the Maninka in Guinea—is similar to the Soninke *gambaré* (four strings), the Bambara *nkoni* (four strings), the Ful6e *hoddu* (three to five strings), and the Wolof *xalam* or *halam* or *khalam* (five strings). Among the Ful6e of Futa Djallon, the *kerona* (two to nine strings) is more common (Coolen 1984:124). In Senegal, the five-stringed plucked lute has a variety of names: *diassare, bappe, ndere*; most groups use it to accompany solo singing of praise songs. Some Manding use the *molo* for divination (Coolen 1984:123).

The harp-lute, *kora* (*soron* among the Maninka of Guinea), is distinctive to the Manding. An instrument at court, it has nineteen or twenty-one strings. Men play it to accompany women's and men's singing of historical songs and praise songs. Mandinka musicians for the hunter's society in Mali use another harp-lute, the *nkoni*, with six to nine strings.

Among the Manding, the large arched harp with three or four strings (*bolon* or *bolombato*) has historical associations with war. The Ful6e use a similarly constructed instrument (also known as *bolon*). Smaller, the Manding six- or seven-stringed arched harp (*simbing* or *simbingo*) serves for the hunter's society. Occasionally, the Jola of The Gambia use it to accompany men's choral singing. The multiple bow-lute (pluriarc), mouthbow, and groundbow are other chordophones of this cluster.

The flute is the most characteristic wind instrument of the Ful6e, particularly herdsmen (figure 1). It has a variety of names: *serndu* (transverse flute, The Gambia), *chorumbal* or *tiorumba* (Ful6e, The Gambia), *tambing* (Ful6e, Guinea). Flutes and horns serve without restrictions of caste in Manding culture in Mali; they appear particularly in chiefs' orchestras (Dalby 1980:575). Among the Maninka of Guinea, several wind instruments (bullroarers, mirlitons, whistles, horns, voice disguisers) served in the *komo* (a secret society) before Islam began suppressing it (Rouget 1980b:821).

FIGURE 1   A Ful6e musician in The Gambia plays a transverse flute (*serndu*).

Emphasis is on solo singing, with one or more instruments in accompaniment. A high-pitched, tense quality is common in both women's and men's voices.

A variety of membranophones occurs, but scholars have done little detailed research on drums in the Western Sudanic cluster. Since drumming rarely has associations with professional musicians, the drummer's musical role is less obvious. Historical accounts suggest the drum was a more common *jali*'s instrument in the past (Knight 1984:67). All groups in the cluster use the double-headed hourglass tension drum (*tama*), first noted in North Africa during the 1300s (King 1980a:309). Other types of membranophones include the cylindrical-shaped (double-headed), the conical-shaped, the bowl-shaped, the barrel-shaped, and the goblet-shaped. Drummers play them with their hands, or with sticks in sets of three, or in combination with other instrumental types in an ensemble. Drums serve a variety of functions: ritual, recreational, laudatory, and ceremonial.

Both melodic and rhythmic idiophones occur in this cluster. The *bala, balo,* or *balafon* (xylophone), an instrument also used by the *jali*, is distinctive among the Manding. In Sierra Leone, other Manding-speakers—Susu, Mandingo, Yalunka, Koranko—call the xylophone *balangi* (Oven 1980:302). The number of keys varies from fifteen to nineteen. The *lala, laala, laalawal,* or *laalagal* (a sistrum, with small pieces of round circular gourds threaded on a stick) and the *horde* (a hemispherical gourd calabash, held against the chest, and struck with finger rings) are common among the Ful6e. All groups use bells, metal scrapers, gourd rattles, slit drums, and water drums. Instruments associated with women include bells (*né* among the Mandinka of The Gambia), gourd rattles, and calabash water drums.

Musical styles

The stylistic features of music among different ethnic groups in the Western Sudanic cluster are similar. Emphasis is on solo singing, with one or more instruments in accompaniment. A high-pitched, tense quality is common in both women's and men's voices. Most songs consist of a soloist's long, rapid declamatory phrases. The melody is melismatic with much ornamentation, and when melodic instruments accompany singing, monophony or heterophony results. If solo singing has a vocal accompaniment, the response is dronelike: a short melodic or rhythmic phrase repeats variously.

The type of instrument used in performance determines the musical scale. The Maninka of Guinea tune xylophones to an equitonal heptatonic scale, but tune the *kora* to a nonequitonal heptatonic scale. Ful6e music, particularly that performed on the one-stringed fiddle, has a pentatonic scale. Wolof drumming is energetic, with complex polyrhythmic combinations of instruments.

People perform music for a variety of occasions. In precolonial times, a highly important context was for royalty. The traditional political structure has broken down, but musicians still perform for important officials and other patrons, singing historical and genealogy praise songs. Music also highlights festive occasions, work, seasonal events, religious rites, wrestling matches, and events of the life cycle—births, weddings, and puberty rites. Exceptions occur with the use of music during Muslim holidays. Wolof drums accent a variety of occasions, but not funerals or Muslim holidays; only the *halam* serves the latter. For other groups, all types of music and instruments serve during the celebration of Muslim holidays, but not in the mosque.

The Central Sudanic cluster

Groups in this cluster include the Songhai, the Djerma, the Dendi, the Hausa, the Fulani, the Kanuri, the Jukun, and the Tiv. Most live in Nigeria, Niger, Mali, and Burkina Faso; some inhabit scattered locations in Benin, Togo, and Ghana.

The Songhai began to dominate large parts of Sudanic Africa during the 1200s, and the Songhai Empire reached its apogee in the early 1500s. It extended from close to the Atlantic in the west to include most of the Hausa states of northern Nigeria in the east. Like their neighbors to the west, the Songhai have felt influence from North Africa. Their language belongs to the Songhai family.

The Hausa were probably not a homogeneous ethnic group. The word *Hausa* had linguistic significance for betokening peoples for whom Hausa was a mother tongue. The Hausa language belongs to the Chad family. Many scholars believe Islam entered the area from Mali in the 1300s, but the religion may have arrived earlier, from the Kanuri of the Bornu Empire. For a while, the Hausa lived within the Songhai Empire, though they also paid tribute to the king of Bornu. Early in the 1800s, the Fulani conquered them and organized their territory into emirates (Mabogunje 1976:20–21).

Because of continuing contacts, much uniformity exists in the music of peoples of the Central Sudanic cluster. Influence from North Africa is most apparent in ceremonial music and types of instruments. Musical relationships between the Hausa and the Fulani are complex. The Hausa have adopted Fulani elements, and the Fulani have adopted Hausa elements, plus those of other local groups. Though the Songhai and Fulani conquered the Hausa (a conquest that resulted in the adoption of musical traditions from both), Hausa music dominates the Central Sudanic cluster with influences that extend to central and southwest Nigeria, the Guinea coast, and Voltaic peoples (King 1980a:309). Cultural contacts between the Hausa and the Kanuri suggest the Kanuri may have introduced North African musical prototypes into Hausa culture. Since no extensive investigation has been done on the music of Bornu, there is no way of knowing the extent the Kanuri may have influenced groups in the Central Sudanic cluster.

Similarities exist in the music of groups in the Western Sudanic and Central Sudanic clusters because of historical links, but several features distinguish the music of the two clusters. As in the Western Sudanic cluster, professionalism is central to the musical culture of Central Sudanic groups. Most musicians are full-time specialists and urbanites. Professional musicians belong to a distinct social class, but the distinctions between musicians and others may not be as rigid as in Western Sudanic areas. Musicians do not take the name of their family: they specialize in vocal or instrumental music, and use a specific term to identify that specialization. Any person who concentrates on acclaiming another is a *marok'i* (pl. *marok'a*), and a professional male singer and/or composer is known as a *mawak'i* (pl. *mawak'a*). *Maka'di* (pl. *maka'da*) is the generic term for players of membranophones, chordophones, and idiophones, but *mai busa* (pl. *masu busa*) denotes performers on aerophones (for other terms, see Ames and King 1971). Female performers bear names that differentiate them from men. A woman specializing in celebratory ululating is a *magu'da* (pl. *magu'diya*), but a professional female singer is a *zabiya* (pl. *zabiyoyi*). A female who acclaims is a *marok'iya* (pl. *marok'a*). Since groups in this cluster did not experience a major dismantling of their traditional social structure as a result of colonial policies,

goge   One-stringed bowed lute of the Hausa

kuntigi   One-stringed plucked lute among the Hausa

kalangu   Double-membrane hourglass tension drum of the Hausa; associated with butchers and recreation

horde   Hemispherical gourd calabash of the Fulani that is held against the chest and struck with finger rings

káakáakii   Long metal trumpet of the Hausa used in ceremonial music

tambari   Large Hausa kettledrum with a resonator of wood; symbol of royalty

patronage in the Central Sudanic cluster has not felt such radical changes as in the Western Sudanic cluster.

Scholars have classified Hausa professional musicians in several ways. Ames (1973:257–268) uses five categories: musicians of occupational classes, musicians in political life, musicians of recreational music, musician-entertainers, and musicians for the *bori* spirit possession religion. King (1980a:311) uses four: ceremonial musicians, court musicians, freelance musicians, and classical praise singers. For most musicians, recruitment is hereditary; musicians permanently attach themselves to certain individuals and organizations, and their status depends on that of their patrons. Among such groups, there also exists a hierarchical structure with one person as the chief of musicians. Because of the ceremonial musicians' association with traditional power, their social status is high; other types of musicians in the society have lower status. Some performers become musicians through achievement, though they may serve a single patron. Praise singers compete intensely for the patronage of officeholders within the traditional government (King 1980a:311). Composers are valued for originality; only ceremonial musicians and musicians who play for spirit possession ceremonies are not judged on this basis. The training of professional musicians is formal, with either kinfolk or an established artist.

Musical instruments

Differences in the types of instruments are clear in the Western and Central Sudanic clusters, most obviously with prototypes based on North African models (like bowed and plucked lutes, and certain types of drums). Within the Central Sudanic cluster, similar terms serve for the one-stringed bowed lute (*goge*, *goje*, and *gogeru* among the Hausa, Songhai, and Fulani, respectively), and the resonating hole of the instrument is on the membrane, rather than on the resonator. The only exception in terminology appears among the Hausa, who call a smaller version a *kukuma* (DjeDje 1980). Fiddles in the Central Sudanic cluster have associations with spirit possession, entertainment, praise, and politics; but no evidence suggests a religious function for the bowed lute in the Western Sudanic cluster.

Plucked lutes in the Central Sudanic cluster have from one to three strings; lutes with more than three strings, used prominently in the Western Sudanic cluster, do not occur in the Central Sudanic cluster. There are terminological similarities between the clusters, but terms relate to different instruments. Both the Fulɓe and the Wolof use the term *molo* for the one-stringed plucked lute; in Hausa and Songhai culture, the *molo* (Hausa) or *moolo* (Songhai) has two or three strings. The one-stringed plucked lute among the Hausa and Songhai is a *kuntigi* or a *kuntiji*, respectively. Ancestors of the two-stringed plucked lute, known as *gurmi* (hemispherical calabash) and *garaya* (oval wood) among the Hausa, date back to the 1300s in the Western Sudanic cluster (Coolen 1984:120; Gourlay 1976:327; Besmer

1983:53–54). That groups in the Central Sudanic cluster use no chordophones but plucked and bowed lutes suggests stringed instruments entered the area from outside.

Little detailed research has been done on membranophones in the Western Sudanic cluster, so it is difficult to be conclusive about similarities and differences between the two clusters. All groups in both clusters prominently use the double-membrane hourglass tension drum (Hausa *jauje*, *kalangu*, and *'dan kar'bi*; Songhai *doodo*). Constructed in a variety of sizes, the instrument has different functions. The Hausa reserve the *jauje* for royalty. They associate the *kalangu* and *'dan kar'bi* with butchers and recreation, though in some areas court musicians use them. Whether the single-membrane hourglass tension drum (Fulani *kootsoo*, Hausa *kotso*) has as wide a distribution as that of the double-membrane prototype is unknown. The Hausa associate the *kotso* with royalty, and regard it as a Fulani instrument (Arnott 1980:24).

Common to the Fulani and groups in the Central Sudanic cluster is the percussion vessel (Fulani *horde*, Hausa *kwarya*, Songhai *gaasay*), a hemispherical gourd, placed against the chest and beaten (with or without finger rings), or placed on the ground and beaten with sticks, hands, or fingers (with or without rings). In both clusters, this instrument usually serves in combination with others to accompany the one-string bowed lute.

Though differences exist in the construction and function of certain instruments, similarities in the types of instruments of the Western and Central Sudanic clusters suggest they entered the Central Sudanic cluster from outside, probably with the Fulani, whose movements had much to do with the spread of lutes (Coolen 1984:121). If the influence had come directly from the Manding, other instruments unique to the Manding—especially xylophones and harps—might have come too. Because instruments common to the Songhai and the Hausa do not occur in the Western Sudanic cluster, the influence cannot have come from the Songhai.

Other instruments based on North African models entered the area through interaction with the Songhai or the Kanuri. The long metal trumpet (*kàakàakii*), used in Hausa ceremonial music, is probably only one of several musical relics of Songhai dominance (Surugue 1980:523; Gourlay 1982:53). This trumpet and an oboe (*algaita*) were "most probably used first in the Bornu empire and subsequently spread to Hausaland" (Erlmann 1983:25). The Hausa *tambari* (large kettledrum), with resonator made of wood, may be a copy of the silver and copper drum the Songhai buried for safety during the Moorish invasions in the 1500s (Harris 1932:106). A symbol of royalty, the *tambari* relates in material form and ceremonial usage to the court at Fez around 1500 (King 1980a:309). Borrowings went both ways. The *shantu*, a percussion tube used by Hausa women, occurs in North Africa as a result of trade in female slaves. The Kanuri *ganga* (double-headed cylindrical drum), and the Hausa and Songhai instrument of the same name, are North African borrowings from West Africa (Hause 1948:23).

Membranophones and idiophones are the most numerous instruments in the cluster. In addition to those discussed above, other single-headed and double-headed drums are bowl-shaped, cylindrical-shaped, goblet-shaped, and circular frame drums. Idiophones include rattles, lamellophones, bells, tube vessels, sistra, clappers, and waterdrums. For personal enjoyment, Fulani cattle herders play end-blown flutes and lamellophones; the latter instruments (Songhai *bamboro*, Hausa *bambaro*, Fulani *bomboro*) are common to most groups in the area.

A variety of wind instruments occurs in Hausaland, including a flute (*sarewa*), a horn (*k'aho*), and several types of pipes (*bututu*, *damalgo*, *farai*, *til'boro*) constructed from guinea corn, wood, and reed. The Songhai use the *dilliara*, a clarinet.

Besides iron bells, rattles, flutes, and vertical drums, the only instrument indige-

In Hausa society, the emir (as traditional head and successor to the king) controls the occasions for the performance of state ceremonial music.

nous to people in central Nigeria is the idiochord raft zither (King 1980b:241–242); the use of the frame xylophone is a result of influence from forest belt groups.

Musical contexts

Professional specializations in Hausa culture involve ceremonial music, court praise song, general praise song, entertainment music, music associated with spirits, and vocal acclamation (King 1980a:309–312). State ceremonial music (*rok'on fada*), court praise (*yabon sarakai*), and rural folk music or popular music stem from nineteenth-century practice. Ceremonial music, probably the most esteemed form of music in Hausa society, is the symbol of traditional power. Two types of praise songs exist: urban classical and popular. Professional musicians who serve a single patron perform urban classical traditions of the past; the music has set stylistic and textual characteristics. Freelance musicians, who may have many patrons, perform popular music of a more recent origin. It rivals court praise song because it appeals to the same audience, and is similar to praise song in the artistry of its leading exponents. The instruments used in popular music—*kalangu, goge, kukuma, kuntigi*—distinguish it from court praise, as does musicians' freedom to praise and ridicule anyone, including rulers.

In Hausa society, the emir (as traditional head and successor to the king) controls the occasions for the performance of state ceremonial music. Ceremonial music thus occurs mostly during *sara*, a weekly statement of authority on every Thursday outside the emir's palace; Babbar Salla or K'aramar Salla, religious festivals at which the emir rides in procession to and from the mosque; *nad'in sarauta*, the installation of the emir and his officials; the emir's departure and return from a journey; visits from other emirs or important people; and weddings and births within the emir's family. The performance of court praise songs occurs at similar occasions, and whenever there is a gathering.

Excepting *bori*, Hausa music and dance have no associations with religion. Music other than the call to prayer is rarely heard in the mosque or during Islamic ritual. *Bori*, a pre-Islamic religion, makes much use of music, which communicates with spirits during the possession ceremony. Freelance musicians perform popular music in all contexts: at work, for entertainment at beer bars and nightclubs, for events of the life cycle, or at any gathering.

Songhai music divides into two types: secular and religious. Secular music includes solo, choral, and instrumental music performed at wrestling matches and dances. While solo songs by men and women accompany work, songs by children and adolescents occur in games and riddles. Songs by adolescents occur during courtship. Choral songs (male, female, mixed voices) may have no accompaniment, or the accompaniment of the *kuntiji*. Texts treat historical events, politics, legends, fables, satire, or praise. Religious music known as *follay*, performed for a hierarchy of divinities, shows links with Hausa *bori*. Each spirit corresponds to a natural force (sky, rain, thunder, earth, river, rainbow), called by special melodies and rhythms.

Also like *bori*, the one-stringed fiddle (*goje*) and calabash gourds (*gaasay*) serve in performances of *follay*.

As court musicians, Fulani performers primarily sing the praises of chiefs and other wealthy patrons. They refer to genealogies, and cite the exploits of ancestors. Some musicians attach themselves to specific patrons, but others travel from one chief's court to another. Besides songs performed for the court, Muslim Fulani enjoy *gime* (sing. *yimre*), poems on religious themes and secular topics, composed in Fulfulde (language of the Fulfulde and the Fulani) since about 1800. The earliest came from Futa Djallon in Guinea and Sokoto in Nigeria. They are sung in private or in small gatherings for the pleasure and edification of the singer or his friends, and on special religious occasions; they have also become a specialty of blind beggars (Arnott 1980:24–25). Secular adaptations of religious poems have begun to appear in performances by nonprofessionals.

Fulani professional drummers have a specialized role in accompanying children's dance songs, and in performing at traditional castigation contests (*soro*, Hausa *sharo*). The latter are a test of manhood; drummers sing the praises of the young men taking part, and provide the instrumental music that helps build up morale and tension (Arnott 1980:24).

Song types performed by Fulani herdsmen resemble those of groups with whom they come in contact, including work songs (like women's pounding songs), lullabies, love songs, herdsmen's songs (in praise of cattle, sung while the cattle are grazing), children's dance songs, and songs associated with traditional dances (*ruume, yake, geerewol*) for young men and girls (Arnott 1980:24–25).

Musical style

In vocal style and melody, music of the Central Sudanic cluster does not differ much from that of the Western Sudanic cluster. Men and women use a tense vocal style, and the melody is usually melismatic with ornamentation. The structure of song forms depends on the text and language, and because Hausa is a tonal and quantitative language, the meaning of texts depends on syllabic pitch and length. Instruments imitate speech. Hausa vocal and instrumental music, melodically and sometimes rhythmically, depends on syllabic tones and quantities. The text is sung or vocally declaimed, or performed nonverbally by instruments. Instrumental music is predominantly for drums or strings with rhythmic accompaniment by an idiophone. In nonprofessional music, the text dominates in the reading and recitation of poems and incantations, and in the calling of praises. Songs are freer, though somewhat dependent on verbal patterns, chants, and acclamations.

The Voltaic cluster

Ethnic groups in the Voltaic cluster have not built empires comparable to those of their neighbors. As a result, the Voltaic cluster consists, not of a few homogeneous nations, but of many culturally distinct groups (Murdock 1959:78)—a fact reflected in the diversity of local music traditions. Throughout the cluster, the impact of Islam and Christianity is slight, though adoption of Islam is increasing among certain groups. Most Voltaic peoples are agriculturalists, and all their languages belong to the Voltaic-Gur subfamily of the Niger-Congo family.

Dispersed within Burkina Faso, Mali, and the northern regions of Côte d'Ivoire, Ghana, Togo, and Benin, the Voltaic cluster further divides into five linguistically, culturally, and musically similar groups: Mossi-Bariba, Senufo, Dogon, Kasena-Nankani, and LoDagaa. In some cases, the linguistic and musical subgroupings do not overlap, and societies fall together in one group solely because of musical considerations. For example, the language of the Birifor belongs to the Mossi group

In the context of performing for royalty and other patrons, specialists usually place emphasis on praise singing.

(Greenberg 1970), but because the Birifor use xylophones, they belong to the LoDagaa musical group (Godsey 1980).

The Mossi-Bariba

The Mossi-Bariba subcluster includes these ethnic groups: Mossi (a complex encompassing the Mamprussi, Dagbamba, and Nanumba), Konkomba, Gourmantché (also called Gurma), Bariba, Kusasi, Frafra, Namnam, some Gonja, and Yarse. Because of common origins, the existence of centralized political structures, and historical links with northern and southern neighbors, societies in the Mossi group are similar. During the 1400s and 1500s, when the Mossi kingdoms rose to power, the Mossi fought several times with the Songhai over control of the Niger Bend. In their campaign against groups in the south, they met the Gourmantché and the Kusasi. By the late 1600s and early 1700s, the growing acceptance of Islam opened communication between the Mossi kingdoms and those in the Western and Central Sudanic clusters, and the isolation that characterized the earlier phases of Islam in the area began to break down (Wilks 1985:476).

The Bariba are distinct because of their location. In the Benin Gap (an area covering roughly present-day Benin, Togo, and southeast Ghana), the savanna breaks through the tropical forest zone, and extends to the Atlantic seaboard. Navigable rivers and coastal lagoons facilitated human movement, and generated contacts and connections that stimulated cultural interchange between the forest and the savanna (Asiwaju and Law 1985:413). The Bariba occupied the land of Borgu (northwest of Yorubaland) during the 1500s, and their kingdom reached its height in the 1700s (Rouget 1980a:492). The Mande and Songhai exercised considerable influence on them, and the Hausa upon the Nupe; in turn, the Bariba and Nupe had a strong formative influence on northern Yoruba groups (Asiwaju and Law 1985:413).

Musical instruments

Influences from groups in the Western and Central Sudanic clusters are clear in the music of Mossi and Bariba groups. Professional musicians belonging to a distinct social class dominate musical life. Because of their attachment to royalty or important persons, most have high status. Instruments associated with North Africa (hourglass tension drum, bowed and plucked lutes, metal trumpets) occur in most cultures. Similar to the situation among the Hausa, these instruments symbolize power. The Bariba associate kettledrums, long metal trumpets, and hourglass tension drums with traditional power; but the Dagbamba associate both the hourglass tension drum (*lunga*, pl. *lunsi*) and the bowed lute (*gonje*; also *gondze* and *goondze*) with royalty (figure 2). There is no evidence that any Mossi group has adopted metal trumpets. The use of the harp-lute and xylophone is proof of Mande influence.

In addition to instruments adopted as a result of contact with outsiders, peoples of the Mossi-Bariba subcluster use a variety of other instruments. Among their

FIGURE 2   A Dagbamba bowed lute (*gondze*) ensemble in Ghana.

stringed instruments are the musical bow, various types of zithers, and various types of flutes. Their aerophones include an ocarina, a clarinet, a trumpet made from wood and animal horn, a bullroarer, a whirling disc, and a mirliton. Drums are made of a variety of materials (gourd, wood, clay), in several shapes: square frame, cylindrical, conical, and barrel. Idiophones include gourd rattles, sticks, lamellophones, and water drums. The Bariba use rock gongs and leg xylophones.

Musical style

The use of a high tessitura is widespread and closely related to the range of melodic instruments that accompany singing (Nketia 1980:329). The ambitus of Dagbamba vocal and instrumental music appears smaller in comparison to the music of groups in the Western and Central Sudanic clusters, where Islamic influence is heavier. Vocal quality is tense, similar to that in other Islamic areas. Most scales are pentatonic, and slight ornamentation occurs in vocal and instrumental styles.

Musical contexts

In the context of performing for royalty and other patrons, specialists usually place emphasis on praise singing. Praise songs in honor of royal persons reinforce the importance of history. Many include references to moral values important to the people. Similar to other groups in the Voltaic cluster, occasions for music making are various, including events of the life cycle (rarely is music used during puberty), work, harvest celebrations, religious rites, and festivals (figure 3). Among the Dagbamba, so much music and dramatic display occurs at funerals, they seem to be festive events. Unlike the Western and Central Sudanic clusters, societies within the Mossi-Bariba subcluster prominently integrate traditional African music at Islamic events. At Islamic occasions in Dagbon, drummers and fiddlers commonly perform historical or genealogy songs.

The Senufo

The Senufo are composed of several different ethnic groups, including the linguistically related Minianka, Tagba, Foro, Tagwana, Dyimini, Nafana, Karabora, and Komona, who live in Côte d'Ivoire, Mali, and Burkina Faso (Greenberg 1970:8; Swanson 1985:10; Zemp 1980:431).

The culture of the Senufo people is in many ways similar to that of their neigh-

ginguru   Harp of the Dogon that is associated with soothsayers

wua   Two- or three-hole flute of the Kasena-Nankani of Ghana; most common melody-producing instrument

FIGURE 3   At a Ramadan festival in Ghana, Dagbamba musicians play hourglass pressure drums (*lunsi,* sing. *lunga*).

bors, but several of their traditions are distinct. They have a caste system for some occupational groups, but do not have a caste of musicians. As with several peoples in Liberia and Sierra Leone, initiation societies for men and women are an important aspect of Senufo culture: music accompanies activities of the Poro, a secret society, especially "the coming-out of a group of initiates and the funeral of a member" (Zemp 1980:434).

The musical instruments of the women's initiation society include a water drum. Those of the men's include double-headed cylindrical drums, large anthropomorphic trumpets with built-in mirlitons, and small mirlitons held in front of the mouth. Ensembles of xylophones and kettledrums play at funerals. Other local instruments include iron scrapers, gourd rattles, trumpets, whistles, and the harp-lute. Senufo music has a pentatonic scale. Other traits include "instrumental polyphony (particularly in the music of the xylophone ensembles)" and "monodic vocal music" (Zemp 1980:434).

The Dogon

The musical culture of the Dogon, whose territory also includes parts of Burkina Faso, has barely felt outside influence: "of all the ethnic groups in Mali, they have probably best preserved their identity, customs," and religions (Schaeffner 1980:575). However, their musical instruments are common to all groups that live in the area.

The performance of drum music is an important aspect of Dogon society. Of the six indigenous types of drums (*boy*), two are single headed. The gourd drum (*barba*) is the only single-headed drum adults use. The double-headed drums are either cylindrical (*boy na, boy dagi*) or hourglass-shaped (*gomboy*); the latter is a tension drum considered foreign. A variety of idiophones includes a slit drum (*korro*), a sistrum (*kebele*), and a rattle. The Dogon associate the harp (*gingiru*) with soothsayers, and its role differs from that of others in Mali: the Dogon do not have a repertory of songs for it. Locally used aerophones are a transverse flute (played by children and youths) and a bullroarer. The latter, because of its association with masked dances and the belief that it is the mother, is central to Dogon culture. The hum of the bullroarer reproduces the voice or cry of *imina na,* the largest mask, and is also believed to imitate the groaning of old men. As a secret instrument, it is usually stashed in a cave with the masks; people play it only at the first and second funeral rites for adult males (Schaeffner 1980:576).

In addition to the performance of music at masked dances, music making occurs at festivals, funerals, initiations, religious observances (rainmaking, divining), and secular activities of children and youths. Collective dancing is important to all music occasions in Dogon society.

The Kasena-Nankani

This subcluster includes the Kasena-Nankani, the Awuna, the Builsa, the Nunuma, the Kurumba, and the Lyela. Only because of James Koetting's (1980) research on the Kasena do we have an idea of the organization of music among these people. Thus, the Kasena will serve as representatives for the area.

Before European contact, the highest office in Kasenaland was earth priest (*tegadu*). Each clan had its own earth priest, who distributed land for farming and settling, and offered sacrifices to spirits of the land. Hereditary political chiefs (*pios*) had authority in domestic and political matters not dealing with the land and shared power with the earth priest, but the clans did not organize themselves into a large union or hierarchy. During British rule, the colonial government appointed chiefs, both earth priests and political chiefs. As their positions became solidified, the chiefs' power grew to equal that of chiefs of centrally organized groups in Ghana.

Musicians in Kasenaland are semiprofessional: they have other jobs, and play music only as needed. Though musicians have high social status as respected and valued members of society, they play for personal enjoyment, rather than prestige (Koetting 1980:121).

The Kasena use several instruments. The *wua,* a two- or three-hole vertical flute, is the most common melody-producing instrument. It is widespread throughout the region, but only the Kasena and Builsa play it in ensembles (Koetting 1980:94). Other wind instruments include the *nabona* (a side-blown ivory trumpet, played in sets of six or seven), the *kaaku* (now used as a toy), and a notched flute. Membranophones or idiophones usually accompany wind instruments. The *gullu* (a cylindrical double-headed drum, played in sets of four), the *kori* (a gourd drum, played in a set of two), and the *gungonga* (hourglass pressure drum) are among the instruments that may combine with flutes. Available idiophones include the *kalenge* (metal pails or large tins) and a metal gong (struck with iron finger rings).

Music is not functional in the sense that an event cannot take place without the proper musical genres; rather, the social nature of the event comes first, and music is an outgrowth of it. The occasions for Kasena music making fall into four overlapping categories (Koetting 1980:57–62): entertainment associated with casual gatherings (children's game playing, gatherings at marketplaces or in private homes); entertainment associated with specific functions (funeral celebrations for elderly men and women, courting, weddings, and festivals); royal and state occasions (durbars, national and regional festivals of the arts, gatherings to honor visiting dignitaries or

Because the xylophone is associated with animism, the local rise of Islam in the late twentieth century has caused a decline in LoDagaa music making with xylophones.

the opening of a school); and ritual and other occasions where music plays a supporting role (agricultural ceremonies and work). Music for royal and state occasions is a tradition that people began to cultivate during colonial rule.

The types of music are not context specific. The same music and dance may mark a variety of social contexts. Some of the most popular genres are the *jongo* (a stomping dance, also called *juntulla*), the *nagila*, the *pe zara*, and the *linle*. Praise songs associated with royalty are the most valued form of Kasena music. Also, people commonly sing work songs.

Music performed by an ensemble of aerophones and membranophones is the distinctive feature among people in this subcluster. Three to six flutes or horns, or a mixed ensemble of both, accompanied by drums, play in a hocket style with polyphonic structures. The music is heptatonic, and polyphony derives from the third as a consonant interval. At final cadences, parts moving in parallel thirds resolve into unison (Nketia 1980:331).

The LoDagaa

This subcluster includes the Lobi (also called LoWilisi), the Birifor, the Lopiel, the Dagaba, the Sisaala, the Nuna, the Puguli, the Gan, the Gouin, and the Wara. Societies in this subcluster live in the northwest tip of Ghana, and in adjacent parts of Burkina Faso and Côte d'Ivoire. The little that is known about the music of peoples in this region comes from two studies of xylophone traditions: Godsey (1980) and Seavoy (1982).

The LoDagaa form a cultural and linguistic continuum that changes from west to east. People in the area acknowledge this situation by using forms of the directional terms *lo* 'west' and *dagaa* 'east' to point up differences between neighboring subgroups (Godsey 1980:xiii–xiv). Most ethnic groups share cultural traits with that of other peoples in the Voltaic region: a belief system based on a cosmic orientation to the land, ancestors, and nature; a social organization based on clans and kinship; and a complex funeral ceremony that involves communal dancing to the music of xylophones and drums (Godsey 1980:1; Seavoy 1982:12). A few participate in curative and protective religious groups such as *bɔɔre*, *dyoro*, and *bire* (Godsey 1980:1–2).

The history of peoples in the region is one of migration and warfare. Since the 1600s, clans migrating in and out of the area have made easy prey for slavers from surrounding states. Only after the British colonial government in Ghana implanted chieftainships did groups become centrally organized (Seavoy 1982:19). In exchange for salt, the Western Sudanic kingdoms of Ghana (to about 1200) and Mali (1200s to 1400s) got gold from unidentified peoples to the south, and Lobi goldfields may have played a role in this trade (Godsey 1980:16–17; Wilks 1971:354). Groups bear some cultural resemblance to the Mande of Senegal, Sierra Leone, The Gambia, and Guinea. The most important of these similarities is the use of xylophones, whose association with funerals, and with dancing at the compound of the deceased, parallel certain funeral practices among the Senufo and other Voltaic peoples (Godsey 1980:17).

Xylophones and drums are the principal instruments of peoples within this subcluster; but because the xylophone is associated with animism (a traditional LoDagaa religious practice), the local rise of Islam in the late twentieth century has caused a decline in LoDagaa music making with xylophones (Mary Hermaine Seavoy, personal communication, 1994). The type of xylophone is unique to the Voltaic and Mande areas. Its distribution extends from Senegambia eastward to northwest Ghana and southern Burkina Faso. The eastern limit of the use of xylophones among the Sisaala is also the eastern limit of its incidence in the Western Sudanic cluster. This distribution is discontinuous with the area of distribution for the next type of fixed-key xylophone found in Sudanic Africa, whose westernmost occurrence is in the Central Sudanic cluster in Nigeria (Seavoy 1982:47). Though a common xylophone is used within the Western Sudanic cluster, two major subtypes correlate with the Mande and Voltaic language groups.

> Xylophones in use by Voltaic-speakers are for the most part tuned pentatonically (in contrast to heptatonic tunings of Mande instruments), have fewer keys, lower register, narrower range, larger size, and greater weight. Their frames incorporate two interstitial poles, inserted between and parallel to the two trapezoidal elements that serve as anchor for the resonator cords. (Seavoy 1982:50)

Even within the Voltaic cluster, there are distinctions. The Sisaala *jengsi* and neighboring Dagaa *gyile* (to the west) are distinguished within the family of Voltaic xylophones by their greater length (about 1.75 meters), sharper keyboard slope (more than twice as high at one end as at the other), and higher number of keys. The *jengsi* has 17 tuned keys; the *gyile* has 17, plus one untuned key (Seavoy 1982:50). Xylophones found farther west, such as those among the Birifor and LoWilisi, have only 14 keys, and performances use only one xylophone. Those in the east (as the Sisaala) normally play xylophones in pairs.

Found throughout the area without any distinct pattern of distribution, drums have a variety of shapes and types: cylindrical drum, conical drum, kettledrum, hourglass tension drum, gourd drum. In addition to the hoe (whose blade commonly serves in accompaniment in xylophone and drum ensembles), people produce sounds from double bells, finger bells, and ankle bells. Among the string and wind instruments are a harp, a musical bow, a raft zither, a flute, and a horn.

The funeral ceremony is one of the most important contexts for the performance of LoDagaa music. As the only large-scale public ceremony, it can have an elaborate organization, with certain songs and dances performed at different points. Funerals for men elicit styles of performance that differ from those for women. Besides funerals, music making also occurs at ceremonies for different curative and protective religious groups. Work songs, games performed by children when they reach puberty, and dances used to commemorate events within the agricultural cycle are nonceremonial occasions for the performance of music. Musicians are semiprofessional (they also participate in farming), but people within the culture identify instrument makers and instrumentalists as specialists.

THE FOREST

Savanna dwellers have had contact with each other through the development of empires, the movement of populations, and the influence of North Africa. As a

The music of groups who live in the Eastern Forest
most often serve as a model to represent the music of
West Africa as a whole.

result, their cultures are similar. In contrast, the cultures of the forest and coast are
diverse. The forest has provided refuge from peoples of the grasslands (Mabogunje
1976:5). Extreme ethnic fragmentation, among more than five hundred ethnic
groups, results in differentiation in political and social organization. Several local
societies evolved into complex nation-states, while others formed loosely organized
confederacies. The linkages established covered small areas, and did not encompass
the scope or size of empires in the Western and Central Sudanic cluster. Also, secret
societies and agegrade associations have served as important institutions within many
forest belt cultures. External influences apparently resulted from contacts with savanna dwellers and Europeans. Traditional African religions are prominent; however,
some members of societies have adopted Islam or Christianity. For subsistence, most
people participate in agriculture and hunting, but a few rely on fishing and livestock
grazing.

Differentiation within the sociopolitical organization of societies is reflected in
music making. Elaborate traditions of court music and masquerades are important.
Features that characterize forest belt music include the use of percussive instruments
and an emphasis on complex rhythms. Because similarities and differences exist (in
how features are manifested and music is socially organized), forest belt music falls
into two regions: eastern and western. The Bandama River, in Côte d'Ivoire, divides
them.

Eastern Forest cluster

The languages of ethnic groups in the east belong to the Kwa and Benue-Congo divisions of the Niger-Congo family (Greenberg 1970). An extensive amount of musical
research has been done on peoples of this region, but gaps remain. Studies exist on
the music of societies in Nigeria, Ghana, and southern Benin, but few investigations
have been done on peoples living in Togo, central Benin, and southeastern Côte
d'Ivoire. The music of groups who live in the Eastern Forest most often serve as a
model to represent the music of West Africa as a whole. Because of cultural diversity,
the region subdivides into several subclusters: (1) the Igbo, (2) the Yoruba, (3) the
Aja, (4) the Gã, and (5) the Akan.

The Igbo

Many ethnic groups whose people speak languages of the Kwa and Benue-Congo
subfamilies live in southeastern Nigeria, but the Igbo will serve to characterize the
area.

Igbo society favors decentralized and nonurban communities. Local rule is largely by councils of elders (Ottenberg 1965:24). No headmen or true chiefs exist. The
agents of the Aro-Chuku Oracle, the final arbiter for intertribal strife, formerly provided a form of supracommunal religiopolitical organization. Age-grade organiza-

tions had importance as a framework for communal administration (Mabogunje 1976:23).

Music making displays the use of different practices in each local area. Proximity to the rural Edo and other communities in Nigeria makes it difficult to distinguish peripheral Igbo music from that of the rural Edo, the Ijo, the Ibibio, and others living to the south and east (King 1980b:239). Music making is not an Igbo class or profession, though individuals specialize according to their talents, and serve as interpreters of the music of the community. Training is informal, and consists of imitating others.

That the Igbo have been receptive to external influences from Central Africa is clear in several musical traits: the equal prominence of membranophones (*igba*) and slit-drums (*ekwe, ufie*); the presence of percussive rhythmic instruments (drums, bells, rattles, percussion vessels, wooden clappers) and melodic instruments (xylophones, lamellophones, flutes, trumpets, musical bows, pluriarcs); the use of a fast tempo with vigorous body movements in religious music and music for dancing; and the preponderance of simple vocal forms, based on the alternation of a solo with a rhythmic choral refrain (King 1980b:239–240; Echezona 1980:20–21).

The contexts for music making include the honoring of a ruler, public assemblies, funeral ceremonies, festivals, and storytelling (Echezona 1980:21–22). The Afikpo Igbo make topical songs by joining new words to old tunes. They sing these songs during performances of masked plays, when members of the local men's society satirize the behavior of persons who have defied tradition or broken customs (Ottenberg 1965:14, 34). Though Igbo is a tonal language, the relationship between music and speech contour is much freer than in Yoruba music.

The Yoruba-Edo-Nupe

Linguistically, groups in this subcluster relate to neighbors in the east; but musically, because of historical contacts, they have more in common with northerners. The Yoruba and the Edo will serve to represent the subcluster.

The Yoruba live mostly in southwest Nigeria, and in settlements scattered throughout the country of Benin toward the Togo border. They have more fully maintained their indigenous culture in Benin than in Nigeria, particularly in religion. With the religious center at Ile-Ife and belief in common descent from Oduduwa, the traditional culture of the Yoruba displays a high degree of homogeneity. Political organization depends on the existence of kingdoms, each under a divine king, ruling with the Ogboni secret society, an elaborate military system, and age-grade organizations. Religious beliefs include both an elaborate cult of ancestors and the worship of Olorun (a sky god), and of lesser gods, such as Şango (the thunder god). Islam has made inroads among the Yoruba; but since the 1840s, the activities of Christian missionaries have checked its advance.

The Yoruba kingdom of Oyo, the most powerful coastal state, rose to prominence before 1500. In the early 1800s, because of an outbreak of civil wars, it began to decline (Asiwaju and Law 1985:446). It had contacts with the Edo-speaking peoples (Benin kingdom) in the east, and by 1700 had involved itself in expansionist policies to the southwest. Its main trading interests were in the north with the Songhai Empire, and with Hausa and Nupe states.

As early as the 1100s, the Edo of Benin had established a nation-state. By the 1500s, it had subjugated most of its neighbors. The administrative organization was of a hierarchical type, with a king (*oba*) at the top. Nobles and groups of nonhereditary chiefs helped him govern. The ruling family, though not the people, claimed a consanguinary relationship with the Ife dynasty of Yorubaland. The Edo state was

As semiprofessionals, Yoruba musicians rely on farming or weaving for their living. Only performers of pop music maintain a livelihood as professionals.

one of the earliest African states to come into contact with Europeans. In the late 1400s, Christian missionaries began work in it, but they had slight success. Edo religious beliefs centered on a high god, and allowed for many lesser gods and quasi-mythological, deified heroes (Mabogunje 1976:23).

As semiprofessionals, Yoruba musicians rely on farming or weaving for their living. Only performers of pop music maintain a livelihood as professionals. The social status of musicians is not uniform. The status of pop musicians and priests is high, but that of some freelance performers is low. Recruitment, particularly of drummers, involves only the male line. Apprentices get their training formally, from kinfolk or established musicians. Most musicians specialize as instrumentalists, or within a specific type of vocal music.

Besides royal occasions, Yoruba music marks events of the life cycle, religious festivals, markets, and work, and serves for recreation and entertainment. The worship of deities (*orisa*), an important and complex context for music making, includes possession and dance with chanted text. Songs for *oro* (the secret society of night hunters, responsible for administering justice) are also central to the culture. People symbolize *oro* by playing a bullroarer—singly, or in combination with mirlitons and drums. The local repertory includes "light entertainment music for informal dancing, royal processional music, and many other types" (Thieme 1970:110).

People formerly made a distinction between urban music (in the royal capital of Benin) and rural Edo music. Though less elaborate, music for commoners no longer differs much from music for the *oba* and his court. Ceremonies celebrating calendrical and religious events (ancestral spirits, hero gods), plus events of the life cycle, occur at court and in rural areas.

In Yoruba society, drums are the dominant instrumental type. Musicians regard instruments within a drum ensemble as members of a family. The leader of the ensemble usually plays the principal instrument, the mother (*iya ilu*, or *iya'lu*). The name repeats as the name for the principal drum in more than one family or group: *iya'lu dundun, iya'lu bata, iya'lu bembe*. Because the system also includes common names for accompanimental or secondary drums within various ensembles, the names *kerikeri* and *isaju* occur in more than one family of drums, specifying instruments of different construction (Thieme 1969:3).

Contact with the north is clearest in the vocal style and the use of instruments. Those influenced by the north use nasalization and an ornamental, melismatic style of singing. Most singers in nonmelismatic areas seldom use ornaments and favor a clear, open, relaxed style. Yoruba instrumental borrowings from the north include the *kàakàakii*; the *famifami* (Hausa *famfami*, a short wooden trumpet); the *kanango*, the *gangan*, and the *dundun* (similar to the Hausa *kalangu*); the *koso* (Hausa *kotso*), the *bembe* (similar to the Hausa *ganga*), the *goje* (Hausa *goge*), and the *duru* (two-stringed plucked lute, similar to the Hausa *garaya* and *gurmi*). Musicians usually play wind instruments only for royalty, but drums have a wider usage; many are played at religious, ceremonial, social, and court events. The *goje* serves for entertainment as an accompanying instrument in *sakara* ensembles. The *duru* accompanies the singing of praise songs to Ogun (god of iron), and of hunting songs.

Besides instruments borrowed from the north, Yoruba families of drums include the *bata* (double-headed conical drum), used at ceremonies honoring Ṣango, and at *egungun* and *agbegijo* masquerades; the *omolu* (three pot drums and two pegged cylindrical wooden drums), used to worship Omolu, god of water and fertility; the *apesin* (single-membrane cylindrical drum), used at masquerades and *oro* festivals; the *kete* (globular cylindrical drum), used for entertainment at events of the life cycle; a variety of pegged cylindrical drums (*apinti, gbedu, igbin, agere*), used at masquerades, religious festivals, and ceremonies for royalty and hunters; and several single-membrane frame drums (*jùjú, samba, sakara, were*), commonly used by youth bands in the performance of urban popular music (Thieme 1969). Performances in Benin include a friction drum. Among the idiophones are the *sekere* or *aje oba* (set of gourd vessel rattles, covered with cowrie nets), *agogo* (externally struck bell, sometimes used in sets), *agidigbo* (box-resonated lamellophone), rhythm sticks, and percussion plaque.

Northern influence on the Edo is clear in the use of an hourglass tension drum, a metal trumpet, and kettledrums. Other Edo instruments include goatskin-covered drums made of hollowed bamboo, cylindrical-shaped drums, rattles, iron bells, wooden clappers, and lamellophones. Edo aerophones include notched flutes, ivory trumpets, and gourd trumpets.

Because Yoruba is a tonal language, Yoruba music depends for its melodic shape on textual tones and intonational patterns. In the reading and recitation of poems and incantations, and in the calling of praises, the text dominates. Though not as strict and sometimes performed more freely, the text is dominant in the performance of chants, praise acclamations, and songs. Instruments serve primarily for the accompaniment of vocal singing. Two vocal types (*orin* 'song', *oriki* 'praise chant'), plus several vocal styles, are available to singers. The Yoruba in the east often sing in unison, and those in the west often sing polyphonically. The use of fourths, which contrasts with polyphony in thirds (as used by the Ashanti and the Baoulé), allows Yoruba voices greater mobility (Rouget 1980a:492).

The Aja

TRACK 6 and 7

The term *Aja* denotes a linguistic group including the Fon of the ancient Dahomey kingdom, the Gun (Egun) of the Porto Novo area, and the Ewe of Togo and modern Ghana. The Ewe use *Aja* as a general term for the Fon and the Gun, though not for themselves. The western Yoruba (such as those of Ketu) use the term *Ewe* as a general name for neighboring Fon and Gun (Asiwaju and Law 1985:414–415). This discussion applies the term *Aja* solely to the Fon and the Gun, and reserves *Ewe* for the Ewe people.

The Aja groups have traditions of a common origin—from Tado (in modern Togo), on the left bank of the river Mono (Asiwaju and Law 1985:429). Immigrants from Ketu to the east, possibly refugees displaced by Yoruba colonization, probably founded the city. In the 1500s, disputes within Tado led to the departure of sections of the community to found settlements of their own. One section, migrating westward, founded Nuatja (Notsie), which became the center for the Ewe's dispersal over the region between the Mono and the Volta rivers in Togo and Ghana. A second section, moving southeastward, settled in Allada, from where factions broke away to found the Fon kingdom of Dahomey at Abomey and the Gun kingdom of Porto Novo.

The Ewe who moved west evolved more than one hundred twenty microstates

axatsevu   Music of the Ewe; characterized by   *akpewi*   Music of the Ewe; dominated by
          rattles   hand clapping or wooden clappers

that differed in dialect and other cultural traits, but their kin who went eastward created much larger and more centralized political units (Asiwaju and Law 1985:432).
In the 1700s, the kingdom of Dahomey had an unusual degree of centralization of
power. The king ruled the country through an administrative hierarchy of governors,
chiefs, and local headmen, and maintained an elaborate court, with palatial ministers
of both sexes (Asiwaju and Law 1985:436; Mabogunje 1976:24).

Bells and drums are the most frequently used instruments among the Fon, the
Gun, and the Ewe. Most ensembles use bells, and a solo bell may provide rhythmic
accompaniment for singing. Among the Fon and the Gun, other instruments include
log xylophones, raft zithers, rattles, water drums, and percussion pots. Among the
winds are the notched flute (believed to be ancient), whistles (used by hunters), and
ivory horns (played by royal musicians in honor of kings and princes). Contexts for
music making vary, and are not particularly different from those of other groups in
the same region—events of the life cycle, seasonal rituals, work, and village festivals.
Other contexts for the performance of music include ceremonies at court, elaborate
ceremonies for *vodun* (in which possession occurs), and the secret society of night
hunters (Rouget 1980a:491), all of which show similarities with Yoruba contexts.

Ewe religious practices resemble those of other Aja speakers and Yoruba speakers.
The worship of Afã (the god of divination) and Yewe (the god of thunder and lightning) requires special drum music. Music for Afã occurs at public occasions in which
nonmembers may participate; but music for Yewe, considered one of the most developed forms of Ewe sacred music, occurs only in festivities nonmembers may not join.
In addition to music performed at religious ceremonies, much of Ewe life focuses on
dance clubs—a context that functions as a form of entertainment, recreation, and
ceremonial activity (Ladzekpo and Ladzekpo 1980:219).

Musicians are not professionals. They play music only when events arise: to welcome a government official or foreign visitor, to promote a political party, to inaugurate a new dance club, to install a new chief, or to perform at a funeral or a social
gathering that might warrant dancing (Ladzekpo and Ladzekpo 1980:219). The
clubs organize their members in age groups, and people expect all local adults
(women and men) to belong to one in their community. Each club has composers
who create music in any of three genres: *axatsevu* (music dominated by rattles),
akpewu (music dominated by hand clapping or wooden clappers), and "specific style"
(drumming and dancing that differs from that of the first two groups).

In addition to idiophones (bells, rattles, clappers), Ewe culture prominently uses
membranophones (cylindrical- or barrel-shaped, played in sets of four or five).
Among the aerophones are wooden flutes, plus trumpets made from elephants' tusks
or bulls' horns. The latter are associated more with royal houses than with dance
clubs (Ladzekpo and Ladzekpo 1980:228).

Important differences in the music of the northern and southern Ewe involve
scales and harmonies. Northern Ewe music has a seven-tone diatonic scale, with

polyphony based on the third as a harmonic interval. The northern Ewe borrowed these features from neighboring Akan groups. The Anlo-Ewe, who live in the south, use a five-tone scale, with harmony based on parallel fourths. They sing in a low tessitura, but the northern Ewe prefer a high one (Ladzekpo and Ladzekpo 1980:229).

The Gã

With the Adangme and the Krobo, the Gã live in southeast Ghana. They probably migrated from Benin in Nigeria and settled in modern Ghana during the 1500s (Hampton 1978a:35). Their music has felt strong influence from neighboring groups. They have adopted many traditions from the Akan (*adowa, asafo, otu, akom*), and share features with other groups in the area (like the Adangme). Song types include work songs, recreational songs for various age groups, music associated with political and military institutions, and songs for social occasions and ceremonies (Hampton 1978b:1; Nketia 1963). Contexts for music making include durbars, harvest festivals, events of the life cycle (but not marriage), celebrations or ceremonies associated with court, hunters, warriors, and cult groups (*otu, akon, me, kple*). People learn music by imitation—girls, from coresident matrikinswomen; boys, from coresident patrikinsmen. Musical ensembles are often unisexual (Hampton 1978b:2).

The Gã use drums prominently, but with limited variety. Excepting double-headed hourglass pressure drums and closed cylindrical drums, membranophones are single-headed open drums. Other instruments include bamboo tubes (*pamploi*), a clapperless iron bell (*nono*), and rattles strung with nets of beads (*fao*).

The Gã use both heptatonic and pentatonic scales. They have borrowed the heptatonic scale from the neighboring Akan. Gã songs are mainly anhemitonic pentatonic. Polyphony occurs in vocal refrains (Nketia 1980:331). Harmonic thirds occur in music using heptatonic scales, and singing in the pentatonic scale may be in unison or in harmony (Nketia 1958:26).

The Akan

Akan-speaking peoples (Ashanti, Brong, Akim, Kwahu, Akwapim, Akwamu, Wasa, Asen, Agona, Fante, Baoulé) inhabit widely dispersed areas in modern Ghana and Côte d'Ivoire (figure 4). The basis of their social organization is rule by matrilineal descent. Political organization, particularly among the Ashanti, is diffuse. The

FIGURE 4   Akan women perform at a deer-hunting festival in Winneba, Ghana.

Many groups in Ghana use the Ashanti talking drum (*atumpan*), and play it in the Akan language.

FIGURE 5   Ashanti women and men dance to the music of large cylindrical drums (*fontomfrom*).

Asantehene is paramount ruler of a confederation of provincial chiefs, and the chiefs in turn exercise authority over subchiefs and headmen of villages under their jurisdiction. The king is not an absolute ruler: a council—the queen mother, the chiefs of the most important provinces, the general of the army—controls him. The symbol of national solidarity is the Golden Stool, which came into being in the time of Osei Tutu (1700–1730), the fourth known king of the Ashanti, and the founder of the Empire. Ashanti religion acknowledges belief in an earth spirit and a supreme god, but lesser gods and ancestor spirits attract popular worship and propitiation (Mabogunje 1976:25).

Performances at the Ashanti royal court are a most important context for music making. Royal musicians permanently attach themselves to the Asantehene and other chiefs, and oral tradition attributes certain chiefs with the introduction of musical instruments, orchestras, musical types, and styles of singing. Such traditions appear in all Akan areas (Nketia 1971:14). The number of musicians, variety of instruments, and musical types are indicators of a king's greatness. Chiefs with a higher status may keep drums and other instruments that lesser chiefs may not.

FIGURE 6   Ashanti men play trumpets (*ntahera*) at a royal funeral in Kumasi, Ghana.

Territorial expansion by conquest, and contact with peoples to the north and west of the Akan area, have led to the adoption of new traditions and musical instruments. Interaction with other peoples also pushed Akan influences into other areas. Many groups in Ghana use the Ashanti talking drum (*atumpan*), and play it in the Akan language. Interactions between Ashanti and the Dahomey kingdom have resulted in common musical types and instruments (Nketia 1971:19). Besides the use of music for royalty (*atumpan, kete, ntahera, kwadwom*), religious cults (*akom*), events of the life cycle (no music occurs at births or marriages), and recreation, there are occupational associations and an elaborate military structure with a highly organized repertory of traditional songs and drum music (Nketia 1963:18; 1980:331).

Akan instrumental types most commonly include drums, as in ensembles of *fontomfrom, kete,* and *atumpan* (figure 5). Rattles and bells accompany drumming, either at court, at events of the life cycle, or during religious and recreational activities. Percussion logs accompany *asonko* recreational music, but percussion vessels occur only sporadically. Membranophones indigenous to the area are usually single-headed and open-ended, but as a result of interaction with neighbors, the Akan have adopted drums from the north: gourd drums (*bentere, pentre*) and the hourglass tension drum (*donno*). Two aerophones have associations with royalty: the *ntahera* (a set of five or seven ivory trumpets [figure 6], played at the court of paramount chiefs), and the *odurugya* (a notched flute, made of cane husk, played at the Asantehene's court). Other aerophones include the *atenteben* (played solo and in ensembles) and the *taletenga* (an idioglot reed pipe). There are few stringed instruments. Among them are the *seperewa* (a six-stringed harp-lute) and the *benta* (a mouth bow). The Baoulé, who live in Côte d'Ivoire, use a wider variety of melodic instruments: the lamellophone, xylophone (with keys laid over the trunks of two banana trees), the forked harp, and the harp-lute. Their use of these instruments may reflect their close contact with neighbors to the north and west.

Use of the heptatonic scale and singing in thirds is distinctive to the Akan. "Clearcut short phrases," phrases of a standard duration, and "longer fluid patterns" can occur within one composition (Nketia 1980:330). Phrasal variation is also apparent in Gã and Ewe drum ensembles.

Western Forest cluster

Of the indigenous groups that live to the west of the Bandama River in Liberia, Sierra Leone, and western Côte d'Ivoire, none evolved into kingdoms or states comparable to the political structures that arose among some forest dwellers in the east. Before about 1400, groups in this area, particularly those in Liberia and Côte d'Ivoire, felt little influence from the savanna empires of Ghana and Mali. This isolation permitted the development of small and widely scattered states, with enough contact to form confederations for defense and trade (Jones 1974:308). However, in the 1400s, with the disintegration of the Mali Empire, Malinke traders and warriors began to move from the savanna into the kola plantations of the forest, bringing merchandise and Islam. Migrations from the north, continuing until the 1800s, resulted in the invention of an indigenous alphabet among the Vai, and in secret societies (Poro for men, Sande for women) that were vehicles for the transmission of culture from one generation to the next (Jones 1974:309). The languages of peoples in this area belong to the Mande, West Atlantic, and Kwa subfamilies of the Niger-Congo family; only the Kwa are probably indigenous to the region.

TRACK 8, 9, and 10   As a result of migrations from the savanna, much unity is clear in the music of groups who inhabit the Western Forest cluster. This unity distinguishes local music making from that of the Eastern Forest. Unlike the eastern area, however, only a few societies in the western area have been the focus of intensive musical research. In a country like Sierra Leone, "musicians listen to each other and learn from each other. . . . There is considerable variety of music even within each group. . . . It would thus be futile to try and cut up Sierra Leone music into tribal sections" (Oven 1981:7). Though detailed information about all ethnic groups is lacking, enough is known for a discussion of the typical features of some societies. This subregion divides into three subclusters, based on linguistic families.

Mande-speakers

The musical traditions of Mande speakers (Susu, Lokko, Koranko, Kono, Krim, Yalunka, Kondi, Gallina, Mende, Kpelle, Vai, Belle, Loma, Mano, Gbandi, Gio,

The Dan attribute to animals or bush spirits the origins of musical instruments. Masks, the personifications of bush spirits, often express themselves in music.

Dan, Guere, Gouro) have had the most dramatic impact on this subregion. Being in the majority, they have heavily affected local social and political institutions. Much information is available on the music of the Dan, the Kpelle, the Mende, and the Vai.

The Dan straddle the borders of Côte d'Ivoire and Liberia. They share several musical characteristics with neighboring groups. Music making is a highly regarded profession, and musicians receive pay for their music. Anyone may become a musician, but usually the children of musicians choose to. Professional musicians formerly attached themselves to a person (like a chief) or an association (warriors, hunters, work groups, secret societies, recreational groups, wrestlers), or traveled from village to village. This type of social organization is moribund; few young professional drummers belong to a work association (Zemp 1980:432).

Musicians use a wide variety of instruments. Idiophones and membranophones are predominant. Among the former are gourd rattles, bells, and slit drums; the latter include mortar drums and cylindrical drums. Chordophones include the musical bow and harp-lute, the latter borrowed from northern neighbors. The most important aerophone is the sideblown ivory trumpet, played in sets of five to seven, and accompanied by drums. The Dan also use a mirliton, a bullroarer, a stone whistle, and a whirling whistle, but they regard these, not as instruments, but as masks, since they express the voice of masks (Zemp 1980:432).

The Dan attribute to animals or bush spirits the origins of musical instruments. Masks, the personifications of bush spirits, often express themselves in music (Zemp 1980:431). A highly important context for music making is puberty. Secluded youths receive musical training. To finish their initiation, they dance and perform music. The Dan have terms for three types of music: *tan* 'dance song' (also 'instrumental music' and 'dance'), *zlöö* 'praise song', and *gbo* 'funeral lament' (Zemp 1980:431). *Tan*, the most widely used, differentiates into the most subtypes, and involves the most instruments.

Most of the music has a pentatonic scale, but some songs (as the *zlöö*) are heptatonic. Polyphony occurs in *tan*; the solo singer usually has as a partner a second voice a fourth lower, and a chorus often joins the soloists responsorially. In larger vocal ensembles, two pairs of soloists (each pair singing in parallel fourths) alternate with the chorus. Singers usually perform *tan* with restraint, and most texts are fixed. A praise song singer uses a more effusive style, a kind of shouting. Improvisation plays an important part in performance (Zemp 1980:432–433).

Kpelle migrations into the area known as Liberia occurred between the 1400s and the 1800s. Most professional musicians work as subsistence farmers or laborers. Known as Kpelle singers, *ngulei-sîyge-nuu* 'the song-raising person', achieve renown for performing at festivals, funerals, and receptions: "Solo singers are often women, but male professional storytellers, and instrumentalists playing the pluriarc, the lamellophone, and the triangular frame zither, are also singers" (Stone 1980:716).

The Kpelle use two words to classify musical instruments: *fée* 'blown' and *ygále* 'struck'—a system similar to that of the Dan. Among blown instruments are a flute (*boo*) and a sideblown horn (*túru*) made of wood, ivory, or horn. Struck instruments include idiophones, membranophones, and chordophones. The Kpelle use a variety of melodic and rhythmic idiophones, including lamellophones (*gbèlee, kónkoma*); a xylophone (*bala*), which consists of free logs resting on banana stalks; slit drums (*kóno, kéleng*); rattles; and bells. Membranophones may be single-headed or double-headed, and are goblet- and hourglass-shaped. Some drums have feet (Stone 1980:717). Chordophones include a triangular frame zither (*konîng*), a multiple bow-lute (*gbegbetêle*), a single-stringed bow lute (*gbee-kee*), a musical bow (*kònkpàla*), and a harp-lute (*kerân-non-konîng*).

The organization of ensembles reflects the social structure of Kpelle culture. The largest and lowest pitched instrument in a slit drum ensemble is the 'mother' (*kóno-lee*), and the medium-sized and smallest slit drums are the 'middle' (*kóno-sama*) and the 'child' (*kóno-long*), respectively (Stone 1980:716–717).

The Kpelle play music on many different occasions. As with the Dan, activities associated with puberty—initiation into Poro and Sande—include more music making than other events of the life cycle. The Kpelle also have music associated with holidays, work, harvest, games, and masked dancing.

Kpelle melody is syllabic and percussive. Repetition is common, and in some traditions hocketing occurs. The scale is usually pentatonic. Ensembles include a combination of pitches with different timbres—voices, drums, rattles, and metal idiophones: "Entries are usually staggered, giving an accumulation of textures" (Stone 1980:718). Men sing in an upper vocal register, but women sing in a lower one. Vocal production, somewhat tight, is "pronounced in the men's voices when they sing bush-clearing songs" (Stone 1980:718).

As a result of common economic and political interests, the Mende (the largest group in the region), the Vai, the Gola, and the Dei, have close cultural interrelationships. Mende institutions of Poro and warfare may have been the main conveyors of musical influence, which passed through the Gola to the Vai and the Dei. The link between the Mende and the Gola is therefore stronger than that between the Mende and the Dei (Monts 1982:103–104). The strongest evidence of influence is in local musical instruments. Excepting the gourd rattle (Mende *segbura*), all of them—slit drums (*kele, kelewa*), lamellophone (*kongama*), drums (*sangboi, mbele*), horn (*bulu*)— are probably of Mende origin.

Though all groups perform the same types of songs, the origin of certain songs within the repertory does not yield such a clear picture of influence from the Mende. Many secret society songs are in Mende (particularly those associated with specific rituals and masked dancing), but "songs used for recreation and entertainment and others of less specific ritual importance" are in Mende, Gola, Vai, and Dei (Monts 1982:108). That initiates' dance troupes perform among the Mende and the Gola suggests "their origins may be with one of these ethnic groups" (Monts 1982:109), but no known evidence specifies which group. Rice songs are mostly in Vai and Mende because they came from the Mande eastern regions, where agricultural practices were more elaborate (Monts 1982:107). Hunting songs tend to be in Gola, for before the migrations of Mende and Vai into the region, the Gola had an economy based primarily on hunting and gathering. Topical songs are exclusively in the languages of the ethnic groups for which musicians perform them. They include "songs for transmitting tribal lore, for storytelling, and for calling attention to violations of social norms" (Monts 1982:112).

Percussive instruments usually accompany singing and dancing. Accompaniments "range in form from the accent of the cutlass striking the bush at regular intervals, as in agricultural labor songs, to the drumming of a professional musician" at masked dances (Monts 1982:106). One instrument usually provides the basic pulse, while another instrument supplies intricate rhythmic patterns. Most songs, particularly those associated with communal activities (social institutions, occupational groups, events of the life cycle) have one- and two-part structures. Songs performed in unison have the one-part structure. Songs based on a two-part structure may have a call-and-response pattern between a solo and a chorus, or between one chorus and another. Occupational groups that have a recognized leader normally make use of the solo-chorus format, but divisions based on sex, age, or no recognizable leader employ the chorus-chorus format.

West Atlantic–speakers

Most speakers of languages in the West Atlantic linguistic subfamily (Temne, Sherbro, Bulom, Limba, Gola, Kissi) live in Sierra Leone; a few live in northern Liberia. Many inhabit areas they have occupied since the 1400s. Though Greenberg associates them with the Senegalo-Guinean ethnic group (which includes the Tukulor, the Fulɓe, the Wolof, and the Serer), their Guinean type of civilization separates them from Senegambians (Boulegue and Suret-Canale 1985:504).

The Temne, who came from the mountainous region of Jallonkadu (an area that later became part of Futa Djallon) and settled on the coast north of the Bulom (Fyle 1981:7–8), are one of the most populous ethnic groups in Sierra Leone. Their music displays characteristics similar to that of other groups in the Western Forest cluster: prominent percussion, masked dancers, secret society music. It also includes features associated with groups in the Western Sudanic cluster: the occasional use of the fiddle (*angbulu, gbulu, rafon*), and the tendency of women to imitate a Sudanic singing style (Christian Horton, personal communication, 19 August 1991). The adoption of these elements may have resulted from interaction with the Fulɓe during Temne territorial expansion toward the east and northeast, and from the dispersal of the Fulɓe in Sierra Leone. Temne song types—dance songs, praise songs, festive songs, songs for chiefs, story songs, love songs, religious songs, work songs, war songs, topical songs—do not differ from those of other groups in the region (Oven 1980:5–6).

Kwa-speakers

Kwa speakers live in Liberia (Dei, Bassa, Gbi, Kran, Padebu [Padebo], Kru, Grebo, Jabo) and Côte d'Ivoire (Bete, Ubi [Oubi], Bakwé, Dida, Godie [Godye]). Data on the music of these groups are cursory and fragmentary, for scholars have not investigated them intensively. The Kwa in Liberia have felt heavy influence from migrants who have become dominant in the region (Monts 1982), and smaller groups (as the Jabo) have adopted elements from stronger Kwa neighbors, the Grebo and the Kru (Herzog 1945). Thus, elements from the indigenous Kwa ethnic groups have survived only minimally.

Kwa-speakers in Côte d'Ivoire have been more selective in their use of elements

FIGURE 7   A Bete masked dancer, Côte d'Ivoire.

from other groups. Masked dancing is an integral part of Bete culture (figure 7). Similar in function to that of the Dan, it serves to cleanse a village of alien forces, officiate at funerals, levy social criticism, greet dignitaries, preside over important trials, prepare men for the hunt, and lead people to war. The Bete, however, do not associate masks with the institution of Poro. Besides influences from the Mande, Bete religious and artistic traditions have close affinities with neighboring Kru and Akan groups. That old Bete songs use Akan-style drumming as accompaniment proves the Bete bridge the gap between the secret societies of Liberia and the Akan kingship traditions from Ghana (Rood 1969:40).

Instrumental types used by Kwa-speakers in the Western Forest cluster include membranophones, idiophones (slit drum, xylophone), chordophones (musical bow, triangular frame zither), and aerophones (wooden horn). Jabo slit drums belong to military organizations, whose members use the instruments during assemblies, social gatherings, and celebrations of war. At social gatherings, young men use a six-key xylophone to perform topical songs.

REFERENCES

Ajayi, J. F. A., and Michael Crowder, eds. 1971. *History of West Africa,* vol. 1. London: Longman

———. 1974. *History of West Africa,* vol. 2. London: Longman.

———. 1976. *History of West Africa,* vol. 1, 2nd ed. London: Longman.

———. 1985. *History of West Africa,* vol. 1, 3rd ed. London: Longman.

Alberts, Arthur S. 1950. *Tribal, Folk and Cafe Music of West Africa.* New York: Field Recordings. LP.

Ames, David. 1973. "A Sociocultural View of Hausa Musical Activity." In *The Traditional Artist*

in African Societies, ed. Warren L. D'Azevedo, 128–161. Bloomington: Indiana University Press.

Ames, David, and Anthony V. King. 1971. *Glossary of Hausa Music and Its Social Contexts.* Evanston, Ill.: Northwestern University Press.

Arnott, D. W. 1980. "Fulani Music." *The New Grove Dictionary of Music and Musicians,* ed. Stanley Sadie. London: Macmillan.

Asiwaju, A.I., and Robin Law. 1985. "From the Volta to the Niger, c. 1600-1800." In *History of West Africa,* vol. 1, 3rd ed., ed. J. F. A. Ajayi and Michael Crowder, 412–464. London: Longman.

Besmer, Fremont E. 1983. *Horses, Musicians, and*

Gods: The Hausa Cult of Possession-Trance. Zaria, Nigeria: Ahmadu Bello University Press.

Boulègue, Jean, and Jean Suret-Canale. 1985. "The Western Atlantic Coast." In *History of West Africa,* vol. 1, 3rd ed., ed. J. F. A. Ajayi and Michael Crowder, 503–530. London: Longman.

Coolen, Michael T. 1984. "Senegambian Archetypes for the American Folk Banjo." *Western Folklore* 43(2):117–132.

Dalby, Winifred. 1980. "Mali: Music and Society / Manding Music." *The New Grove Dictionary of Music and Musicians,* ed. Stanley Sadie. London: Macmillan.

DjeDje, Jacqueline Cogdell. 1980. *Distribution of the One String Fiddle in West Africa.* Los Angeles: UCLA Program in Ethnomusicology, Department of Music.

———. 1982. "The Concept of Patronage: An Examination of Hausa and Dagomba One-String Fiddle Traditions." *Journal of African Studies* 9(3):116–127.

Duran, Lucy, et al. 1987. "On Music in Contemporary West Africa: Jaliya and the Role of the Jali in Present Day Manding Society." *African Affairs: Journal of the Royal African Society* 86(343):233–236.

Echezona, W. W. C. 1980. "Igbo Music." *The New Grove Dictionary of Music and Musicians,* ed. Stanley Sadie. London: Macmillan.

Eno Belinga, Samuel-Martin. 1972. "The Traditional Music of West Africa: Types, Styles, and Influences." In *African Music: Meeting in Yaoundé (Cameroon) 23–27 February 1970,* 71–75. Paris: La Revue Musicale.

Erlmann, Veit. 1983. "Notes on Musical Instruments among the Fulani of Diamare (North Cameroon)." *African Music* 6(3):16–41.

Fyle, C. Magbaily. 1981. *The History of Sierra Leone: A Concise Introduction.* London: Evans Brothers.

Godsey, Larry Dennis. 1980. "The Use of the Xylophone in the Funeral Ceremony of the Birifor of Northwest Ghana." Ph.D. dissertation, University of California at Los Angeles.

Gourlay, Kenneth A. 1976. Letter to the Editor. *Ethnomusicology* 20(2):327–332.

———. 1982. "Long Trumpets of Northern Nigeria—In History and Today." *African Music* 6(2):48–72.

Gray, John. 1991. *African Music: A Bibliographical Guide to the Traditional, Popular, Art, and Liturgical Musics of Sub-Saharan Africa.* New York and Westport, Conn.: Greenwood Press.

Greenberg, Joseph. 1970. *The Languages of Africa,* 3rd ed. Bloomington and The Hague: Indiana University and Mouton.

Hampton, Barbara. 1978a. "The Contiguity Factor in Gã Music." *The Black Perspective in Music* 6(1):32–48.

———. 1978b. *Music of the Gã People of Ghana: Adowa,* vol. 1. Folkways FE 4291. LP disk and descriptive notes.

Harris, P. G. 1932. "Notes on Drums and Musical Instruments Seen in Sokoto Province, Nigeria." *Journal of the Royal Anthropological Institute* 62:105–125.

Hause, Helen E. 1948. "Terms for Musical Instruments in the Sudanic Languages: A Lexicographical Inquiry." *Journal of the American Oriental Society* 7:1–71.

Herzog, George. 1945. "Drum-Signaling in a West African Tribe." *Word: Journal of the Linguistic Circle of New York* 1(3):217–238.

Jones, Abeodu Bowen. 1974. "The Republic of Liberia." In *History of West Africa,* vol. 2, ed. J. F. A. Ajayi and Michael Crowder, 308–343. London: Longman.

King, Anthony. 1980a. "Hausa Music." *The New Grove Dictionary of Music and Musicians,* ed. Stanley Sadie. London: Macmillan.

———. 1980b. "Nigeria." *The New Grove Dictionary of Music and Musicians,* ed. Stanley Sadie. London: Macmillan.

Knight, Roderic C. 1984. "Music in Africa: The Manding Contexts." In *Performance Practice: Ethnomusicological Perspectives,* ed. Gerard Béhague, 53-90. Westport, Conn.: Greenwood Press.

Koetting, James Thomas. 1980. "Continuity and Change in Ghanaian Kasena Flute and Drum Ensemble Music: A Comparative Study of the Homeland and Nima/Accra." Ph.D. dissertation, University of California at Los Angeles.

Ladzekpo, Alfred Kwashie, and Kobla Ladzekpo. 1980. "Anlo Ewe Music in Anyako, Volta Region, Ghana." In *Musics of Many Cultures: An Introduction,* ed. Elizabeth May, 216–231. Berkeley: University of California Press.

Mabogunje, Akin L. 1976. "The Land and Peoples of West Africa." In *History of West Africa,* vol. 1, 2nd ed., ed. J. F. A. Ajayi and Michael Crowder, 1–32. London: Longman.

Monts, Lester P. 1982. "Music Clusteral Relationships in a Liberian–Sierra Leonean Region: A Preliminary Analysis." *Journal of African Studies* 9(3):101–115.

Murdock, George P. 1959. *Africa: Its Peoples and Their Culture History.* New York: McGraw-Hill.

Nketia, J. H. Kwabena. 1958. "Traditional Music of the Gã People." *African Music* 2(1):21–27.

———. 1963. *African Music in Ghana.* Evanston, Ill.: Northwestern University Press.

———. 1971. "History and the Organization of Music in West Africa." In *Essays on Music and History in Africa,* ed. Klaus P. Wachsmann, 3–25. Evanston, Ill.: Northwestern University Press.

———. 1980. "Ghana." *The New Grove Dictionary of Music and Musicians.,* ed. Stanley Sadie. London: Macmillan.

Ottenberg, Phoebe. 1965. "The Afikpo Ibo of Eastern Nigeria." In *Peoples of Africa,* ed. James L. Gibbs, Jr., 1–39. New York: Holt, Rinehart and Winston.

Oven, Cootje van. 1980. "Sierra Leone." *The New Grove Dictionary of Music and Musicians,* ed. Stanley Sadie. London: Macmillan.

———. 1981. *An Introduction to the Music of Sierra Leone.* Wassenaar, Netherlands: Cootje van Oven.

Rood, Armistead P. 1969. "Bété Masked Dance: A View from Within." *African Arts* 2(3):37–43, 76.

Rouget, Gilbert. 1980a. "Benin." *The New Grove Dictionary of Music and Musicians,* ed. Stanley Sadie. London: Macmillan.

———. 1980b. "Guinea." *The New Grove Dictionary of Music and Musicians,* ed. Stanley Sadie. London: Macmillan.

Schaeffner, André. 1980. "Mali: Dogon Music." *The New Grove Dictionary of Music and Musicians,* ed. Stanley Sadie. London: Macmillan.

Seavoy, Mary Hermaine. 1982. "The Sisaala Xylophone Tradition." Ph.D. dissertation. University of California at Los Angeles.

Stenning, Derrick J. 1960. "Transhumance, Migratory Drift, Migration: Patterns of Pastoral Fulani Nomadism." In *Cultures and Societies of Africa,* ed. Simon and Phoebe Ottenberg, 139–159. New York: Random House.

———. 1965. "The Pastoral Fulani of Northern Nigeria." In *Peoples of Africa,* ed. James L. Gibbs, Jr., 363–401. New York: Holt, Rinehart and Winston.

Stone, Ruth M. 1980. "Liberia." *The New Grove Dictionary of Music and Musicians,* ed. Stanley Sadie. London: Macmillan.

Surugue, B. 1980. "Songhay Music." *The New Grove Dictionary of Music and Musicians,* ed. Stanley Sadie. London: Macmillan.

Swanson, Richard Alan. 1985. *Gourmantche Ethnoanthropology: A Theory of Human Being.* Lanham, Md.: University Press of America.

Thieme, Darius. 1969. "A Descriptive Catalogue of Yoruba Musical Instruments." Ph.D. dissertation, Catholic University of America.

———. 1970. "Music in Yoruba Society." In *Development of Materials for a One Year Course in African Music for the General Undergraduate Student (Project in African Music),* ed. Vada E. Butcher, 107–111. Washington: Howard University Press.

Wilks, Ivor. 1971. "The Mossi and the Akan States, 1500 to 1800." In *History of West Africa,* vol. 1, ed. J. F. A. Ajayi and Michael Crowder, 344–386. London: Longman.

———. 1985. "The Mossi and the Akan States, 1400 to 1800." In *History of West Africa,* vol. 1, 3rd ed., ed. J. F. A. Ajayi and Michael Crowder, 465–502. London: Longman.

Zemp, Hugo. 1980. "Ivory Coast." *The New Grove Dictionary of Music and Musicians,* ed. Stanley Sadie. London: Macmillan.

Yoruba Popular Music
Christopher A. Waterman

General Features
Muslim Genres
Yoruba Highlife
Jùjú
Afro-Beat
Fùjí
"Traditional" and "Popular" Styles

About 30 million Yoruba live in southwestern Nigeria and parts of the Benin Republic and Togo. The term *Yariba* appears in written form in the early 1700s, in Hausa-Fulani clerics' accounts of the kingdom of Ọyọ, one of a series of some twenty independent polities (including Ile-Ifẹ, Ọyọ, Ibadan, Ilọrin, Ẹgba, Ẹgbado, Ijẹbu, Ilẹṣa, Ondo, Ekiti). Expansion of the Ọyọ Empire and its successor state, Ibadan, encouraged the application of this term to a larger population. The spread of certain musical instruments and genres—including the *dùndún,* an hourglass-shaped pressure drum ("talking drum"), now among the most potent symbols of pan-Yoruba identity, and the *bàtá,* an ensemble of conical, two-headed drums, associated with the thunder god Ṣango—played a role in Ọyọ's attempt to establish a cultural underpinning for imperial domination.

Inter-Yoruba wars of the 1700s and 1800s encouraged the dispersal of musicians, especially praise singers and talking drummers. We might regard such performers as predecessors of today's popular musicians, since their survival as craft specialists depended largely upon creating broadly comprehensible and appealing styles. Some performers, linked exclusively to particular communities, kin groups, or cults, were responsible for mastering secret knowledge, protected by supernatural sanctions; but other, more mobile musicians, exploiting regional economic networks, had to develop a broader and shallower corpus of musical techniques and verbal texts.

In the late 1800s and early 1900s, a pan-Yoruba popular culture emerged, but perceptions of cultural differences among regional subgroups survived. Dialect and musical style continued to play a role in maintaining local identities and allegiances, providing a framework for criticism of regional and national politics (Barber 1991; Apter 1992). Yoruba popular musicians have often drawn upon the traditions of their natal communities to create distinctive "sounds," intended to give them a competitive edge in the marketplace.

In the early 1900s, in and around Lagos (port and colonial capital), syncretic cultural forms—including religious movements, plus traditions of theater, dance, and music—reinforced Yoruba identity. By 1900, the heterogeneous population of Lagos included culturally diverse groups: a local Yoruba community, Sierra Leonean, Brazilian, and Cuban repatriates, Yoruba immigrants from the hinterland, and a

The practice of "spraying"—in which a satisfied praisee dances up to the bandleader or praise singer and pastes money to his forehead—provides the bulk of musicians' profits.

sprinkling of other migrants from Nigeria and farther afield. Interaction among these groups was a crucial factor in the development of Yoruba popular culture during the early 1900s. Lagos was also a locus for importing new musical technology, and, beginning in 1928, for commercial recording by European firms. Since the late 1800s, continual flows of people, techniques, and technologies between Lagos and hinterland communities have shaped Yoruba popular culture.

GENERAL FEATURES

Performances of most genres of Yoruba popular music occur at elaborate parties after rites of passage, such as namings, weddings, and funerals, and at urban nightspots ("hotels"). Recorded music of local and foreign origin is played, often at high volume, in patrilineal compounds, taxicabs, barbershops, and kiosks. Some genres of popular music are associated with popular Islam, and others with syncretic Christianity; some praise the powerful, and others critique social inequality; some have texts in Yoruba, and others in pidgin English; some are fast, vigorous, and youthful in spirit, and others are slow and solemn, "music for the elders."

Yoruba popular music fuses the role of song (a medium for praise, criticism, and moralizing) and the role of rhythmic coordination in sound and physical movement (an expression of sociability and sensory pleasure). As tradition is important to Yoruba musicians and listeners, so are the transnational forces that shape their lives. Yoruba popular culture—not only music, but also styles of dancing, televised comedies and dramas, tabloids, sports, gambling, slang, and fashion in clothing and hair—incorporates imported technologies and exotic styles, thus providing Yoruba listeners with an experiential bridge between local and global culture.

The organization of instruments in Yoruba popular music generally follows the pattern of traditional drumming (Euba 1990): an *iyá'lù* 'mother drum' leads the ensemble, and one or more *omele* 'supporting drums' play ostinatos, designed to interlock rhythmically. In *jùjú,* electric guitars are organized on this pattern. Another practice associated with deep Yoruba (*ìjinlèé Yorùbá*) tradition is the use of musical instruments to "speak." Yoruba is a tonal language, in which distinctions of pitch and timbre play important roles in determining the meaning of words. *Jùjú, fújì,* and most other popular genres employ some variant of the *dùndún,* which articulates stereotyped contours of pitch, representing verbal formulas such as proverbs (*òwe*) and epithets of praise (*oríkì*). Imported instruments—such as congas, electric guitars, and drum synthesizers—also serve to articulate proverbs and epithets of praise, though musicians say such instruments are less "talkative" than pressure drums.

In most genres, the bandleader (often called a captain) is a praise singer who initiates solo vocal phrases (*dá orin* 'creates song alone'), segments of which a chorus doubles. He also sings responsorial sequences, in which his improvised phrases alternate with a fixed phrase, sung by the chorus. His calls are *elé,* the nominal form of the verb *lé* 'to drive something away from or into something else'. Both the responses and the vocalists who sing them are *ègbè* (from *gbè* 'to support, side with, or protect someone'). The social structure of popular music ensembles is closely linked to traditional ideals of social organization, which simultaneously stress the "naturalness" of hierarchy and the mutual dependency of leaders and supporters.

The practice of "spraying"—in which a satisfied praisee dances up to the bandleader or praise singer and pastes (*lè*) money to his forehead—provides the bulk of musicians' profits. Cash advances, guaranteed minimums, and record royalties are, except in the case of a handful of superstars, minor sources of income. The dynamics of remuneration are linked to the musical form, which is often modular or serial. Performances of *jùjú* and *fújì* typically consist of a series of expressive strategies—proverbs and praise names, slang, melodic quotations, and satisfying dance grooves—unreeled with an eye toward pulling in the maximum amount of cash from patrons.

Song texts

Some genres—and even segments of particular performances—are weighted more toward the text-song side of the spectrum, others more to the instrument-dance side. Colloquial aesthetic terminology suggests a developed appreciation of certain aural qualities—dense, buzzing textures, vibrant contrasts in tone color, and rhythmic energy and flow. Nevertheless, Yoruba listeners usually concentrate most carefully on the words of a performance. One of the most damning criticisms listeners can level against a singer or drummer is that he speaks incoherently, or does not choose his words to suit the occasion.

Yoruba song texts are centrally concerned with competition, fate (*orí* 'head'), and the limits of human knowledge in an uncertain universe. Invidious comparison—between the bandleader and competing musicians (who seek to trip him up), or between the patron whose praises are sung and his or her enemies—is the rhetorical linchpin of Yoruba popular music. Advertisements for business concerns are common in live performance and on commercial recordings. Musicians praise brands of beer and cigarettes, hotels, rug makers, football pools, and patent medicines.

Prayers for protection—offered to Jesus, or to Allah, or to the creator deity Eledumare—are another common rhetorical strategy. *Ayé* 'life, the world' is portrayed as a transitory and precarious condition, a conception evoked by phrases like *ayé fèlè- fèè* 'flimsy world' and *ayé gbègi* 'world that chips like wood or pottery'. Song texts continually evoke the conceptual dialectic of *ayínikè* and *ayínipadà*—the reality that can be perceived and, if one is clever and lucky, manipulated; and the unseen, potentially menacing underside of things. Competition for access to patrons and touring overseas is fierce, sometimes involving the use of magical medicines and curses. Yoruba pop music stars have often carried out bitter rhetorical battles on a series of recordings. This practice harnesses the praise-abuse principle to the profit motive, because to keep up with the feud, audiences have to buy each record.

Another major theme of the lyrics of popular songs is sensual enjoyment (*igbádùn* 'sweetness perception'). Singers and talking drummers often switch from themes of religious piety and deep moral philosophy to flirtatious teasing, focused on references to dancers' bodily exertions. Many musicians have adopted good-timing honorifics, such as "minister of enjoyment," "father of good order," "ikebe [butt] king." The images of pleasure projected in *jùjú* and *fújì* are related to the themes of praise and the search for certainty. The subject of praise singing is rhetorically encased in a warm web of social relationships: surrounded by supporters and shielded from enemies, her head "swells" with pride (*iwúlórí*) as she sways to "rolling" (*yí*) rhythms.

wáka   Usually performed by women and originally intended for the spiritual inspiration of participants in Muslim ceremonies

sákárà   Music for social dancing and praising that is performed and patronized mostly by Muslims; also, a frame drum

gòjé   Single-stringed bowed lute made of a calabash and covered with skin

móló   Three-stringed plucked lute commonly used in sákárà ensembles in the 1920s and 1930s

àpàlà   Yoruba popular music that developed from music performed on *gángan* talking drums to entertain women

MUSLIM GENRES

Performing styles associated with Islam and Christianity have strongly influenced Yoruba popular music. One group of genres—*wáka*, *sákárà*, *àpàlà*—is associated with Muslim people and social contexts. Though Islamic authorities do not officially approve of indulgence in music, the success of Islam among the Yoruba (as elsewhere in West Africa) has depended on its ability to adapt to local cultural values. Many traditional drummers are Muslims, and some of the biggest patrons of popular music are wealthy Muslim entrepreneurs. Examples of the genres discussed in this section are included on the compact disc *Yoruba Street Percussion* (1992).

Wáka

The Yoruba adopted *wáka* music from the Hausa, probably in the early 1800s. Usually performed by women, these songs were originally intended for the spiritual inspiration of participants in Muslim ceremonies. They were performed unaccompanied, or with hand clapping. In the early 1920s, tin cymbals with jingles (*sèlí* or *pèrèsèkè*) became their preferred accompaniment. Soon after the mid-1940s, drums and other percussive instruments were introduced. By the 1970s, the typical ensemble included five or six singers, a pressure drum (*àdàmò*), one or more *àkúbà* or *ògìdo* (conga-type drums, based on Latin American prototypes), a bottle-gourd rattle (*sèkèrè*), and a bass lamellophone (*agídìgbo*). This development appears to have been centered in the Ijebu area. By the mid-1990s, *wáka* had come to be regarded as a specialty of the Ijebu, though Muslims in all the Yoruba subgroups performed and patronized them. The combination of instruments added to *wáka* groups after 1945—*dùndún, àkúbà, sèkèrè, agídìgbo*—and the rhythmic patterns they played on recordings suggest the influence of *àpàlà*, another popular genre associated with the Ijebu.

Though *wáka* songs were first recorded in Lagos in the late 1920s, only after 1945 did professional specialists perform them. Their lyrics increasingly dealt with secular matters, earning the approbation of orthodox Muslims. By the mid-1960s, the producer in charge of Muslim religious broadcasts for the Western State Service of the Nigerian Broadcasting Corporation had begun to refer *wáka* musicians to the corporation's music department (Euba 1971:178). *Wáka* bandleaders downplay the Islamic associations of the genre, claiming to have many Christian patrons. Though this stance is in part a matter of public relations, the most popular *wáka* singers have expanded their networks of patronage to include many non-Muslims. Popular *wáka* singers have included Majaro Acagba (popular in the 1920s and 1930s), Batile Alake (1950s–1960s), and the contemporary superstar Queen Salawa Abeni (b. 1965), who has brought aspects of *fújì* into her style.

Sákárà

A genre of music for social dancing and praising, *sákárà* is performed and patronized mostly by Muslims. Oral traditions attribute its origins to Yoruba migrants in Bida, a Nupe town (Ojo 1978:1–4), or to Ilorin, the northernmost major Yoruba town, a prominent center of Islamic proselytization in Yorubaland (Euba 1971:179; Delano 1973[1937]:153). Examples of the genre were being performed in Ibadan and Lagos during or soon after the Great War (1914–1918). Many influential *sákárà* musicians have come from the Egba Yoruba town of Abeokuta.

The term *sákárà* denotes an instrument, a musical genre, and a style of dancing. The instruments used in a typical *sákárà* ensemble include a single-membrane frame drum, with a body consisting of a circular ring of baked clay (*sákárà*); an idiophone made from a gourd cut in half (*ahá*), or a whole gourd held in both hands and struck with ringed fingers (*igbá*); and a single-stringed bowed lute, made of a calabash and covered with skin (*gòjé*). The ensemble is led by a praise singer, who often also plays the *gòjé*. The *gòjé* shares a melodic line with the lead *sákárà* drummer and the lead singer, and plays short variations on the melodic line in a highly ornamented style (Thieme 1969:393). The lead drummer cues changes in tempo and style, and plays praise names, proverbs, and slang phrases.

The *móló*, a plucked three-stringed lute, was commonly used in *sákárà* ensembles during the 1920s and 1930s (Delano 1937:153–157), but was eventually displaced by the *gòjé*. The *gòjé*'s greater volume and penetrating timbre made it the preferred instrument for live performance and recording. During the same period, the acoustic guitar displaced the *móló* in informal, small-group settings. The *móló* has virtually disappeared in Yorubaland (Thieme 1969:387–390).

Sákárà is regarded as a "solemn" style—a term denoting stateliness of tempo and demeanor, with a philosophical depth of lyrics. It has come to be regarded as a traditional genre, despite its association with Muslim contexts, performers, and patrons. This regard is partly due to singers' eloquence in using Yoruba poetic idioms, and partly to the fact that stylistic features of *sákárà* associated with Islamic cantillation—vocal tension and nasality, melodic ornamentation, melisma—have been reinterpreted as indigenous traits.

The first star of *sákárà* was Abibu Oluwa, popularly known as *Oniwáàsì* 'The Preacher'. In the late 1920s and 1930s, he was recorded by Odeon, His Master's Voice, and Parlophone Records. The biggest star on recordings of the 1940s was Ojo Olewale; in the 1950s and 1960s, S. Aka, Ojindo, and Yusufu Ọlatunji ("*Baba l'ẹgbà*") competed for supremacy, often engaging in thinly veiled character attacks, preserved on commercial recordings. In the 1960s, youths in towns throughout Yorubaland still performed *sákárà*, competing on the mass market with styles such as *jùjú* and *àpàlà*. However, by the 1970s, it was regarded primarily as a music for old people, and Yusufu Ọlatunji had been enshrined as the genre's founder.

Àpàlà

This genre originated in the Ijẹbu area, probably in the early 1940s. According to one practitioner, it developed from music performed on *gángan* talking drums to entertain women. It may have represented a conscious effort on the part of professional *gángan* drummers to counter growth in the popularity of *sákárà* and *ẹtikẹ,* a secular genre of *dùndún* drumming (Euba 1990:441). The effort was successful: during the 1960s and 1970s, as the popularity of *sákárà* faded, *àpàlà* became the dominant genre of popular music among Yoruba Muslims. Though the leaders of *àpàlà* groups were originally drummers, by the 1960s the most popular and influential bandleaders—Ligali Mukaiba, Kasumu Adio, Alhaji Haruna Iṣọla—were singers. By the 1970s, Iṣọla and Alhaji Ayinla Ọmọwura (an Ẹgba musician) were the brightest stars of *àpàlà* music.

The typical *àpàlà* group includes a lead singer (usually the bandleader) and

The tradition of highlife dance bands originated in the early 1900s in Accra, capital of Gold Coast (Ghana).

several choral singers, two or more drums from the *àdàmò* pressure-drum family (called *àpàlà* drums by some musicians), one or more *àkúbà* or *ògìdo*, an *agídìgbo*, and a *s̩èk̩èr̩è*. *Àpàlà* varies in tempo, and, as with other styles of social dance drumming, there are specialized styles for younger and older people. *Àpàlà* rhythms are organized along the basic principles of *gángan* drumming: one drummer takes the role of the lead drum *(iyá'lù)*, others act as the *omele*, and the *ògìdo* and the *agídìgbo* anchor the bass. A metal idiophone—an *agogo* 'iron bell', or a truck muffler or wheel—plays a repeated timeline. One of the rhythms commonly used in *àpàlà* is *wòrò*, a social dance style of drumming that spread throughout Yorubaland during the political rallies of the 1950s.

The lyrics of *àpàlà* fit into the praise song mold. The recorded output of Haruna Is̩ola, for example, includes hundreds of songs named after benefactors and important personalities (*gbajúmò* 'a thousand eyes know them'). Many of the human subjects of *àpàlà* lyrics are Muslims, but to attract a larger Yoruba-speaking audience, singers explore topics of broad interest. In 1959, Is̩ola recorded a song on the Nigerian boxer Hogan Bassey's bout with David Moore:

L'ójó Sátidé l'Améríkà,
Máas̩ì ojó kejìdínlógún ni wón f'arésí,
Ni naintin-fiftinain-i nìjá'bósí.
Sé er̩ójú ayé-o?
Hogan Bassey pélú David Moore ni wón mà forí gbárí,
Níbi tí wón ti ńjà l'ójó yen.
Éjè lódí l'ójú kò r̩ènì kan.
Òkan ò ri ojú inú ló ńlò.
David Moore bá fi èrú gba taitulù lo tempoari.
Nwón tonra won je l'ásán nii.
Kìnìún kò ní'jà k'éran wéwé ta féle-fèle.
T'órí e bá gbóná, t'o bá to gùrì alè,
Eran t'ó bá lo débè ló mí a yámútù [Hausa word].

On a Saturday in America,
It was on the 18th of March that the contest was held.
The fight took place in 1959.
Do you see the eyes of the world? [Do you see what happened?]
Hogan Bassey and David Moore, they knocked their heads together,
Where they were fighting that day.
He had blood in his eyes, didn't see anybody.
Nobody saw him, it is his inner mind that he used.
David Moore used tricks to take the title away from him temporarily.
They [the Americans] are fooling themselves: it was vanity.

The lion will not fight; small animals start scattering (when the fight begins).
If he should get angry, if he should piss copiously,
Any small animals that go to that place must die.

To explain Bassey's loss, regarded as an international embarrassment for Nigeria, Iṣọla uses a tale about the power of the lion and popular beliefs concerning the efficacy of talismans. Vocalized in a nasal, melismatic style, and supported by interlocking rhythms, his song is at once Yoruba, Muslim, and cosmopolitan.

The golden age of *àpàlà* was the 1950s. By the 1990s, a few groups were still working in cities such as Ijẹbu-Ode and Ibadan, but *àpàlà*, like *sákárà*, was no longer a music for youths. The two charismatic stars of the genre, Iṣọla (of Ijẹbu-Igbo) and Ọmọwura (of Abẹokuta), died in the 1980s.

YORUBA HIGHLIFE

The tradition of highlife dance bands originated in the early 1900s in Accra, capital of Gold Coast (Ghana). Before the 1940s, Ghanaian bands (such as the Cape Coast Sugar Babies) had traveled to Lagos, where they left a lasting impression on local musicians. In the 1920s and 1930s, Lagos was home to the Calabar Brass Band, which recorded for Parlophone as the Lagos Mozart Orchestra. The core of the band was martial band instruments: clarinets, trumpets and cornets, baritones, trombones, tuba, and parade drums. The band played a proto-highlife style, a transitional phase between the colonial martial band and the African dance orchestra.

During the 1930s and 1940s, Lagos supported several African ballroom dance orchestras, including the Chocolate Dandies, the Lagos City Orchestra, the Rhythm Brothers, the Deluxe Swing Rascals, and the Harlem Dynamites. These bands played for the city's African élites, a social formation comprised largely of Sierra Leonean and Brazilian repatriates, whose grandparents had returned to Lagos in the 1800s. Their repertory included foxtrots, waltzes, Latin dances, and arrangements of popular Yoruba songs.

The 1950s are remembered as the Golden Age of Yoruba highlife. Scores of highlife bands played at hotels in Lagos and the major Yoruba towns. Bobby Benson's Jam Session Orchestra (founded in 1948) exerted a particularly strong influence on Yoruba highlife. A guitarist who had worked as a dance band musician in England, Benson brought the first electric guitar to Lagos (1948), opened his own nightclub (Caban Bamboo), and employed many of the best musicians in Nigeria. His 1960 recording of "Taxi Driver, I Don't Care" (Philips P 82019), was the biggest hit of the highlife era in Nigeria. During the 1950s and 1960s, many of his apprentices—Victor Ọlaiya ("the evil genius of highlife"), Roy Chicago, Edy Okonta, Fela Ransome-Kuti—went on to form their own bands.

The typical highlife band included from three to five winds, plus string bass, guitar, bongos, conga, and maracas. Though the sound of British and American dance bands influenced the African bands, the emphasis was on Latin American repertory, rather than on swing arrangements. Unlike *jùjú* bands, highlife bands often included non-Yoruba members, and typically performed songs in several languages, including Yoruba, English, and pidgin English.

By the mid-1960s, highlife was declining in Yorubaland, partly as a result of competition from *jùjú*. Some highlife bandleaders, including Roy Chicago, incorporated the *dùndún,* and in an attempt to compete with *jùjú* began to use more deep Yoruba verbal materials. Musicians such as Dele Ojo, who had apprenticed with Victor Ọlaiya, forged hybrid *jùjú*-highlife styles. Soul, popular among urban youth from around 1966, attacked highlife from another angle. The Nigerian civil war

jùjú   Named for the tambourine, this popular music genre of the Yoruba emerged in
Lagos around 1932

aṣíkò   Dance drumming style, performed
mainly by Yoruba Christian boys' clubs

sámbà   Square frame drum that may have
been introduced to the Yoruba by the
Brazilians

ògìdo   Bass conga drum of the Yoruba

(1967–1970), which caused many of the best Igbo musicians to leave Lagos, delivered the final blow. By the mid-1990s, highlife bands had become rare in
Yorubaland.

JÙJÚ

This genre, named for the tambourine (*jùjú*), emerged in Lagos around 1932. The
typical *jùjú* group in the 1930s was a trio: a leader (who sang and played banjo), a
ṣèkèrè, and a *jùjú*. Some groups operated as quartets, adding a second vocalist. The
basic framework was drawn from palm wine guitar music, played by a mobile population of African workers in Lagos (sailors, railway men, truck drivers).

The rhythms of early *jùjú* were strongly influenced by *aṣíkò*, a dance drumming
style, performed mainly by Christian boys' clubs. Many early *jùjú* bandleaders began
their careers as *aṣíkò* musicians. Played on square frame drums and a carpenter's saw,
aṣíkò drew upon the traditions of two communities of Yoruba-speaking repatriates
who had settled in Lagos during the 1800s: the Amaro were *emancipados* of Brazilian
or Cuban descent, and the Saro were Sierra Leonean repatriates (who formed a
majority of the educated black élite in Lagos). *Aṣíkò* rhythms came from the Brazilian
samba (many older Nigerians use the terms *aṣíkò* and *sámbà* interchangeably), and
the associated style of dancing was influenced by the *caretta* 'fancy dance', a Brazilian
version of the contredanse. The square *sámbà* drum may have been introduced by the
Brazilians (known for their carpentry), or from the British West Indies, perhaps via
Sierra Leone. Though identifying a single source for the introduction of the frame
drum is impossible, this drum was clearly associated with immigrant black Christian
identity.

Early styles

The first star of *jùjú* was Tunde King, born in 1910 into the Saro community.
Though a member of the Muslim minority, he learned Christian hymns while
attending primary school. He made the first recordings with the term *jùjú* on the
label, recorded by Parlophone in 1936. Ayinde Bakare, a Yoruba migrant who recorded for His Master's Voice beginning in 1937, began as an *aṣíkò* musician, and went
on to become one of the most influential figures in postwar *jùjú*. Musical style was an
important idiom for the expression of competitive relationships between neighborhoods. During the 1930s, each quarter in Lagos had its favorite *jùjú* band.

The melodies of early *jùjú*, modeled on *aṣíkò* and palm wine songs and Christian
hymns, were diatonic, often harmonized in parallel thirds. The vocal style used the
upper range of the male full-voice tessitura, and was nasalized and moderately tense,
with no vibrato. The banjo—including a six-stringed guitar-banjo and a mandolin-
banjo—played a role similar to that of the fiddle in *sákàrà* music, often introducing
or bridging between vocal segments, and providing heterophonic accompaniment for
the vocal line. *Jùjú* banjoists used a technique of thumb and forefinger plucking
(*krusbass*) introduced to Lagos by Liberian sailors.

From the beginning, *jùjú* lyrics drew heavily upon deep Yoruba metaphors. In "Association" (recorded by Parlophone in 1936), Tunde King sings:

> Agbe ló l'áró; kìí ráhùn áró.
> Àlùkò ló l'ósùn; kìí ráhùn osùn.
> Lékéléké, kìí ráhùn ẹfun
> Ìyàwó àkọ́fé, kìí ráhùn ajé
> Òkèlẹ́ ẹ̀bà, kìí ráhùn ọbẹ̀
>
> K'árìrà máà mà jẹẹráhùn owó.
> K'árìrà máà mà jẹ́ẹ ráhùnọmọ.

> The blue touraco parrot is the owner of indigo dye; it doesn't usually complain
>   for want of indigo dye.
> The red aluko bird is the owner of rosewood; it doesn't usually complain for
>   want of rosewood.
> The white cattle egret doesn't usually complain for want of chalk.
> The first wife one marries doesn't usually complain for want of money.
> The first morsel of cassava porridge doesn't usually complain for want of soup.
>
> Good fortune, don't let us complain for want of money.
> Good fortune, don't let us complain for want of children.

Here, King draws on Yoruba oral tradition to forge a metaphoric correspondence between a natural relationship (birds, bright colors) and a cultural one (beginnings, abundance). Other examples of his style are on the compact disc *Juju Roots: 1930s–1950s* (1993).

After the mid-1940s, *jùjú* underwent a rapid transformation. The first major change was the introduction, in 1948, of the *gángan,* attributed to bandleader Akanbi Ege. Another change was the availability of electronic amplifiers, microphones, and pickups. Portable public-address systems had been introduced during the war, and were in regular use by Yoruba musicians by the late 1940s. The first *jùjú* musician to adopt the amplified guitar was Ayinde Bakare. He experimented with a contact microphone in 1949, switching from ukulele-banjo to "box guitar" (acoustic), because there was no place to attach the device to the body of the banjo. Electronic amplification of voices and guitar catalyzed an expansion of *jùjú* ensembles during the 1950s. In particular, it enabled musicians to incorporate more percussion instruments without upsetting the aural balance they wanted between singing and instrumental accompaniment.

In the postwar period, *jùjú* bands began to use the *agídìgbo* and various conga-type drums (*àkúbà, ògìdo*). This reflects the influence of a genre called *agídìgbo* and mambo music, a Yoruba version of *konkoma* music, brought to Lagos by Ewe and Fanti migrant workers (Alájá-Browne 1985:64). According to *jùjú* musicians active at the time, the *agídìgbo* and *ògìdo* (bass conga) provided a bass counterbalance for the electric guitar and *gángan.*

The instrumentation of Bakare's group shifted from one stringed instrument and two percussion instruments (before the war), to one stringed instrument and five percussion instruments (in 1954). By 1966, most *jùjú* bands had eight or nine musicians. Expansion and reorganization of the ensemble occurred simultaneously with a slowing of tempos. Slower tempos and expanded ensembles were in turn linked with changes in aural texture. Western technology was put into the service of indigenous aesthetics: the channeling of singing and guitar through cheap and infrequently serviced tube amplifiers and speakers augmented the density and buzzing of the music.

The birth of later jùjú can be traced to the
innovations of Isiah Kehinde Dairo, an Ijesa Yoruba
musician, who had a series of hit records around the
time of Nigerian independence (1960).

The practice of singing in parallel thirds continued to dominate, but there were
notable exceptions. Ekiti Yoruba bandleader C. A. Balogun utilized the distinctive
polyphonic vocal style of his natal area, in which the overlap between soloist and chorus produces major seconds and minor sevenths. Many bandleaders produced records
with a song in standard Yoruba dialect and mainstream *jùjú* style on the A side, and a
local Yoruba dialect and style on the B side. Most *jùjú* singing shifted from the high-
tessitura, nasalized style of the 1930s and 1940s to a lower, more relaxed sound closer
to traditional secular vocal style and the imported model of the crooner. Tunde King's
distinctive style of singing was continued by Tunde Western Nightingale, "the bird
that sings at night," a popular Lagosian bandleader of the 1950s and 1960s.

Later styles

The birth of later *jùjú* can be traced to the innovations of Isiah Kehinde Dairo
(1930–1996), an Ijẹṣa Yoruba musician, who had a series of hit records around the
time of Nigerian independence (1960). His recordings for the British company
Decca were so successful, the British government in 1963 designated him a member
of the Order of the British Empire. In 1967, he joined *àpàlà* star Haruna Iṣọla to
found Star Records. His hits of the early 1960s, recorded on two-track tape at Decca
Studios in Lagos, reveal his mastery of the three-minute recording. Most of his
records from this period begin with an accordion or guitar introduction, plus the
main lyric, sung once or twice. This leads into a middle section, in which the *dùndún*
predominates, playing proverbs and slogans which in turn the chorus repeats. The
final section usually reprises the main text.

The vocal style on Dairo's records was influenced by Christian singing of hymns.
(Dairo was pastor of a syncretic church in Lagos.) It also reflects the polyphonic
singing of eastern Yorubaland (Ilẹṣa, Ekiti). His lyrics—in Standard Yoruba, Ijẹṣa
dialect, and various other Nigerian and Ghanaian languages—were also carefully
composed. By his own account, he made special efforts to research traditional poetic
idioms. Many of his songs consist of philosophical advice and prayers for himself and
his patrons, as in the song *"Elele Ture"* (1962):

> Òṣùpá roro, l'ójú òrun toòrò,
> Orí mi ọmọ j'áyé mi toòrò.
> Olú sọjí ọrun, ọmọ j'áyé mi toòrò.
> Ọba tí ómí pẹ́sẹ́ f'éku, ọmọ j'áyé mi toòrò.
> Ọba tí ómí pẹ́sẹ́ f'ẹyẹ, ọmọ j'áyé mi toòrò.
> T'ó ńpẹ́sẹ́ f'érà t'ù mí rìn l'álẹ́, ọmọ j'áyé mi toòrò.

> Moon shining in the peaceful sky,
> My destiny ["head"], let my life be peaceful.
> King who wakes in heaven, let my life be peaceful.

King that provides for rats, let my life be peaceful.
King that provides for birds, let my life be peaceful.
That provides for ants that walk on the ground, let my life be peaceful.

Jùjú continued to develop along lines established by Bakare and Dairo's experiments. The oil boom of the 1970s led to a rapid, though uneven, expansion of the Nigerian economy. Many individuals earned enough money from trade and entrepreneurial activity to hire musicians for neotraditional celebrations, and the number and size of *jùjú* bands increased concomitantly. By the mid-1970s, the ideal *jùjú* ensemble had expanded beyond the ten-piece bands of Bakare and Dairo to include fifteen or more musicians. Large bands helped boost the reputation of the patrons who hired them to perform at parties, and helped sustain an idealized image of Yoruba society as a flexible hierarchy (Waterman 1990).

Jùjú of the 1990s

Jùjú bands of the mid-1990s fall into three basic sections: singers, percussionists, guitarists. The singers stand in a line at the front of the band. The "band captain" stands in the middle, flanked on either side by choral singers. The percussion section includes from one to three talking drums (*àdàmò*), several conga-type drums, a set of bongos played with light sticks ("double toy"), *ṣẹ̀kẹ̀rẹ̀*, maracas, *agogo*, and in the larger and better-financed bands, a drum set ("jazz drums").

The leader's guitar is tuned to an open triad. He uses it to play simple motifs, which function as the leader's trademark, and cue changes in rhythm or texture. The guitar section also includes a lead guitar, which takes extended solos; two or three "tenor guitars," which serve as *omele* 'supporting instruments'; and a Hawaiian (pedal steel) guitar, which may play solo or add coloristic effects. Melodic patterns come from hymns, Yoruba songs, the old palm wine guitar tradition, and various other sources, including African-American popular music, country, and Indian film music.

Sunny Ade

One star of *jùjú* is King Sunny Adé. Born in Ondo in 1946, he started his musical career playing a *sámbà* drum with a *jùjú* band. He formed his own ensemble, the Green Spot Band, in 1966. He modeled his style on that of Tunde Nightingale, and his vocal sound represents an extension of the high-tessitura, slightly nasalized sound established by Tunde King in the 1930s. His first big hit was "Challenge Cup" (1968), a praise song for a football team, released on a local label, African Songs. In 1970, he added electric bass guitar (displacing the *agídìgbo*), and began to record with imported instruments, purchased for him by his patron, Chief Bọlarinwa Abioro. Adé quickly developed a reputation as a technically skilled musician, and his fans gave him the informal title *Àlùjànuń Onígítà* 'The Wizard of Guitar'. One of his earliest recordings, "*Bolarinwa Abioro*" (1967), is a praise song for Chief Abioro:

> Jẹ́ jẹ́ jẹ́ jẹ́ jẹ́ jẹ́,
> Bọ́lárìnwá mi, ọmọ Abíórò
> Ọkọ Múyìbátù mi, jẹ́jẹ́ ló l'ayé.
> Bọ́lá t'ó bí Bọ́láńlé ló b'Ádébáyọ̀ uṇ lẹ́ ló bí Ọláẹ́ẹ̀yẹ àti Ọláwùnmí pẹ́lú
>   Ọládọṣù.
> Ìpókíá n'ílé l'area Ẹ̀gbádò.
> Bọ́lárìnwá-o, l'àwá ḿbá lọ-o; ibi amí rẹ́ l'àwá dé yìí-o.
> Má mà yún oko n'ígbà òjò;
> Má mà f'ẹsẹ́ kan nini.
> Abíórò, jọ̀-gbọ̀dọ́-e-e-e,
> Aláyé yẹ ẹ́-o.

Apart from Fela Anikulapo Kuti, King Sunny Adé—
"Golden Mercury of Africa, Minister of
Enjoyment"—is the only Nigerian popular musician
who has had significant success in the international
market.

Gently, gently, gently, gently, gently, gently,

My Bọlarinwa, child of Abioro,

Husband of Muyibatu, softly, softly, so is the world.

Bọla that fathered Adebayọ has fathered Ọláléyẹ and Ọlawunmi with Ọladosu.

Ipokia is your area, Egbado (region).

Oh Bọlarinwa, we are following you; the place we're going to, that's where we've
  reached.

Don't go to the farm in the rainy season;

Don't step on the wet ground.

Abioro, important person,

The world is going to be good for you.

In 1972, splitting with Chief Abioro, Adé changed the name of his band to the
"African Beats." The LP *Synchro System Movement* (1976) artfully blended the vocal
style he had adopted from Tunde Nightingale with aspects of Afro-Beat, including
minor tonality, slower tempos, and a langorous bass. This LP was one of the first
long-play recordings to feature a continuous thirty-minute performance, a move
away from the three-minute limit of most previous recordings, and toward the typical
extended forms of live performances. By 1979, Adé had expanded his band to
include sixteen performers, including two tenor guitars, one rhythm guitar, Hawaiian
guitar, bass guitar, two talking drummers, ṣẹ̀kẹ̀rẹ̀, conga (àkúbà), drum set, synthesizer, and four choral vocalists.

Apart from Fela Anikulapo Kuti, King Sunny Adé—"Golden Mercury of Africa,
Minister of Enjoyment"—is the only Nigerian popular musician who has had significant success in the international market. For release by Island Records in 1982, he
recorded the album *Juju Music* in Togo, under the direction of French producer
Martin Meissonnier. The LP reportedly sold 200,000 copies, impressive for African
popular music. Later releases were less successful, and Island Records dropped Adé in
1985. In the mid-1990s, he continued to play to mass audiences in Nigeria, and to
make an occasional tour of the United States and Europe.

Ebenezer Obey

Born in the Ẹgbado area of western Yorubaland in 1942, Chief Commander
Ebenezer Obey is the other star of *jùjú*. He formed his first band, the International
Brothers, in 1964. His early style, strongly influenced by I. K. Dairo, incorporated
elements of highlife, Congolese guitar style, soul, and country. His band expanded
during the years of the oil boom. In 1964, he started with seven players; by the early
1970s, he was employing thirteen; and by the early 1980s, he was touring with eighteen. He is praised for his voice, and for his philosophical depth and knowledge of
Yoruba proverbs. Like Dairo, he is a devout Christian, and many of his songs derive
from the melodies of hymns.

In the 1980s, decline in the economy, devaluation of the currency, and increased competition from *fújì* bands put many of the *jùjú* groups formed during the 1970s out of work. Adé and Obey's only serious competitor is Sir Shina Peters, whose album *Ace* was a big hit in 1990. Peters's style represents an attempt to bring dance rhythms from *fújì* music into *jùjú*. The history of *jùjú* provides many examples of strategic borrowing from competing genres.

AFRO-BEAT

Centered on the charismatic figure Fela Anikulapo Kuti (born in 1938 in Abeokuta), Afro-Beat began in the late 1960s as a confluence of dance band highlife, jazz, and soul. Though in style and content it stands somewhat apart from the mainstream of Yoruba popular music, it has influenced *jùjú* and *fújì*.

Fela is the grandson of the Reverend J. J. Ransome-Kuti (a prominent educator, who played a major role in indigenizing Christian hymns). His mother was Funmilayo Ransome-Kuti (a political activist, founder of the Nigerian Women's Union). It is said that Fela received his musicality from his father's family, and his temperament from his mother's. In the mid-1950s, he played with Bobby Benson's and Victor Olaiya's highlife orchestras. In 1958, he traveled to London to study trumpet at Trinity College of Music. While there, he joined with J. K. Braimah to form Koola Lobitos, a band that played a jazz-highlife hybrid. Fela returned to Lagos in 1963, and by 1966 had been voted the top jazz performer in a readers' poll, held by *Spear Magazine*. Though his reputation grew among musicians in Lagos, his music appealed primarily to an audience of collegians and professionals.

The popularity of soul among young people in Lagos during the late 1960s strongly influenced Fela. In particular, the success of Geraldo Pino, a Sierra Leonean imitator of James Brown, caused him to incorporate aspects of soul into his style. A 1969 trip to the United States, where he met black activists, changed his political orientation and his concept of the goals of music making. In 1970, on returning to Lagos, he formed a new group, Africa '70, and began to develop Afro-Beat, a mixture of highlife and soul, with infusions of deep Yoruba verbal materials.

In the early 1970s, Fela's style centered on Tony Allen's drumming, Maurice Ekpo's electric-bass playing, and Peter Animaṣaun's rhythm-guitar style (influenced by James Brown's playing). The band also included three congas, percussion sticks, *ṣèkèrè*, and a four-piece horn section (two trumpets, tenor sax, baritone sax). Jazz-influenced solos were provided by trumpeter Tunde Williams and the brilliant tenor saxophonist Igo Chico. Like many Lagos highlife bands of the 1950s, Fela's early bands included Ghanaians and non-Yoruba Nigerians. The original Africa '70 stayed together until the mid-1970s, when Fela's increasingly autocratic behavior led Allen and Chico to quit.

Over more than twenty years, the organizational principles of Afro-Beat have remained remarkably constant. The basic rhythm-section pattern divides into complementary strata: a bottom layer, made up of interlocking electric-bass and bass-drum patterns; a middle layer, with a rhythm guitar, congas, and a snare back beat; and a top layer, with percussion sticks and *ṣèkèrè* playing ostinatos. The horn section provides riffs in support of Fela's singing, and its members play extended solos.

Fela's early recordings included love songs ("Lover"), risqué songs in pidgin English ("*Na Poi*"), and Yoruba songs based on proverbs and tales ("*Alujọn jọn ki jọn*"). In the mid-1970s, Fela composed increasingly strident lyrics, attacking the excesses of foreign capitalism and Nigerian leaders. It was then that the textual content of Afro-Beat clearly separated from the mainstream of Yoruba popular music. Fela's political goals—shouted by his trademark slogan, "Music is a weapon"—led him to compose more in pidgin English, to reach a wider international audience.

fújì   Popular genre of Yoruba music in the
      1990s; grew out of Muslim practices but
      also gained a Christian audience

ajísáàrì   Music customarily performed before
      dawn during Ramadan by young men
      among the Yoruba

Records such as *Zombie* (ridiculing the Nigerian military), and *Expensive Shit* (recounting the efforts of police to recover drugs from Fela's feces) established his reputation as a fearless rebel, and consolidated his audience, composed largely of urban youth and members of the intelligentsia.

Fela was first arrested by the Nigerian secret police in 1974. Three years later, the military attacked his compound, the "Kalakuta Republic," and threw his mother from a window, causing internal injuries from which she died. Fela responded with the LP *Coffin for Head of State,* covered with a montage of newspaper clippings reporting his mother's death and funeral. Continued run-ins with the Nigerian government stiffened his resistance to authority.

In the early 1980s, Fela developed a mystical philosophy, based on reconstructed Yoruba religion, Afrocentrism, Egyptology, and the teachings of a Ghanaian prophet, Professor Hindu. He changed the name of his band to Egypt '80. In the mid-1980s, his band included nine horn players (three trumpets, one alto sax, three tenor saxes, two baritone saxes), two guitarists, two bassists, a drum set, three congas, two *şèkèrè,* and around a dozen singers and dancers. His typical composition became longer and more complex—"a song with five movements . . . a symphony but in the African sense" (Fela, quoted in Stewart 1992:117). The sound of the ensemble shifted toward a denser texture. In some subsequent recordings (like *Teacher Don't Teach Me Nonsense,* 1986), Fela experiments with polytonality: while the rhythm section stays near one tonal center, the horns explore another (a fourth or a fifth away).

Fela's music continues to exert influence on Yoruba musicians, though it achieves far fewer local record sales than *jùjú* or *fújì.* Fela's biographers have depicted him as a paradoxical figure: a revolutionary traditionalist, a materialist mystic, an egalitarian dictator, a progressive sexist. Yet for all his idiosyncrasies, he is as much a product of Yoruba historical experience as King Sunny Adé.

FÚJÌ

This genre, the most popular one in the early 1990s, grew out of *ajísáàrì,* music customarily performed before dawn during Ramadan by young men associated with neighborhood mosques. *Ajísáàrì* groups, made up of a lead singer, a chorus, and drummers, walk through their neighborhood, stopping at patrilineal compounds to wake the faithful for their early morning meal (*sáàrì*). *Fújì* emerged as a genre and marketing label in the late 1960s, when former *ajísáàrì*-singers Sikiru Ayinde Barrister and Ayinla Kollington were discharged from the Nigerian Army, made their first recordings, and began a periodically bitter rivalry. In the early 1970s, *fújì* succeeded *àpàlà* as the most popular genre among Yoruba Muslims, and has since gained a substantial Christian audience.

The instrumentation of *fújì* bands features drums. Most important are various sizes of talking-drum (*dùndún, àdàmọ,* and sometimes a smaller hourglass-shaped drum, the *kànàngó*, two or three of which may be played by a single drummer). Bands often include *sákárà* drums (still associated with Muslim identity), plus the conga-type drums used in *àpàlà* and *jùjú*. Commonly, they also use *ṣèkèrè*, maracas, and a set of *agogo* attached to a metal rack. In the mid-1980s, *fújì* musicians borrowed the drum set from *jùjú*. The wealthiest bands use electronic drum pads connected to synthesizers.

Other experiments represent an attempt to forge symbolic links with deep Yoruba traditions. In the early 1980s, Alhaji Barrister introduced into his style the *bàtá* drum, associated with the Yoruba thunder god Ṣango. He named the drum "Fújì Bàtá Reggae." He dropped the *bàtá* after influential Muslim patrons complained about his using a quintessentially pagan instrument. On other recordings, he employed the *kàkàkí*, an indigenous trumpet, used for saluting the kings of northern Yoruba towns.

Later appropriations of Western instruments—the Hawaiian or pedal steel guitar, keyboard synthesizers, and drum machines—have largely been filtered through *jùjú*. Some *jùjú* musicians complain that *fújì* musicians, whom they regard as musical illiterates, have no idea what to do with such instruments. In fact, imported high-tech instruments are usually used in *fújì* recordings to play melodic sequences without harmonic accompaniment, to signal changes of rhythm or subject, and to add coloristic effects—techniques consistent with the norms of the genre.

Though *fújì* has to a large degree been secularized, it is still associated with Muslims, and record companies time the release of certain *fújì* recordings to coincide with holy days, such as Id-al-Fitr and Id-al-Kabir. Segments of Qur'ānic text are frequently deployed in performance, and many *fújì* recordings open with a prayer in Yoruba Arabic: "*La ilaha illa llahu; Mohamudu ya asuru lai* 'There is no god but Allah; Mohammed is his prophet'."

Fújì music is an intensively syncretic style, incorporating aspects of Muslim recitations, Christian hymns, highlife classics, *jùjú* songs, Indian film-music themes, and American pop, within a rhythmic framework based on Yoruba social-dance drumming. To demonstrate knowledge of Yoruba tradition, *fújì* musicians also make use of folkloric idioms, like proverbs and praise names. On his 1990 LP and music video *Music Extravaganza*, Barrister borrows from an animal fable to denigrate his rivals:

> Tí Àwòko bá ńṣeré, kẹ́yẹ-kẹ́yẹ má à fóhùn l'ẹyẹ oko.
> Àròyé n'iṣẹ́ ìbákà-o; igbe kíkẹ́ ni ṣ'éyẹ.
> B'ólóògbùrọ́ ṣél'óhùn tó, ó yí foríbalẹ̀ f'ọba Orin.
> Ati àròyé ìbákà-o, at'igbe kíkẹ̀ ni ṣ'éyẹ̀,
> B'áwòko ò m'órin wá,
> Àròyé kín'ìbákà máa ríwí?
> Igbe kíl'ẹyẹ owulẹ́ kẹ́ lásọ́n-làsọ̀n?
> Kíni ol'óbúrò ó fi ohùn orin kọ?

> When *Awoko* is singing, all these lesser birds shouldn't make a sound.
> Incessant yammering is Canary's work; hoarse shouting is the birds' work.
> Even the speckled pigeon with a beautiful voice must prostrate before the King of Song.
> With Canary's babbling and the birds' chattering,
> If *Awoko* doesn't bring songs,
> What kind of babbling will the Canary do?
> What noise would the birds bother to make?
> What song would a speckled pigeon use her voice to sing?

If Yoruba popular music is a product of markets, it is also, in important ways, unlike other commodities. Yoruba musicians and audiences regard music as a potent force with material and spiritual effects.

Awoko, a local bird (known for the complexity and beauty of its call), is Barrister. Canary and Speckled Pigeon are his rivals. The melody to which these words are sung is modeled on that of "*Malaika,*" an East African song, composed by Fadhili Williams, copyrighted by Pete Seeger, and introduced to Nigeria in a cover version by Boney M. (a German-based Eurodisco band).

References to the overseas tours of successful bandleaders are also common. On the 1991 release *New Fuji Garbage Series III,* Barrister opens with a description of his success on a recent visit to London, narrated in the present tense:

> We dey for [are in] Great Britain, where we perform for people's enjoyment.
> We dey for Great Britain, where we perform for people's enjoyment.
>
> Òyìnbo [European] people dey dance Fújì Garbage for every corner.
> Naija [Nigerian] people dey dance Fújì Garbage for every corner.
> Jamò [German] people dey dance Fújì Garbage for every corner.
> Akátá [African-American] people dey dance Fújì Garbage for every pub house.
> DJs dem dey play [they are playing] Fújì Garbage for British-i radio.
>
> When I dey [dare] sing, people dey [they] dance-i-o.
> When I dey sing, people dey dance-i-o.

Later in the recording, Barrister sings the praises of Akeem Olajuwon, center for the Houston Rockets (of the National Basketball Association), describing in pidgin English and Yoruba the art of dribbling:

> Baki-ball eré félèé.
> Awa gbá sókè, a tún gbá sílè:
> Baki number 1, baki number 2, baki number 3, baki number 4.
> O yára jù bóòlù sínú èwòn,
> Bí t'Akim omo Olajuwon.
> Awa gbà basketball.
>
> Basketball is an energetically flapping [cool] game.
> You bounce it up, then you bounce it down:
> Basket number 1, basket number 2, basket number 3, basket number 4.
> You quickly throw the ball into the chains [net],
> Just like Akeem, son of Olajuwon.
> We receive [dig] basketball.

On another album, Barrister transports the listener to Orlando, Florida, to visit a theme park he calls Destney World and describes the wonders of Western technology: "We all entered a big lift; suddenly the lights went out, and all the whites screamed, 'Oh, my mother!'" Verbal snapshots of adventures overseas allow listeners to share vicariously the superstar's transnational movements, and provide a medium for evaluating aspects of life in the West (*ìlú òyìnbo* 'land of the whites').

"TRADITIONAL" AND "POPULAR" STYLES

To draw a sharp boundary between "traditional" and "popular" music in Yoruba society is impossible. The criteria most commonly invoked in attempts to formulate a cross-cultural definition of popular music—openness to change, syncretism, intertextuality, urban provenience, commodification—are characteristic even of those genres Yoruba musicians and audiences identify as deep Yoruba. The penetration of indigenous economies by international capital and the creation of local markets for recorded music have shaped Yoruba conceptions of music as a commodity. Musical commodification did not, however, originate with colonialism and mass reproduction. Yoruba musicians have long conceived of performance as a form of labor, a marketable product. The notion of the market as a microcosm of life (captured in the aphorism *ayé l'ọjà* 'the world is a market') and a competitive arena, fraught with danger and ripe with possibilities, guides the strategies of musicians, who struggle to make a living under unpredictable economic conditions.

If Yoruba popular music is a product of markets, it is also, in important ways, unlike other commodities. Yoruba musicians and audiences regard music as a potent force with material and spiritual effects.

Though the foregoing genres of music vary in instrumentation, style, and social context, each invokes deep Yoruba tradition while connecting listeners to the world of transnational commerce. Taken as a whole, Yoruba popular music provides a complex commentary on the relationship between local traditions and foreign influence in an epoch of profound change.

REFERENCES

Adé, Sunny. 1967. "*BGlarinwa Abioro.*" *African Songs* 21A. 45-rpm single.

———. 1976. *Synchro System Movement.* African Songs AS26. LP disk.

———. 1982. *Jùjú Music.* Island Records CID 9712. Compact disc.

———, and his Green Spots. 1967. *African Songs.* LP disk.

Alájá-Browne, Afọlábi. 1985. "Jùjú Music: A Study of its Social History and Style." Ph.D. dissertation, University of Pittsburgh.

Anikulapo Kuti, Fela. 1986. *Teacher Don't Teach Me Nonsense.* Polygram 833 525–2 Q-1. Compact disc.

Apter, Andrew. 1992. *Black Critics and Kings: The Hermeneutics of Power in Yoruba Society.* Chicago: University of Chicago Press.

Barber, Karin. 1991. *I Could Speak until Tomorrow: Oriki, Women and the Past in a Yoruba Town.* Washington, D.C.: Smithsonian Institution Press.

Dairo, Isiah Kehinde, and his Blue Spots. 1962. *Elele Ture.* Decca NWA 5079.

Delano, Isaac. 1973 [1937]. *The Soul of Nigeria.* Nendeln: Kraus Reprints.

Euba, Akin. 1971. "Islamic Musical Culture among the Yoruba: A Preliminary Survey." In *Essays on Music and History in Africa,* ed. Klaus P. Wachsmann, 171–184. Evanston, Ill.: Northwestern University Press.

Jùjú Roots: 1930s–1950s. 1993. Cambridge, Mass.: Rounder Records. CD 5017. Compact disc.

———. 1990. *Yoruba Drumming: The Dùndún Tradition.* Bayreuth: Bayreuth University. Bayreuth African Studies, 21–22.

Isọla, Haruna. 1959. "Hogan Bassey." 78-rpm 10-inch disk. Decca WA 3120.

Ojo, Ọlaṣebikan. 1978. "Sakara Music as a Literary Form." Senior honors thesis, University of Ibadan.

Stewart, Gary. 1992. *Breakout: Profiles in African Rhythm.* Chicago: University of Chicago Press.

Thieme, Darius. 1969. "A Descriptive Catalog of Yoruba Musical Instruments." Ph.D. dissertation, Catholic University of America.

Waterman, Christopher A. 1990. *Jùjú: A Social History and Ethnography of an African Popular Music.* Chicago: University of Chicago Press.

Yoruba Street Percussion. 1992. Original Music. OMCD016. Compact disc.

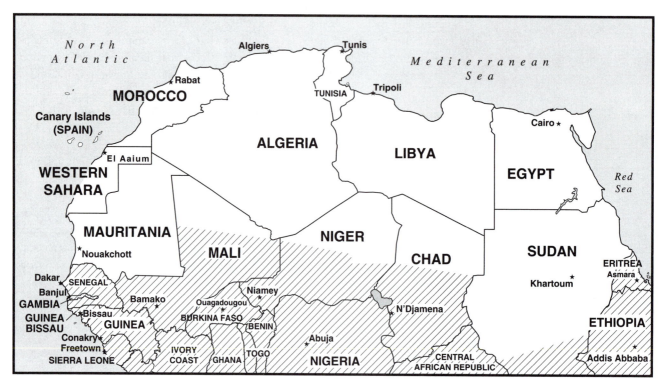

North Africa

North Africa

The music of North Africa—played by Arabs, Berbers, and black Africans—combines elements from the Middle East with those from sub-Saharan cultures. Blends of northern and southern musical practice are common throughout this region.

North Africa: An Introduction
Caroline Card Wendt

The People
Culture History
The Arab-Andalusian Tradition
Music and Islam
Music in Folk Life
Popular Music

As a culture area, North Africa extends eastward from the Atlantic coast to encompass the Mediterranean nations of Morocco, Algeria, Tunisia, and Libya, known as the Maghrib, to the western desert of Egypt. The area reaches southward into the Sahara to include Mauritania and northern sections of Mali and Niger. The Atlas Mountains, which extend from Morocco to Tunisia, divide a narrow stretch of fertile and densely populated agricultural land along the Mediterranean coast from the sparsely populated, arid expanses of the Sahara. Major elements unifying the peoples of this area are the religion of Islam and the Arabic language—the official language of each country except Mali and Niger. All the countries were formerly subject to one or another of the European powers, which in varying degrees influenced their present economies, educational systems, and development. Because the political boundaries are often inconsistent with ethnic distributions, some groups (such as the Tuareg) divide into several different nationalities.

THE PEOPLE

The population consists principally of Caucasoid Arabs and Berbers, and of negroid Africans known in the Maghrib as Gnawa. The Arabs are descendants both of early Muslim invaders from the Arabian Peninsula and of native Berber inhabitants long assimilated into their society and culture. The Berbers, whose ancestors may be the earliest inhabitants of Mediterranean North Africa (Murdock 1959), comprise numerous groups who speak related dialects of a Hamito-Semitic language (Greenberg 1966) and exhibit similar traits. The largest Berber populations are located in Morocco and Algeria. The black Africans are descendents of indigenous Saharans and immigrants from the broad intermediate zone at the southern edge of the Sahara known as the sahel or Sudan. Though black Africans are a minority in the Maghrib, they form a noticeable portion of the population of Mauritania and the Saharan regions of the other countries. The musical traditions of the Arabs, Berbers, and negroid Africans, though not untouched by acculturation, stem from different cultural heritages, which merit separate consideration. Of relevance, also, are patterns of nomadic, village, and urban ways of living that often cut across ethnic and regional categories.

CULTURE HISTORY

The early Berber tribes dwelled on the coast until the arrival of Phoenician traders, about 1200 B.C. Together, the Phoenicians and Berbers built Carthage and a civilization that spread across western North Africa and the Mediterranean, from Sicily to Spain. In 202 B.C., the Romans took Carthage. By A.D. 40, they controlled an area from the Atlantic coast to present-day eastern Libya. About six hundred years of Roman rule ended with the invasion of Vandals from Scandinavia, soon followed by Christian Byzantines. In 688, at the time of the first Muslim Arab invasion, North Africa was widely, if superficially, Christian. Within a century, the Arabs were masters of all Mediterranean North Africa and Spain, and though their empire eventually receded, most of the lands and peoples they subjugated were irreversibly changed, in language, religion, and culture. Subsequent European conquests hardly affected Arabic cultural patterns.

The character that distinguishes North Africa from the Arabic-speaking Muslim Near East arises in large measure from its Berber subculture. While urban Berbers were receptive to the culture of their conquerors, rural and nomadic Berbers were much less so. Withdrawing into mountain villages or retreating deep into the desert, they remained resistant and even hostile to foreign intrusion. As a result, Berber language, culture, and tribal patterns have persisted in the Moroccan Atlas, in the Algerian high plateaus, in desert towns in Mauritania and Libya, and in oasis communities and nomadic encampments across the Sahara. In remote areas, Islam and the accompanying Arab traditions penetrated slowly, forming a veneer of Muslim culture over pre-Islamic customs and beliefs. In the Ahaggar region of the Algerian Sahara, long an impenetrable mountain stronghold of warrior Berber Tuareg tribes, Muslim religion and culture had little effect until the latter part of the 1800s.

Gradually, the Arab culture of the Maghrib filtered southward to permeate the Sahara with Islamic character. Over centuries the trans-Saharan trade routes, mainly under control of the Berber Tuareg, carried Mediterranean arts and technology southward. The northern Berbers introduced methods of irrigation, fertilization, and animal husbandry that enabled sahelian cultivators to grow crops farther north into the arid zone (Murdock 1959:125–126). In varying degrees, many Sahelian cultivators were incorporated into Tuareg society and culture, and elements of sub-Saharan music became part of Tuareg traditions.

Sahelian arts and music have also moved northward. In cultivation centers throughout the Sahara, rhythms, vocal styles, and dances of sub-Saharan origin predominate. In the Maghrib, black Muslim brotherhoods perform Sahelian-style music for exorcisms, rituals of curing, and Muslim celebrations and festivals. Blends of northern and southern musical practices are clear, also, in the Mauritanian bardic tradition, which, combining modal structures akin to Arab tradition with rhythmic patterns related to those of West Africa, forms styles the musicians term white and black ways (Guignard 1975a, 1975b; Balandier and Mercier 1952; Nikiprowetzky 1961, 1964; Duvelle 1966). Since the 1960s, recurring drought, increasing population, and political strife have prompted migrations in many directions: herders drive their animals farther in search of water and pasture, and pastoralists and cultivators abandon rural areas for employment in towns and cities. The musical result of these migrations is the rapid evolution of new genres from older and borrowed sources. For source material and inspiration, composers of urban music have turned increasingly to rural repertories and foreign music. Radio broadcasts and cassette recordings convey to the most remote areas a wide range of musical styles.

The musics of the region, therefore, do not form ready categories. As modern composers and arrangers adapt old traditions to new performance situations, the distinctions among classical, folk, and popular genres are often blurred. Due to the per-

nuba   A suite of songs, in five movements in
   Morocco, each in one of five rhythmic
   modes performed in fixed order

rabab   Two-stringed fiddle in North Africa

'ud   Plucked lute with pear-shaped resonator

tar   Hand-held frame drum with attached
   cymbals

derbuka   Single-headed, goblet-shaped drum
   of North Africa

vasiveness of the media, some repertories once specific to particular villages or regions are now more widespread. Conversely, urban styles and instrumentation, with their special appeal to youth, increasingly influence the performance of traditional musics in rural communities. The distinctions between religious and secular genres are equally unclear, for the texts of many songs sung for secular purposes have religious content or sentiment, and some religious music collectively performed exhibits folk genre traits. Furthermore, some genres performed exclusively by traditional specialists at folk-life celebrations straddle the categories of folk and professional, and of religious and secular. Musical styles, subject matter, and performance practices continually interplay with the social contexts and histories that underlie and inform the musical cultures.

THE ARAB-ANDALUSIAN TRADITION

In A.D. 711, Arabs crossed the Mediterranean to conquer Spain (el-Andalus), beginning a period of Muslim rule on the Iberian Peninsula that endured for nearly eight hundred years. Arab music flourished at Córdoba, Seville, Granada, and other Andalusian cities. Though modeled on the seventh- to ninth-century music of the court of the Umayyad dynasty in Damascus and that of the early Abbasid dynasty in Baghdad, it soon developed a distinctly Andalusian character. The reconquest of Spain by the Christians, beginning in the 900s, resulted in the retreat of the Muslims to North Africa in three large migrations: Seville to Tunis (Tunisia) in the tenth to twelfth centuries, Córdoba to Tlemcen (Algeria) and Valencia to Fez (Morocco) in the twelfth, and Granada to Fez and Tetuan (Morocco) in the fifteenth. Andalusian music, stemming from diverse locations and periods, further evolved into regional Moroccan, Algerian, and Tunisian schools, each differing slightly in terminology, modal practice, theory, and repertory. The environment proved less favorable than the Andalusian to the cultivation of the arts, and much of the old music was subsequently lost; less than half the original repertory is presently known. Nevertheless, musicians regard the music they perform as a continuation of the Andalusian tradition.

Since independence (in the 1960s), Algerians and Tunisians have made efforts to revive old music, and to move it from an esoteric sphere into that of public education. Their movement has succeeded in stimulating interest among the younger generation. In 1972, a professional four-year program in Arab-Andalusian music, employing traditional oral methods of instruction, was established at the School of Music at Fez (Loopuyt 1988). Other schools throughout the Arab world offer programs directed toward the preservation and continuing development of the tradition.

The original Andalusian repertory consisted of twenty-four *nubat* (sing. *nuba*), each based on one of twenty-four melodic modes. A *nuba* in Moroccan tradition is a suite of songs (*sana'i*; sing. *san'a*) in five movements (*miyazen*; sing. *mizan*), each in one of five rhythmic modes performed in a fixed order. Each vocal movement follows an instrumental prelude. An Algerian *nuba* consists of nine alternating instrumental and vocal movements; the Tunisian counterpart, ten (Pacholczyk 1980:265–266). The meters and sequences differ in each of the schools. Essentially monophonic, the music contains no harmony other than an occasional drone accompaniment.

Though the music stems from oral tradition, the poetic texts come from literate sources. The principal poetic forms are the *qasida*, the *muwashshah*, and the *zajal*. The *qasida* is a solo improvisation of earlier Near Eastern tradition. The *muwashshah*, a court poetry, and *zajal*, a popular form, developed in Spain concurrently with the Andalusian *nuba*. Strophic texts with instrumental refrains are characteristic of *muwashshah* and *zajal*. The subject matter is romantic in its praise of human love, beauty, nature, and earthly pleasures. The texts of some *nubat*, notably "*Ramal al-Maya*," praise Muhammad and divine love. As many as forty poems may occur within a single movement of a *nuba*, which can last for more than an hour. A complete *nuba* is rarely heard; more common are abbreviated versions, or selected movements from several *nubat*.

The modal structure, vocal style, and phrasing characteristic of the Arab-Andalusian *nuba* are attributed to the legendary ninth-century musician and theorist Ziryab. Educated in Baghdad, and trained in Persian and Arab traditions, Ziryab brought to el-Andalus not only expertise in performing and teaching, but also a musicotherapeutic system, known as the "tree of modes," or the "tree of temperaments." The system was based on concepts then prevalent in Arab medicine: relationships between parts of the body and elements of earth and Heaven believed to underlie human physical and psychological states and behaviors. Ziryab's system, which he presented as a revelation rather than a theory, associated specific modes (*tubu'*; sing. *tab'*), with body organs (heart, liver, brain, spleen) and human temperaments (anger, calm, joy, sadness). The musical modes were further linked with natural elements (air, fire, water, earth), colors (red, yellow, white, black), and conditions (heat, cold, humidity, dryness). Ziryab's system contained twenty-four modes, one for each hour of the day; particular modes were performed at set hours. From this elaborate scheme evolved the rules on which the twenty-four *nubat* were constructed and performed.

Ziryab and his followers' concern with the cosmic and ethical qualities of music outlasted that of their Near Eastern counterparts, who, influenced by Greek theorists, became more occupied with modal analysis, an area of less concern in Andalusia and North Africa. Also, cultivation of the musical arts in Andalusia depended more on urban support, as the less powerful Andalusian courts were unable to provide the degree of patronage afforded artists and performers in the East. The Arab-Andalusian tradition thus evolved in more popular directions, with greater emphasis on composed orchestral and choral forms, and less on the solo improvisation favored in the Eastern courts (Pacholczyk 1976:3). Later performance practices in North Africa reinforced the divergence of the idiom from its Eastern source.

Male professionals perform Arab-Andalusian music, mainly for state functions and private celebrations for those who can afford the orchestra. The size of the ensemble varies according to the occasion, the patron's wishes, and regional custom. Normally included are a two-stringed fiddle (*rabab*), several violins or violas (sing. *kamanja*) held vertically on the knee, one or two four-stringed plucked lutes (sing. '*ud*), a hand-held frame drum with attached cymbals (*tar*), and a single-headed, goblet-shaped drum (*derbuka*). If the instrumentalists do not double as vocalists, the ensemble may also include one or two solo singers. The *rabab* is traditionally played by the leader, though its use has declined since the introduction of the violin (in the 1700s). In modern practice, it is often replaced by a violin, viola, or other melodic instrument. Since the 1930s, orchestras have grown in size to include as many as thirty or forty musicians (Saada n.d.:2). Doublings and additions of new instruments

Music occupies an ambiguous position in Muslim life. Since the beginning of Islam, Muslim authorities have disputed the question of whether music should be permitted in worship.

(such as mandolin, guitar, piano, and saxophone), with increased use of metal strings, equal temperament, and higher tunings, now produce qualities of sound unlike those of earlier ensembles (Saada n.d.:2; Schuyler 1984:17).

MUSIC AND ISLAM

The Muslim call to prayer (*adhan*), intoned five times daily, is a familiar sound in local towns and cities. Its style varies according to regional tradition and the personal style of the muezzin (*mu'adhdhin*), or caller. The calls range from stylized recitation on one or two tones to highly melismatic renditions based on specific melodic formulas (*maqamat*) of the Middle Eastern Arab tradition. Familiar, also, are the sounds of children intoning memorized verses from the Koran at neighborhood mosques and religious schools. Children are rewarded for precise and artful recitation, which may follow, depending on local custom, one of several established methods of Qur'ānic chant (Anderson 1971:154–155). The calls to prayer and the scriptural recitations are performed in Arabic, the language of the Qur'ān. Whether simply spoken or elaborately sung, they emphasize clarity of pronunciation and strict adherance to the rules of Arabic.

Music occupies an ambiguous position in Muslim life. Since the beginning of Islam, Muslim authorities have disputed the question of whether music should be permitted in worship. Because music, especially instrumental music, was associated with pagan practices and sensual entertainments, early authorities declared the act of listening to music "unworthy" of a Muslim. The debate continues. To avoid secular associations, references to music are usually avoided in mention of calls to prayer, Koranic recitations, and other forms of religious expression (Anderson:146–147). In some communities, music making of any kind—religious or secular—is discouraged in the name of Islam. A few forbid music altogether, as do members of the puritanical Mozabite sect of Algeria (Alport 1970:228, 234–235). Nevertheless, the sung praise of the Islamic deity is standard practice in most of the region.

The annual departure and return of pilgrims to Mecca (*hajj*), the beginning and ending of a journey every Muslim tries to make at least once, are occasions for singing religious songs. In the holy month of Ramadan, during which the faithful fast in the daylight hours, families sing religious songs as they gather for the evening or predawn meal. Special Ramadan songs also occur in street processions. Muhammad's birthday (*mawlid*) is celebrated with hymns of praise and epic songs depicting events in his life. The best known of these is *el-burda* 'the Prophet's mantle'. The religious music is mainly vocal, but instruments are used in certain contexts, as in the ceremonial Thursday evening proclamations of the holy day in Morocco, with trumpet (*nfir*) or oboe (*ghaita*) accompaniment. Pairs of oboes or trumpets, in ensemble with drums, such as the double-headed cylindrical types (*gangatan*; sing. *ganga*) played in Niger, herald the beginning and end of Ramadan.

Pre-Islamic beliefs and unorthodox practices of Sufi mystics have mingled with canonic precepts to produce a unique form of Islam, in which the veneration of saints (*marabutin*; sing. *marabut*) is a feature. The concept of saints as mediators between divinity and humanity, and as sources of good health and fortune, became a feature of Islamic worship in western North Africa after A.D. 1200. Religious brotherhoods (sing. *zawiya*) arose around legendary holy figures, often revered as patron saints or village founders. The activities of the brotherhoods center on small cupolaed mosques, which enclose the tombs of the saints. Some of these structures also contain facilities for lodging and teaching. Each year, thousands of worshipers make pilgrimages to the tombs of locally revered saints.

Hymns are regularly sung at the tombs. In Tunisia, canticles of praise are performed to the accompaniment of *mizwid* (bagpipe) and *bendir* (single-headed frame drum) (Erlanger 1937:9). In the Atlas Mountains of Morocco, Friday, the holy day, is celebrated weekly at the tomb with a procession of oboes and drums. The musicians, by virtue of their close identification with the saint, are believed to possess some of the holy man's spiritual power (*baraka*), enabling them to aid the sick and offer protection to the community (Schuyler 1983:60–64).

Featured in the rituals of the religious brotherhoods are songs and recitations of Sufi origin, known collectively as *zikr* (or *dhikr*), meaning "in recollection" of Allah. Though the *zikr* is usually sung in Arabic, vernaculars are occasionally used, as is the custom among the Berber Tuareg. Some practices include the repetition of raspy, guttural utterances on the syllable *he*. These increase in intensity, and lead the participants into states of trance (Rouget 1985:271–273).

On Muhammad's birthday or other occasions deemed appropriate, the *zikr* may be part of a larger ceremony known as *hadra*, a term meaning "in the presence of," with allusion to the supernatural. Though the *hadra* takes many forms, it typically includes special songs and rhythms, rigorous dancing, and altered states of consciousness. In trance, a participant may become possessed or may express emotional fervor with acts demonstrating extraordinary strength or oblivion to pain. In other instances, participants seek exorcism of unwanted spirits believed to be the cause of illness or misfortune (Rouget 1985:273–279; Saada 1986:46–48, 80–82). In Libya, where the *hadra* is a curing ceremony, a ritual specialist performs exorcisms to an accompaniment of songs and drums—a procedure that, if the illness is severe, may be repeated for seven days or more (El Miladi 1975:3–4). In Morocco, the music for the *hadra* is played on the *ghaita* and *tbel* (kettledrum) by professional musicians (Schuyler n.d.:2). In Algeria, use of melody instruments is rare (Saada n.d.:8–9). In the *hadra*, Islamic concepts of spirits (*jinn*), as described in the Qur'ān, merge with pre-Islamic beliefs and practices.

The Gnawa brotherhoods specialize in the manipulation of spirits, and are much in demand for exorcisms, curing rites, circumcision ceremonies, and purification rituals after funerals. Their ceremonies appear to consist mainly of a blend of Islamic and pre-Islamic black African beliefs and practices. Prominent is their use of the *qarqabu* (or *qarqaba*), an instrument, likely of Sudanic origin, found in Hausa communities in many parts of North Africa. It consists of two pairs of iron castanets, joined by a connecting bar; the player uses two of these instruments, one in each hand. The Gnawa also play a *gumbri*, a three-stringed plucked lute, known by different names to black musicians throughout North and West Africa. The possession and curing ceremonies of the Gnawa, in particular, resemble those of Sudanic practice, though cultural elements from other sources may also be present. At annual celebrations of the Tunisian Gnawa in honor of their patron saint, Sidi Marzuk, the ritual texts are sung in a language, *ajmi*, apparently neither of Arabic nor Berber derivation and unknown to the present participants (Laade 1962:4).

The Tuareg of Niger conduct curing ceremonies, known as *tende n-guma*, in

The pastoral Tuareg of Niger customarily hold weddings after summer rains, when they assemble their herds of camels on the plains near In-Gall—an event known as the *cure salée*.

which men's raspy, gutteral sounds, uttered on the syllable *he*, mingle with women's songs and the rhythms of a mortar drum (*tende*) and hand clapping. The men's vocal sounds are similar to those heard in performances of the *zikr*, to which they may be related. Sudanese Sufi orders practice an African form of *zikr*, in which repetitions of certain syllables, including the breathy *he*, appear to have replaced most of the original texts (Trimingham 1965:213–217). The Tuareg deny, however, that the curing ceremonies are religious. Secular songs are sung, though always in duple meter and in slower than normal tempo (about M.M. 75–96) to accommodate the swaying movements of entranced patients (a behavioral feature also of Sudanese *zikr*). Though local Muslim leaders denounce the rituals as pagan and contrary to the teachings of Islam, the Tuareg view them as psychotherapeutic, and exhibit no conflict between their concepts of a spirit-filled world and their Islamic faith. If these rituals once had religious associations, they are unknown.

MUSIC IN FOLK LIFE

Religious festivals, national holidays, and life cycle celebrations are major occasions for music making in folk life. The Muslim holidays, local saints' festivals, and political or national holidays are the most important annual events; weddings and circumcisions are the most celebrated moments of the life cycle.

Annual events

Muslim festivals follow a lunar calendar, containing about 354 days. Because of the shorter annual cycle, the religious holidays rotate through the seasons, arriving about eleven days earlier each year in contrast with the solar cycle. The religious observances normally contain no music, but the accompanying festivities are occasions for music and dance. On 'Aid el-Fitr (Id al-Fitr), the festival marking the end of Ramadan, the townspeople of Agadez, Niger, gather in the courtyard of the Sultan's palace to hear the ceremonial oboes and kettledrums (sing. *ettebel*) played by the court musicians. When this ceremony is completed, the musicians, mounted on horseback, lead the Sultan's parade through the streets of the city, playing the oboes and large cylindrical drums suspended from their shoulders. On the tenth day of the twelfth month occurs the feast of 'Aid el-Adha (also known as 'Aid-el-Kbir and Tafaski), which commemorates Abraham's sacrifice of a sheep in place of his son, at God's command. This holiday provides an occasion for Algerian Tuareg women to gather around a mortar drum to sing from a repertory of festival songs. The community crowds around them, emitting shouts and shrill cries of approval while clapping rhythms in synchrony or in hemiolic contrast with those of the drum. On Mawlid (the twelfth day of the third month), townspeople in Libya have musical gatherings and fireworks after the religious observances (El Miladi 1975:3–4).

Saints' festivals (*moussem* or *ziara*, sing.) are often linked to dates in the Muslim lunar calendar. The annual pilgrimage to the tomb of Mouley Abdallah in Tazruk, Algeria, occurs fifteen days after 'Aid el-Fitr (Saada 1986:50–51). In the Moroccan

Rif, the Aith Waryaghar make an annual pilgrimage to the tomb of Sidi Bu Khiyar on the day before 'Aid-el Adha (Hart 1970:4). Such events, which often draw thousands of people, typically last two days. In the hope of obtaining personal good health and fortune through exposure to the spiritual power of the saint and the holy area surrounding his tomb, people say prayers and perform rituals. Social reunions, feasting, and music follow the ritual observances.

Many of the saints' festivals follow a seasonal schedule, occurring regularly during the summer months. Some of them have an economic role and religious and social functions. The *moussem* of Imilchil in central Morocco, held annually at the autumnal equinox, attracts thousands of pilgrims to the tomb of Sidi Mohamed el-Merheni. After devotions, the participants turn to bartering goods and animals, performing music, dancing, and carrying on courtships (Bertrand 1977:115–127). *Tazz'unt*, a Berber festival in the Moroccan High Atlas, occurs on 31 July, in accordance with the Julian calendar (12 August by the Gregorian). Though the functions of the festival resemble those of a *moussem*, the event is limited to the inhabitants of neighboring villages who share bonds of lineage. The rituals performed are for the collective well-being of the community, rather than for individuals (Jouad and Lortat-Jacob 1978:50–60).

Political or patriotic celebrations follow a solar calendar. Each country in the region commemorates its independence and important historical moments with annual holidays featuring military parades and the singing of patriotic songs. Public presentations of regional music and dance that highlight the nation's ethnic heritage often have a part.

Life cycle celebrations

Weddings normally occur during favorable periods in agricultural or pastoral cycles, which govern the lives of the people. In the Moroccan Atlas, Berber weddings usually occur during the festival season in late summer, after the first harvest (Lortat-Jacob 1980:23). The pastoral Tuareg of Niger customarily hold weddings after summer rains, when they assemble their herds of camels on the plains near In-Gall—an event known as the *cure salée*.

The sequence of rituals constituting a traditional Muslim wedding gives rise to several kinds of music, some of it performed or led by professionals. Special wedding songs are sung by women to the bride and by men to the groom, seeking blessings on the union and instructing each in the duties of marriage. Ritual verses are sung, also, during the ceremonial application of henna to the bride's and groom's hands and feet. Professional praise singers extol the virtues of the couple and comment on the generosity of the guests. Musicians with tambourines, oboes or flutes, and drums—the sizes and shapes varying with local custom—lead the bride and groom in processions. Separate musical entertainments are provided for male and female guests. A professional bard may sing traditional poetry to the men on religious, heroic, or romantic themes, while female specialists lead the women in lively songs and dances to their accompaniment of hand-held drums or tambourines (Westermarck 1914, chapters 3–8; Jamous 1981:268–276).

Circumcision is regarded as a young boy's first step toward manhood. As a rite of passage, it is both a sacred and a festive occasion. Though the preferred age is four or five or younger, the event is often postponed because of the cost of the ceremony and attendant feast. To minimize expenses, several families with boys of an appropriate age may collaborate in a collective ceremony, or a family may choose to perform the rituals as part of a larger, annual festival. In Algerian tradition, the event consists of several stages: a ceremonial haircutting (*tahfifa*), attended by men only; a ritual application of henna and the bestowal of gifts, attended by women only; a ceremonial

The professional singer-poets, ritual specialists, praise singers, and instrumentalists are commonly members of hereditary musician clans or artisan castes who specialize in particular traditions.

feast for relatives and guests; and finally, the actual surgical operation. During the henna ritual, the women sing the child's praises, and exhort the nervous mother to be joyous and proud. Their songs and activities are interspersed with shrill ululations of approval. The henna ceremony concludes with singing, which may last for hours, of songs dedicated to Muhammad (Toualbi 1975:91–95). Moroccan village custom contains similar elements, but in a different order. The surgery, which precedes the feast, is announced with intermittent volleys of gunfire. During the operation, men recite prayers and women sing special ritual songs (*urar*), similar to those sung for marriage, but with other texts (Lortat-Jacob 1980:83–84). Ceremonies for circumcision may also include the services of Gnawa musicians, who perform special ritual songs and dances of mystical or magical significance.

Musical specialists

The professional singer-poets, ritual specialists, praise singers, and instrumentalists who perform at festivals and family celebrations are commonly members of hereditary musician clans or artisan castes who specialize in particular traditions. Gifted singer-poets were formerly attached to the courts of tribal chiefs or other persons of power and wealth. Their heroic ballads and songs of praise enhanced their patrons' status and imbued the surrounding community with a sense of shared history and identity. Though the patronage system has almost disappeared, the traditions and functions of praise and epic singing are perpetuated by musicians who perform at weddings, religious festivals, and private parties.

In Mauritania, professional, hereditary poet-musicians (*griots*) sing panegyric poetry to the accompaniment of an elongated four-stringed lute (*tidinit*), played by men, and a harp-lute (*ardin*), played by women. In addition, a large, hand-struck kettledrum (*tbel*), played by women, is occasionally used. The tradition is sometimes termed *classical*, as it demands not only instrumental virtuosity and a command of classical Arabic and Moorish poetry, but also mastery of an elaborate and complex body of theory. In Mali, Niger, and southern Algeria, Tuareg *griots* of the artisanal caste practice a related tradition. Known to the Tuareg as *aggutan*, they typically entertain at weddings, celebrations for births, and small, private parties. Their repertory similarly consists of heroic legends and praise poetry, sung to the accompaniment of the *tahardent*, a lute similar to the Mauritanian *tidinit*. Their tradition embraces a system of rhythms and modes, serving as the material for improvisation, and a set of rules (though less explicit than the Mauritanian) that govern composition and performance. In the late 1960s, the *tahardent* tradition of the Tuareg of Mali began spreading to urban centers throughout the Sahara.

Many musical specialists are itinerant. During the festival months of late summer, the *imdyazn*, professional musicians native to the eastern regions of Morocco, travel in small bands through the villages of the High Atlas. A typical group consists of a singer-poet and several accompanists, whose instruments include a double clarinet (*zammar*) or a flute (*talawat*), one or two frame drums (sing. *daf*), and an alto fiddle (*lkmnza*), similar to a European viola (Lortat-Jacob 1980:41–42). The *rways*, itinerant musicians from southern Morocco, wander throughout the country performing an acculturated music derived from Arab-Andalusian, European, Arab-popular, and West African styles. These musicians often perform at Djemma el Fna, the grand square in the heart of Marrakesh, which for centuries has been a center for traditional musical entertainments (Grame 1970:74).

For the sedentary performer, music is more often a part-time activity, supplemented by some other line of work, and payment for services is frequently in gifts, rather than in money. In this category are the women who as ritual specialists perform at weddings, births, and circumcisions. Some of them are also professional mourners and singers of funeral laments. In Morocco, female entertainers (*haddarat*) accompany their songs with *bendir, tbel*, and the clay cylindrical drum *ta'riya* (Chottin 1938:9–10). In Algeria, urban female professionals (*msam'at*) accompany their songs and dances with *derbuka* and *tar* (Saada n.d.:5). Tuareg singers, traditionally members of artisanal clans, employ small, double-headed, hand-held drums (*gangatan*; sing. *ganga*) or a kettledrum (in Algeria, *tegennewt*; in Niger, *tazawat*).

Poetry and song

Vocal music, except when used for dancing, functions primarily as a vehicle for poetry, a highly developed and esteemed art in North Africa. Frequent topics are love (always in allusive or idealized form) and current or historical events. The texts are interspersed with praises and evocations of Allah, or exclamations such as "O my soul!" or "O my mother!"; the singing of poetry is largely improvisatory. Singers much in demand are those who can set to a familiar melody a spontaneously composed, rhyming text, concerning persons and events of immediate interest. Equally in demand are singer-poets who draw their material from traditional lore, embellishing and adapting well-known themes to suit each occasion. From one performance to the next, however, songs for ritual purposes vary little in melody or text. In this category are the Berber *urar* (also *ural*) verses, sung usually by women at weddings and ceremonies for circumcisions (Lortat-Jacob 1980:51).

Topics pertaining to valor in battle, actual or allegorical, form an important part of the *tesîwit*, a repertory sung solo by pastoral Tuareg men. *Tisiwit* consists of strophic poems sung to formulaic melodies or motifs of corresponding rhythm. Though some texts are customarily sung to particular melodies, the poetry and music are essentially independent and do not form fixed units. The songs may be sung unaccompanied or with *imzad*, a bowed lute, played by Tuareg women. Without imitating the singer's style or synchronizing with the singer's melody, the instrumentalist reinforces the vocal line with a rendering of the same melody. Interludes between strophes provide instrumentalist opportunities for improvisation on the melodic material. Performances of *tesîwit* poetry with *imzad* by legendary artists of the past reached high levels of artistic achievement.

Songs for dancing belong to a separate category. Instruments, infrequently used with other vocal genres, hold an important role in dance music. They typically include the *bendir*, the *tabl*, and the *ghaita*. The texts, of secondary importance, usually consist of formulaic verses, often with ostinato or vocable responses.

The characteristics of song vary by territory, ethnic group, genre, and occasion. Melodies range from little-ornamented, repetitive forms, to complex and highly melismatic structures. Much of the regional character derives from the rhythms, which adhere closely to the meters of regional poetry. The repertories of village and nomadic Berbers are possibly the least acculturated of local traditions. Pentatonicism of various types is common, and melodic use of an augmented fourth above the tonic

The dance begins slowly, with barely perceptible steps, and builds to a climax, when a high-pitched ascending glide on the flute coincides with a sharp cry by the solo singer and a formulaic ostinato by the chorus.

is often prominent. Microtonicism in melodic structure and ornamentation occurs in Berber song, but is more characteristic of Arab styles. Though Arab song is similarly linked with poetry, it is less closely associated with dance. In Tunisia, Andalusian songs and customs have been preserved in the traditions of particular occupational groups, such as the fruit and vegetable merchants of Tunis (Erlanger 1937:10). The songs of the Gnawa, like those of black cultivators in the Sahara, make occasional use of thirds and fourths, intervals rarely heard in Arab or Berber music. Furthermore, the vocal styles and repertories characteristic of sedentary and nomadic groups often cut across regional and ethnic divisions. Agricultural and other types of work songs are prominent among sedentarists, while songs for caravans and ballads about warriors are characteristic of nomads. Within the same group, the vocal styles of men often differ from those of women (see Nikiprowetzky 1964:81–83).

Instrumental music

Instrumental music, played for the primary purpose of listening, is uncommon in the folk life of towns and villages. Instruments serve mainly for dances and ceremonial purposes, such as wedding processions and the proclamation of a holy day or the onset of Ramadan. Instrumental improvisations serve as interludes between verses sung by professional bards, but they are rarely performed apart from vocal contexts. It is principally in the traditions of pastoral groups that purely instrumental music has a prominent place.

FIGURE 1   Jima (Ajo) wult Emini plays an *imzad*. Agadez, Niger.

Music for solo flute is common among herdsmen and others in lonely occupations. An end-blown flute, held in oblique position, with finger holes arranged in two groups, is played by Arab shepherds in the Maghrib and Mauritania, and by Tuareg herders in Algeria and Niger. The Arab *gasba* (or *qasaba*), made of a hollow reed, has five or more finger holes; the four-hole *zaowzaya* of Mauritania is made from an acacia root or bark; the four-hole Tuareg *tazammart* (also *tasensigh* and *sarewa*) is made from a reed or a metal tube (Card 1982:63–65; Guignard 1975a:172; Nikiprowetzky 1961:6; Saada 1986:92–95). *Tazammart* players in the Algerian Sahara sometimes accompany their melodies with a vocal drone produced in the throat while blowing into and fingering the instrument; the drone functions as a pedal point to the melody. Flute music, though traditionally played for solitary pleasure or the entertainment of a few companions, is now heard by a wider audience through recordings and radio broadcasts of accomplished performers.

Another instrumental genre is the music for *imzad* played by Tuareg women (figure 1). The melodies for solo *imzad* belong to a genre apart from the vocal music accompanied by it. The chief purpose of this music was formerly to inspire men before combat and to honor heroes on their return. Played mainly by women of the dominant or "noble" caste, the *imzad* symbolized the values of the traditional society. The music also embodied Tuareg concepts of gallantry toward women; thus, the music of the *imzad* was a featured part of courtship. Though the *imzad* was less often heard after the 1980s, it retains an esteemed position in Tuareg musical culture. Its repertories are regional, closely associated with local persons and events. Its styles of playing differ by region: those of the Algerian Sahara are believed to be older than those of the southern and western areas. Instruments similar to it are found among neighboring peoples, but played by men, often to accompany the player's own singing.

The regional traditions often bear the imprint of a celebrated local performer, whose personal style has been much emulated. During the late 1900s, the scope of such influence increased, in town and country, with the availability of cassette recordings (Card 1982:102–109). The result is a reduction in local musical activity. The trend toward homogeneity is constrained, however, by the strength of tradition.

Dance

The most widely known Berber dances of Morocco are the *ahidus* (also *haidous*) of the middle and eastern High Atlas, and the *ahwash* of the western High Atlas. The dancers stand shoulder to shoulder in a circle, or in two incurved, facing lines. The musicians, who both accompany and direct the dances, stand in the center. Musicians for the *ahidu*s include a singer-poet (*ammessad*), one or more assisting singers, and drummers with instruments of diverse sizes and pitches. The rhythms, which include solo improvisations, are frequently in quintuple meter. The songs (*izlan*, sing. *izli*) contain short verses with choral responses, sung to melodies composed of small intervals within a narrow range (Chottin 1938:5–6; Jouad and Lortat-Jacob 1978:86; Lortat-Jacob 1980:68–69). The structure of the *ahwash* is more complex. The drumming begins slowly, in duple or quadruple meter, but is transformed at midpoint into a rapid, asymmetric rhythm. The songs, sung to pentatonic melodies, consist of two-line verses, exchanged between the men and women. The *ahwash*, involving an entire village, is a highlight of festivals. Care is lavished on a performance, for its quality is said to determine the success or failure of the festival (Lortat-Jacob 1980:65–70, 120–124). Another Moroccan Berber dance is the *tamghra*, specific to weddings. To a men's accompaniment of *bendir*, it is performed for or by the bride and her attendants. The rhythms are similar to those of *ahidus*, but include no solo improvisations (Jouad and Lortat-Jacob 1978:86; Lortat-Jacob 1980:124–125).

Some dances are specific to particular villages or areas. An example is the *ahelli*, a nocturnal festival dance unique to Gourara, Algeria. It features the use of a six-hole wooden flute (*temja*). Standing in close formation, the dancers encircle the flutist, a solo singer, and several dance leaders. An introductory flute prelude sets the pitch for a drone, hummed by the dancers. An additional prelude precedes each of a series of songs with choral responses, sung in a high vocal register. The dance begins slowly, with barely perceptible steps, and builds to a climax, when a high-pitched ascending glide on the flute coincides with a sharp cry by the solo singer and a formulaic ostinato by the chorus (Augier 1972:307–309; Saada n.d.:8). Another example is the *guedra*, performed at Goulimine and certain oases in the Bani area of southern Morocco. The principal solo dancer begins on her knees, and as the encircling musicians gradually quicken the tempo, rises to her feet. The dance takes its name from a pottery drum used in accompaniment (Sheridan 1967:45).

Dances of the same name often assume different regional forms. The *sa'dawi* of Tunisia is a scarf dance, usually performed by women, featuring rhythmic movements of the hips and undulating gestures with a hand-held scarf. The dance is accompanied by a large kettledrum, *tbel*, and a mouth-blown bagpipe, *zukra*

The Arab *fantaziya* (or fantasy) of the Maghrib is a choreographed spectacle involving horses and men. To an accompaniment of drums, mounted riders armed with swords maneuver and race their horses.

(Erlanger 1937:9). Among the Ouled Naïl of Algeria, this dance involves both men and women. The men, armed with rifles, fire intermittent salvos above the heads of the women, who with small steps leap and turn (Saada n.d.:5).

Movements emulating the gestures of battle are a part of many local dances. Some dances incorporate religious elements. Popular is the gun dance (*baroud*, also *berzana*), of which variants occur throughout the region. In the Algerian form, male dancers armed with loaded muskets arrange themselves in a circle or in facing lines. The dancers turn shoulder against shoulder, taking small steps as they respond to the melody of the *ghaita* and rhythms of the *qallal* or *dendun*. Alternating vocal soloists chant invocations of Muhammad in the form of brief couplets with choral responses. On cue, the participants point their muskets to the earth and fire in synchrony, bringing the dance to a noisy, smoky climax. The gun dance is performed at any time (Augier 1972:305–306; Pottier 1950:120, 122; Saada n.d.:7).

Similar dances are performed with swords and sticks. In the *zagara*, a Tunisian saber dance, men perform in pairs. Each brandishes a sword in the right hand, while making shielding motions with the left. The dance has the accompaniment of *zukra* and *tbel* (Erlanger 1937:9). Stick dances in imitation of swordplay, said to be of ancient origin, are often a part of saints' festivals and other large celebrations. In the Algerian Sahara, men perform the *'lawi* dance with large sticks or batons. As they weave past one another in response to the orders of a leader, they strike their batons in intricate patterns. Musicians accompany the dance with kettledrums, tambourines, vase-shaped pottery drums, and double-headed cylindrical drums, which impart variety of pitch and timbre to intricate hemiolic interchanges of duple and ternary rhythms.

The *sebiba*, unique to the oasis of Djanet in southeastern Algeria, is a choreographed spectacle that once a year or more involves the entire town. The origins of the event are obscured in conflicting legends. Costumed inhabitants of opposite sectors of the town, representing rival lineages, engage in stylized battle. The musicians and dance leaders are women, who play small drums (sing. *tobol*) struck with curved beaters (sing. *takurbat*). Any woman who can play a drum may participate. Two columns of women in close formation, each with its leader and followed by dancers, follow a circular path, which defines the arena. The participants, their number limited only by the availability of costumes, form two circles. Armed with mock lances and mock swords, they begin the gyrations of the dance. Incited by the leaders and encouraged by the songs, claps, shouts, and shrill cries of the spectators, the dancers continue for hours. The ensuing revelry continues throughout the night (Gay 1935:61–66; Pottier 1950:161–165).

Dance in North Africa is not limited to human beings (figure 2). The Arab *fantaziya* (or fantasy) of the Maghrib is a choreographed spectacle involving horses and men. To an accompaniment of drums, mounted riders armed with swords maneuver and race their horses. The maneuvers culminate in elaborate displays of horseman-

FIGURE 2   Tuareg camel parade at a festival. Ahaggar region of Algeria.

ship and swordplay. The *fantaziya* symbolically reenacts battles waged by the warriors who carried the "sword of Islam" to establish the Muslim Empire in North Africa (Saada n.d.:5). A similar spectacle, involving camels, is the Tuareg *ilugan* (or *ilujan*), sometimes termed a "camel fantasy." To an accompaniment of women's *tende* singing and drumming, the camels, under the direction of their riders, perform a series of stylized movements. The rhythms of the women's songs, usually in duple meter with ternary subdivisions, are said to imitate the gait of the camels. The warrior elements, infused with Tuareg concepts of gallantry, often lead to flirtatious exchanges between the men and the women. Though *ilugan* is an important part of Tuareg weddings, it is occasionally performed also at saints' festivals and other large gatherings (Blanguernon 1955:115; Nicolaisen 1963:104–105; Saada 1986:55–56, 59).

POPULAR MUSIC

The rapid growth of the media in the early 1900s spurred development of new genres and hybrid styles. The recording industry, present in North Africa as early as 1910, promoted widespread dissemination of regional and foreign styles (Danielson 1988:160). Young urban composers and singers, infused with nationalist spirit, began to turn to regional repertories for material and inspiration. The attraction of modern styles from the Middle East and Europe led them to experiment with foreign tonalities, instruments, and methods of arranging.

The Arab-Andalusian repertories provided further material. Popularized versions of the classic repertory were in evidence early in the century. In 1913 on a visit to Biskra, Algeria, Béla Bartók documented simplified renditions of *nubat* (1920: 489–501). Continuing popularization of this music produced genres that adhere in varying degrees to the classical models. Citing Algerian examples, Saada identifies several levels of transformation from Arab-Andalusian music to popular urban versions. *Arabi*, a music consisting of poems sung in local dialects to well-known classical melodies, resembles traditional sources, but adheres less strictly to the rules of classical composition. Departing further from the tradition is *hawzi*, a genre popular in the Tell region, consisting of love poems sung in the regional dialect to highly simplified versions of Arab-Andalusian melodies; its singers are usually men. Representing a third step is *sha'bi*, a music widely popular throughout the Maghrib, containing a blend of Arab-Andalusian formal elements and nonclassical rhythms, accents, ornaments, and harmony. Foreign instruments (such as guitar, organ, accordion) are commonly used. The texts, which contain topical, down-to-earth subject

In the 1980s, a cabaret music, *rai*, derived from bedouin Arab recitations, emerged in northern Algeria.

matter, are often sung in common street dialect. Finally, a music of more remote derivation is *zendani*, played and sung by urban female professionals who entertain in small groups at family festivals. The songs, consisting of strophic love poems sung to melodies accompanied by *derbuka* and *tar*, are performed for dancing (Saada n.d.:4–5).

A modern Moroccan music, *azri*, rooted in Middle Eastern traditions but influenced by others, first gained popularity in the early days of radio, when broadcasts of urban music from the Middle East began to reach the Maghrib. Composers of *azri* draw from many sources, including Moroccan, European, and American traditions. Western influence is evident mainly in the instrumentation, and in the occasional use of diatonic intervals imposed by such instruments as piano and organ (Schuyler 1977:n.p.).

In the late 1960s, *tahardent* music of the Malian Tuareg began to move eastward with the migration of drought refugees into Niger (figure 3). Among the migrants were artisanal specialists, *aggutan*, whose former patrons could no longer support them. Finding little success in singing Tuareg legends of Mali to mixed urban audiences in Niger, they quickly turned their talents to more marketable material. Most successful was the setting of new strophic texts with romantic and risqué themes to

FIGURE 3   Hattaye ag Muhammed Ahmed plays a *tahardent* left-handed. Agadez, Niger.

takumba, an existing rhythmic-modal formula of Malian origin. Many *aggutan* further augmented their opportunities by learning to sing in several local languages. The instrumental interludes between strophes, a traditional practice, provided attractive displays of virtuosity with appeal to urban audiences. Astute performers emphasized particular stylistic elements common to several related traditions, thus making their music more accessible to audiences of diverse ethnic backgrounds. Itinerant musicians gradually carried the music across Niger into southern Algeria. Though verses of heroism and praise continue to be sung for those who request them, *takumba* and its stylistic successors are the mainstay of modern Tuareg professionals (Card 1982:161–182).

In the 1970s, a hybrid music emerged in Morocco, derived from Arab, Berber, and Gnawa sources, mingled with Western elements. The music was begun by urban youths concerned both with the preservation and modernization of Morocco's traditional musics (Danielson 1988:160). Spurred by the Moroccans, youths in western Algeria initiated a similar movement. Simultaneously, a modern music rooted in the traditions of the Kabyle region spread throughout Algeria. In the 1980s, a cabaret music, *rai*, derived from bedouin Arab recitations, emerged in northern Algeria. At first denounced because of its sensual texts, *rai* became accepted as an expression of the yearnings and sufferings of modern youth (Saada n.d.:10). In the 1990s, recordings included trumpet, accordion, guitar, keyboards, and rhythm instruments.

REFERENCES

Alport, E. A. 1970. "The Mzab (Algeria)." In *Peoples and Cultures of the Middle East*, ed. Louise E. Sweet. New York: Natural History Press.

Anderson, Lois Ann. 1971. "The Interrelation of African and Arab Musics: Some Preliminary Considerations." In *Essays in Music and History in Africa*, ed. Klaus P. Wachsmann, 143–169. Evanston, Ill.: Northwestern University Press.

Augier, Pierre. 1972. "Ethnomusicologie saharienne: les documents sonores recueillis récemment en Ahaggar et au Gourara." *Libyca* 20:291–311.

Balandier, G., and P. Mercier. 1952. "Notes sur les théories musicales maures à propos de chants enregistrés." *Reports of International Conference of West Africanists*, II, Bissau, 1947 (Lisbon: Ministério das Colónias, Junta de Investigações Coloniais), V, pp. 137–191.

Bartók, Béla. 1920. "Die Volksmusik der Araber von Biskra und Umgebung." *Zeitschrift für Musikwissenschaft* 2:489–501.

Bertrand, A. 1977. *Tribus Berberes du Haut Atlas.* N.p.: Vilo.

Blanguernon, Claude. 1955. *Le Hoggar.* Paris: Arthaud.

Card, Caroline. 1982. "Tuareg Music and Social Identity." Ph.D. dissertation, Indiana University.

Chottin, Alexis. 1938. *Tableau de la musique marocaine.* Paris: Geuthner.

———. 1948. "Les visages de la musique marocaine." In *Maroc: Encyclopédie coloniale et maritime,* ed. E. Guernier, 543–560. Paris: Editions de l'Empire français.

Danielson, Virginia. 1988. "The Arab Middle East." In *Popular Musics of the Non-Western World,* ed. Peter Manuel, 141–160. New York: Oxford University Press.

Duvelle, Charles. 1966. *Musique maure.* OCORA, OCR 28. LP disk.

El Miladi, Salem. 1975. "Music and Magic in Year Cycle Rites in Libya." Unpublished manuscript.

Erlanger, Rodolphe de. 1937. *Mélodies tunisiennes.* Paris: Librairie orientaliste Paul Geuthner.

Gay, Le Capitaine. 1935. "Sur la Sébiba." *Journal de la Société des Africanistes* 5:61–66.

Grame, Theodore. 1970. "Music in the Jma al-Fna of Marrakesh, Morocco." *Music Quarterly* 56: 74–87.

Greenberg, Joseph. 1966. *The Languages of Africa.* Bloomington: Indiana University Press.

Guignard, Michel. 1975a. *Musique, honneur, et plaisir au Sahara.* Paris: Geuthner.

———. 1975b. *Mauritanie: Musique traditionnelle des griots maures.* SELAF/ORSTOM Collection Tradition Orale. ORSTOM CETO 752–3. 2 LP disks.

Hart, David Montgomery. 1970. "Clan, Lineage, Local Community and the Feud in a Rifian Tribe [Aith Waryaghar, Morocco]." In *Peoples and Cultures of the Middle East*, vol. 2, ed. Louise E. Sweet, 3– 75. Garden City, N.Y.: Natural History Press.

———. 1976. *The Aith Waryaghar of the Moroccan Rif: An Ethnography and History.* Tucson: University of Arizona Press.

Jamous, Raymond. 1981. *Honneur et baraka: Les structures sociales traditionnelles dans le Rif.* London: Cambridge University Press.

Jouad, Hassan, and Bernard Lortat-Jacob. 1978. *La saison des fêtes dans une vallée du Haut-Atlas.* Paris: Seuil.

Laade, Wolfgang. 1962. *Tunisia*, vol. 2, "Religious Songs and Cantillations." Folkways FW 8862. LP disk.

Loopuyt, Marc. 1988. "L'enseignement de la musique arabo-andalouse à Fes." *Cahiers de musiques traditionnelles* 1:39–45.

Lortat-Jacob, Bernard. 1980. *Musique et fêtes au Haut-Atlas.* Paris: Ecole des Hautes Etudes en Sciences Sociales.

Murdock, George Peter. 1959. *Africa: Its People and Their Culture History.* New York: McGraw-Hill.

Nicolaisen, Johannes. 1963. *Ecology and Culture of the Pastoral Tuareg.* Copenhagen: National Museum.

Nikiprowetzky, Tolia. 1961. *La musique de la Mauritanie.* Paris: Radiodiffusion Outre- Mer Sorafom.

———. 1964. "L'ornémentation dans la musique des Touareg de l'Aïr." *Journal of the International Folk Music Council* 16:81–83.

Pacholczyk, Jozef M. 1976. *Andalusian Music of Morocco.* Ethnodisc ER 45154. LP disk.

———. 1980. "Secular Classical Music in the Arabic Near East." In *Music of Many Cultures*, ed. Elizabeth May, 253–268. Berkeley: University of California Press.

Pottier, René. 1950. *Le Sahara.* Paris: Arthaud.

Rouget, Gilbert. 1985. *Music and Trance: A Theory of the Relations between Music and Possession.* Chicago: University of Chicago Press.

Saada, Nadia Mécheri. 1986. "La musique de l'Ahaggar." Ph.D. dissertation, University of Paris.

———. N.d. "La musique d'Algérie." Unpublished manuscript.

Schuyler, Philip. 1983. "The Master Musicians of Jahjouka." *Natural History*, October, 60–69.

———. 1984. "Moroccan Andalusian Music." In *Maqam: Music of the Islamic World and its Influences*, ed. Robert H. Browning, 14–17. New York: Alternative Museum.

———. 1977. *Morocco: The Arabic Tradition in Moroccan Music.* EMI Odeon 3C 064-18264. LP disk.

———. N.d. *The Music of Islam and Sufism in Morocco.* Bärenreiter-Musicaphon BM 30 SL 2027. LP disk.

Sheridan, Noel. 1967. *Morocco in Pictures.* New York: Sterling Publishing.

Toualdi, Noureddine. 1975. *La circoncision: blessure narcissique ou promotion sociale.* Alger: Sociétée Nationale D'Edition et de Diffusion.

Trimingham, John Spencer. 1965. *Islam in the Sudan.* London: Frank Cass.

Wendt, Caroline Card. 1994. "Regional Style in Tuareg *Anzad* Music." In *To the Four Corners*, ed. Ellen Leichtman. Warren, Michigan: Harmonie Park Press.

Westermarck, Edward. 1914. *Marriage Ceremonies in Morocco.* London: Macmillan.

Tuareg Music
Caroline Card Wendt

The Musical Culture
The *Anzad*
The *Tende*
Musical Curing Ceremonies
The *Tahardent*
Other Instruments
Other Vocal Genres
Dance Traditions

For more than a thousand years, Saharan travelers have reported encounters with the Tuareg people. From the pens of Arab and European explorers come tales of tall, veiled, camel-riding warriors who once commanded the trade routes from the Mediterranean to sub-Saharan Africa. Most of the reports dwell on the appearance and ferocity of the warriors, but those who looked more closely noted distinctive cultural traits, such as matrilineal kinship and high status among unveiled women, rarities in the Muslim world. As Saharan travel became easier, observers from many backgrounds—missionaries, militaries, colonial administrators, traders, scholars, tourists—ventured among the Tuareg and reported their findings. The result is a large, varied, and often contradictory, body of literature.

The name *Tuareg*, a term outsiders conferred on the people, suggests a sociopolitical unity that has probably never existed. The people constitute eight large units or confederations, each composed of peoples and tribal groups with varying degrees of autonomy. These groups and their locations are: Kel Ahaggar (Ahaggar mountains and surrounding area in southern Algeria, southward to the plains of Tamesna in northern Niger); Kel Ajjer (Tassili n-Ajjer region of southeastern Algeria, eastward into southwestern Libya); Kel Aïr (Aïr mountains of northern Niger, and plains to the west and south); Kel Geres (southern Niger, south of Aïr); Kel Adrar (Adrar n-Foras mountains of Mali, southwest of Ahaggar); Iwllimmedan Kel Dennek, or "eastern Iwllimmedan" (plains between Tawa and In-Gal in western Niger); Iwllimmedan Kel Ataram, or "western Iwllimmedan" (along the Niger River, southwestern Niger); Kel Tademaket (along the bend of the Niger River, between Timbuktu and Gao, Mali). The word *Kel* denotes sovereign status.

Censuses, like much other information on the Tuareg, show little agreement. In addition to the difficulties of conducting a census in the Sahara is the question of Tuareg identity. Lloyd Cabot Briggs dealt with the problem by limiting his work to an estimated ten to twelve thousand Tuareg in the "Sahara proper," excluding large numbers in the south, whom he regarded as assimilated in varying degrees with sub-Saharan peoples and thus not "true Tuareg" (Briggs 1960:124). Most surveys, however, have included the southern Tuareg: Francis Nicolas estimated the population at 500,000 (1950:foreword, n.p.), Henri Lhote at 300,000 (1955:157), and George

Peter Murdock at 286,000 (1959:405–406). The differences in these and other estimates arise in part from divergent opinions on whom to count. Some observers regarded as "true" Tuareg only the camel-herding warrior-nomads (*imuhagh, imajaghan, imushagh*), often called nobles, who formerly held the dominant position within the social hierarchy. More commonly, scholars have included the subordinate goatherds (*imghad,* or Kel Ulli), sometimes called vassals, who physically and culturally resemble the dominant Caucasoid Tuareg. Only occasionally have observers paid attention to the artisans (*inadan*), including those specializing in music, whose origins are uncertain and whose social position is often ambiguous. Not until late in the 1900s did the designation *Tuareg* extend to Negroid agricultural and domestic workers, descendants of formerly subjugated peoples, who live among or in association with the pastoral Tuareg, sharing their language, identity, and many aspects of culture. Late-twentieth-century governmental estimates of the population, reflecting an official emphasis on national unity, usually ignore ethnic divisions, and therefore offer few specific data on the Tuareg and other minorities.

The question of identity is further compounded by regional differences in self-designated terms. The regional cognates *imuhagh, imajaran,* and *imushagh,* for example, vary as to whom they include (Card 1982:30–34). Tuareg musical traditions and other cultural traits vary by region. The dialects of the Berber language spoken by the Tuareg—*tamahaq* (north), *tamajag* (south), *tamashaq* (west)—are sufficiently different as to be mutually unintelligible to many speakers.

Countering the cultural diversity is the cohesion generated by a set of ancient ideals and values flowing from the nomadic traditions that form the society's cultural core. The heroic images reach outward from their source, endowing on all within their sphere a shared identity and the legacy of a glorious past. The perseverance of the Tuareg as a people has been due less, perhaps, to the prowess of its warriors than to the ability of the dominant group to impose its culture on others. Thus, Tuareg identity endures, only slightly diminished by the cessation of warfare and raiding, economic hardship, and loss of sovereignty. Ancient values, expressed in modified forms, continue to give Tuareg culture its character.

THE MUSICAL CULTURE

Music occupies a prominent position in the social, political, and ceremonial life of the Tuareg. It plays an important role in celebrations of birth, adulthood, and marriage, and in religious festivals, customs of courtship, and rituals of curing. It is the focus of many informal social gatherings. Tuareg music and poetry are well developed arts: some traditions reach far into the cultural past. The Tuareg highly esteem the verbal arts, of which they consider music an extension; and they recognize and respect outstanding composers and performers. They look down on professionalism, in the sense of a livelihood earned from musical performance; it is limited to specialized members within the artisanal caste. Musical ability, however, wherever it emerges, does not go unrecognized, and the people much admire skillful musicians of all social ranks.

Most Tuareg music is vocal; but much includes instruments, primarily a one-stringed fiddle (*anzad*), a mortar drum (*tende*), and a three-stringed plucked lute (*tahardent*). Though few in kind and number, these instruments have greater cultural significance than their quantity might suggest, for each has an association with specific poetic genres and styles of performance, and each serves as the focal point of particular social events.

THE *ANZAD*

The one-stringed fiddle (*imzad* in northern dialect, *anzad* in southern, *anzhad* in western), played only by women, is basic to the traditional culture. Its use has

anzad   One-stringed fiddle of the Tuareg,
          played by women

ahal   A courtship gathering that features love
         songs, poetical recitations, jokes, and
         games of wit

declined markedly since about 1900, but it continues to enjoy a symbolic place in the culture. The Tuareg have long believed it a mighty force for good, a power capable of giving strength to men and of inspiring them to heroic deeds. Its playing formerly encouraged men in battle and ensured their safe return; in the late 1900s, women play it, though much less often, for the benefit of men working or studying in distant places. For all Tuareg listeners, its music evokes images of love and beauty. Charles de Foucauld, foremost among early Tuareg scholars and field workers, eloquently summarizes Tuareg feelings about it:

> The *imzad* is the favored musical instrument, preeminently noble and elegant; it is preferred above all others, sung of in verse, and yearned for by those absent from the land it symbolizes and the sweetness it recalls. (Foucauld 1951–1952, trans.)

Much of its power was in reality the power of the women who played it. Tuareg society required repeated recognition of heroic acts, and constant revalidation of the behavioral ideals that motivated them; its melodies and accompanying songs of praise were a potent force toward that end. In 1864, warriors in combat strove always to act courageously, lest their women deprive them of music: the prospect of silent fiddles on their return renewed their courage in the face of defeat (Duvéyrier 1864:450; see also Lhote 1955:329).

To play the *anzad* well requires years of practice. The Tuareg say a woman cannot acquire the necessary skill under the age of about thirty. Formerly, a mature woman of talent and imagination could command respect, and if she combined these endowments with noble lineage, she would enjoy high status. Tuareg women of all social levels have been known to play the instrument, but it was mainly those of the camel-herding warrior aristocracy with slaves to attend them who had the leisure to learn to play the instrument well. In the early 1900s, during the economic decline that followed a defeat by the French and the abolition of slavery, most women of noble lineage lost this advantage over their lower-born sisters; and consequently, the number of highly accomplished fiddlers diminished. The end of warfare as a noble occupation probably reduced some of the incentive to play, for the Tuareg look upon most types of modern work as degrading and little worthy of celebration in music and poetry.

In addition to its significance in the ethos of warfare, the *anzad* symbolizes youthfulness and romantic love. Musical evenings with it usually continue to function as occasions for unattached young people's courting. An *ahal* 'courtship gathering' features love songs, poetical recitations, jokes, and games of wit. Presiding over the event is an *anzad* player, whose renown may attract visitors from far away. So closely associated is the *anzad* with the *ahal* that "the name of one brings to mind the other." Attendance at an *ahal* carries no shame, but discretion requires that young people not mention the word *ahal* in the presence of their elders. For similar reasons, they must speak the word *anzad* discreetly (Foucauld 1951–1952:1270–71).

For religious leaders among the Tuareg, who are mostly Muslim, the *anzad* distracts the mind from thoughts of Allah and the teachings of Muhammad. They claim it aggrandizes the position of women and encourages licentious behavior. Worse, the mystical powers they believe the instrument and its music contain do not derive from their scriptures, but hark back to animistic beliefs. They therefore discourage fiddling; in some communities, they forbid it. Responding to the demands of fundamentalist movements, some elders who played the fiddle in their youth have voluntarily put it aside. Instead of claiming the celebrated role of musical and social leader that might once have been theirs, they have chosen a more submissive and pious role. For centuries, the preservation of Tuareg culture has rested with women, whose undisputed authority on cultural matters was enough to counteract most outside influences. The undermining of that authority thus threatens, not only the *anzad* tradition, but the continuity of all Tuareg traditions.

According to context and point of view, the *anzad* has diverse meanings. It symbolizes intellectual and spiritual purity and traditional behavioral ideals. It connotes gallantry, love, sensuousness, and youth. It evokes images of a distant, pre-Islamic past. The traditions surrounding it reflect the high status of Tuareg women, unusual in the Muslim world. Yet within this diversity there is no contradiction: the *anzad* is a multifaceted symbol of Tuareg culture and identity.

Techniques of construction and playing

The *anzad* is a one-stringed bowed lute, commonly found among West African peoples (DjeDje 1980:1–8). The name, glossable as 'hair', refers to the substance of the string. The body of the instrument is a hollow gourd 25 to 40 centimeters in diameter, cut to form a bowl. Tightly stretched leather, usually goatskin, covers the opening; lacings usually attach it to the gourd. A slender stick, inserted under the leather top at opposite edges, extends 30 to 36 centimeters beyond the body on one side, and serves as a neck. One or two large sound holes—the number varying with local tradition—are cut into the leather near the perimeter of the gourd. The string, formed of about forty strands of horsehair, is attached at each end of the inserted stick. Short twigs, crossed and bound with leather, positioned beneath the string near the center of the skin surface, form a bridge. As the string tightens, the neck arches forward. The bow consists of a slender stick, held in an arc by the tension of the attached hair. To improve contact, people rub resin on both bow hair and string. In the northern regions, people often finger-paint the fiddle and the bow with colorful geometric designs; such decoration is rare in the south, though some instruments sport ornamental leather fringes. Players tune the instrument by moving a leather strip that binds the string to the neck near the tip, thereby adjusting the length of the vibrating portion of the string. Players vary in choosing a pitch for tuning the string; but from one performance to another, a player's pitches are consistent.

The player sits, holding the fiddle in her lap with the neck in her left hand. Rarely during the performance of a single piece does she change the position of her hand, though she may do so in preparation for another piece, using her thumb as a stop to effect a new tuning without changing the tension of the string. She fingers the string with a light touch. (Women do not try to press the string to the neck, which does not function as a fingerboard.) By extension of the little finger, the performer can readily gain access to the secondary harmonic, which sounds an octave above the open string. A few performers employ additional harmonics. By exerting light pressure on the string, they produce brilliant tones, and can increase the pitch

Many Tuareg think the *anzad* originated in Ahaggar, the northernmost Tuareg region, now a part of Algeria; and it undoubtedly has deep roots in the region's warrior traditions.

range beyond an octave. The result is a rich musical texture, a kaleidoscope of tone colors.

To exploit the instrument's imitative possibilities, a skillful fiddler may vary the speed and length of the bow strokes. Slow strokes combined with rapidly fingered notes can suggest a melismatic singing style, and short strokes paired with single notes can produce a syllabic effect. Short, light strokes coupled with harmonics may simulate the tones of a flute; rapid use of the bow in tremolo style may depict animals in flight; halting, interrupted strokes may portray a limping straggler. Storytellers use these techniques, which can support a singer's text or vocal style.

Music for solo *anzad*

The *anzad* is both a solo instrument and an accompaniment for voice. Though performers occasionally play vocal melodies as instrumental pieces, the melodies they most often perform as solos are airs (*azel*; pl. *izlan*), composed specifically for the instrument.

The styles of playing and composing for the *anzad* exhibit distinctive regional characteristics. Many Tuareg think the instrument originated in Ahaggar, the northernmost Tuareg region, now a part of Algeria; and it undoubtedly has deep roots in the region's warrior traditions. The music, often called old style, exhibits distinctive traits from an earlier period, traceable at least to the 1920s. During much of the twentieth century, to a degree not found among other groups, the Ahaggar Tuareg guarded their musical traditions against change. Domination by the French, which began about 1900, evoked a highly conservative response from the Ahaggar Tuareg— a response later intensified by opposition from the colonial government. In 1962, after Algeria attained independence, exposure to different political ideologies, educational policies, and national media intensified cultural differences between the Ahaggar Tuareg and their southern kinfolk. The division of the Tuareg into separate nationalities thus reinforced the cultural isolation of the Ahaggar Tuareg and encouraged the conservation of older musical traits and repertory (Card 1982:85–97).

Characteristic of the Ahaggar style of composition for the fiddle is a formulaic structure. Short melodic formulas, or motifs, are linked together in phrases of varying lengths. A typical unit consists of a rapid cluster of tones centered on one or more pitches. The basic unit may be further elaborated with acciaccaturas, mordents, turns, and other ornaments. Many of the melodies structured in this manner, such as "*Tihadanaran*" (figure 1), have become fixed in the repertory, with minimal variation. In Ahaggar style, rhythm is usually subordinate to melody; in many compositions, the pulse is difficult to discern.

In tribute to an old tradition that has continued to grow and change, the Tuareg describe *anzad* music in the Aïr region of Niger as "a still-flowering plant." Though French domination brought an end to traditional fighting there (as it had in Ahaggar), it did not evoke the same reactionary response. The features that distinguish the Aïr style from that of Ahaggar are due largely to individual variation, a vital part of the old *anzad* tradition that has continued to thrive in Aïr. As in Ahaggar style, rhythm is subordinate to melody, and is based on formulaic motifs; however, the units join more smoothly, to the extent that it is often more difficult to determine where one ends and another begins. The phrases tend to have simpler structures, with less profuse ornamentation. Notable, too, are long phrases of original or developed material, particularly in recent compositions. Newer pieces are often through composed, in contrast to older compositions. In general, people more readily accept musical innovations in Aïr than in Ahaggar.

In marked contrast is the rhythmic style of Azawagh, a region of Niger west of Aïr. There, *anzad* music has strongly accented rhythms, metric melody, short phrases, and regularly recurring pulses. Though the music is constructed of formulaic material, the melodic elements, unlike those of Aïr and Ahaggar, are subordinate to rhythm. Performance often has an accompaniment of hand clapping, and sometimes of dancing; both rarely occur in connection with *anzad* music elsewhere. The distinctive style and performance practices of the *anzad* tradition in Azawagh suggest an unusual degree of acculturation has occurred between the pastoral Tuareg and the region's Sudanese peoples, of whom many are former Tuareg captives or clients. In the music of other Tuareg regions, evidence of acculturation turns up, but it is more pronounced in Azawagh.

The styles discussed are but three of many regional traditions. Traits characteristic of one area often appear in another. Interregional borrowing of repertories and genres has long been a part of the *anzad* tradition.

Anzad n-asak: music for fiddle and voice

A large portion of the *anzad* repertory is designed for performance with voice. When accompanying a vocalist, the fiddler reinforces the vocal line with a heterophonic rendering of the melody. Each performer expresses it in a personal style, emphasizing different aspects of the melody or rhythm, and each makes little effort to synchronize the lines. Interludes between the strophes of the texts provide opportunities for instrumental display and for improvisation on the thematic material (figure 2). If accompanying herself, a woman may play but a single drone, reserving for the instrumental interludes a display of her musicianship. Men, however, are the preferred vocalists, and if male singers are available at a gathering, women seldom sing. It is possible that women once sang more in mixed company, for there are many references in the older literature to women's songs of praise and encouragement for warriors.

The texts constitute a genre known as *tesîwit*, which represents the highest achievement in Tuareg poetic arts. The principal subjects are love and heroism. In diction rich in imagery, the poems extol the virtues of courage in battle and gallantry in love, ever confirming the ideals of the warrior aristocracy. People may sing *tesîwit* alone, or to the accompaniment of the *anzad*; but they never sing it with any other instrument. The *anzad*, in turn, is rarely heard with other poetic genres. A *tesîwit* may take one of several meters traditional to a region; composers then set it to a new or existing melody that corresponds with the meter (Foucauld 1925:I:iii–x; Nicolas 1944:9–18). The subject matter, also regional, refers frequently to local persons and events. New texts and melodies continually come into being; the repertory retains many older ones, with the names of the composers.

The male vocal style in singing *tesîwit* is typically high pitched, tense, and much ornamented with mordents, shakes, and other graces, unlike the usual male singing of other genres. The nomadic Tuareg admire high-pitched singing, produced with high tension of the throat muscles, and singers often strain to attain the ideal. A

When accompanying a vocalist, the fiddler reinforces the vocal line with a heterophonic rendering of the melody. Each performer expresses it in a personal style, emphasizing different aspects of the melody or rhythm.

FIGURE 1 *"Tihadanaren,"* an *anzad* melody in Ahaggar style. Soloist: Bouchit bint Loki ag Amilan. Tamanrasset, Algeria, 1976.

range extending to an octave above middle C is common. When women sing *tesîwit,* they do so at a more relaxed midrange, thereby exhibiting none of the piercing quality that characterizes the style of male singers.

FIGURE 1 (*continued*)

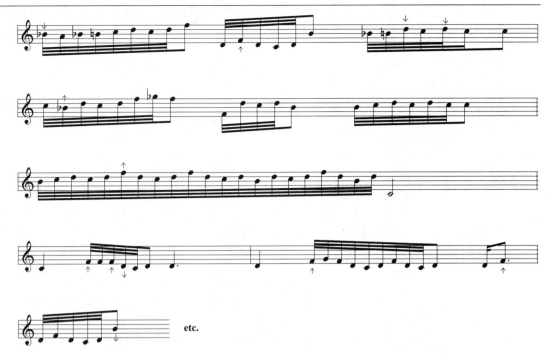

The song "*Chikeshkeshen* 'Girls'," an example of *tesîwit* from the Aïr region, conveys the anguish of a young man who feels unjustly ignored by the women of his community, for in their recognition of him as a valiant warrior lies his sense of self-worth. The text also conveys his need to reconcile the ancient values with the principles of Islam (Nikiprowetzky 1963:B1; trans. Dominique Casajus, Mahmoudan Hawad, Caroline Card).

Girls, today I am ill.
My illness is not the fever,
Nor even a pain in the stomach or a chill;
These days I do not hear my name.
Even though a great blow of the sword could not penetrate my shield,
This eats into my legs up to the calves.

When it occurs, women are indifferent to me, and
I am no longer a cause for jealousy among my age-brothers.
Unloved, my camel's spirit [my prowess] will be broken.
It will destroy my saddle [riding ability] and cut my arms,
Like breaking off the branches of an acacia tree.
I, myself, am greater than a great tree trunk, or at least equal to it.
My proud bearing is like that of the trunk of the largest acacia.

These are the words of a young man filled with pride,
Carrying at his side his gun and his threatening sword.
By day, when our enemies swept down upon our tents,
I fired the gun from behind the saplings that support the tent.
With it I put to flight hundreds of horsemen.
I with my sword, that dog of combat,
Remained standing, sword in hand, refusing to mount my steed.
By the mosques of Takreza and Aglal, and by the marabout of Rayan,
And by the one who dwells at Tin-Wasaran,
Allah, don't make me love my enemies!

tende   Mortar drum, the music performed to
its accompaniment, and the social event
that accompanies it

May those who hate me with a vengeance never pass my way!
They have no desire but to cut my throat.
If they cut my throat, they would be jubilant.
Let them not look to Allah to vilify me!
Let them not look to Satan to pursue me!
It is an evil spell that they have spread over the earth for me,
But I have avoided it. I have the help of the marabouts.
By heaven and earth, we are in the hands of Allah!

THE *TENDE*

The word *tende* (in northern dialect, *tindi*) refers to a mortar drum, the music performed to its accompaniment, and the social event that features it. Though the Tuareg hold *anzad* music in higher esteem, *tende* is the music they more often perform. It is central to Tuareg camel festivals and curing ceremonies, and is also a part of certain dance traditions. In addition to drumming, both men and women take part—by singing, dancing, clapping, and shouting. Unlike the *anzad*, the mortar drum does not require years to learn acceptable skills, and the person who plays it, unless unusually gifted, receives little special attention. A singer of *tende* occasionally gains recognition, but most performers are nonspecialist members of the community. *Tende* is a music of ordinary people; its appeal is immediate and communal. Residents of urban areas increasingly employ its various forms, but it remains a music of the bush, a symbol of earthy values.

Construction

The *tende* is a single-headed mortar drum, named for the wooden vessel from which people make it. Because it is constructed of a mortar and pestles—items used daily in the preparation of food—the drum appears only on festive occasions, when people assemble it for a few hours of use. Its construction requires a footed wooden mortar, two heavy wooden pestles about $1\frac{1}{4}$ meters long, a piece of moistened goatskin, and a length of rope. The ends of dampened goatskin wrap around the pestles, which serve as grips for stretching the skin over the opening of the mortar. In some traditions, people discard the pestles as soon as they have secured the skin with rope. Commonly, however, they attach the pestles to the drumhead as part of the instrument, providing for later tuning and adjustment. To hold the ends of the pestles parallel, and to form seats (on which women, stones, or bricks may sit), people tie rope between the ends of the pestles. (For photos of the construction of *tende*, see Borel 1981:112–114.) The weight on the pestles increases the tension on the attached drumhead, thus tuning it: the heavier the weight, the higher the pitch and the brighter the timbre. This form of mortar drum is unique to the Tuareg.

Periodically during performance, to keep the goatskin moist and pliable, people sprinkle water onto the drumhead. In some traditions, they fill the mortar with water

FIGURE 2 "*Ezzel n oufada aoua etteb ales ou n abaradh* 'Young man's song about a man leading a camel'." Performers unidentified. Holiday and Holiday 1960:A3.

Songs of love and praise form a large portion of the traditional repertory, and criticism and scorn have their place too. Nearly any topic of interest is fitting subject matter.

before stretching the skin over it; by tipping the mortar, they can then moisten the head from the inside. This use of water in the drum has led some to identify it mistakenly as a water drum.

The rise of *tende*

The use of the mortar as a drum may be a recent development. The earliest report of such an instrument is that of Francis Rodd, who in Aïr in 1926 described and sketched a *tende* with attached pestles weighted with stones (1926:272). In Timbuktu in 1934, Laura Boulton made a recording of a Tuareg drum that, though she said it was a water drum, appears to have been a *tende* of the type without attached pestles (Boulton 1957:A:86b). In Ahaggar, a *tende* first appears in a text collected by Ludwig Zöhrer in 1935. His collection from that period includes several recordings of what may have been *tende*. In his later writing, based on this material, he speaks of *tende* as the only "truly Tuareg drum" other than the ceremonial *attebel* of the chief (1935, item 11; 1940:141). Despite the earlier southern references, some believe that the instrument originated among vassal tribes in the Adrar n-Foras region of northeastern Mali, and that it spread from there into Ahaggar and Niger (Mounier 1942:155; Blanguernon 1955:154). Others believe its use to have been introduced or strongly influenced by sub-Saharan slaves (Holiday and Holiday 1960:4; Lhote 1955:184). Whatever its origin, the *tende* did not become prominent in Tuareg musical life until after 1930.

If *tende* was indeed originally a vassal tradition, its emergence may have accompanied the shifts of wealth and power that in the late nineteenth and early twentieth centuries favored the vassal tribes of the north. During that period, the vassals of Ahaggar gained greater control over the camels (Keenan 1977:56–61), and were consequently able to take a more prominent role in camel festivals. Mounier states that about 1930 the vassal drum began to replace a small hand-held drum formerly used by noblewomen at the Ahaggar festivals (1942:155). In the southern regions, the *tende* as a Tuareg festival instrument appears to have merged with Hausa dance traditions. In a 1944 publication on the Tuareg of Azawagh, Francis Nicolas mentions *tende* as a Tuareg alternative to a Hausa drum, *ganga*, used to accompany the dance songs of Tuareg slaves (Nicolas 1944:3, 7). In Niger by the 1950s, the mortar drum had become an established part of musical culture (Holiday and Holiday 1960:4). The diversity of the *tende* traditions that have developed may best be understood in the light of these cultural fusions. For further discussion, see Card (1983:155–171).

Camel-festival *tende*

The mortar-drum music most often mentioned in the literature is *tende n-əmnas* 'mortar drum of the camels'. These events celebrate weddings, births, honored visits, and other joyous occasions. Featured are camel races and dances. In its classic form, women sing and play the drum, while men parade or race their camels around them, in a fashion sometimes described as a "fantasy," and known in Tuareg dialects as *ilu-gan*, *ilujan*, and *ilaguan*. The races and displays of precision riding, combined with the men's flirtatious behavior toward the women, perpetuate the traditional virtues of male prowess and gallantry. In the late 1900s, as the nomadic herders become urbanized, the music of *tende n-əmnas* is increasingly performed out of context; and in some areas, male artisan-specialists play the drum.

The texts of *tende n-əmnas* burgeon with personalized references to camels, extolling with esteem and affection their beauty and merits. Mere ownership of a superb riding camel is often sufficient for a man's commemoration in song, and texts praise good riders for their skill and rapport with their animals. But though the references to camels are numerous, the real subjects are people. Songs of love and praise form a large portion of the traditional repertory, and criticism and scorn have their place too. Nearly any topic of interest is fitting subject matter. Some texts, set to familiar tunes, develop extemporaneously, and include the singer's commentary on local persons and current events. Such songs function in a journalistic capacity, and performers skilled in this kind of improvisation attract an appreciative following.

Characteristic of the style of northern *tende n-əmnas* is the women's choral drone, which functions as a pedal point to the solo line (figure 3). People rarely use the drone south of Tamesna, except in the rainy season during the period known as the Cure Salée, when cameleers from many regions assemble their herds on the salty plains of Niger near In-Gal. This is a time for weddings and social gatherings with much celebrating and music making, especially *tende*. In the southern regions, a choral ostinato in responsorial style replaces the uninterrupted drone. The rhythms, said to imitate the gaits of the camels, are of two types: those based on equal beats in duple meter with syncopated duple or ternary subdivisions, and those based on unequal beats of 3+4+3 in several variations (Saada 1986:186–194). The drummed rhythms may actually direct the movements of the camels, for the riders take their cues from the women at the drum (Borel 1981:120–123). Characteristic, also, are pentatonic structure and quick tempos (typically about M.M. 132–146), usually faster than those of other types of *tende* (figure 3).

Dance *tende*

In Niger, people perform *tende n-tagbast* 'dance *tende*', at many birth and marriage celebrations, and at other special events. Only artisans, sedentary blacks, and (to a lesser extent) vassals dance it. Traditionally, noble Tuareg do not dance (Lhote 1951: 98–103). The word *tagbast* is the nominal form of the verb *egbas* 'circle the waist with a belt'. By extension, it bears the sense of "elegant attire" or "stylish dress," and with *tende*, denotes a musical occasion celebrated with fine clothes and dancing. Dancers perform within a circle of spectators. Dancers, alone or in groups, enter the circle and perform a few steps, then retreat, to be followed by others. Men's shouts and women's flutter-tongued cries of approval reward expert exhibitions.

Women sing the texts, but the *tende* is usually played by men of the artisanal caste, whom women accompany on an *assakalabu* (a gourd upturned in a basin of water). The instrumental ensemble may also include a frame drum, *əkänzam*, which men or women play. The use of instruments with the dance may be a recent addition to a formerly unaccompanied dance tradition; and if instruments are not readily available, the dances take an accompaniment of singing and hand clapping only. Dance music without instruments is known as *ezele n-tagbast*. Artisan-musicians familiar with the tradition of *tende n-əmnas* may have introduced the mortar drum into the dance. The texts praise and commemorate good dancers, much as texts of *tende n-əmnas* praise good riders; and many of the texts similarly speak of love.

Duple meter with duple subdivisions, occasionally syncopated, are characteristic

assakalabu Instrument created by upturning a gourd in a basin of water that is struck with a stick

tende n-əmnas Events where the mortar drum is played and that feature personalized references to camels

FIGURE 3 *Tende n-əmnas* song for the Tuareg celebration of the annual Muslim festival of sacrificial sheep. Vocal soloist: Lalla bint Salem. Tamanrasset, Algeria, 1976.

of the genre. Ternary subdivisions are rare, except for brief hemiolic exchanges within the melody, or between parts. The pulse, strongly marked and accompanied by hand clapping, receives further reinforcement from steady, equal beats struck on the *assakalabu*. Though slower than *tende n-əmnas*, the tempos of *tende n-tagbast* vary according to the dance. The formal structure can be either antiphonal or responsorial. In the former, a melodic line alternates between two choruses, or between a soloist and a chorus; in the latter, a solo line follows or overlaps a choral ostinato, as is characteristic of the southern *tende n-əmnas* tradition.

MUSICAL CURING CEREMONIES

The use of music to cure certain types of illnesses is widespread throughout the Sahara. Musical curing practices have an origin in ancient beliefs in good and evil spirits, known to the Tuareg as *Kel Asuf* 'People of the Solitude'. The spirits, believed to inhabit fire, water, wind, caves, darkness, and empty places, are responsible for most Tuareg mental illnesses, and for other sufferings from unseen causes. The pre-Islamic animism of the Tuareg has merged with Muslim concepts of the spirit world, and in some regions the curing ceremony is known by the Arabic name *el janun* (in Ahaggar, *alhinen*) 'possession, madness'. The term derives from the Arabic word *jinn*, denoting earth-dwelling spirits (described in the Qur'ān), which aid or hinder the lives of mortals. In the Tuareg traditions of Niger, the ceremony is known as *tende n-gumatan*. The word *guma* (pl. *gumatan*) refers to the patient—more often a woman—for whom people hold the ceremony (Rasmussen 1985). The origin of the term is uncertain, but Tuareg from the Aïr to Niamey recognize its sense as "*tende* of the possessed" or "*tende* of the emotionally ill."

Because the Tuareg believe music—especially strong rhythms—attracts spirits, curing ceremonies feature singing, clapping, and drumming. In some cases, music entices unwanted spirits from the body; in others, it restores harmony between the patient and his or her personal spirit. The ceremonies, always held late at night, include a chorus of women, a *tende* player (male or female), and often an *assakalabu* player (always a woman). Necessary, also, are male participants, who utter raspy, rhythmic grunts (*tahəmahəmt*). At the center sits or stands the *guma*, who sways to the rhythms of the drum. Members of the family and community, who contribute with hand clapping and cries of encouragement, surround the immediate group. The spirited songs, rhythms, and raspy grunts of the men lead the patient and some participants into altered states of consciousness. People may repeat the ceremony for as many consecutive nights as necessary. The Tuareg say that because the spirits' natures are well known to the community, they can usually project at the outset how many nightly rituals they will need to effect a cure.

In the past, the rituals of curing probably had specific texts, and possibly special music, but current practices permit the use of any songs the patients or their families desire. The tempos of the songs conform to a *tende n-gumatan* standard (about M.M. 73–96), slower than usual for either *tende n-əmnas* or *tende n-tagbast* (Borel 1981:124; Card 1982:150). The slower tempos and the gutteral utterances of the men, who force their breath rhythmically through constricted throats, are the major features that distinguish the music of the curing ceremonies from other types of *tende*.

THE *TAHARDENT*

A popular music and dance associated with the three-stringed lute *tahardent*, is performed in urban centers across the Sahara from Mali to Algeria. Men of the artisanal caste, many of whom earn their living as professional musicians (*aggu*; pl. *aggutan*),

tahardent   Three-stringed lute played in urban centers across the Sahara from Mali to Algeria

takɔmba   New Tuareg genre where seated listeners respond to rhythms with undulating movements of the torso

perform the music. Such men once performed as bards in the courts of chiefs, singing the praises of their noble patrons and reciting tales of battles and heroes of local Tuareg legend to the accompaniment of the plucked lute. But the *tahardent* repertory that is now popular among urban Tuareg is not the heroic music of the past; it is music for entertainment, which friends and acquaintances of diverse ethnic backgrounds can share.

The *tahardent* has long been a part of Tuareg traditions in Mali, but not until the late 1960s did the instrument begin to spread into other Tuareg areas. The movement of *tahardent* music from its source (between Timbuktu and Gao) began about 1968, when Malian Tuareg suffering from drought began to seek relief across the border, in Niger. Among the refugees were many artisan-musicians whose traditional patrons could no longer support them. To increase their opportunities, the itinerants quickly altered their repertories to appeal to a more diverse, multiethnic audience. Crowded conditions in the refugee centers forced many to continue their migration northeastward. By 1971, *tahardent* music began to be heard in Agadez, and in 1974 it reached Tamanrasset, Algeria. Since 1976, Malian *tahardent* players have been active in most urban centers across the Sahara and Sahelian borderlands, and recordings of *tahardent* music are in wide circulation throughout West Africa.

The *tahardent* is not unique to the Tuareg, and it almost certainly did not originate among them. The Hausa and Djerma of Niger call the same instrument *molo*; throughout West Africa, it goes by other names; in Mauritania, professionals play the *tidinit*, a similar instrument with four strings. In all the traditions, the music is performed exclusively by musicians whose professions are normally hereditary, and whose social roles and statuses are similar. The close resemblance of the Tuareg tradition to its neighboring counterparts accounts for much of its present popularity in the multicultural urban areas. Hausa, Djerma, Fulani, Songhay, Tuareg, and other West Africans can find shared enjoyment in the music, for the similarities of the styles, repertories, and performance practices, particularly in their modern forms, are greater than the differences.

The new genre, popularly known as *takɔmba*, consists of accompanied songs and instrumental solos. To provocative rhythms, seated listeners (both men and women) respond with undulating movements of the upper torso and outstretched arms. People exchange prized recordings of star performers and hit songs, and copy them from one tape to another. The texts are sensuous. At vital moments, people express approval in rhapsodic exclamations of "*ush-sh-sh!*"—as in the following translation (Card 1977: tape XVII, track 1, item 3).

TRACK 12

> My soul loves what it will,
>   O my Khadisia!
> The best woman is one who is fat,
>   Not one who is thin!

Or else a woman who has a low stomach
  Which is soft, nice to touch,
Or one who has fleshy arms and calves,
    Ush-sh-sh-sh!

Songs of this type appeal most to Tuareg who have accepted urban life and contemporary values. Those who adhere to traditional ways are often vehement in their disdain for the instrument, the music, and its devotees: they denounce *tahardent* music as a corrupt, urban product, and not a true Tuareg art. To them, it matters little that the *tahardent* represents an old and respected Tuareg tradition in Mali. Their attitudes toward it highlight an emerging division between conservatives and progressives.

Construction and playing

The instrument has an oblong body covered with cowhide or goatskin. Artisans carve the body from a single block of wood, and cover it with cowhide or goatskin, which they attach with tacks or lacings. A length of bamboo, inserted under the skin, and extending beyond the body, serves as a neck. A large sound hole is cut into the skin just below the bridge. The instrument comes in two sizes. The larger (and more commonly used) has a body length of about 51 to 53 centimeters, a width of about 18 to 20, and a neck of about 30. Three strings, of differing lengths and thicknesses, are attached to a mounting just above the sound hole. They stretch over the bridge, where they are fastened to the end of the neck with leather bindings that are adjustable for tuning. The strings, nowadays made of nylon, are collectively called hairs. Individual strings bear animal names: the lowest is *ahar* 'lion'; the middle, *tazori* 'hyena'; and the highest, *ebag* 'jackal', or *awokkoz* 'young animal'. The two lower strings are tuned to a perfect fourth or perfect fifth, depending on the music. The upper string—occasionally plucked, but not fingered—sounds an octave above the lowest; its principal function is sympathetic vibration. A metal resonator (*tefararaq*) dangles from the end of the neck, where it buzzes.

The player sits cross-legged, and normally holds the neck in his left hand. On his right index finger he wears a plectrum (*esker*), made of bone and leather. He plucks the middle string with the index finger, the lower with his thumb. With the other fingers he taps accompanying rhythms on the instrument's surface. With his left-hand fingers he stops the strings against the (unfretted) neck. As the melodic range rarely exceeds an octave, hand shifts during the course of a composition are unnecessary. A player may occasionally slide a finger along the string in a glissando, but normally the fingering is crisp, and the pitches clearly articulated. Esteemed performers exhibit virtuosity in their improvisations on the basic rhythmic patterns, particularly in the instrumental interludes between vocal strophes. People do not perform separately or with other instruments the poetry they sing or recite to the accompaniment of the *tahardent*, whether of the old tradition or the new.

Musical styles

Many Tuareg, unaware of historical and stylistic distinctions, refer to all *tahardent* music as *takəmba*. To the performers, however, *takəmba* is but one of several compositional formulas, which they call rhythms. Each rhythm has a name, is suitable for a specific context, and may bear distinctive modal and rhythmic characteristics. The rhythms *n-geru* and *yalli* (figure 4) serve only in the performance of heroic ballads, a tradition that may be several hundred years old; both have five-pulse rhythms, but

FIGURE 4   Rhythmic structure of *n-geru* and *yalli*.

FIGURE 5   Twelve-pulse patterns in several configurations as they appear in *abakkabuk*, *ser-i*, *jaba*, and *takǝmba*.

different tonal (or modal) structures. *Yalli* was first recorded by Laura Boulton in Timbuktu in 1934 (African Music item 86A). In her documentation, the term *yalli* (given as *Yali*) became confused with subject matter; musical analysis, however, confirms the identity of the rhythm. The rhythms *abakkabuk*, *ser-i*, *jabâ*, and *takǝmba* (figure 5) serve for light entertainment and dancing. All rely on twelve-pulse patterns in various configurations. *Abakkabuk* is an old rhythm unique to the Tuareg. *Ser-i* 'toward me' is a traditional pattern played for the enjoyment of members of the artisanal caste, to which the musicians belong. *Jabâ* and *takǝmba*, of more recent origin, are rhythms that praise youth and youthful pleasures; according to performers, *jabâ* is the product of a commission in 1960 by wealthy patrons of the Kel Tamoulayt; similarly, *takǝmba* is a rhythm composed for the chief of the Malian village of that name near Bourem.

Few outsiders have studied *tahardent* music, and recordings are scarce. Comparison of the limited data with that of similar neighboring traditions points to relationships between the heroic forms (*yalli*, *n-geru*) and Arabic music of North Africa and the Middle East, particularly in tonal structures and sociomusical meanings. The dance music, with its twelve-pulse horizontal hemiolas, shows greater affinity with sub-Saharan Africa (Duvelle 1966; Anderson 1971:143–169; Card 1982:166–174). The *tahardent* tradition of the Tuareg thus reflects the intercultural status of its artisan-creators, who, more than other musicians, have drawn freely upon both Middle Eastern and sub-Saharan sources.

OTHER INSTRUMENTS

Tuareg musical culture also includes a variety of drums and a herdsman's flute. Some of these instruments are limited to particular regions, others to particular persons or events.

Drums

The *assakalabu*, or *aghalabo*, consists of a hemispherical calabash floating in a basin of water. The earliest written reference to the instrument is that of Francis Rodd, who observed a basin filled with milk, rather than water (1926:272, plate 22). The player, always a woman, strikes the calabash with a stick. Slight variation in timbre is possible by regulating the depth of the gourd in the liquid; the more forceful the stroke, the deeper the tone. The instrument, used only with *tende* and *tazâwat*, appears at camel festivals and other celebrations, dances, and curing ceremonies. Because it serves only to reinforce basic beats (women play no rhythmic subdivisions on it), it offers opportunities for young women to take part in ensembles, and to become acquainted with the drumming traditions.

The *tazâwat* is a medium-sized kettledrum, played by women in the Azawagh region of Niger. Accompanied by *assakalabu*, hand clapping, and occasionally *anzad*, the drum frequently serves in the curing ceremonies of this region, where people deem it especially effective in treating illnesses attributed to *jinn*. The (seated) player rests the drum on the ground before her, and strikes it with her hands. Some *tazâwat* players exhibit rhythmic versatility and virtuosity. People construct the drum from a half calabash, covered with cowhide or goatskin. Lacings threaded through eyelets in the leather, and knotted at the bottom of the bowl, hold the drumhead taut. A northern variant, *tegennewt*, occasionally seen in Ahaggar, is made from a wooden or enameled metal bowl (Saada 1986:99–100). One of the few recorded collections of *tazâwat* is in the archives of the Musée d'Ethnographie, Neuchatel, Switzerland (Borel 1981:116).

The *əttebel*, a large ceremonial kettledrum, is the traditional symbol of Tuareg chieftainship—and formerly, of tribal sovereignty. Selected people play it on important ceremonial occasions, such as the installation of a chief or the celebration of an annual Muslim festival, and formerly played it to summon men to battle (Nicolas 1939:585). The *əttebel* is similar in construction to the *tazâwat*, but it is wider and deeper, and is played differently. Two men suspend the drum by ropes above the ground, and strike it alternately. Because the Tuareg believe the drum has mystic powers, its handling, playing, storage, and repair, are traditionally subject to rituals and taboos (Nicolaisen 1963:396). Since the end of tribal sovereignty, however, the ceremonial drums, though still played occasionally, have lost much of their former significance, and people less rigorously observe the traditions concerning them.

The *əkänzam* (pl. *iəkänzaman*) is a single-headed, shallow frame drum, similar in appearance to the European tambourine, but without jingles. Hand held and played by either a man or woman, it typically measures 25 to 30 centimeters in diameter. Southern *tende* ensembles, especially those in which artisan-musicians are the principal performers, may include one or more.

In Hausa, the term *ganga* (pl. *gangatan*) is a generic 'drum'. For the Tuareg, it has assumed regional meanings: in Ahaggar, it refers to a hand-held, shallow, double-headed drum, played by women to accompany the singing of songs for weddings; in Aïr, it refers to a suspended, double-headed cylindrical drum, played by musicians attendant on the Sultan of Agadez, who serves as chief of certain Tuareg groups in the Aïr and southern Niger.

When a mortar drum is unavailable or too much trouble to prepare, a plastic or metal container popularly known as a "jerry can" often substitutes for it. Some Tuareg actually prefer a jerry can to the traditional mortar drum. In Ahaggar, as a result of an inscription ("made in Germany") that appeared on the first cans imported into the region, people began to call the container *jermani* (Saada 1986:103). Though not properly a musical instrument, the wide use of the jerry can in this manner justifies its inclusion among Tuareg musical instruments. Jerry cans are readily available, and have the advantage of needing no preparation. When used as a drum, the jerry can is often called a *tende*.

The flute

For private pleasure or as an aid in controlling animals, herdsmen traditionally play an obliquely held flute, termed *tazammart* in the north and *tasansagh* or *sarewa* (Hausa) in the south. The instrument, about 1 meter long and 2 to 5 centimeters in diameter, contains four holes. Formerly made from a hollow stalk or from the root of the acacia tree, it is now more commonly constructed of metal or plastic tubing. The flutes sometimes sport a traditional decoration: a dyed-leather fringe.

Flute repertories vary regionally, and have no accompanying vocal texts. In the Algerian Sahara, the music of the flute is often accompanied by a vocal drone produced in the throat of the player as he blows into and fingers the instrument. The

The Tuareg regard any type of rhythmic movement as dance, whether they perform it standing or sitting. The stylized movements of camels under the control of their riders are also called dance.

drone, like that accompanying *tende* songs in this region, serves as a pedal point to the melody.

People play the flute in small groups, but rarely at large social gatherings. The urbanization of herders, and increasing media exposure of outstanding performers, are gradually giving new status to the flute as a solo instrument. Some performers, recorded and broadcast by Radio Niger (which regularly includes flute music in its programming) have become well known for musicianship and virtuosity.

OTHER VOCAL GENRES

Aliwen

A large body of wedding songs (*aliwen*), sung by women, constitutes a major musical genre in the Ahaggar and Tassili-n-Ajjer regions of Algeria. The poetic texts are one of the finest and most elaborate of the region's traditions, second only to the *tesîwit* poetry associated with the *anzad*. The wedding songs, which frequently take the accompaniment of *gangatan*, may represent a tradition dating from the mid-1600s or earlier. Many of the older texts, having retained their ceremonial character, appear little changed over time. People occasionally add new songs, but the songs conform to the older metric, rhythmic, and semantic traditions: they continue to emphasize the communal and social aspects of marriage (Saada 1986:71–74, 212–234). That little new composition of *aliwen* has occurred in the late 1900s reflects the conservatism characteristic of this Tuareg area.

Specific *aliwen* mark the ceremonial stages of the wedding. The singing begins in the bride's quarters on the first morning of the festivities, which usually last for a week. Special songs further celebrate the grooming of the bride, the erection of the nuptial tent, the parade of camels (*ilugan*), and the processions of the bride and bridegroom to the tent. Two groups of women sing verses antiphonally, or a soloist and chorus sing responsorially. In Tassili n-Ajjer, believed to be the source of the tradition, the songs are always accompanied by the *ganga*, and vocal and drum rhythms synchronize rigorously. The rhythms consist of complex combinations of beats of unequal length. In Ahaggar, where people use the drum less regularly, the rhythms are less complex. When the drum is used, the rhythms are usually independent of the melodic line (Augier 1972:298; Saada 1986:115–127, 181–182).

Religious music

Orthodox Muslims frown on music for worship. Religious vocal music, unaccompanied by instruments, is an accepted practice in much of the Sahara and the southern borderlands. Religious performance was not a part of ancient Tuareg culture, and though it is increasing in importance with the growth of urban populations and the spread of fundamentalist Muslim movements, the entire population does not perform it. The men participate in all types of Muslim observances more than the women, who, as traditional guardians of culture, are more supportive of pre-Islamic beliefs and practices.

The religious music takes two forms: *azziker* and *amadikh*. The former, a term derived from Arabic *dhikr*, is a ritual music sung in recollection of Allah in the less orthodox mosques and improvised places of worship along the desert routes. Though the *dhikr* is common to all Muslim peoples, the Tuareg form is unique in musical style, which resembles that of the dance traditions and curing ceremonies, its use of Tuareg dialects (rather than Arabic), and its perspective (said to express the special manner in which the Tuareg envision Allah). *Amadikh* is panegyric poetry sung in praise of Muhammad. Both men and women sing this music anywhere, away from places of worship. The texts, like those of *azziker*, are in the vernacular; and the music, though strongly regional in style, exhibits distinctive traits, such as triple meter, uncommon in most Tuareg music. Commercial recordings of *azziker* and *amadikh* are rare. For programming, however, Radio Niger has made a sizable collection.

Children's songs

The unaccompanied songs that mothers sing to their children include a wide variety of styles and subjects. Some lie partway between speech and song; some consist of vocables sung to simple, repetitive melodies of two or three pitches; and others have elaborate structures and contain many verses. Lullabies seem to differ from other women's songs in their more supple style, the use of semitones, and a dissymmetric structure subordinate to the demands of improvised texts (Augier 1972:298–299). Zöhrer says the texts consist of a mixture of endearments and religious matter (1940:145–146). Many women, however, amuse their children with any music that comes to mind. The song may be taken from a repertory of dances, or it may describe a men's hunt. In Ahaggar, women sing a song to children about an ostrich, a bird that has not been seen in that area for a century. As they sing and clap, they prompt the children to imitate the imagined movements of the bird. At an early age, however, parents encourage children to participate in their elders' music making.

DANCE TRADITIONS

The Tuareg regard any type of rhythmic movement as dance, whether they perform it standing (as in *tende n-tagbast*, *tehemmet*, *tehigelt*, *tazengherit*, and *arokas*), or sitting (as in *takamba* and often *tende n-gumatan*). The stylized movements of camels under the control of their riders (*ilugan*) are also called dance. Standing dances, once performed exclusively by slaves for the entertainment of the nomads, are now more widely performed, though usually by men of lower-than-noble rank. Women, especially those of noble lineage, rarely participate in such dances. Seated men and women of all social ranks respond to the rhythms of *tahardent* music with undulating movements of the arms and shoulders, and patients being treated in *tende n-gumatan* may respond vigorously, standing or sitting, with swaying movements described as head dancing.

Tehigelt and *tehemmet*

The dance called *tehigelt* in Ahaggar and *tehemmet* in Tassili n-Ajjer (where people say it began) is accompanied by songs, hand clapping, and one or more drums. The event always occurs at night, in celebration of a joyous occasion. The dance, formerly performed only by slaves, is now joined by men of all ranks, and occasionally by women, who participate with modest movements. The dancers form a large circle. As performed by men, the movements consist of hopping steps, with knees lifted high and arms outstretched. Sometimes the men engage in mock-battle gestures. The

tazengherit   Ecstatic form of music and
dance performed in Ahaggar, particularly
at the oases of Tazruk and Hirafok

arokas   A dance performed in the Agadez
area of Niger with a women's chorus,
soloist, and spirited hand clapping

musical accompaniment, similar to *tende n-ɘmnas*, includes a chorus of women, a vocal soloist, and drummers. The rhythms of *tehigelt* and *tehemmet* are distinct, but the antiphonal and responsorial styles of singing differ little from those of *tende* (Augier 1972:295; Saada 1986:79–80). In Tassili n-Ajjer, the ensemble may include several *gangatan* and jerrycans; in Ahaggar, the use of a single drum (traditionally a *tegennewt*, but now more commonly a *tende* or jerry can) is more common. Increasingly, the dances are performed to recorded music taped at previous events and replayed on portable players, or over loudspeakers.

Tazengherit

Tazengherit is an ecstatic form of music and dance performed in Ahaggar, particularly at the oases of Tazruk and Hirafok, where certain groups specialize in it. Men dance exclusively to the accompaniment of a women's chorus, one or two female soloists, hand clapping, and their own gutteral utterances (similar to those of *tende n-gumatan*). No instruments are used. People sing *tazengherit* songs in sets of three to five, following an established pattern, each more intense and structurally elaborate than the preceding. For many of the participants, the event culminates in frenzied dancing and altered states of consciousness (Augier 1972:295–296).

Arokas

Arokas, a dance performed in the Agadez area of Niger, involves the accompaniment of a women's chorus, a female soloist, and spirited hand clapping. The songs and movements are nearly identical to those of *tende n-tagbast*, but no instruments are used. The word derives from *erked* 'to dance'.

REFERENCES

Anderson, Lois. 1971. "The Interrelation of African and Arab Musics: Some Preliminary Considerations." In *Music and History in Africa,* ed. Klaus P. Wachsmann, 143–169. Evanston, Ill.: Northwestern University Press.

Augier, Pierre. 1972. "Ethnomusicologie saharienne: les documents sonores recueillis récemment en Ahaggar et au Gourara." *Libyca* 20:291–311.

Blanguernon, Claude. 1955. *Le Hoggar.* Paris: Arthaud.

Borel, François. 1981. "Tambours et rythmes de tambours Touaregs au Niger." *Annales Suisses de Musicologie* 1:107–129.

Boulton, Laura. 1957. *African Music.* Folkways Records, FW 8852. LP disk.

Briggs, Lloyd Cabot. 1960. *Tribes of the Sahara.* Cambridge, Mass.: Harvard University Press.

Card, Caroline. 1977. Field collection. Archives of Traditional Music, Indiana University.

———. 1982. "Tuareg Music and Social Identity." Ph.D. dissertation, Indiana University.

———. 1983. "*Tende* Music among the Tuareg: The History of a Tradition." In *Cross Rhythms, Occasional Papers in African Folklore,* ed. Kofi Anyidoho et al., 155–171. Bloomington, Ind.: Trickster Press.

DjeDje, Jacqueline Cogdell. 1980. *Distribution of the One String Fiddle in West Africa.* Los Angeles: Program in Ethnomusicology, Department of Music, University of California. Monograph in Ethnomusicology 2.

Duvelle, Charles. 1966. *Musique Maure.* OCORA Records, OCR 28. LP disk and notes.

Duvéyrier, Henri. 1864 [1973]. *Les Touareg du nord*. Liechtenstein: Nendeln [New York: Krauss].

Foucauld, Charles de. 1925. *Poésies touarègues: dialecte de l'Ahaggar*. 2 vols. Paris: Editions Ernest Leroux.

———. 1951–1952. *Dictionnaire touareg-français: dialect de l'Ahaggar*. 4 vols. Paris: Imprimerie national de France.

Holiday, Geoffrey, and Finola Holiday. 1960. *Tuareg Music of the Southern Sahara*. Folkways Records, FE 4470. LP disk.

Keenan, Jeremy H. 1977. *The Tuareg: People of Ahaggar*. London: Allen Lane.

Lhote, Henri. 1951. "Un peuple qui ne danse pas." *Tropiques* 337(December):99–103.

———. 1955. *Touaregs du Hoggar*. Paris: Payot.

Mounier, G. 1942. "Le travail des peaux chez les Touareg Hoggar." *Travaux de l'Institut des recherches sahariennes* 1:133–169.

Murdock, George Peter. 1959. *Africa: Its Peoples and Their Culture History*. New York: McGraw-Hill.

Nicolaisen, Johannes. 1961. "Essai sur la religion et la magie touarègues." *Folk* 3:113–162.

———. 1963. *Ecology and Culture of the Pastoral Tuareg*. Copenhagen: National Museum.

Nicolas, Francis. 1939. "Notes sur la société et l'état chez les Twareg du Dinnik." *Bulletin de l'Institut français d'Afrique noire* 1:579–586.

———. 1944. "Folklore Twareg: poésies et chansons de l'Azawarh." *Bulletin de l'Institut français d'Afrique noire* 6(1–4).

———. 1950. *Tamesna: les Iullemmeden de l'Est, ou Touareg "Kel Dinnik."* Paris: Imprimerie nationale.

Nikiprowetzky, Tolia. 1963. *Nomades du Niger*. OCORA Records, OCR 29. LP disk.

Rasmussen, Susan. 1985. "Gender and Curing in Ritual and Symbol: Women, Spirit Possession, and Aging among the Kel Ewey Tuareg." Ph.D. dissertation, Indiana University.

Rodd, Francis Rennel (Lord Rennel of Rodd). 1926 [1966]. *People of the Veil*. Oosterhut, Netherlands: Anthropological Publications.

Saada, Nadia Mécheri. 1986. "La musique de l'Ahaggar." Ph.D. dissertation. University of Paris.

Wendt, Caroline Card. 1994. "Regional Style in Tuareg *Anzad* Music." In *To the Four Corners*, ed. Ellen Leichtman. Warren, Mich.: Harmonie Park Press.

Zöhrer, Ludwig. 1935. "Protokoll zu den Phonogrammen Ludwig Zöhrers von den Tuareg der Sahara."

———. 1940. "Studien über die Tuareg (Imohag) der Sahara." *Zeitschrift für Ethnologie* 72:124–152.

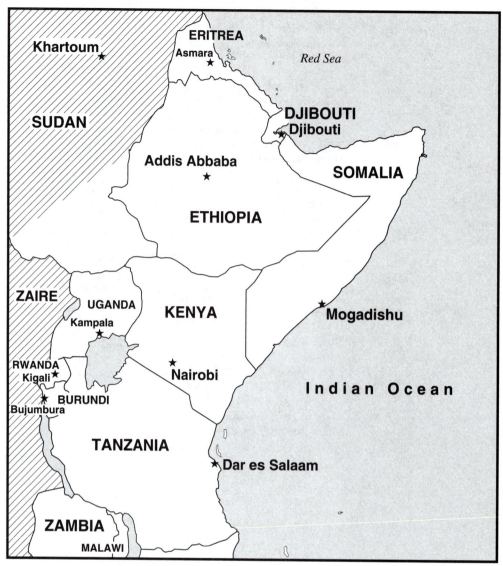

East Africa

East Africa

East African musical performances reveal practices from the Arab world to the north as well as South and Southeast Asian musical elements from the east. Royal ensembles of drums, flutes, trumpets, and xylophones—historically connected to the courts of rulers from Ethiopia to Kenya—persist in a variety of contemporary settings.

East Africa: An Introduction
Peter Cooke

The Settled Peoples
Nomadic and Seminomadic Peoples
Indonesian, Arabic, Islamic, and European Influences
Late-Twentieth-Century Developments and Urban Music

East Africa ranges from the dry scrubland of northern Mozambique to the empty deserts of northern Sudan and Eritrea, and from the seasonally dry savanna bordering the Indian Ocean inland to the mountain–rain-forest mosaic of Rwanda and Burundi.

More than 100 million people live in this area, and their life-styles and origins vary as much as anywhere else in Africa, though they exclude large areas of Sudan, Ethiopia, and Somalia. About 118 different languages have been identified in the Sudan alone, and almost as many in Ethiopia; and since language and musical style are often closely related, it is not surprising to find that musical traditions vary as much as languages and dialects.

In contrast with anthropological research, musical research in this area has been patchy, often nonexistent, and the task of attempting an overview is complicated, as elsewhere in Africa, by a past that has known considerable population movement but has produced little or no historical documentation. Theories about the origins and movements of whole societies remain speculative; myths are often the only available evidence.

From time to time, debate on the extent to which Indonesian peoples penetrated and colonized East Africa (bringing their cultural practices, including music, with them) still surfaces (Jones 1964). Archaeologists and historians are uncertain about the origins of the Cwezi, powerful cattle folk, who probably in the 1300s appeared in the area around the northwestern shores of Lake Victoria, where they established dynasties that ruled until 1966.

Changes in religious practices have affected traditional music and dance. Islam continues to gain converts throughout East Africa—a spread that in earlier centuries was associated with trade with the Arab world, rather than conquest, but which need not always have been connected with the introduction of the Arabic language. Islamic prohibitions on musical practices, though important in some countries, have little effect in many parts of Africa. Western missionaries, initially antipathetic to almost all aspects of traditional culture, have had a greater impact on musical practices by introducing harmonized hymns to cultures that had nurtured primarily monophonic styles of singing. This process has been intensified since the 1970s through partnership with the tools of the Western media, which floods Africa with Western popular music. In the twentieth century too, students and urban migrant workers who maintain links with their home villages are ensuring the spread of modern town-music styles into the most distant villages.

Leaving aside questions of Western musical influence, it is possible to comment generally on the similarities and differences of traditional musical style and function among three principal groups of peoples. The first are the traditionally nomadic and pastoral peoples, many of whom are said to have moved southward and westward out of the region of the Horn of Africa during the past several centuries. They include groups such as the Baggāra (wandering the deserts and scrubland of the Sudan); the Karamojong, the Jie, the Pokot, and the Turkana of eastern Uganda and neighboring parts of Kenya; and the Maasai of the rift-valley plains farther south in Kenya and Tanzania. The second group are sedentary agriculturalists, such as the Nilotes of Sudan and the Bantu-speaking peoples who many centuries ago moved southward and then eastward and northward, it is thought from a Bantu heartland on the west side of the continent. Third are the Cushitic-speaking Amhara and Tigre, and other peoples of present-day Ethiopia and Somalia.

Within these cultural divisions there is considerable musical diversity, often linked to contacts between peoples. The Bantu-speaking Meru and Gogo of Tanzania have absorbed elements of musical style from their pastoralist Maasai neighbors who came from northern Kenya; and the Kuria, a small, Bantu-speaking group of pastoralists in northwestern Kenya, only late in the twentieth century have turned to agriculture.

But all these peoples tend to have the same uses for music as do Africans elsewhere in the continent: providing an essential ingredient in most rituals and ceremonies, and accompanying the daily tasks of men and women.

THE SETTLED PEOPLES

In East Africa, the so-called Bantu line, marking the northern limit of the northward and eastward movement of Bantu-speaking agriculturalists from the forests of the southern Congo, runs irregularly from east to west across central Uganda; it then dips south around the dry, central plains of Kenya and northern Tanzania. Farther east, pockets of Bantu-speaking peoples inhabit east-central Kenya, parts of the coast, and inland river valleys as far north as southern Somalia.

In a detailed historical survey of East African music, Gerhard Kubik (1982) divides the area south of the Bantu line into four smaller areas: first, the interlacustrine region, formerly comprised of kingdom-states in southern and western Uganda, Rwanda, Burundi, and northwestern Tanzania; then a Tanzanian area, divided into eight smaller music-style areas because of the variety of peoples living there; third, the Swahili-speaking coastal area, where Swahili and other coastal groups have absorbed Arabic and Islamic influence; and last, the Nyasa-Ruvuma area, stretching from Lake Nyasa down to the coast on either side of the Tanzania-Mozambique border, whose peoples (which include the Makonde) Kubik considers, in the light of historical, linguistic, and other evidence, are related to the Shaba of southern Zaïre, and so have more in common with other central African peoples.

North of the Bantu line in southeastern Sudan and southern Ethiopia live many groups of Nilotic- and para-Nilotic-speaking peoples who, though settled in small villages, practice a good deal of pastoralism. In the Sudan in particular, there is increasing Islamization, with varying effects on older musical practices.

Klaus Wachsmann and Kathleen Trowell's survey of the sound-producing instruments of Uganda (1953) illustrates the variety of musical instruments in use in

begana   Box lyre that was an instrument of the Amharic aristocracy in Ethiopia

omulanga   Harpist for the rule of Buganda in the area of Lake Victoria

akadinda   Xylophone associated with the Uganda court and played by several players

entenga   Drum chime associated with the Uganda court

southern and western parts of East Africa. It lists stringed instruments, such as musical bows, zithers, arched harps, lyres, and tube fiddles; end-blown flutes (mostly of the notched type), cone flutes (of clay, bamboo, wood, or horn), vessel flutes (often made from spherical seed shells and small gourds), end-blown and side-blown trumpets (often played in sets); idiophones of many kinds, including several types of xylophone; and lamellophones (known generically as *sanza* or *mbira* in southern and central Africa, but by neither of these names in the area under discussion, where names using the roots -*embe* or -*dongo* are more common). Last, there is a variety of drums, including tall single-headed ones, usually hand beaten, and the cylindroconical "Uganda drum," which, though it has two skins, is beaten by hand, or with sticks or clubs, usually on one head only.

TRACK 13

Many of these instrumental types are also found among the settled Nilotic peoples of the southern Sudan, some of whom (the Luo) migrated south through northern and eastern Uganda as far as the Kavirondo gulf on the eastern side of Lake Victoria. The lyre is such an example. Its distribution in Africa is limited to the northeast of our area. The presence of lyres in the Arabian peninsula, as far north as Iraq—and even on the western coast of India—are a reminder of the extent of the movement of African sailors and slaves to the Arab ports of the Near East and India. Many musicians active in professional and semiprofessional ensembles in the coastal areas of the Arabian peninsula have African origins.

The box lyre known as *begana* was formerly an instrument of the Amharic aristocracy in Ethiopia. Box lyres are also used in northern Kenya and in the region around Mount Elgon on the Kenya-Uganda border, but bowl lyres are more widespread, not only throughout Ethiopia, but also in the Sudan and around the northern shore of Lake Victoria. Lyres are popular instruments among young men in large areas of the Sudan and Ethiopia, and the Bantu-speaking Ganda and Soga of Uganda apparently adopted their bowl lyre after the mid-1800s from their Nilotic (Luo) neighbors to the east.

Styles of playing vary greatly: in much of the Sudan, the popular technique is to strum across all strings with a plectrum held in one hand, while using the fingers of the other hand to mute all but one string at a time. The result is that the unmuted pitches, usually comprising the basic pattern of the song (lyres usually accompany singing), ring out through the dry rhythmic texture of sound created by the muted strings. Ganda and Soga musicians prefer rapid plucking by fingers and thumbs, and the notes of the scale, as in the case of many lamellophones, are divided out on both sides of the instrument so each hand can pluck patterns that interlock.

Political institutions greatly affect the music of both the settled peoples of highland Ethiopia and those of the interlacustrine highland region, which extends south like a spine from the headwaters of the Nile. In both areas, the "Sudanic" concept of kingship took root: powerful kingdom-states evolved, and music flourished within their courts. Specially named drums symbolizing chiefly power were carefully guarded as part of the royal regalia, to be sounded only at coronations and other important state occasions.

This is true among certain Sudanese pastoralist peoples also. Among the Murle, four sacred drums represent the four separate "drumships" of the tribe, the instruments being sounded only in two circumstances: to invoke divine assistance in time of feud, and to announce the outlawing of a wrongdoer.

The former emperor of Ethiopia included in his processions forty-four pairs of kettledrums (*nagarit*), and allowed his princes only twenty-two pairs each. More important, perhaps, than the symbolic nature of such music is the fact that rulers through their patronage made possible the growth of professional classes of musicians.

The former kabaka of Buganda, like other rulers in the area of Lake Victoria, maintained several ensembles at court. He had a private harpist (*omulanga*), and his palatial ensembles included a flute consort (requiring flutes of six sizes, accompanied by four drums), two xylophones (the larger instrument, an *akadinda,* requiring a team of six players), a drum-chime (*entenga*), a bowl lyre ensemble, and a band of trumpeters—in addition to large numbers of royal drums.

Trumpet ensembles were formerly part of the music at the courts of other East African kings and rulers. These trumpets are usually side blown, made from wood, bamboo, or sections of calabash. Each instrument sounds one or two pitches; the performer produces the second by opening a small tip in the narrow end near the mouth hole. The trumpeters combine their pitches in hocket to produce multipart pieces usually derived from well-known songs, whose texts convey chiefly praise and recall royal histories. In many cases, royal musicians were accorded special privileges, such as grants of land, and they usually kept their skills within their own family or their own clan. In Uganda, royal patronage ended in 1966, when the autonomy of the kingdom-states was overthrown.

Trumpets played in hocket style are common in other parts of Africa, and in East Africa many smaller societies (such as the Waza of southern Sudan and the Alur of northwestern Uganda) perform in similar ensembles for dances they regard as having central importance in reinforcing social cohesion. Gerd Baumann has detailed the importance of the *sorek,* a dance performed during the ritual harvest festivals of the Miri of the Nuba Mountains (Sudan), when the entire community participates, dancing in concentric circles around the trumpeters, who play instrumental transformations of songs which in other contexts are for the ears of men only. At such times, virtually all "are carried away by the intricate beauty of the gourds' interlocking sounds, the supple rhythm of tension and relaxation in the dancing, and the physical experience of being 'in tune' with others" (Baumann 1987:85, 182). He sees the "moral power" of such music and dancing as "essential to the reintegration of Miri communities" struggling to preserve their ethnicity in the face of growing political and economic integration into the Islamic state of Sudan.

There is a good case for regarding other hocketing ensembles as performing essentially similar roles. Sets of end-blown flutes played in hocket also appear in many parts of East Africa. They consist of sets of single-note flutes of graded length, made from reeds or bamboo, most of which are closed at the lower end by a natural node or a movable plug. They are reported to accompany the communal circle dances of various peoples in the central highlands and valleys of Ethiopia, among the Ingessana of Sudan (Kubik 1982) and along the western rift valley as far south as the Transvaal in southern Africa and the desert areas of Botswana and Namibia.

A sample shows the basic structure of a song recorded from a group of young adolescents in Madi, in the West Nile district of northern Uganda. The whole group sang the text first, indulging in improvisation that produced occasional harmonies in

The use of music to entertain and enhance the dignity and status of rulers in East Africa must have contributed to the richness of musical traditions. Not all the ensembles have ceased to function; some were recruited to serve new political leaders.

fourths and fifths. The men then began blowing their one-note flutes to outline the melody in more than one octave. Almost before the melody was established among the flutes, a good deal of variation making in individual parts had appeared, as players inserted single notes at extra points in the basic pattern, elaborating their own one-note rhythms. The result was a lively harmonic and polyrhythmic ostinato, absorbing and surrounding the vocal line, with the texture further enriched by drumming and hand clapping. More research needs to be done before one could confidently say this style is essentially representative of other stopped-flute– and trumpet-playing traditions in East Africa.

Given the social and ritual importance of such ensembles, it was perhaps not surprising that powerful chiefs frequently took control of them. In addition to royal trumpet ensembles, powerful chiefs in Rwanda, Burundi, and western Uganda maintained smaller ensembles—of cone-shaped flutes, made of clay, wood, or short lengths of bamboo. These ensembles were known as *esheegu* among the Banyankore of Uganda, and *isengo* among the musicians of the former king of Rwanda. Though the institution of kingship no longer exists in these regions, the clans responsible for these ensembles maintain the tradition.

Interlocking techniques are further exemplified in traditions of playing xylophones and drums in Uganda. In the Ganda *amadinda* style, two players, seated one on each side of a twelve-key log xylophone, beat out, each in octaves, two isochronous pentatonic patterns, derived from the melody of a song. By listening to the pattern the first two players sound on the two bottom notes of the instrument, and by reduplicating it two octaves higher on the top two keys of the instrument, a third player extracts another part. Ganda musicians have expressed wonder at the unknown inventors of such a simple and beautifully logical means of realizing their songs on this instrument.

The use of music to entertain and enhance the dignity and status of rulers in East Africa must have contributed to the richness of musical traditions; and though the political upheavals of the 1960s and 1970s saw the demise of royal power and its associated music in East African countries, not all the ensembles have ceased to function. Some were recruited to serve new political leaders. Musicians from others teach their art in schools and colleges, or have joined "national" music and dance ensembles. Hence it was possible to record the *amakondeere* trumpet band of the former omukama of Bunyoro performing at a trade fair in Hoima (Bunyoro, western Uganda) in 1968, two years after the disbanding of the kingdoms in Uganda, and several key members of Heartbeat of Africa, a national troupe, were formerly musicians in the palace of the kabaka of Buganda.

Indigenous political institutions did not always monopolize music and dance traditions. During the colonial period, the formal parades and military bands of the ruling colonial powers inspired the rise of competitive associations known as *beni* (from the English word "band"), *kingi* (from the English word "king"), or *scotchi* (imitating Scottish kilts and bagpipes). Originating on the East African coast in imitation of the regimentation of the Royal Navy (and later the regiments of the King's African Rifles), *beni ngoma* 'dance, feast, drum' and its derivatives eventually spread throughout East Africa. Wherever they were performed, precision of movement seems to have been an ever-present concept, combined with the use of European instruments (wherever possible) and formal European dress. *Beni* was an expression of competitiveness within nontribal society (Ranger 1975).

In British East Africa, native recruits readily learned skills on European band instruments: the kabaka of Uganda established a military band for his private army, and several police regiments also formed similar bands, playing European tunes from sheet music. Immediately after independence, the same bandsmen began composing their own music and arranging traditional melodies for their bands.

In contrast to the official institutions, these associations were small independent organizations. They originally appeared in the ports of the East African coast, among the Swahili. Where their musicians were unable to obtain European trumpets and bugles (or, in the case of *scotchi,* sets of bagpipes), locally made kazoos or gourd trumpets and drums sufficed. A Ugandan poet and writer, Okot p'Bitek, reported how the concept of "armyness" was introduced to the Acooli Jok cult, and its possessed participants behaved in a characteristically military way.

Ex-members of the King's African Rifles took the idea of *beni* and its music, dress, and choreography back to their home villages in many parts of British East Africa, and though the original *beni, kingi,* and *scotchi* have been superseded among the urban coastal communities where they originated, stylistic features of *beni* survive in the *goma,* a men's dance with slow, precise movements, using walking sticks, dark glasses, and other "European" accoutrements (Campbell and Eastman 1984). Furthermore, one can find stylistic features of *beni* in the choreography of village dances in many inland areas of East Africa, where quite often the dances are regarded as "traditional." Examples are the *mganda* in Tanzania, the *malipenga* of northern Malawi (Kubik 1985:194–195), the *beni* of the Yao, and the *dingidingi* (a girls' dance) of Acooli, Uganda—the last no doubt a product of the parallel development of women's associations.

Summarizing a survey of *beni* and related associations Ranger considered these "societies were not pantomimes of white power, nor protest movements set against it . . . but concerned with survival, success and reputation of their members, acting as welfare societies, as sources of prestige, as suppliers of skill (1975:75). Though *beni* seem to have stood for features of twentieth-century music in Eastern Africa normally explained as the result of Europeanization, "the brass band itself had extra-European origins, and apparent exoticisms, like danced drill and mimed combat, were in fact derived from the long-standing competitive dance traditions of the Swahili coast" (Ranger 1975:164).

Religious institutions

Evidence suggests that the repertory and style of music at court paralleled, as one might expect, the high conservatism of the royal institutions. Royal music itself was often perceived as having a quasi-religious function, associated with the notion of the king's divinity.

Such conservatism is even truer of the music of the Monophysite Christian church of highland Ethiopia, founded in Axum in the fourth century. Its liturgy (*zema*) and religious poetry (*qene*) is chanted in the classical Sabean language known as Ge'ez, and in the shaking of the sistrum to mark the ends of lines, it has parallels with religious performances in Jewish synagogues. Ecstatic liturgical dance (*aquaquam*) is another feature of this worship.

enswezi   Cult in southern Uganda whose music is marked by the use of four drums interlocking in fast triple rhythms

emibala   'Drum texts' that accompany special songs addressed in turn to specific spirits

A similar complex liturgy (also in Ge'ez) was the subject of recent research among the Falasha of northern Ethiopia, where Kay Shelemay (1986) has established with convincing musical evidence that the religious tradition of the so-called Black Jews was strongly influenced by contact with Christian monasticism in the fourteenth and fifteenth centuries—and, indeed, that its very Jewishness may have stemmed from such contacts. In 1984, Operation Moses took most of the Falasha community to Israel, where the Falasha ritual will probably not survive.

Many traditional religious cults are based, as in many other parts of sub-Saharan Africa, on ancestor worship and a belief that ancestral spirits and other spirits have the power to intervene in the affairs of mortals. Examples are the *zār* cults of Sudan and parts of Ethiopia and Somalia, and the *bacwezi* cults of western Uganda. In southeastern Uganda, traditional healers of the *enswezi* cult use songs invoking individual spirits (*lubaale* 'gods' or *mayembe*), and these songs combine with dancing, drumming, and the use of loud rattles to help induce a variety of states of possession. Those who become possessed may be the sick persons, professional mediums, or even the officiating priest-healer.

Such religious music is usually distinguishable from secular music. In Busoga, southern Uganda, music of the *enswezi* cult is marked by the use of four drums interlocking in fast triple rhythm, and with the lead drummer (who beats the three lower-pitched drums) inserting appropriate *emibala* 'drum texts' while accompanying special songs addressed in turn to specific spirits. Another ingredient in the musical texture is provided by women cult members known as "daughters of Kintu." (Kintu was the chief ancestor of the cult, the legendary first king of the Ganda.) They join in the wordless refrains with voices disguised by singing into their kazoos (*engwara*), made from narrow conical sections of dried gourds.

Most systems of musical tuning in East Africa are pentatonic, and among the people of southern Sudan and Uganda there is a strong tendency toward equipentatonicism (Wachsmann 1950, 1967). The Wagogo of central Tanzania sing, often in parallel harmony, melodies that are basically tetratonic, and which Kubik (1985) considers are based on selective use of the sequence of natural harmonics from partials four to nine.

Kubik's own most recent research, however, suggests that interval size differences in such pentatonic scales are probably not emically significant. When presented with a wide range of pentatonic tunings of sample xylophone scales and melodies, even the most skilled traditional musicians (Ganda, Soga, Teso) judged them acceptable. The implications of such tests of perception require further investigation.

NOMADIC AND SEMINOMADIC PEOPLES

TRACK 15 and 16

Vast areas of the Sudan, nearly all of Somalia, and parts of Ethiopia and the plains of inland Kenya, Tanzania, and northeastern Uganda, consist of desert or dry scrubland, thinly inhabited by pastoral peoples. They include the Cushitic-speaking Somali and

Oromo (sometimes known as "Galla") of southern Ethiopia, para-Nilotic peoples such as the Karamojong, Turkana, and Pokot to the southwest of Lake Rudolph, and the Samburu and Maasai of the rift-valley plains of Kenya and Tanzania. For many of these peoples, musical instruments would be an encumbrance. Their music is purely vocal, save for the occasional rhythmic accompaniment of hand clapping, or the sounds of stamping feet, sometimes enhanced by the jingling of ankle bells or other items of personal adornment. In Arab-influenced areas, frame drums or kettledrums may accompany such singing.

Historical traditions, war, and—above all—cattle are common subjects in nomads' repertory of songs. The melodies, like those of most Bantu- and Nilotic-speaking peoples, are mostly pentatonic; but unlike the melodies of these peoples, the phrase tends to be longer and more undulating, with frequent use of long-held tones. An example shows the refrain of a song performed by men of the Jie tribe in Karamoja, northeastern Uganda. Different soloists took turns to sing out brief utterances in a rapid speech rhythm between refrains. A wide range of nonlexical vocal utterances, some using explosive sounds from the diaphragm, typify the refrains.

Though call-and-response form is ubiquitous in Africa, among pastoralists the choral response tends to be longer than the call, and sometimes overlaps the soloists' parts to produce simple part singing, or includes ostinati, creating harmonies of fourths and fifths. However, such generalizations can be faulted. Kenneth Gourlay (1972) has shown the relative proportions of soloists' parts among the singing of Karimojong men's songs can vary greatly, depending on the genre. He has distinguished two categories of men's song, personal "ox songs" and choral songs, and has demonstrated how in the former the soloist's part can dominate the structure, while in the latter the choral refrains make up the major part of the pattern. Part singing in long choral refrains is a feature of the Nandi and Kipsigis peoples of western Kenya.

INDONESIAN, ARABIC, ISLAMIC, AND EUROPEAN INFLUENCES

The coastal peoples of East Africa have long had contact with the Arabic world, and with other cultures around the shores of the Indian Ocean. However, in a critical survey of the evidence (presented by Leo Frobenius, Erich M. von Hornbostel, Arthur M. Jones, and Jaap Kunst), R. Blench plays down the degree to which Indonesian influence penetrated the African continent. He concludes that while there is ample reason to suppose there was an influx of a people from some part of Indonesia to the Malagasy Republic (Madagascar) and the neighboring African coast, the evidence for Indonesian colonization and influence on parts of the interior (as suggested by Jones, who cites a good deal of musical and organological evidence) is "thoroughly insubstantial." Nevertheless, the *valiha,* the tube zither with wire strings fitted around a large tube of bamboo and played in Malagasy and in other parts of Tanzania, is a striking example of Indonesian importation. The *marimba,* a box-resonated xylophone, played in the islands of Zanzibar and Pemba and on the mainland nearby, is possibly additional evidence of cultural contact with Indonesia.

Myths sometimes provide tantalizing glimpses into the past. The "national" dance of the Baganda, most commonly performed for feasts, and said to have long been associated with the court of the former kabaka, is the *baakisimba*—a term derived from the verb *okusimba* 'to plant', and the steps are said to symbolize pressing the offshoots of plantains into the ground, and this action in turn is associated with the ancestor-god-king Kintu, who supposedly brought the plantain to Buganda. Plantains became not only the staple diet of the area, but also the chief ingredient of the beer and spirits necessary for celebrations and feasts (personal communication A. Ssempeke, 1988).

Most of the Sudan is Arabic-speaking, and Islam is the official religion of that

Quite apart from Arab contacts, the East African coast has long had a history of contact with the outside world.

country. The practice of Qur'ānic chanting in schools has accompanied the spread of Islam south into all the other countries of East Africa. Arabic poetry is enjoyed by the Arabic-speaking communities of the north and along the East African coast, and men of the Sudanese Sufi order perform the ecstatic ritual known locally and elsewhere in the Islamic world as *zikr* or *dhikr* 'remembrance'. The participants use a special, rhythmic, deep-breathing technique, combined with rhythmic movement and utterances of the name of Allah, to help them achieve communally their aim of communicating directly with their deity.

In many areas, however, musical practices associated with pre-Islamic cults, such as *zār* often flourish alongside Islamic practices. Young Miri women living in the Nuba mountains of Sudan enjoy singing commercially produced Arabic *dalūka* songs, which for them stand for, celebrate, and allow access to and indulgence in, "much of what they think best in the urban Sudan," while relishing the performance of their traditional rituals (Baumann 1987).

Early in the first millennium, Arab traders set up stations along the East African coast. Arabic influence is particularly noticeable on the islands of Zanzibar and Pemba, and to a lesser extent in the music of the coastal Swahili peoples, where epic songs (*utenzi*) and lyrical poems (*shairi*) use meters and strophic structures similar to those of Arabic poetry. Swahili heptatonic melodies, delivered with a certain amount of melisma, differ distinctly from the songs of most other Bantu-speaking peoples (Jones 1975–1976).

Descriptions of the types of *ngoma* performed in and around the port of Lamu (Campbell and Eastman 1984) show that Swahili culture has a mixed nature. Excepting the *goma*, these *ngomas*, while using the *nzumari* (an Arabic shawm) or the *tarompet* (a Western cornet) and Arab-derived tambourines, feature styles of dancing that, with an emphasis on circular hip movements, are similar to the styles of dancing of other Bantu-speakers of inland East Africa. Farther inland, the Nyamwezi, a Bantu-speaking people of central Tanzania, who for centuries controlled the ivory trade routes to the interior, also sing in "Arabic" style—with diatonic melodies that have a certain amount of melisma. In the extreme southwest of East Africa, the Yao appear to have absorbed considerable Islamic influence.

Without other evidence of culture contact, it would be a mistake to assume Arab influence wherever diatonic or melismatic structures appear. For example, it would be difficult to show Arab musical contacts with the Konzo, who inhabit the Ruwenzori mountains along the Uganda-Zaïre border, despite their use of heptatonic songs and instruments, such as harps, flutes, zithers, and xylophones (Cooke and Doornbos 1982). The same is true for the Makonde of northern Mozambique and southern Tanzania, whose music is primarily hexatonic, based on roughly equal steps of 160–180 cents, and who in ensembles sing parallel thirds. The Makonde and their neighbors may be related more to the peoples of the Shaba province of southern Zaïre than to their Tanzanian neighbors farther north (Kubik 1982).

A highly melismatic and tense-voiced style, used by Hima pastoralists in western Uganda and their Tutsi counterparts of Rwanda and Burundi, is more problematic. These peoples have absorbed the language, but neither the musical style nor the diet and life-style, of the Bantu peoples they live among, and over whom they established ruling hegemonies.

Instruments have traveled more easily than musical styles. In the past century, the tube fiddle (a bowed lute, probably derived from the Arabic rebab) has migrated across Kenya, through southern Uganda, and as far west as Rwanda and Burundi. In the mid-to-late-twentieth century, townsfolk adopted Western instruments in considerable numbers, but rural people less frequently used them.

LATE-TWENTIETH-CENTURY DEVELOPMENTS AND URBAN MUSIC

Quite apart from Arab contacts, the East African coast has long had a history of contact with the outside world. Madagascar was extensively colonized by Indonesians. In the 1500s, Portuguese traders came to the coast of East Africa, but in the 1600s, they were ejected from Fort Jesus at Mombasa: their musical legacy may perhaps be the violin, still used alongside lutes and frame drums in small Arab orchestras playing the hybrid music known as *taarabu.*

Taarabu is found along the whole of the east coast of Tanzania and Kenya, particularly in the larger towns—Dar es Salaam, Malindi, Mombasa—where large instrumental ensembles perform music obviously based on that of Arabic orchestras. Indeed, in Dar es Salaam one of the first groups to be formed called itself "The Egyptian Music Club." Indian influences, mostly derived from Hindi film sound tracks, are also heard in the music of these groups. Indian harmoniums and Arabic instruments (notably the *'udi,* an unfretted lute derived from the Arabic *'ud*) appear in the ensembles and in Lamu Island songs, sung in either of three languages—Swahili, Arabic, Hindi.

The harmonized hymns that Christian missionaries introduced to British and German East Africa after the 1850s are tending to be replaced. Christian Africans, sometimes called "Sunday composers," are experimenting in composing, for educational and religious choirs, traditional African-style melodies, not all of them harmonized in four parts in hymnbook style. Some are performed to accompaniments of drums and rattles, but in many newer churches in towns like Kampala, electric organs, bass guitars, and synthesizers are coming into use, and sects such as the Baptist and Free Presbyterian churches are popularizing the gospel-hymn repertory.

In the 1960s, the Roman Catholic Church in western Uganda adopted Benedicto Mubangizi's hymnbook, *Mweshongorere Mukama* (1968), which contains ninety-five hymns, many of them composed in call-and-response form. Its preface enjoins users not to introduce harmonies other than those produced by overlapping refrains in some of the hymns. Like other composers—such as Joseph Kyagambiddwa, a Muganda, whose *Uganda Martyrs' Oratorio* has been published, performed, and recorded in Europe and East Africa—Mubangizi takes care to compose in a way that does not disregard the traditional rules controlling the relationship between speech tones and melodies. During the 1980s, however, more and more of his hymns were being performed in four-part harmony.

In Kenya, Uganda, and Tanzania, school-music festivals have stimulated the production of innumerable secular and religious compositions in quasi-traditional style, staged alongside the performance of traditional tribal songs and dances, European scholastic songs, madrigals, and Christian spirituals. Arrangements of traditional songs are now part of the repertory of village cultural societies, which meet to rehearse and perform traditional songs and dances of the community in new contexts, grouped and sometimes acted out as miniature dramas.

In the 1960s, Zaïrean bands mingled with bands performing a new wave of *kwela* music, Congolese jazz, and popular European and American styles in the nightclubs of Kenya.

One would expect Western influence to be found in the popular urban music of East Africa. The guitar is ubiquitous. Even in rural districts it often vies for popularity with traditional stringed instruments, such as lyres and zithers. African radio networks are accountable for much of this development, though the first guitar music recordings appeared around 1945. J. Low (1982) identified the successive adoption of a variety of styles of playing in Kenya—from the simple vamping of Swahili-language town music to the complex finger styles of Congolese musicians like Mwenda-Jean Bosco and Musango. This variety gave some indication of the degree to which popular musicians circulated around East Africa.

The appearance of electric guitar bands in the 1960s allowed other Western instruments to join the ensembles, and at that time Zaïrean bands (whose musicians had migrated from their hometowns during the civil wars there) mingled with bands performing a new wave of *kwela* music, Congolese jazz, and popular European and American styles in the nightclubs of Kampala, Nairobi, and Mombasa. In the 1970s, singers tended to become more important in such bands, with much part singing and call-and-response patterns using local languages, while guitar parts were tending to become more rhythmic than melodic. Though Western popular music is continually making inroads, much of this music includes African-American, Caribbean, and Latin American styles—all of which owe much to an African heritage.

In rural areas most distant from towns (though such music is readily available on transistor radios), any imitations of Western popular music have tended to be dominated by essentially African features. Intervillage competitions held in Acooli (northern Uganda) during the late 1960s featured groups of youths playing three sizes of *likembe*, lamellophones, in ensembles of up to fifteen. Though the *likembe* itself was a newcomer to Acooli (having traveled northeast from the Congo during the previous thirty years), and though the youths' repertory included pieces entitled "Rumba" and "Vals" and "Foxtrot," plus tunes said to have been inspired by the white American country singer Jim Reeves, the way each instrumental part was composed, and the way it interlocked with the other parts, were purely Acooli in style, closely related to the style of music played on the Acooli trough zither (*nanga*).

REFERENCES

Baumann, Gerd. 1987. *National Integration and Local Integrity.* Oxford: Oxford University Press.

Blench, Roger. 1982. "Evidence for the Indonesian Origins of Certain Elements of African Culture: A Review with Special Reference to the Arguments of A. M. Jones." *African Music: Journal of the International Library of African Music* 6(2):81–93.

Campbell, C. A., and C. M. Eastman. 1984.

"Ngoma: Swahili Adult Song Performance in Context." *Ethnomusicology* 27(3):467–494.

Cooke, Peter, and Martin Doornbos. 1982. "Rwenzururu Protest Songs." *Africa* 52(1):37–60.

Gourlay, Kenneth A. 1972. "The Making of Karimojong Cattle Songs." Nairobi: Institute of African Studies, University of Nairobi. Discussion paper 18.

Jones, Arthur M. 1964. *Africa and Indonesia: The Evidence of the Xylophone and Other Musical and Cultural Factors.* Leiden: E. J. Brill.

———. 1975–1976. "Swahili Epic Poetry: A Musical Study." *African Music: Journal of the African Music Society* 5(4):105–129.

Kubik, Gerhard. 1982. *Ostafrika: Musikgeschichte in Bildern,* vol. 1: *Musikethnologie,* part 10. Leipzig: VEB Deutscher Verlag für Musik.

———. 1985. "African Tone Systems: A Reassessment." *Yearbook for Traditional Music* 17:31–63.

Low, John. 1982. "A History of Kenyan Guitar Music: 1945–1980." *African Music: Journal of the International Library of African Music* 6(2):17–36.

Mubangizi, Benedicto. 1968. *Mweshongorere Mukama* [*Sing to the Lord*], 2nd edition. Kisubi, Uganda.

Ranger, Terence O. 1975. *Dance and Society in Eastern Africa 1890–1970: The Beni Ngoma.* Berkeley: University of California Press.

Shelemay, Kay Kaufman. 1986. *Music, Ritual and Falasha History.* East Lansing: Michigan State University Press.

Wachsmann, Klaus P. 1950. "An Equal-Stepped Tuning in a Ganda Harp." *Nature* 165:40–41.

———. 1967. "Pan-Equidistance and Accurate Pitch: A Problem from the Source of the Nile." *Festschrift für Walter Wiora,* ed. Ludwig Finscher and Christopher-Hellmut Mahling, 583–592. Cassel: Bärenreiter.

Wachsmann, Klaus P., and Kathleen Margaret Trowell. 1953. *Tribal Crafts of Uganda.* New York: Oxford University Press.

Music in Tanzania
Stephen H. Martin

People and Language
History
Areas of Musical Style
Musical Instruments
Neotraditional Music Forms

After a succession of colonial occupations (Arab, German, British), Tanganyika achieved independence in 1961. Zanzibar, consisting of the islands of Zanzibar and Pemba, achieved independence from Great Britain in 1963. For several centuries, these states had had close cultural ties. In 1964, their political union established the United Republic of Tanzania.

With a land area of nearly a million square kilometers, Tanzania is the largest country in East Africa. It is one of the least urbanized African countries: only 15 percent of its people live in urban areas. Its largest cities include the coastal capital of Dar es Salaam, Zanzibar (on Zanzibar Island), Mbeya (in the eastern highlands), Mwanza (on the southern shore of Lake Victoria), Dodoma (the new capital, in the center of the country), and Tanga (a port, north of Dar es Salaam). In 1990, the national population was about 26.3 million.

Geographical regions

Tanzania has three major geographical regions: narrow coastal lowlands and islands, central plateaus, and highlands. The first lies along an 800-kilometer coastline on the Indian Ocean. It is Tanzania's most densely populated region, and its hottest and wettest. Included in it, several kilometers northeast of Dar es Salaam, are Zanzibar (the largest coral island off the coast of East Africa) and Pemba.

A gradual rise from the coastal region to the central plateaus causes the climate to become drier and cooler. The character of the central plateaus ranges from grasslands (of the Maasai Steppe, in the north), to a grassy plateau (which covers about a third of the country's area). Drought is common, and the poverty of the soil limits agriculture.

The northern highlands contain the country's highest mountains, among them Kilimanjaro, the highest peak in Africa. The Rufiji, Tanzania's principal river, flows out of the southern highlands; scrub woodlands characterize the eastern highlands. In the central highlands, mild temperatures and abundant rainfall encourage high population density.

PEOPLE AND LANGUAGE

About one hundred twenty diverse, mainly Bantu-speaking, ethnic groups populate

In music making, traditional sex roles persist most strongly in rural areas. An increased involvement of women in music making is visible in such urban musical forms as *taarab* and jazz.

Tanzania. A unique feature of the country's demography is that no single group makes up a majority. The largest is the Sukuma, about 13 percent of the national population. Most of the remaining groups make up no more than 3 percent to 4 percent each; several groups, among them the Maasai, equal less than that.

Other language groups include some derived from the Khoisan family (like the Sandawe), some Nilotic groups in the north, and various nonindigenous groups (Arabs, Indians, Pakistanis, Europeans), mostly in urban areas. Though some ethnic groups (Sukuma, Nyamwezi, Makonde, Haya, Gogo, Chaga, Nyakyusa, Ha) have exerted influence politically, the general ethnic balance of the country has aided governmental efforts to build a national character, thus avoiding major ethnic upheavals and political rivalries.

Another important unifying factor in Tanzanian culture is the national language, Swahili. Though people speak it alongside English, Tanzania is one of a handful of African nations that use an indigenous African language for official communication. Swahili is a lingua franca; it developed through active commercial interchange among Arabs, Portuguese, and Bantu-speaking inhabitants of the Tanganyikan interior. That the language does not come from a specific ethnic group has helped lessen tribal rivalries.

Despite the impact colonial governments made on urban growth and national rule, Tanzania has principally an agrarian economy. Its only large city, Dar es Salaam, is a legacy of the colonial presence. Nevertheless, several forces have wrought changes in people's life-styles. The introduction of Western education, the spread of Islam and Christianity, the establishment of *ujamaa* villages (relocation habitats, established under President Nyerere's régime), and the building of roads and railways, have been agents of social and cultural change. To deal with intertribal marriages, the temporary absence of males from villages (while seeking employment in urban areas), and rapid urban growth, traditional tribal customs have had to change. The music of urban Tanzania reflects many of these issues.

Though Tanzanian law treats women the same as men, traditional values of male dominance still have social effects, especially in villages. In music making, traditional sex roles persist most strongly in rural areas. An increased involvement of women in music making is visible in such urban musical forms as *taarab* and jazz.

The religious culture of Tanzania consists of three strata, each of which represents about one-third of the population: indigenous practices centering on ancestor worship, Islam, and Christianity. Indigenous religions predate the arrival of colonialism. Islam came by way of Zanzibar through Arab traders, documented from the tenth century at the latest. Its impact is visible mostly in the coastal region and on the islands, and to a lesser extent in some of the interior regions, into which it penetrated during the 1800s. Christianity arrived in the 1840s. It brought an emphasis on Western education and health. It also exerted some political influence: most of the country's leaders got their education in mission schools.

HISTORY

The East African coast has a long and well-documented history. The earliest document in print, the *Periplus of the Erythrean Sea*, is a guidebook to the Indian Ocean, written by a Greek merchant in the first century (Blankaart 1683). It describes the interaction between the Arab traders and the coastal inhabitants. In the first century, many of the Bantu-speaking peoples of Tanzania arrived; by the twelfth, the intermarriage of Arab traders and African women created an Arab-African culture, and produced the beginnings of Swahili culture and language.

The arrival of the ancestors of the Bantu- and Nilotic-speakers of the interior may have begun in the first millennium. The migrations of the Bantu were probably from the south, southwest, and west; the Nilotes came from the north or northwest, southern Sudan, and possibly western Ethiopia. Before these migrations and the beginning of the Iron Age, Bushman hunters and gatherers inhabited most of Tanzania. Evidence of their presence is visible the rock paintings of central Tanzania, near the territory of the Sandawe, Khoisan (click language) descendants of the Bushman population. Eric Tenraa's studies (1963, 1964) of the music of the Sandawe give further evidence of this connection. Kubik (1967, 1968) has posited that musical scales based on portions of the natural harmonic series also show relationships between living cultures and those of early inhabitants. He points out that elements such as polyphonic vocal music, yodeling, and the use of tetratonic and pentatonic scales (derived from partials of the harmonic series) are features of Bushman music. According to his analysis, these features appear in the music of the Gogo. Though the Gogo are linguistically unrelated to Bushmen, he says they may have absorbed these musical elements from earlier occupants of the land.

From this point, the development of Tanzanian history is visible in several stages, beginning with the development of Zanzibar as a center of trade and the seat of the East African Arab sultanate, the arrival of the Portuguese explorers, and the colonial occupations of the German and British regimes, followed by independence and unification.

The development of Zanzibar followed the success of Kilwa, a community on the Tanganyikan coast. By the early 1300s, it was a prominent Arab center of trade; its contacts reached as far eastward as India and Persia. With the Kenyan coastal town of Mombasa, Zanzibar soon overtook Kilwa as a major commercial center.

At the end of the 1400s, the arrival of Portuguese traders boosted Zanzibar's commercial status. Though the impact of the foreign presence in Zanzibar and Mombasa was important, the Portuguese exerted little influence on the Tanganyikan mainland. Their primary interest was in India.

By the mid-1800s, Omani sultans had seized power in Zanzibar, and were controlling a lucrative trade in slaves and ivory. Meanwhile, the incursion of Arab slavers created unrest in the interior, and led to political realignments and the reshuffling of power. From the north, invasions by the Maasai, and the resistance of the Hehe, took place; from South Africa, the Ngoni began migrating.

Europeans were also present on the mainland in the 1800s. Richard Francis Burton, John Hanning Speke, David Livingstone, and Henry Morton Stanley—all explored or lived in Tanganyika in the mid-to-late 1800s. By the 1870s, British representatives were pressuring the Omani sultanate to end its trade in slaves, but until well into the 1880s, they had little effect on independent traders, like Tippu Tib, who created a virtual Arab empire west of Lake Tanganyika, an area rich in ivory; he also completed the first known coast-bound caravan from central Africa to Dar es Salaam.

German influence began in 1890, with the establishment of the German East Africa Protectorate. Treaties worked out by Karl Peters with the interior inhabitants

Drums reveal, or hold the key to, historical information about earlier Tanzanian societies. In Iramba, where prehistoric rock shelters and caves exist, archaeologists have found seventy-eight drums, which predate by two hundred years or more the current inhabitants of the area.

laid the groundwork. Nonetheless, such groups as the Hehe and the Chagga vigorously resisted further German incursion into the mainland.

The Great War had major effects on East Africa. More than two hundred fifty thousand Africans died in Tanganyika alone. The Treaty of Versailles placed Tanganyika under mandate to the League of Nations, which assigned it to British administration. The biggest impact of World War II was the movement toward independence. In 1954, the Tanganyikan African National Union (TANU), led by Julius Nyerere and others, brought Tanganyika closer to independence.

Musical scholarship

Little is known of the music history of Tanzania. Terence O. Ranger's study (1975) of dance clubs, and Hartwig's study (1969) of the Kerebe of northwestern Tanzania, are important examples of musical scholarship. Ranger takes a comprehensive look at a single musical style as it occurs throughout East Africa. Hartwig examines the music of a single area: he tries to reconstruct Kerebe culture history. He focuses on a zither, the only chordophone the Kerebe used before 1900. It originally accompanied a beer-drinking ceremony. Over time, it and the social context of its performance evolved. Instead of accompanying elders with songs having historical texts, it began to serve purely for entertainment, in association with hand clapping and dancing. On the arrival of colonialism, young men and women became the principal performers.

AREAS OF MUSICAL STYLE

Tanzania has eight areas of musical style, some of which spill over into other nations (Kubik 1982:38). These areas include (1) the coastal regions along the Indian Ocean, and the islands of Zanzibar and Pemba; (2) the areas of the WaNyamwezi and WaSukuma, north-central Tanzania; (3) the area of the WaGogo, central Tanzania; (4) the area of the WaChagga, Kilimanjaro; (5) the area of the Karagwe and Buhaya, northwestern Tanzania (with cultural ties to the royal traditions of southern Uganda, Burundi, and Rwanda); (6) the western area, including the Wafipa and others; (7) the area around the Ruvuma river valley, extending into the northern part of Mozambique; (8) the area of the Ubena and the Upangwa (southwestern highlands), and the area around Lake Nyasa.

MUSICAL INSTRUMENTS

Unlike other parts of Africa, especially West Africa, the documentation of music and musical activity in Tanzania is sparse. Perhaps the largest body of available knowledge pertains to musical instruments and their geographical distribution throughout the country. Such studies, many based on collections of instruments in the National Museum in Dar es Salaam, have been undertaken by both Tanzanian and non-Tanzanian researchers. Some remain unpublished. The following organological overview summarizes this information.

Membranophones

Membranophones occur throughout Tanzania in a variety of forms and sizes. Certain drums have an association with specific regions. For drums, the most important shapes include kettle, cylindrical, barrel, conical, hourglass, footed, and goblet-shaped versions. How the heads are attached varies from region to region. Larger drums usually have heads made of cow skin, goat skin, or zebra skin; smaller drums have heads made from the skin of reptiles.

In the West Lake area, a typical type of drum is the braced conical drum, the "Uganda drum." Like most Tanzanian drums, it is made of wood, though some examples have copper bodies. The tops are open; the bottoms, closed. Cowhide, braced with narrow leather strips, covers both. The top half of the drum is cylindrical, and the bottom tapers like a cone with the point sliced off. The tops are open; the bottoms, closed. Cowhide, braced with narrow leather strips, covers both. The Haya drum (*ng'oma*) comes in several sizes. The same drum occurs in Uganda, Rwanda, and Burundi. Among the Kerebe (on Lake Victoria), a similar instrument occurs in royal sets, believed to have been made by Haya and Ganda slaves. Another drum is the *iduffu*, a large, circular, frame drum, used by the Haya in the *kuzikiri*, a Moslem ritual dance. With Islam, this drum penetrated the interior.

In the central plateaus of the country, drumming conforms with Islamic principles. In the Tabora area, for the installation of new chiefs, the Nyamwezi formerly used a set of royal drums. These drums—large, round, bowl shaped, footed—were traditionally played only on special occasions. For royal ceremonies, the Nyamwezi also used other, nonfooted, and smaller drums. In rituals connected with secret societies, the Sukuma still use large, double-headed, cylindrical drums. Near Dodoma, among the Gogo, drumming occurs only in women's ceremonials, and only women play the instruments. The drums, used to accompany *ng'oma* dances, are large, hourglass types, with only one end covered with skin; the other end is open. Pegs fix the skins to the drums, whose body sometimes has a carved handle at the waist. To play, women hold the drums between their legs, and hit the heads with their hands. The largest of the set, played by the master drummer, is the *ng'oma fumbwa*; the smaller ones are *nyanyulua*.

In the coastal region, in areas like Mtwara, Lindi, and Dar es Salaam, cylindrical drums in a variety of sizes are characteristic. Also found are differently sized goblet drums, with pegged membranes. To accompany the *mbeta* dance, the Zaramo (of the Dar es Salaam area) use drums and other percussive instruments with flutes. A variety of *msondo* (cylindrically shaped drums), with pegged or tacked-on heads, also occur along the coast, and in Morogoro and the south. In dances such as the *gombesugu* and the *sindimba*, the Makonde (southern region) and Zaramo use a large hourglass drum. In the coastal areas, and to the north from Morogoro to Tanga, braced cylindrical drums accompany the *selo* dance.

Among the Fipa (Rukwa, southern highlands), a low, goblet-shaped instrument has a pegged drumhead of snakeskin. On the head, several lumps of beeswax act as a paste for tuning. The drum specially accompanies marimba music.

In addition to being musical instruments, Tanzanian drums have symbolized power and authority, as the variety of royal drum sets shows. Also, drums reveal, or hold the key to, historical information about earlier Tanzanian societies. In Iramba, where prehistoric rock shelters and caves exist, archaeologists have found seventy-eight drums, which predate by two hundred years or more the current inhabitants of the area (Hunter 1953:28). Hidden in sixteen caves, these drums were concealed with rocks, possibly to protect them from an imminent invasion. Nothing is known of the original tribes to which they belonged, but these caves are a place of wonder to the Nyampala, a subgroup of the Nyisanzu, who inhabit the area.

Idiophones

Among the major classes of instruments in Tanzania, idiophones are the oldest and most numerous. This class divides into two groups: untuned and tuned idiophones.

Untuned idiophones

Untuned idiophones group as bells, rattles, scrapers, and shakers. These instrument-types are found widely throughout the country. In general, they serve as part of percussive batteries, or are used alone to provide rhythm for otherwise unaccompanied singing (as with the bells used in the *msunyunho* choral singing of the Gogo). Additionally, dancers wear some idiophones.

The Swahili term *njuga* denotes a string of small bells, which dancers wear around the ankles. Bean shaped, the bells are iron, with one or several metal balls inside. Dancers string together about fifteen bells; shaken, each bell chimes at a unique pitch. The Gogo stitch these bells onto strips of leather about 20 centimeters long. The Maasai Moran have a larger set of bells, the *ol-tnalan*. Worn on elaborate leather bands, sometimes decorated with cowrie shells, these bells are iron, and have several iron balls inside. Among the Chagga, male dancers wear on their backs *shimo-lo*, sets of bells.

In southern Tanzania, the Mawia and the Mwera wear ankle rattles, made of small, hard fruit shells, strung together in rows. With the dancers' foot stomping in performance, these musical adornments provide a distinct cross-rhythmic pattern against the patterns of the accompanying battery of drums.

In southern Tanzania, scraped idiophones, like the *tatarizo,* are often used. The *tatarizo* is made of a bamboo stem, with twenty or more serrations carved around it. In several musical contexts, people play it by scraping a small wooden stick across the serrations.

The Swahili term *manyanga* is the generic name of an array of shaken, seed-filled rattles, mostly made of dried calabashes or coconuts, and spread widely around the country. Their shells often have perforations, which serve the functions of decoration and sound amplification. They are often played in pairs, but they may be played singly. The Sukuma and the Haya use them in trance-inducing rites.

Another kind of shaken idiophone is the *kayamba*, a reed rattle, two layers of reeds stitched together, with small seeds in the space between the layers. Used in a variety of contexts, it is found in southern Tanzania—among the Burungi, the Luguru, the Ngoni, the Sukuma, and others. It is shaken with both hands, whose thumbs provide additional rhythms by slapping against it.

Tuned idiophones

Tuned idiophones are of two types: mbiras and xylophones. In Tanzania, the term *marimba* often specifies either of these groups, and the Swahili phrase *marimba madogo* 'small marimba' refers to the mbira.

Mbira

A range of mbiras occurs throughout the country: some are boards, mounted in gourd resonators; others are box resonated. The number of lamellae may vary from as few as six to several dozen. The keys are usually metal, bamboo, or rattan, and their vibrations resonate in a box resonator (among the Gogo, the Makonde, and the Mwera); or the keys, attached to a board, resonate in a calabash (among the Makua). Often, to add a buzz, each key has a loosely attached metal ring, or the resonating cavity contains idiophonic modifiers, like a small hole covered with the membrane of a spider's nest.

Among the Tanzanian mbiras are the Makonde *ulimba*, possibly the oldest mbira in Tanzania (Kubik 1985:5); the Makua *rumpa*, a flatboard mbira with eight iron keys and a calabash as a resonator; and the Gogo *marimba*, a box-resonated form, which has versions with nine to forty-five keys (Nketia 1968:80). Young men play the nine-key version for personal enjoyment; the larger versions have thirty-four to forty-five keys; one uses fifty-six (Hyslop 1976:2).

The instruments with thirty-four to forty-five keys are played in an ensemble of six musicians, three of whom play the *marimba* in a responsorial relationship: one player acts as leader, and each player also sings. Each performer plays slightly different ostinato patterns, which utilize tones about a third apart. The part of the lead singer-player overlaps constantly with the part of the responsorial chorus of player-singers.

The tuning of the instruments is pentatonic, with tones that roughly equate the sequence D–F–G–A–B. For the simultaneous sounding of any of these tones to be consonant in Gogo terms, they must be a third or a fourth apart. The typical sound of the ensemble gives the impression of a constantly sounding dominant-seventh chord (figure 1). The other three performers include two who play hand-held rattles, and a dancer who wears ankle bells.

The significance of the Gogo *marimba* in Tanzanian musical culture is shown by the fact that in 1970 it was chosen to represent the nation in a special issue of four postage stamps, illustrating musical instruments of East Africa.

Xylophones

Among the xylophones in Tanzania are log xylophones and box-resonated xylophones. The Makua play the *mangolongondo*, a log xylophone that has nine keys that vibrate freely on two logs, on which they rest. Along the coast, the Zaramo play a box-resonated xylophone, which they simply call *marimba*. It has eight or nine keys, and in performance is usually paired with a similar instrument. In such instances, one instrument, the *marimba ya kuanza*, starts the piece; the other, *marimba ya kugenkizia* 'marimba that turns the tune around', elaborates on the basic pattern. Three drums of different pitches—*boi, msondo, seberea*—complete the ensemble, which normally accompanies songs. Box xylophones also occur among the Sambaa and Bondei, and on Zanzibar and Pemba. Frame xylophones (such as the Mandinka *balofon* or the Chopi *timbila*) are not traditional in Tanzania, though in the mid-1970s, after a tour of West Africa, members of the national troupe brought them into the country.

FIGURE I   Vocal harmony of the Wagogo people: *a,* basic vocal harmonies; *b,* extended vocal harmonies.

Only women play mouth bows, often for lullabies. The women's bow is a small, straight piece of split bamboo, with a copper wire or fiber string.

Chordophones

A large assortment of chordophones occurs throughout Tanzania. They range from simple musical bows to unusual and sophisticated lutes, one of which is simultaneously bowed and plucked. Typical also are lyres and bow harps, chordophones common throughout all of East Africa.

Musical bows

Only women play mouth bows, often for lullabies. One example is the *nganga* of the Fipa, who live southeast of Lake Tanganyika. This bow, and many others used only by women, show little resemblance to the hunting bow: the women's bow is a small, straight piece of split bamboo, with a copper wire or fiber string.

Braced bows—with gourd resonators attached to the center of the stick, and a wire noose attached to the same spot on the stick, subdividing the string—are found in western and central Tanzania. In Tabora, the Nyamwezi use the *igubu,* a large example, to accompany songs. To accompany dances, young Sukuma men and women play a musical bow, the *yazoli.* Another example is the *donondo,* found among the Nyaturu. Unbraced musical bows also occur in the southern areas of Tanzania, among the Pangwa and Sangu.

Zithers

Bar zithers are generically known as *zeze* (as are bows and lutes), while board zithers are called *bango.* The latter, which occur mainly in coastal and southern areas, use calabash resonators. One Gogo musician, Lubeleje Mkasa Chiute, has developed a unique version of the board zither, the *chipango* (Gogo for *bango*). He invented it while a student at the College of Art, Bagamoyo.

In Iranga District (south central highlands), where the population is mostly Wahehe, a board zither, the *kipango,* has six strings, with a gourd resonator at one end. It occurs throughout this area, and in Malawi and Mozambique. Traditionally, a musician sits, and sets it between his thighs. However, guitar music has affected its playing: many of its musical patterns resemble those of guitar music. Young performers actually play the instrument like a guitar.

The Hehe zither is the *ligombo,* a narrow, three-stringed, trough zither. Its most famous performer, Pancras Mkwawa, played for recordings made by Hugh Tracey in 1951. For a resonator, the *ligombo* has at its base an open gourd.

Two other types of trough zither also occur: the Sandawe *tloto* has six strings, derived from wrapping a single strand through holes on the high ends of the trough. The trough ends in a handle on one side of the instrument. The other type is the *inanga.* It is larger and proportionately much wider, with a rim around the entire trough, and carved notches for the wrappings of the single stand at each end. This version occurs in the West Lake area, and in Tabora.

Lutes

The term *zeze* also covers lutes. Of the ethnic groups that play lutes, the Gogo have probably the richest musical heritage—a fact most Tanzanians readily acknowledge. Known as the *izeze* among the Gogo, these instruments come in a variety of sizes, with different numbers of strings (from one to twelve). Musicians pluck or bow them, and sometimes perform both ways at once. Gogo musicians are also famous for virtuosity in performance.

In the 1970s and 1980s, Tanzanian fiddles began to undergo innovation, especially at the hands of Hukwe Zawosi, one of the nation's most celebrated musicians. The largest *izeze* is more than a meter long. Attached to tuning pegs, the strings extend rearward from the neck; the skin of a dik-dik covers the body, a calabash shell. The lengths of the pegs vary, and the strings keep clear of each other. The body bears burned etchings and ornamental tacks. The tuning of this instrument (as with other pitched Gogo instruments) uses "the 4th to the 10th partials of the harmonic series, with a diminished 5th occurring between the 5th and 7th partials" (Kubik 1980:567–571) (figure 2).

Harps

Bow harps are seven-stringed, boat-shaped instruments. Cowhide covers their resonators, intricately decorated with burned-in parallel and diagonal lines. The Ha traditionally use bow harps; people of the Morogoro and Iringa areas call them *kinubi*.

In Tanzania, the bowl lyre, typical in East African cultures, occurs only among the Kuria (Mara area), who know the instrument as the *litungu*, an eight-stringed version. People formerly made the bodies of bowl lyres from a carved wooden bowl; by the late 1900s, a metal bowl, of a kind common in households, served the same purpose. Sections of zebra skin, lashed together, cover both sides of the resonator. The use of gut for its strings has given way to the use of nylon, which permits greater stability in tuning. Werema Masiaga Chacha, a Kurian musician, is Tanzania's leading performer on the *litungu*.

Aerophones

Many kinds of aerophones occur in Tanzanian traditional music (Gnielinski 1985). They range from simple flutes to composite trumpets. In traditional contexts, aerophones are often associated with magical practices and beliefs, as in the land around Lake Victoria, where they serve as rainmakers or storm deterrents (Wachsmann 1961:48), or as symbols of authority in connection with war, hunting, or convening communal gatherings.

FIGURE 2   Comparison of Wagogo tuning and harmonic partials of the overtone series: *a,* basic four-tone scale with the number of the harmonic overtone series (top number) and the number of cents between overtones (bottom number); *b,* extended scale, with same numerical indicators as above.

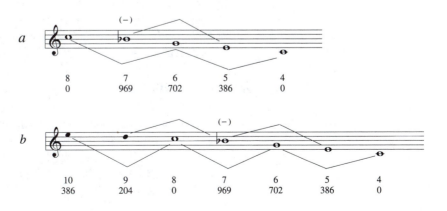

imbutus   Horn used by the Kumbu as the emblem of the chief and considered the most sacred possession of chiefdom

beni ng'oma   Social dance clubs of East Africa with dance steps that reinterpreted military drills of European models

Trumpets

The most striking indigenous aerophones are trumpets (Swahili *baragumu*). In some societies, they serve both musical and nonmusical functions. Fishermen in Bukoba and Zanzibar use them to call customers. The Butu and Maasai used them as a part of military campaigns. The Kimbu used a horn called *imbutu* as the emblem of the chief, and considered it the most sacred possession of every Kimbu chiefdom.

Other trumpets include the *ntandara* (also *ntanduka*), end-blown wooden trumpets of the Ukerewe. About 1.8 meters long, these were played in sets. They resemble the Ugandan *amakondere*. Side-blown trumpets, made of kudu horns (*nzamba*), occur in the West Lake area. The *lilandi*, a deep-sounding trumpet, is a composite, made of seven to fourteen gourds, attached by stitches and special gum; the largest gourd serves as the bell. The Kabwa (Mara area) use this trumpet in wedding rituals, and play it all night before circumcisions (Hyslop 1976:54). They also use it to accompany singing, and they play it in ensembles with membrane drums and stringed instruments. In central Tanzania, bamboo trumpets (*mputa*) occur. These are side-blown instruments, with a round gourd attached as a bell.

Flutes and reeds

Flutes in Tanzania tend to be side blown—like the Hehe *kilanzi*, the Makua *npeta*, and the Makonde *mwanzi* (Swahili for 'bamboo')—and occur throughout the country. These instruments are mostly bamboo, but are occasionally stalks of millet. Those made of the latter are often played by children. Many traditional flutes have begun to be displaced by modern versions, even those imported from China. Traditional flutes, however, continue to play an important role in more traditional songs and contexts, where musicians are still reluctant to use nontraditional flutes. Flutes are apparently used to express personal feelings, and in traditional settings often add rather individual touches to the musical fabric. They are also used by shepherds herding cattle, and by children playing in fields.

Reed instruments, though found in parts of the country, are not indigenous to Tanzania. Along the coast, and on Zanzibar and Pembe, an Arabic reed import—the *zumari*, a single-reed clarinet—is found. In the area of Dar es Salaam, the Zaramo people use the *zumari* in some religious musical activities, but elsewhere in Tanzania, it is rare or not seen at all.

NEOTRADITIONAL MUSICAL FORMS

After 1945, music in Tanzania, as in other parts of East Africa, began to undergo a series of changes that pointed toward the development of a new cultural consciousness. This change was roughly parallel to the political changes that began to surface in the country: the mutual recognition, by both Africans and Europeans, of the inevitability of political independence (Kubik 1981:83). Africans who had participated in World War II returned from Europe, having seen and heard unfamiliar musical forms. By the 1950s, recordings of Cuban rumbas and other Latin American styles began to become popular in Zaïre, where local bands adapted and imitated these rhythms, and eventually developed them into Congolese jazz, which became highly influential in Tanzania.

Beni ng'oma

The impact of Western influence on Tanzanian music took many forms. One of the most revealing absorptions of this influence into the African cultural framework involved the European brass band. In the early 1900s, East Africans became familiar with the music of German and British brass bands. As early as 1906 in Dar es Salaam, German bands recruited Africans. In 1919, when the British entered the city after the war, they found among Africans an abundant supply of trained brass-band performers. The impact of British brass bands had already been felt elsewhere in East Africa, with the formation of the King's African Rifles (KAR) in Kenya and Uganda in 1906.

The degree to which Tanzanians admired the regalia of European military ensembles and metaphorically reinterpreted this phenomenon in their own terms is visible in the array of musical and social adaptations their own traditional culture made, in the form of social dance clubs, *beni ng'oma*. These clubs, originating along the Kenyan coast as competitive dance associations, have a deep-rooted history, and actually date from the 1890s. Some of the features of this tradition were European military titles for officers and dance steps that imitated military drills. Despite these traits, *beni ng'oma* is essentially African in character, and the meanings of its dance steps and titles are quite different from those of its European models (Ranger 1975). The language used was Swahili. The popularity of *beni ng'oma* penetrated well into the interior, but by the 1930s it began to wane. By 1945, interest was beginning to shift toward dance bands. The decline of *beni ng'oma*, coinciding with the end of the colonial era, became a sociomusical token of the decline of colonialism. The demise of the dance clubs revealed the acculturative forces that were exerting themselves on Tanzanian music.

Christian music

From the earliest presence of Christian missionaries until the 1930s, the music of the Christian Church in Tanzania was merely Western music performed on Tanzanian soil. To European and American hymns, missionaries added texts in indigenous languages, without regard for tonal inflection and other linguistic subtleties. Despite missionaries' early resistance to change, the efforts of young missionaries and enterprising African Christians eventually Africanized the church. Within rituals, they included African musical elements, and they encouraged the composition of liturgical pieces that incorporated African elements.

The first use of African music in Christian worship was among the Ngoni people of Malawi in the late 1800s (Jones 1976:39). But this situation was exceptional. In Tanzania, African music began to appear in Christian churches in the early 1950s. Various articles discussing this development began to appear in the *Journal of the African Music Society* in 1956. Tanzanian composer and clergyman Stephen Mbunga published a list of records of music composed by Africans, including music for Christian worship (1963:125–164, 209–211).

An example of ecclesiastical Africanization is Mbunga's *Missa Baba Yetu* 'Mass of Our Father' (1959), a work whose vocal parts have typically African harmonic and rhythmic relationships, especially in the Gloria. In addition to composing, Mbunga acted as a spokesman for Africanizing the music of Tanzanian churches. In an article on musical reform (1968), he called for educational reorientation, like the kind out-

> Tanzanian jazz bands emerged most prominently in Dar es Salaam. Their development was fostered not only by the Africanization of European musical instruments and musical concepts, but also by the impact of African-American music and culture.

lined by Nyerere, Tanzania's first president. In his 1967 speech "Education for Self-Reliance," Nyerere had called on the nation to move, educationally and culturally, toward an African mentality. Mbunga claimed the same reorientation was necessary in music. He cited the need for a "cultural self-adjustment," and made suggestions for future directions in the nation's policy on music. He also wrote a book on music in the Christian churches of Africa (1963).

Training centers

In the 1960s, to spark a sense of musical nationalism, the Tanzanian government set up official agencies. One such agency was the Music Conservatoire of Tanzania, Limited, founded in 1967 in Dar es Salaam. This conservatory helped Tanzanians rediscover their musical heritage, and provided musical training in Western musical performance and composition. However, it emphasized the European classical tradition, and thus did not reach the goal of creating a nationalistic framework.

In the 1970s, other training centers began to appear around the country. At Bukoba, the Ruhija Music Centre, under the direction of Mr. W. Both and the Lutheran Church, primarily trained local musicians. On the coast, the Bagamoyo College of Arts also began a program in musical training. At the University of Dar es Salaam, such scholars as Graham Hyslop, a British musician and musicologist who specialized in East African music, began teaching courses in music and working with African choirs. In 1974, to oversee the development of a nationalized cultural pride, President Nyerere reestablished the Ministry of National Culture and Youth.

Jazz

Tanzanian jazz bands emerged most prominently in Dar es Salaam. Their development was fostered not only by the Africanization of European musical instruments and musical concepts, but also by the impact of African-American music and culture, which, by the 1960s, was being felt in many parts of the continent. Another important musical influence was the new music coming out of Zaïre. This style, derived from the Latin American rumba, entered Tanzania by way of 78-rpm records, and later by an influx of Congolese bands, which dominated popular music in East Africa for more than a decade. Eventually, Tanzanian bands, aided by the government, began to borrow some of the stylistic features of the Zaïrian bands, and developed a Tanzanian style of jazz.

Tanzania's lack of facilities for commercial recording and manufacturing limited the commercial production of jazz. Nevertheless, people elsewhere in Africa managed to hear this music on records and tape dubs pirated from Radio Tanzania broadcasts. During the 1970s and 1980s, this station recorded local bands, and thereby generated dynamic musical activity. In 1979, the station recorded more than 6,000 traditional-music ensembles, 120 jazz bands, 60 *taarab* groups, 50 choirs, and 30 brass bands (Wallis and Malm 1984). Using its library, more than 1,500 tapes (as of 1980), which featured more than 60 bands, Radio Tanzania's national radio broadcasts helped preserve the uniqueness of Tanzanian jazz as it aided its development.

Three socioeconomic factors affected the development and proliferation of the new popular musical forms: the availability of European instruments, the rise of panethnic communities in urban areas, and European discovery of the commercial viability of African popular music (Kubik 1981). Companies like Odeon, Victor (His Master's Voice), and Columbia were the first to record popular music in East Africa. Even the packaging of the recordings appealed to a specific African market—the emerging, but sparse, African middle class.

In the mid-1970s, the jazz bands of Dar es Salaam reflected the variety of cultural and musical influences that for two decades had affected popular music. Three bands performing in Dar es Salaam in the mid-1970s prove this point: the Orchestre Maquis du Zaïre, a Zaïrian band, included Tanzanian female dancers (figure 3); NUTA Jazz Band represented the National Union of Tanganyika Workers; Sunburst consisted of native Tanzanians, African-Americans, and a Jamaican. Each of these bands performed music that reflected different spheres of musical influence: the first played Congolese style, the second favored a style more closely related to Tanzanian traditional music, and the third displayed influences from African-American culture and the West Indies.

Taarab

A musical style popular throughout coastal East Africa, *taarab* centers principally in Zanzibar. Related more closely to Egyptian café music than to music of the Tanzanian mainland, this style finds its roots in the same soil as Swahili. In addition to serving as social entertainment, *taarab* reinforces, preserves, and elevates, the position of Swahili. Its music, a heterophonic orchestral style, traditionally accompanies Swahili love poetry known as *mashaira*. The typical *taarab* orchestra consists of a trapezoidal zither (*kanuni*), violins, cellos, string basses, accordion, lute (*udi*), end-blown flute (*ney*), a battery of percussion, and sometimes an electric guitar and electric keyboard or organ. A chorus and vocal soloists join the instrumentalists, so a typical Zanzibari ensemble consists of twenty-five to thirty-five performers.

Taarab developed about 1950. It grew out of Egyptian *firqah* orchestras, which, during the 1940s, provided sound tracks for Egyptian films. By the mid-1950s, *taarab* music clubs had sprung up in every district of urban Zanzibar. They played mainly for local weddings and other festive activities. After the revolution of 1964,

FIGURE 3 Orchestre Maquis du Zaïre, a Congolese-style band with Tanzanian female dancers.

the song texts became politicized to reflect the ideology of the Afro-Shirazi Party, and several ensembles received governmental sponsorship. On the Tanzanian mainland, song texts often reflected the ideology of President Nyerere. In the 1980s, some *taarab* groups went back to performing Swahili love poems.

In Zanzibar, *taarab* clubs were not exclusively a male domain. Women's clubs, though not initially so prominent, existed as a network of smaller ensembles. Unlike the male groups, the female clubs had loose structures, and were small. The most famous *taarab* singer was a woman, Siti binti Saad.

Nationalization

Utamaduni, the Tanzanian National Dance Troupe (founded in 1964), is possibly the clearest embodiment of the notion of neotraditional music in Tanzania. Authorized by the Ministry of National Culture and Youth, it was the means by which the ministry tried to develop a nationalized form of music—one that amalgamated musical styles from the nation's ethnic groups. This ensemble assembled a corps of some of the nation's finest musicians from a variety of ethnic backgrounds.

In 1974, to accelerate the process of musical nationalization, the government set up Baraza la Muziki la Taifa, the National Music Council. Other institutions involved in nationalization are the Tanzanian Film Company (to which the government granted sole rights to release recordings of Tanzanian music), and Radio Tanzania.

REFERENCES

Blankaart, Stephen. 1683. *Periplus Maris Erythræi*. Amstelodami: Apud Jansonnio-Waesbergios.

Gnielinski, Anneliese von. 1985. *Traditional Music Instruments of Tanzania in the National Museum*. Dar es Salaam: National Museums. Occasional paper 6.

Hartwig, Gerald W. 1969. "The Historical and Social Role of Kerebe Music." *Tanzania Notes and Records* 70:41–56.

Hunter, G. 1953. "Hidden Drums in Singida District." *Tanganyika Notes and Records* 70:41–56.

Hyslop, Graham. 1976. "Musical Instruments of Tanzania." Manuscript.

Jones, Arthur Morris. 1976. *African Hymnody in Christian Worship: A Contribution to the History of Its Development*. Gwelo, Zimbabwe: Mambo Press.

Kubik, Gerhard. 1967. "The Traditional Music of Tanzania." *Afrika* 8(2):29–32.

———. 1968. *Mehrstimmigkeit und Tonsysteme in Zentral- und Ostafrika*. Vienna: Österreichischen Akademie der Wissenschaft.

———. 1980. "Tanzania." *The New Grove Dictionary of Music and Musicians*, ed. Stanley Sadie. London: Macmillan.

———. 1981. "Neo-Traditional Popular Music in East Africa since 1945." *Popular Music* 1:83–104.

———. 1982. *Musikgeschichte in Bildern: Ostafrika*. Leipzig: VEB Deutscher Verlag für Musik.

———. 1985. "Tanzania Music Areas." Manuscript.

Martin, Stephen H. 1991a. "Brass Bands and the Beni Phenomenon in Urban East Africa." *African Music* 8(1):72–81.

———. 1991b. "Popular Music in Urban East Africa." *Black Music Research Journal* 11(1):39–53.

Mbunga, Stephen B. G. 1963. *Church Law and Bantu Music.* Schoeneck-Beckenried, Switzerland: Nouvelle Revue de Science Missionaire. Supplement 13.

———. 1968. "Music Reform in Tanzania." *African Ecclesiastical Review* 10:47–54.

Nketia, J. H. Kwabena. 1968. "Multi-Part Organization in the Music of the Gogo of Tanzania." *Journal of the International Folk Music Council* 19:79–88.

Ranger, Terence O. 1975. *Dance and Society in Eastern Africa 1890–1970.* Berkeley: University of California Press.

Simon, Artur, ed. 1983. *Musik in Afrika.* Berlin: Staatliche Museen Preussischer Kulturbesitz, Museum für Völkerkunde.

Tenraa, W. F. E. R. 1963. "Sandawe Musical and Other Sound Producing Instruments." *Tanganyika Notes and Records* 60:23–48.

———. 1964. "Sandawe Music and Other Sound Producing Instruments: Supplementary Notes." *Tanganyika Notes and Records* 62:91–95.

Wallis, Roger, and Krister Malm. 1984. *Big Sounds from Small Peoples.* New York: Pendragon Press.

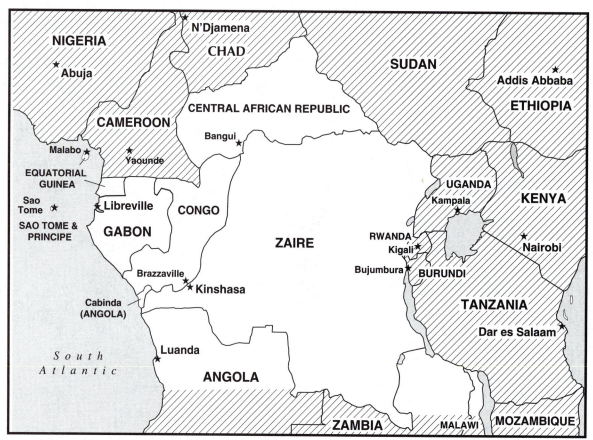

Central Africa

In 1997, a new government in Zaïre changed the name of the nation to "Democratic Republic of the Congo."

Central Africa

In Central Africa, music reflects interchanges with styles from such distant sources as Portugal and Latin America. Within the region, the polyphonic singing of the Pygmies has influenced—and been influenced by—the music of their neighbors. Royal chiefdoms, secret societies, migrant laborers, and European Christian evangelization have all added to the richness of the musical palette.

Central Africa: An Introduction
Gerhard Kubik

Musical Cultures in the Adamawa-Eastern Subregion
Musical Cultures in the Bantu Subregion

Since the mid-1800s, perceptions about the identity and location of the central part of the African continent have changed repeatedly. For David Livingstone (1857), the center lay near the Zambezi River; for Georg Schweinfurth (1875), it occupied Mangbetu country, in the northeast of what in the late 1900s was the Republic of Zaïre. In 1960, Ubangi-Shari, one of the four territories of French Equatorial Africa, proclaimed independence under the name "Central African Republic"; in 1966, it became an empire; and in 1979, after a coup d'état, it became a republic again.

Thus, "Central Africa" is not an observational fact, but a geographical concept, with social and cultural implications. Such concepts change over time. They vary from culture to culture, and from author to author; compare the notion of "West-Central Africa" (Murray 1981:154).

For descriptive purposes here, Central Africa is the portion of Africa where people speak languages belonging to either of two divisions:

(1) Adamawa-Eastern languages, or family I.A.6 (Greenberg 1970), spoken mainly in Cameroon, the Central African Republic, and northeastern Zaïre.
(2) Bantu languages of zones A, B, C, H, L, K, and (in part) D and M (Guthrie 1948).

The Bantu languages fall together with the Semi-Bantu and Bantoid languages of the Cameroon grassland, in family I.A.5, or Benue-Congo languages (Greenberg 1970).

There are good reasons for correlating cultural-geographical boundaries with languages, rather than with other aspects of culture. First, as J. H. Kwabena Nketia and others have noted, language joins intimately with music. In Central Africa, people do not merely conceptualize sounds, but often verbalize them. Instrumental patterns produced on the Azande harp and box-resonated lamellophone evoke verbal associations, which inspire musician-composers to find new text lines (Kubik 1964:51–52). By repeating mnemonic syllables (which may or may not constitute lexically meaningful words), performers learn timbral sequences and rhythmic patterns; and in the rain forest from Cameroon to Congo and Zaïre, large slit drums

In 1997, a new government in Zaïre changed the name of the nation to "Democratic Republic of the Congo."

Central African linguistic zones

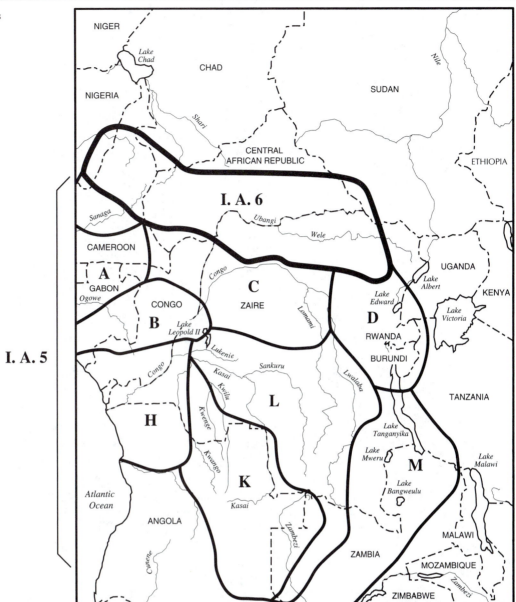

have served as "talking drums," to send messages in speech tones (Carrington 1949, 1956, 1975). Second, the languages of the African continent have been much better and more systematically researched than the musics; linguistic relationships unlock important chapters in African history, and throw indirect light on music history.

On a map of Central Africa, the line between the I.A.6 and I.A.5 languages marks a stylistic divide between Central African musical subregions. Most of Zaïre, all of Gabon, Equatorial Guinea, the islands of São Tome and Principe, Congo, most of the Central African Republic, and large parts of Cameroon, Angola, and the northern parts of Zambia, make up what I call Central Africa. This grouping acknowledges a combination of linguistic and cultural affinities, patterns of migration, and musical styles. Because of a historical migration of pastoral peoples from the East African Horn, and the presence of specific patterns of political organization in the interlacustrine area, Rwanda and Burundi are properly perceived as belonging to East Africa, rather than to Central Africa. On similar grounds, I exclude the southwestern part of Angola (particularly the Province of Huila), which, as Guthrie's zone R (1948), includes the cultures of the Nkhumbi, the Handa, and others.

Three women, pestles in hand, stand around a mortar. They strike alternately into the mortar, to produce an interlocking beat. Sometimes, between the main working strokes, each woman lightly taps her pestle on the rim of the mortar, to create accents and rhythmic patterns within a twelve-pulse cycle.

So defined, Central Africa is a vast region, diverse in musical cultures. In large expanses of the rain forest, the musical cultures of Bantu-speakers have supplanted an ancient culture, which survives in pockets, dispersed from southern Cameroon across the Congo to the Ituri Forest: that of the Pygmy hunter-gatherers. Though the Pygmies adopted Bantu languages long ago, their musical culture retained distinctive traits, which influenced the later arrivals. Wherever contact occurred among the three ethnic-linguistic entities (I.A.6-speakers, Bantu I.A.5-speakers, Pygmy I.A.5-speakers), cultural exchange and adaptation followed. In addition, cultures from outside Central Africa repeatedly made inroads into the region.

MUSICAL CULTURES IN THE ADAMAWA-EASTERN SUBREGION

This area lies north of the equator. It extends from the border of northeastern Nigeria, across Cameroon and the Central African Republic, into parts of the southern Sudan, including northern parts of Zaïre (see map).

The people who settled in this subregion can be classed in the following cultural clusters, proceeding from west to east (Murdock 1967).

(a) Chamba-Yungur (cluster 66), in the west; with individual peoples such as the Chamba, the Kutin, the Longuda, the Yungur, the Ndongo, the Vere.
(b) Adamawa (cluster 68), also in the west; including the Mundanga, the Fali, the Mumuye, the Mbum, the Lakka, the Namshi.
(c) Banda-Gbaya (cluster 71); including the Gbaya, the Banda, the Manja, the Ngbandi.
(d) Azande (cluster 72); including the Azande, with all their subdivisions, plus the (related) Nzakara.

The ecology of this broad area draws on a uniform savanna landscape, which supports a small population. Intermittently mountainous areas (especially the Adamawa massif) have often served as a retreat for invaded autochthonous peoples.

Certain stylistic and structural traits in music occur saliently throughout this subregion, as an extensive sample of recordings, obtained during the mid-1960s, shows (Kubik 1963–1964). These traits encompass tonal systems, singing in parts, patterns of movement, and instrumental resources. Some of them occur in the whole subregion, and some in parts of it.

Possibly all these peoples use pentatonic tonal systems. In western areas, the typical scale is often a plain anhemitonic pentatonic one, with seconds and minor thirds. In the more eastern areas, narrower intervals occur, as in some forms of Zande music (Kubik 1964). In several cultures, this scale combines with a homophonic two-part style of singing, with a predilection for simultaneous fourths and fifths. Despite differences in the intervals actually preferred in different areas—even within a homogeneous musical culture, like that of the Azande—simultaneous fourths and fifths are

Elementary pulsation: ca 430 M.M.

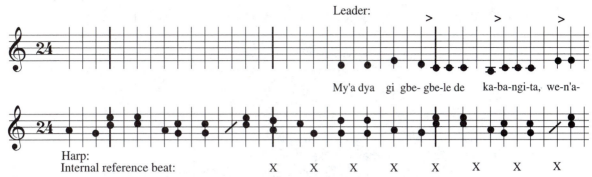

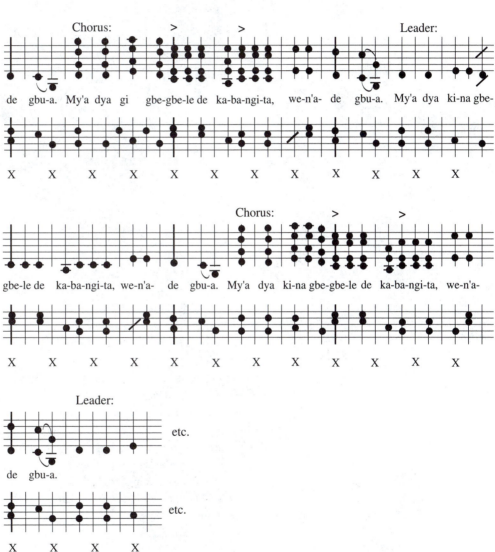

FIGURE 1 *Wen'ade gbua:* Zande song, performed by Antoine Gbalagume (about thirty years old) on the harp, with a leader and a chorus of men and women, at Djema, Central African Republic, May 1964 (Kubik 1963–1964:R47/B). In this notational system, a note head on the staff marks the impact point of a note to be sung or played; in singing, the note is held until it is revoked by the sign for a stop (/). Thus, duration is expressed indirectly, by marking the moment on the timeline when sound production stops.

perfect (that is, aimed at 498 and 702 cents, respectively). In this subregion, no evidence for the use of a tempered tonal system has turned up. Figure 1 shows typical Zande style: a leader and a chorus homophonically perform a multipart song, accompanied by a five-stringed harp.

In the western part of this subregion, some cultural anthropologists have considered the peoples who inhabit highland or mountainous areas an old Sudanic or pale-

kundi   Term for the tanged type of harp in
the Central African Republic

FIGURE 2   Kutin performers on double bells.
Kontcha, northern Cameroon, 1963.

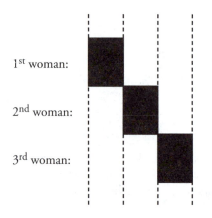

FIGURE 3   Three Chamba women rhythmically
organize their work. Northeastern Nigeria, 1963.

1st woman:

2nd woman:

3rd woman:

FIGURE 4   Interlocking patterns of beats produced by millet-pounding strokes.

onigritic stratum: these peoples are the descendants of long-established agriculturalists of the savanna. Music may retain survivals from the remote past. Therefore, it is
significant that here we find evidence of the presence of kinetic patterns combined in
interlocking style. In figure 2, Gonga Sarki Birgui and Hamadjan, who live at
Kontcha (a Ful6e-dominated area), play together on *toŋ ito*, two double iron bells of
the Central African flange-welded type, with bow grip (Kubik 1963–1964:B8910,
B8920). The bells are individually called *toŋ senwa* 'the higher' (1=B_M+40 cents,
2=F_H+5), and *toŋ deni* 'the lower' (1=F_M−5, 2=A_M+30, Korg Tuner readings).
Subscripts in these readings indicate the octave range: M, middle; H, high. The bells,
positioned with their openings toward the chest, are played in a two-tone pattern
with a softwood beater held in the right hand. The patterns interlock. By varying the
distance between the opening and the chest, the musicians modify the timbre of the
bells. Both these techniques of structuring are probably ancient in African music;
they also occur in the instrumental music of other regions, as in the *mvet* of zone A.

Among the Chamba, who are related to the Kutin, evidence of tripartite interlocking has turned up in the organization of women's millet-pounding strokes (figure
3). Three women, pestles in hand, stand around a mortar. They strike alternately into
the mortar, to produce an interlocking beat (figure 4). The photograph shows the
technique: one woman has just struck, the second one has lifted her pestle to the ver-
tex, and the third is halfway down her stroke. But the total action is more complex:
sometimes, between the main working strokes, each woman lightly taps her pestle on

FIGURE 5   Watched by children, Lazaro Tourgba of Zemio, Central African Republic, plays a Zande harp, 1964.

the rim of the mortar, to create accents and rhythmic patterns within a twelve-pulse cycle. From time to time, with lips, palate, and tongue, the women also produce sucking and clicking sounds; they thereby add to the percussion another timbre-melodic line (Kubik 1963–1964: B 8609). Figures 3 and 4 show an approach to patterning that is basic to much African music: they suggest, in tandem with the known history of these populations, the antiquity of the concept.

From northernmost Cameroon (which falls partly into Greenberg's family of III.E, or Chadic languages), across the Central African Republic, into southern Sudan, stretches what can be called Africa's most cohesive harp territory. The harp, an ancient Egyptian-Saharan heritage, found widespread footholds in the savannas at the northern fringes of the rain forest. From the specimens played among the Ngbaka, south of Bangui (Arom 1967), to those of the Nzakara and Azande (Dampierre 1963; Kubik 1964), most of the peoples mentioned under (c) and (d) above, except for the Gbaya in the west, play harps (figure 5).

In the Central African Republic, the harps belong to what Wachsmann (1964) called the tanged type of African harp. Ancient connections are still visible in stylistic analogies in harp music across this subregion, including nomenclature, with the frequently heard term *kundi* (Zande, Nzakara) and its variants, like *kundeŋ* (the Karre at Bozoum). In the northwesternmost areas of the Adamawa-Eastern division of languages, harps accompany iron smelting, and are played by associates—often close family members or junior apprentices—of a blacksmith working at the furnace (Gardi 1974). In the southeast of this subregion, harps have spread into the land of the Mangbetu, speakers of a Central Sudanic language, whom outsiders have often erroneously associated with the Azande. In the early 1900s, Mangbetu carvers, exploiting what were the beginnings of a lucrative colonial trade in touristic art, produced thousands of ivory harps with carved motifs and body coverings made of reptile skin. (A large collection reposes at the Musikinstrumentenmuseum, Munich.)

kponingbo   A twelve- or thirteen-key log
    xylophone, accompanied by a slit drum
    (*guru*) and a double-skin membrane drum

FIGURE 6   A sequence of bichords in Zande music.

European tourists bought these specimens of Mangbetu harps, which ended up in the international trade of African art, or in public collections.

Harp music of the Azande, Nzakara, and Banda has been studied by several authors (Giorgetti 1957; Dampierre 1963; Kubik 1964 and 1967). In the older styles of the Azande, one often finds asymmetric patterns within a regularly cyclical number, such as twelve or twenty-four pulses (figure 1). Harmony in Zande music for the harp includes sequences of four bichords (figure 6), which also appear in vocal harmony. The tonal-harmonic system of Zande music strictly regulates the occurrence of each of these bichords; the relationship to the referential beat usually follows the same scheme as in figure 1. The scale is a descending pentatonic one, which musicians memorize with the aid of a text they often play to check the tuning at the beginning of a piece (figure 7); here is its translation.

> Little by little, that's work.
> One must play the harp, and sing its song.
> The ancient things implicate work.

Zande tunings, however, vary; two notes in particular, identified in figure 7 by a parenthesized macron, may be lowered by almost a semitone.

The harp is not the only prominent Zande instrument; the Azande have a wide range of instrumental resources. Three types of xylophone appear in this area: the *manza*, the *longo*, and the *kponingbo*. The first of these, associated with Zande royalty, has a pentatonic tuning, in two large, one medium, and two small intervals. A specimen documented by Kremser (1982) in Zaïre had gourd resonators; another, found at Chief Zekpio's place in Dembia, Central African Republic, had five logs placed over banana stems. A chief's relative played it, to accompany the chief's harp music (figure 5). The term *manza* may connect with other xylophone terminology in the northern part of Central Africa. Though no evidence on Indonesian origins has presented itself (compare Jones 1964:151–52), relationships with xylophone names farther west from the Azande are likely: *mɛndzáŋ* in Ewondo (southern Cameroon), and *mɛntʃaŋa* in Mpyɛmɔ́ (southwestern Central African Republic). These cognates imply historical relationships in the distribution of xylophones in this subregion. The *longo* (also pronounced /rongo/) is a portable, gourd-resonated xylophone. The specimen documented among the Azande at Dembia (figure 8) resembles types found in Chad, and falls clearly within the northernmost area of gourd-resonated xylophones in Africa.

FIGURE 7   A Zande phrase for checking the tuning of the harp (*kundi*). It is performed in free speech rhythm.

FIGURE 8   For a recording, a Zande musician plays a gourd-resonated xylophone (*longo*). Djema, Central African Republic, 1964.

FIGURE 9   The military-inspired notched flute and drum ensemble of Rafai, Central African Republic, 1964.

The *kponingbo*, a twelve- or thirteen-key log xylophone, accompanied by a slit drum (*guru*) and a double-skin membrane drum in the *kponingbo* circle dance, is likely an Azande import from farther south, possibly as far as language zone L. In pieces for *kponingbo*, this origin is suggested by a rhythmic pattern that seems to be a remolding of a timeline associated with music in Katanga and eastern Angola (zones L and K). Characteristically, the Zande xylophones are not played in interlocking style, though those of Uganda and northern Mozambique are.

The instrumental resources of the Azande also include one flute ensemble, which consists of a set of notched flutes, with four finger holes each, and accompanied by marching-style drums. Based in Rafai (Central African Republic), it was first reported by Mecklenburg (1912); it still existed in 1964 (figure 9). All the evidence available suggests it was a late-nineteenth-century adaptation of military music that bands had performed on expeditions in the southern Sudan during the Mahdi rebellion.

MUSICAL CULTURES IN THE BANTU SUBREGION

Pygmy cultures

The linguistic and cultural map of the tropical–rain-forest areas of Central Africa in 3000 B.C. differed distinctly from that of the late 1900s (Murray 1981:26). Before about 1000 to 500 B.C., when speakers of early Bantu languages migrated from the Bantu Nucleus (a zone embracing parts of western Cameroon and eastern Nigeria) to western parts of Central Africa, the equatorial forest was inhabited by bands of hunter-gatherers, who differed racially from other speakers of Niger-Congo languages, namely the Pygmies. Despite some authors' repeated claims to have discovered an original Pygmy tongue, no such claim has survived scrutiny. All the sylvan hunter-gatherers that remain speak Bantu languages believed to be adaptations of the ancient Bantu tongues spoken by the first migrants with whom the Pygmies had con-

luma   Reed pipes that are popular among the Ituri Forest Pygmies of central Africa

jenge   Men's society, featuring masking, of the Bangombe Pygmies along the Sangha River

tact. In music, however, a pre-Bantu Pygmy musical culture may have survived. Pygmy music distinctively combines a polyphonic style of singing with an extremely developed technique of yodeling. These traits appear in the music of Pygmy groups in widely separated areas, as shown by a comparison of recordings: in the Ituri Forest, Zaïre (Tracey 1973); among the Bangombe and Bambenjele of the Upper Sangha, Central African Republic (Djenda and Kubik 1964, 1966 Phonogrammarchiv Vienna); and among the Bambenjele (Ba-Bénzélé) and the Aka, south of Bangui (Arom 1967). Even outposts of Pygmy culture prove the persistence of a Pygmy musical style, as witness recordings by barely a dozen individuals staying at Ngambe (in the Cameroon grasslands), and associating with the Tikar chief of that town (Kubik 1963–1964: B 8650).

The strength of Pygmy musical culture also shows in the fact that the Pygmies' neighbors have almost invariably borrowed, however imperfectly, the Pygmies' vocal polyphony. In one musical genre or another, these neighbors adopt a Pygmy style of singing, which quite often associates with hunting songs. Bantu-speakers such as the Mpyɛmɔ and Mpompo, in the southwestern Central African Republic and southeastern Cameroon, have adopted Pygmy musical traits; but so have semi-Bantu-speakers, such as the Tikar, notably in a dance called *ngbānya* and in hunting songs called *nswē*. The Mangbetu, speakers of a Central Sudanic language in northeastern Zaïre, have also adopted some elements of Pygmy polyphony. Therefore, on finding Pygmy-style vocal polyphony among any sedentary population in Central Africa, a listener can conclude there has been Pygmy contact in the past, even if none occurs at present.

Similarly, Pygmies have adopted musical traits from their neighbors, with whom they have economically associated themselves since the early contact era. These traits include playing reed pipes, such as the *luma*, popular among the Ituri Forest Pygmies (Tracey 1973); playing various types of drums, and even the polyidiochord stick zither, used by the Pygmies of the Upper Sangha (and borrowed from Bantu speakers of zones A and B); and performing pieces drawn from the expressive repertory of secret societies, such as the *jenge* (Djenda 1968). Practiced in the area of the Ogowe River, Congo, *jenge* was first documented and recorded by André Didier and Gilbert Rouget (1946); it was later studied extensively by Maurice Djenda. Among the Bangombe Pygmies (along the Sangha River), *jenge* is a men's society, which centers on a "masked monster" (also *jenge*). The mask boasts strips of raffia leaves; it resembles a moving bell or robe. In public performance, accompanied by drums, the monster performs rapid twisting movements in front of women and children. Noninitiates believe the monster lives in the forest, where it controls hunters' luck. Totemistic ideas also play a role in the perception of *jenge*, since the people considered the monster the ancestor of one of the oldest members of the group in the camp (Djenda 1968:40). While the songs sung at public *jenge* performances correspond in style with general Upper Sangha Pygmy traits (as in dances like *wunga* or *moyaya*), an unusual song for rituals in homophonic harmony uses simultaneous fifths: members of the secret society sing it, while they carry raffia leaves back from the river, to build the mask. The members run through the village, where they end the song with shouts.

Some scholars, in particular Grimaud (1956) and Rouget, have claimed to have found similarities between Pygmy and San polyphony. They have taken inspiration from evolutionary perspectives on African music history, rather than from systematic comparisons of data. Independent inquiry has not confirmed the existence of a musical culture shared by African hunters, despite the findings of the Cantometrics Project (Lomax 1968). Most likely, the musical styles of Pygmies in Central Africa, and of San in southwestern Africa, have in common only two general traits: yodeling and vocal polyphony (in the African definition of the term). But Pygmy polyphony clearly derives from different principles and a different tonal system from that of the San; it possibly makes use of extracts of the harmonic series over a single fundamental, while !Kung' and other San tonal resources makes use of two fundamentals, at varying intervals, with their harmonics up to the fourth partial. San tonal material clearly derives from experience with the harmonics of braced musical bows, but no instrumental inspiration for Pygmy polyphony has been traced, and Pygmy tonal sequences differ from those of the San.

Bantu musical cultures in zones A, B, C, H, L, K

These musical cultures are diverse. This diversity is partly explained by the complex patterns of successive migrations, cultural divergence, and cultural convergence, during the past two thousand years. The tentative division of the Bantu languages into zones (Guthrie 1948) is still a useful yardstick, because it reflects, if only imperfectly, cultural dividing lines.

Zones A and B

These zones cover southern Cameroon, Equatorial Guinea (mainly a Faŋ-speaking area, with a certain absorption of Spanish culture), Gabon, and parts of the Congo. Zone A is situated in the northwesternmost Bantu area, where evidence proves contact with (a) the Semi-Bantu and other (non-Bantu) cultures of the Cameroon grasslands, and (b) West Africa, notably eastern Nigeria. Included in zone A on the Cameroon coast are the Duala (group 20), who had early contact with the Germans; the Basa (group 40); and the Yaounde (Ewondo-speaking), Bulu, Beti, and Faŋ (group 60), a large group, which extends far south into Gabon.

Musical documentation of this area began in colonial times, with the arrival of German administrators and missionaries: after July 1884, the diplomat Gustav Nachtigal established the Deutsch-Kamerun Schutzgebiet (German-Cameroon Protectorate). Early collections of musical instruments date back to the late 1800s (Ankermann 1901), including notes on the music of ethnic groups, particularly the Faŋ, or "Pangwe" (Hornbostel 1913). Establishing Christian missions in this area had, from the beginning of the 1900s, a notable influence on musical traditions. By the 1950s, this influence had given rise to an indigenous Christian music, such as Pie-Claude Ngumu's *Maîtrise des Chanteurs à la Croix d'Ébène* in the Cathedral of Yaoundé (1971). Ngumu later turned musicologist, and wrote (1976b) on the structure of *mendzaŋ* xylophone music, which he had also used in his ecclesiastical compositions. Another Cameroonian specialist, Albert Noah Messomo (1980), concentrated on the social and literary side of *mendzaŋ*.

Stick zithers

A prominent musical instrument that particularly characterizes language zone A, and overlaps slightly into zones B and C, is the "Cameroonian" or "Gabonese" polyidio-

With the impact of Latin American phonograph records and highlife from West Africa, music for xylophones in southern Cameroon changed considerably. Starting in the 1960s, xylophone bands played increasingly for young people's parties in dance halls. Their tuning became uniformly diatonic.

chord stick zither, called *mvet* in more northerly areas. Probably an autochthonous instrument of the Bulu-Beti-Faŋ group, it gives this culture area an unmistakable identity, since *mvet* is not only an instrument, but also a genre of oral literature. We do not know how far back in history it was invented, but it is one of those Central African instrumental traditions that has a small and compact geographical distribution: the instrument is not known in any other part of Africa.

The *mvet* is made from a stick of a raffia frond, from which idiochord strings are lifted and hooked into a notched bridge placed in the middle of the stick. From one to five gourd resonators are attached to the stick. By adjusting rings made of raffia, a musician can accurately tune the instrument. A *bom-mvet* 'stick zither poet' uses the zither for accompanying epic poetry, and sometimes for the narration of tales. In the area east of Nanga-Eboko (Cameroon), this zither is known under the name *ebenza*. A full performance in public often includes mime and dance.

In cultures outside the Bulu-Beti-Faŋ cluster, the stick zither is often known as *ngombi*, which among the Faŋ is the term for another stringed instrument, the harp. Surprisingly, Pygmy hunter-gatherers have adopted these zithers in the northern Congo and in the southwestern Central African Republic, where in the mid-1960s they appeared in Pygmy camps that were otherwise nearly devoid of nonutilitarian material wealth (Djenda and Kubik 1964; Djenda 1968).

Xylophones

Another instrument widely found in zones A and B is the gourd-resonated portable xylophone, whose presence is perhaps explained by diffusion from areas of southwestern Zaïre and northwestern Angola (zone H), during the sixteenth to eighteenth centuries. Until the late 1900s, such instruments, often called *mēnjyāŋ* or *m~endzaŋ* in southern Cameroon, were associated with chieftainship, and served as chiefly representatives; they were sometimes played during processions, as was usual, for instance, in the ancient kingdom of Congo. Among peoples such as the Ewondo-speaking groups (Ngumu 1976a, 1976b), four such xylophones usually constituted an ensemble, accompanied by drum and rattle. The names for the individual xylophones vary from language to language. Among the Mvele (at Minkolong, near Andom, between Nanga-Eboko and Bertoua, southern Cameroon), the following names were used in Daniel Mbeng's group, from the highest to the lowest pitched: *ololoŋ* (with ten keys), *ombek* (with six keys), *gboŋgboŋ* (with six keys), *eduma* (with three keys). Some of these names are onomatopoeic; all of them relate to musical functions in the ensemble.

The tunings of southern Cameroon xylophones have sparked controversy. Ngumu (1976a:14–18) gives intracultural evidence about the conceptualization of the process of tuning. According to him, tuning begins with a note in the center of the (middle-range) *omvək*, transcribed as note 1 in figure 10. Musicians consider this note analogous to the head of a family. Tuning then proceeds in descending tonal

FIGURE 10   Schematic design of a ten-key southern Cameroon xylophone (*omvɔk*).

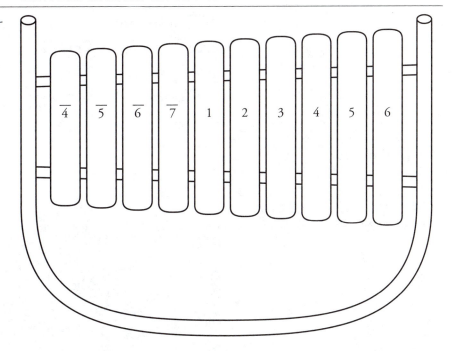

order: 1–2–3–4–5–6. Next, the octaves (sometimes called the wives) are found for notes 6, 5, and 4; in figure 10, these are notes #6, #5, and #4, in ascending order. Ngumu states that, in Ewondo-speaking areas, *omvɔk*-type xylophones originally had nine notes and hexatonic tuning. His main informant, however, told him some musicians had begun to introduce an additional note (#7 in figure 10), from an area called the Etenga country. Local musicians accept this note, called spoilsport (*esandi*), with reluctance (Ngumu 1976a:15). Thus, while the original tuning of the southern Cameroonian xylophone was probably hexatonic, after some time—perhaps at the beginning of the twentieth century, and possibly under the influence of German scholastic music—it gained a seventh note. Though Ngumu thinks *mendzaŋ* tunings were locally variable in their exact intervals, the cents figures of some old tunings may point to a predilection for neutral thirds between notes spaced one key apart (1 and 3, 2 and 4, and so on). In this style, thirds and octaves are the harmonic sounds of the xylophone parts and the vocal parts. In contrast to Ngumu, Jones believed, on the basis of Stroboconn measurements, that the hexatonic tunings were gapped equi-heptatonic scales (1971, 1978).

After the 1940s, with the impact of Latin American phonograph records and highlife from West Africa, music for xylophones in southern Cameroon changed considerably. Starting in the 1960s, xylophone bands played increasingly for young people's parties in dance halls. Their tunings, as in the case of the Richard Band de Zoetele (which traveled overseas, and achieved fame in the Cameroonian mass media) became uniformly diatonic. From the 1970s on, the repertory of many southern Cameroon xylophone dance bands consisted of popular rumba, cha-cha, and pachanga tunes, taken from Zaïrean, Congolese, and Cuban records. A case in point was the xylophone band at the Miami Bar (figure 11), performing in what was the red-light district near the port of Douala; sailors from many nations frequented the bar.

Harps and pluriarcs

Little material remains to elucidate the remote history of the musical cultures of zones A and B. The most remarkable evidence, however, is in a seventeenth-century European source (Praetorius 1620), which depicts two musical instruments that

Harps with carved heads are used for religious instruments by Faŋ priests. The people consider the harp the deity's "house." In Faŋ cosmogony, it symbolizes the female principle.

could have been collected only on the coast of Gabon: a seven-stringed harp and a pluriarc, described as *Indianische Instrumenta am clang [sic] den Harffen [sic] gleich* 'Amerindian instruments, in sound like the harp'. The illustrator drew them from life, and his grouping of instruments implies he had access to a collection of specimens, probably in a German nobleman's house.

Comparison with late-twentieth-century instruments suggests the pluriarc is likely to have come from the Gabon-Congo border (language zone B)—perhaps from the population cluster that later fanned into the Nzabi (group 10), Fumu (group 30), Mbede (group 20), or even Mfinu, Yanzi, and Mbunu (all in group 40). Alternatively, it could have come from the ancestors of the present Bateke, who in the late 1800s still used pluriarcs similar to the one Praetorius depicted (Wegner 1984:82).

The harp depicted by Praetorius provides more important evidence for the music history of western Central Africa. It falls organologically within Wachsmann's type III, or "shelved type" of African harp (1964). Most probably, a sixteenth-century Kele maker produced it. The Bakele group are considered long-established on the coast of Gabon. By 1470, European sailors had landed on the Gabon coast, where they gradually built up trading contacts. In the nineteenth and twentieth centuries, Kele harps sported a hook or extension, which in some specimens looks like a "7," and in others like the high heel of a shoe. Normally, Gabonese harps have eight strings. Praetorius's specimen may not even be an exception, since an enlargement of the drawing reveals what looks like a loose string with a peg on its end.

Praetorius's illustration, compared with late nineteenth- and early twentieth-century Gabon harps in museum collections, reveals an organological stability over more than 370 years. Gabon is the southernmost distribution area of harps in Africa. Some authors associate Gabonese harps with the origin of the Faŋ people, who are said to have come from the northeast, that is, somewhere in non-Bantu-speaking areas of the Central African Republic. The Faŋ migrants, probably limited in number, are supposed to have mixed with the local population in northern Gabon, and to have adopted a Bantu language. While there is no doubt Gabonese harps originated in the northeast, their presence in Gabon by the early 1600s (as suggested by Praetorius's illustration) predates the supposed Faŋ migration. Moreover, this illustration proves Wachsmann's type III was already developed four hundred years ago, and probably much earlier; it may have originated in type II ("tanged type"), by the absorption of organological ideas from local stringed instruments in Gabon and the Congo, notably the pluriarc.

The "shelved type" of African harp has a strictly defined distribution, concentrated in the territory of the Republic of Gabon. The northern subtype, called *ngombi* in Faŋ, has a carved head instead of the shoe heel; the head represents an important female deity, *Nyiŋgɔn Möböγɔ*, often translated by Faŋ informants as *Esprit Consolateur* (Consoling Spirit). Harps with carved heads are used for religious instruments by Faŋ priests, such as André Mvome in Oyem. The people consider the harp the deity's "house." In Faŋ cosmogony, it symbolizes the female principle; it contrasts with the male principle, betokened by the color white (to the Faŋ, the color of sperm), and by the *bɛŋ* 'mouth bow'.

Zone C

This is a large, diversified ethnic-linguistic zone, which covers mainly the northern parts of Zaïre and the Congo. It extends through much of the rain forest, from the borders of southeastern Cameroon and Gabon, across the northern Congo into Zaïre, down to Lake Léopold II, and to the Lwalaba River. It includes speakers of languages such as Buŋgili and Kota (group 10), Ŋgombe (group 30), Moŋgo-Ŋkundu (group 60), Tetela (group 70), and many others. In this zone, there are no less than thirty-eight distinguishable languages (Guthrie 1948).

This zone has supported the fieldwork of many cultural anthropologists, historians, and ethnomusicologists, including Alan P. Merriam (1959); Erika Sulzmann, among the Ekonda (1959); Jan Vansina, among the Kuba (1969); and J. F. Carrington (1949, 1956, 1975), who studied the relationship between tone and tune in message drumming, particularly on slit drums. For the northern Congo and adjacent areas, there are recordings by Didier and Rouget (1946), and by Djenda and Kubik (1964, 1966), and scattered recordings of later dates.

Typical harmonies

One of the characteristics of this zone is the presence of rich harmonic styles of singing, which, among the Bakota and Buŋgili in the northern Congo, result in three-part homophonic chord clusters. Buŋgili harmonic patterns derive from triads that shift along three steps of a diatonic heptatonic scale, as recordings Kubik made in the northern Congo in 1964 prove.

The basic chords, written over F and G in the notation of figure 12, could be mouthbow-derived. From Gabon across the northern Congo into Zaïre, Western Central African tunings for mouth bow usually have two fundamentals a whole tone apart, and the performer almost always makes use of the sound spectrum up to partials 5 or 6 of both fundamentals. This combination creates a basically hexatonic system, consisting of the clusters F–A–C and G–B–D.

For reasons not yet fully understood, this system extends, in Buŋgili and neigh-

FIGURE 12   Melodic and harmonic mouth bow progressions.

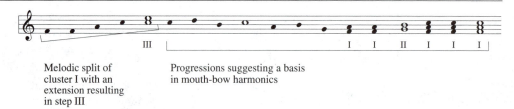

III

I   I   II   I   I

Melodic split of cluster I with an extension resulting in step III

Progressions suggesting a basis in mouth-bow harmonics

boring peoples' vocal music, to include one more third on top of the deeper chord, in the cluster F–A–C–E. Hence in Buŋgili and Bakota vocal performances, one finds melodic and harmonic patterns like the scheme of figure 12, abstracted from recordings made near Liouesso, northern Congo, in 1964. The background in these harmonic patterns is also revealed by the fact that the tonal center is F.

Farther north, among the Mpyɛmɔ ethnic group, living in the southwestern corner of the Central African Republic, songs show comparable harmonic clusters. The Mpyɛmɔ have oral traditions that claim the people migrated from northern parts of the Republic of the Congo, up the Sangha River, to their present habitat, about the beginning of the 1800s (Djenda 1967). Mpyɛmɔ harmonic patterns often employ two roots a semitone apart. The result is simultaneous vocal sounds, as in the story-song "Atɛndɛ" (figure 13).

This harmonic progression, however, is only one aspect of the conglomerate of styles and techniques that make up Mpyɛmɔ music. The Mpyɛmɔ had various contacts with other musical cultures, both during their migration north, and in their present homeland (Djenda and Kubik 1964, 1966), as four traits show:

1. *Harmonic patterns exclusively use major triads, and shift between two basic notes a semitone apart.* This type of organization, which occurs only in *ɟya* 'chantefables', is probably an ancient heritage from the Congo. The tonal system associated with these harmonic patterns is hexa- or heptatonic, with the melodic compass of individual voices never reaching an octave.
2. *Parallel fourths, in a pentatonic system*, whose origin is unknown; the trait was possibly introduced by contact with nearby non-Bantu peoples, such as the Gbaya and the Karre.
3. *Pygmy-style polyphony*, showing the close contacts this group has had with the Pygmies of the Upper Sangha.
4. *Unison singing*, to the accompaniment of gourd-resonated xylophones (mɛntʃaŋa) and the box-resonated lamellophone (*kembe*), introduced in the 1920s by migrant workers returning from employment in railway construction between Point Noire and Brazzaville.

Among the Mpɛmɔ, the *kembe* is tuned to a tempered (possibly equidistant) pentatonic system, and is accompanied by a well-known five-stroke twelve-pulse timeline.

Musical instruments

Musical instruments in zone C illustrate the full use of the natural resources of the rain forest. The slit drum (*kuli* or other names) plays an important musical role; it also serves to send standardized messages (Carrington 1975). There is a variety of membrane drums, with two prevailing kinds of tension (Wieschhoff 1933): (a) in the

FIGURE 13   *"Atɛndɛ"*: Mpyɛmɔ story-song, with leader and chorus. Performed by Nyaŋgɔ-Bɛbɛnisaŋgɔ, a woman about fifty years old, at Bigene, Nola District, Central African Republic, June 1964.

Elementary pulsation: 375 M.M.

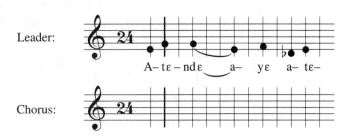

Leader:

A–tɛ–ndɛ   a– yɛ a–tɛ–

Chorus:

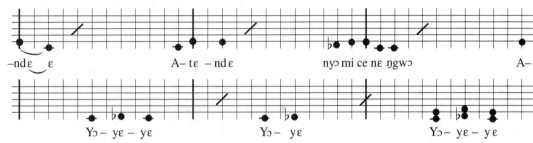

–ndɛ   ɛ   A–tɛ –ndɛ   nyɔ mi ce nɛ ŋgwɔ   A–

Yɔ–yɛ–yɛ   Yɔ– yɛ   Yɔ–yɛ–yɛ

Hand clapping: X . . X . X . .

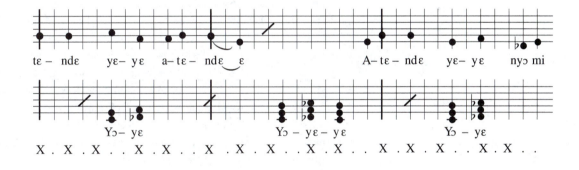

tɛ – ndɛ   yɛ– yɛ   a–tɛ– ndɛ   ɛ   A–tɛ– ndɛ   yɛ– yɛ   nyɔ mi

Yɔ– yɛ   Yɔ – yɛ– yɛ   Yɔ– yɛ

X . X . X . . X . X . . X . X . . X . X . . X . X . . X . X . .

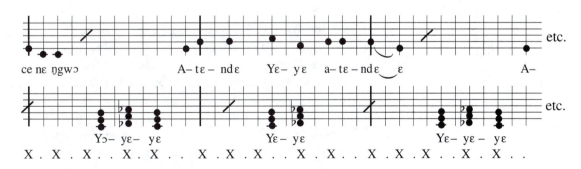

ce nɛ ŋgwɔ   A–tɛ – ndɛ   Yɛ– yɛ   a–tɛ–ndɛ   ɛ   A–   etc.

Yɔ– yɛ– yɛ   Yɛ– yɛ   Yɛ– yɛ– yɛ   etc.

X . X . X . . X . X . . X . X . X . . X . X . . X . X . . X . X . .

west of zone C, the predominant form is wedge-and-ring tension (*Keilringspannung*), characterized by a wedge-tensioned girdle attached to leather lacings around the body of the drum (figure 14); (b) in the southern parts of zone C, "Kasai tension" (*Kassai-Spannung*) seems restricted to a single area in Zaïre, and is especially common in drums of the Bakuba.

In museum collections, the tall drums from the "Kingdoms of the Savannah" (Vansina 1966) are famous for elaborate relief carvings with abstract, often ideo-

"When all the instruments are played together, a truly harmonic effect is produced from a distance; nearby one can hear the sticks rattling, which causes a great noise."—from seventeenth-century account of music in Congo

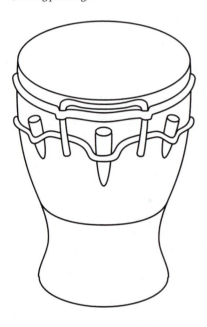

FIGURE 14   A membrane drum of zone C, tuned by wedge-and-ring tension (*Keilringspannung*).

graphic, motifs, and sometimes with the depiction of a hand on the side of the drum. Catalogues often record such instruments as "Kuba king's drums," though the number of kings must have been small, compared with the number of extant drums. As elsewhere, a lucrative trade in ethnographica developed by about 1910; and the fame of Kuba royalty made a market for these drums, so long as they bore appropriate labels.

Zone C also favors a single-note, asymmetric, rhythmic pattern, which accompanies many musical performances. The area where this timeline occurs in Central Africa may indicate migratory patterns, because timelines are diachronically stable. For structural reasons (which can be expressed mathematically), they cannot change the relationship of their beats without instantly losing their identity. Secondary traits, like accentuation and speed, can change more easily.

A five-stroke, twelve-pulse pattern, x . x . x . . x . x . . (with x meaning a stroke, and a period meaning an empty pulse), is found in much of zone C; it extends eastward into zone D, where it appears in music of the Lega, group 20 in zone D (Kishilo w'Itunga 1976). But farther south, in zones L and K, it is mostly replaced by its inverted mirror image, the seven-stroke, twelve-pulse pattern. Wherever in Central Africa one of these timelines occurs, the other is excluded, hidden, or reduced to a complementary pattern, struck simultaneously with the first.

The five-stroke, twelve-pulse pattern links Central Africa to West African cultures of the Kwa (I.A.4) linguistic family (Greenberg 1970), where timelines are also prominent; the pattern separates Central Africa from most of East Africa, except the Nyasa-Ruvuma cultures and the Zambezi valley.

Zone H

Thanks to early contacts established between Portugal and the kingdoms of Congo, Ndongo, and Matamba, zone H is unique on the map of Central African musical cultures: a large amount of written and pictorial sources date from the 1500s on. If nowhere else, music history can be at least partially reconstructed there for the last four hundred years.

The major language of the zone is Kikoongo (group 10), including related languages such as Yombe and Sundi, spoken in southwestern Zaïre; other languages of the zone include Ndoŋo (group 20), and Taka and Mbaŋgala (group 30). Kimbundu is the most important language spoken in Luanda (Angola), and in the hinterland into the Province of Malanji. The zone includes southwestern Zaïre, southern Congo, Cabinda (with the Loango coast), and northwestern Angola.

European influences and research
The kingdom of Congo was an area of early Christian evangelization. Whether by the 1600s missionaries had affected the music of Kikoongo-speaking peoples is difficult to assess; but there were probably considerable influences, not only from

Christian religious music, but also from military and ceremonial music. European wind instruments came into use at that time (Schüller 1972), and their knowledge spread far into the interior of Angola, where wooden trumpets figure among the paraphernalia of secret societies. The smaller types have a separate mouthpiece, similar in size and bore to sixteenth-century European trombones (Kubik 1981). The introduction of church bells into the kingdom of Congo spawned an industry that produced small clapper bells with local metallurgical techniques.

During the late 1600s, detailed accounts of music, musical instruments, organology, and musical sociology, came from the research of two Capuchin missionaries: António Giovanni Cavazzi and Girolamo Merolla. Cavazzi went to what is now northern Angola in 1654; for thirteen years, he lived and traveled in the kingdom of Congo and adjoining areas. Many of the illustrations in his book (1687) depict musical scenes. One shows warriors playing a bell and a "double bell" (Hirschberg 1969:15). Since the discovery of his original paintings, new sources on the music of the Congo and neighboring kingdoms have opened up. Merolla traveled to Luanda from Naples in 1682; he worked for five years in the town of Sonyo, traveled up the Zaïre River, and visited Cabinda. Some historians have considered his information on musical instruments (1692) secondary and largely based on Cavazzi, but it is probably more independent. Similarities or identities with Cavazzi's account are likely explained by the fact that these missionaries were near contemporaries, and had contact with the same cultures, albeit at a distance of more than a decade.

Merolla's testimony, written with obvious love for African music, equals that of Cavazzi. One famous etching shows several musical instruments: a gourd-resonated xylophone (*marimba*), a pluriarc (*nsambi*), two types of scraper (*kasuto, kilondo*), a double bell (*longa*), a goblet-shaped single-skin drum (*ngamba*), and an end-blown horn (*epungu*).

Referring to the kingdom of Congo and neighboring areas, Merolla describes some of these instruments:

> One of the most common instruments is the *marimba*. Sixteen calabashes act as resonators and are supported lengthwise by two bars. Above the calabashes little boards of red wood, somewhat longer than a span, are placed, called *taculla*. The instrument is hung round the neck and the boards (keys) are beaten with small sticks. Mostly four *marimbas* play together; if six want to play, the *cassuto* is added—a hollowed piece of wood four spans long, with ridges in it. The bass of this orchestra is the *quilondo*, a roomy, big-bellied instrument two and a half to three spans in height which looks like a bottle towards the end and is rubbed in the same way as the *cassuto*. When all the instruments are played together, a truly harmonic effect is produced from a distance; nearby one can hear the sticks rattling, which causes a great noise. The *nsambi* is a stringed instrument consisting of a resonator and five small bows strung with strings of bark fiber, which are made to vibrate with the index finger. The instrument is supported on the chest for playing. The notes sound weak but not unpleasant. (Hirschberg 1969:16, 18)

The four-piece xylophone ensemble described by Merolla does not survive in the territory of the former kingdom of Congo; in fact, xylophones seem to have disappeared from there. Some people have thought, therefore, that Cavazzi and Merolla were describing xylophones from one of the neighboring kingdoms, possibly Matamba, in the present Malanji Province of Angola, where large, gourd-resonated xylophones appear in association with chiefs. However, present-day Malanji xylophones, played on the ground and not carried on a strap around the musicians' shoulders, are probably not related historically to the depicted seventeenth-century specimens.

kakoxa   Two-stringed bowed lute that was inspired by seventeenth- or eighteenth-century Iberian stringed instruments

madimba   Gourd-resonated xylophones from central African area that probably derive from southeast African models

musique moderne zaïreoise   Guitar-based music that emerged after the 1940s in the Brazzaville and Kinshasa area

Survivals

The xylophone tradition seen by Cavazzi and Merolla does survive, however—though not in the kingdom of Congo, but farther north, where, in organology, attitude of playing, and other traits, including the fact that four xylophones play together, the xylophones of southern Cameroon provide the closest parallel to what Merolla described. This situation exemplifies a pattern frequently met in cultural history: a tradition migrates away from its original center of distribution, but survives in lands on the periphery, while it disappears from its original home.

The same consideration applies to the other instruments depicted by Merolla. The "quilondo" (*kilondo*) survives in some Latin American music, as in the type of *reco-reco* used during the Festa de Santa Cruz in Carapicuiba village, State of São Paulo, Brazil, though it is smaller than the specimen Merolla depicts (*Folclore de São Paulo*, n.d.:2). The slave trade exported the *nsambi*—and its name—to Brazil, where several nineteenth-century painter-authors reported its use.

In zone H, scrapers (*cassuto*) survive, particularly among Kimbundu-speakers in Angola. In Luanda, these scrapers (*dikanza*) have served particularly in novel twentieth-century ballroom dance traditions, such as the *rebita* and *semba*, dances characterized by the belly bounce, a light abdominal touch or shock. In Angola, scrapers also accompany military-music-inspired dances, such as *kalukuta*.

Not much of the sixteenth-to-seventeenth-century tradition has probably survived in zone H. Extensive contact with the outside world—via sea links to West Africa, Europe, and Brazil; via trade links to the interior of Africa, from the 1700s on, especially by the *pombeiros* (Portuguese-African traders who crossed Africa from Luanda to Mozambique)—has many times remodeled the musical cultures of the zone.

Bell-resonator lamellophones

Among the traditions of the Loango coast (Cabinda and adjacent areas), one tradition that has aroused considerable interest is the "Loango-sanza" (Laurenty 1962). It is a type of lamellophone belonging to the broad category classed by Tracey as having a bell-type resonator: the resonator, made of wood, is hollowed out from below. In Loango lamellophones, the cavity is usually in the shape of a half moon; the number of notes is small (usually only seven); in contrast to many other lamellophones in Africa, the notes lie in ascending scalar order from left to right.

Loango-type lamellophones have a narrow distribution area in Central Africa; they appear mainly along the Loango coast. By chance, however, the oldest specimen preserved in collections is of the Loango type; it was collected, not on the Loango coast, but in Brazil, where it was undoubtedly made by a slave from the Loango coast, not later than 1820. Together with a collection of ethnographic objects belonging to a North American furrier who was (1827–1848) American consul to the Habsburg Empire, it was acquired by the Museum für Völkerkunde, Vienna, where it remains (Janata 1975; Kubik 1977). It has a carved head—a trait that must have been common in the 1800s, because Stephen Chauvet (1929) prints a photograph of another specimen with a carved figure on top, in contrast to many later-collected specimens, which have only a somewhat extended top. Compare the instruments in the collections of the Musée Royal de l'Afrique Central (Laurenty 1962). The symbolic presence of a carved head, and the half-moon shape of the cavity of the resonator, are elements that imply strong cultural contacts with zones A and B.

There could be a historical sequence from the Loango-type lamellophones to what is a later (and possibly mid-nineteenth-century) development in the lower Congo-Zaïre area: the *likembe* (with a box resonator), though this type has a V-shaped or N-shaped arrangement of the lamellae. The *likembe* is a development that originated in zone H. With Belgian colonial penetration up the Zaïre River, it spread rapidly: by the 1920s, it had reached all of Zaïre and Congo, most of Uganda and northeastern Angola, and a few areas beyond.

Instrumental innovations

Widespread innovations in instrumental technology and musical style have their origins in zone H, which has absorbed and modified many exogenous traditions. The *kakoxa* 'two-stringed bowed lute' took inspiration from seventeenth- or eighteenth-century Iberian stringed instruments. The *madimba* 'gourd-resonated xylophones', found in Malanji Province, probably derive from southeast African models, whose techniques of playing and manufacture were carried to northern Angola by personnel who regularly traveled with the *pombeiros*. These traders followed the route from Luanda to Malanji, to the Lunda Empire, to Kazembe near Lake Mweru, and down south, through the Maravi Empire, to the Portuguese trading posts Tete and Sena, on the Zambezi in Mozambique.

Musical innovations that emerged from zone H also include developments in urban music, in the area of the twin cities of Brazzaville (Congo) and Kinshasa (Zaïre). After the 1940s, these municipalities, separated only by the Zaïre River, witnessed the rise of a new guitar-based music, generally called *musique moderne zaïreoise* and *musique moderne congolèse* (Kazadi wa Mukuna 1973), or Western-Congolese guitar style (Kubik 1965a). According to verbal accounts by Wendo, a guitarist of the 1950s, guitars first came to Matadi and Kinshasa (then Léopoldville) in the 1930s, brought by Kru sailors from West Africa.

Local music for solo guitar, with performers such as Wendo and Polo Kamba singing in Lingala (the Congolese trade language), developed; it was recorded on the Ngoma label by the Firme Jeronimidis, based in Kinshasa. An ensemble style of music for guitar also developed; it was heavily influenced by Latin American records, which brought to Central Africa African-American music from Latin America and the Caribbean.

This infusion culminated in the development of electric-guitar styles in the 1960s, advanced by bands that achieved international renown: O.K. Jazz, Rochereau Tabu Ley and his African Fiesta, and others. Some bands, such as that of Jean Bokilo, with his celebrated "Mwambe" series of recordings of many versions of one song, tried to integrate into the new styles "traditional" patterns—in Bokilo's case, harmonic patterns. Though these styles originated in zone H, they cannot be considered extensions of Kikoongo "traditional" music, because they include elements from many regions of Zaïre and the Congo, in reflection of the ethnic mix in cities like Kinshasa and Brazzaville.

Zone L and (in part) zone M

This area extends from central parts of Zaïre, across Katanga, into northwestern

FIGURE 15   A *mukupela* 'double-skin hourglass drum' (Zambia, 1971).

Zambia; it includes languages of the Pende (group 10), Luba (group 30), Kaonde (group 40), Lunda (group 50), and Mbwera-ŋkoya (group 60). It has been well researched, particularly by musicologists associated with the Musée Royal de l'Afrique Centrale, Tervuren (Belgium), including Gansemans (1978, 1980), Gansemans and Schmidt-Wrenger (1986), and Laurenty (1971, 1972). It is also one of the rare areas in Central Africa where archaeological evidence of musical practices is available. South of the equatorial forest, several Iron Age cultures developed; they produced a surplus population, which, beginning about A.D. 1000 to 1100, began the Third Bantu Dispersal, from a wide area in northern Katanga, with migration taking effect to the southwest (Angola), south (Zambia), and southeast (Malawi, Mozambique). From graves at Sanga and Katoto (in Katanga), single iron bells and other iron objects have been dated to about A.D. 800, and coincide in time with findings farther south, especially at the site of Ingombe Ilede.

Iron bells in this area, as elsewhere in Central Africa, figure among the regalia of chiefs and other officials of centralized states. Their study therefore has relevance to the broader history of the "Kingdoms of the Savannah." Other musical instruments associated with chieftainship or kingship in this area include the *mukupela* 'double-skin hourglass drums' (figure 15), of the Luba-Lunda population; because of their materials (wood, skin), there is little chance any can be recovered from archaeological deposits.

Merriam's study of a Songye village in the Lwalaba River area (in 1959–1960) became a classic example of an approach that linked music with the broader cultural and social panorama, and focused on the status and the creativity of individuals. Later, research on the music and dance ethnography of the Hemba by Pamela Blakely (1993) garnered a large amount of data on one of the lesser-known peoples of group 30 in zone L. In precolonial times, trade routes going through Katanga from both west and southeast left their mark on the music of zones L and M. Small, board-shaped lamellophones known in Shiluba as *cisanji* (Tracey 1973) probably developed from southeast African models that had been reduced in size for use by long-distance porters coming up the Zambezi. The Maravi Empire (1600s and 1700s), through which the trade route passed, was the source of single-note xylophones called *limba*, used in religious contexts that similarly became known farther north. East African trade routes ending in Katanga led, not only to the rise of a sizable Kiswahili-speaking population there (speaking Kingwana, a Swahili dialect), but also to the introduction of instruments such as the flatbar zither (Shiluba *luzenze*) and the board zither (*ngyela*), played in "vamping style" with a pendular motion of the right index finger (Laurenty 1960, 1971). The friction drum (*ng'oma wa bimrunku* or *tambwe ng'oma* in Shiluba) points to contacts with the Lunda cluster of peoples and eastern Angola; for description of this instrument, see Laurenty (1972:44–45).

The presence of centralized political structures among the peoples of zones L and M found expression in the royal music associated with traditional rulers, such as the drums called *cinkumbi* by the peoples of Mwata Kazembe, in the Lwapula Valley near Lake Mweru. Mwesa I. Mapoma (1974) studied royal musicians among the Bemba in Luapula and Northern Provinces of Zambia. The importance of music for initiations in this zone, particularly for the initiations of girls—such as the *cisungu* rites among the Lenje, the Soli, and others in Zambia—stresses the continuation of a social structure with a matrilineal system of descent.

Christian evangelization

In the twentieth century, both southern Zaïre and northeastern Zambia proved to be fertile areas for establishing Christian missions. The result was two byproducts that have affected the musical cultures of those areas: scientific research by Christian missionaries, and indigenous acquaintance with Christian hymnody.

Many missionaries interested themselves in the local musical cultures; their efforts led to the study and development of the music. A. M. Jones worked from 1929 to 1950 as a missionary and principal of St. Mark's College (Mapanza, Zambia); he studied the musical cultures of the Bemba, the Nsenga, and other groups. Also in Zambia, Father Corbeille collected musical instruments, which remain in the University of Zambia.

Introducing Christian hymns and school music had many effects, and eventually stimulated the emergence of a new ecclesiastical music, both in the established churches (for example, the work of Joseph Kiwele, who in the 1950s composed *Messe Katangaise*; see Kishilo w'Itunga 1987), and in the separatist ones.

For Zambia, Mwesa I. Mapoma (1980:20:630) says

> music among Christian denominations has consisted mostly of Western hymns set to local languages, usually taking little account of the tonal inflection or the rhythmic structure of the text, provided the religious text fits the meter. Earlier some denominations introduced religious texts set to traditional Zambian music, but Western hymns were substituted as soon as more people had been attracted to the church. In the early 1950s African-led Christian churches such as the Emilio and Lumpa appeared. The worship of the Emilio sect, led by a former Roman Catholic seminarian, resembled Catholic church practice but used African music and vernacular languages. The Lumpa sect led by Alice Lenshina, a self-styled prophet, also used traditional music in worship, but because of the increasing fascination of the Lumpa followers the sect was banned in 1964. The example set by these two churches has since been followed by the Roman Catholic and other churches. . . . In some churches even dancing has been introduced and the interior of the church adapted accordingly.

Zones L and M have also seen the emergence of a new, guitar-based, popular music for dancing, in response to multiple factors, including urbanization and migrant labor. This process started in the 1930s, particularly along the copper belt on both sides of the Zaïre-Zambia border, an area that attracted miners from many parts

In the dark of night, men of the secret society bring the tubes up to the village, and emit into the mouthpiece fearful vocal sounds, which the tubes seemingly amplify.

FIGURE 16   The Katanga guitarist Mwenda-Jean Bosco, 1982.

of Central Africa. A township culture soon developed around the emerging major centers (Kolwezi, Likasi, Lubumbashi, Ndola), where a Katanga "guitar style" arose (Kubik 1965b, 1966; Kazadi wa Mukuna 1980; Low 1982). Hugh Tracey (1973) first recorded pieces in this style; he also discovered Mwenda-Jean Bosco, alias Mwenda wa Bayeke (figure 16), a Luba-Sanga guitar composer, who in the 1950s and 1960s rose to be one of Africa's foremost guitarists (Rycroft 1961, 1962).

Zone K

This zone covers all of eastern Angola, northwestern Zambia, and adjacent areas in Zaïre. Musicologically, it is one of the most thoroughly studied parts of Central Africa, and it has also been one of the most attractive to researchers in art, because of the intimate interrelationships among music, masked dancing, and visual art. It is a zone of highly institutionalized musical practice connected with initiation schools and secret societies. Included in zone K are the following languages: Cokwe, Lwena, Luchazi, Mbwela, Nkhangala (group 10); Lozi (group 20); Luyana (group 30); and Totela (group 40). The latter two groups have perhaps more links with southern Africa than to Central Africa.

Within zone K, the cultures of group 10 show clearly ancient affinities with the Luba-Lunda cultural cluster (zone L). The Lunda-related cultural history of the Cokwe, the Lwena, and the so-called Ngangela peoples (including the Lucazi, the Mbwela, the Nkhangala, the Nyemba, and others) is obvious; their history explains it, as do the patterns of migration from the ancient Lunda Empire after the 1500s. Migration of the Cokwe to new lands continued until late in the twentieth century. In the 1800s, Cokwe families penetrated farther and farther south from their original homes (in northeastern Angola); they settled on river grasslands in the Kwandu-Kuvangu Province of Angola. They have had much cultural influence on the Ngangela-speaking peoples, with whom they developed close affinal relationships. Cokwe masks, such as *Cikŧza* or *Kalelwa* (figure 17)—the latter depicting a nineteenth-century Cokwe king, Mwene Ndumba wa Tembo—appear all over eastern Angola and in northwestern Zambia. In musical performances, these masks proceed to the public dance place (*cilende*) in a village, stop in front of the set of long, goblet-shaped drums (*vipwali* or *zing'oma*), and speak a recitation (*kutangesa*), which drum strokes guide, cue, and interrupt (Kubik 1965b, 1971, 1981).

In zone K, most music is performed within the traditional institutions of education for the young, the secret societies, and the context of royalty. Among the Lozi or "Barotse" on the Zambezi (southwestern Zambia), the paramount chief presides over the *kuomboka* ceremony, a picturesque festival, marked yearly by a procession with boats. Every year, when the Zambezi inundates the plains up to the highlands, the Lozi people migrate ceremonially to the dry places, to the accompaniment of instrumental music and dancing (Kalakula 1979). Their music stands stylistically apart from most of the music in zone K, because of the historical links of the Lozi people

FIGURE 17   Two prominent Cokwe masked characters: above, *Kalelwa;* above right, *CikŁza.*

with the south, and because of their proximity to Ndebele culture in Zimbabwe. In contrast to the multipart singing style of the group 10 peoples in zone K, their style emphasizes fourths and fifths as simultaneous intervals, structured in a manner comparable to Shona-Nsenga harmonic patterns (Jones 1959; Kubik 1988). The tunings and chords of Lozi gourd-resonated xylophones called *silimba* reflect the nature of this tonal system.

Among the peoples of group 10 in zone K, the performance of certain musical works marks royal events, especially the death or installation of a chief. Luchazi, Cokwe, and Lwena chiefs keep in their assortment of regalia the *mukupele* or *mukupela* drum, and sometimes a double bell. The *mukupele* is played only at a royal death or installation. The sound owes its loudness to an ingenious device, a small piece of calabash neck covered with a mirliton (a spider's nest covering), and inserted into a hole on the side of the drum.

Megaphones

Another ritual for dead kings or chiefs that involves sound is in the Ngangela languages called *vandumbu*, a term that also refers to the principal musical instrument of the occasion, a megaphone; its sound is not considered *mwaso* 'song, music' (pl. *myaso*): it represents the voices of the dead kings. Its production is a secret, whose knowledge is reserved to those who have passed an initiation ceremony; those persons keep the *vandumbu* under water all year long, in a shallow place in the riverine marshlands. Individual megaphones, up to 4 meters long, consist of wooden tubes with a round mouthpiece, cut from tall trees; the orifice often takes the shape of a crocodile's mouth, or that of some other ferocious riverine animal. The body of each tube is wrapped with plant fiber.

In the dark of night, men of the secret society bring the tubes up to the village, and emit into the mouthpiece fearful vocal sounds, which the tubes seemingly amplify (Kubik 1981). Three megaphones are normally used during the ceremony. In front of them, as in a procession, walk the players of three smaller instruments, real trumpets (*nyavikali*), about 1.5 meters long; by overblowing, the players can produce the harmonic series. During the event, people make a sacrifice of millet beer: while they dip one of the horns into a mortar, they pour the beer onto its teeth. The ceremony tries to guarantee the fertility of the village, by gaining the dead kings' goodwill. The

The characteristic vocal tendency is to proceed by step, as in a song that expresses the secluded initiates' yearning for their return home, at the beginning of the rainy season.

salient aspects of this procession resemble those of royal receptions in the kingdom of Congo in the 1600s, as described by seventeenth-century authors.

Initiations

Other musical performances in group 10 of zone K highlight the public aspects of age grade rites of initiation. Every year during the dry season, from about May to October, *mikanda* 'circumcision schools' for young boys, aged six to twelve, are established outside the villages. In that season, one can probably find a *mukanda* (sing.) every six to twelve miles through the more densely populated areas across eastern Angola, northwestern Zambia, and adjacent border areas in Zaïre.

The circumcising surgery marks the beginning of a *mukanda*, and precedes the building of the lodge in which the recuperant boys will stay in seclusion for several months. In the *mukanda*, besides other subjects, music and dance instruction play an important role (Kubik 1981). In a Luchazi *mukanda*, three kinds of musical instruction occur.

1. *myaso yatundanda* 'songs of the initiates', performed with the *kuhunga* and *kawali* dance-actions, accompanied by *vipwali* drums. There are also songs for the initiates to perform on specific occasions—when receiving food, at sunrise, and at sunset ("greeting the sun").
2. *kutangesa* 'recitations by the initiates'. The music teacher, sitting astride a *cipwali* drum, cues the group of initiates, who recite long texts, sometimes with historical content.
3. *myaso yakukuwa* 'songs performed at night by initiates' (and their teachers and guardians), accompanied with concussion sticks.

The songs performed at night display three- or four-part harmony. Vocal music among the Cokwe, Lwena, Luchazi, and related peoples in group 10 of zone K, exemplifies a homophonic multipart style, in a hexa- or heptatonic system, which emphasizes simultaneous sounds in triads, either in thirds plus fifths, or in fourths plus thirds.

A song for circumcision

The movement of individual voices can be parallel, oblique, or contrary; the characteristic tendency is to proceed by step, as in a song that expresses the secluded initiates' yearning for their return home, at the beginning of the rainy season (figure 18).

The singers of figure 18 accompany themselves on concussion sticks in two groups: *mingonge* 1 and *mingonge* 2. Each person holds two sticks, one in each hand. The letter "A" indicates that the right-hand stick strikes the left-hand stick from above; the letter "B" indicates that the left-hand stick strikes the right-hand stick from above. This motion is achieved, not by the individual action of one hand alone, but by an even and absolutely regular left-right, up-down alternation of the move-

FIGURE 18 (below and opposite)   "*Tangwa ilombela mity'e* 'The day the trees will sprout'": song in Luchazi, as performed in the lodge of a circumcision school (*mukanda*). Mikula village, Kabompo District, Zambia; 29 July 1971. Mingonge I & II and Tutanga I are concussion sticks.

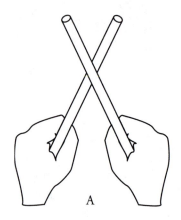

A

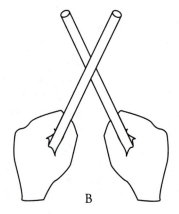

B

ment of both hands. The sticks then hit each other at a point in the middle of the path described by the hands.

The performance of figure 18 includes a third rhythmic part: two or three *tutanga* players hold in the left hand a wooden slat (*katanga*) about 6 decimeters long, and strike it with a stick (*mungonge*) held in the right.

The text of the song of figure 18 expresses yearning for the village. A *mukanda* is normally closed at the end of the dry season, when the trees begin to sprout. So the boys in seclusion, and their guardians and teachers, are looking forward to that day:

FIGURE 18 (continued)   Elementary pulsation: 430 M.M.

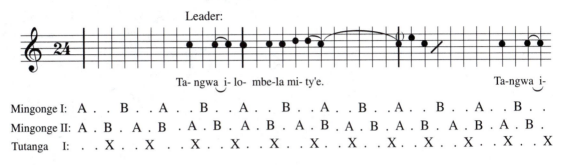

```
Leader:
Ta- ngwa i- lo- mbe-la mi- ty'e.                    Ta-ngwa i-

Mingonge I:   A . . B . . A . . B . . A . . B . . A . . B . . A . . B . . A . . B . .
Mingonge II:  A . B . A . B . A . B . A . B . A . B . A . B . A . B . A . B .
Tutanga  I:   . . X . . X . . X . . X . . X . . X . . X . . X . . X . . X . . X
```

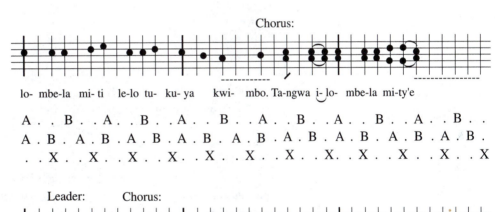

```
Chorus:
lo- mbe-la mi- ti  le-lo tu- ku- ya  kwi- mbo. Ta-ngwa i- lo- mbe-la mi-ty'e

A . . B . . A . . B . . A . . B . . A . . B . . A . . B . . A . . B . .
A . B . A . B . A . B . A . B . A . B . A . B . A . B . A . B .
. . X . . X . . X . . X . . X . . X . . X . . X . . X . . X . . X
```

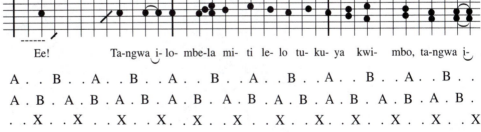

```
Leader:      Chorus:
Ee!          Ta-ngwa i- lo- mbe-la mi- ti le- lo tu- ku- ya kwi- mbo, ta-ngwa i-

A . . B . . A . . B . . A . . B . . A . . B . . A . . B . . A . . B . .
A . B . A . B . A . B . A . B . A . B . A . B . A . B . A . B .
. . X . . X . . X . . X . . X . . X . . X . . X . . X . . X . . X
```

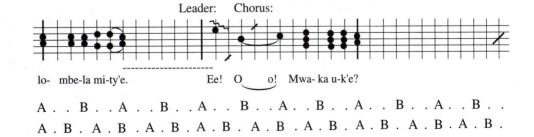

```
Leader:      Chorus:
lo- mbe-la mi-ty'e.           Ee! O   o! Mwa- ka u-k'e?

A . . B . . A . . B . . A . . B . . A . . B . . A . . B . . A . . B . .
A . B . A . B . A . B . A . B . A . B . A . B . A . B . A . B .
. . X . . X . . X . . X . . X . . X . . X . . X . . X . . X . . X
```

All masks are made in a *mukanda* by the guardians of the secluded initiates. It is the guardians who appear disguised as masks in front of the women of the village, to reassure them of their children's well-being.

LEADER	Tangwa ilombela mity'e—
	Tangwa ilombela miti,
	   lelo tukuya kwimbo.
			LEADER	The day the trees will sprout—
				The day the trees will sprout,
				   that day we return to the village.

CHORUS	Tangwa ilombela mity'e.		CHORUS	The day the trees will sprout.
LEADER	Ee!		LEADER	*Ee!*

CHORUS	Tangwa ilombela miti,
	   lelo tukuya kwimbo.
	Tangwa ilombela mity'e.
			CHORUS	The day the trees will sprout,
				   that day we return to the village.
				The day the trees will sprout.

LEADER	Ee!		LEADER	*Ee!*
CHORUS	Oo! Mwaka uk'e?		CHORUS	*Oo!* Which year?

As in this song, each singer can form his own voice by choosing any of the notes shown in the transcribed chord cluster, and he can vary it from one repetition to another. Each singer must follow a basic rule, however: the melody of any voice line must move strictly stepwise.

Neutral thirds

The older harmonic singing style of the Cokwe- and Ngangela-speaking peoples incorporates the use of thirds that can be described as neutral, while fifths and fourths tend to be sung as perfect intervals. The neutral thirds seem to fluctuate between the values of 330 and 380 cents, according to measurements of instrumental tunings (Kubik 1980). Whether they derive from the idea of equidistance or not is difficult to ascertain. They probably result from continual adjustments in intonation, whereby singers try to maintain throughout a song a uniformly euphonic consonance—a consonance that creates consistent "major" triads on adjoining steps of the scale (figure 18).

Adjusting intonation to conform with the euphonic expectation of the Cokwe and Ngangela ear has also been noted in songs of the women's secret *tuwema* society. The term *tuwema* (sing. *kawema*) 'flames' refers to a show staged by women at night. In the darkness, while the women sing and dance, they wave glowing bark cloth strips attached to their arms. This action creates an impressive display: sparks fly in vivid patterns. How the women effect the show is their secret. For this area, it illustrates the intimate relationship of aural, visual, and kinetic arts.

This interrelationship also informs masked dancing, both by the *makisi a vampwevo* 'masks of the women', in which body paint is used, and by the *makisi a vamala* 'masks of the men'. Every year, the men construct individual masked characters. Most of the masks are anthropomorphic; some are zoomorphic. All are made in a *mukanda* by the guardians of the secluded initiates, and it is the guardians who appear disguised as masks in front of the women of the village, to reassure them of their children's well-being. During the *mukanda* season, many public mask fests take place. A performance late in the evening, after supper, may feature the individual appearances

FIGURE 19   The young woman (*mwanaphwo*), a famous carved mask of the Cokwe.

of the *cileya* 'court fool', or of the *mwanaphwo* 'young woman', one of the famous carved masks of the Cokwe (figure 19).

Recent innovations, such as the wig (*ciwiki*), with its Afro hairstyle, can also appear. These masks appear singly; but in contrast, a dramatic masquerade takes place in the daytime, at the *cilende*, or village danceplace. It features a dozen masked characters in succession, until the feast closes with the appearance of the madman, a spectacular mask, taking the highest rank; it is variously called *mpumpu* (in Mbwela), *lipumpu* (in Lucazi), and *cizaluke* (in Lwena-Luvale). In southeastern Angola, the person wearing this mask sports a simulated penis, which he wags during the performance. The madman represents an ancient king, Mwene Nyumbu, who after his sister insulted him is said to have instituted circumcision by circumcising himself.

All masked performances are accompanied by the standard *vipwali* or *zing'oma* drums, sometimes three of them played by one person. In the latter case, this set of instruments is called *tumboi* among the Mbwela and Nkhangala of southeastern Angola.

Musical instruments

In instrumental resources, zone K is characterized by the predominance of percussion—strangely reminiscent of the situation on the Guinea coast (West Africa)—from the families of idiophones and membranophones.

Stringed instruments include only the friction bow (*kawayawaya*), imports such as the *kalyalya* (two- or three-stringed bowed lute, based on the *kakoxa* of zone H), and, beginning in the mid-1900s, homemade banjos and guitars.

Mnemonic patterns

Rhythmic patterns are taught by syllabic or verbal mnemonic structures, such as *macakili, macakili, kuvamba kuli masika* 'in the circumcision lodge there is coldness', and *mu cana ca Kapekula* 'in the river grasslands of Kapekula'. These mnemonics are almost notations of the accentual, rhythmic, and conceptual characteristics associated with the patterns they represent. Plosive sounds, such as /p/, /t/, and /k/, represent accented strokes, the affricate sound /tʃ/ (orthographically spelled "*c*," and pronounced as in English "church") usually shows the position of the referential beat, while nasal sounds tend to represent silent or unaccented pulse-units. The mnemonics transcribed in figures 20 and 21 come from the Ngangela repertory of eastern Angola, where these patterns serve as accompaniment and timeline in several genres of music and dance.

FIGURE 20   A Ngangela mnemonic pattern (*macakili macakili*, for rattles).

$$\binom{8}{}\left[\uparrow \quad \circ \quad \blacktriangle \quad \downarrow \quad \uparrow \quad \circ \quad \blacktriangle \quad \downarrow \right]$$

Mnemonics: ma–ca–ki–li   ma–ca–ki–li

Reference beat: 1   2   3   4

FIGURE 21   A Ngangela mnemonic pattern (*mu cana ca Kapekula*, struck on any object with two sticks). For the symbols, see figure 20.

$$\binom{8}{}\left[\begin{array}{cccccccc} \cdot & X & \cdot & \cdot & X & \cdot & X & \cdot \\ \cdot & X & \cdot & X & \cdot & X & \cdot & X \end{array} \right]$$

Mnemonics: mu–ca–na   ca–Ka–pe–ku–la

Reference beat: 1   2   3   4

FIGURE 22   The *kachacha* timeline. The referential beat starts on the stroke over the numeral 1, but the pattern begins on the first stroke of the mnemonics as written. This notation captures both concepts: top line, in mnemonics; bottom line, in the pattern's relationship with the referential beat.

either

(16)

Mnemonics: x • x • x • x x • x • x • x x •

ɔlɔc cɔ ŋ bɔ ŋ bɔ ŋ bɔ ŋ bɔlɔ ŋ bɔ ŋ bɔ ŋ bɔlɔ

Reference beat: 2   3   4   1

or

Right-hand stick: x • x • x • x x • x • x • x x •

Left-hand stick: • x • x • x • • x • x • x • • x

(16)   2   3   4   1

FIGURE 23   The *muselemeka* timeline, transcribed in mnemonics with a referential beat.

(12)

Mnemonics: x • x • x x • x • x x •

ŋ bɔ c ŋ bɔ c ŋ bɔlɔ ŋ bɔ c ŋ bɔlɔ

Reference beat: 2   3   4   1

Timelines

Two standard asymmetric timelines (figures 22 and 23) are most prominent for steering performances with drums, lamellophones, or other instruments. In Luvale, they are called *kachacha* or *muselemeka,* respectively, because of their association with the kinetic pattern of dances of the same name. Among the Lwena-Luvale, *kachacha* is a dance genre that involves a set of single-skin goblet-shaped drums (*jing'oma*), and sometimes a two-note xylophone (*jinjimba*). It also accompanies masked dancing.

In contrast to the Guinea coast, where this pattern also plays a dominant role in many musical genres (Jones 1959), its relationship to the dance beat, or musicians' referential beat, is different in southern Central Africa. Beat 1 coincides here with the second *lɔ* in the mnemonics.

By contrast, in Yoruba usage of the same pattern, beat 1 coincides with the first *lɔ*, which falls off the beat in *muselemeka*. Both timelines in zone K are usually struck with two sticks on the body of a drum. When accompanying a *likembe*, a second performer strikes the sticks against the body of the *likembe*; when accompanying some other types of lamellophones, the second performer strikes the resonator. When a friction drum (*pwita*)—always characterized by internal friction (as in figure 24)— plays with other drums, the timeline is struck on the body of the *pwita*. The friction stick is rubbed with wet hands; performers keep a water vessel beside them, to wet their hands intermittently.

Among the instrumental resources within zone K, lamellophones have also played an important role; among the Cokwe, five different types are distinguishable.

1. *cisaji cakele* often refers to lamellophones with a board-shaped composite body, made of material from the raffia palm, from which the lamellae also derive.
2. *cisaji cakakolondondo* has a board-shaped body, with ten iron lamellae arranged in a V-shape. Tuning is often achieved by attaching differently sized lumps of black wax to the underside of the playing-ends of each lamella.
3. *cisaji calungandu* has a board-shaped body, with two interspersed ranks of lamellae, six in each, in ascending order from left to right. Tuning is with wax, as above.
4. *mucapata* has 17, 19, or more, iron lamellae, arranged in sections according to tonality. The body is hollowed out from the end facing the player (the "bell-shaped" resonator in Tracey 1948). Tuning is carried out exclusively by adjusting the length of the lamellae that extend over the bridge.

FIGURE 24   Friction drum (*pwita*) of the Luvale and Lwena (northeastern Angola), showing internal friction; a *lihongo*, a kind of reed, is the friction stick.

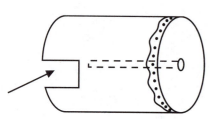

5. *likembe* has a box resonator, normally (in this area) with eight notes, arranged in an N shape—that is, with two deep notes, one in the middle, one on the right (as seen from the player's viewpoint). A trait of the playing technique of this type of lamellophone is the extensive use of the sound hole at the back of the box; opening and closing it gives a "wow" effect.

The history of these lamellophones, like the history of Central African music in general, involves the forces of diffusion, adaptation, and innovation. The *likembe* is a twentieth-century introduction to zone K, for which its history has been reconstructed (Kubik 1980). The raffia lamellophones are either ancient, and linked with cultures across Central Africa (such as Central Cameroon, where they play a prominent role), or imitative of lamellophone types with iron lamellae, now found among the Cokwe. One of the raffia lamellophones in the collections of the Museu de Etnologia, Lisbon (no. AH–622), is clearly modeled after the *mucapata*. The *cisaji cakakolondondo* and the *cisaji calungandu* may have remote connections with the Lower Zambezi Valley; and from the 1700s, the ideas leading to their invention may have spread from there to Angola, with the trading of the *pombeiros*. Alternatively, *mucapata*—undoubtedly an original Cokwe or Cokwe-Mbangala invention—may have some historical connection with the Loango-type lamellophones. This possibility is suggested by the shape of the top part (where the backrest is often missing), the presence of a bell-type resonator, and certain patterns in the arrangement of the notes.

REFERENCES

Ankermann, Bernhard. 1901. "Die afrikanischen Musikinstrumente." *Ethnologisches Notizblatt* 3:I–X, 1–32.

Arom, Simha. 1967. "Instruments de musique particuliers à certaines ethnies de la Republique Centrafricaine." *Journal of the International Folk Music Council,* 19:104–108.

Blakely, Pamela A. 1993. "Performing Dangerous Thoughts: Women's Song-Dance Performance Events in a Hemba Funeral Ritual (Republic of Zaïre)." Ph.D. dissertation, Indiana University.

Carrington, John F. 1949. *A Comparative Study of Some Central African Gong-Languages.* Brussels: Institut Royal Colonial Belge.

———. 1956. "Individual Names Given to Talking Gongs in the Yalemba Area of Belgian Congo." *African Music* 1(3):10–17.

———. 1975. *Talking Drums of Africa.* New York: Negro Universities Press.

Cavazzi, Giovanni António. 1687. *Istorica Descrizione de 'tre' Regni Congo, Matamba et Angola.* Bologna: Giacomo Monti.

Chauvet, Stephen. 1929. *Musique Nègre.* Paris: Société d'éditions géographiques, maritimes et coloniales.

Dampierre, Eric de. 1963. *Poètes Nzakara.* Paris: Institut d'Ethnologie, Université de Paris. Classiques Africains.

Didier, André, and Gilbert Rouget. 1946. *Musique pygmée de la haute-Sangha.* Paris: Boîte à Musique, BAM LD 325. LP disk.

Djenda, Maurice. 1967. "Les anciennes danses des Mpyèmo." *African Music* 4(1):40–46.

———. 1968. "Les Pygmées de la Haute Sangha." *Geographica* 14:26–43.

Djenda, Maurice, and Gerhard Kubik. 1964. Field-Research Notes: Central African Republic. Vienna: Phonogrammarchiv.

———, and Gerhard Kubik. 1966. Field-Research Notes: Central African Republic. Vienna: Phonogrammarchiv.

Erlmann, Veit. 1981. *Populäre Musik in Afrika.* Berlin: Staatliche Museen Preußischer Kulturbesitz. Veröffentlichungen des Museums für Völkerkunde Berlin, Neue Folge 53, Abteilung Musikethnologie 8.

Folclore de São Paulo. n.d. Brochure. São Paulo: Secretaria de Cultura, Esportes e Turismo.

Gansemans, Jos. 1978. *La musique et son rôle dans la vie sociale et rituelle Luba.* Tervuren, Belgium: Musée Royal de l'Afrique Centrale. Sciences Humaines, 95.

———. 1980. *Les instruments de musique Luba.* Tervuren, Belgium: Musée Royal de l'Afrique Centrale. Sciences Humaines, 103.

Gansemans, Jos, and Barbara Schmidt-Wrenger. 1986. *Zentralafrika.* Leipzig: Deutscher Verlag für Musik. Musikgeschichte in Bildern, 1, part 12.

Gardi, René. 1974. *Unter afrikanischen Handwerkern.* Graz: Akademische Druck- und Verlagsanstalt.

Giorgetti, Filiberto. 1957. *Musica Africana.* Bologna: Editrice Nigrizia.

Greenberg, Joseph H. 1970. *The Languages of Africa.* Bloomington, Ind.: Research Center for the Language Sciences.

Grimaud, Yvette. 1956. "Note sur la musique vocale des Bochiman !Kung' et des pygmées Babinga." *Colloques de Wégimont* 3:105–126.

Guthrie, Malcolm. 1948. *The Classification of Bantu Languages.* London: International African Institute.

Hirschberg, Walter. 1969. "Early Illustrations of West and Central African Music." *African Music* 4(3):6–18.

Hornbostel, Erich Moritz von. 1913. "Musik." In *Die Pangwe,* ed. G. Tessman, 320–357. Berlin: E. Wasmuth.

Janata, Alfred. 1975. *Musikinstrumente der Völker.* Vienna: Museum für Völkerkunde.

Jones, Arthur M. 1959. *Studies in African Music.* 2 vols. London: Oxford University Press.

———. 1964. *Africa and Indonesia: The Evidence of the Xylophone and Other Cultural and Musical Factors.* Leiden: E. J. Brill.

———. 1971. *Africa and Indonesia: The Evidence of the Xylophone and Other Cultural and Musical Factors,* 2nd ed. Leiden: E. J. Brill.

———. 1978. "Review of 'Les mendzaŋ des chanteurs de Yaoundé' by Pied-Claude Ngumu." *Review of Ethnology* 5(2–3):23–24.

Kalakula, Likando. 1979. *Kuomboka: A Living Traditional Culture among the Malozi People of Zambia.* Lusaka: National Educational Company of Zambia (Neczam).

Kazadi wa Mukuna. 1973. "Trends of Nineteenth and Twentieth Century Music in the Congo-Zaïre." In *Musikkulturen Asiens, Afrikas und Ozeanien im 19. Jahrhundert,* ed. Robert Günther, 267–284. Regensburg: Gustav Bosse.

———. 1980. "The Origin of Zaïrean Modern Music: A Socio-economic Aspect." *African Urban Studies* 6:77–78.

Kishilo w'Itunga. 1976. "Structure des chansons des Lega de Mwenga." *Revue Zaïroise des Arts* no. 1 (Sept.), 7–22.

———. 1987. "Une analyse de la 'Messe Katangese' de Joseph Kiwele." *African Music* 6(4):108–125.

Kremser, Manfred. 1982. "Die Musikinstrumente der Azande: Ein Beitrag zur Musikgeschichte Zentralafrikas." In *Bericht über den 15. Österreichischen Historikertag in Salzburg, 14. bis 18. September 1981,* Referate und Protokolle der Sektion 7, 295–300.

Kubik, Gerhard. 1963–1964. Field-Research Notes: Nigeria, Cameroon, Central African Republic, Congo, Gabon. Vienna: Phonogrammarchiv.

———. 1964. "Harp Music of the Azande and Related Peoples in the Central African Republic." *African Music* 3(3): 37–76.

———. 1965a. "Neue Musikformen in Schwarzafrika: Psychologische und musikethnologische Grundlagen." *Afrika heute* (Bonn), Sonderbeilag 4, 1 March, 1–16.

———. 1965b. Field-Research Notes: Angola. Vienna: Phonogrammarchiv.

———. 1966. "Die Popularität von Musikarten im Afrika südliche der Sahara." *Afrika heute* (Bonn), 15 December, 370–375.

———. 1967. "La musique en République Centrafricaine." *Afrika* (Bonn) 8(1):43–47.

———. 1971. Field-Research Notes: Zambia. Vienna: Phonogrammarchiv.

———. 1977. "Die 'brasilianische Sanza' im Museum für Völkerkunde, Wien." *Archiv für Völkerkunde* 31:1–5, plates 1–2.

———. 1980. "Likembe Tunings of Kufuna Kandonga (Angola)." *African Music* 6(1):70–88.

———. 1981. *Mukanda na makisi— Circumcision school and masks.* Berlin: Museum für Völkerkunde, MC 11. LP disk and notes.

———. 1988. "Nsenga / Shona Harmonic Patterns and the San Heritage in Southern Africa." *Ethnomusicology* 32:39–76.

Laurenty, Jean-Sebastien. 1960. *Les cordophones du Congo Belge et du Ruanda-Urundi.* Tervuren: Musée Royal du Congo Belge.

———. 1962. *Les Sanza du Congo.* Tervuren: Musée Royal de l'Afrique Centrale.

———. 1971. "Les cordophones des Luba-Shankadi." *African Music* 5(2):40–45.

———. 1972. "Les membranophones Luba-Shankadi." *African Music* 5(2):40–45.

Livingstone, David. 1857. *A Narrative of Dr. Livingstone's Discoveries in South-Central Africa.* London: Routledge.

Lomax, Alan. 1968. *Folk Song Style and Culture.* Washington, D.C.: American Association for the Advancement of Science.

Low, John. 1982. *Shaba Diary: A Trip to Rediscover the 'Katanga' Guitar Styles and Songs of the 1950's and 60's.* Vienna: Föhrenau. Acta Ethnologica et Linguistica, 54.

Mapoma, Mwesa I. 1974. "Ingomba: The Royal Musicians of the Bembe People of the Luapula and Northern Provinces of Zambia." Ph.D. dissertation, University of California, Los Angeles.

———. 1980. "Zambia." *The New Grove Dictionary of Music and Musicians,* ed. Stanley Sadie. London: Macmillan.

Mecklenburg, Adolf Friedrich, Herzog zu. 1912. *Vom Kongo zum Niger und Nil.* Leipzig. Berichte zur Deutschen Zentralafrika-Expedition 1910–11.

Merolla, Girolamo. 1692. *Breve, e Succinta Relazione del Viaggio nel Regno di Congo Nell' Africa Meridionale,* ed. Angelo Piccardo. Naples.

Merriam, Alan P. 1959. "The Concept of Culture Clusters Applied to the Belgian Congo." *Southwestern Journal of Anthropology* 15:373–395.

Messomo, Albert Noah. 1980. *Mendzan: Etude ethno-littéraire du xylophone des Beti Yaounde.* University of Yaoundé.

Murdock, George Peter. 1967. *Ethnographic Atlas.* Pittsburgh: University of Pittsburgh Press.

Murray, Jocelyn, ed. 1981. *Cultural Atlas of Africa.* Oxford: Elsevier.

Ngumu, Pie-Claude. 1971. *Maîtrise des Chanteurs à la Croix d'Ébène.* Victoria, Cameroon: Presbook.

———. 1976a. "Les mendzaŋ des Ewondo du Cameroun." *African Music* 5(4):6–26.

———. 1976b. *Les mendzaŋ des chanteurs de Yaoundé.* Vienna: Föhrenau.

Pinto, Tiago de Oliveira, ed. 1986. *Brasilien.* Mainz: Schott.

Praetorius, Michael. 1620. *De organographia.* Wolfenbüttel: Praetorius. *Syntagma Musicum,* 2.

Rycroft, David. 1961. "The Guitar Improvisations of Mwenda Jean Bosco [I]." *African Music* 2(4):81–98.

———. 1962. "The Guitar Improvisations of Mwenda Jean Bosco [II]." *African Music* 3(1):86–102.

Schüller, Dietrich. 1972. "Beziehungen zwischen west- und westenzentralafrikanischen Staaten von 1482 bis 1700." Ph.D. dissertation, University of Vienna.

Schweinfurth, Georg. 1875. *Im Herzen von Afrika: Reisen und Entdeckungen im Centralen Aequatorial-Afrika während der Jahre 1868 bis 1871.* Leipzig: F. A. Brockhaus.

Sulzmann, Erika. 1959. "Les danseurs ekonda à 'Changwe yetu'." *Zaïre* 13:57–71.

Tracey, Hugh. 1948. *Handbook for Librarians.* Roodepoort: African Music Society.

———. 1973. *Catalogue of the Sound of Africa Recordings.* Roodepoort: International Library of African Music.

Vansina, Jan. 1966. *Kingdoms of the Savannah.* Madison: University of Wisconsin Press.

———. 1969. "The Bells of Kings." *Journal of African History* 10(2):187–197.

Wachsmann, Klaus Peter. 1964. "Human Migration and African Harps." *Journal of the International Folk Music Council* 16:84–88.

Wegner, Ulrich. 1984. *Afrikanische Saiteninstrumente.* Berlin: Museum für Völkerkunde. N.S., 41.

Wieschhoff, Heinz. 1933. *Die afrikanischen Trommeln und ihre außerafrikanischen Beziehungen.* Stuttgart: Strecker und Schröder. Studien zur Kulturkunde, 2.

Musical Life in the Central African Republic

Michelle Kisliuk

Sounds of the City: *Zokela*
Sounds of the Forest: BaAka Pygmies
Conclusion

This essay laces together two musical narratives set in Centrafrique (Central African Republic) in the early 1990s. The introductory narrative focuses on an urban dance music based in the capital, Bangui. The second description, by contrast, addresses the performative, political, and social circumstances within which BaAka pygmies—who live mostly in the rain forest area in the southwest of the country—are negotiating their daily lives.

A link between these two musical domains might at first seem unlikely, but the urban music is in fact stylistically rooted in the Lobaye River region, which overlaps with the home area of BaAka (Aka) and other pygmies (see map). These domains also connect as performances of modernity—how people situate themselves within a changing world. As I shall describe, the BaAka among whom I lived include within their repertory a form that mixes together hymns from various Christian sects, pop-song snippets from the radio, and rhythms and melodies from neighboring Bolemba pygmies (whose lives and culture, unlike BaAka, are relatively integrated with those of their nonpygmy counterparts). BaAka meld all these aspects into a dance form that is about being modern. Concurrently, urban musicians in a collection of bands called *zokela* draw on local song styles—including Bolemba and Mbati pygmy styles—situating their electric sound in regional culture.

I write in the first person here because I want to emphasize that ideas and information about musical performance are by nature embedded within personal experience, bound and defined by moment and circumstance. This viewpoint is particularly appropriate for addressing African performance, intimately tied in most cases to the socioaesthetic moment (Chernoff 1979; Stone 1982). My descriptions are based on several years of research among BaAka pygmies, spanning eight years (1986–1994) and including a two-year stay. The material on urban music in Bangui is culled from the same period.

SOUNDS OF THE CITY: *ZOKELA*

It is a weeknight in Fatima, a section of Bangui. Fatima is the neighborhood where people originally from the Lobaye region tend to gather (the Lobaye river area is in the southwest of the country). In an open-air dance bar, the disk jockey switches

zokela   An urban dance music based in the
Central African Republic city of Bangui

soukous   Urban music style from Zaïre
makossa   Urban music style from Cameroon

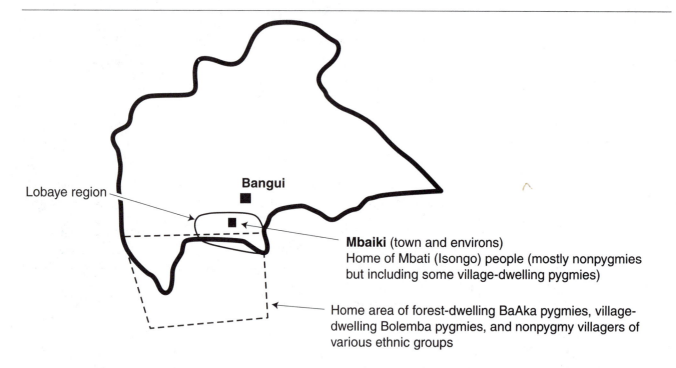

Lobaye region

Bangui

Mbaiki (town and environs)
Home of Mbati (Isongo) people (mostly nonpygmies
but including some village-dwelling pygmies)

Home area of forest-dwelling BaAka pygmies, village-
dwelling Bolemba pygmies, and nonpygmy villagers of
various ethnic groups

Central African Republic
(Centrafique). This map
highlights only areas mentioned in this article. The
Central African Republic is
bordered to the south by the
Republic of Congo, to the
north by Chad, to the west
by Cameroon, and to the
east by Zaïre (now Demo-
cratic Republic of the
Congo).

from a current *soukous* hit from Zaïre to a tune by *zokela*—musicians who play and sing in a vigorous style based on multiethnic rhythms, harmonies, melodies, and topical themes from the Lobaye. Though the dance floor had been far from empty before, suddenly just about everybody seated at the little wooden tables leaves beers and sodas behind, grabbing friends to get up and dance *motengene,* the loose, ribcage-rotating, regional dance.

Originally the name of a band, *zokela* has burgeoned into a full-fledged style. On a weekend, those in search of an evening of energetic dancing, social commentary, and proverbs set to the rhythms of the Lobaye might find one of the *zokela* bands playing at a club (only one band would be playing at a time, since three or more bands must share instruments). Inside an open-roofed club, after paying a fee of 500 francs (about $1.50 in 1996), one would find the musicians and patrons warmed up by about 9:00 P.M. Four singers standing in a row, each behind a stationary microphone, would be trading lead lines and overlapping choral responses with tight harmonies. Occasionally a singer might withdraw, replaced by one who had been waiting casually at the sidelines.

Though overshadowed internationally by neighboring urban musical styles from Zaïre and Cameroon (like *soukous* and *makossa*), musicians from Centrafrique, and the Lobaye region in particular, have been developing their own style of electrified band music since the late 1970s, and their popularity with the Centrafrican people is high.

This story of the genesis of the *zokela* sound is based on my conversations with members of the original band, and on discussions with Lobayans who form the core of the listening and dancing community for *zokela*.

The origins of *zokela*

Several people I spoke with began the story of *zokela* by recounting an incident from 1981. Musiki, an established rumba-style band from Bangui, was touring the country. For a few days, Musiki stayed in the town of Mbaïki, where they discovered aspiring boy-musicians calling themselves *zokela* (Mbati) 'noise'—a noise like water gurgling down a stream, or like women ululating at a funeral dance, or, less literally, like the sound of the life-force.

Kaïda Monganga, the leader of the original *zokela*, later narrated his recollections of how *zokela* began (my translation):

> I learned music from my mother. When she would take me to the fields, she would sing, so she taught me how to sing. In Mbaïki, at the age of eight I got together with some friends to sing Mbati songs from traditional legends, funerals, and ceremonies—songs that were part of our upbringing—and we also began to interpret music from Zaïre on homemade guitars. This was at the age of about 10, between 1970 and 1974. We were actually imitating the Centrafrican bands who were themselves imitating the rumba style from Zaïre; but as kids, we could not enter the local nightclubs. Then Piros, a composer among us, arranged an interpretation of a traditional song, and each time we would sing it, lots of people would gather on the path to listen, and they would encourage us. We formed two little groups, and after several more years of encouragement we got together as one and decided to choose the name Zokela, meaning in the Mbati language 'acclamation, joy, heat, ambience, noise.'
>
> One night in Mbaïki, an *orchestre* came to play at a dance bar. They played from 8 p.m. until 2 a.m. And we youngsters, with our little group, we came there to ask them to let us play, but they made us stay outside. . . . We really suffered out there until 2 a.m. But when the evening was over, and the people began to leave, they said "there's a little group here, you should let them come in and play." And we went and played only one song, and it was that traditional song. When we played it there was pandemonium, and even though we'd only been allowed to play one song, we were very happy because it was the first time we had ever picked up an electric guitar and mic. Oh! That was the end! Oo-la-la, we were overjoyed.

Everyone who heard the young members of Zokela that night in Mbaïki was stunned that they had captured on modern instruments the insistent and vital sound of ceremonies and funeral dances. Accented by a trap set, the bass guitar and glass bottle (tapped with a stick) caught the texture of village drums. The bass emphasized high-low contrasts (like the open and muted strokes of a low-pitched drum), while the bottle added the syncopated triplets of a matching high-pitched drum. Two lead guitars built on that rhythmic base, playing interlocking, repeating riffs—brighter sounding than in *soukous*—jumping octaves and rolling in cycles like a tumultuous brook.

Though this was not the first time a band had tried to integrate musical elements from the Lobaye into an urban sound, it was the first time a group had succeeded in getting the melodies, harmonies, vocal quality, and especially the *motengene* dance rhythms and energy into the music. After the leader of Musiki heard Zokela for the first time (in 1981), he and a financially successful music lover from the

While *zokela* musicians continue to compose their own tunes and lyrics, they are delving progressively deeper into local traditions and creatively elaborating on urban culture

Lobaye invited the young men to Bangui to perform several club concerts there. This exposed the band to the Bangui public, and they exploded onto the cultural scene, soon beginning to play regularly at Club Anabelle, in the Fatima neighborhood. Over the following months, the band struggled to remain in Bangui, all of the musicians living in one house—at least four singers, two lead guitarists, drum set player, and bassist.

Kaïda continues:

In 1982, we were invited to make our first recording, and when we introduced that rhythm, Zokela took Bangui by storm. We wanted to stay in Bangui because that way we'd at least have access to instruments and to repairs. So since 1983, we have been in Bangui.

At that time, we began to expand our repertory, to compose, to create, based on traditional music. But we also began to compose some songs in the national language [Sango], instead of only in our regional languages from the Lobaye, so the people who did not understand would no longer feel excluded, and we were very successful. To attract attention, we costumed ourselves in animal skins, traditional dress—that is, panther skins—and when I came out on stage: boom! the people were very interested.

Since then, the band has remained popular.

Zokela began singing not only about their experience as Lobayains, but also about urban life in Bangui, to which people from all regions of the country could relate. In rhythm, vocal style, and lyric, Zokela voiced the contemporary and complex experience of urban Centrafricans, melded with ethnic roots. Nevertheless, the band was at a disadvantage because the government would not aid a group from the Lobaye (birthplace of the deposed Emperor Bokassa), and because their songs, like the traditional forms that inspired them, contained social commentary unlike the beautiful but unthreatening love songs of most of the other rumba-style bands in Bangui.

According to several of the members of Zokela, there was a problem of tribal jealousy. Kaïda recalls, "Some people wanted Zokela to disappear. Even our songs on the radio were censored because we were very successful. They were afraid we would develop our region, and then come again to dominate. We went along for 10 or 11 years with that tribalistic regime [of President André Kolingba], but it seems that now there will be a change. [The new president, Ange] Patassé promised to support Centrafrican artists."

While Zokela were staying in Bangui during their initial entrance onto the scene in the early 1980s, several of the more established Bangui bands (including Musiki, Makembe, Cannon Stars, Cool Stars) began tempting the singers to join them—and they succeeded to some extent because they had instruments and some money. A growing core group of singers and players was so large, there were still many musicians left to fill the places of those who had moved on. As a result, rather than seeing their sound and energy become diffused and destroyed by recruitment from other bands, Zokela not only continued on their own, but infiltrated to varying degrees the sound of most of the other bands in Bangui.

Kaïda continues the story:

> We did not have our own instruments, we were renting instruments, and to put up a concert was very expensive. But for us it wasn't just the money, but our future. We needed to make ourselves known on a national level so we could develop as artists. We didn't concern ourselves with earning money; women loved us, and life was beautiful. The important thing was to produce, to perform.
>
> In 1985, a local producer who wanted to work with us approached us. He provided instruments, a makeshift studio, but then he began to want to dominate us. We were the creators of the music, but he wanted everything to pass his approval first. . . . But how could he do that? This was our group; we were the ones who formed it.
>
> So the rest of us, those of us who had brought the music from Mbaïki in the first place, we decided to look for other people to help us. And so those who stayed with that producer for the sake of the instruments formed the subgroup Zokela Motike ['Orphans'], and we became Zokela Original. We were the four founders of Zokela: Mabele, Ilonga, Degoumousse, and Kaïda. The rest went with that producer.
>
> So I took other new singers, and we mounted a coup again, in 1986, and we put out an album [homemade cassette] . . . that was very, very successful. We recorded and toured a lot throughout 1988–89, . . . but we were still renting instruments. Then there was another disagreement within Zokela Motike. Luanza, the head of Motike, decided to break and form yet another Zokela. . . . So I accepted that there be many Zokelas because I wasn't afraid: I know my position; I know the secret of this music. I'm not afraid to share it with the youngsters. . . . So Luanza made "Zokela National" in late 1992, and it was very successful, even more so than Motike. And it gave me a lot of pleasure to see the youngsters that we trained.

The members of all the *zokela* groups, despite their conflicts, continue to cooperate, covering each other's songs without hesitation, and by necessity sharing instruments. One of the musicians explained that the reason Zokela keeps splitting off into new bands is that they are all like brothers, having grown up together in the same town, and therefore nobody can really boss anybody else around. Instead of following a leader when conflicts arise, they just split off. This situation accommodates the younger musicians from Mbaïki and elsewhere in the Lobaye who want to be connected with the *zokela,* and has strengthened the style and its influence, moving *zokela* further toward becoming a national style.

In January 1993, a French-owned beer company sponsored an event that the announcers on Radio Bangui called a concert of *la musique traditionelle moderne* 'modern traditional music' (figures 1 and 2). All three *zokela* bands, plus a potential fourth band, played at this concert, held at the upscale nightclub Punch Coco. The Banguisois audience, of mixed ethnic background, crowded in to hear and see the latest *zokela* compositions and *motengene* dancing, and responded enthusiastically to songs that captured the collective experience of economic and political crisis in the country.

FIGURE 1   Mixed *zokela* bands perform at club Punch Coco in Bangui, 1993. The singers break for an interlude of dancing, while bassist Maurice Kpamanda stands behind them. Photo by Justin Mongosso.

"... We go to work in the fields, a long walk away, to survive. I talk to my dead relatives, who can no longer help me; I cry."—from a *zokela* song

FIGURE 2 Lead *zokela* guitarists and percussionists, with the bottle player seated behind the drum set. The beer company slogan, *la blonde qui fait courire l'Afrique* 'the blonde that makes Africa chase after her', is displayed behind the musicians. Photo by Justin Mongosso.

While *zokela* musicians continue to compose their own tunes and lyrics, they are delving progressively deeper into local traditions and creatively elaborating on urban culture (weaving in references to Christian religious music or advertising jingles), much in the way that the Mbati songs elaborate and comment on social surroundings. For example, in 1995, a hit by Zokela National—"*Essa Messa* 'I Call You'"—used several regional languages, plus Sango, to express a proverb whose theme is reciprocal assistance: "During tough times, you can call on a real friend to help you, but I called you and you did not answer." (This may covertly criticize the government—something *zokela* is known for.) "But what befalls me now will befall you later. If you need my help, I must help you." The song goes on to name all the musicians in the band, who will be there to help each other.

Another song, "*Exode Rurale* 'Rural Exodus',", warns villagers not to leave their fertile earth behind and move to the city. It describes the difficulties of survival in Bangui. But many *zokela* songs—like that first one they played as boys—are modern arrangements of the exact melodies and words of traditional songs. In Mbaïki and in villages throughout the Lobaye, one can hear *zokela* tunes playing regularly on family tape players, while next door at a funeral or a ceremony people may be singing the songs that form the basis of that style. One important difference in the urban musical setting is that musical performance there is dominated by men, while in the village, women have an equal or greater role.

Another *zokela* song, a hit by Zokela Original, is "*Motike* 'Orphans'" (on CD track 17). The text, in the Mbati language, laments the difficulty of being musicians:

Zokela nzonga mawa.
Ngo si mbi ko Bangui ngo ke sio na Isongo.
Ngo simba tene ngo kpoua na lele.
Nya kolo eti.

Zokela is unhappy, pitiable.
We go to work in the fields, a long walk away, to survive.
I talk to my dead relatives, who can no longer help me; I cry.
And I have crippled feet [a reference to a guitarist (figure 2)].

As you listen to the audio example, try isolating the bass, played by Maurice Kpamanda of Zokela Original, said to be the only bassist who truly captures village rhythms. The lead singer at the opening of the song is Kaïda Monganga.

Partly as an effort to escape the paralysis of ever-deepening poverty, *zokela*'s latest move has been toward what Kaïda calls spectacle—an international pop-show style that emulates *soukous* bands touring from Zaïre. Holding a movable microphone, the lead singer, or "star" (Kaïda himself, in this case), is separated from the "chorus." And whereas in a club setting the singers dance *motengene* informally, occasionally adding a small choreographed bit to an instrumental interlude (figure 1), the spectacle introduces highly choreographed dance numbers with female dancers.

In the Bangui soccer stadium in 1994, during a spectacle showcasing Centrafrican superstar singers, Kaïda tried to add a folkloric-show aspect to the spectacle. As one of several singers who performed that evening, he brought pygmies from the Mbaïki area to come on stage with him and imitate their forest-dwelling BaAka cousins, whose styles of music and dance differ widely from those of the Mbati pygmies. Mbati pygmies normally dance a version of *motengene* as their traditional dance, while BaAka generally do not (the hip swiveling and rib rotating of *motengene* contrasts with the square-hipped chugging and buttock-bobbing steps of most BaAka dancing). During this spectacle, however, the Mbati pygmies were asked to provide an introduction, wearing BaAka leaves and loincloths, and singing in BaAka style (which they could only approximate). Kaïda himself could then explode onto the stage with his modern sound, spurring the "pygmies" to drop everything and dance *motengene* instead. These Mbati pygmies were at first so reticent to perform in front of the crowd that the organizers had to get them drunk before they were willing. Their dancing was nonetheless impressive, if unsteady, and the crowd, of mostly urban Lobayans (many of whom do not distinguish between BaAka and Mbati pygmies), cheered wildly.

This incident highlights both the creative tension and the possible pitfalls when a visceral identification with local roots meets an enticing modernity. Extending that tension, *zokela*'s struggle to find footing as a regional, urban, then national style was almost eclipsed here by a simultaneous wish for dramatic impact and international appeal. Kaïda, who had at first refused to give up his autonomy to a producer in exchange for some measure of security, now, even while making explicit the roots of his style, blurred the realities of those roots for the sake of spectacle.

The story of *zokela* resembles that of many urban musics developing throughout Africa. In their very sound, they have been reclaiming and redefining experience in the postcolonial era, first by experimenting with electric instruments and a "modern" sound, then expanding to a national public with a regionally or ethnically based style; then, some of them have leaped toward an international market. But the consequences of an international leap for a music like *zokela*—potent mainly for its localness—are uncertain in the climate of worldbeat.

The music of African pygmies has held a special place in ethnomusicological imagination. The yodeling and hocketing of pygmy singing has served as an icon of social and musical utopia.

SOUNDS OF THE FOREST: BAAKA PYGMIES

The music of African pygmies has held a special place in ethnomusicological imagination. In the writings of Colin Turnbull (1962), Alan Lomax (1976), Robert Farris Thompson (1989), and Simha Arom (1978, 1985), the yodeling and hocketing of pygmy singing has served as an icon of social and musical utopia. Pygmies who call themselves BaAka (sometimes Bayaka, depending on the regional accent) live between the Sangha and Oubangui rivers in the southwestern Central African Republic, and extend as far south as Imfondo in the Republic of the Congo. They live mostly in densely forested areas, and their culture is based largely on hunting and gathering. Since the 1960s and 1970s, however, these pygmies (like most other pygmies of equatorial Africa) have become more involved in farming—either as seasonal laborers for village-based farmers of other ethnic groups, or, increasingly, on their own plots cut in the forest.

I use the term *pygmy* (French *pygmée*) with reluctance. It derives via Middle English *pigmei* and Latin *Pygmæi* from Greek *Pygmaîoi* 'people pertaining to the *pygmé* (the distance from the elbow to the knuckles)', denoting a mythical dwarfish people, who repeatedly warred with and were defeated by cranes. H. M. Stanley had applied the term to them in 1887, but Paul Schebesta (1933) introduced the term formally, replacing an older term, *Negrillo*. An alternative term, such as *forest people*, while at first preferable to pygmy, inadvisedly attaches to a people an essentialized place. (What happens when pygmies move out of the forest? or when the forest recedes?) While awaiting a more neutral alternative, or at least a time when *pygmy* will be free of pejorative connotations, it is preferable to use the term each group uses for itself (Efe, Mbuti, Twa, Baka, BaAka, and others), reserving pygmy for general use.

The BaAka whom I came to know best in Centrafrique live near Bagandou, a rural community in the Lobaye region south of Mbaïki, crossing the border with the Republic of the Congo. The Bagandou have a long-standing, hereditary exchange relationship with the BaAka of the region. Various terms have been used to characterize this relationship—*clientship, symbiosis, parasitism, servitude* (Bahuchet 1985:554–555). These conceptions betray the complexity and variability of relationships between pygmies and their neighbors across equatorial Africa. The BaAka term for Bagandou villagers and other Africans is *milo* (pl. *bilo*). By itself, the term simply designates nonpygmy dark-skinned Africans, whom BaAka see as separate and distinct from themselves. When I refer generally to non-BaAka Africans, I use either *milo* (*bilo*), or Turnbull's term *villagers*.

BaAka dances: *mabo* and *dingboku*

During my initial research (1987–1989), I became familiar with, and participated in, the current repertory of BaAka hunting dances and women's dances in the Bagandou area (Kisliuk in preparation). I spent most of my time living with one particular

FIGURE 3 The theme of "*Makala,*" the basic melody, from which spring variations, elaborations, and counter-melodies.

Ee ya ee ya Ma – ka la eh (ah) ee ya na le la oh – ho ho

extended family, but I also traveled as far as the northern Congo to gain a sense of the flow and exchange of new *beboka* 'singing, dancing, drumming' (sing. *eboka*) coming in and out of the area. Below, I describe two of the BaAka dance forms (*beboka*) that I came to know well during that period.

A popular hunting dance

One of the most popular BaAka dances of the late 1980s is *mabo,* a hunting dance. Because it was new (new dances emerge every few years, some survive for generations, and others fade away), I was able to learn the songs. Whereas songs for older dances have been elaborated over the years to the point where the underlying melodic themes often completely drop away (though people still hear the themes in their minds), with new songs, people sing basic melodic themes from time to time, and therefore improvisations and elaborations are easier for newly initiated ears to recognize.

One of the most frequently performed songs at the time is one I call "*Makala,*" the name of an unknown person, probably a deceased BaAka child from the Congo. (BaAka do not actually name their songs, as they have no occasion to objectify them in that way.) I learned to recognize a basic "theme" of "*Makala*" by chance. I was walking along a path with some BaAka teenagers, who suddenly sang out the theme in isolation. I then recognized that theme and others during dances, when I would hear a whole chorus of singers elaborating.

During a dance in my home camp, several young women gathered by the recorder to play with the level-indicator lights by singing into the microphone. This playful moment makes their various improvisations easier to hear. The basic theme of "*Makala,*" as transcribed into conventional Western notation (figure 3), shows interlocked and yodeled sections. You will be able to pick out this theme on the recording.

Each BaAka dance form has particular rhythms, played on at least two (often three) drums, made from hollowed tree trunks. On each end, each drum has a head made from antelope skin—a type of drum borrowed from Isongo villagers. One drummer will sit straddling a drum, while another man behind him might play a cross-rhythm with a stick on the side of the drum. The basic rhythm for *mabo,* played on the smaller of two drums, is a triplet pattern played steadily with alternating hands, thus implying a three-against-two feeling.

In the following excerpt, adapted from an ethnography of BaAka performance (Kisliuk 1991 and in preparation), I describe a particular instance of how it feels to dance and sing *mabo:*

My senses tingled; I was finally inside the singing and dancing circle. The song was "*Makala,*" and singing it came more easily to me while I danced. As I moved around the circle, the voices of different people stood out at moments, affecting my own singing and my choices of variations. Ndami sang a yodeled variation (*mayenge*) I had not heard before. I could feel fully the intermeshing of sound and motion, and move with it as it transformed, folding in upon itself. This was different from listening or singing on the sidelines because, while moving with the circle, I became an active part of the aural kaleidoscope. I was part of the changing design inside the scope, instead of looking at it and projecting in.

The physical task of executing the dance step melded with the social interac-

dingboku   A dance performed by a line of women related by residential camp or clan

mabo   A hunting dance that was one of the most popular BaAka dances of the late 1980s

mokondi   General name for dances involving BaAka spirits

beboka   Singing, dancing, and drumming of the BaAka

tions of looking, listening, smiling, reacting, that kept us all dancing. Since our camp was built on a hill, it took extra effort to dance the full-soled steps while going up or down hill. Running the bottom of my foot inchwormlike across the ground required the sturdy support of all the muscles in my leg. All this while trying to stay loose enough to follow through with my whole body and keep up with the beat. As I continued to dance, trying to refine my step, I noticed more fully the inward and delicately grounded concentration of the movements, like the blue duiker (*mboloko*, a small antelope). Someone cried out "*Sukele!*" (an interpretation of the French *sucré* 'sweet').

Suddenly, a few people shouted rhythmic exclamations that suggested a shift to the *esime* (the intensified rhythmic section), and the singing stopped. Tina stepped into the center of the circle and walked in the opposite direction to the one in which we were dancing. He shouted "*Pipi!*" (imitating a carhorn), and the group answered "*Hoya!*" (an exclamation). He continued, "*O lembi ti?* 'Are we tired?'," and we answered "*O lembi (o)te!* 'We aren't tired!'" As the *esime* continued, people "got down" in their dancing, crying "heeya, heeya" repeatedly on the beat, and sometimes jumping forward with a scoot instead of stepping to the beat.

At one point, the women grabbed the shoulders of those in front of them in line, and began chugging ahead on the beat. I joined in, finding it hard to jump all the way up the hill while staying as close as possible to Ndoko, whose shoulders I held onto in front of me. Someone was behind me, I don't recall who, but she had to grab my waist because she could not reach my shoulders comfortably. It was unavoidably clear at this moment that I was bigger than everybody else.

A women's dance

Ongoing, informal negotiation and disputed expectations, as part of BaAka social dynamics, are highlighted in performance. An egalitarian sensibility, coupled with individual autonomy, make for a cultural climate of constant negotiation (Dumont 1986; Turnbull 1962; Moise 1992). In the context of BaAka women's dances, gendered wills intensify the social fray. *Dingboku* is a dance performed by women in a line (often several lines—of women related by residential camp or clan). They stand linked at the shoulder, and then step forward and back together (figure 4). The subject of *dingboku* is a celebration of women's sexuality, and some of the songs mock men. But only male BaAka play drums, and therefore drumming sometimes becomes a focus of tension during the women's dances—even in *dingboku*, which has no drum accompaniment.

In a performance I witnessed, Sandimba and Djongi (two women from my home camp), who knew the dance best, gestured cues to the other women, indicating how they should link up in line and how to proceed. For fifteen minutes within the hullabaloo of chatting, milling around, and extemporaneous drumming, they tried to establish two lines. Finally, throngs of men, and some women, stood aside to watch.

FIGURE 4   BaAka women dancing *dingboku*. Sandimba is at the end of the line, on the left.

When the second line of dancers was ready to begin, someone started a song, "*Ooh Leh.*" Short and syncopated, the phrases in this song established a driving beat, to which the women, in two lines, hopped percussively from foot to foot. The lines repeatedly approached each other and then separated. The line of less experienced dancers got tangled, and Sandimba called out, "*Hoya!*" a signal to end the song, and the group responded unanimously, "*Ho!*"

Then Sambala, a man, stepped in to try to reorganize the women, but they managed to get themselves in line and ready to continue. Sandimba introduced a slower, less syncopated song, emphasizing the dance beat; this intervention helped unify the company. The lines faced each other, an arm's length apart, and moved together as a unit across the space and back.

Several minutes later, after dancing energetically, the women were tired, and Sandimba called up a final, slower song. The lines faced each other and moved as a group across the space at close range, one line stepping forward, the other backward. This song had no words, only vocables (*eeya oh eeye*), with a lush interlock and harmonious overlap. The central melody, based on three descending phrases that form an asymmetrical repeating pattern, produced a gentle tension and cyclic drive. The performance coalesced now to a solid groove, the slowed stepping and lush harmonies making some of the women seem to fall into a dreamy, trancelike state.

Amid this euphoria, some drummers began to play *mabo* triplets in the background, but actually fell into time with *dingboku*. Maybe the drumming men wanted to participate in this mood, or else they hoped to move the event along into *mabo*. The effect, intentional or not, was to articulate a cross-rhythm that heightened the intensity of the moment.

BaAka responses to missionization

In 1989, some BaAka encountered Christian evangelism for the first time. The most concentrated episode began in late 1988, when American missionaries from the Grace Brethren Church, a fundamentalist sect based in Wonona Lake, Indiana, started a campaign to plant churches among the BaAka of the Bagandou region. This was my first significant encounter with missionaries too, and I was not sure how to react. I tried my best to keep an open mind, believing that most missionaries have good intentions, and often give in positive ways. Besides, I knew of many instances where missionized peoples reinterpret the lore of the missionaries, resulting in a spirited resistance to the "colonization of consciousness" (Comaroff and Comaroff 1989).

Komba   Creator god of the BaAka

gano   Traditional legends in which Komba, the creator god, is a friend and caretaker

nzapa   The term for the Christian God in the Sango language of Central Africa

BaAka in this region (with the Baka pygmies of Cameroon) recognize the creator god Komba, but they cite him mostly as a character in *gano*—traditional legends, in which Komba is a friend (*beka*) and caretaker (*kondja*). Otherwise, I did not hear people refer to Komba except in an occasional exclamation like "Komba's mother!" or, when someone's luck was down, "Komba is a bad person." But once I asked my friend Sandimba if Komba and *nzapa* (the Sango word used for the Christian God) were the same entity. She hesitated slightly, then answered they were. Linking Komba and *nzapa* had likely circulated to Sandimba from BaAka who had been exposed to an evangelist strategy of paralleling Christian beliefs as much as possible with indigenous ones, then "explaining" where indigenous beliefs go wrong.

The god dance

An earlier wave of Christian influence among local BaAka had started about a year before. Cousins from one family had migrated to the west, toward the town of Nola, where they were "converted" by Baptist missionaries. When these cousins came back to Bagandou to visit, they began convincing their relatives to take up *nzapa*. The idea slowly spread through the forest. In the camp where I was living, one evening after a *mabo* had ended, I saw Tina lead some men in a brief burst of preaching and hymn singing. They mixed songs and practices from various Christian sects observable in the village, calling all of it the god dance (*eboka ya nzapa*), and made up their own form of preaching; anyone could decide to play the role of preacher on the spur of the moment.

A common expression I heard while BaAka prayed was *ame* 'amen'. Diaka *ame* can be glossed as English 'me', and repeating "me" at the ends of phrases became part of their version of praying. BaAka children started singing songs about *nzapa* during their play, and a parent sometimes absentmindedly sang along *alleluya ame* 'alleluia, me'. Early one morning, Sandimba's boy Mbaka was distractedly singing in falsetto a song with the words *eeya, Malia, oh, na nzapa,* from a local Roman Catholic hymn. When I asked Sandimba what the song was about, she said it did not refer to anything, but was just a song heard around lately.

Nevertheless, during the following coffee harvest season (when many BaAka converged in temporary camps near Bagandou to help with the harvest), little by little rumors began to circulate that some BaAka thought dances like *mabo* were satanic (*ba sata*). Then suddenly some of the most ardent followers of *nzapa* refused to dance and started accusing other BaAka of being satanic. A split developed between those who had been mildly interested before, but were now becoming suspicious of the *nzapa* craze, and those who were following what an increasing number of *nzapa* fanatics were saying.

One weekend early in this heated controversy, I missed a big dance in a neighboring camp because I had to go to Bangui. When I returned, Sandimba told me that during that dance she had challenged the *nzapa* fanatics in front of everybody. She had told them:

> We BaAka have dances, like *elio* [a curing dance], like *monjoli, djoboko* [both older dances, associated with spearhunting], *mabo, monina* [another women's dance], all belonging to us, to BaAka. But *nzapa* is a *bilo* thing, it comes from far away. It's for the *bilo* because they can read and write, but a Moaka has never written the name of his friend [Komba]. . . . I yelled at them, "You are liars, big liars." I yelled, "Liars, liars!" and the others applauded. We haven't changed our decision.

Sandimba said that after her speech they danced both *mabo* and *dingboku,* but the *nzapa* followers refused to participate. In our camp that evening, we could hear the *nzapa* people having a "god dance" in the distance. From inside a hut, Sandimba grumbled: "That's the *nzapa* of monkeys." Always ready with witty insults, she continued, "They wear clothes like monkeys with tails. They're dirty and always wear the same dirty outfits that smell of urine"—instead of the white robes that some "real" Christians wear.

BaAka traditionally believe in ancestral spirit entities, *bedjo*, some of which are personalized and belong to families, and others of which are more general and nameless (Hewlett 1986:92). As proprietors (*bakondja*) of the forest, *bedjo* play a role in the success of the hunt. Many of the rituals and protocols around the hunt focus on securing their help (Bahuchet 1985:451). Related to the *bedjo* are *mokondi*. Most BaAka understand *mokondi* to be a grouping of ancestral *bedjo* connected to a dance form efficacious for the hunt, or for the purpose of redressing social conflicts within the hunting group. *Mokondi* is also a general name for dances involving any of these spirits, including *edjengi,* a category of spirits. (Elanga, my friend and a respected elder, explained to me that for the dance *edjengi,* each family has its personalized *bedjo*). One day, my youthful friend Ndanga was sitting next to me looking at a religious pamphlet and casually praying in Sango, reproducing actions he had seen among village Christians and thinking, perhaps, that I might approve of his efforts. To his mumbled monologue, he added the word *Christo.* When I asked him what *Christo* is, he said it is a spirit (*edjo*).

The firstfruits of Balabala's work

The most focused evangelical activity of this period was sponsored by the Grace Brethren Church. I had heard that this project was led by an American woman known locally as Balabala. Balabala devoted much of her energy—in the form of brief but intense appearances—at Dzanga, a permanent BaAka settlement west of the area where I was spending most of my time. As yet unaware of any details, I set out to visit Dzanga—to compare *beboka* repertories, and to get a sense for the choices BaAka in different areas were making in response to missionization.

At Dzanga, I was shocked by what I saw. The BaAka there had stopped performing their traditional repertory of music and dance (such as *mabo* and *dingboku*). Whereas in neighboring areas BaAka had been hotly debating the value of what the Christians were saying, at Dzanga all of the BaAka had been convinced by Balabala and her Centrafrican evangelists that their own music, dance, and traditional medicine were satanic. BaAka at Dzanga told me proudly—assuming I would approve, since I am white, like Balabala—that they now performed only one kind of *eboka.* Now they would only sing hymns to the Christian god in church. These hymns were not in their own language, but in Sango, which many BaAka, especially women, do not understand.

The church at Dzanga was not quite finished. It consisted of support poles and the beginnings of a thatch roof, but rows of log seats were in place (figure 5). On

I saw the god dance as a means of addressing modernity. These BaAka were claiming any "otherness" that surrounded them and usually excluded them, and mixing it into a form they could define and control.

FIGURE 5 BaAka of Dzanga hold a Christian religious service in 1989. The choir sings at left, while the preachers consult their Bibles in Sango.

Sunday morning, the BaAka of Dzanga gathered in churchlike clothing, wearing it as close to the style of villagers as they could manage. One woman had a matching blouse, cloth, and head wrap in a bright green and white pattern. Other women were not so fancy, but covered their heads with an old cloth. Several men sat at the front of the enclosure: one wore a long, white Muslim gown (*bubu*) and huge sunglasses; another man, the choral director, wore jeans and a corduroy vest, and no shoes. The choir consisted of women and girls, who in enthusiastic harmony sang hymns in Sango.

A Moaka stood in front of the congregation. In Diaka, he told the story of Adam and Eve from Genesis, using the word "Komba" for "God," as he had likely been instructed to do. Another Moaka, sitting at the front of the church with a copy of the Bible, read a few words haltingly in Sango. A third man, the one wearing the sunglasses, sat next to the preacher with a second copy of the Bible, which he held upside down. The man who had been reading then proceeded to catechize the congregation, asking repeatedly "Who created us?" and they answered halfheartedly "Komba created us." He continued, "Where did we come from?" There was no answer, just confused murmuring. He repeated, "Where did we come from?" and a voice piped up, unsure, "From earth" (*sopo* 'ground, earth'). Then the choral director struck up another hymn, to the accompaniment of a homemade guitar—perhaps emulating Balabala, who plays guitar.

I had been traveling (by foot) with my longtime friend and assistant, Justin Mongosso of Bagandou. When the service was over, Justin asked if he could comment. Everyone stayed to listen, expecting, perhaps, that he would constructively critique their praying technique, as the evangelists do. But instead, he began by saying that he wondered what would happen now that they had stopped using their traditional medicine. Many of the listeners, especially the elders, nodded with concern. Where would they get treatment? There was no clinic anywhere nearby, Balabala was not providing care (we found at Dzanga an especially large clientele for our first aid), and praying was not going to cure them. Why were they abandoning their medicine? They answered that they worried that if they continued, they would die among bad spirits (*sata* and *goundou*). Gone were the vacant smiles of moments earlier. Brows were furrowed, and for the moment, people leaned forward in their seats, listening intently.

Three years later

In 1992, when I next returned to Centrafrique, I saw a somewhat different picture. At the Dzanga settlement, though BaAka were still rejecting BaAka song forms and dance forms, people had begun to significantly recontextualize the Grace Brethren Church material. The BaAka church was no longer standing. Apparently the *nzapa* leaders among them had traveled to Balabala's field school at another BaAka settlement, Moali, and those remaining at Dzanga had not bothered to maintain the church.

The evening of my arrival at Dzanga, the BaAka held a god dance similar to what I had seen years earlier at my home camp, but this one was more elaborate. The dancers, mostly children and teenagers, moved in a circle, using *motengene*-type steps with the singing style and drum rhythms of Bolemba pygmies. Bolemba recreational dances are also emulated by nonpygmy Bagandou teenagers in nearby villages (and by *zokela* in Bangui)—which is probably how these BaAka, in turn, became familiar with the style. Many adults stood by, some joining in the dancing, others watching enthusiastically and singing along. Grace Brethren songs were preceded and followed by Bolemba-style interpretations of hymns from various Christian sects represented in Bagandou village, including Baptist, Apostolic, and even Roman Catholic hymns. They not only blended all that into the same dance, but mixed in Afro-pop snippets in Lingala (from radio tunes from Zaïre and the Congo).

🎧 TRACK 19   Audio example 19 is an excerpt from this event. The man calling out the solo line sings an alleluia, and adds a few disconnected words in Sango; the chorus responds in Bolemba-style harmonies with an initial alleluia, followed by pygmy singing sounds, which jump large intervals on the syllables *oh* and *eh*.

Confused about this transition from hymns in church to dancing, I asked a man whether, as some claimed, Balabala had taught them this dance. He said yes, and when I asked if she actually dances, he answered in the affirmative, demonstrating by imitating her bouncing movements as she played the guitar to accompany hymns. Balabala and the Grace Brethren do not allow dancing in their religious practice, but since no one was present to enforce a European-style distinction between music and dance, the hymns had become the basis for a new dance form.

As I witnessed this performance, I saw the god dance as a means of addressing modernity. In an effort to reinvent themselves as competent in a changing world, these BaAka were claiming any "otherness" that surrounded them and usually excluded them, and mixing it into a form they could define and control. Three years earlier, the BaAka I had come to know best, unlike those at Dzanga, had been heatedly arguing the validity of the Christian material. But by 1992, the controversy had subsided. My old friend Djolo explained to me then that the god dance is just one among many *beboka*; they could dance their own dances and still pray to god. They had placed the god dance within a BaAka system of value, poised uneasily within a wider, dynamic repertory vying to define an emerging identity.

Though those BaAka most directly affected by the missionaries could be left without the tools to renew a solid sense of identity with which to construct a future, many BaAka have the resilience to use the missionaries' presence to their advantage. Vast distances, difficult terrain, widely varying reactions, and dynamic cultural trends help subvert the missionary influence. In the most positive possible scenario, the missionary effort will have given some BaAka the foreknowledge to face other challenges ahead—including the depletion of the forest by loggers and farmers, the diminishment of the supply of game, and state pressure to make pygmies conform to an official image of modernity.

CONCLUSION

Scholars, artists, journalists, missionaries, politicians, and profiteers have repeatedly placed African pygmies in a timeless cultural box. Each to a different purpose, and even in dialogue with each other, they have marked the forest people as utopian or backward, savage or sublime. At the same time, urban African bands like Zokela, hurtling into a realm of marketable worldbeat, have faced the prospect of being stripped of regional potency to survive.

The overlapping musical spheres described in this essay illustrate that categories like "traditional," "popular," and "modern" are metaphors for ways of seeing, defined by local politics and creative circumstances. This view of cultural processes can challenge categories that become oppressive if left unquestioned. In a flourishing and ever-changing expressive world, teenagers in Bagandou village enjoy performing the dances of their Bolemba pygmy neighbors, and those village children in turn inspire BaAka pygmies in the forest and *zokela* musicians in the city to interpret similar styles—all to different, though thoroughly modern, rooted, and relevant ends.

REFERENCES

Arom, Simha. 1978. *Anthologie de la Musique des Pygmées Aka.* 3 OCORA 558.526.27.28. LP disks and notes.

———. 1985. *Polyphonies et Polyrhythmies Instrumentales d'Afrique Centrale.* 2 vols. Paris: SELAF.

Bahuchet, Serge. 1979. "Notes Pour L'Histoire de la Region de Bagandou." In *Pygmées de Centrafrique: Etude Ethnologique, Historique, et Linguistique sur les Pygmées "Ba-binga" (Aka, Baka) du Nord-Ouest du Basin Congolais,* ed. S. Bahuchet. Paris: SELAF.

———. 1985. *Les Pygmées Aka et la Forêt Centrafricaine.* Paris: SELAF.

Chernoff, John Miller. 1979. *African Rhythm and African Sensibility.* Chicago: University of Chicago Press.

Comaroff, Jean, and John L. Comaroff. 1989. "The Colonization of Consciousness in South Africa." *Economy and Society* 18(3):267–296.

Dumont, Louis. 1986. *Essays on Individualism.* Chicago: University of Chicago Press.

Hewlett, Barry. 1986. "The Father-Infant Relationship among Aka Pygmies." Ph.D. dissertation, University of California, Santa Barbara.

Kisliuk, Michelle. 1991. "Confronting the Quintessential: Singing, Dancing, and Everyday Life among Biaka Pygmies (Central African Republic)." Ph.D. dissertation, New York University.

———. In preparation. *"Seize the Dance!" Performance and Modernity among BaAka Pygmies.*

Lomax, Alan. 1976. *Cantometrics: An Approach to*

the Anthropology of Music. Berkeley: University of California Extension Media Center.

Moise, Robert. 1992. "'A Mo Kila!' (I Refuse!): Living Autonomously in a Biaka Community." M.A. thesis, New York University.

Mouquet, Eric, and Michel Sanchez. 1992. *Deep Forest*. Celine Music and Synsound (Dance Pool). Sony Music Entertainment (France) / Columbia Records DAN 4719762. Compact disk.

Schebesta, Paul. 1933. *Among Congo Pygmies*. London: Hutchinson.

Stone, Ruth M. 1982. *Let the Inside Be Sweet: The Interpretation of Music Event among the Kpelle of Liberia*. Bloomington: Indiana University Press.

Thompson, Robert Farris. 1989. "The Song That Named the Land: The Visionary Presence of African-American Art." In *Black Art: Ancestral Legacy: The African Impulse in African American Art*, 97–138. Dallas: Dallas Museum of Art.

Turnbull, Colin M. 1962. *The Forest People: A Study of the Pygmies of the Congo*. New York: Simon and Schuster.

Southern Africa

Southern Africa

Music in southern Africa, as elsewhere on the continent, has long been associated with political power and royal musicians. During the colonial and apartheid eras, music provided a crucial means of communication for people with limited means of social expression. Today, popular music here still has important social and political implications.

Southern Africa: An Introduction

John E. Kaemmer

Indigenous Music of Southern Africa
Issues Concerning Indigeous Music in Southern Africa
Impact of the Wider World

Studies of southern Africa usually define their subject as the southern tip of the continent. However, to focus on the music requires special consideration of the northern boundary of the area, often considered the Zambezi River. This boundary does not include the area west of the Zambezi, nor does it help clarify matters by dividing Mozambique. The people of northern Mozambique are culturally related to central African peoples, and unlike other peoples of southern Africa, most of them have been influenced by the Arabic cultures of East Africa. Madagascar is geologically a part of southern Africa, but its culture, including its music, derived from cultures of Southeast Asia, whence came its languages and the ancestors of most of its inhabitants.

Modern political and economic divisions are also relevant to the definition of southern Africa. The Southern Africa Development Council consists of Angola, Botswana, Lesotho, Malawi, Mozambique, Namibia, Swaziland, Tanzania, Zambia, and Zimbabwe. Many of these countries include areas with cultural and linguistic characteristics of central or eastern Africa. A common feature of the countries of southern Africa is involvement with the mines of South Africa, where miners from all of them have migrated to work. The cooler climates in southern Africa enable people to raise cattle; but because of problems with tsetse fly and sleeping sickness in central Africa, cattle are not common there. The presence or absence of cattle relates historically to wealth and social stratification, which in turn affect musical activities.

Languages are another important criterion in delineating this area. All speakers of the Khoisan languages in the southwestern part of the continent are in southern Africa. All of the non-Khoisan languages are classed as belonging to the Niger-Congo branch of the Congo-Kordofanian family of languages (Greenberg 1970:30–38), more commonly referred to as Bantu. Following Guthrie's classification of Bantu languages (1948), southern Africa includes those ethnic groups in language zones R (southern Angola and Namibia), S (Venda, Sotho, and Nguni of South Africa), and T (Zimbabwe and southern Mozambique), plus those in parts of Zones M (southern Zambia) and N (southern Malawi). The Ovimbundu of Angola speak a southern Bantu language, even though they are not oriented to cattle raising, as are most speakers of southern African Bantu languages.

Musical criteria also play an important part in defining southern Africa. All groups south of the Zambezi sing with harmonies in octaves and/or fifths, but groups that sing in thirds are farther north (Jones 1959:222). Included in southern Africa for this article are the areas of the "south-central African tonal-harmonic belt," including southern Zambia, much of Zimbabwe, and central Mozambique (Kubik 1988:46). Harmonic patterns in these areas are distinct from the music farther north, and from the styles of most of the peoples of South Africa.

Since music is a part of human culture, the cultural traits of southern Africa are relevant to the study of music there. George Peter Murdock (1959) has not used the term "southern Bantu" to label any of the groups he describes, but he notes several features that distinguish southern Africans from his Central African Bantu group. Central African societies have traditionally been matrilineal in social organization, but most of the societies in southern Africa have been patrilineal. The societies included in southern Africa in this article are basically those listed in Murdock's chapters "Bushmen and their kin" (9), "Middle Zambezi Bantu" (47), "Southwestern Bantu" (48), "Shona and Thonga" (49), "Nguni" (50) and "Sotho" (51). A good working definition for general consideration of southern Africa is to include those areas south of the fifteenth parallel of southern latitude.

INDIGENOUS MUSIC OF SOUTHERN AFRICA

The peoples of southern Africa share many musical traits with other African peoples, particularly the Bantu. These include the ubiquity of polyrhythms, various degrees of influence of linguistic tones upon melody, and numerous instruments, particularly drums, plucked lamellophones, and xylophones. The prevalence of some sort of rattling or buzzing arrangement on instruments is another common feature. Also widespread is the use of cyclic form, with variations and extensive improvisation, both in music and in text.

Southern Africa shares with much of central Africa a history of hierarchical societies with similar traits. In southern Africa, as elsewhere in the continent, music has been important as a symbol of political power. The symbols by which kings maintained power included ritual fires, an important female secondary ruler, and the sponsorship of royal musicians. The history of these kingdoms is in part the history of colonialism. Many of these kingdoms were destroyed during interethnic fighting and the impact of Europeans in the last two hundred years, but many headmen of small groups maintain symbolic drums or xylophones. Music has played an important part in areas with puberty-initiation rites, particularly where control of the rituals is a mark of political strength.

Many peoples in southern Africa define music in terms of the presence of metered rhythm. This means that drumming alone is considered music, and chanting or speaking words is singing, so long as it is metrical. When the singing voice is used without rhythm, the resulting vocalization is not usually considered singing. Many of the groups have no word which would accurately be glossed as 'music'; most of them have distinct words for singing, for playing an instrument, and for dancing.

Languages are an important and fascinating part of the story of southern African music, but they will be dealt with here only as they affect music. Like other African languages, those of southern Africa are tonal, so the nature of the language tones restricts to some degree the freedom to move melodically. The languages of southern Africa are not so highly dependent upon tones as are the languages of West Africa, so the match of speech tone with melody is more a matter of aesthetics than comprehension. Among the Venda, singing adheres to the linguistic tones most closely at the beginning of phrases, and with rising more than falling melodic intervals; adherence to linguistic tones is stronger in the beginning line of a song than in later ones

One feature distinguishing southern Africa is that the musical bow is the major chordophone.

FIGURE I   A boy plays a gourd-resonated bow in southern Mozambique, Johannesburg, 1953.

(Blacking 1967:166–70). Studies of the musical effects of linguistic tones have been done by Jones (1959:230–251) and Rycroft (1971:223–224).

One feature distinguishing southern Africa is that the musical bow is the major chordophone. A few general comments on musical bows will enable the reader to follow more easily the discussions of bows found in the subareas. Musical bows commonly have one string, fastened with tension at each end of a curved stick, so the string makes a sound when put into motion. One of the basic differences between bows is how the string is caused to vibrate. It can be struck by something, usually a small stick, or it can be plucked by one finger, or by the thumb and index finger together. Indirect action on the string also puts it into vibration, including scraping a stick across notches carved into the bow (friction bow) or blowing onto a feather attached to a bow (*gora* or *lesiba*). Scraping the string, as in bowing any chordophone, has also been practiced in the area.

The sound of a bow is resonated in different ways. With a mouth bow, part of the bow is inserted in the player's mouth, and movements of the player's mouth and throat emphasize different overtones. With a gourd bow, the resonator is a gourd fastened to or held against the bow; the player can produce tunes by moving the gourd against his or her body, emphasizing different overtones by varying the volume of air resonating in the gourd.

Musical bows are made so that they can produce more than one fundamental tone. Sometimes, as with a braced bow, a thread links the string to the bow somewhere along the length of the string, making the string vibrate in two sections. Other bows produce different fundamentals as the player stops the string with a finger or an object (figure 1).

Southern African societies exchanged cultural and musical features far back in the past (Johnston 1970:95). The most accurate term for referring to this music is *indigenous*—a term applicable, for example, to the Khoisan adoption of Bantu lamellophones, but not to their use of the guitar. Though the following treatment of different groups gives the impression of distinct differences, the actual situation consists of ethnic boundaries that are frequently indistinct. The same is true of differences between musical traditions.

A survey is heavily dependent on the literature, and a problem in gaining an accurate view of the area is the extreme variability of sources. Some ethnic groups have been thoroughly studied by people whose principal interest and skill lies in music and anthropology; many other groups have not been adequately described at all, or available descriptions focus on nonmusical matters. The varying ages of studies are also important, since the musical traits of societies studied fifty years ago may differ profoundly from the practices of those societies today.

Khoisan peoples

At the end of the 1400s, when Europeans first found the southern tip of Africa, that area was already inhabited by several diverse peoples. The pastoral groups in the area around the Cape of Good Hope were called Hottentots by the Europeans; the hunter-gatherers farther north were called Bushmen. Both of these peoples differ physically from the rest of the people in Africa. Their languages, which exploit several clicking sounds, have been classified as either click languages or Khoisan languages. The latter term comes from the names these people use for themselves: Khoi or Khoikhoi for the Hottentots, and San for the Bushmen.

In the late 1400s, the people who spoke Bantu languages were living farther to the north and east of the Cape, and were interacting with the Khoisan peoples. Archæological and linguistic evidence indicates that the Bantu-speaking peoples of southern Africa arrived there from the north within the last thousand years, and either overran or pushed aside the indigenous peoples (Phillipson 1985:208). Many of the Khoikhoi were enslaved by the European settlers, and eventually mixed with Europeans and workers brought from Asia to form what are now called the colored people of South Africa. Though the San were traditionally hunters and gatherers, they are increasingly becoming cattle herders and farmers.

The Khoikhoi

The Khoikhoi included four major groups: the Cape Hottentots, the Eastern Hottentots, the Nama (or Namaqua), and the Korana. These groups no longer exist; most of these people either disappeared or became assimilated into the colored population of South Africa. A few groups speaking dialects of Khoi languages are still found in Namibia. The musical practices of the Khoikhoi as recorded in early documents are important because of their influence on later developments. Many of their songs were reportedly based on a descending four-note scale, equivalent to D–C–A–G (Rycroft 1980a:730–731).

Among the major instruments of the Khoikhoi were musical bows, of which they played several types. Men played a braced mouth bow. Women played a longer bow, *kha:s.* Seated, a woman secured the instrument by one foot, resting its center on a hollow object serving as a resonator; she held the upper part of the bow near her face, touching it with her chin to obtain a different fundamental tone. She could also modify that tone by touching the center of the string (Kirby 1934:211–212).

The most notable Khoikhoi bow was the *gora,* used to accompany cattle herding. It consisted of a string that the player put into motion by forcefully inhaling and exhaling over a feather connecting the string to one end of the bow. Variations in the way it was blown would make the instrument bring out different tones of the harmonic series. The *gora* was borrowed by neighboring Bantu speakers (Kirby 1934:171–192).

Single-tone flutes were important to the Khoikhoi, especially the Nama and the Korana. These flutes were about 40 centimeters long, made from reeds with all the nodes removed, or from the bark of a particular root (Kirby 1934:139, 145). In either case, a plug was inserted in the bottom, which could be raised or lowered to modify the pitch. The flutes were played in ensembles for dancing, with each man sounding his note as needed to create a melody in hocket. Seventeenth-century descriptions indicate that men and women danced in separate, concentric circles; which sex danced on the inside varied from one group to another.

The Khoikhoi made drums by placing skins over their cook pots. The Europeans called this instrument a *rommelpot,* though the *rommelpot* in Europe is a type of friction drum (Kirby 1934:16).

The San

The San live in scattered places in Botswana, Namibia, and southern Angola. As

FIGURE 2   Rhythms played on the San group bow (after Kubik 1970:29).

hunter-gatherers, they did not have complex musical institutions. Much of their music was for self-expression, dealing with everyday topics, such as the success of the hunt. Songs also accompanied curative dances, in which men would go into a quivering trance representing internal heat, which could cure the sick (Katz 1982).

In the 1960s, the San in the Cuito-Cuanavale area of southeastern Angola and nearby areas of Namibia were the only ones who could give a clear idea of their indigenous musical styles (Kubik 1970:12). Their most widely used indigenous instrument was the bow; classifiable in four musical-bow complexes, of which three used the common hunting bow. The player resonated the bow by putting one end in his or her mouth, resting the other on the ground. By changing the shape of the mouth, the player emphasized certain overtones, creating melodic interest. By stopping the string, the player obtained different fundamental tones. Because the bows were long, they were stopped near the end, thus producing two fundamental tones, separated by intervals of a second, a minor third, or a major third (Kubik 1970:22, 26). The bows were also used with a gourd resonator, not fastened to the bow, but held against it; the gourd was moved in contact with the bare chest, causing a variety of overtones to resonate.

A third tradition, the group bow, involved three individuals who played on one bow (Kubik 1970:27–33). The bow was laid with one end on the ground and the center resting on an upended pan or gourd, serving as a resonator. The first player (A) secured the bow with his foot, and held a piece of gourd with which he stopped the string at either of two places, depending on the song; with a short stick, he beat the string in steady triplets. The second performer (B), at the upper end of the bow, played an irregular rhythm with his stick, with duplets on one part of the string and triplets on another. The third player (C), sitting between the other two, beat the stick in duple rhythms (figure 2). The name of the instrument when used this way was *kambulumbumba*. The same technique was used by children among surrounding Bantu-speakers. For a variety of reasons, including the name of the instrument, it is probable that this bow was originally a Bantu instrument. The San also have a tradition of mouth-resonated friction bows made especially for musical purposes with a palm leaf ribbon, rather than with a string (Kubik 1970:33–35).

The musical bow produces multipart music in the interplay between the fundamental tone and overtones. San vocal multipart music becomes a type of counterpoint as singers are encouraged to sing individual variants on a basic line. Singers also employ techniques of canon and imitation, singing with few words (England 1967:59–61).

In San multipart music, tones that can be used interchangeably or occur simultaneously are always in the same harmonic series (Kubik 1970:66). Many San songs have a tetrachordal structure, in which two tones at the interval of a fifth are used with another fifth, placed a second or a third above the first pair. The most common occurrence of this involves the use of the first, second, fifth, and sixth scalar tones (*do, sol, re, la*). This structure would naturally result from playing two bows together if they were tuned a second or a third apart.

A prehistoric use of hunting bows for music making is indicated by a San rock painting whose location is now unknown (Kirby 1934:193). The painting shows one person playing seven bows lined up on the ground.

The San also use raft zithers (*kuma*) and a form of stamping tube (*bavugu*) (Kubik 1970:35–44). The latter instruments were made with three gourds or mock oranges assembled one above the other and held with wax. A hole was cut through all three, which were then beaten against the upper thigh with the top of the instrument struck with the hand. This instrument was played only by women, who were reticent about showing it to the researchers. It probably had something to do with female initiation or fertility (Kubik 1970:42).

The San are using more and more of the musical resources of the people surrounding them. In addition to the group bow, they have adopted the plucked lamellophone (*likembe* or *mbira*).

The San sing with multipart and hocket techniques. San singing differs from responsorial singing elsewhere in Africa because San soloists in a group interweave their singing without necessarily responding to each other (Kubik 1970:53). When players of a mouth-resonated bow begin to sing, they must temporarily stop bringing out melodic overtones with the mouth, so the alternation of vocal and instrumental sections results in a kind of two-part form. Both Khoikhoi and San yodeled as they sang. Yodeling is not commonly found in Africa, other than among the Shona of Zimbabwe.

Nguni peoples

Nguni is a term scholars use to denote the southernmost Bantu-speaking people in Africa. That they interacted extensively with earlier non-Bantu inhabitants of southern Africa is shown by the fact that unlike Bantu farther north, they have clicks in their languages.

Two Nguni groups, the Xhosa and Zulu, constitute a major part of the indigenous population of South Africa. The Xhosa were closest to the Cape of Good Hope, and at least some of them settled among Khoisan peoples and mixed with them (Dargie 1991:33). They were also the first Bantu-speakers to come into conflict with Europeans as the latter spread beyond the cape. These conflicts weakened them, so they did not form strong kingdoms as did the Zulu and Swazi, their neighbors to the northeast. The Zulu are descendants of clans united into a nation by Chaka, who ruled from 1816 to 1828 (Joseph 1983:54). They fought against the Boers and the British, finally being defeated in 1879. The Swazi were also organized as a kingdom, eventually becoming a British protectorate, and later the independent nation of Swaziland.

During the early 1800s, the Boers emigrated north to escape the English, and the indigenous peoples became involved in wars with the whites and with each other. Various groups separated themselves from the Zulu kingdom and fled, conquering others as they went. A branch of the Nguni went north, to become the Ndebele of northern Transvaal and Zimbabwe. People now called Ngoni invaded what is now Malawi, mixing with other peoples there. The Shangaan (or Shangana) in Mozambique, and along its border with Zimbabwe and South Africa, are also descendants of the Zulu dispersion. Thus, the ethnic configuration in these countries is complex, with traits of Nguni culture often appearing in non-Nguni contexts.

General traits of Nguni music

Several features typify Nguni musical culture. In communal musical events, choral

Among Xhosa women and girls, a form of overtone singing occurs. This technique involves singing a low fundamental tone while shaping the mouth to emphasize different overtones.

singing is the most important form of music. Singing is considered best when done with an open voice, "like the lowing of cattle" (Tracey 1948b:46). Singing is polyphonic and responsorial, with the divergence of parts occurring as phrases begin and end at different points. The Zulu language causes sung tones to be lowered in pitch when the vowels follow voiced spirants and stops except the phoneme /b/ (Rycroft 1975–1976:44).

Another typical feature is the traditional prominence of the musical bow. Scales are based on the natural tones of the musical bow, often omitting the seventh. Nguni musical cultures have diverse scalar systems; the seventh is often missing, and perfect fourths and fifths are often important (Rycroft 1971:230). The use of semitones may be due to the traits of the bow (Rycroft 1971:218–219). Among the Nguni people, a "tonality shift" or "tonality contrast" is important (Rycroft 1971:235). This feature is noteworthy farther north, and would seem consistent with the practice of using the overtone series from nonidentical fundamentals, as is often done with the musical bow.

Though drums are not commonly used in many Nguni traditions, they are known. The friction drum and double-headed drum are used in some rituals (Joseph 1983:67).

Among the Zulu, the major form of communal music consists of choral dance songs (Rycroft 1975–1976:63; Joseph 1983:60). This form of communal music occurs in many rituals, including puberty ceremonies, weddings, and divinations (Joseph 1983:64–77). Drinking songs and work songs are also in this style. Men's praise poetry is performed without meter; therefore it is not considered music, though the clearly pitched singing voice is used (Rycroft 1980b:201).

Individualistic forms of song, such as lullabies and songs for personal enjoyment, were traditionally accompanied on the musical bow—a practice that has long been declining. One of the musical bows used by the Zulu was the *ugubhu,* an unbraced gourd-resonated bow more than a meter long. Another bow, the *umakhweyana,* was braced near the center and gourd resonated; it is thought to have been borrowed from the Tsonga, to the north (Rycroft 1975–1976:58). Braced bows have the main string divided in different ways, so the differences in the fundamental tones range from a whole tone to a minor third.

Among Xhosa women and girls, a form of overtone singing, *umngqokolo,* occurs (Dargie 1991). This technique involves singing a low fundamental tone while shaping the mouth to emphasize different overtones. This kind of singing is said to sound somewhat like a performance on the *umrhubhe,* a bow, played by scraping a string with a stick. The style may have developed from a practice of small boys: they impale a beetle on a thorn, put it in their mouths, and isolate various overtones produced by the insect's buzzing (Dargie 1991:40–41).

The Xhosa have a quivering dance (Rycroft 1971:215), which calls to mind the curative dances of the San.

Single-tone flutes are found among the Zulu and Swazi. The latter use them during their first-fruit rituals. These flutes are long, tuned by means of plugs—as was the practice among the Khoikhoi (Kirby 1934:112–117).

Sotho peoples

Murdock included many ethnic groups in the Sotho cluster (1959:386–387), but in the ethnomusicological literature, only three major groups regularly appear: those living in Lesotho (the southern Sotho), those living in Botswana (the Tswana or Chwana, or western Sotho), and those living in South Africa (the Pedi, or eastern Sotho). The Sotho of Lesotho are a mixture of refugees who in the mid-1800s were united into a state. Their leader, Moshoeshoe I, asked for missionaries in 1833, and sought status for his kingdom as a British protectorate in 1868. This action led to strong European influences and to Lesotho's becoming politically, but not economically, separate from South Africa. This branch of Sotho is the only one whose language incorporates clicks from the Khoisan languages (Adams 1974:387).

The Sotho peoples share many musical features with the Nguni, such as the importance of choral singing (*mahobelo*) and the use of one-stringed chordophones and reed flutes. The Tswana, who originally lived on open plains with few trees, have a strong tradition of choral singing. Their vocal music is primarily pentatonic (Mundell 1980:89). Unlike Nguni musical textures, the Sotho responsorial parts do not often overlap.

Dancing to instrumental sounds may be a twentieth-century development in Lesotho (Adams 1974:142), but not with other Sotho peoples. The Sotho outside Lesotho have customarily performed flute dances. Perhaps the people of Lesotho lacked such dances because they were drawn from many ethnic backgrounds. Reed-flute dances occurred among the Tswana, possibly adopted from the Khoikhoi (Kirby 1934:146). Reed-flute ensembles are among the prerogatives of a chief. Though the Sotho in Basutoland do not have the flute dances, they do have flutes, which resemble those of the Nguni. Pedi boys also use a one-tone flute, but when they play it, they whistle with their lips while they inhale (Kirby 1934:90).

The southern Sotho have adapted an instrument from the Khoi *gora.* They call it *lisiba,* from their word *siba* 'feather'; it may well be called an air-activated stick zither (Adams 1974:89, 109). Both inhaling and exhaling, players cause air to move past the feather; they produce most overtones while inhaling. Exhaling often produces laryngeal sounds, except during an expert's performance. Changes of pitch can be caused by changes in breath pressure and changes in the shape of the oral cavity (Kirby 1934:188–191).

The songs the southern Sotho sing with the *lesiba* have a special name, *linon'.* The instrument is connected with cattle herding, as it was among the Khoikhoi, and the Sotho use its sounds to control their cattle (Adams 1974:111). The feather from the instrument ideally comes from the cape vulture, the bird the instrument represents.

Sotho peoples use rattles made from cocoons and animal skins, but not from gourds (as used by people farther north). Pedi cocoon rattles are worn by women only; their dance skirts, made of reeds, rattle during dancing (Kirby 1934:10).

Southeastern African peoples

Several groups in southeastern Africa appear to have lived in the same area for several hundred years. These include the Venda in the eastern Transvaal, the Chopi in southern Mozambique, and the Shona between the Limpopo and Zambezi rivers. The Thonga include several groups formed when the Zulu wars of the early 1800s sent

makhololo   Rulers of the Venda who are distinguished from common people

tshikona   National music of the Venda produced by an ensemble of one-pitch pipes
   played in hocket

bepha   Among the Venda and the Tsonga,
   collective visits by youthful performers sent
   by one chief to another

conquerors and refugees eastward into the coastal lowlands; these groups include the Tswa, the Ronga, the Tsonga, and the Shangaan (Tracey 1980:662).

Because the Zulu dispersion brought many Zulu-speakers into southeastern Africa, the area is now characterized by a mixture of languages. Many of these languages (and Shona) pronounce sibilant fricatives, /z/ or /s/, with something of a whistle. The Venda have been influenced by the Sotho, but they share many aspects of language and culture with the Shona.

The musical cultures of southeastern Africa emphasize instruments, rather than choral singing. The separation between the two parts of responsorial forms is more distinct, and polyrhythms occur both in the accompaniment and in its relation to the singing. Musical bows among the San and the Nguni are usually played with fundamentals a second or a third apart, but Shona and Tsonga bows usually have fundamentals a fourth or fifth apart. Southeast African single-toned flutes are played in hocket, but they are constructed differently from those of the San and Nguni. Instead of having plugs for tuning, the nodes are retained in the bamboo or the reeds, and the instruments are tuned by being shortened or by receiving extra sections.

The musical cultures of southeast Africa have several instruments in common, including a variety of drums, mbiras (lamellophones), and xylophones. Since the Shona are the topic of another article in this volume, the treatment given here will focus on other southeastern Bantu, and will include comparisons with the Shona.

The Venda

The Venda, living in a mountainous area of northeastern South Africa, submitted to European rule in 1899. When John Blacking did research among them (in the 1950s), they were still performing many of their traditional musical events. They distinguish sharply between commoners and rulers (*makhololo,* a term used in western Zambia for the Sotho conquerors of the Lozi).

The Venda are believed to have crossed the Limpopo river from the north several hundred years ago; their language and culture closely resemble those of the Karanga branch of Shona. Though Venda musical skills are widespread, public performances require some form of payment. The Venda assume that any normal person is capable of performing music well (Blacking 1973:34).

The national music of the Venda is the *tshikona,* an ensemble of one-pitch pipes played in hocket. Traditionally, men played pipes, and women played drums. Each chief had his *tshikona,* which would perform on important occasions, such as first-fruit ceremonies. The chiefs vied with each other to create the best ensemble, sometimes using it to further their own political ends. Venda men working in the mines of South Africa perform the dance there, doing their own drumming. The tonalities of *tshikona* music are the most important feature of Venda tonal organization (Blacking 1965:182).

Tshikona is not the only music sponsored by chiefs. The Venda share with the

Tsonga the practice whereby each chief sends youthful performers on collective visits (*bepha*) to other chiefs to perform and bring back gifts. Thus, each chief succeeds in building up a corps of devoted followers (Blacking 1965:35). Among the Tsonga, such performing groups are competitive (Johnston 1987:127).

The nature of musical sponsorship means that little social commentary is expressed through song. However, in individual musical performances, people may express their feelings and frustrations, including criticism of other people, without fear of negative consequences (Blacking 1965:28).

The Venda have a wide variety of instruments. Differential tuning—some instruments using heptatonic scales, and others using pentatonic scales—indicates different origins for different instruments. The pipes used in *tshikona* are ideally made from bamboo from a secret grove in eastern Venda country, and are heptatonic within a range of three octaves; metal and plastic pipes are also used. The Venda also play reed pipes, pentatonically covering two octaves.

Venda instruments include a twenty-one-key xylophone, the *mbila mutondo* (nearly obsolete), plus a twenty-seven-key lamellophone, the *mbila dzamadeza.* They also have a friction bow (*tshizambi*), obtained from the Tsonga, and the *dende,* a braced gourd-resonated bow. The *ng'oma* is a huge pegged drum with four handles, played with *tshikona* and in rainmaking rituals (Kirby 1934:34, 38).

The Venda have borrowed some of their musical practices from neighboring peoples. Circumcision schools with their related music have come from the Sotho. These schools are sponsored by individuals, who from them gain financial and political advantages. Venda possession cults have come from the Karanga, one of the Shona groups to the north.

An important feature of Venda music is the "principle of harmonic equivalence" (Blacking 1967:168). Though the rise and fall of tones in various verses may differ objectively, the Venda consider them the same, so long as the notes involved are within the same harmonic series. By substituting pitches in this way, the Venda can allow for variations in the rise and fall of linguistic tones in different parts of the text.

The Chopi

One of the most important musical traditions in southern Africa is that of the Chopi. They seem to have inhabited their lands, just east of the mouth of the Limpopo, since the early 1500s (Tracey 1948a:122), and they were not subjugated by the Zulu invasions of the 1800s. To accompany dance cycles (*ngodo*), they use large ensembles of xylophones.

The ideal Chopi ensemble consists of xylophones (*timbila*) in five sizes, covering a range of four octaves. The slats are fixed to the framework, each with a resonator attached below it (figure 3). Originally the resonators were gourds, each being

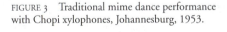

FIGURE 3   Traditional mime dance performance with Chopi xylophones, Johannesburg, 1953.

The Tsonga believe that individuals can become possessed of evil spirits of people from outside ethnic groups, usually people thought to have died outside their home territory.

matched to resonate best with the slat to which it was attached. Carefully checking the tuning of these xylophones by using a set of tuning forks and asking the players which fork most closely matched each slat resulted in a scale that approximated an equidistant heptatonic scale (Tracey 1948a:124).

Each chief formerly sponsored a xylophone ensemble. The lyrics often related to popular social concerns, and could criticize wrongdoing. To keep the messages up to date, new compositions were created every few years, with the lyrics created before the music. A complete dance cycle, lasting about forty-five minutes, had nine to eleven movements.

The Tsonga

The Tsonga formerly inhabited the coastal lowlands of southern Mozambique. Pressed by the Zulu wars, they moved to the eastern Transvaal. They now live south of the Venda, or interspersed with them.

The Tsonga share many musical practices with their neighbors, particularly the Shona and the Venda. They have a mouth-resonated braced bow (*chipendana*), which resembles the Shona *chipendani* in having a thick handle carved onto the center of the bow. Both groups use a friction bow (Tsonga *xizambe,* Shona *chizambi*). Instead of a string, these bows employ a palm leaf ribbon; it can be stopped in as many as four places by one player's fingers, and the player's mouth brings out a variety of overtones. When two bows are played in duet, they are tuned a fifth apart (Johnston 1970:86). In playing this bow, melodic notes are sometimes displaced an octave higher, so they will not be in the range of feebly heard low notes—a form of harmonic equivalence. Mnemonic syllables help teach *xizambe* rhythms, and indicate the rhythmic complexity found in other Tsonga music (Johnston 1970:83).

With the Shona, the Tsonga believe that individuals can become possessed of evil spirits of people from outside ethnic groups, usually people thought to have died outside their home territory. The Tsonga become possessed of spirits of Zulu or Ndau origin. Rituals are designed to rid these individuals of the spirits, using music bearing a resemblance to the musical styles of the Zulu or the Ndau people. The quasi-Zulu songs are pentatonic with the *mandhlozi* rhythm, in rather straightforward duple time; the quasi-Ndau songs are heptatonic with a triplet drumming the *xidzimba* rhythm (Johnston 1972:10). The Shona become possessed with spirits of the Ndebele, or of the light-skinned traders who formerly connected them with the Zambezi valley. The Shona traditionally value possession by ancestral spirits, and rituals for these other spirits tend to emphasize dealing with the spirit properly, rather than exorcising it.

The national dance of the Tsonga, the *muchongolo,* is known in the eastern part of Zimbabwe as the *muchongoyo.* It represents the actions of warriors in battle, and features asymmetrical rhythms.

Like all southeastern Bantu peoples, the Tsonga have a variety of drums: the *xigubu,* a double-headed drum, made of metal containers; the *ndzumba,* used for puberty school; and the *ng'oma,* for beer drinks. *Ncomane,* a type of tambourine, are used for rituals of exorcism. Drumming is also taught by the use of mnemonic syllables. Drums are used in communal music associated with specific events.

The Tsonga have instruments that they do not share with the Shona. They use a three-hole transverse flute (*xitiringo*), a mouth-resonated cane bow (*mqangala*), a large gourd-resonated braced bow (*xitende*), and a ten-slat xylophone (*mohambi*) (Johnston 1971:62).

The Sena and the Nyungwe

In the Shire and Zambezi river valleys of southern Malawi and central Mozambique live several groups whose culture is seldom classed as southern African, but whose music is closely related to that of the southeastern area as a part of Kubik's "southcentral African tonal-harmonic belt." The most prominent traditions in this area are Sena xylophones (*valimba*) and zithers (*bangwe*), and Nyungwe reed-pipe dances. As a result of many peoples' flights from civil war during the 1980s in Mozambique, some of these traditions have been studied in southern Malawi.

The xylophones of the Sena use the musical structure characteristic of Shona mbiras, but some features indicate that the tuning of the instrument is intended to be equiheptatonic. Andrew Tracey found a wide discrepancy in the tuning of an instrument he was studying, but he also noted that the musicians cared little what tone they started their songs on—an indication of equidistant tuning (1991:88). The tuning of the *bangwe* was closer to equiheptatonic, as are the tunings of Sena lamellophones (*malimba*) (van Zanten 1980:109).

Nyungwe reed-pipe dances are of two types: *nyanga* have only one instrumental tune, with which singers improvise their parts; *ngororombe* have many different tunes played on the pipes. These dances differ from Sotho flute dances in that each performer has two to five pipes. These dances are performed for enjoyment, including when performers are hired for weddings, funerals, or parties. The music follows the chordal sequence typical of mbira music of the Shona. The rhythmic structure is similar also, with twenty-four-pulse or forty-eight-pulse segments. Male players alternate a sung note, a blown note, and an inhalation. They also dance, and are accompanied by a lead singer and a women's chorus (Tracey 1971).

Middle Zambezi peoples

To the north of the Zambezi River in Zambia are several ethnic groups culturally considered a part of southern Africa: the Tonga live in the area bordering the river to the east of Victoria Falls; the Ila live farther to the northwest, along the Kafue River; still farther west are the Lozi and the Nkoya, groups that have consistently maintained stratified societies, with kings and royal musical ensembles.

The Ila and the Tonga

In the 1800s, both the Ila and the Tonga, particularly the latter, suffered from raids by the Lozi and the Ndebele. As a consequence, they no longer have symbolic African kingdoms within the modern state. Their musical practices relate more to communal events and individual enjoyment.

In the 1930s, Arthur M. Jones found many types of songs among the Ila and the Tonga. It is important to these people that individuals, both young men and young women, compose songs that are distinctively theirs. Some songs sung on informal occasions are specific to each sex: *impango* for females, and *ziyabilo* for males.

Three kinds of songs were sung for dancing, specific ones for the *cin'ande* (a dance for young people) and the *mucinko* (a dance for young women), and others for *ngongi*   Double bells, which can be used only by royal ensembles of the Lazi and Nkoya

kuomboka   A ceremony the Lozi perform to mark the retreat from the floodplain as the river rises seasonally

dances involving all ages. Other kinds of song include the *mapobolo* for slow, gentle singing; the *mapobaulo,* formerly used for fighting; and the *zitengulo,* for mourning (Jones 1949:14–19).

Among the Ila, who were less susceptible to raids, chiefs controlled the performance of the double-flange-welded clapperless bells resembling those of West Africa. In seclusion during puberty, girls used to play horns. Flutes were used to call cattle.

The Ila have two types of lamellophones: the larger (*ndandi*), with fourteen keys, and the smaller (*kankobela*), with about eight (Jones 1949:28). The *ndandi* resembles the instruments of Lozi commoners and the Nkoya (Brown 1984:378). Ila xylophones are tuned to the same notes as the *ndandi* (Jones 1949:30). The keys of the *kankobela* and the lower eight keys of the Lozi xylophone (*silimba*) contain the same tones as the *kalimba* that Andrew Tracey considers the "original African *mbira*" (Kubik 1988:64–65).

The Lozi and the Nkoya

The Lozi (also called Barotse, formerly Luya) and the Nkoya are neighbors along the Zambezi near the Zambian border with Angola. Both have a strong monarchy, whose leaders are thought to have come from the Lunda kingdoms in Zaïre. The Lozi inhabit the floodplain, where annual runoff from the rainy season brings silt that enriches the soil; the Nkoya inhabit the hills, depending less on agriculture and more on livestock and hunting. The richness of the soil has led to differences in the wealth of the two groups—differences that influence the relationship of their royal families and their musical practices (Brown 1984).

In 1840, the Lozi were conquered by the Kololo, a Sotho group; they freed themselves in 1868. In the late 1800s, their king negotiated for his kingdom status as a British protectorate. This status helped keep the kingdom intact; in fact, both the king and the royal musicians received salaries from the colonial government (Brown 1984:63). The Lozi language is a mixture, basically Southern Bantu Luyana with heavy borrowing from Sotho. The Nkoya have a Central Bantu language.

In both groups, royal music is distinct from commoners' music. Royal ensembles, consisting of a xylophone and three drums, always accompany the king and symbolize his status. Only the chiefs can use double bells (*ngongi*)—a usage common in West Africa, but usually found farther south only in archaeological excavations. Unlike most xylophones, Lozi and Nkoya xylophones are played by only one person each. To facilitate being carried in processions, each instrument is secured by straps around its performer's neck, held away from his body by a bowed piece of wood. The drums used in royal ensembles include the *ng'oma* (the most important one), which has tuning paste added to the head to deepen its sound. The other two drums are double-headed pegged drums; they have higher pitches than the *ng'oma,* with a buzzer arrangement; the *ng'oma* player does the major improvisations (Brown 1984: 126–128).

Instruments are not the only feature that distinguishes royal music from commoners' music. Linguistic distinctions are important: Lozi royal musicians sing in Luyana, the archaic language, but commoners sing in Lozi (Brown 1984:393). Nkoya beliefs concerning sources of music help strengthen the differences of status between royalty and commonalty. The Nkoya believe that spirits taught royal music to the people, but nonroyal music is not of divine origin; royal dances are more restrained than those of commoners (Brown 1984:141–142, 472).

Music also highlights the differences between the Lozi and the Nkoya: Nkoya instruments are pitched higher (Brown 1984:358). The Lozi have a special kind of music, *lishoma,* which they consider their national music (Brown 1984:329). Lozi songs concern cattle, including raids and conquest; Nkoya royal songs emphasize death and dying (Brown 1984:44, 170). Lozi texts are the more detailed and organized (Brown 1984:221).

Lozi xylophones usually have eleven keys, with the lower three separated by thirds. The other keys approximate the diatonic scale, but with a flat third and no seventh. The vocal range is a fourth or less, but that may be simply the nature of certain songs. The songs are polyrhythmic, with certain types of songs having sixteen-pulse units and others having twelve-pulse units; the latter type facilitates duple and triple rhythmic mixes (Brown 1984:407–427, 434).

Music plays a big part in an important Lozi ritual, the *kuomboka,* a ceremony that occurs as the people retreat from the floodplain to higher ground when the river rises. An important feature of this ceremony is the royal barge, which carries the king to his palace on higher ground. In his entourage is the *maoma,* the national drum. It is unusually large, about a meter in diameter. Its head is painted with dots, and its side bears carvings of human and animal figures. Only royal men play it. During the *kuomboka,* the ancient Luyana language is used. After it come two days of dances: the *liwale* for women and the *ng'omalume* for men (Brown 1984:326). The latter includes dancing to drumming without singing (Brown 1984:30–41). Because the Nkoya do not live on a floodplain, their major ritual is a first-fruits ceremony, the *mukanda* (Brown 1984:271).

Lozi music is not limited to royal ensembles. Music called *makwasha* is sung by everyone. It deals with various subjects, including hunting, and also serves for paddling canoes. It is played on fifteen-key lamellophones (*kahanzi*), with lower keys tuned like royal xylophones (Brown 1984:159).

Southwestern Bantu peoples

The Bantu-speakers living in southern Angola and northern Namibia are classed as Southwestern Bantu (Murdock 1959:369–374). The major groups in this area are the Ovimbundu in central Angola, and the Ovambo and Herero in Namibia. Information on the music of these groups is sketchy, largely because the political climate has not been conducive to research by outsiders. Smaller, related groups in southern Angola include the Humbi. Gerhard Kubik made a short visit there in 1965, from which he produced recordings and an article (1975–1976).

The Ovimbundu

The Ovimbundu appear to be Central Bantu, since they do not raise cattle, and they lack the almost mystical focus on cattle that typifies most of the people of southern Africa; however, they are the northernmost people who speak a Southern Bantu language. The railway passing through their area connects them economically and culturally with the copper belt of Zaïre and Zambia, and with South Africa. They may be transitional between the cultures to the north and those in the southwestern part of Angola (Kubik 1980:432).

The Ovambo share with other groups in this area a pluriarc (multiple bow lute), consisting of a board with five to eight curved sticks fastened to one end, and strings fastened from the ends of the sticks to the opposite end of the board.

The Ovimbundu once maintained a distinction between aristocrats and commoners, but it has weakened, reducing its effect on musical activities. A signal feature of the society is that for recreation, rituals, and court cases, each village has a central area, the *ocila,* from the word *okucila* 'to dance' (Childs 1949:26). The Ovimbundu danced most often during the full moon, and also at funerals. They had work songs and road songs, presumably for walking on their trading expeditions.

The Ovambo

The Ovambo live along the border between Namibia and Angola. They share with other groups in this area a pluriarc (multiple bow lute), consisting of a board with five to eight curved sticks fastened to one end, and strings fastened from the ends of the sticks to the opposite end of the board; South Africans called this instrument an Ovambo guitar. The Ovambo call an eight-stringed form of it *chihumba.* Kubik attributes the instrument to sources in northern Angola; Kirby suggested a possible historic relationship with a row of hunting bows depicted in a prehistoric cave painting (1934:243–244).

The Nkhumbi

The music of the Nkhumbi differs distinctively from the music of west-central Africa, especially regarding "vocal style and motional patterns" (Kubik 1975–1976:98). However, though most of the groups in southern Africa sing in octaves and fifths, the Nkhumbi sing and play the pluriarc in parallel thirds—a trait that tends to indicate a northern origin of the instrument.

It is not surprising that musical bows would be important among these people. They have a gourd-resonated bow (*mbulumbumba*), whose two fundamental tones are produced by increasing tension on the string, and by stopping it with the thumb (Kubik 1975–1976:103–104). Unlike the San *kambulumbumba,* this bow is played by one individual.

Two mouth-resonated bows differ in the way the bow is placed at the mouth. The *sagaya* is braced with a short thread, dividing the main string into two parts, giving fundamentals about a whole tone apart; it is loosely held across the mouth. The *ohonji* is a hunting bow, braced in the center to form "two not quite equal parts" (Kubik 1975–1976:102). Its end is pressed against the inside of the player's right cheek. Performers do not sing with it, but associate bow tunes with language. They play the bows so the paired fundamentals are a whole step apart.

Other musical instruments found by Kubik among the Nkhumbi were drums (including a friction drum), a pluriarc, gourd rattles, lamellophones, percussion sticks, and bullroarers. Performers in this area often accompany their instrumental music with various vocalizations.

The Herero

The Herero are a primarily pastoral people in northeastern Namibia, with some groups in Botswana. While women sing and clap, men dance. The Herero customarily sing dirges at funerals. New songs are composed by professional singers, often dealing with cattle or horses. During colonial wars with Germany (1903–1908), the Herero suffered a disastrous military defeat; crossing the desert as refugees, many perished. People still remember this experience, which they commemorate in their songs, especially those that concern death and mortuary rituals (Alnaes 1989).

ISSUES CONCERNING INDIGENOUS MUSIC IN SOUTHERN AFRICA

Several important theoretical questions about African music are raised by musical practices in southern Africa. One of the most complex issues is the tuning of musical instruments. Indications are that in southeast Africa, some xylophones and lamellophones are tuned with equiheptatonic scales. The widespread use of musical bows, however, has led in many places to tunings based on the harmonic series. The pitches of the tones of the equiheptatonic scale do not match the pitches defined by the harmonic series. Several reasons for the use of equiheptatonic tunings have been suggested, including origin in Southeast Asian musical practices (Jones 1964), and development from singing in thirds (Kubik 1985:35). Another possibility is that, like the tempered scale (whose pitches are also equidistant), it provides a way of being able to sing at any convenient pitch level without having to retune an instrument.

The nature of the influence of the San and their music upon the music of southern Africa is also an important question. Dealing with it in detail, Kubik has argued for a relationship between San musical bows and the nature of harmonic progressions in the musical traditions of the southcentral African tonal-harmonic belt. This belt represents practices distinct from those of other parts of Africa. These practices, however, are not so distinct from those of many groups in southern Africa. The music of the tonal-harmonic belt shares many features with that of the Nguni-Sotho peoples, who use two- or three-bow fundamentals and their overtones, resulting in a "tonality shift" or "tonality contrast" (Rycroft 1971:235). All these traditions share an overriding intonational trait, Blacking's principle of harmonic equivalence: tones that can be sounded simultaneously, or that can be substituted for each other, must belong to the same harmonic series. All these practices exemplify harmony in the sense of progressions of prescribed aural combinations (Kaemmer 1993:105). Perhaps the tonal-harmonic belt represents the result of interplay between the chorus-bow traditions of South Africa and the xylophone-mbira traditions of the southeast.

There is also the possibility that certain African musical traits originated in Indonesia. If people from Indonesia could discover and settle the island of Madagascar, it is highly possible that they could have landed on the mainland of Africa. Whether they actually did or not is the issue. The nature of Chopi xylophones raises this question, especially the equidistant tuning. Moreover, the nature of the Chopi ensembles differs from that of xylophone ensembles elsewhere in Africa. The theory of Indonesian origins includes cultural and musical features all over Africa (Jones 1964). Compelling evidence to settle this issue may never be found.

Another issue concerns the origin of the lamellophones, used all over Africa for entertainment. Only among the southeastern Bantu are lamellophones regularly used for ritual. In that area, they are also larger and more complex. These lamellophones (mbira) may have originated from xylophones (Jones 1964). This possibility is argued from the fact that one xylophone is commonly played by two players, one on each side—which means that for one player, the low notes are on the left, and for the other, they are on the right. Many *mbira* have low notes in the center, meaning they

TRACK 20 and 21

mbila   Chopi word for a xylophone key;
          closely related to the term *mbira*, which
          designates a lamellophone

are on the left for one hand, and on the right for the other hand. However, if Andrew Tracey's theory about the original *mbira* is valid, the layout of tones may more closely relate to the notes of the harmonic series than to any of the equitonic xylophones. It is possible that the low notes are often in the center because of the way the instrument lies under the hands.

Africans talk about xylophones and lamellophones with closely related words. Many of the languages of the area use a type of retroflex /r/, which if moved somewhat farther back in the mouth sounds something like /l/. For example, the term Maravi is used by Murdock (1959:294) to denote a cluster of people in Malawi, but the two terms differ only in the orthography of the /r/ and the /l/ (and of the bilabial fricative). The term for lamellophone in southeastern Africa is *mbira*, a word closely related to the Chopi word for a xylophone key (*mbila*), but with the same phonetic difference. It is also possible that the words *mbila* and *mbira* are related to *limba* and *rimba*, as in *ulimba* and *marimba*—all of which in some places denote both xylophones and lamellophones. These various noun stems can receive prefixes—like *ma-* and *ti-* for plural, and *ka-* for diminution—that add to their meaning. In many Bantu languages, the verb-stem for the concept 'to sing' is *-imba,* and the relational suffix that relates the verb to something else is *-ila* or *-ira.* Thus, *-imbira* or *-imbila* would mean 'to sing for'. Recognizing such closely related sounds is important in determining possible historical relationships.

The issue of the origins of the mbira is complicated by the fact that the lamellophone is played in West Africa with the free ends of the lamellae away from the player. This has been considered a case where the instrument diffused from one area to another without the related playing skills. Since the origins of the mbira lie in antiquity (lamellae having been found in archaeological sites), the details of its prehistoric development may never be known.

IMPACT OF THE WIDER WORLD

Though interethnic borrowing of cultural features has occurred in southern Africa as far back in time as we can determine, it is only in the last three hundred fifty years that the impact of non-African societies is clear and overwhelming. The impact of non-African societies comes partly from the musical practices themselves, but the impact of social and cultural changes brought about by European conquest has been paramount.

The musical practices of all of southern Africa have been heavily influenced by unique factors emanating from the Republic of South Africa, which has the largest proportion of Europeans of any country in Africa, largely because of the temperateness of its climate and the wealth of its minerals. Settlers sent by the Dutch East India Company landed in Cape Town in 1652. Before long, they had brought in Asians to help work their farms. English settlers arrived after armed forces had defeated the Dutch. All these immigrants brought musical traditions with them.

Mining

In the 1800s, with the discovery of diamonds in Kimberly and gold in the Transvaal, the European influence in southern Africa intensified. Conflict developed between the English and the descendants of the Dutch, who had precipitated devastating wars by moving into areas occupied by Africans. The impact of the British spread with the colonization of Southern Rhodesia (now Zimbabwe) and the discovery of copper in Northern Rhodesia (now Zambia). The explorations of David Livingstone brought Malawi into the British orbit, leaving Angola and Mozambique to the Portuguese and Southwest Africa (now Namibia) to the Germans.

The wealth in the mines lured many African men from their communities. Most had no choice but to leave their wives and families behind. Their absence from home meant that village rituals, with their associated music, had to be adapted to weekends or holidays, or else they died out. The communities that grew up around the mines provided meeting places where people of many ethnic groups heard each other's music, including that of Africans of European descent.

The companies that ran the mines often sponsored indigenous African dances as entertainment on Sundays, the miners' day off. These dances helped maintain differences of ethnic identity among the men, and gave them an outlet for entertainment and self-expression. These dances also catered to tourists, providing outsiders with convenient views of exotic music and dance.

In nonmining areas, Africans who worked for Europeans were either people educated in Western knowledge (who became clerks and household help), or people uneducated in Western forms (who worked on plantations). Many Africans who worked in the big mining centers were not Western educated, but became permanently urban. They sought to become recognized as city dwellers, rather than "tribesmen," and used skills in European music to demonstrate their claims (Coplan 1985:12).

Apartheid

South Africa was unique in having such strong European influence so early. In most of southern Africa, intensive European domination did not occur until after the Treaty of Berlin (1885). Major wars of colonial conquest occurred in Namibia, Zimbabwe, and South Africa. Africans were subject not only to military activity, but also to the presence of military bands, with instruments that seemed new and exciting to them. Since African tradition viewed musical spectacles as an important symbol of political power, military bands were seen as a new type of power, and were often imitated as a new kind of dance (Ranger 1975).

The policy of apartheid, strict racial separation, heavily influenced music in both South Africa and Namibia, which from 1915 to 1990 was under South African control. Racial separation was a continentwide practice; but in South Africa in 1948, after the Afrikaner party had taken electoral power, it became official policy. Until then, musical events mixed Africans and Europeans, with Africans often providing the music.

Under apartheid, Africans were eventually forbidden to perform at European nightclubs, thus losing economic opportunity and a means of interracial communication. The lack of resources devoted to African education meant that African schoolchildren had less formal training in music than European schoolchildren. Songs in African theatrical performances became a major form of social commentary in South Africa, where theater was seen as a form of communication, rather than an aesthetic activity (Coplan 1985:225).

Missions and education

An important feature of musical change in southern Africa was the activity of

The stigma attached to Africans and their culture by European racism and ethnocentrism directly influenced musical practices in a variety of ways.

Christian missionaries, both as proponents of new religious doctrines, and as purveyors of European education. Most missionaries had difficulty distinguishing between Christian doctrine and European culture. They tended to disparage African customs and African music, which they believed not only inferior, but also sinful.

Many Africans viewed religion as a form of power that equaled spears and guns. Consequently, they viewed Christianity as an important reason for European domination and thus a more effective religion. New converts who accepted the rituals also adopted the music that accompanied them. They turned away from indigenous forms of music, accepting the notion that they were sinful and inferior. Missionaries often translated their hymns into African languages, unaware of the importance of linguistic tones to the understandability and aesthetic quality of the music.

Some missionary agencies, recognizing the importance of indigenous forms of expression to their converts, created hymns and songs in indigenous styles. The Livingstonia mission in northern Malawi did so from the beginning. In the 1960s, the Methodist mission in Zimbabwe began a program of fostering the use of indigenous musical idioms in the church, but older people had already formed negative opinions about them. Workshops on indigenization of the arts have been held regularly since then, with many churches cooperating. After the second Vatican Council (1962–1965), the Roman Catholic church began using vernacular languages in services—a change that afforded an opportunity to adopt indigenous musical styles to accommodate the new languages of worship.

Education, fostered by the missions until the various countries became independent, was oriented to European culture. Its aim was preparing workers for government and business; training in music played only a small part in it. The curriculum used in the schools of the colonial power was also taught in Africa, including the songs. Being related to the missions, schools usually promoted choral singing.

One type of music became popular all over southern Africa: the *makwaya,* from the word "choir." It involved singing, complex marching routines, and special costumes. Adaptations of jazz in responsorial form, accompanied by drumming and dancing, have become popular with young people.

In the Anglophone areas of southern Africa, schools commonly sponsored musical contests. The judges were usually Europeans, who formed their judgments on the basis of European musical criteria. Having African judges was avoided in South Africa, for fear that African judges would be biased in favor of their kinsmen (Coplan 1985:154).

Sociopolitical factors

In the twentieth century, during struggles for political liberation, songs served to politicize people and motivate fighters. In Zimbabwe's struggle, composers and performers emphasized the indigenous aspects of culture; during the 1960s and 1970s, the mbira became more popular than the guitar among young people, but since independence, the situation seems to have reversed.

The stigma attached to Africans and their culture by European racism and ethnocentrism directly influenced musical practices in a variety of ways. In most of southern Africa, the mastery of European music was seen as prestigious—resulting in considerable decline of indigenous traditions. The Venda of South Africa, however, refused to use European music because they resented foreign control over their lives (Blacking 1973:38). In most parts of the country, the performance of indigenous music was often seen as implying support of "separate development" (that is, apartheid), and was thus avoided.

That socioeconomic factors play an important role in musical change does not mean that musical interest is irrelevant in itself. From the earliest days of European settlement, the Khoikhoi at the cape were utilizing Malay and Dutch musical idioms (Coplan 1985:9–11). Black vaudeville entertainers from the United States not only helped improve Africans' self-respect, but also served as musical models for African musical entertainers (Coplan 1985:70). As early as 1890, African-American choirs were traveling to South Africa to perform (Erlmann 1991:21–53). That the Nguni peoples valued choral singing helped them relate to African-American singing. The improvisational nature of African-American music also struck a responsive chord with them (Coplan 1985:146).

Musical instruments

The adoption or imitation of European instruments has been significant in southern African music. Simply adopting the instruments has not necessarily meant that Africans have played European music on them (Kirby 1934:257; Rycroft 1977; Kauffman 1973.) Double-headed drums are common in southern Africa, especially in separatist religious groups. Both the use of round metal tins in the manufacture of these drums and their style of playing indicate that they were copied from the European bass drums used in military bands. In the early days of the Cape Colony, the Khoikhoi were copying violins and guitars, creating the *ramkie,* a homemade lute (Kirby 1934:246–256).

Commercially produced European instruments were found to be not only louder than indigenous instruments, but also more versatile. The most important of these was the guitar, which became a major instrument all over southern Africa. Though the acoustic guitar was popular for many years, the electric guitar is taking its place. Guitars have often supplanted musical bows because the latter are soft in sound, and much of their appeal is only to the performer. Among Xhosa girls, imported lamellophones took the place of bows (Rycroft 1994:132). Pennywhistles experienced a surge of popularity in the 1950s in South Africa because they were not only versatile, but cheap (Coplan 1985:62, 155–156).

Independence and international relations

Independence has changed the situation in many southern African countries. A major development has been in the amount of readily available modern education. While pedagogy has not usually covered music in depth, the increasing consciousness brought about by Western education has carried over into music. Many traditional African musicians can perform superbly on their instruments, but cannot explain, in Western terms, what they are doing and how they are doing it; younger musicians who have been to school, however, have become aware of what is happening in their musical traditions—such as young Shona mbira players, able to explain the four sections of a cycle of their music.

Political changes have affected the organization of indigenous music. In

Mozambique, chiefly power was curtailed, so chiefs no longer sponsor xylophone ensembles. Though to many people these ensembles represent Mozambican music, other governmental agencies now sponsor them. They are also being integrated with European instruments (Celso Paco, personal communication, 1993)—a process that will doubtlessly modify the tradition.

Increased contacts with the outside world have led young people to see the possibility of producing records as a way of building a successful career. With some exceptions, young musicians tend to imitate the popular music stars they hear, apparently shunning the music of their elders. Both South Africa and Zimbabwe have active recording industries, serving local and international markets; however, the control of production is in the hands of international corporations, who seek to market worldbeat on the basis of technical simplicity and exotic appeal. European producers and technicians in South Africa tend to impose their own values and criteria on African performers, whom they have often considered merely laborers (Meintjes 1994). Some studios are beginning to pay the performers royalties instead of a onetime fee.

REFERENCES

Adams, Charles R. 1974. "Ethnography of Basotho: Evaluative Expression in the Cognitive Domain Lipapali (Games)." Ph.D. dissertation, Indiana University.

Alnaes, Kirsten. 1989. "Living with the Past: The Songs of the Herero in Botswana." *Africa* 59(3):267–299.

Blacking, John. 1965. "The Role of Music in the Culture of the Venda of the Northern Transvaal." In *Studies in Ethnomusicology,* ed. Mieczeslaw Kolinski, 2:20–53. New York: Oak Publications.

——. 1967. *Venda Children's Songs: A Study in Ethnomusicological Analysis.* Johannesburg: Witwatersrand University Press.

——. 1973. *How Musical Is Man?* Seattle: University of Washington Press.

Brown, Ernest Douglas. 1984. "Drums of Life: Royal Music and Social Life in Western Zambia." Ph.D. dissertation, University of Washington.

Childs, Gladwyn Murray. 1949. *Umbundu Kinship and Character.* London: Oxford University Press.

Coplan, David B. 1985. *In Township Tonight! South Africa's Black City Music and Theatre.* London: Longman.

Dargie, David. 1991. "Umngqokolo: Xhosa Overtone Singing and the Song Nondel'ekhaya." *African Music* 7(1):32–47.

England, Nicholas. 1967. "Bushman Counterpoint." *Journal of the International Folk Music Council* 19:58–66.

Erlmann, Veit. 1991. *African Stars: Studies in Black South African Performance.* Chicago: University of Chicago Press.

Greenberg, Joseph H. 1970. *The Languages of Africa,* 3rd ed. Bloomington: Indiana University Press.

Guthrie, Malcolm. 1948. *The Classification of the Bantu Languages.* London: International African Institute.

Johnston, Thomas. 1970. "Xizambi Friction-Bow Music of the Shangana-Tsonga." *African Music* 4(4):81–95.

——. 1971. "Shangana-Tsonga Drum and Bow Rhythms." *African Music* 5(1):59–72.

——. 1972. "Possession Music of the Shangana-Tsonga." *African Music* 5(2):10–22.

——. 1987. "Children's Music of the Shangana-Tsonga." *African Music* 6(4):126–143.

Jones, Arthur M. 1949. *African Music in Northern Rhodesia and Some Other Places.* Livingstone, Zambia: Rhodes-Livingstone Museum.

——. 1959. *Studies in African Music.* London: Oxford University Press.

———. 1964. *Africa and Indonesia.* Leiden: E. J. Brill.

Joseph, Rosemary. 1983. "Zulu Women's Music." *African Music* 6(3):53–89.

Kaemmer, John E. 1993. *Music in Human Life: Anthropological Perspectives on Music.* Austin: University of Texas Press.

Katz, Richard. 1982. *Boiling Energy: Community Healing among the Kalahari !Kung.* Cambridge, Mass.: Harvard University Press.

Kauffman, Robert. 1973. "Shona Urban Music and the Problem of Acculturation." *Yearbook of the International Folk Music Council* 4:47–56.

Kirby, Percival R. 1934. *The Musical Instruments of the Native Races of South Africa.* London: Oxford University Press.

Kubik, Gerhard. 1970. *Musica tradicional e aculturada dos !Kung de Angola,* trans. João de Freitas Branco. Lisbon: Junta de Investigações do Ultramar, Centro de Estudos de Antropologia Cultural. Estudos de Antropologia Cultural, 4.

———. 1975–1976. "Musical Bows in South-Western Angola, 1965." *African Music* 5(4):98–104.

———. 1980. "Angola." *The New Grove Dictionary of Music and Musicians,* ed. Stanley Sadie. London: Macmillan.

———. 1985. "African Tone Systems—A Reassessment." *Yearbook of Traditional Music* 19:31–63.

———. 1988. "Nsenga / Shona Harmonic Patterns and the San Heritage." *Ethnomusicology* 32(2):39–76.

Meintjes, Louise. 1994. "Mediating Difference: Liveness in the Production of Mbaqanga Music in Johannesburg." Seminar paper presented to the Institute for Advanced Study and Research in the African Humanities, Northwestern University, 9 November 1994.

Mundell, Felicia H. 1980. "Botswana." *The New Grove Dictionary of Music and Musicians,* ed. Stanley Sadie. London: Macmillan.

Murdock, George Peter. 1959. *Africa: Its Peoples and Their Culture History.* New York: McGraw-Hill.

Phillipson, David W. 1985. *African Archaeology.* Cambridge: Cambridge University Press.

Ranger, Terence O. 1975. *Dance and Society in Eastern Africa: 1890–1970.* London: Heinemann.

Rycroft, David K. 1971. "Stylistic Evidence in Nguni Song." In *Essays on Music and History in Africa,* ed. Klaus P. Wachsmann (Evanston, Ill.: Northwestern University Press), 213–241.

———. 1975–1976. "The Zulu Bow Songs of Princess Magogo." *African Music* 5(4):41–97.

———. 1977. "Evidence of Stylistic Continuity in Zulu 'Town' Music." In *Essays for a Humanist: An Offering to Klaus Wachsmann,* 216– 260. New York: Town House Press.

———. 1980a. "Hottentot Music." *The New Grove Dictionary of Music and Musicians,* ed. Stanley Sadie. London: Macmillan.

———. 1980b. "Nguni Music." *The New Grove Dictionary of Music and Musicians,* ed. Stanley Sadie. London Macmillan.

———. 1994. "African Arts, Music: Musical Instruments." *Encyclopaedia Britannica,* 15th ed. 13:132–135.

Tracey, Andrew. 1971. "The Nyanga Panpipe Dance." *African Music* 5(1):73–89.

———. 1972. "The Original African Mbira?" *African Music* (2):85–104.

———. 1980. "Mozambique." *The New Grove Dictionary of Music and Musicians,* ed. Stanley Sadie. London: Macmillan.

———. 1991. "Kambazithe Makolekole and his Valimba Group: A Glimpse of the Technique of the Sena Xylophone." *African Music* 7(1):82–104.

Tracey, Hugh. 1948a. *Chopi Musicians: Their Music, Poetry, and Instruments.* London: International African Institute.

———. 1948b. *Ngoma: An Introduction to Music for Southern Africans.* New York: Longmans, Green.

van Zanten, Wim. 1980. "The Equidistant Heptatonic Scale of the Asena in Malawi." *African Music* 6(1):107–125.

Popular Music in South Africa
David B. Coplan

The study of popular musical traditions in South Africa stretches over three centuries of cultural turbulence, across linguistic and political boundaries, to the far reaches of the subcontinent, and to the capitals and colleges of Europe and America. It encompasses the contributions made by South Africans of European and African origin, and by Americans of African descent.

From the late 1600s, increasingly dominant European colonists overwhelmed the cultures of the majority population. Popular musical forms emerged and spread within a colonial context: European settlers, mainly from the Netherlands and Britain, developed an industrialized economy, based on the exploitation of an indigenous, slave-labor force. Since the 1860s, the growth of urban centers accompanied that development and produced environments where intensive interethnic and interracial contacts took place, amid institutionalized racial segregation and the processes of class formation.

In the late 1800s and early 1900s, South African mining and manufacturing grew prodigiously and created a demand for labor that, reaching nearly to the equator, transformed the face of southern Africa. The African communities most affected by Christian missionization responded readily to the prospect of better employment in Kimberley or Johannesburg; yet colonial taxes and seductive labor recruiters also drew to the mines thousands of cattle keepers and farmers. So it was that black people arriving with circumscribed provincial patterns of African and Afro-Western (African Christian) culture found themselves at once enmeshed, not only in what people described as "a welter of the tribes," but in a welter of races, values, customs, languages, nationalities, social conditions, levels of education, and world views.

In those circumstances, performances and styles played a crucial role in black people's social self-definition and cultural reintegration. Traditionalist or Christian, rural rooted or urbanized, Africans moved continuously between town and country. Their movements assured that urban and rural performance cultures would continue to influence each other. By the mid-1800s, white townspeople were beginning to fear the increase of Africans and people of mixed race, who crowded into ghettos or "locations" (as people termed black residential areas attached to every town). In the late 1800s, after the discovery of the world's largest known deposits of diamonds and gold

Founded in 1652 as a refreshment and refitting station for the Asia-bound ships of the Dutch East India Company, Cape Town is aptly called South Africa's "Mother City."

in South Africa, the government institutionalized in a migrant labor system the permanent oscillation of tens of thousands of black workers between country homes and urban workplaces. In the decade after the Great War, despite the increasing severity of influx-control regulations (designed to slow the movement of black people to the cities), black urban communities swelled.

Those conditions provided the context for the development of a stylistically diverse, but strongly interactive, popular-performance culture. The forms that appeared were tied to the expressive and recreational preferences of a given ethnic, regional, or class-based audience, yet coexisted with newly incorporative styles and performance venues, designed by their performers to attract an unrestricted clientele (figure 1). Both the audiences and the influences involved in developing a particular music-and-dance form usually varied more than popular stereotypes supposed. While in rural areas new forms often evolved in the context of changing realities, urban spaces—"locations," mine compounds, factory hostels, schools, churches, welfare centers, union halls—became the crucibles of creativity and dissemination. The cities, in particular Johannesburg, also became the centers of local recording and broadcasting industries, the largest in Africa after the 1940s. So the cultural history of South Africa's cities and towns frames the description of the country's indigenous popular music.

CAPE TOWN

Founded in 1652 as a refreshment and refitting station for the Asia-bound ships of the Dutch East India Company, Cape Town is aptly called South Africa's "Mother

FIGURE 1   Gabriel Thobejane of the group Malombo, 1977.

City." Race relations there, under a system of chattel slavery (which accommodated communities of free blacks), set the pattern for the development of South African society. Cape Town, too, gave birth to South African popular music, the styles that arose among the people of the colony's farms and thoroughfares. There, the resident population—Dutch burghers; displaced Khoikhoi and San ("Hottentot" and "Bushman"); slaves from Madagascar, Mozambique, the Dutch East Indies, the Malabar coast of India—grew with new arrivals, transient merchant-sailors, and adventurers. The interbreeding of that population, in particular the mating of Dutch males with Khoi-San, south Asian ("Malay"), and Malagasy slave females, gave rise to South Africa's "coloured" (mixed-race) people. Earning a place in Cape society as skilled artisans and craftsmen, coloured performers (both slave and free) became South Africa's first professional popular musicians.

In seaport taverns, at white colonial balls and banquets, and on country plantations, slave musicians learned to play European instruments for the delectation of their masters' families, guests, and customers. As early as 1676, the Dutch governor had an orchestra of slaves. Music became a marketable trade, and musical ability enhanced a slave's value. Formal instruction was minimal, but slave musicians displayed a talent for playing by ear. Performing European dance music led coloured musicians to create musical blends, accommodating black and white musical cultures. Surviving examples are the Cape white "picnic song" and the Cape Malay "drum song," with texts in Afrikaans (South African creole Dutch): except for the race of the performers, these songs are stylistically indistinguishable.

Coloured musicians also played for their own communities. In the 1700s, British influence at the Cape grew; and in 1806, the British took the colony over. Among both whites and their servants, English country dances then became fashionable. From the 1730s, servants held "rainbow balls," whose grace, glamour, and spectrum of skin color bore comparison with antebellum New Orleans.

Less formal entertainments that flourished among coloureds took place in city backyards, on beachfronts, and on country farms, where Afrikaans trade-store instruments—violin, guitar, concertina—formed the basis of coloured folk musical culture. Eventually, coloureds, Bantu-speaking blacks, and white tenant farmers (*bywoners*), would introduce these instruments into all the folk-musical cultures of South Africa. The ubiquity of these instruments led not only to the blending of indigenous and European dance musics, but to new developments within indigenous musical traditions. These developments included neotraditional styles: elaborations and reinterpretations of African traditional music, made possible by the enhanced technical capacities of the imported instruments. Africans referred to this process by coining terms for its products, such as the Zulu *maskanda* (from Afrikaans *musikant*), showing the new instruments' local culture of origin. Neotraditional music also involved the invention of new instruments based on European models. These included a four-stringed plucked guitar (the Khoi *ramkie*), and two homemade violins (*t'guthe* and *velviool*). Black Africans later developed their own versions, including the *igqonqwe* (a Zulu *ramkie*), and the *mamokhorong* or *sekhankure* (a one-stringed Basotho violin). By about 1900, people had reconceptualized the trade-store instruments as "traditional African instruments"; in the late twentieth century, musicians referred freely to the music of the "Zulu traditional guitar" and of the "Basotho traditional concertina" (later, accordion).

KIMBERLEY

The late 1800s saw striking developments in urban popular music. In the 1870s, in the remote north of the Cape Colony, a diamond rush led to the rise of Kimberley, an "instant city." To its opportunities flocked fortune hunters, whites and blacks

sefela   Long, musical poetic narratives devel-
    oped by the Bosotho veteran migrants on
    their travels to the mines

tickey draai   Dance that was accompanied by
    the guitar and popular until the 1940s

oorlams   Popular working-class musicians
    who were coloured or black Africans and
    served as cultural brokers

abaphakathi   South African popular per-
    formers whose competence and versatility
    secured a free existence for them

alike: workers and professionals came from all over southern Africa. Many rural
Africans were target workers, people who intended to stay only until they had earned
enough to buy a rifle and other sought-after European goods, and to pay the taxes
that would permit them to keep their lands. The innovations they made in their
musical culture went far beyond instruments and dances. Thoroughly transforming
their forms of expression, they created new genres of dance, song, and oral poetry. In
those genres, they assimilated to familiar cultural categories and social values new
experiences and conditions. Among the familiar genres was the traditional praise
poetry of the Xhosa, which served to flatter and satirize overseers in the mines (both
black and white), and to apostrophize rural chiefs. Another such genre was the Zulu
men's walking-and-courting song (backed now by the guitar, the concertina, and the
violin), which pilloried the moral shallowness of friendship and romantic love.
Among the richest examples were the Basotho's veteran migrants' songs (*sefela sa lit-
samaea-naha*), long musical poetic narratives, developed on "long walks" from
Basutoland to Kimberley (Coplan 1988).

In the migrants' texts, Kimberley became a symbol of immorality. In 1984, more
than a century after the Basotho first ventured there, Majara Majara of Lesotho could
sing, in his *sefela*:

Ke buoa ka Kemele;   I speak of Kimberley;
Ke buoa ka Sotoma.   I speak of Sodom.

It was not only the male migrants who found themselves singing new songs:
women, their lives disrupted by the prolonged absence of their men, also migrated.
In the canteens of Kimberley, some of them became famed singers and dancers.

Except for the privileged colonial élite and entrepreneurial class, life in early
Kimberley was so rough and disorganized, the government could not enforce South
Africa's usual pattern of racial segregation. In time, whites built closed compounds,
which imprisoned African male migrant workers. Other black people crowded into
"locations." At first, however, the poorer classes of all races and nationalities lived
jumbled together in shantytowns, which resounded with the music of canteens, concerts, dance halls, honkytonks, and house parties. Black and white "diggers" caroused
together to the music of banjos, guitars, pianos, concertinas, and violins; the men
enjoyed the companionship of camp followers, mostly black women, drawn from the
countryside. Among the prospectors were Americans (both white and black), who
brought to the canteens their own instrumental styles.

Among the most popular performers were coloured musicians. Some were itinerant professionals; others, artisans with profitable musical avocations. On the violin
and guitar, these players obligingly created blends of Khoi, Cape-Malay-Afrikaans,
British, and American popular melodies. One genre that emerged from this musical

mix was the dance *tickey draai* (Afrikaans) 'turn on a tickey [threepence]'; played on the guitar, it was popular until the 1940s.

The social identity of Kimberley's popular working-class musicians was significant, because it set the pattern for artistic leadership in black popular music elsewhere in the country. The musicians were mainly proletarian coloureds or black Africans who spoke Afrikaans or English, which they learned in workplaces, rather than in mission schools. Called *oorlams* in Afrikaans, or *abaphakathi* 'those in-between' in Xhosa, they served as cultural brokers, or middlemen between black and white. In the process, they earned a reputation for being too clever by half. Many discovered that musical (in addition to linguistic and cultural) competence and versatility could secure a free and independent, if itinerant, existence. From their ranks came more than one generation of innovative black popular musicians. It may have been among such musicians in nineteenth-century Kimberley that the tonic–dominant–subdominant harmonic progression became established as the signature of South African black popular music.

CHRISTIAN RELIGIOUS MUSIC

European Christian hymnody first became a factor in the development of black South African music in the early 1800s. Strife between white settlers and Xhosa pastoralists led to the uprooting of many African communities in the eastern Cape. As early as 1816, Ntsikana, a Xhosa prophet and visionary, prescribed for the cultural reformulation of Xhosa society a blend of African and Christian religious beliefs, values, and practices. For his congregation, he composed several Afro-Christian hymns, which choirs performed and transmitted orally. In 1876, a mission newspaper published in Tonic Sol-fa notation his hymn "*Ulo Tixo Mkulu* 'Thou, Great God'." In 1884, John Knox Bokwe, renowned Xhosa composer and Presbyterian choirmaster, republished it, with three of Ntsikana's other hymns. Ntsikana's style strikingly infuses Protestant hymnody with the stateliness of Xhosa melody, harmony, and rhythm.

On mission stations, refugees from successive frontier wars in the eastern Cape and from the rapid expansion of the Zulu kingdom to the north found shelter, farms, work, and access to the religious and educational requirements of life in colonial society. There, the choral part singing that became the foundation of all indigenous southern Bantu music making achieved a fit with Christian hymnody.

Blacks thought congregational singing one of the most attractive aspects of Christian ritual. African choirs made harmonies, not on the basis of a dominant melodic line, but by polyphonically embellishing a bass ostinato. Though Western concepts of tonality were foreign, blacks enshrined as a choral set piece Handel's "Hallelujah Chorus" (*Messiah*, 1742). More importantly, the melodic direction of southern Bantu part songs tends to follow the tonal patterns of the words. To Bantu-speakers' ears, the violation of traditional tone-tune relationships and patterns of syllabic stress made many of the early translations of European hymns unlovely, but converts eventually got used to it. In the mid-1800s, Tiyo Soga, the first ordained black minister in South Africa (Free Church of Scotland), adapted several Scottish melodies to Xhosa texts.

By the 1880s, a movement toward cultural revitalization and nationalism was growing among mission blacks disappointed with their lack of social advancement. John Bokwe, a leader in the movement, preserved semantic tones while achieving a high musical and literary quality—a happy marriage of African and European compositional principles. His efforts pioneered a new black South African choral style, widely known as *makwaya* (choir), which he used in Scotland to support his studies for the ministry, and to gain for black South African Christians a sympathetic hearing. Since then, many illustrious figures in black South African choral music—

In Cape Town, the Virginia Jubilee Singers'
appearances led to the emergence of the minstrel
parades of the "Cape Coon Carnival," which became
a permanent institution of coloured performances.

Benjamin Tyamzashe, A. A. Khumalo, Hamilton Masiza, Marks Radebe, Reuben
Caluza, Joshua Mohapeloa, Michael Moerane—have appeared.

Several outstanding songs exemplify the *makwaya* style. One is "*Nkosi Sikelel'
iAfrika* 'God Bless Africa'," composed in 1897 by a Johannesburg teacher, Enoch
Sontonga; S. E. R. Mqayi, the Xhosa national poet, later added more stanzas. In the
early 1900s, Reuben Caluza's Ohlange Institute Choir popularized this song, which
in 1925 became the anthem of the African National Congress, South Africa's most
active antiapartheid organization; in the 1990s, it was the national anthem of several
central and southern African countries. Though rhythmically stolid, its perceived
combination of melancholic yearning and spiritual grandeur made it a musical
embodiment of the thirst for freedom.

At least until the 1960s, *makwaya* must be considered popular music, because of
its distribution among choirs, civic and political organizations, unions, wedding parties, and community concerts. In evolving contexts, it supported the traditional
attachment of black South Africans to choral song. Reflecting the secular use of the
emotional and spiritual catharsis provided in sacred pieces (such as Methodist
hymns), it influenced other forms of vocal and instrumental music, including working-class choral forms—the sonorous *ingoma ebusuku* (Zulu) 'night music', more
recently known as *isicathamiya* 'sneaking up', and the lighter school songs, known as
mbholoho (Mthethwa 1980:24–26)—and South African ragtime and early jazz, plus
the rearrangement of indigenous folk songs for choral performance in four-part harmony.

INFLUENCES FROM THE UNITED STATES

Makwaya was not the only musical form or trend that in the late 1800s and early
1900s influenced the Western-educated African élite. Since the 1860s, blackface
minstrelsy had been popular with urban whites in South Africa; and as a representation (however distorted) of the performances of black Americans, it had an impact
on Anglicized black South Africans, who admired the achievements of Booker T.
Washington and other black American leaders. Many black South African leaders
(including John Dube, Solomon Plaatjie, Reuben Caluza, and Charlotte Manye
Maxexe) visited or received education in the United States.

No less important were the activities of the African Methodist Episcopal
Church, based in Philadelphia. With other black American denominations of the
very late 1800s, it sent missionaries to South Africa, where they set up schools and
churches, whose most important musical contribution was teaching and performing
Negro spirituals, an art form that delighted black South Africans, and stunned local
composers into recognizing what they might accomplish in Afro-Christian hymnody.
American performers, recordings in the first decade of the twentieth century, and
Tonic Sol-fa sheet music were also making black Americans' music available; and

coon songs, ragtime, and close-harmony quartet singing all made significant impressions on the Afro-Western cultural models of South Africa's black educated élite.

These trends came together in the tours Orpheus "Bill" McAdoo's Virginia Jubilee Singers made in Cape Town and other cities during the 1880s and 1890s (Erlmann 1991:21–53). McAdoo patterned his company after the Fisk Jubilee Singers and other black American troupes. By that time, black American performers had long since appropriated minstrelsy, which they infused with a representation of African-American culture. Their performances made a big impact on South African audiences, black as well as white; and their music helped revive the popularity of minstrelsy as a local genre. Amateur companies patterned after McAdoo's troupe sprang up among members of African civic and cultural organizations, and at secondary schools such as Lovedale and Healdtown in the Cape, and the Lyndhurst Road School in Kimberley. Notable among these companies were Kimberley's Diamond Minstrels and the Philharmonic Society, which included McAdoo's original pianist, Will Thompson, who had decided to stay in South Africa. Reflecting the revaluation of indigenous culture taking place among African intellectuals, the Philharmonic Society's programs featured several *makwaya* arrangements of traditional African folk songs. Another result was the formation of the South African Native Choir, patterned after McAdoo's company, but featuring an extensive selection of *makwaya* songs; in the 1890s, that choir toured Britain and the United States.

In Cape Town, the Virginia Jubilee Singers' appearances led to the emergence of the minstrel parades of the "Cape Coon Carnival," which became a permanent institution of coloured performances. Following the custom in which Cape Town became "the kingdom of the coloured man" for the duration of New Year's Day, coloured men's clubs began marching through the streets in American minstrel costume, performing for the amusement of riotous crowds a mix of minstrel and Afrikaans favorites. Before the 1970s, when the government quarantined the Coon Carnival in a football stadium, the parades gave Cape Town's best-known reed and brass jazzmen opportunities to display their talents.

Until about 1930, black South African urban popular music developed in mission schools, community and voluntary organizations, and neighborhood social events. Regionally, the most important centers that fostered the emergence of a new Afro-Western performative culture were in the Cape, among Xhosa-speaking élites in Queenstown, Port Elizabeth, and Cape Town itself, and at Lovedale and the other mission institutions. School concerts and community concerts included lively groups of "student coons," vocal quartets, choirs, solo balladeers, and "minstrels," who bore a closer resemblance to British "concert-parties," or to early vaudeville musical-variety shows, than to the blackface format. Missions and mission schools also sponsored brass bands of the type favored by evangelical ministries in Britain in the late 1800s. In addition, the parlors of many educated Cape Africans housed a piano, or a small harmonium or pedal organ, around which families gathered to sing hymns and popular ballads and "evergreens."

As American ragtime and jazz attained popularity in South Africa, mission-trained instrumentalists from popular "coon troupes," both coloured and Xhosa, came together to form some of South Africa's first jazz bands. Among the best known were the Blue Rhythm Syncopators of Queenstown, led by pianist Meekley "Fingertips" Matshikiza; it featured William "Sax-O-Wills" Mbali, one of the Cape's first professional tenor saxophone players and ballroom dancers. Bands, choirs, and variety troupes sprang up wherever there were missions, schools, and urban centers; and so, while coloureds and Cape Africans were leaders in early-twentieth-century Afro-Western musical performance, similar developments with a local cultural flavor occurred among the Zulu of Durban and Natal, and among the Tswana of

In the early 1900s, American ragtime, dixieland, and jazz became popular among westernizing coloureds and Africans, whether educated or not.

Rustenburg and Pretoria in the Transvaal. Developments in Kimberley reflected the community's multiethnicity, though even there the educated black élite was mainly Xhosa-speaking.

JOHANNESBURG

In 1886, the discovery of the world's largest known gold deposits, beneath a desolate ridge in the South African Republic of the Transvaal, upstaged the Kimberley lode. Again, work seekers from all over the subcontinent gravitated to the spot, soon to be the "Golden City" of Johannesburg, which by about 1900 sheltered at least fifty thousand whites, forty thousand urbanized blacks, and one hundred thousand black miners. To Johannesburg flocked educated African professionals, frustrated by smaller communities' limited opportunities, low pay, and isolation; by 1904, the census reported 25 percent of the permanent black population was literate. The range of regional, ethnic, class, and educational backgrounds that municipal regulation crowded together within a black community (and away from whites) created in turn a musical mix that became the basis for black show business in South Africa.

Like other towns in South Africa, turn-of-the-century Johannesburg was racially segregated as much by custom as by law. The city's atmosphere, duplicating on a larger scale that of Kimberley a quarter-century before, gave blacks opportunities to circulate more freely than in the older, settled towns of the Cape, Natal, and Transvaal. Some of the poorer residential areas on the eastern and western fringes of the city were racially mixed: Africans, coloureds, whites, Indians, and Chinese lived together. In addition to drinking houses frequented by blacks only, musical entertainment was available at many of the city's 118 unsegregated canteens. The harshness and insecurity of black life in early Johannesburg accompanied cultural disorientation. Musical performances became workshops in which musicians fashioned new models of urban African and African-Western culture, and devised new patterns of social identity and behavior. In the context of recreational socialization, interpersonal and community relationships formed and strengthened, and people enacted and celebrated the process of collective self-definition.

Probably the most familiar setting for informal music making was the shebeen, an unlicensed business (usually a private residence), whose owners illegally brewed and sold beer and liquor. The origins of this institution apparently go back to seventeenth-century Cape Town, where Dutch colonists sold liquor to black servants and slaves, and sometimes provided rooms to drink it in. The term *shebeen* apparently came from the speech of immigrant Irish vice police in early-twentieth-century Cape Town. Transvaal law decreed prohibition for blacks in 1896, but government-run distilleries produced cheap brandy for black workers. In addition to African home-brewed beer, the supply of strong drink led to the illegal sale of several near-lethal concoctions. Different shebeens attracted different kinds of patrons, as people sought each other's company on the basis of ethnic or geographical origins, occupational and class memberships, neighborhood and friendship ties, shared self-images and aspirations, and the forms of dance and music they implied.

So a group of Basotho migrants at a shebeen might hold an impromptu performance of young men's *mangae* songs or *mohobelo* dances, or listen to the improvisations of a concertina virtuoso; Zulu domestics and manual workers enjoyed guitar and violin duos, plus songs for walking and weddings; Shangaans (from Mozambique) displayed their (Portuguese-influenced) solo guitar styles; and the Bapedi excelled at accompanying melodies on the autoharp, or dancing in a circle, beating rhythms on rubber or oxhide stretched over the top of a 44-gallon petrol drum. Much of that music was neotraditional, as rural-born musicians discovered what they could do with trade-store instruments. The instruments themselves provided a natural vehicle for importing American, British, and even Afrikaans songs, rhythms, and styles of playing.

JAZZ, *MARABI*

For new arrivals from the countryside, the ability to incorporate black American and European elements and items into their performances expressed knowledge of, and a certain mastery over, the dominant exogenous culture and the new social environment. Africans returning home injected urban tunes, rhythms, and steps into country dances. Laborers who set their sights on permanent urban residence began buying American-style clothes, sending their families to church and school, and seeking popular music at neighborhood concerts and shebeens. All black people in the towns lived close together—well off and poor, educated and illiterate, Christian and animist, Zulu and Basotho, coloured and African. Ethnic musical traditions began to blend with Afro-Western and Western ones. An early generation of professional and semiprofessional black musicians, who by supplying musical modes of adaptation intended to earn good money, syncretized the new styles.

In the vanguard of that generation were solo "pianomen," primarily from the Cape, but not uncommonly from other towns in Natal, the Free State, and the Transvaal. In the early 1900s, American ragtime, dixieland, and jazz became popular among westernizing coloureds and Africans, whether educated or not. Queenstown, in the Cape midlands, produced so many leading players (like "Fingertips" Matshikiza), it earned the nickname "Little Jazz Town." Whether pianomen performed at school and community concerts and élite social affairs, or in rough canteens at railway junctions and in periurban shantytowns, they soon found they could lessen or cut their dependence on pay from menial jobs, provided they kept moving and played a variety of popular styles for diverse audiences. The shebeens belonged mostly to women, who had transformed into a profitable business their traditional skill at brewing. The "shebeen queens" often bought their own instruments, and vied for the services of popular pianists and organists, who attracted patrons to parties. In Johannesburg, their competition produced an unstable stylistic blend of Xhosa melodies, *tickey draai*, and ragtime. This was *thula n'divile* 'keep quiet, I've heard it', a three-chord harmonic format, which served as an exhortation for others to cease their noise, so the player might flaunt something new.

Whenever black people tried to create stable, ordered communities, with functioning social institutions and viable patterns of urban culture, the government moved in to destroy them. By the 1920s, authorities scheduled the "black spots" ("locations") for removal. Yet these places, which in Johannesburg included Doornfontein, Prospect Township, and Malay Camp–Vrededorp, and in Pretoria included Marabastad and Lady Selbourne, were centers of social and cultural inventiveness. Though slums, they were the settings for the emergence of professional black stage entertainment, and for the birth of an indigenous kind of jazz.

shebeen   Unlicensed bar, often a private home, where patrons gather to drink and perform neotraditional music

marabi   Hybrid music, dance form, and a social occasion that was both indigenous and urban

abaqhafi   "Street cowboys" who wandered the cities and played Zulu guitar songs

famo   A wild and risqué version of *marabi* that appeared among Basotho migrants

indunduma   A Zulu piano-vamp style of *marabi*

makwaya   Choral song that became a form of South African popular music until the 1960s

In the dance halls and shebeens, the pianomen's efforts at devising a musical formula that would please a diverse patronage led them to work into a repetitive three-chord version of American ragtime and jazz the melodies and rhythms of black ethnic groups. By the late 1920s, that music was known in the Transvaal towns as *marabi*, a term whose origins are uncertain, but whose incorporative flexibility and lively danceability gave listeners the sense of a music at once indigenous, urbanized, African, up to date, worldly. *Marabi* often develop a four-bar progression of polyphonic chords ending on the dominant: I–IV–I$_4^6$–V^7. In *marabi*, the use of a recurrent sequence of chords offset with varying melodic phrases simulates traditional choral part songs. "Fingertips" Matshikiza and his like were renowned *marabi* pianists, but in Johannesburg the most famous of all was Tebetjane, whose 1932 composition "*uTebetjana Ufana ne'Mfene* 'Tebetjane looks like a baboon'" became the emblem of the style. In accordance with African holistic concepts of performance, and the close identification of performance genres with their practitioners and social settings, *marabi* was not merely a hybrid instrumental music, but a dance form, a social occasion, and a category of participants (urbanizing proletarians). So pervasive a part of life did it become that music critic and jazz composer Todd Matshikiza (Fingertips's nephew) proclaimed it "the name of an epoch." True to its inclusive purpose, its rhythmic and chordal structure was rigid, and there was little of the "free" improvisation that characterized American jazz; but because it blended into the river of American honkytonk so many streams of indigenous music, it became the reservoir of a uniquely South African jazz.

Pianomen and pedal organists were not the only instrumentalists who spawned *marabi*: the brass and fife-and-drum bands of British forces sent to South Africa during the Boer War (1899–1902) had much impressed Africans. Later, African brass and reed players trained in the marching bands of the Native Military Corps and the Salvation Army began to form their own ensembles. They played at weddings and church festivals, and for women's neighborhood and religious organizations and the coins of outsiders seeking excitement in the "locations." Theirs was a process that added to European marches African polyrhythm and polyphonic improvisation. Soon, however, untrained bandsmen, especially Bapedi domestic servants exposed to brass by the Lutheran missions of the Transvaal, joined trained players. Their method was to repeat short segments of European tunes in combination with African melodies, worked out by trial and error on the new instruments, and orchestrated polyphonically by ear. During the 1920s and 1930s, *marabi*—including the famous *tamatie saus* (Afrikaans) 'ketchup', and the antipolice satire "Pick-up Van"—became staples of marching band repertories. In time, small ensembles of piano, brass, reed, violin, banjo, and drums began to play at shebeens and neighborhood social occasions, leading to the emergence of *marabi* dance bands like the Japanese Express.

Stylistic exchange between rural neotraditional African music on the one hand and *marabi* on the other took place in both directions. Rural dances (like Xhosa *mabokwe*), neotraditional forms (like the Zulu guitar songs of roving *abaqhafi*, "street cowboys"), and incipient syncretic urban styles (like Xhosa *itswari* 'soiree' and *thula n'divile*), all flowed into *marabi*, which, in turn, contributed new rhythms and inventive, often deliberately comical, footwork. In Johannesburg, *famo*, a wild and risqué version of *marabi*, appeared among Basotho migrants and proletarians; combined with neotraditional Basotho dance, it became a staple of working-class entertainment in the towns and rural villages of the Orange Free State and Lesotho. Zulu guitar and violin players quickly assimilated into their walking, courting, and wedding songs *marabi*'s vamp. In Durban, workers danced to a Zulu piano vamp style of *marabi* called *indunduma* 'mine dumps'—a reference to Johannesburg, where people disappeared amid mountains of slag.

Indeed, for people trying either to maintain traditional family systems and codes of social behavior, or to construct new Afro-Western Christian ones, *marabi* represented the dangers and the depths of anomic urban immorality and hedonism; but the children of the "locations," loving the ragtime love songs and *marabi* favorites of the day, sneaked to the parties and dances with many a joy-seeking husband or wife. Rural-oriented traditionalists, urbanized elitists, and those trying to keep one foot in both social environments developed self-defining styles and occasions of performance.

JAZZ: THE "RESPECTABLE RESPONSE"

Through Christian preparatory schools, teachers' colleges and associations, membership in churches, urban professional employment, and even newspapers (such as *Isigidimi sama Xhosa*, *Ilanga lase Natal*, *Imvo Zabantsundu*, and *Tsala ea Bechuana*), educated African élites had long possessed social institutions and networks connecting rural areas, small towns, and "locations." By the 1920s, their culture was a century old. During the years between the world wars, several important developments occurred in it, in conscious opposition to ragtime, jazz, and *marabi*. First, a generation of *makwaya* composers arose, more innovative and influential than any before. Benjamin Tyamzashe enhanced the contribution of Xhosa folk song to *makwaya*. Joshua Mohapeloa, a talented tunesmith, used his facility with Tonic Sol-fa notation to arrange Basotho folk songs for Western four-part choral performance, and to compose choral songs that stretched and snapped the rigid rules of Western harmony to weld it to Basotho polyphony. A choir leader himself, Mohapeloa helped perfect the local method, whereby choirs are led rather than conducted: the leader sets up the foundation melody in the bass, and the other three parts enter above, in polyphonic relation to the bass (lead), though not necessarily to each other. For the representation of African part songs, Mohapeloa saw he could turn to advantage the rigidity and insufficiency of Tonic Sol-fa. While encouraging the free use of African tonality, ornamentation, timbre, and polyphonic "part agreement," choral leaders used Tonic Sol-fa as a skeletal sign of the general direction and organization of parts.

The greatest composer of *makwaya* was Reuben T. Caluza, of Natal (Erlmann 1991:181–236). His promotion of music as a fundraiser for the Ohlange Institute, a trade school, led him to experiment with a range of ensembles and styles. He went so far as to found student pennywhistle-and-drum bands, which paraded in the streets of small towns around Natal. More important was the Ohlange choir, whose performances under his direction became, before the Great War, major cultural events in Durban, Johannesburg, and other towns. Their performance of Enoch Sontonga's *Nkosi Sikelel' iAfrika* at early meetings of the South African Native National Congress (later the African National Congress) led to the adoption of that song as the ANC's organizational anthem. Caluza composed in Tonic Sol-fa dozens of songs, many of which had social and political themes, such as "*iLand Act*" (to protest the Land Act of

By the 1940s, ballroom and swing-jazz orchestras on the American big band model dominated black show business in the cities, especially Johannesburg.

1913), "Influenza" (to mourn deaths in the flu epidemic of 1918), and *Ingoduso* (to deplore a perceived loss of moral responsibility among young Zulu immigrants to Johannesburg). By variously combining indigenous Zulu melodies, ragtime, and hymnodic *makwaya*, he objectified three distinct categories of Afro-Western choral song: *isiZulu*, traditional folk songs arranged in four-part harmony; *imusic*, strongly Westernized "classical" *makwaya*; and *ukureka*, ragtime. In 1932, for His Master's Voice (London), he recorded more than one hundred twenty of his arrangements and compositions; Lovedale Press published several in Tonic Sol-fa. Caluza had no hesitation about performing for working-class audiences, or any audience that cared to hire him; and he was not, despite his exalted status, above composing a choral *marabi* or two. What apparently astonished audiences was his ability to synchronize harmoniously voices, onstage movements, and keyboard. He earned musical degrees at Hampton Institute (Virginia) and Columbia University (New York), and passed the later part of his musical career as director of the music school at Adams College (Amanzimtoti, Natal). His influence on popular composition and performance in Zulu was lasting and profound, from school concerts to élite and workers' choral competitions to jazz bands like J. C. P. Mavimbela's Rhythm Kings, which, in the late 1930s, specialized in swing-jazz arrangements of Caluza songs.

Another major development in élite performance was the development of polished semiprofessional variety song-and-dance companies (still called minstrels) out of the school and neighborhood amateur concerts of the 1920s. Minstrel companies like the Erie Lads, Darktown Negroes, Africans Own Entertainers, Hiver Hyvas, and Darktown Strutters, drew on British "concert-party" and black American vaudeville, made available through films, recordings, and sheet music. Their performers offered a mix of ragtime and dixieland vocals in African languages, American popular standards (like "Can't Help Lovin' Dat Man"), *makwaya*, step-dancing, tap-dancing, comic turns, and dramatic sketches—all wearing matching tuxedos.

At the same time, admiration for American jazz and big-band music, combined with a desire to upgrade the image of local entertainment created by the Japanese Express and other *marabi* bands, led to the formation of several black "society" jazz bands. Coloured dance bands of the 1920s, such as Rayner's Big Six and Sonny's Revellers, were the first to answer this need; but by the late 1930s, the Merry Blackbirds, Rhythm Kings, and the somewhat jazzier Jazz Maniacs, were providing the music for all-night concert and dance occasions at élite venues (such as the Bantu Men's Social Center and the Inchcape Hall's Ritz Palais de Danse). There, well-dressed, literate domestic servants and professionals immersed themselves in the turns of American ballroom dancing. Putting on evening dress to dance to the Jazz Maniacs' rendition of "Tuxedo Junction" or the Merry Blackbirds' ragtime favorite "MaDlamini" (a famous shebeen queen) was more than just good entertainment: it was a conscious effort to acquire the performative dimensions of (Western) "civilization" (especially its African cousin, black American show business), while projecting

FIGURE 2   Jazz at the Odin, 1950s. *Left to right:* Kippie Moeketsi, Banzi Bangani, Mackay Darashe, Elijah Nkonyane (trumpet), Ntemi Piliso.

FIGURE 3   Pinoccio Mokgaleng, founder of the Sophiatown Modern Jazz Club, and vocalist Dolly Rathebe, in the late 1950s.

oneself as an accomplished representative of it. Promoter and talent scout Griffiths Motsieloa brought the two forms of élite performance together in 1937, when, by teaming the Darktown Strutters with the Merry Blackbirds Orchestra, he created the Pitch Black Follies, a popular traveling concert and dance company.

By the 1940s, ballroom and swing-jazz orchestras on the American big band model dominated black show business in the cities, especially Johannesburg. Despite laws that did not recognize "musician" as a legitimate category of employment for blacks, dozens of such bands toured the country, often teaming up for concert and dance performances with variety troupes. Once begun, shows had to carry on until at least four or five A.M., since curfew laws and an absence of public transportation made it impossible for black concertgoers to go home at night. Some bands, like the Jazz Maniacs and Harlem Swingsters, avoided touring by securing regular engagements around Johannesburg. Few musicians, however, could manage exclusively on their musical earnings. For example, Wilson "King Force" Silgee, saxophonist and leader of the Jazz Maniacs, was for a lengthy period a "tea boy" in the Johannesburg municipal clerk's office. The Jazz Maniacs were among those bands who for many years refused to make recordings, stating that the flat fees of a few pounds per side weren't worth the effort, and helped competing bands copy their compositions and style. Others, however, especially the top vocal soloists and groups, viewed records as a useful medium for increasing their audience. It was common for people to attend shows expressly to hear their favorite recording artists perform current hits. In the late 1940s, The Band in Blue, starring virtuoso clarinet and alto saxophonist Kippie Moeketsi (figure 2), backed an all-black ensemble in Ike Brooks's musical variety film *Zonk* (unreleased, in private hands).

Among the most popular vocal groups were the male close-harmony quartets (patterned after the Mills Brothers and the Inkspots) such as the Manhattan Brothers, the African Inkspots, and the Woody Woodpeckers. Similar female soloists included Dolly Rathebe (figure 3), Dorothy Masuku, and Susan Gabashane. In the 1950s and early 1960s, female quartets, such as the Dark City Sisters and Miriam Makeba's Skylarks, sang jazz with a local flavor. Much of the jazz the singers and bands popularized was arrangements of American songs and local compositions in

As for *mbaqanga*, South Africa's own jazz, there is no more characteristic a composition than Miriam Makeba's "*Patha Patha* 'Touch Touch'."

the American swing idiom, with lyrics in African languages. Local music made its mark, however, in jazz orchestrations of African folk songs and popular *marabi*, and in the use of African rhythms in original compositions.

Many songs engagingly combined American and African melodic and rhythmic motifs. An important performative aspect of this process occurred in the late hours of live shows, when players would put away their American sheet music and "let go." A more *marabi*-based, African shebeen jazz took over; and the brass, reeds, and piano took improvised solo choruses over a pulsating beat. Not all audiences adored American popular culture, and many patrons demanded from the bandsmen a more local jazz idiom. Some bands, like the Chisa Ramblers, specialized in "backyard" party engagements, for which they supplied *marabi*.

From that kind of playing and the vocals that accompanied it arose *mbaqanga*, a Zulu name for a stiff corn porridge, which jazzmen regarded as their professional staple, a musical daily bread. The dance of the period was the *tsaba-tsaba*, a big-band successor to the *marabi*. The best-known song in this style was "*Skokiaan*" (named after a deadly drink), composed in the late 1940s by a Rhodesian, August Musurugwa, and first recorded by his African Dance Band of the Cold Storage Commission of Southern Rhodesia (later the Bulawayo Sweet Rhythm Band). This hit was eventually released as sheet music in seventeen European and African languages; in the United States, it topped the Lucky Strike Hit Parade in 1954, in a rendition by Louis Armstrong titled "Happy Africa." As for *mbaqanga*, South Africa's own jazz, there is no more characteristic a composition than Miriam Makeba's "*Patha Patha* 'Touch Touch'," the signature tune of a popular and playfully sexy dance of the 1950s.

As the example of *marabi* proves, much of what was African in local jazz was bubbling up from the music of migrants, urban workers, and people of the "location" streets—music performed in shebeens, in workers' hostels, in community halls, at backyard feasts, at weddings. At least as early as the Great War, Zulu workers arriving in Durban from smaller communities in Natal formed male choirs, modeled on church and school concerts, amateur coon variety shows (*isikunzi*), and Caluza's ensembles. The music of these choirs, a blend of ragtime and indigenous part singing, was first known as *ingoma ebusuku* 'night music', after all-night competitions among choirs. Performers wore matching blazers and sharply pressed trousers, and made synchronous movements with their arms, torsos, and bodies. Their styles of step dancing—*isicatamiya*, and later *cothoza 'mfana* (Zulu) 'sneak up, boy'—later became standard terms for the music and dance of Zulu workers' choirs (Erlmann 1991:156–174). By the 1940s, a range of styles within that idiom had evolved. The most traditional were the *mbombing* choirs, named after loud, high-pitched, choral yells, sung antiphonally with low-pitched parts, said to imitate the whine of bombs falling from airplanes in newsreels of World War II. The most sophisticated were the songs of Solomon Linda, a brilliant composer and arranger, whose Original Evening

Birds were the acknowledged champions of *isicatamiya*. Under the title "Wimoweh" (a mnemonic for the guitar vamp, which survived American transformation), Pete Seeger and the Weavers later rearranged and recorded his hit song "*Mbube* 'Lion'." Because of its popularity, *mbube* survived for many years as a term for a style of Zulu male singing.

The same rhythm that found its way to America in "Wimoweh" put a characteristic stamp on South African jazz through the interposition of *kwela*, a style of street jazz that sprang up in the 1940s. While several etymologies compete in explaining this term (which in its aspirated form, *khwela*, means 'to climb on' in both Zulu and Sotho), there is a clear association with petty criminality, youth gangs, and other forms of socially resistant street life. The central instrument of a *kwela* ensemble, the pennywhistle (a six-hole fippled metal recorder or flageolet), has antecedents in the *phalafala* and other indigenous aerophones. Its most noticeable early appearance in South Africa seems to have been with fife-and-drum corps of Scottish regiments, which paraded in Johannesburg and Pretoria during the Second Boer War. Early in the 1900s, groups of young Northern Sotho domestics and street toughs known as *amalaita* formed their own pennywhistle-and-drum bands, and on weekends marched in the streets. Later, the pennywhistle became the favored instrument of proletarian hustlers and crapshooters, who, whenever the police pickup van, known as a *kwela-kwela*, passed by, would hide their dice, and take out their pennywhistles for an innocent-looking jam session.

"OUR KIND OF JAZZ": *MBAQANGA*

During the 1940s and 1950s, for the coins of admiring passersby, aspiring young musicians (many only ten years old), formed street bands to play pennywhistles, acoustic guitars, and one-stringed washtub basses. Their music was *kwela*, a blend of American swing and the African melodies and guitar-vamp rhythms of the "locations." *Kwela* became a popular downscale version of *mbaqanga*, and eventually several of its most talented pennywhistle soloists found their way into recording studios. Since no system for paying royalties to black musicians existed in South Africa until 1964, they made little money; but they did achieve publicity. Famous pennywhistle virtuosos included Spokes Mashiyane (whose revenues from recording helped build Gallo into South Africa's largest recording company), and Little Lemmy Mambaso (who, when, in 1960, the black musical *King Kong* toured to London, played for Queen Elizabeth II). *Kwela* featured an ostinato vamp sequence of chords (C–F–C–G^7) on guitar, under a pennywhistle melody divided into an antiphonal AABB phrase pattern. This pattern also occurs in *mbaqanga*; its phrasing originates in traditional Nguni songs, which consist of a single musical sentence divided into two phrases (Kirby 1937:286–288). *Kwela* studio bands typically featured a soloist backed by four pennywhistles playing the theme in unison, plus bass and drums. In the early 1950s, Aaron "Jake" Lerole used such a unit to record his classic *kwela* hit, "Tom Hark," a song that made hundreds of thousands of pounds for Gallo, and became popular in Britain in a version by Ted Heath, a clarinetist. Many studio reed players got their start as pennywhistlers, and even the famous virtuosos eventually wound up in the studios playing saxophone *mbaqanga*. In the early 1990s, Mambaso and Lerole still made a living that way. Spokes Mashiyane said the simplicity of the pennywhistle allowed him greater freedom to bend and blend notes in the near-vocalized African manner. Improvised jazz solos on recordings such as "Kwela Kong" attest to Spokes' genius for making an aesthetic virtue out of technical limitations: he acrobatically shaded, warped, and vocalized a torrent of timbres and tones.

Black studio musicians had at first little respect for the street pennywhistlers, but the latter's popularity forced acceptance and encouraged musical exchange. By the

Under "separate-amenities" legislation, black and white musicians could not perform together, or play for multiracial audiences, without special permits.

late 1950s, a blend of *kwela*, *mbaqanga* and American big-band jazz, had emerged in recordings such as "Baby Come Duze" by Ntemi Piliso and the Alexandra Allstar Band. That form of *mbaqanga*, sometimes known as *majuba* (after the Jazz Maniacs' recording of the same name), characterized South African jazz at its popular height. American jazz was also popular, especially among sophisticates. In the United States, the big bands were dying out, and jazz as a broadly popular music was in decline.

These developments influenced black South African jazzmen profoundly, and the honor roll of local musical giants such as Kippie "Morolong" Moeketsi, Dollar Brand, Mackay Davashe, Elijah Nkonyane, Sol Klaaste, Hugh Masekela, Jonas Gwangwa, Chris MacGregor (a white pianist and leader of a multiracial band), and Gideon Nxumalo is too lengthy to summarize here. Female singers (such as Miriam Makeba, Dolly Rathebe, Abagail Khubeka, Peggy Phango, and Thandi Klaasens) and close-harmony quartets (such as the Manhattan Brothers and LoSix) helped maintain the popularity and compositional productivity of both *mbaqanga* and American-style vocal jazz.

A series of jam sessions organized at the Odin Cinema by the Modern Jazz Club in Sophiatown, a vigorous black suburb known as Johannesburg's "Little Harlem," epitomized and energized interest in American mainstream jazz. As in the United States, smaller units, such as Mackay Davashe's Shantytown Sextet and the King Force Quintet (Wilson Silgee's successor to the Jazz Maniacs), were replacing big bands. Those ensembles played bebop *mbaqanga*, combining the melodic and rhythmic motifs and two-part, two-repeat phrasing of the latter with the virtuosic improvising of the former. Almost indistinguishable from their American counterparts were the Jazz Epistles, featuring Dollar Brand on piano, Hugh Masekela on trumpet (figure 4), Jonas Gwangwa on trombone, and Kippie Moeketsi on clarinet and alto saxophone. Except for Moeketsi, who toured to London only with Mackay Davashe's Jazz Dazzlers Orchestra and *King Kong* in 1960–1961, these players, and a good many others of South Africa's most prominent musicians, fled from apartheid into exile, where they enjoyed outstanding careers overseas. Most of the Jazz Epistles, Miriam Makeba, all four of the Manhattan Brothers, drummer Louis Moholo, singer Letta Mbuli, composer and author Todd Matshikiza, and countless other stars settled outside South Africa. Their decision to leave the country was not based on the declining popularity of jazz. Despite their departure, the 1960s saw spirited developments in South African jazz. During the first half of the decade, a series of major "Cold Castle" jazz festivals, sponsored by South African Breweries in Soweto, helped focus urban blacks' attention on established and rising vocalists and players.

BLACK SHOW BUSINESS UNDER APARTHEID

Voluntary exile was a response to increasingly restrictive conditions imposed by the Nationalist Party government, which came to power in 1948 and set about implementing a system of rigid measures to enforce the separation of the races. Under

FIGURE 4   A jazz concert in Sophiatown, 1950s;
center stage, trumpeter Hugh Masekela.

"separate-amenities" legislation, black and white musicians could not perform together, or play for multiracial audiences, without special permits. To make way for white settlement, the government removed black suburbs close to urban centers, which had often served as centers of black cultural life. The residents relocated to distant new townships. In the late 1950s, Sophiatown was bulldozed out of existence—at its cultural and political apogee. In 1960, the musical *King Kong*, based on the downfall of black heavyweight boxing champion Ezekial "King Kong" Dhlamini, appeared. It was a result of collaboration between African performers and composers and white directors, choreographers, and producers. It featured the music of Todd Matshikiza, with arrangements by Stanley Glasser, Mackay Davashe's swinging Jazz Dazzlers Orchestra, Miriam Makeba, and the Manhattan Brothers' Nathan Mdledle in the leading roles, and a host of Johannesburg's top black performers. With both black and white audiences in Johannesburg, it was a big success; it served to define an era, in opposition to the government's good-fences-make-good-neighbors vision of apartheid. But when the show toured to London, many members of the cast chose to stay abroad, and returnees found the basis of black show business had severely eroded. Cut off from the city, the black communities like Soweto turned inward, and dissention and violence plagued concert and dance hall stages. Beginning in the 1960s, community halls, and even the black cinemas in Johannesburg, where African music was staged, instituted a no-dancing policy, lest physical high spirits lead to physical violence.

Frustrated in one direction, black popular musicians turned their energies in others. Neotraditionalists were still active, and electric amplification of their favored instruments provided opportunities for increased technical sophistication, a broader range of outside influences, and access to a wider popular audience. In the 1960s, the guitar became the dominant instrument in all Western popular music. In West and Central Africa, syncretic styles of guitar playing, such as highlife and Congo beat, dominated local scenes. In South Africa, a new electrified-guitar *mbaqanga* (accordion, violin, pennywhistle-cum-saxophone, backed by electric bass and trap drums) emerged, also known by the American loanword "jive." Musically, *mbaqanga* jive borrowed from the old *mbaqanga* and *tsaba-tsaba* to create a new up-tempo rhythm, played in 8/8 time on high hat, but with a strong internal feeling of 2/4 and syncopated accents on offbeats. The melodic theme was in the bass, which, with the back-up vocalists, became the lead instrument, representing the chorus in traditional vocal

This format became known as *simanjemanje* ("now-now things"), a form that at once celebrated and burlesqued Western manners, material culture, and indigenous heritage.

music. The lead guitar, saxophone, violin, accordion, and solo vocal took the upper parts in antiphonal fashion. The phrase structure was the familiar AABB repeat of the old *mbaqanga*. Hence, the sound of *mbaqanga* jive derived more from traditional and neotraditional African music than from the earlier, more Western and jazz-influenced *mbaqanga* of the 1950s. The leading figures in its innovation and development were Simon Nkabinde, a Swazi composer and vocalist (known as Indoda Mahlathini), and John Bhengu, a Zulu guitarist (known as Phuzhushukela).

The audience for this music was not the sophisticated, English-speaking, urbanized, American-jazz and popular-ballad fans of "Little Harlem," but the thousands of semiliterate domestic servants, industrial workers, and mineworkers who retained rural values. With the clearing of the "locations" under the group-areas legislation of the early 1950s, influx-control regulations reinforced the migrant-labor system, and denied most recent arrivals the right to bring their relatives, or to settle permanently in urban areas. In the same decade, the Land Acts of 1913, 1936, and 1945, which had reserved 87 percent of South Africa's territory for white ownership, uprooted and impoverished rural life. The remaining 13 percent became the basis for the infamous "Bantustans" or homelands, which South Africa began to declare independent, starting in 1963 with the Transkei. The government pursued on a new level the policy of preventing the formation of either a stable urban work force or a landed rural peasantry. By law, many black South Africans found themselves citizens of reserves they had never seen.

In such an atmosphere, urban workers turned their eyes from the ecological devastation, poverty, and hopelessness of their rural districts. In sound, text, and choreographic display, the music they preferred, *mbaqanga* jive, provided symbolic images of once independent African cultures, in which men and women possessed their full *ubuntu* (Zulu) 'humanity'. Indoda Mahlathini had a thrilling bass register, which he employed to develop the role of solo male "groaner" in front of a chorus of four female voices, the legendary Mahotella Queens. Mahlathini and his Queens developed a kind of variety show, which included fast changes among traditional dance movements in beads, feathers, and skins; athletic turns in shorts, sneakers, and baseball caps; and svelte ballads in evening dress. This format for *mbaqanga* became known as *simanjemanje* ("now-now things"), a form that at once celebrated and burlesqued Western manners, material culture, and indigenous heritage. Phuzushukela, who combined electrified Zulu guitar with bass, drums, saxophones, and all-male backup singers, dressed his band entirely in traditional Zulu leopard skins.

The texts of Mahlathini's songs created a vision of an autonomous rural African past, when people daily honored cohesive moral and political values, not just in the breach, but in the observance. The songs favorably compared these values to the supposed individualism and immorality of "now-now," but the comparison was less important than Mahlathini's presentation of forceful images of a heroic, independent African past, and of a self-sufficient African idyll. In the face of dependency and dehumanization, these images contributed to a sense of resistant nationalism and self-regard, and were less a mystification of African tradition than a mobilization of its remaining psychocultural resources. By the late 1960s, the major recording companies had recruited or formed dozens of *simanjemanje* ensembles, which sang in a variety of local languages, each with a groaner and a chorus. Until the mid 1970s, *simanjemanje* dominated sales of locally made recordings and the airwaves of the African-language services of the South African Broadcasting Corporation ("Radio Bantu"). Concerts and extended tours of groups like Mahlathini's, sponsored by their recording companies, were among the most frequent professional performance events for blacks. Educated Africans cared little for these events and preferred jazz or the rock and soul arriving from North America and England.

In 1954, the proceeds from a farewell concert for Father Trevor Huddleston, a social activist, went to set up, at Dorkay House in Johannesburg, a permanent home for the Union of Southern African Artists, a multiracial organization, which, in the "Dorkay Jazz" series of the late 1950s, first brought local jazz players and jazz singers to large white audiences, and produced *King Kong*. One Dorkay associate, Gibson Kente, a songwriter from the eastern Cape, who had studied social work at the Jan Hofmeyr School (Cape Town), took from *King Kong*'s success inspiration to start a theatrical company in Soweto. In 1963, his first production, *Manana, the Jazz Prophet*, introduced urban black audiences to musical theater with a mix of energetic dance-melodrama and solo and choral *mbaqanga*, backed by a swinging band. Over the years, his music style created an audience for theater in the black townships. The training he gave his cast produced a new generation of black theatrical performers, many of whom went on to create important companies and productions of their own. While he continued to produce major works, his disciples brought to international attention the energy of his music and dance. Mbongi Ngema, creator of *Sarafina!*, a success in 1988–1989, both in Johannesburg and on Broadway (New York), trained under him.

During the 1970s, township-jazz musical theater expanded to become the preeminent local showcase for new black talent. The *simanjemanje* style of *mbaqanga* or *mqhashiyo* (Zulu) 'fly off, like chips from the ax', as people then called it, continued to command a large following, rivaled only by imported Anglo-American popular hits, and by the latest and most professionally polished and talented of the *cothoz' mfana* or *isicatamiya* groups, Ladysmith Black Mambazo. People consider the leader of that group, Joseph Shabalala, a masterful composer and singer. Ladysmith Black Mambazo, who usually performed *a cappella* and in Zulu, were among the top-selling groups in South Africa, more than a decade before Paul Simon, an American musician, recruited them for his *Graceland* album and tour of 1986. In 1987, they won a Grammy, for best folk album (*Shaka Zulu*).

Another phenomenon of the late 1960s and 1970s whose popularity lasted two decades was the group Malombo, a unique fusion of the indigenous African musics of northern South Africa and progressive, "free" jazz and rock influences from North America. Malombo began with Philip Thabane on guitar, Abbie Cindi on flute, and Julian Bahula on African drums; but the band soon divided. For ten years, Thabane, the guiding genius of the group, and originator of its style, teamed up with Gabriel Mabee Thobejane, percussionist and dancer. They derived their vocals, melody, and percussion from the Northern Sotho, Amandebele, and Venda cultures of the Transvaal; and they took guitar arrangements and improvisatory style from such Americans as Wes Montgomery and John McLaughlin. Their music, though not explicitly political, came to occupy a special place in the vanguard of local progressive music, where it embodied a blend of African cultural nationalism and modernism known as the Black Consciousness Movement. Other groups that performed in the

Another innovator was Jonathan Clegg, a young white folk guitarist, who learned the Zulu language and Zulu traditional and neotraditional guitar playing.

Malombo style, such as Dashiki, were explicitly political; they played at rallies of the South African Students Organization. Curiously, Malombo established a loyal following among young white listeners. They probably spent more time touring in the United States than any other South African band. In the 1980s, Thobejane teamed up with Sakhile, an African jazz-fusion group, while Thabane recruited two young percussionists to carry on Malombo, who recorded their latest album, *Uhh!*, in New York and London (figure 5). The Malombo style, though a singular sensation in South African music, influenced other, more mainstream, jazz-fusion groups: Sakhile, Bayete, Amampondo, and Malopoets.

In the late 1970s, *simanjemanje*'s market dominance declined, as working-class listeners demanded a more worldly and less ethnically oriented music to accompany their political demands. The most successful new groups were local interpreters of popular international soul and reggae styles, though few could compete with Earth, Wind, and Fire; or with Bob Marley; or with Harold Melvin and the Blue Notes. "Wake Up Everybody," the last-named group's soul hit, was among the popular anthems of the Soweto Uprising of 1976–1977. Among the South African groups who managed to compete with the imports were soul-*mbaqanga* singers Babsi Mlangeni, Steve Kekana, Mparanyane, and the Soul Brothers. That blend of *mbaqanga* and American pop and soul led to the main musical developments and commercial successes in township music in the 1980s.

Among the most significant developments outside the "township soul" and the reggae mainstream was a revival of slow-tempo *marabi*, effected by pianist Dollar

FIGURE 5   The author, David Coplan, performing with Malombo; percussionist Gabriel Thobejane; guitarist Philip Thabane.

Brand (now Abdullah Ibrahim) on his album *Mannenburg.* His success inspired older jazz pioneers, such as Zakes Nkosi, Victor Ndlazilwane, and Ntemi Piliso, to return to the studio, and younger jazzmen, such as pianist Pat Matshikiza (Todd's nephew), guitarist Sandile Shange, and saxophonist Barney Rachabane, to record in the older style. Meanwhile, mainstream jazz musicians, such as Winston Mankunku Ngozi and Michael Makgalemele, helped revive the local popularity of American jazz, with arrangements of local melodies on landmark albums, *Yakhal' Inkomo* and *The Bull and the Lion.* At local festivals, a style of soul and jazz fusion with only few local characteristics attained considerable popularity, because of the musical excellence of representative groups such as the Drive, Spirits Rejoice, and the Jazz Messengers.

Another innovator was Jonathan Clegg, a young white folk guitarist, who, from fatherly mentors at Johannesburg's Wemmer Hostel for black migrant industrial workers, learned the Zulu language and Zulu traditional and neotraditional guitar playing. Among his close associates was young Sipho Mncunu, a domestic worker, dance-song composer, dance-team leader, and neotraditional guitarist from Zululand, with whom he formed Juluka, a group that combined Anglo-American folk with Zulu traditional and neotraditional music and instruments. A fine dancer and team leader, Clegg introduced multiracial Zulu dancing and stick fighting to South African audiences. Influenced by guitarist Phuzushukela, Juluka began their recording career in the Zulu *mbaqanga*-jive style, and soon evolved toward a more international form of Zulu rock. South African Broadcasting banned Juluka's recordings, stating that Clegg was insulting the Zulu people by claiming to play their music; but the ban did not prevent the Zulu monarch, King Zwelethini, from appointing Clegg a "royal minstrel." After the 1970s, Mncunu and Clegg split up, and Clegg achieved success with his new Zulu hard-rock ensemble, Savuka. Through statements, political songs, and leadership in the South African Musicians Association, Clegg maintained his good faith with the freedom movement in South Africa. He and his fellow members of Juluka and Savuka represented a new wave of musically bicultural black and white musicians, whose success signaled the emergence of a national South African popular culture.

The 1980s in South Africa saw an effloration of popular groups and musicians, fueled by the dramatic improvement in locally available electronic musical technology, and by a new international interest in African popular music. The styles described here maintained a particular following, and stars such as Ladysmith Black Mambazo, Jonathan Clegg, Mahlathini, Sakhile, and Ray Phiri's *mbaqanga*-rock band Stimela developed a diverse national audience. The most popular representatives of local music were the township funk-rock groups playing what people commonly call "bubblegum," a term that identifies the youthful, bouncy, top-40, party-music aspect of balladeers and funk-dance bands, though it suggests nothing of their stylistic innovations, or political lyrics and musical metaphors. The top township party-dance groups in the early 1990s were Brenda Fassie (with or without the Big Dudes), Steve Kekana, Chicco, Yvonne Chaka Chaka, Lazarus Kgakgudi, Condry Ziqubu, and Sipho "Hot Sticks" Mabuse. In the 1970s, it was the last, working with the group Harari, who developed the blend of South African rhythm and melody with "progressive" American rock music that became the basis for the most profound of the bubblegum artists. Since 1988, Chicco and Condry Ziqubu produced powerfully political songs about friends and relatives in exile, police brutality, and communal concerns like drunkenness and domestic violence. Sipho Mabuse's album *Chant of the Marching* was banned in South Africa. The music proved more experimental and inventive than many more "serious" listeners might have expected, and there was no music more danceable than the heavy-bass and synthesizer-bubblegum version of the old township rhythm.

Township theater, with its music-and-dance component, remained the most potent form of the artistic expression of black South African social experiences and aspirations.

White South African bands kept current with international trends, and several, following the lead of Jonathan Clegg, blended local African influences into rock. Among Afrikaners, the popular social commentary of balladeer David Kramer led to the appearance of outré hard-rock and blues bands, such as the Kerkorrels and Gereformeerde Blues Band, who shocked conservative Afrikaner parents, but delighted their offspring.

The old traditions of choral dance music, continuing to flourish in performance among black South Africans, played an important role in the mobilization of the antiapartheid movement. The Congress of South African Trade Unions, and other major organizations, sponsored frequent cultural days and festivals, when amateur groups, through political dance and song, gave audiences emotional inspiration and unifying catharsis. Township theater, with its music-and-dance component, remained the most potent form of the artistic expression of black South African social experiences and aspirations. Meanwhile, the international focus on South Africa, and Paul Simon's Graceland project, gave greater recognition to South African performers. Celebrated artists in exile, such as Hugh Masekela and Miriam Makeba, revitalized their careers. In the early 1990s, these artists, plus Abdullah Ibrahim, returned home and achieved success in local tours.

REFERENCES

Andersson, Muff. 1981. *Music in the Mix.* Johannesburg: Ravan Press.

Coplan, David B. 1985. *In Township Tonight! South Africa's Black City Music and Theatre.* London and New York: Longman. Johannesburg: Ravan Press.

———. 1988. "Musical Understanding: The Ethnoaesthetics of Migrant Workers' Poetic Song in Lesotho." *Ethnomusicology* 32:337–368.

Erlmann, Veit. 1991. *African Stars.* Chicago: University of Chicago Press.

Kirby, Percival R. 1937 [1967]. "The Musical Practices of the Native Races of South Africa." In *Western Civilization and the Natives of South Africa,* ed. I. Schapera, 131–140. New York: Humanities Press.

Mthethwa, Bongani. 1980. "Zulu Children's Songs." In *Papers Presented at the Symposium on Ethnomusicology: Rhodes University, Grahamstown, October 10–11, 1980,* ed. Andrew Tracey, 23–25. Grahamstown: Rhodes University.

Glossary

Words beginning with special characters are alphabetized according to pronunciation:

6 follows *b*

ɗ follows *d*

ə follows *e*

ɔ follows *o*

ʋ follows *v*

Page numbers in *italic* type indicate pages on which illustrations appear.

ORTHOGRAPHY

ɛ or ę = "eh" as in **bet**

ɔ or ǫ = "aw" as in **awful**

ŋ or ṇ = "ng" as in **sing**

γ or yg = "ch" as in German **ach**

ʃ or ṣ = "sh" as in **sh**out

6 = implosive "b"

ɗ = implosive "d"

! = click sound

ˊ = high tone

ˋ = low tone

^ = high-low tone

˜ = nasalized sound

---

abaphakathi South African popular performers whose competence and versatility secured a free existence for them (336, 337)

abaqhafi "Street cowboys" who wandered South African cities and played Zulu guitar songs (318, 343)

aboakyere Festival of the Brong and Effutu of Ghana, in which local residents may criticize the chief (45)

abofoo Dance performed by Akan hunters to cleanse the hunter who killed the animal (44)

adaha Style of highlife that grew out of colonial military-band music (121)

adakem Struck box idiophone of West Africa (80)

àdàmọ̀ Yoruba pressure drum (172, 174, 179, 182)

adhan North African Muslim call to prayer (192)

aerophone Musical instrument whose sound is produced by vibrating air, often a column of air (9)

Afã Ewe god of divination (160)

Afikpo A people living in Nigeria (157)

African Fiesta A brass-heavy big band that became publicly acclaimed in Congo and Zaïre in the 1950s and 1960s (87, 122)

African Jazz Joseph Kabasele's band, which defined and popularized Congo-Zaïre rumba (85, 86–87, 110, 122)

Afrikaans Language spoke by the Afrikaner people of South Africa (3, 335)

afrobeat Yoruba musical genre deriving in the late 1960s from highlife, jazz, and soul, and influential in *jùjú* and *fújì* (87, 180, 181–82)

afrodisco A disco-based style of African music, influenced in the 1980s by Angelique Kidjo (120)

afrojazz A style of jazz popular in Africa in the mid-1990s (126)

afroma A style of jazz popular in Africa in the mid-1990s (126, 134)

agbegijo Masquerade of the Yoruba people of Nigeria (159)

agbekor Energetic dance of the Anlo-Ewe of Ghana, employing intricate steps (47)

aggu (pl. ***aggutan***) Tuareg griot of the artisanal caste, who performs music professionally (196, 202–203, 219)

agídìgbo (1) Large box-resonated Yoruba lamellophone that resembles a Cuban lamellophone; (2) Yoruba version of konkoma music, brought to Lagos by Ewe and Fanti migrant workers (80, 159, 172, 174, 177)

agogo 'Iron bell', struck clapperless bell of the Yoruba of Nigeria that plays the timeline (159, 174, 179, 183)

Agona An Akan-speaking people of Ghana (161)

ahá Yoruba idiophone made from a gourd cut in half (173)

ahal A courtship gathering that features love songs, poetical recitations, jokes, and games of wit (208–209)

ahelli Nocturnal festival dance of Gourara, Algeria (199)

ahidus (also ***haidous***) Berber dance of the middle and eastern High Atlas (199)

ahwash Berber dance of the western High Atlas (199)

Aïr Subgroup of the Tuareg, nomadic peoples of the Sahara and Sahel regions of Africa (141, 206)

ajísáàrì Yoruba music customarily performed before dawn during Ramadan by young men associated with neighborhood mosques (182)

akadinda A xylophone of the Buganda in Uganda, having seventeen to twenty-two notes, played by several players, and associated with the court (232, 233)

Akan A people speaking the Akan language in Ghana, West Africa (161–63)

Akim An Akan-speaking people of Ghana (161)

akpewu Music of the Ewe, dominated by the clapping of hands or wooden clappers (160)

Aksumite Empire (or **Axum**) A political structure centered in territory that has become the modern state of Ethiopia (25)

àkúbà Yoruba conga, based on Latin American prototypes (172, 174, 177)

Akwamu An Akan-speaking people of Ghana (161)

Akwapim An Akan-speaking people of Ghana (161)

aladura 'Owners of prayer', an indigenous Yoruba syncretic religious movement (5)

algaita (also ***algeita***) Oboe of the Hausa and other peoples in North Africa (147)

aliwen Nuptial song performed by women in the Ahaggar and Tassili-n-Ajjer regions of Algeria (224)

Alur A people of Uganda (233)

amadikh Tuareg panegyric poetry sung in praise of the prophet Muhammad (225)

amadinda Twelve-key log xylophone of the Ganda style in Uganda; two players sit on each side of it (234)

amakonde[e]re Royal trumpet ensemble of the Buganda in Uganda (234, 252)

Ambassadeurs Internationales, Les Name of Les Ambassadeurs after 1978, when it moved to the capital of Côte d'Ivoire (119)

Ambassadeurs, Les Twelve-piece band established by Salif Keita in Mali for combining modern urban pop with indigenous African instruments and Islamic vocals (89, 119)

Amhara Peoples who speak the Amharic language of Ethiopia (231)

ammessad Berber singer-poet who performs for *ahidus* and *ahwash* (199)

analytical records Recordings in which each performer plays separately so that parts can be more easily transcribed (34)

Anlo-Ewe A subgroup of the Ewe-speaking people of the southeast coast of Ghana (161)

anzad (also *anzhad*; *imzad*) Tuareg one-stringed fiddle (207–14, 222)

àpàlà Yoruba musical genre that originated in the Ijẹbu area, probably in the early 1940s (172, 173–75, 183)

apesin Single-membrane cylindrical drum of the Yoruba of Nigeria (159)

apoo Festival of the Brong and Effutu of Ghana, in which participants may criticize the chief (45)

aquaquam Ecstatic liturgical dance performed in the Monophysite Christian Church of highland Ethiopia (235)

arabi Genre of Algerian popular music (201)

Aro-Chuku oracle Final arbiter for intertribal strife among the Igbo of Nigeria (156)

arokas Tuareg dance performed in the Agadez area of Niger (226)

Asantehene Paramount ruler of a confederation of provincial chiefs in Ghana (162)

Asen An Akan-speaking people of Ghana (161)

Ashanti An Akan-speaking people of Ghana (161)

aṣíkò Yoruba dance-drumming style of early *jùjú*, performed mainly by Christian boys' clubs (176)

asonko Percussion logs played to accompany recreational music by the Akan of Ghana (163)

assakalabu (also *aghalabo*) Tuareg gourd upturned in a basin of water and struck with sticks (217, 218, 222–23)

atenteben Bamboo flute played by Akan peoples of Ghana (163)

atumpan Asante single-headed barrel drums played in pairs tuned a perfect fourth apart (162)

axatsevu Ewe music dominated by rattles (160)

azan Muslim call to prayer (56, 57, 65, 66, 67)

Azande (1) A people living in the Central African Republic and Zaïre; (2) A people of southern Sudan, living south of the Bongo (262–63)

azel (pl. *izlan*) Tuareg air composed for performance on the *anzad* (210)

azri Genre of modern Moroccan popular music (202)

baakisimba National dance of the Baganda, most commonly performed for feasts (237)

BaBenzele A Pygmy people of Central Africa (268)

bala A Mande xylophone with wooden keys fastened to a frame of gourd resonators (37, 88–89, 118, 144, 165)

balangi Manding xylophone with fifteen to nineteen keys (144)

Bamana (also **Bambara**) A northern Mande-speaking people of Mali (143)

Bambara A trade language of Senegal, developed from the Mande subfamily of the Niger-Congo family (2)

bambaro (also *bamboro*) Hausa and Songhai lamellophone (147)

Banda Culture group in the Central African Republic (266)

BaNgombe A Mongo people of Zaïre (268)

bangwe Equiheptatonically tuned Sena zither (321)

Bankalawa A Plains Jawara people of northern Nigeria (47, 50)

Bantous, Les A brass-heavy big band that became publicly acclaimed in Congo and Zaïre in the 1950s and 1960s (122)

Bantu Group of more than five hundred languages in central and southern Africa (245)

Baoulé An Akan-speaking people of Ghana (161, 163)

bappe Senegalese five-stringed plucked lute (143)

baroud (also *berzana*) North African men's dance with guns, climaxed by synchronized shooting toward the earth (200)

bāsān-kōb (also *basamkub*) Five-stringed lyre of the Hadendowa of eastern Sudan

basarake Titled Nyamalthu men of the former Bauchi State in Nigeria (46)

bàtá Yoruba ensemble of conical, double-headed drums, associated with the thunder god Sango (159, 169, 183)

bavugu !Kung bamboo stamping tubes (315)

Bayete Internationally acclaimed South African pan-African-playing group of the mid-1990s (126, 352)

beboka BaAka singing, dancing, and drumming (299, 303, 305)

begena (also *begana*) Amhara lyre with a box resonator (232)

Bemba A people living in Zambia (281)

bendir Tunisian single-headed frame drum, used with mizwid to accompany canticles of praise (193, 197, 199)

benga The definitive popular music of Kenya, developed by the Luo of western Kenya (89, 125)

beni (also *beni ngoma*) (1) Competitive associations in East Africa that used European instruments and stressed precision of movement; (2) Interethnic style of playing kazoos and moving associated with British marching bands from the Great War (1914–1918); (3) A synthesis of dance and competitive modes, influenced by colonial brass-band music in East Africa (13, 28, 29, 124, 234–35, 253)

bentere Gourd drums adopted by the Akan of Ghana from their northern neighbors (163)

bepha Collective visits by youthful performers sent by one chief to another among the Venda and Tsonga (318, 319)

berimbau Brazilian chordophone, possibly derived from the mbulumbumba, an Angolan gourd-resonated bow (133)

Bété A people of Côte d'Ivoire (45, 167)

bira Shona spirit-possession ceremony in which participants seek assistance from their deceased ancestors (132)

bolon Manding and Fulɓe large three- or four-stringed arched harp, associated with war (142, 143)

bomboro Fulani lamellophone (147)

boo Kpelle flute (165)

borii (also *bori*) Hausa groups organized around possession-trance performances (48, 146, 148)

Bowu Vai male masquerader in Liberia (53)

Bɔtɔndɔ Vai term for Muslim observance of Id al-Fitr (55)

braced bow A musical bow in which a thread (sometimes called a tuning noose) links the string to the bow, making the string vibrate in two sections (250, 312, 316)

bubblegum South African synthesized dance music, originating in the 1980s (129, 353)

bywoners White tenant farmers in South Africa who introduced the concertina, guitar, and violin (335)

ɓeli Vai men's secret society, Poro (52)

C-natural A Nigerian guitar-fingering pattern (77)

cabildos Cuban term for social brotherhoods of slaves (102)

call and response Structural form in which phrases performed by a soloist alternate with phrases performed by a choir or ensemble (10)

Cannon Stars Band of Bangui, Central African Republic, popular in the early 1980s (294)

Cape Coon Carnival Minstrel parades on New Year's Day in Cape Town, accompanied by jazz musicians (339)

caretta 'Fancy dance', Brazilian contredanse that influenced dancing in Yoruba *jùjú* (176)

cassuto Scrapers, particularly among Kumbundu-speakers of Angola (277, 278)

caste Rigid social class, one of which is designated for musicians in parts of West Africa (142)

chegbe Struck idiophone made of a bottle or kerosene can and played to accompany palm-wine guitar music (100)

Chewa A culture group of Malawi (44)

chihumba Ovambo eight-stringed multiple-bow lute (324)

chimurenga 'Songs of liberation', mbira-derived songs related to the uprising in Zimbabwe, or to modern Shona political processes in Zimbabwe (88, 89, 130–31)

chipendani Shona mouth-resonated braced bow with a thick handle carved onto the center of the bow (320)

chisungu Nubility rite for Bemba girls in which scenes of grinding maize and collecting potatoes are enacted (44)

Chopi A culture group of southern Africa (37, 319–20)

chordophone musical instrument whose sound comes from the vibrations of a stretched string (9)

chorumbal Transverse flute of the Fulɓe of The Gambia (143)

cisanji (also *cisaji*) Small, board-shaped lamellophones in the Shiluba area of Zaïre (280, 288–89)

Columbia Major recording label, which by the 1930s was distributing its products across Africa (115, 255)

Congo Success A brass-heavy big band that became publicly acclaimed in Congo and Zaïre in the 1950s and 1960s (122)

Cool Stars Band from Bangui, Central African Republic of the early 1980s (294)

crossrhythms Rhythms of two or more voices that create distinctively different and opposing patterns (34)

dadɛwɛ 'Bush spirit' or nature divinity of the Vai Poro society (53)

daf Moroccan frame drum (197)

Dagbamba Culture group of northern Ghana (150–51)

dagomba Kru guitar style influenced by early highlife music of Ghana (77, 101–102)

dako Community unit in Kru settlements, with territorial, dialect, and social identity (96–97)

dalūka Sudanese single-headed cup-shaped clay drum (238)

dan Nyamalthu dance of the brave in the former Bauchi State in Nigeria (46)

Dan Southern Mande culture group in eastern Liberia (Gio) and western Côte d'Ivoire (Yacouba) (164)

dance ring A circular space defined by the placement of audience and dancers (45)

dansi A non-Islamic popular music that developed in East Africa by the 1940s (124)

Daura Hausa state (49)

dayirigaba Dance of Nyamalthu or Terawa youths in the former Bauchi State in Nigeria (46)

dazoo Head of Poro activities in Vai communities (61)

Dei A people living in Liberia (165)

dende Venda braced gourd-resonated bow (319)

derbuka North African single-headed goblet-shaped drum (190, 191, 197, 202)

dhikr (also *zikr*) 'Remembrance', ecstatic ritual of the Sufi Islamic sect (68–69, 193, 225, 238)

diassare Senegalese five-string plucked lute (142, 143)

dilliara Songhai clarinet (147)

dingboku BaAka dance performed by a line of women related by residential camp or clan (300–301)

direct transcription Writing down music notation during live performances or from memory (32, 33)

djembe Wassoulou goblet-shaped drum (118)

dodo Hausa masked dancer in northern Nigeria (47)

Dogon Speakers of a Gur language in the Boundiagara region of Mali (152–53)

donno Hourglass drum adopted by the Akan from their northern neighbors (163)

doodo Songhai double-headed hourglass tension drum (147)

down the coast The area south and east of Liberia, including Fernando Po and other West African countries (98–99)

dumbah (also *dumbak*) Arabic goblet drum, used in taarab orchestras of Zanzibar in the 1950s (125)

dùndún Yoruba double-headed, hourglass-shaped, pressure drum, can produce glides of speech; a symbol of pan-Yoruba identity (169, 170, 172, 175, 178, 182)

duru Yoruba two-stringed plucked lute (158–59)

dyeli (also French *griot*) A professional musician among the Manding of Mali, often belonging to a specific caste (142)

ɗaa (Vai) Islamic fortieth-day death feast (56, 58, 69)

ɗaabo kulɛ 'Arabic voice', Vai stylistic designation for Qur'ānic recitation (54, 55, 66, 71)

ɗɔŋ (Vai) 'Song' (71)

ebenza Stick zither in the area of Nanga-Eboko in Cameroon (270)

Edo Culture group that includes the Bini and other related peoples of Nigeria (157–60)

egungun Formal theatrical association for masquerades that reincarnates deceased ancestors in Nigeria (159)

ekwe Igbo struck log idiophone (157)

emibala Drummed texts that accompany special songs addressed to specific spirits in turn (236)

engwara Kazoos made from narrow conical sections of dried gourds and played for the enswezi cult performance (236)

enswezi Cult in southern Uganda whose music is marked by the use of four drums interlocking in fast triple rhythm (236)

entenga Buganda drum chime (232, 233)

esime The intensified rhythmic section in BaAka performance (300)

Espagnol Zambian guitar tuning, D–a–d–f♯–a–c♯' (84)

Ewe A Kwa-speaking people of Ghana and Togo (159–61)

Eyuphoro Mozambican band that became internationally popular in the 1980s (134)

ǝkänzam (pl. *iǝkänzaman*) Tuareg shallow frame drum (217, 223)

ættebel Large ceremonial kettledrum, symbol of Tuareg chieftainship (223)

æzziker (from Arabic *dhikr*) Tuareg ritual music sung recollecting Allah in mosques and improvised places of worship (225)

Falasha Jewish cultural group of Ethiopia (236)

famifami Yoruba short wooden trumpet, borrowed from the Hausa famfami (158)

famo A wild and risqué version of marabi that appeared among Basotho migrants (342, 343)

fantaziya 'Fantasy', Maghrib spectacle involving choreographed movements by

horses and men, accompanied by drums (200–201)

fao Gã rattles strung with nets of beads (161)

fidao Vai ceremony of redemption held for the deceased (57, 69)

field recordings Recordings made by ethnomusicologists on location as people perform in various events (33–34)

fireman Guitar-fingering pattern associated with Kru styles (77, 101)

firqah An Egyptian kind of orchestra, whose style led to that of modern Egyptian film music (125, 255)

follay Songhai religious music (148)

Fon A people of the Republic of Benin (159–60)

fontomfrom Genre of Akan music characterized by slow, dignified movements and played by royal orchestras (44, 162)

Foulah (see **Fulɓe**)

friction bow Instrument in which scraping a stick across notches carved into the bow indirectly vibrates the string (312)

fújì The most popular Yoruba musical genre of the early 1990s, using a lead singer, a chorus, and drummers, a development from *ajísáàrì* (171, 172, 181, 182–85)

Fula, Fulani (see **Fulɓe**)

Fulɓe A pastoral people scattered throughout the western Sudan region (141–42)

Fulɓeni Hausa term for Fulɓe, used in the Central Sudanic and Voltaic clusters (141)

Gã A people of southeastern Ghana (161)

gabusi Plucked lute of the Comoro Islands (75)

gagra Higi dance that tests men's bravery (46)

Galambawa A people of northern Nigeria (47)

gambaré Soninke four-stringed plucked lute (143)

ganga (pl. *gangatan*) (1) Tuareg drum; (2) double-headed cylindrical drum played in Niger to herald the beginning and end of Ramadan; (3) northern Nigerian double-headed cylindrical drums with a snare string (147, 192, 197, 216, 223, 224, 226)

gángan Yoruba "talking drum" (173, 177)

gano Traditional BaAka legends in which Komba, the creator god, is a friend and caretaker (302)

garaya (also *gàraayàa*) Hausa two-stringed lute (146)

Gay Gaieties A Zimbabwean all-female jazz band (131)

gbee-kee Kpelle single-stringed bow-lute (165)

gbegbetêle Kpelle multiple bow-lute (165)

gbèlee Kpelle lamellophone (165)

gbo Dan funeral lament (164)

Ge'ez Liturgical language of the Christian church in Ethiopia (25)

gewel (pl. *awlu'be*) Name for a musician among the Wolof and Fulɓe of The Gambia and Senegal (142) *ghaita* Moroccan oboe (192, 193, 197, 200)

Ghorwane A large Mozambican band, with a lineup of three guitars, trumpet, sax, and percussion (127, 134)

gime Poems on religious themes and secular topics composed in Fulfulde (149)

gingiru Dogon four-stringed lute, made only by physicians and used to provide rhythm for the spirit to heal (152, 153)

gogeru Fulani one-stringed bowed lute (146)

goje (also *goge, gòjé*) (1) Hausa one-stringed bowed lute with resonating hole on the membrane, not the body; (2) Yoruba single-stringed bowed lute, made of a calabash and covered with skin (146, 149, 158–59, 172, 173)

Gola A people of western Liberia (165)

goma Men's dance with slow, precise movements, using European accoutrements, including dark glasses (235)

gomboy Dogon hourglass-shaped tension drum (153)

gome (also *gombay*) The earliest popular music of West Africa, believed to have developed in Freetown, Sierra Leone (117)

gora Southern African musical bow in which the musician vibrates the string by blowing onto a feather attached to the bow (312, 313)

gourd bow Musical bow that has as its resonator a gourd fastened to or held against the bow (312, 314)

Graceland Long-playing album released in 1986 featuring Paul Simon's crossover collaboration with South African musicians (88, 116, 129, 351, 354)

Grebo A Kru-speaking people of southeastern Liberia (166)

griot (French) West African musical specialist, usually a custodian of important historical and cultural knowledge (8)

group bow A musical bow played by three individuals and known as kambulumbumba (314)

guedra (1) Moroccan pottery drum; (2) pottery-drum-accompanied dance performed in southern Morocco (199)

gullu Kasena-Nankani cylindrical double-headed drums, played in sets of four (153)

gumbri Gnawa three-stringed lute (193)

gungonga Kasena-Nankani hourglass-shaped pressure drum, playable with flutes (153)

gurmi Hausa two-stringed plucked lute with a hemispherical calabash resonator (146)

gyile A xylophone used in Ghana (155)

Ha Cultural group of Rwanda and Burundi (251)

haddarat Moroccan female singer-instrumentalists (197)

hadj Pilgrimage to Mecca that devout Muslims are encouraged to make (54, 69, 192)

Ham (Jaba) A people of northern Nigeria (47)

Hannibal A small, independent British recording label (116)

harp, shelved type Harp found in a small area of Gabon and in southernmost Central African Republic (272–73)

harp, tanged type Azande *kundi* (264, 265–66, 273)

Hausa A people of northern Nigeria and Ghana; their language is a trade language of the region (2, 145)

Hawaiienne (French) 'Hawaiian' A tuning used by Masengo guitarists (84)

hawzi Musical genre popular in the Tell region of Algeria (201)

Haya A cultural group of Tanzania (247)

heavy-lift songs Kru mariners' songs for unloading ships and handling other hard jobs (95)

Hehe A cultural group of Tanzania (245, 246, 250)

heptatonic equitonal scale Pitch inventory with seven pitches that are equally spaced within the octave (144)

highlife Genre of West African popular music that originated in Ghana in the early 1900s featuring clarinets, trumpets, cornets, baritones, trombones, tuba, and parade drums (7, 101, 103, 175–78)

Higi A people of northern Nigeria (46–47)

Hima Pastoralists of western Uganda (239)

His Master's Voice (HMV) London-based recording label, which by the 1930s was distributing its products across Africa (80, 85, 109, 115, 124, 255)

hocket The distribution of a melody among several voices so that each voice performs only intermittent notes (154, 165, 233)

hoddu Ful6e three- to five-stringed lute (143)

horde Fulani hemispherical gourd calabash held against the chest and struck with finger rings (144, 146, 147)

hosho Shona seed-filled gourd rattle that accompanies singing, mbira dzavadzimu ensembles, and panpipes (130)

Hottentots Old European name for pastoral peoples around the Cape of Good Hope, now known as Khoi and living in South Africa and Namibia (313, 335)

Ibibio A people of Nigeria (157)

idiophone Musical instrument whose principal vibrating substance is not a membrane, a string, or the air but the material of the instrument (10)

iduffu Haya large, circular frame drum used in a Moslem ritual dance, kuzikiri (247)

igba Igbo membranophone (157)

igbá Yoruba gourd held in both hands and struck with ringed fingers (173)

Igbo (see also **Ibo**) A cultural group of southern Nigeria (156–57)

Ijo A culture group of Nigeria (157)

Ile-Ife Religious center of the Yoruba peoples (157)

ilugan (also *ilujan, ilaguan*) Tuareg spectacle involving choreographed movements of camels and men (201, 217, 224, 225)

imam Islamic teacher, doctor, scribe, musical leader, and interpreter of the Qur'ān (54)

imbutu Kumbu horn used as a chiefly emblem and considered the most sacred possession of the chiefdom (252)

imdyazn Professional musicians native to the eastern regions of Morocco (196)

imzad (also *anzad*) Tuareg bowed lute, played by women (197, 198–99, 207–208)

indunduma Zulu piano-vamp style of marabi in South Africa (342, 343)

inherent rhythms Rhythms that may be heard by a listener, but are not played as such by any of the performers (32, 33)

isicat[h]amiya Step dancing of choirs that blended ragtime and indigenous part singing in South Africa (338, 346–47, 351)

isikunzi Amateur variety shows in South Africa (346)

Island Records Company whose Mango label signed Salif Keita, launching his international career on a monumental scale (88, 119)

Ituri Forest Large tropical forest in central Africa (262, 268)

iyá'lù (also *iya ilu*) Yoruba 'mother drum', principal instrument in a Yoruba drum ensemble (158, 170, 174)

izli (pl. *izlan*) Berber songs performed for ahidus and ahwash (199)

Jabo A subgroup of the Kru-speaking peoples of Liberia (166)

jali (pl. *jalolu*) Professional musicians among the Maninka of Guinea and Mandinka of Gambia (118, 142)

jaliya-type ensembles Groups featuring a jali or professional singer (83, 90)

Jarawa A people of northern Nigeria (47)

jauje Hausa double-headed hourglass-shaped tension drum, reserved for royalty (147)

jazz bands Street bands in Kinshasha playing music unlike American jazz (109)

jeke Vai basket rattle (53, 58)

jenge BaNgombe Pygmies' men's society, featuring masking (268)

jengsi Sisaala seventeen-keyed xylophones, normally played in pairs (155)

Jie A Karamojong people of Uganda (231)

Johannesburg International Arts Alive Festival Musical festival established in 1992 to encourage experimental interchanges between international and local artists (129)

Johnny Walker Guitar-fingering pattern used in Nigeria (77)

Jola (Diola) A cultural group of the Cassamance region of Senegal (141, 143)

jongo Kasena-Nankani stamping dance (154)

Joobai Vai male masquerader (53)

jùjú (1) Yoruba tambourine; (2) Yoruba musical genre originating in Lagos around 1932 featuring a singer-banjoist, a *ṣèkèrè*, and a *jùjú* (88, 101, 111, 121, 176–81)

Juluka South African musical duo formed by Johnny Clegg and Sipho Mchunu; it disbanded in 1985 (128, 353)

kàakàakii (also **kakaki**) Hausa long trumpet, made from thin brass or metal from a kerosene tin (146, 147)

kabosa (also **kabosy**) Plucked lute of Madagascar that is identical to the qubuz, played in Arabia from about A.D. 500 to about A.D. 1500 (75, 91)

kachacha Dance that involves a set of single-headed goblet-shaped drums and sometimes a two-note xylophone (288)

k'aho Hausa horn (147)

kakoxa Two-stringed bowed lute that took inspiration from the seventeenth- or eighteenth-century Iberian stringed instruments (278, 279, 287)

kalangu Hausa double-headed hourglass-shaped tension drum, associated with butchers and recreation (146, 147)

kalela Zambian name of the genre beni (124)

kalenge Kasena-Nankani metal pails or large tins (153)

kamanja North African bowed lute, held vertically on the knee (191)

kamele ngoni Wassoulou six-stringed harp (118)

kànàngó Yoruba small hourglass-shaped drum, used singly or in sets of two or three to accompany *fújì* (183)

Karamojong A cultural group of Uganda (231, 237)

Karanga A Shona subgroup of Zimbabwe (319)

Karoo Festival Afrikaans-language musical festival, which in the mid-1990s gained mass public appeal (129)

Kasena-Nankani A cultural group of northern Ghana (153–54)

kawayawaya A central African friction bow (287)

kebele Dogon sistrum (153)

keleŋ Vai struck log idiophone (53)

kéleng Kpelle struck log idiophone (165)

kembe Lamellophone of the Mpyɛmɔ́ (Nola District, Central African Republic) (274)

kengai Vai women who supervise Sande musical activities; expert Vai dancers and singers (61, 62)

kerân-non-koning Kpelle harp-lute (165)

kerona Fulɓe two-to-nine-stringed plucked lute (143)

kete (1) Asante master drum; (2) Yoruba globular cylindrical drum (159, 162)

kha:s Braced mouth-resonated bow played by Khoikhoi women (313)

Khoisan "Click" languages of southern Africa; speakers of any of these languages (312–313)

khomba A Tsonga "turning" dance to make women fertile (44, 45)

kingi Competitive association in East Africa that emphasized precision of movement and European instruments (234–235)

kipango Board zither in the Iranga District of Tanzania, with six strings and a gourd resonator at one end (250)

kirikiri A name for Zaïrean rumba (121)

kithara Greek term for guitar (possibly via Arabic qitara) that appears in European texts from the thirteenth century (74)

Kituxe e os Acompanhantes Angolan band that performs a mix of merengue, rumba, and rural Angolan styles (133)

kologo Internal-spike lute of Ghana (91)

Komba BaAka creator god (302, 304)

komo Maninka secret society that uses wind instruments (143)

kòn-kpàla Kpelle musical bow (165)

koni Maninka four-stringed lute (143)

konîng Kpelle triangular frame zither (165)

kónkoma Kpelle lamellophone (165)

kóno Kpelle hand-held struck log idiophone (165)

konting Five-string plucked lute of the Mandinka of The Gambia (142, 143)

koŋgoma Large lamellophone with three or four metal tongues and a box resonator (53, 58, 80, 165)

kootsoo (also **kotsoo**) Fulani or Hausa single-headed hourglass-shaped tension drum (147)

kora Manding harp-lute with nineteen or twenty-one strings that traditionally accompanies singing of praises and historical songs but has been incorporated into international styles (8, 36, 37, 161, 88–89, 118, 119–20, *135*, 142, 143)

Koranko A northern Mande-speaking people of northern Sierra Leone (144)

kori Kasena-Nankani gourd drums, played in sets of two (153)

korro Dogon struck log idiophone (153)

Kɔlɔpɔ Vai male masquerader (53)

kponingbo A twelve- or thirteen-keyed log xylophone, accompanied by a struck hollow-log idiophone (*guru*) and a double-headed drum (266)

Kru Liberian speakers of Kru or Krao, a language of the Kwa group, who worked on ships up and down the West African coast (94–106)

Krusbass Yoruba two-finger guitar style in which all right-hand passages were played with the thumb and index fingers (77, 101, 176)

kuji A Nyamlthu chief in the former Bauchi State in Nigeria (46)

kukuma Hausa small one-stringed bowed lute (146)

kuma San raft zither (315)

kundi (1) Bongo anthropomorphically carved harp, probably adopted from the Azande; (2) tanged harp in the region of the Central African Republic (264, 265–66)

kuntigi Hausa one-stringed plucked lute (146, 148)

kuntiji Songhai one-stringed bowed lute (148)

kuomboka Lozi ceremony marked yearly by a procession of boats as the people migrate ceremonially to dry land (282, 322, 323)

Kuria A cultural group of Kenya (231)

Kutin A culture group of Cameroon (264)

Kuyate Originally the name of Manding families of professional musicians in Mali (142)

kwasa kwasa A name for Zaïrean rumba (110, 111, 121)

kwela A style of street jazz that sprang up in southern Africa in the 1940s and 1950s and featured pennywhistles, the precursor of mbaqanga (111, 125, 128, 347)

Ladysmith Black Mambazo South African band that achieved major international distribution partly as a result of the success of Paul Simon's album *Graceland* (116, 129, 351, 353)

lala Sistrum with small pieces of round circular gourds threaded on a stick (144)

'lawi Algerian Saharan dance performed by men striking sticks or batons (200)

lesiba Southern Sotho musical bow played by blowing air past a feather to vibrate the string (312, 317)

ligombo Hehe narrow three-stringed trough zither with a gourd resonator at one end (250)

likembe East African lamellophone, played in ensembles of up to fifteen, also known as mbira (240, 288–79)

lilandi A composite trumpet, made of seven to fourteen gourds and used in nuptial rituals in Tanzania (252)

Limba A cultural group closely related to the Temne of Sierra Leone (143)

Lingala Dominant language of Congo-Zaïre (109, 123)

litungu East African eight-stringed lyre (251)

lkmnža Moroccan alto fiddle (197)

Lobi A cultural group of northeastern Côte d'Ivoire (154)

locations Black residential areas attached to towns in South Africa (336)

LoDagaa A subgroup of the Dagari-speaking people of Ghana (154–55)

longo A central African portable, gourd-resonated xylophone (266)

Lozi Dominant cultural group of the Barotse kingdom of Zambia (282–83, 321–23)

Lucazi (also **Luchazi**) A cultural group of eastern Angola and northwestern Zambia (28–29, 282–86)

Lugbara A cultural group of eastern Angola and northwestern Zambia (44)

luma Reed pipes popular among Ituri Forest Pygmies of central Africa (268)

maazo Head of women's secret society, Sande, among the Vai (64)

mabo A hunting-related dance that was one of the most popular BaAka dances of the late 1980s (299–300, 302)

madiaba Popular music in Kinshasa from 1988, based on a variant of the rumba (110, 111)

madimba Central African gourd-resonated xylophones, probably deriving from southeast African models (278, 279)

magu'da A woman specializing in celebratory ululation in West Africa (145)

Maguzawa A people of northern Nigeria (45, 47, 49)

mahobelo Choral singing of the Sotho peoples of southern Africa (317)

Mahodi Vai term for the Muslim observance of Mawlid (55, 69–70, 72)

mahon'era (also *mahonyera*) Zimbabwean basslike singing, primarily on roots of bichords, with yodeling (130)

Mahotella Queens Female mbaqanga chorus, one of the most internationally celebrated South African groups of the 1990s (128, 350)

mai busa Performer on an aerophone in West Africa (145)

mainline Guitar-fingering pattern associated with Kru sailor styles (77, 83, 101)

majika Indigenous Mozambican rhythm that is the basis of *marrabenta* (134)

maka'di Generic term for players of membranophones, chordophones, and idiophones (145)

Makembe Band from Bangui, Central African Republic, popular in the early 1980s (294)

makhololo Venda rulers, as distinguished from common people (318)

Makonde A people of Mozambique (238)

makossa Cameroonian style of urban music (111, 120, 292)

makwaya A music whose name is derived from the word choir and featuring songs, marching routines, and special costumes (328, 337, 343–44)

malaila A genre performed in Zambia to honor a dead warrior (45)

malimba A Sena equiheptatonically tuned lamellophone (321)

Malinke A group of northern Mande-speakers of Mali, Guinea, and Côte d'Ivoire (163)

malipenga Malawian name of the genre beni (124, 235)

mamokhorong A one-stringed Basotho violin, developed in South Africa (335)

Manding Speakers of northern Mande languages (140, 143–46)

Mandingoes A group of northern Mande-speakers of Liberia (143)

Mandinka A people including the Manding, Malinke, Mandingo, and Maninka (141)

Mangbetu Speakers of a Central Sudanic language in northeastern Zaïre (265, 268)

mangologondo Makua loose-log xylophone with nine keys (249)

Maninka A group of northern Mande-speakers in Guinea and Liberia (143)

manyanga Generic Swahili name for an array of shaken seed-filled rattles, mostly calabashes or coconuts (248)

manza Zande pentatonically tuned xylophone associated with royalty (266)

marabi A South African hybrid of indigenous and urban music, dance, and context (111, 128, 341–43)

marabout An itinerant Muslim cleric who possesses special powers (68)

Margi A people of northern Nigeria (47)

marimba Box-resonated xylophone played in the islands of Zanzibar and Pemba and on the nearby mainland (248–49)

maringa (1) Variant of the palm-wine-guitar style, using more strumming and incorporating West Indian rhythms; (2) Intertribal social dance, popular on the west coast of Africa from Sierra Leone to Zaïre (77, 101, 104–105, 110–12)

marok'i (female *marok'iya*) West African professional singer of praises (145)

marokaa (also *maroka*) Nigerian Hausa singers of praises (49)

marrabenta Mozambican topical music, performed on three guitars and danced in a sexually suggestive style (134)

MASA (Marche des Arts et Spectacles Africains) Important musical trade fair held in Abidjan every other year (117–18)

masabe A Tonga dance (43)

mashaira Swahili love poetry accompanied by *taarab* music (255)

mawak'i A West African professional male singer and/or composer (145)

mbalax (Wolof) 'percussion-based music' Senegalese popular music, mixing Cuban rhythms with kora-based traditional melodies, sung in a high-pitched style (89, 119–20)

mbaqanga A South African jazz idiom that took its name from a stiff corn porridge (88, 89, 128, 130, 131, 346, 347–48)

mbila Chopi word for a xylophone key and closely related to the term *mbira*, which designates a lamellophone (326)

mbila dzamadeza Venda twenty-seven-keyed lamellophone (319)

mbila mutondo Venda twenty-one-keyed xylophone (319)

mbira Shona plucked lamellophone, played singly or in ensembles (10, 325–26, 327)

mbira dzavadzimu 'Mbira of the ancestral spirits', Zimbabwean lamellophone with twenty-two or more wide keys (31, 127, 130, 131–33)

mbombing South African choirs with high-pitched yells imitating falling bombs as seen in newsreels of World War II (346)

mbube Style of Zulu male singing in South Africa (347)

mbulumbumba Angolan gourd-resonated bow, recognized in Brazil as the berimbau (133, 324)

melekket A system of musical notation invented by Ethiopian clerics in the mid-1500s (25–27, 29, 30, 37)

membranophone Musical instrument whose sound comes from the vibrations of a stretched membrane (9–10)

Mende A people of western Liberia and eastern Sierra Leone (165)

mendzaŋ A central African xylophone (269, 270–71)

merengue A Haitian and Dominican ballroom dance, popular in Africa as a result of dissemination on gramophone records (85, 102, 122, 133)

mganda Tanzanian name of the genre beni (124, 235)

Milaji Vai term for the Muslim observance of Miraj (55, 69)

milo BaAka term for non-Pygmy dark-skinned Africans, whom the BaAka see as separate and distinct from themselves (298)

mirliton An object or membrane made to sound by the indirect action of the vibration of an instrument to which it is attached; its sound is often described as a buzz (143, 152, 158, 283)

mizwid Tunisian bagpipe, used with bendir to accompany canticles of praise (193)

mokondi General BaAka name for dances involving spirits (303)

molo Senegalese one-stringed plucked lute (47, 143, 146)

mólò Yoruba three-stringed lute, commonly used in *sákàrà* ensembles during the 1920s and 1930s (172, 173)

motengene Hip-swiveling, rib-rotating dance that is traditional among the Mbati Pygmies (292)

mɔli Sande Muslim version of a women's secret society among the Vai (61–62, 63–65, 72)

msam'at Algerian urban female professional singer-dancers (197)

msondo Cylindrical drum with pegged or tacked-on head that is played along the coast of Tanzania (247)

mucapata Lamellophone with a bell-type resonator that is probably of Cokwe or Cokwe-Mbangala invention (289)

muchongolo A Tsonga dance representing warriors' actions in battle and featuring asymmetrical rhythms (320)

mukanda Boys' age-grade circumcision schools established outside villages in central Africa (284)

mukupela Drum played only at the royal death or installation in central Africa (280, 283)

muqaddam Muslim leader of a sect (68)

musical bow Instrument having a string fastened with tension at each end of a curved stick, that can be plucked or struck (312)

Musiki Band from Bangui, Central African Republic, of the early 1980s (293–94)

musique moderne zaïroise Guitar-based music that emerged after the 1940s in the Brazzaville and Kinshasa area (110, 278, 279)

muwashshah North African court poetry, developed in Spain and having strophic texts with instrumental refrains (191)

mvet Stick zither with idiochord strings lifted from the raffia; genre of oral literature in the central African region (264, 270)

myaso yakukuwa Lucazi or Luvale songs performed at night during circumcision ceremonies, accompanied by concussion sticks (284)

nabona Kasena-Nankani side-blown ivory trumpets, usually played in sets of six or seven (153)

Nafali Vai male masquerader (53)

nagarit The emperor of Ethiopia's kettle-drums, of which forty-four pairs played in his processions (233)

nai An obliquely blown flute of Zanzibar (125)

nations Term used in Brazil for slaves' social brotherhoods (102)

native blues A guitar-playing idiom practiced in interior villages (77)

ncomane A Tsonga tambourine, played for exorcism-related rituals (321)

ndere Senegalese five-stringed lute (143)

né Mandinka bells in The Gambia (144)

nfir Moroccan trumpet (192)

nganga Musical bow of Fipa women, who live southeast of Lake Tanganyika (250)

ngodo Chopi dance cycles accompanied by large ensembles of xylophones (319)

ngoma (also *ng'oma, ngʻoma*) (1) East African performances that feature dancing with an emphasis on circular movements of the hips; (2) East African term for drums and performances; (3) 'Drum', a membranophone; a healing complex of central, southern, and parts of equatorial Africa (238, 247, 319, 322)

Ngoma Greek-owned recording studio in Kinshasa that began operating in the 1940s (83, 85, 109)

ngombi Fan term for the harp; stick zither outside the Bulu-Beti-Fan cluster (270, 273)

ngongi Double bells, which can be used only by royal ensembles of the Lozi and Nkoya of southern Africa (322)

ngorda Dance of the nobility of the former Bauchi State in Nigeria (46)

ngororombe Shona panpipes played in ensemble in hocket for entertainment (321)

ngulei-siyge-nuu 'Song-raising-person', Kpelle solo singer (164)

Nilotes Peoples of the northeast Sudan (231, 245)

njuga Swahili term that denotes a string of small iron bells that dancers wear around their ankles (248)

nkangala (also *nqangala*) Women's mouth-resonated bow, of Zulu origin (3, 128)

nkoni Bambara six- to nine-stringed harp-lute played by members of the hunter's society (143)

nono Gã clapperless iron bell (161)

notation Written use of a system of signs or symbols (24)

nsambi Central African multiple-bow lute (277)

Nsenga A subgroup of Maravi peoples of Malawi (44, 283)

nsogwe Dance of the Nsenga and the Southern Chewa after the birth of a woman's first child (44)

ntahera Set of five or seven ivory trumpets associated with Akan royalty (163)

nuba North African suite of songs: (1) Moroccan, in five movements, each in one of five rhythmic modes and performed in a fixed order; (2) Algerian, in nine alternating instrumental and vocal movements; (3) Tunisian, in ten movements (190–91)

Nyamwezi A cultural group of Tanzania (247)

nyanga Nyungwe reed-pipe dances with one instrumental tune, within which singers improvise their parts (321)

nyanyuru Fulɓe and Tukulor one-stringed bowed lute (142, 143)

nyavikali Central African trumpets (283)

nyia kulɛ (Vai) 'Fine voice' (66, 71)

nzapa The Sango term for the Christian God in central Africa (302–305)

nzumari Double-reed aerophone of the coastal Bantu peoples of Kenya (238)

oba Edo king in Benin and Nigeria (157, 158)

Odeon Major recording label, which by the 1930s was distributing its products across Africa (115, 255)

odonso Guitar-playing idiom practiced in West African villages (77)

odurugya Notched flute made of cane husk and played at the Asantehene's court (163)

Ogboni A Yoruba secret society (157)

ògìdo Yoruba bass conga, based on Latin American prototypes (172, 176, 177)

ohonji (also *onkhonji*) Nkhumbi or Luhanda term for hunting bow or mouth-resonated musical bow, braced in the center, with the end pressed against the inside of the player's cheek (324)

ohugua Guitar-playing idiom practiced in West African villages (77)

O.K. Jazz Zaïrean band that achieved international renown in the 1960s (84–85, 110, 279)

OK Success A brass-heavy big band that became publicly acclaimed in Congo and Zaïre in the 1950s and 1960s (122)

ol-tnalan Set of bells worn on elaborate leather bands by Maasai Moran (248)

Olodumare (or **Olorun**) The supreme being of the Yoruba people of Nigeria (157)

omele Yoruba 'supporting drums', which play ostinatos designed to interlock rhythmically (170)

omolu Three pot drums and two pegged cylindrical wooden drums used to worship Omolu (159)

Omolu Yoruba god of water and fertility (159)

omulanga Harpist for the ruler of Buganda in the area of Lake Victoria (232, 233)

omvɔk Note in the center of the xylophone where tuning begins, considered head of the family (270)

oorlams Popular working-class musicians who were coloured or black Africans and served as cultural brokers in South Africa (336–37)

opim Guitar-playing idiom practiced in West African villages (77)

Orchestra Ethiopia Ethiopian ensemble founded in 1963 for the modern presentation of traditional music (28, 29)

Orchestra Makassy Tanzanian band joined by Remmy Ongala in 1964 (125)

Orchestra Matimila Tanzanian band joined by Remmy Ongala in 1981, after Orchestra Makassy had disbanded (125)

Orchestra Super Matimila Tanzanian band formed by Remmy Ongala in the 1990s (125)

oriki Yoruba poetry praising an individual, a deity, a town or even an inanimate object (159, 170)

orisha (also *orisa*) Yoruba intermediate deities below the high god, Olodumare (158)

oro Yoruba secret society of night hunters, symbolized by the playing of a bullroarer (158, 159)

oud A North African plucked lute with pear-shaped resonator; a short-necked plucked lute of Zanzibar (125)

Oyo Yoruba kingdom, the most powerful coastal state that rose to prominence before 1500 (157, 169)

pachanga Cuban dance made famous in Africa by Aragon and Johnny Pacheco (111, 120)

palm-wine guitar style (also called **sea-breeze music**) Music played with a guitar and a bottle or hollowed-log idiophone (77, 100–101, 121)

pamploi Gã bamboo tubes (161)

Pathé-Marconi Major recording label, which by the 1930s was distributing its products across Africa (115)

pennywhistle A usually cheaply manufactured and sold metal whistle with several holes for fingering (100, 103–104, 128, 329, 347)

pennywhistle jive An alternate name for *kwela* (128)

pluriarc Multiple-bow lute (143, 324)

pombeiros African-Portuguese traders (278, 279, 289)

Poro General term for men's secret societies of West Africa (5, 52–53)

prempresiwa Large lamellophone with three or four metal tongues and a box resonator (80)

prescriptive transcription Notation that indicates to performers how to create specific musical sounds (32)

principle of harmonic equivalence Feature of Venda music where notes of the same harmonic series are substituted (319, 325)

Pullo, Pulo (see **Fulɓe**)

Qaddiriyya Islamic brotherhood that traces its roots to Sufi sects of North Africa (68)

qarqabu (also *qarqaba*) North African instrument consisting of two pairs of iron castanets joined by a connecting bar, one pair held one in each hand (193)

qasaba Arab flute played by Tuareg herders in Algeria and Niger (198)

qasida North African solo vocal improvisation deriving from West Asian traditions (191)

qene Ethiopian Christian religious poetry chanted in Ge'ez (235)

qitara Arabic term for guitar (74)

rabab North African two-stringed fiddle (190, 191)

rabi al-'awwal Third month of the Islamic Hijra calendar (69)

Radio Congo Belge pour les Indigènes Governmental station that opened in 1948 (109)

Radio Congo Belge First government-controlled station in Kinshasa, which opened in 1940 (109, 122)

Radio Congolia Privately owned radio station in Kinshasa, which began broadcasting in 1939 (109)

Radio-Léo Jesuit-owned radio station in Kinshasa, which broadcast 1937–1948 (109)

rai A North African Arabic style of cabaret music (120, 203)

Rail Band Guitar-based band that flourished in Mali in the late twentieth century (119)

Ramadan Islamic month of fasting (5, 54, 55)

ramkie Lute with three or four strings, played by southern Africans in Cape Town (75, 329, 335)

rika A tambourine of Zanzibar (125)

riti Wolof bowed lute with a holed gourd resonator (143)

rok'on fada Hausa state ceremonial music (148)

rommelpot European term for a Khoikhoi drum made by placing skins over a pot (313)

rways Itinerant musicians of southern Morocco who perform Arab-Andalusian, European, Arab popular, and West African acculturated styles (197)

sa'dawi Tunisian dance usually performed by women featuring hip movements and gestures with a hand-held scarf (199)

SADC Music Festival (Southern African Development Community Music Festival) A regionally cooperative festival, first held in October 1995 (126)

Sahel zone Dry borderland region between the savanna and the Sahara Desert (140)

sákárà (1) Yoruba single-membrane clay-bodied frame drum; (2) Yoruba musical genre for dancing and praising, performed and patronized mostly by Muslims (172–73, 176, 183)

salsa A Latin American musical fusion of rhythm and blues, jazz, and rock, popular in Africa as a result of dissemination on gramophone records (114, 122)

sámbà Yoruba square drum, derived from Latin American or Caribbean models and associated with immigrant black Christians (176)

San A people of southern Africa (269, 313–15)

Sandawe A cultural group of Tanzania (245)

Sande Generic term for women's secret societies in West Africa (5, 52–53)

saŋgba Vai conical single-headed drum (53)

sapeur Member of the Society of Ambienceurs and Persons of Elegance (122–23)

saransara Maguzawa feast with dancing in northern Nigeria (45)

sarewa Hausa four-holed flute, made of a reed or metal tube (147, 223)

sasa-ture Dance for chaotic social situations in the former Bauchi state, Nigeria (44, 45)

sasaa Vai gourd rattle (53, 62, 63, 64)

Savuka South African duo formed by Johnny Clegg after 1985 (129, 353)

scotchi Competitive associations in East Africa that utilized bagpipes or locally made representations for performance (234–35)

sebiba Choreographed spectacle held at the oasis of Djanet, southeastern Algeria (200)

sefala (also *sefela*) Long, musical poetic narratives developed by Sotho veteran migrants on their travels to South African mines (336)

ṣèkèrè (also *sekere*) Yoruba bottle-gourd rattle (159, 172, 176, 179, 181, 183)

sèlí (also *pèrèṣèkè*) Yoruba tin cymbals with jingles, used to accompany *wákà* (172)

Semba Tropical Angolan national orchestra, founded after 1975 by the Ministry of Culture (133)

Senegambians People living west of the Mandinka in West Africa (141)

Sensacional Maringa da Angola Angolan fifteen-piece band that performs a mix of merengue, rumba, and rural Angolan styles (133)

Senufo A Gur-speaking cultural group of north-central Côte d'Ivoire (29–30)

seŋ feŋ Vai term for instrumental performance (71)

seperewa (also *sanku*) Harp-lute of the Guinea Coast (75, 80, 91, 101, 163)

Serer A cultural group of north-central Côte d'Ivoire (141)

serndu Transverse flute of The Gambia (143)

sha'bi Genre of Maghrib popular music (201)

Shango (also *Ṣango*) Yoruba god of thunder (157, 159, 169)

shantu Hausa women's percussion tube (147)

shebeen Unlicensed bar, often a private home, where patrons gather to drink and perform music (127, 340–41, 342)

shimolo Set of bells that Chagga male dancers of Tanzania wear on their backs (248)

Shirati Jazz Band founded by D. O. Misiani to play benga (125)

simanjemanje (1) Urban dance-song type, drawing from South African choral music; (2) The soft female chorus that backs up a male "groaner" in South African mbaqanga (128, 131, 350–51)

simbing Manding six- or seven-stringed arched harp that is smaller than the *bolon* (143)

sistrum A shaken idiophone consisting of rattles attached to a stick or frame (144, 153)

Society of Ambienceurs and Persons of Elegance Trend set by the Zaïrean musician Papa Wemba, who in the 1970s culti-

vated a style of dress reminiscent of 1950s Paris fashion and eighteenth-century dandyism (122)

son Traditional musical genre of Cuba, popular in Africa as a result of dissemination on gramophone records (109, 114, 122)

Songhai A people of West Africa (145)

Soninke A group of Mande-speakers of northern Mali (143)

sorek A dance performed during the ritual harvest-festivals of the Miri of the Nuba Mountains in Sudan (233)

soron Maninka harp-lute with nineteen or twenty-one strings (143)

soukous A name for Zaïrean rumba, featuring three guitar parts and a solo singer (88, 89, 110, 111, 117, 121, 122, 292)

Southern African Development Community Cooperative forum that economically and culturally links twelve countries of southern Africa (126)

staff notation Notation utilizing the lines and spaces common to the representation of Western art music (35)

Standard Bank Grahamstown Arts Festival Largest and most securely established musical festival in South Africa (129)

Sterns A small, independent British recording label (116)

suku-ba Vai professional Qur'ānic reciter (66, 70, 72)

Sunburst A Tanzanian jazz band that included native Tanzanians, African-Americans, and a Jamaican (255)

Swahili An East African cultural group; a trade language that draws on the structures and vocabularies of Bantu languages and Arabic (2–3, 123–24, 245)

taarab (Arabic 'joy, pleasure, delight') Popular coastal East African music that traditionally accompanied Swahili love-related poetry, often played at weddings (113, 124, 125–26, 239, 255–56)

tablature Notational system that places numbers or letters on a diagram that resembles the strings or keys of an instrument (36)

tahardent (1) Tuareg three-stringed lute, resembling the Mauritanian tidinit; (2) Tuareg musical genre that has become popular in Niger (196, 202, 207, 219–22, 225)

take Nyamalthu praise-name performance in the former Bauchi State in Nigeria (46)

takəmba New Tuareg genre in which seated listeners respond to rhythms with undulating movements of the torso (220–21)

talawat Moroccan flute (197)

taletenga Idioglot reed pipe of the Akan of Ghana (163)

talk-men Kru sailors who served as interpreters for their ability with pidgin English (96)

tama Double-headed, hourglass-shaped tension drum of the Western Sudanic cluster (120, 144)

tambari Hausa large kettledrum with a resonator of wood, symbolizing royalty (146, 147) *tambing* Fulɓe transverse flute (143)

tamghra Berber dance performed for or by a bride and her attendants (199)

tan Dan dance-song (164)

tar North African frame drum with attached cymbals (190, 191, 197, 202)

ta'riya Moroccan clay cylindrical drum (197)

tarompet Western cornet played in *ngoma* performances (238)

tasabia (Arabic) String of prayer beads (68)

tatarizo A scraped bamboo idiophone of southern Tanzania (248)

tazammart (also *tasansagh* and *tasensigh*) Tuareg four-holed flute, made of a reed or metal tube (198, 223–24)

tazâwat Medium-sized kettledrum, played by women in the Azawagh region of Niger (197, 222–23)

tazengherit Tuareg ecstatic music and dance, performed especially at Tazruk and Hirafok oases, Ahaggar (226)

tbel Moroccan kettledrum (193, 196, 197, 199, 200)

tegennewt Algerian kettledrum, made from a wooden or enameled metal bowl and occasionally played by the Tuareg (197, 223, 226)

tehemmet Tuareg dance of Tassili-n-Ajjer, accompanied by songs, clapping, and one or more drums (225–26)

tehigelt Tuareg dance of Ahaggar, accompanied by songs, clapping, and one or more drums (225–26)

temja Algerian six-holed wooden flute (199)

Temne A cultural group of Sierra Leone (143, 166)

tende (also *tindi*) Tuareg single-headed mortar drum (194, 201, 207, 214–19, 226)

tende n-əmnas Events where the mortar drum is played and that feature personalized references to camels (217–19)

tesîwit Pastoral Tuareg strophic poems sung solo to formulaic melodies or motifs (197, 211–13, 224)

tickey draai Dance accompanied by the guitar and popular until the 1940s in South Africa (75, 336–37, 341)

tidinit Mauritanian lute (196, 220)

Tijaniyya Islamic brotherhood that traces its roots to Sufi sects of North Africa (68)

timbila South African Chopi xylophones played in large ensembles (127, 134, 319–20)

timeline Any of several repeating rhythmic patterns underlying much West African ensemble music and usually played by a high-pitched struck idiophone, such as a double clapperless bell (174)

tirtir Chadian circular dance performed by the Zaghawa and characterized by solemn hopping

tobol Small drum played for the sebiba (200)

Tonic Sol-fa (also known as **solfège**) Verbal syllables that represent relative pitches (38)

toŋ ito Two double iron bells of the Central African flange-welded type, with a bow grip (264)

tɔmbɔ Vai word for dance (71)

tɔmbɔ kɛ bɔɔniɛ-nu Vai troupe of Sande society young initiate dancers (62, 63)

tsaba-tsaba Urban popular dance-song genre, drawing from South African choral music (346, 349)

tshikona Venda music produced by an ensemble of one-pitch pipes played in hocket (318–19)

tshizambi Venda friction bow, obtained from the Tsonga (319)

Tuareg Nomadic people of Algeria, Mali, and Niger (193, 206)

TUBS Time Unit Box System of notation, developed in 1962 for teaching African drumming (35, *36*)

tuku Single-headed wooden goblet drum that accompanied music of the Kru of Liberia (98, 99)

turu Daura dance, for which singers praise the royal ancestors (49)

túru Kpelle side-blown horn (165)

tusona Graphic configurations of dots circumscribed by lines of the Luchazi culture of Angola and Zambia (28–29)

Tutsi A cultural group of Rwanda and Burundi (239)

'ud North African four-stringed lute (190, 191)

'udi Swahili plucked lute of East Africa (75, 239)

ugubhu Zulu unbraced gourd-resonated musical bow more than a meter long (316)

ujamaa Villages that served as resettlement habitats under President Nyerere's regime in Tanzania (244)

ulimba Makonde-Mwera type lamellophone with broad iron tongues with no bridge (249)

umakhweyana Zulu gourd-resonated musical bow braced near the center (88, 316)

umngqokolo A form of overtone singing performed by Xhosa women and girls in southern Africa (316)

umrhubhe A bow played by scraping a string with a stick in southern Africa (316)

urar (also *ural*) Berber ritual verses, sung usually by women at weddings and circumcision ceremonies (196, 197)

Utamaduni Tanzanian National Dance Troupe, founded in 1964 to amalgamate music styles in Tanzania (256)

Vai (Vey) Northern Mande-speakers of northwest Liberia (51–73, 165)

valiha Wire-stringed tube zither, the best-known instrument of Madagascar; also played in Tanzania (237)

valimba A Sena xylophone in south-central Africa (321)

valimba (or *ulimba*) Gourd-resonated large xylophone of southern Malawi (321)

vodoun (vodun) Deities of the people of Dahomey (160)

Wagogo A people of central Tanzania (236)

wákà Yoruba musical genre, adopted from the Hausa and usually performed by women (172)

wala (Vai) Wooden boards on which Qur'ānic inscriptions are written (54)

Wasa An Akan-speaking people of Ghana (161)

wasan bòorii Spirit-possession dance that occurs in many Hausa communities (48)

wasan maharba Dance in which hunters reenact personal experiences of going on hunts (46, 47)

wedge-and-ring-tension drum Drum with a wedge-tensioned girdle attached to leather lacings around its body (275, 276)

Wolof A cultural group of Senegal (119, 142)

WOMAD (World of Music Arts and Dance) Festival conceived by the British rock musician Peter Gabriel in 1980 (116)

World Circuit A small, independent British recording label (116)

wua Kasena-Nankani two- or three-hole vertical flute, the most common melody-producing instrument of Ghana (152, 153)

xalam (also *halam* or *khalam*) Wolof five-stringed plucked lute (90, 142, 143)

Xhosa A cultural group of South Africa (315–17, 329, 336–40, 341, 342–343)

yabon sarakai Hausa court-praise music (148)

Yalunka A cultural group of Guinea and Sierra Leone (144)

yaponsa (from the Ghanaian song "Yaa Amponsah") Guitar-fingering pattern of Nigeria (77)

Yavi Vai male masquerader in Liberia (53)

Yellow Blues A Zimbabwean all-female jazz band (131)

Yewe Ewe god of thunder and lightning (160)

yodeling Rapid shifting between a singer's upper and lower registers (130, 245, 268, 315)

Yoruba Dominant cultural group of southwest Nigeria (158–59)

zabiya Professional female singer in West Africa (145)

zagara Tunisian dance performed by paired men brandishing swords (200)

Zaiko Langa Langa Congo-Zaïre rumba band that in the 1970s popularized soukous (122)

zajal Popular North African court poetry, developed in Spain and having strophic texts with instrumental refrains (191)

zammar Moroccan double clarinet (197)

zaowzaya Mauritanian four-holed flute, made of acacia root or bark (198)

zār Northeast African curing ceremony involving singing, dancing, and drumming (236, 238)

zekete-zekete Popular music from 1977 to 1987 in Kinshasa, based on a variant of the rumba (110, 111)

zēmā Ethiopian Christian chant liturgy (25, 235)

zendani Genre of Maghrib popular music, played and sung by urban female professionals at family festivals (202)

zeze Generic Tanzanian term for bar zithers, bows, and lutes (250, 251)

zhita Higi boys' inititiation ritual in northern Nigeria (46)

zikr (see ***dhikr***)

Zimbos, Os Angolan band that performs a mix of merengue, rumba, and rural Angolan styles (126, 133)

zlöö 'Praise song', a musical genre of the Dan of West Africa (164)

zokela An urban dance-music based in the Central African Republic city of Bangui (291–97)

Zooba Sande masked dancer who impersonates a male ancestor water-dwelling spirit (53, 59–65)

zukra Tunisian bagpipe, used to accompany a scarf dance (199, 200)

Zulu A cultural group of South Africa (316–18)

A Guide to Publications on African Music

Reference Works

Aning, Ben Akosa. 1967. *An Annotated Bibliography of Music and Dance in English-Speaking Africa.* Legon: Institute of African Studies.

Gaskin, Lionel John Palmer. 1965. *Select Bibliography of African Music.* London: International African Institute.

Gray, John. 1991. *African Music: A Bibliographical Guide to the Traditional, Popular, Arts, and Liturgical Musics of Sub-Saharan Africa.* New York and Westport, Conn.: Greenwood Press.

Greenberg, Joseph H. 1966. *The Languages of Africa.* Bloomington, Ind.: Research Center for the Language Sciences.

Guthrie, Malcolm. 1948. *The Classification of Bantu Languages.* London: International African Institute.

Merriam, Alan P. 1970. *African Music on LP.* Evanston, Ill.: Northwestern University Press.

Murdock, George Peter. 1967. *Ethnographic Atlas.* Pittsburgh: University of Pittsburgh Press.

Murray, Jocelyn, ed. 1981. *Cultural Atlas of Africa.* Oxford: Elsevier Publishers.

Stone, Ruth M., and Frank J. Gillis. 1976. *African Music and Oral Data: A Catalog of Field Recordings, 1902–1975.* Bloomington and London: Indiana University Press.

Thieme, Darius L. 1964. *African Music: A Brief Annotated Bibliography.* Washington, D.C.: Library of Congress.

Tracey, Hugh. 1973. *Catalogue of the Sound of Africa Recordings.* Roodepoort, South Africa: International Library of African Music.

Varley, Douglas H. 1936. *African Native Music: An Annotated Bibliography.* London: The Royal Empire Society.

General

Anderson, Lois Ann. 1971. "The Interrelation of African and Arab Musics: Some Preliminary Considerations." In *Essays in Music and History in Africa,* ed. Klaus P. Wachsmann, 143–169. Evanston, Ill.: Northwestern University Press.

Ankermann, Bernhard. 1901. "Die afrikanischen Musikinstrumente." *Ethnologisches Notizblatt* 3:I–X, 1–32.

Arom, Simha. 1976. "The Use of Play-Back Techniques in the Study of Oral Polyphonies." *Ethnomusicology* 20(3):483–519.

————. 1991. *African Polyphony and Polyrhythm,* trans. Martin Thom et al. Cambridge and Paris: Cambridge University Press and Editions de la Maison des Sciences de l'Homme.

————. 1992. "A Synthesizer in the Central African Bush: A Method of Interactive Exploration of Musical Scales." In *Für Gyorgy Ligeti: Die Referate des Ligeti- Kongresses Hamburg 1988,* ed. Peter Petersen, 163–178. Hamburg: Laaber-Verlag; Hamburger Jahrbuch für Musikwissenschaft, 11.

Ballanta, Nicholas George Julius. 1926. "Gathering Folk Tunes in the African Country." *Musical America* 44(23):3–11.

Bebey, Francis. 1975. *African Music: A People's Art,* trans. Josephine Bennett. Westport, Conn.: Lawrence Hill.

Blacking, John. 1955. "Some Notes on a Theory of African Rhythm Advanced by Erich von Hornbostel." *African Music* 1(2):12–20.

Bowdich, Edward T. 1821. *An Essay on the Superstitions, Customs, and Art Common to the Ancient Egyptians, Abyssinians, and Ashantees.* Paris: J. Smith.

Carrington, John. 1949. *Talking Drums of Africa.* London: Carey Kingsgate.

Collins, John. 1985. *African Pop Roots.* London: W. Foulsham.

Curtin, Philip. 1964. *The Image of Africa: British Ideas and Action, 1780–1850.* Madison: University of Wisconsin Press.

Danielson, Virginia. 1988. "The Arab Middle East." In *Popular Musics of the Non-Western World,* by Peter Manuel: 141–160. New York: Oxford University Press.

Davidson, Basil. 1966. *African Kingdoms.* New York: Time-Life Books.

Erlmann, Veit. 1981. *Populäre Musik in Afrika.* Berlin: Staatliche Museen Preußischer Kulturbesitz. Veröffentlichungen des Museums für Völkerkunde Berlin, Neue Folge 53, Abteilung Musikethnologie 8.

Faruqi, Lois I. al. 1986. "Handashah al Sawt or the Art of Sound." In *The Cultural Atlas of Islam,* ed. Isma'il al Faruqi and Lois Lamya' al Faruqi, 441– 479. New York: Macmillan.

———. 1986. "The Mawlid." *The World of Music* 28(3):79–89.

Finnegan, Ruth. 1970. *Oral Literature in Africa.* Nairobi: Oxford University Press.

Gibb, H. A. R. 1929. *Ibn Battuta, Travels in Asia and Africa.* London: Darf.

Hampton, Barbara. 1980. "A Revised Analytical Approach to Musical Processes in Urban Africa." *African Urban Studies* 6:1–16.

Herzog, George. 1934. "Speech-Melody and Primitive Music." *Musical Quarterly* 20(4):452–466.

Hornbostel, Erich M. von. 1928. "African Negro Music." *Africa* 1:30–62.

———. 1933. "The Ethnology of African Sound Instruments." *Africa* 6:129–154, 277– 311.

Jones, Arthur M. 1971 [1959]. *Studies in African Music.* 2 vols. London: Oxford University Press.

———. 1964. *Africa and Indonesia: The Evidence of the Xylophone and Other Musical and Cultural Factors,* 2nd ed. Leiden: E. J. Brill.

———. 1976. *African Hymnody in Christian Worship: A Contribution to the History of Its Development.* Gwelo, Zimbabwe: Mambo Press.

Kauffman, Robert. 1980. "African Rhythm: A Reassessment." *Ethnomusicology* 24:393– 415.

Kubik, Gerhard. 1962. "The Phenomenon of Inherent Rhythms in East and Central African Instrumental Music." *African Music* 1:33–42.

———. 1965. "Transcription of Mangwilo Xylophone Music from Film Strips." *African Music* 3(4):35–41.

———. 1972. "Transcription of African Music from Silent Film: Theory and Methods." *African Music* 5(1):28–39.

———. 1977. "Patterns of Body Movement in the Music of Boys' Initiation in South-East Angola." In *The Anthropology of the Body,* ed. John Blacking, 253–274. London: Academic Press.

———. 1985. "African Tone Systems—A Reassessment." *Yearbook for Traditional Music* 17:31–63.

———. 1986. "Stability and Change in African Musical Traditions." *The World of Music* 27:44–69.

Livingstone, David. 1857. *A Narrative of Dr. Livingstone's Discoveries in South-Central Africa.* London: Routledge.

Manuel, Peter. 1988. *Popular Musics of the Non-Western World.* New York: Oxford University Press.

Merriam, Alan P. 1959. "African Music." In *Continuity and Change in African Cultures,* ed. William R. Bascom and Melville J. Herskovits, 49–86. Chicago: University of Chicago Press.

———. 1964. *The Anthropology of Music.* Evanston, Ill.: Northwestern University Press.

———. 1972. *The Arts and Humanities in African Studies.* Bloomington: African Studies Program, Indiana University.

———. 1981. "African Musical Rhythm and Concepts of Time-Reckoning." In *Music East and West: Essays in Honor of Walter Kaufmann,* ed. Thomas Noblitt, 123–142. New York: Pendragon Press.

———. 1982. *African Music in Perspective.* New York: Garland.

Mudimbe, V. Y. 1988. *The Invention of Africa: Gnosis, Philosophy, and the Order of Knowledge.* Bloomington: Indiana University Press.

Mukuna, Kazadi wa. 1992. "The Genesis of Urban Music." *African Music* 7(2):72–74.

Murdock, George P. 1959. *Africa: Its People and Their Culture History.* New York: McGraw-Hill.

Nketia, J. H. Kwabena. 1962a. "The Hocket Technique in African Music." *Journal of the International Folk Music Council* 14:44–55.

———. 1962b. "The Problem of Meaning in African Music." *Ethnomusicology* 6(1):1–7.

———. 1974. *The Music of Africa.* New York: Norton.

———. 1982. "On the Historicity of Music in African Cultures." *Journal of African Studies* 9(3):1–9.

Nketia, J. H. Kwabena, and Jacqueline C. DjeDje. 1984. "Trends in African Musicology." In *Selected Reports in Ethnomusicology V: Studies in African Music* (UCLA), ix–xx.

Omibiyi, Mosunmola. 1973–1974. "A Model for the Study of African Music." *African Music* 5(3):6–11.

Rouget, Gilbert. 1985. *Music and Trance: A Theory of the Relations between Music and Possession,* trans. Brunhilde Biebuyck. Chicago: University of Chicago Press.

Serwadda, Moses, and Hewitt Pantaleoni. 1968. "A Possible Notation for African Dance Drumming." *African Music* 4(2):47–52.

Simon, Artur, ed. 1983. *Musik in Afrika.* Berlin: Museum für Völkerkunde.

Stapleton, Chris, and Chris May. 1990. *African Rock: The Pop Music of a Continent.* New York: Dutton.

Stone, Ruth M. 1985. "In Search of Time in African Music." *Music Theory Spectrum* 7:139–158.

Stone, Ruth M., and Verlon Stone. 1981. "Event, Feedback, and Analysis: Research Media in the Study of Music Events." *Ethnomusicology* 25(2):215–225.

Thompson, Robert Farris. 1974. *African Art in Motion.* Berkeley and Los Angeles: University of California Press.

Vansina, Jan. 1969. "The Bells of Kings." *Journal of African History* 10(2):187–197.

Wachsmann, Klaus P. 1964a. "Human Migration and African Harps." *Journal of the International Folk Music Council* 16:84–88.

———. 1964b. "Problems of Musical Stratigraphy in Africa." In *Colloques de Wégimont* 3:19–22.

———. 1966. "The Trend of Musicology in Africa." In *Selected Reports in Ethnomusicology* (UCLA), 1(1):61–65.

———. 1970. "Ethnomusicology in Africa." In *African Experience,* ed. John N. Paden and Edward W. Soja, 128–151. Evanston, Ill.: Northwestern University Press.

———, ed. 1971. *Essays on Music and History in Africa.* Evanston, Ill.: Northwestern University Press.

Wallaschek, Richard. 1893. *Primitive Music: An Inquiry into the Origin and Development of Music, Songs, Instruments, Dances, and Pantomimes of Savage Races.* London: Longmans, Green.

Waterman, Richard A. 1952. "African Influence on the Music of the Americas." In *Acculturation in the Americas,* vol. 2, ed. Sol Tax, 207–218. Chicago: University of Chicago Press.

Wegner, Ulrich. 1984. *Afrikanische Saiteninstrumente.* Berlin: Staatliche Museen Preußischer Kulturbesitz. Museum für Völkerkunde Berlin, Abteilung Musikethnologie, new series, 41.

West Africa

Agawu, Kofi. 1986. "'Gi Dunu,' 'Nyekpadudo,' and the Study of West African Rhythm." *Ethnomusicology* 30(1):64–83.

———. 1987. "The Rhythmic Structure of West African Music." *Journal of Musicology* 5(3):400–418.

———. 1990. "Variation Procedures in Northern Ewe Song." *Ethnomusicology* 34(2):221–243.

Akpabot, Samuel. 1972. "Theories on African Rhythm." *African Arts* (Los Angeles) 6(1):59–62, 88.

Ames, David W. 1973. "A Sociocultural View of Hausa Musical Activity." In *The Traditional Artist in African Societies,* ed. Warren d'Azevedo, 128–161. Bloomington: Indiana University Press.

Ames, David W., and Anthony V. King. 1971. *Glossary of Hausa Music in Its Social Contexts.* Evanston, Ill.: Northwestern University Press.

Amu, Ephraim. 1933. *Twenty-Five African Songs.* London: Sheldon Press.

Anyidoho, Kofi. 1982. "Death and Burial of the Dead: Ewe Funeral Folklore." M.A. thesis, Indiana University.

Arntson, Laura. 1992. "The Play of Ambiguity in Praise-Song Performance: A Definition of the Genre through an Examination of its Practice in Northern Sierra Leone." Ph.D. dissertation, Indiana University.

Avorgbedor, Daniel Kodzo. 1986. "Modes of Musical Continuity among the Anlo-Ewe of Accra: A Study in Urban Ethnomusicology." Ph.D. dissertation, Indiana University.

———. 1992. "The Impact of Rural-Urban Migration on a Village Music Culture: Some Implications for Applied Ethnomusicology." *African Music* 7(2):45–57.

Besmer, Fremont. 1972. *Hausa Court Music in Kano, Nigeria.* Ann Arbor, Mich.: University Microfilms.

———. 1974. *Kídàn Dáràn Sállà: Music for the Muslim Festivals of Id al-Fitr and Id al- Kabir in Kano, Nigeria.* Bloomington: African Studies Program, Indiana University. Indiana University Monographs.

———. 1983. *Horses, Musicians, and Gods: The Hausa Cult of Possession-Trance.* South Hadley, Mass.: Bergin and Garvey.

Bird, Charles S., and Martha B. Kendall. 1980. "The Mande Hero." In *Explorations in African Systems of Thought,* ed. Ivan Karp and Charles S. Bird, 13–26. Bloomington: Indiana University Press.

Bird, Charles S., Mamadou Koita, and Bourama Soumaoro. 1974. *The Songs of Seydou Camara, Volume One: Kambili.* Bloomington: African Studies Center, Indiana University.

Bosman, William. 1967 [1705]. *A New and Accurate Description of the Coast of Guinea.* Facsimile of the 1705 (English) edition. London: Frank Cass.

Burton, Sir Richard Francis. 1966 [1893]. *A Mission to Gelele, King of Dahome.* London: Routledge and Kegan Paul.

Chernoff, John M. 1979. *African Rhythm and African Sensibility: Aesthetics and Social Action in African Musical Idioms.* Chicago: University of Chicago Press.

Collins, E. John. 1977. "Post-War Popular Band Music in West Africa." *African Arts* 10(3):53–60.

———. 1985. *Musicmakers of West Africa.* Washington: Three Continents.

———. 1986. *E. T. Mensah, King of Highlife.* London: Off the Record Press.

———. 1987. "Jazz Feedback to Africa." *American Music* 5(2):176–193.

———. 1989. "The Early History of West African Highlife Music." *Popular Music* 8(3):221–230.

Collins, E. John, and Paul Richards. 1982. "Popular Music in West Africa." In *Popular Music Perspectives,* ed. David Horn and Philip Tagg, 111—141. Goteborg, Exeter: International Association for the Study of Popular Music.

DjeDje, Jacqueline Cogdell. 1980. *Distribution of the One String Fiddle in West Africa.* Los Angeles: UCLA Program in Ethnomusicology, Department of Music.

————. 1982. "The Concept of Patronage: An Examination of Hausa and Dagomba One-String Fiddle Traditions." *Journal of African Studies* 9(3):116–127.

Duran, Lucy, et al. 1987. "On Music in Contemporary West Africa: Jaliya and the Role of the Jali in Present Day Manding Society." *African Affairs: Journal of the Royal African Society* 86(343):233–236.

Ekwueme, Lazarus. 1975–1976. "Structural Levels of Rhythm and Form in African Music with Particular Reference to the West Coast." *African Music* 5(4):105–129.

Euba, Akin. 1970. "New Idioms of Music-Drama among the Yoruba: An Introductory Study." *Yearbook of the International Folk Music Council* 92–107.

————. 1971. "Islamic Musical Culture among the Yoruba: A Preliminary Survey." In *Essays on Music and History in Africa,* ed. Klaus P. Wachsmann, 171–184. Evanston, Ill.: Northwestern University Press.

————. 1977. "An Introduction to Music in Nigeria." In *Nigerian Music Review,* no. 1, ed. Akin Euba, 1–38. Ife: Department of Music, University of Ife.

————. 1990. *Yoruba Drumming: The Dùndún Tradition.* Bayreuth: Bayreuth University. Bayreuth African Studies, 21–22.

Fiagbedzi, Nissio. 1976. "The Music of the Anlo: Its Historical Background, Cultural Matrix, and Style." Ph.D. dissertation, University of California, Los Angeles.

Gourlay, Kenneth A. 1982. "Long Trumpets of Northern Nigeria—In History and Today." *African Music* 6(2):48–72.

Hampton, Barbara L. 1992. "Music and Gender in Gã Society: Adaawe Song Poetry." In *African Musicology: Current Trends,* vol. 2, ed. Jacqueline Cogdell Djedje, 135–149. Los Angeles: University of California Press.

Harper, Peggy. 1970. "A Festival of Nigerian Dances." *African Arts* 3(2):48–53.

Herzog, George. 1945. "Drum-Signaling in a West African Tribe." *Word: Journal of the Linguistic Circle of New York* 1(3):217–238.

Keil, Charles. 1979. *Tiv Song.* Chicago: University of Chicago Press.

Kinney, Esi Sylvia. 1970. "Urban West African Music and Dance." *African Urban Notes* 5(4):3–10.

Knight, Roderic. 1972. "Towards a Notation and Tablature for the Kora." *African Music* 1(5):23–35.

————. 1974. "Mandinka Drumming." *African Arts* 7(4):25–35.

————. 1984a. "Music in Africa: The Manding Contexts." In *Performance Practice: Ethnomusicological Perspectives,* ed. Gerard Béhague, 53–90. Westport, Conn.: Greenwood Press; Contributions in Intercultural and Comparative Studies, 12.

————. 1984b. "The Style of Mandinka Music: A Study in Extracting Theory from Practice." In *Selected Reports in Ethnomusicology V. Studies in African Music,* ed. J. H. Kwabena Nketia and Jacqueline Cozdell Djedje, 3–66. Los Angeles: University of California.

Koetting, James. 1970. "Analysis and Notation of West African Drum Ensemble Music." *Selected Reports in Ethnomusicology,* ed. J. H. Kwabena Nketia and Jacqueline Cozdell Djedje, 1(3):115–146. Los Angeles: Institute of Ethnomusicology, University of California.

————. 1984. "Hocket Concept and Structure in Kasena Flute Ensemble Music." In *Selected Reports in Ethnomusicology V. Studies in African Music,* ed. J. H. Kwabena Nketia and Jacqueline Cozdell Djedje, 161–172. Los Angeles: University of California.

Ladzekpo, S. Kobla. 1971. "The Social Mechanics of Good Music: A Description of Dance Clubs among the Anlo Ewe-Speaking People of Ghana." *African Music* 5(1):6–22.

Little, Kenneth. 1965. *West African Urbanization: A Study of Voluntary Associations in Social Change.* Cambridge: Cambridge University Press.

Locke, David. 1982. "Principles of Offbeat Timing and Cross-Rhythm in Southern Eẽe Dance Drumming." *Ethnomusicology* 26(2):217–246.

————. 1987. *Drum Gahu.* Crown Point, Ind.: White-Cliffs Media.

Locke, David, and Godwin K. Agbeli. 1980. "A Study of the Drum Language in Adzogbo." *African Music* 6(1):32–51.

Mensah, Atta Annan. 1958. "Professionalism in the Musical Practice of Ghana." *Music in Ghana* 1(1):28–35.

Monts, Lester P. 1982. "Music Clusteral Relationships in a Liberian–Sierra Leonean Region: A Preliminary Analysis." *Journal of African Studies* 9(3):101–115.

Nketia, J. H. Kwabena. 1962. "The Problem of Meaning in African Music." *Ethnomusicology* 6:1–7.

————. 1963. *Drumming in Akan Communities of Ghana.* London: University of Ghana and Thomas Nelson.

————. 1973. "The Musician in Akan Society." In *The Traditional Artist in African Societies,* ed. Warren d'Azevedo , 79–100. Bloomington: Indiana University Press.

Nzewi, Meki. 1974. "Melo-Rhythmic Essence and Hot Rhythm in Nigerian Folk Music." *The Black Perspective in Music* 2(1):23–28.

Omibiyi, M. A. 1981. "Popular Music in Nigeria." *Jazzforschung* 13:151–168.

Parkin, David. 1969. "Urban Voluntary Associations as Institutions of Adaptation." *Man* 1(1):90–95.

Peil, Margaret. 1972. *The Ghanaian Factory Worker: Industrial Man in Africa.* Cambridge: Cambridge University Press.

Phillips, Ekundayo. 1953. *Yoruba Music.* Johannesburg: African Music Society.

Phillips, Ruth B. 1978. "Masking in Mande Sande Society Initiation Rituals." *Africa* 48:265–277.

Robertson, Claire. 1984. *Sharing in the Same Bowl: A Socioeconomic History of Women and Class in Accra.* Bloomington: Indiana University Press.

Smith, M. G. 1957. "The Social Functions and Meaning of Hausa Praise Singing." *Africa* 27:26–45.

———. 1959. "The Hausa System of Social Status." *Africa* 29:239–252.

Stone, Ruth. 1982. *Let the Inside Be Sweet: The Interpretation of Music Event among the Kpelle of Liberia.* Bloomington: Indiana University Press.

———. 1988. *Dried Millet Breaking: Time, Words, and Song in the Woi Epic of the Kpelle.* Bloomington: Indiana University Press.

Thieme, Darius. 1967. "A Descriptive Catalog of Yoruba Musical Instruments." Ph.D. dissertation, Catholic University of America.

Thompson, Robert F. 1966. "An Aesthetic of the Cool: West African Dance." *African Forum* 2(2):85–102.

———. 1974. *African Art in Motion: Icon and Act in the Collection of Katherine Coryton White.* Los Angeles: University of California Press.

Turay, A. K. 1966. "A Vocabulary of Temne Musical Instruments." *Sierra Leone Language Review* (Freetown) 5:27–33.

Ward, William Ernest. 1927. "Music in the Gold Coast." *Gold Coast Review* 3(2):199–223.

Waterman, Christopher A. 1990. *Jùjú: A Social History and Ethnography of an African Popular Music.* Chicago: University of Chicago Press.

Yankah, Kwesi. 1983. "To Praise or Not to Praise the King: The Akan *Akpae* in the Context of Referential Poetry." *Research in African Literatures* 14(3):381–400.

———. 1985. "Voicing and Drumming the Poetry of Praise: The Case for *Aural Literature.*" In *Interdisciplinary Dimensions of African Literature,* ed. Kofi Anyidoho et al., 137–153. Washington, D.C.: Three Continents Press.

Zemp, Hugo. 1967. *Musique Dan.* Paris: Mouton.

North Africa

Carlisle, Roxane. 1975. "Women Singers in Darfur, Sudan Republic." *The Black Perspective in Music* 3(3):253–268.

Daw, Ali al-, and Abd-Alla Muhammad. 1985. *Traditional Musical Instruments in Sudan.* Khartoum: Institute of African and Asian Studies, University of Khartoum.

———. 1988. *Al-mūsīqa al-taqlīdīya fī maǧtamáʿa al-Berta* [*Traditional Music in al-Berta Society*]. Khartoum: Institute of African and Asian Studies, University of Khartoum.

Deng, Francis Mading. 1973. *The Dinka and Their Songs.* Oxford: Oxford University Press.

Erlmann, Veit. 1974. "Some Sources on Music in Western Sudan from 1300–1700." *African Music* 5(3):34–39.

Farmer, Henry George. 1924. "The Arab Influence on Music of the Western Soudan." *Musical Standard* 24:158–159.

———. 1939. "Early References to Music in the Western Sūdān." *Journal of the Royal Asiatic Society of Great Britain and Ireland,* part 4 (October):569–579.

Ismail, Mahi. 1970. "Musical Traditions in the Sudan." *La Revue Musicale* 288–289:87–93.

Saada, Nadia Mécheri. 1986. "La musique de l'Ahaggar." Ph.D. dissertation, University of Paris.

Schmidt-Wrenger, Barbara. 1979. *Rituelle Frauengesänge der Tshokwe: Untersuchungen zu einem Säkularisierungsprozess in Angola und Zaire.* 3 vols. Tervuren: Musée Royal de l'Afrique Centrale.

Simon, Artur. 1989a. "Musical Traditions, Islam and Cultural Identity in the Sudan." In *Perspectives on African Music,* ed. Wolfgang Bender, 25–41. Bayreuth: Bayreuth African Studies, series 9.

———. 1989b. "Trumpet and Flute Ensembles of the Berta People in the Sudan." In *African Musicology: Current Trends,* ed. Jacqueline C. Djedje and William G. Carter, 1:183–217. Los Angeles: Crossroad Press; Festschrift J. H. K. Nketia.

———. 1991. "Sudan City Music." In *Populäre Musik in Afrika,* ed. Veit Erlmann, 165–180. Berlin: Museum für Völkerkunde.

Tucker, A. N. 1932. "Music in South Sudan." *Man* 32:18–19.

———. 1933a. "Children's Games and Songs in the Southern Sudan." *Journal of the Royal Anthropological Institute of Great Britain and Ireland* 63:165–187.

———. 1933b. *Tribal Music and Dancing in the Southern Sudan (Africa) at Social and Ceremonial Gatherings.* London: W. Reeves.

Wendt, Caroline Card. 1994. "Regional Style in Tuareg *Anzad* Music." In *To the Four Corners,* ed. Ellen Leichtman. Warren, Mich.: Harmonie Park Press.

East Africa

Abokor, Ahmed Ali. 1990. "Somali Pastoral Work Songs: The Poetic Voice of the Politically Powerless." M.A. thesis, Indiana University.

Anderson, Lois. 1967. "The African Xylophone." *African Arts / Arts d'Afrique* 1:46–49.

———. 1977. "The Entenga Tuned-Drum Ensemble." In *Essays for a Humanist: An Offering to Klaus Wachsmann*, 1–57. New York: Town House Press.

Campbell, C. A., and C. M. Eastman. 1984. "Ngoma: Swahili Adult Song Performance in Context." *Ethnomusicology* 28(3):467–494.

Cooke, Peter. 1970. "Ganda Xylophone Music: Another Approach." *African Music* 4(4).

———. 1990. "Report on Pitch Perception Carried Out in Buganda and Busoga (Uganda) August 1990." *ICTM Study Group* 33:2–6.

Cooke, Peter, and Martin Doornbos. 1982. "Rwenzururu Protest Songs." *Africa* 52(1):37–60.

DeVale, Sue Carole. 1984. "Prolegomena to a Study of Harp and Voice Sounds in Uganda: A Graphic System for the Notation of Texture." In *Selected Reports in Ethnomusicology*, vol. 5, ed. J. H. Kwabena Nketia and Jacqueline Cogdell DjeDje, 284–315. Los Angeles: University of California.

Giannattasio, Francesco. 1983. "Somalia: La Terapia Coreutico-Musicali del Mingis." *Culture Musicali* 2(3):93–119.

———. 1988a. "Strumenti Musicali." In *Aspetti dell' Espressione Artistica in Somalia,* ed. Annarita Puglielli, 73–89. Rome: University of Rome.

———. 1988b. "The Study of Somali Music: Present State." In *Proceedings of the Third International Congress of Somali Studies,* ed. Annarita Puglielli, 158–167. Rome: Il Pensiero Scientifico Editore.

Gnielinski, Anneliese von. 1985. *Traditional Music Instruments of Tanzania in the National Museum.* Dar es Salaam: National Museums. Occasional paper 6.

Gourlay, Kenneth A. 1972. *The Making of Karimojong Cattle Songs.* Nairobi: Institute of African Studies, University of Nairobi. Discussion paper 18.

Hartwig, Gerald W. 1969. "The Historical and Social Role of Kerebe Music." *Tanzania Notes and Records* 70:41–56.

Kavyu, Paul. 1978. "The Development of Guitar Music in Kenya." *Jazzforschung* 10:111–119.

Kimberlin, Cynthia. 1978. "The Baganna of Ethiopia." *Ethiopianist Notes* 2(2).

Kubik, Gerhard. 1967. "The Traditional Music of Tanzania." *Afrika* 8(2):29–32.

———. 1981. "Popular Music in East Africa since 1945." *Popular Music* 1:83–104.

Low, John. 1982a. "A History of Kenyan Guitar Music: 1945–1980." *African Music* 6(2):17–36.

———. 1982b. *Shaba Diary: A Trip to Rediscover the 'Katanga' Guitar Styles and Songs of the 1950's and '60's.* Vienna: Fohrenau. Acta Ethnologica et Linguistica, 54.

Martin, Stephen H. 1991a. "Brass Bands and the Beni Phenomenon in Urban East Africa." *African Music* 8(1):72–81.

———. 1991b. "Popular Music in Urban East Africa." *Black Music Research Journal* 11(1):39–53.

Omondi, Washington A. 1984. "The Tuning of the Thum, the Luo Lyre, A Systematic Analysis." In *Selected Reports in Ethnomusicology V. Studies in African Music* (UCLA), 263–281.

Ranger, T. O. 1975. *Dance and Society in Eastern Africa.* Berkeley and Los Angeles: University of California Press.

Roberts, J. S. 1968. "Popular Music in Kenya." *African Music* 4(2):53–55.

Shelemay, Kay Kaufman. 1983. "A New System of Musical Notation in Ethiopia." In *Ethiopian Studies Dedicated to Wolf Leslau,* ed. Stanislav Segert and Andras J. E. Bodrogligeti, 571–582. Wiesbaden: Otto Harrassowitz.

———. 1989 [1986]. *Music, Ritual, and Falasha History.* East Lansing: Michigan State University Press.

Wachsmann, Klaus P. 1971. "Musical Instruments in Kiganda Tradition and Their Place in the East African Scene." In *Essays on Music and History in Africa,* ed. Klaus P. Wachsmann, 93–134. Evanston, Ill.: Northwestern University Press.

Central Africa

Arom, Simha. 1967. "Instruments de musique particuliers à certaines ethnies de la République Centrafricaine." *Journal of the International Folk Music Council,* 19:104–108.

Blakely, Pamela A. 1993. "Performing Dangerous Thoughts: Women's Song-Dance Performance Events in a Hemba Funeral Ritual (Republic of Zaïre)." Ph.D. dissertation, Indiana University.

Brandel, Rose. 1961. *The Music of Central Africa.* The Hague: Martinus Nijhoff.

Carrington, John F. 1949. *A Comparative Study of Some Central African Gong-Languages.* Brussels: Institut Royal Colonial Belge.

Dehoux, Vincent, and Frédéric Voisin. 1992. "Analytic Procedures with Scales in Central African Xylophone Music." In *European Studies in Ethnomusicology: Historical Developments and Recent Trends,* ed. Max Peter Baumann et al., 174–188. Wilhelmshaven: Florian Noetzel; Intercultural Music Studies, 4.

———. 1993. "An Interactive Experimental Method for the Determination of Musical Scales in Oral Cultures: Application to the Xylophone Music of Central Africa." *Contemporary Music Review* 9:13–19.

Gansemans, Jos. 1978. *La musique et son rôle dans la vie sociale et rituelle Luba*. Tervuren, Belgium: Musée Royal de l'Afrique Centrale. Sciences Humaines, 95.

———. 1980. *Les instruments de musique Luba*. Tervuren, Belgium: Musée Royal de l'Afrique Centrale. Sciences Humaines, 103.

Gansemans, Jos, and Barbara Schmidt-Wrenger. 1986. *Zentralafrika*. Leipzig: Deutscher Verlag für Musik. Musikgeschichte in Bildern, 1, part 12.

Kubik, Gerhard. 1964. "Harp Music of the Azande and Related Peoples in the Central African Republic." *African Music* 3(3):37–76.

Laurenty, Jean Sébastien. 1960. *Les Cordophones du Congo Belge et du Ruanda-Urundi*. Tervuren: Musée Royale de l'Afrique Centrale.

———. 1962. *Les Sanza du Congo Belge*. Tervuren, Belgium: Musée Royale de l'Afrique Centrale.

———. 1968. *Les Tambours à fente de l'Afrique Centrale*. Tervuren, Belgium: Musée Royale de l'Afrique Centrale.

———. 1974. *La Systematique des aérophones de l'Afrique Centrale*. Tervuren: Musée Royale de l'Afrique Centrale.

Merriam, Alan P. 1973. "The Bala Musician." In *The Traditional Artist in African Societies*, ed. Warren d'Azevedo, 23–81. Bloomington: Indiana University Press.

Mukuna, Kazadi wa. 1973. "Trends of Nineteenth and Twentieth Century Music in the Congo-Zaïre." In *Musikkulturen Asiens, Afrikas und Ozeanien im 19. Jahrhundert*, ed. Robert Günther, 267–284. Regensburg: Gustav Bosse.

———. 1980. "The Origin of Zaïrean Modern Music: A Socio-economic Aspect." *African Urban Studies* 6:77–78.

Schweinfurth, Georg A. 1873. *In the Heart of Africa: Three Years' Travels and Adventures in the Unexplored Regions of Central Africa from 1868–1871*. London: S. Low, Marsten, Low, and Searle.

Voisin, Frédéric. 1994. "Musical Scales in Central Africa and Java: Modeling by Synthesis." *Leonardo Music Journal* 4:85–90.

Southern Africa

Adams, Charles R. 1974. "Ethnography of Basotho: Evaluative Expression in the Cognitive Domain Lipapali (Games)." Ph.D. dissertation, Indiana University.

Brown, Ernest Douglas. 1984. "Drums of Life: Royal Music and Social Life in Western Zambia." Ph.D. dissertation, University of Washington.

Berliner, Paul. 1978. *The Soul of Mbira: Music and Traditions of the Shona People of Zimbabwe*. Berkeley and Los Angeles: University of California Press.

Blacking, John. 1967. *Venda Children's Songs*. Johannesburg: Witwatersrand University Press.

———. 1985. "Movement, Dance, Music, and the Venda Girls' Initiation Cycle." In *Society and the Dance: The Social Anthropology of Process and Performance*, ed. Paul Spencer, 64–91. Cambridge: Cambridge University Press.

Colson, Elizabeth. 1969. "Spirit-Possession Among the Tonga of Zambia." In *Spirit Mediumship in Society in Africa*, ed. John Beattie and John Middleton, 69–103. London: Routledge and Kegan Paul.

Coplan, David B. 1985. In *Township Tonight! South Africa's Black City Music and Theatre*. London: Longman.

———. 1988. "Musical Understanding: The Ethnoaesthetics of Migrant Workers' Poetic Song in Lesotho." *Ethnomusicology* 32:337–368.

Erlmann, Veit. 1991. *African Stars: Studies in Black South African Performance*. Chicago: University of Chicago Press.

Johnston, Thomas. 1970. "Xizambi Friction-Bow Music of the Shangana-Tsonga." *African Music* 4(4):81–95.

———. 1971. "Shangana-Tsonga Drum and Bow Rhythms." *African Music* 5(1):59–72.

———. 1972. "Possession Music of the Shangana-Tsonga." *African Music* 5(2):10–22.

———. 1987. "Children's Music of the Shangana-Tsonga." *African Music* 6(4):126–143.

Joseph, Rosemary. 1983. "Zulu Women's Music." *African Music* 6(3):53–89.

Kauffman, Robert. 1969. "Some Aspects of Aesthetics in Shona Music of Rhodesia." *Ethnomusicology* 13(3):507–511.

———. 1972. "Shona Urban Music and the Problem of Acculturation." *IFMC Yearbook* 4:47–56.

Kirby, Percival R. 1937 [1967]. "The Musical Practices of the Native Races of South Africa." In *Western Civilization and the Natives of South Africa*, ed. Isaac Schapera, 131–140. New York: Humanities Press.

———. 1965. *The Musical Instruments of the Native Races of South Africa*, 2nd ed. Johannesburg: Witwatersrand University Press.

Kubik, Gerhard. 1964. "Harp Music of the Azande and Related Peoples in the Central African Republic." *African Music* 3(3):37–76.

———. 1971. "Carl Mauch's Mbira Musical Transcriptions of 1872." *Review of Ethnology* 3(10):73–80.

———. 1988. "Nsenga / Shona Harmonic Patterns and the San Heritage in Southern Africa." *Ethnomusicology* 32(2):39–76 (211–248).

———. 1989. "The Southern African Periphery: Banjo Traditions in Zambia and Malaŵi." *The World of Music* 31:3–29.

Kubik, Gerhard, Moya Aliya Malamusi, Lidiya Malamusi, and Donald Kachamba. 1987. *Malaŵian Music: A Framework for Analysis*. Zomba, Malaŵi: University of Malaŵi, Department of Fine and Performing Arts.

Malamusi, Moya Aliya. 1984. "The Zambian Popular Music Scene." *Jazzforschung* 16:189–195.

Marshall, Lorna. 1969. "The Medicine Dance of the !Kung Bushmen." *Africa* 39(4):347–381.

McLeod, Norma. 1977. "Musical Instruments and History in Madagascar." In *Essays for a Humanist: An Offering to Klaus Wachsmann.* New York: Town House Press.

Mthethwa, Bongani. 1980. "Zulu Children's Songs." In *Papers Presented at the Symposium on Ethnomusicology: Rhodes University, Grahamstown, October 10–11, 1980,* ed. Andrew Tracey, 23–35. Grahamstown: Rhodes University.

Rycroft, David. 1961. "The Guitar Improvisations of Mwenda Jean Bosco." *African Music* 2(4):81–98.

———. 1962. "The Guitar Improvisations of Mwenda Jean Bosco (Part II)." *African Music* 3(1):86–102.

———. 1971. "Stylistic Evidence in Nguni Song." In *Essays on Music and History in Africa,* ed. Klaus P. Wachsmann, 213–241. Evanston, Ill.: Northwestern University Press.

Tracey, Andrew. 1971. "The Nyanga Panpipe Dance." *African Music* 5(1):73–89.

Tracey, Hugh. 1970. *Chopi Musicians: Their Music, Poetry, and Instruments.* London and New York: International African Institute, Oxford University Press.

Tsukada, Kenichi. 1988. "Luvale Perceptions of Mukanda in Discourse and Music." Ph.D. dissertation, Queen's University of Belfast.

———. 1990. "*Kukuwa* and *Kachacha:* Classification and Rhythm in the Music of the Luvale of Central Africa." In *People and Rhythm,* ed. Tetsuo Sakurai, 229–276. Tokyo: Tokyo Shoseki. In Japanese.

———. 1991a. "*Mukanda* Rites and Music: A Study of Initiation Rites in Central Africa." In *Ritual and Music,* vol. 2, ed. Tomoaki Fujii, 177–228. Tokyo: Tokyo Shoseki. In Japanese.

———. 1991b. "*Kalindula* in *Mukanda:* The Incorporation of Westernized Music into the Boys' Initiation Rites of the Luvale of Zambia." In *Tradition and Its Future in Music,* ed. Yoshihiko Tokumaru et al., 547–551. Tokyo: Mita Press.

Turner, Victor. 1968. *The Drums of Affliction: A Study of Religious Processes among the Ndembu of Zambia.* Oxford: International African Institute.

Westphal, E. O. J. 1978. "Observations on Current Bushmen and Hottentot Musical Practices." *Review of Ethnology* 5(2–3):9–15.

Zenkovsky, S. 1950. "Zar and Tambura as Practiced by the Women of Omdurman." *Sudan Notes and Records* 31:65–85.

A Guide to Recordings of African Music

Catalogs and Audiographies

Catalogue of Zonophone West African Records by Native Artists. 1929. Hayes, Middlx.: British Zonophone Company.

Merriam, Alan P. 1970. *African Music on LP: An Annotated Discography.* Evanston, Ill.: Northwestern University Press.

Tracey, Hugh. 1973. *Catalogue: The Sound of Africa Series.* Roodepoort, South Africa: International Library of African Music.

General

Africa Dances. 1980. Authentic Records, ARM 601C Authentic. Audiocassette.

Courlander, Harold, and Alan P. Merriam. 1957. *Africa South of the Sahara.* Folkways Records FE 4503. 2 LP disks.

Discover a Whole New World of Music. 1991. Newton, N. J.: Shanachie Records 9101, CD 124. Compact disc.

Hood, Mantle. 1969. *Africa East and West.* Los Angeles: Institute of Ethnomusicology, University of California. IER 6571.

Kronos Quartet and Judith Sherman. 1992. *Pieces of Africa.* Elektra / Nonesuch 979275–2. Compact disc.

Tracey, Hugh. 1953. *The Guitars of Africa.* London LB-829. Music of Africa, 5. LP disk.

West Africa

Adé, Sunny. 1976. *Synchro System Movement.* African Songs AS26. LP disk.

———. 1982. *Juju Music.* Island Records CID 9712. Compact disc.

Aingo, George Williams. 1992. *Roots of Highlife–1927.* Heritage HT CD 17. Compact disc.

Ames, David. 1964. *The Music of Nigeria, Hausa Music,* vol.1. Bärenreiter- Musicaphon Records BM 30 SL 2306. LP disk.

———. 1976? *Nigeria III: Igbo Music.* Bärenreiter-Musicaphon Records BM 30 SL 2311. LP disk.

Amoaku, W. K. 1978. *African Songs and Rhythms for Children.* Folkways Records FC 7844. LP disk.

Arom, Simha. 1975. *The Music of the Peuls.* EMI Odeon. LP disk.

Bebey, Francis. 1978. *Francis Bebey: ballades africaines: guitare.* Paris: Ozileka 3306. LP disk.

———. 1984. *Akwaaba.* Tivoli, N. Y.: Original Music OMCD 005. Compact disc.

Camara, Ladji. 1993. *Les ballets africains de Papa Ladji Camara.* Lyrichord. LP disk.

Dairo, I. K., and his Blue Spots. 1962. *Elele Ture.* Decca NWA 5079.

Dieterlen, Germaine. 1957. *Musique Dogon Mali.* Ocora OCR 33. LP disk.

———. 1966. *Musique Maure Mauritania.* OCR 28. LP disk.

Diamonds, Black. 1971? *Songs and Rhythms from Sierra Leone.* New Rochelle, N. Y.: Afro Request SRLP 5031. LP disk.

Duran, Lucy. 1985. *Jaliya / Malamini Jobarteh and Dembo Konte.* London: Stern's Africa. LP disk.

———. 1990. *Boubacar Traoré: Mariama.* London: Stern's Africa 1032. LP disk.

Forster, Till. 1987. *Musik der Senufo, Elfenbeinkuste.* Berlin: Musikethnologische Abteilung, Museum für Völkerkunde MC 4. 2 LP disks.

Freire, João. 1992. *Travadinha: The Violin of Cape Verde.* Buda Records 92556–2. Compact disc.

Işola, Haruna. 1959. "Hogan Bassey." Decca WA 3120. 78-rpm, 10-inch disk.

Jenkins, Jean. 1985. *Sierra Leone: Musiques traditionnelles.* Paris: OCORA 558- -549. LP disk.

Johnson, Kathleen. 1983. *Rhythms of the Grasslands: Music of Upper Volta,* vol. 2. Los Angeles: Elektra / Asylum / Nonesuch 72090. 2. LP disk.

Kouyate, Tata Bambo. 1989. *Tata Bambo Kouyate.* London: Globestyle ORB 042. LP disk.

Kroo Young Stars Rhythm Group. 1953. *O Gi Te Bi.* Decca DKWA 1335. LP disk.

Leigh, Stuart. 1981. *Music of Sierra Leone: Kono Mende Farmer's Songs.* Folkways Records FE 4330. LP disk.

Maal, Baaba. 1991. *Baayo.* New York: Island Records, Mango Records 162 539907–2. Compact disc.

Rouget, Gilbert. 1971. *Musique Malinke, Guinée.* Paris: Vogue LDM 30 113. LP disk.

———. 1981. *Sénégal: musique des Bassari.* Paris: Chant du Monde LDX 74 753. LP disk.

Okie, Packard, ed. 1955. *Folk Music of Liberia.* Folkways Records FE 4465.

Weka-Yamo, Aladji, and Ayivi Go Togbassa. 1992. *Togo: Music from West Africa.* Rounder CD 5004. Compact disc.

Stone, Ruth M., and Verlon L. Stone. 1972. *Music of the Kpelle of Liberia.* Folkways FE 4385. LP disk.

Zemp, Hugo. 1971. *Musique Guère: Côte d'Ivoire.* Paris: Vogue LD 764. LP disk.

North Africa

Atiya, Aziz S. 1960. *Coptic Music.* Folkways Records. LP disk.

Deng, Francis M. 1976. *Music of the Sudan: The Role of Song and Dance in Dinka Society.* Folkways Records FE 4301–03. 3 LP disks.

Duvelle, Charles. 1966. *Musique maure.* Paris: OCORA OCR 28. LP disk.

Gottlieb, Robert. N.d. *Sudan I: Music of the Blue Nile Province: The Gumuz Tribe.* Cassel: Bärenreiter Musicaphon BM 30L 2312. LP disk.

———. N.d. *Sudan II: The Ingessana and Berta Tribes.* Cassel: Bärenreiter Musicaphon BM 30L 2313. LP disk.

Guignard, Michel. 1975. *Mauritanie: Musique traditionnelle des griots maures.* SELAF / ORSTOM (Collection Tradition Orale) CETO 752–3. 2 LP disks.

Laade, Wolfgang. 1962. *Tunisia,* vol. 2, "Religious Songs and Cantillations." Folkways Records FW 8862. LP disk.

Lortat-Jacob, Bernard, and H. Jouad. 1979. *Berbères du Maroc: ahwach.* Collection du Centre National de la Recherche Scientifique du Musée de l'Homme LDX 74705. LP disk.

Lortat-Jacob, Bernard, and Gilbert Rouget. 1971. *Musique berbère du haut atlas.* Paris: Disques Vogue LD 786. LP disk.

Musiciens du Nil. 1988. Paris: OCORA D559006. Compact disc.

Pacholczyk, Jozef M. 1976. *Andalusian Music of Morocco.* Tucson, Ariz. Ethnodisc ER 45154. LP disk.

Schuyler, Philip. N.d. *The Music of Islam and Sufism in Morocco.* Bärenreiter- Musicaphon BM 30 SL 2027. LP disk.

———.1977. *Morocco: Arabic Tradition in Moroccan Music.* UNESCO Collection. EMI Odeon 3C 064-18264.

Simon, Artur. 1980a. *Musik der Nubier / Nordsudan (Music of the Nubians / Northern Sudan).* Berlin: Musikethnologische Abteilung, Museum für Völkerkunde MC 9. 2 LP disks.

———. 1980b. *Ḍikr und Madiḥ. Gesänge und Zeremonien: Islamisches Brauchtum im Sudan.* Berlin: Museum Collection MC 10.

Yassin, H. M., and Amel Benhassine. 1986. *Sounds of Sudan, Vol. 3: Mohamed Gubara.* London: Record World Circuit, WCB 005. LP disk.

Yurchenco, Henrietta. 1983. *Ballads, Wedding Songs, and Piyyutim of the Sephardic Jews of Tetuan and Tangier, Morocco.* 1983. Folkways Records FE 4208. LP disk.

East Africa

Abana Ba Nasery. 1992. *!Nursery Boys Go Ahead! The Guitar and Bottle Kids of Kenya.* Green Linnet GLCD 4002. Compact disc.

African Acoustic. 1988. Tivoli, N.Y.: Original Music OMA 110C. Audiocassette.

Boyd, Alan. 1985. *Music of the Waswahili of Lamu, Kenya.* Folkways Records, FE 4093–4095. 3 LP disks.

Burundi Drums: Batimbo-Musiques et Chants. 1992. Auvidis, Playa Sound PS 65089. Audiocassette.

Graebner, Werner. 1989. *Nyota: Black Star and Lucky Star Musical Clubs.* Globestyle CDORBD 044. Compact disc.

———. 1990. *Zein Musical Party: Mtindo Was Mombasa / The Style of Mombasa.* Globestyle CDORBD 066. Compact disc.

Kenya: Musiques du Nyanza. 1993. Paris: OCORA C 560022/23. 2 compact discs.

Mandelson, Ben, and Werner Graebner. 1990. *Mombasa Wedding Special: Maulidi and Musical Party.* Global Style CDORBD 058. Compact disc.

The Nairobi Sound. 1982. Brooklyn, N.Y.: Original Music OMA 101C. Audiocassette.

Nzomo, David. 1976. *Gospel Songs from Kenya: Kikamba Hymns.* Folkways FR 8911. LP disk.

Roberts, John Storm. 1988? *The Kampala Sound: 1960s Ugandan Dance Music.* Tivoli, N. Y.: OMA 109C. Audiocassette.

Songs the Swahili Sing: Classics from the Kenya Coast. 1980. Brooklyn, N.Y.: Original Music OMA 103C. Audiocassette.

Ssalongo, Christopher Kizza, and Peter Cooke, arr. and ed. 1988. *The Budongo of Uganda.* Edinburgh: K and C Productions KAC 1001. Audiocassette.

The Tanzania Sound. 198-. Tivoli, N.Y.: Original Music OMA 106C. Audiocassette.

Tanzania Yetu. 1985. Terra 101. London: Triple Earth Records. LP disk.

Central Africa

Arom, Simha. 1965. *Ba-Benzélé.* UNESCO Collection. Bärenreiter Musicaphon BM 30 L 2303. LP disk.

———. 1980. *Anthologie de la Musique des Pygmées Aka.* Paris: OCORA 558.526.27.28. 3 LP disks and notes.

———. 1992. *République Centrafricaine: Banda Polyphony.* UNESCO/Auvidis D 8043. Compact disc.

Arom, Simha, and G. Dournon-Taurelle.1971. *Musiques Banda: République Centrafricaine.* Disques RA 558.526–528. LP disk.

Bourgine. Caroline. 1991. *Congo: Cérémonie du Bobé.* OCORA W 560010.

Dehoux, Vincent. 1992. *Centrafrique: Musique Gbáyá—Chants à penser.* Paris: OCORA C 580008.

Fernandez, James W. 1973. *Music from an Equatorial Microcosm: Fang Bwiti Music from Gabon Republic, Africa, with Mbira Selections.* Folkways Records FE 4214. LP disk.

Gabon: pygmées bibayak et chantres des bapounou et des fang. 1980. Paris: OCORA 4.504.515. Audiocassette.

Gansmans, Jos. 1981. *Zaïre: musique des Salampasu.* Paris: OCORA 558.597. LP disk.

Jangoux, Jacques. 1973? *Music of Zaïre: Peoples of the Ngiri River.* Folkways Records FE 4241–4242. 2 LP disks.

Kisliuk, Michelle. 1992. *Mbuti Pygmies of the Ituri Rain Forest.* Recordings by Colin Turnbull and Frances S. Chapman. Smithsonian / Folkways CDSF 40401. Compact disc.

Mouquet, Eric, and Michel Sanchez. 1992. *Deep Forest.* Compact disk. Sony Music Entertainment (France) / Columbia Records DAN 4719762.

Papa Wemba: Le voyageur. 1992. Filament Music Publishers/WOMAD, Real World CD RW 20. Compact disc.

Roots of O.K. Jazz: Zaïre Classics 1955–56. 1993. Cramworld Crammed Discs Craw 7. Compact disc.

Sallée, Pierre. 1968? *Gabon: musiques des Mitsogho et des Batéké.* Paris. OCORA 84. LP disk.

Zaïre: musiques urbaines à Kinshasa. 1987. Paris: OCORA 559.007. LP disk.

Zaïre: la musique des Nande. Geneva. 1991. VDE-Gallo CD-652. Compact disc.

Southern Africa

Barkaak, Odd Are, and Pearson Likukela. *Kuomboka Music [Zambia].* Nayuma Museum. Audiocassette.

Chimurenga Songs: Music of the Revolutionary People's War in Zimbabwe. 1988. Harare, Zimbabwe: Gramma Records L4VZ5. Audiocassette.

Chiweshe, Stella. 1990. *Stella Chiweshe: Ambuya?* Newton, N. J.: Shanachie 65006. Compact disc.

D'Gary. *Malagasy Guitar: Music from Madagascar.* 1992. Newton, N. J.: Shanachie 65009. Compact disc.

Dube, William (William Dube Jairos Jiri Sunrise Kwela Band). 1980. *Take Cover.* Bulawayo, Zimbabwe: Teal Record Company ZIM 32. LP disk.

Erlmann, Veit. 1986. *Zulu Songs of South Africa.* Lyrichord LLST 7401. LP disk.

———. 1988. *Mbube Roots: Zulu Choral Music from South Africa, 1930's–1960's.* Rounder CD5025. Compact disc.

Gesthuisen, Birger, and Henry Kaiser. 1992. *A World Out of Time: Henry Kaiser and David Lindley in Madagascar.* Shanachie 64041. Compact disc.

Hanna, Marilyn, ed. 1985. *Ephat Mujuru: Master of Mbira from Zimbabwe.* Lyrichord LLST 7398. LP disk.

Hallis, Ron, and Ophera Hallis. 1980. *Music from Mozambique.* Folkways Records FE 4310. LP disk.

Homeland 2: A Collection of Black South African Music. 1990. Rounder CD 5028. Compact disc.

Kachamba, Donald, Moya Aliya Malamusi, Gerhard Kubik, and Stuwadi Mpotalinga. *Malawi: Concert Kwela.* Le Chant du Monde CDM LDX 274972. Compact disc.

Kivnick, Helen, and Gary Gardner. 1987. *Let Their Voices Be Heard.* Rounder Records 5024. LP disk.

Kubik, Gerhard. 1981. *Mukanda na makisi— Circumcision school and masks.* Berlin: Museum für Völkerkunde MC 11. LP disk and notes.

Kubik, Gerhard, and Moya Aliya Malamusi. 1989. *Opeka nyimbo: Musician-Composers from Southern Malaŵi.* Museum für Völkerkunde, Musikethnologische Abteilung. Museum Collection MC 15. Two LP disks and notes.

Laade, Wolfgang. 1991. *Zimbabwe: The Ndebele People.* Westbury, N. Y.: Koch International, Jecklin-Disco JD 654-2. LP disk.

Mapoma, Isaiah Mwesa. 1971. *Inyimbo: Songs of the Bemba People of Zambia.* Tucson, Ariz.: Ethnodisc ER 12103. LP disk.

Mazai Mbira Group. 1989?. Harare, Zimbabwe: Gramma Records L4AML. Audiocassette.

Mujuru, Ephat. 1980? *Rhythms of Life.* Lyrichord LLCT 7407. Audiocassette.

Project Grassworks. 1990. *Sounds Sung by South African Children.* Athlone: Grassroots Educare Trust. Audiocassette.

Randafison, Sylvestre, and Jean-Baptiste Ramaronandrasana. 1989. *Madagascar: Le valiha.* Harmonia Mundi Playa Sound PS 65046. Compact disc.

Tchiumba, Lilly. 1975. *Angola: Songs of My People.* Monitor Records MFS 767.

Tracey, Hugh. 1956. *International Library of African Music.* Roodepoort, South Africa.

Tracey, Hugh, and John Storm Roberts. 1989a. *Siya Hamba!* Tivoli, N. Y.: Original Music OMCD 003. LP disk.

————. 1989b. *From the Copperbelt: Zambian Miners' Songs.* Tivoli, N. Y.: Original Music OMCD 004. Compact disc.

Wood, Bill. 1976. *Music of Lesotho.* Folkways Records FE 4224. LP disk.

A Guide to Films and Videos

GENERAL

Katsumori, Ichikawa, prod. 1990. *The JVC Video Anthology of World Music and Dance.* Tokyo: JVC, Victor Company of Japan. Vols. 17, 18, and 19. Videocassettes.

WEST AFRICA

Chevallier, Laurent, and Nicole Jouve. 1991. *Djembefola.* New York: Interama. 16mm.

Cohen, Hervé. 1991. *Sikambano: The Sons of the Sacred Wood.* Paris: Les Films du Village. Videocassette.

Haas, Philip. 1990? *Seni's Children.* New York: Milestone Film and Video. Videocassette.

Hale, Thomas A. 1990. *Griottes of the Sahel: Female Keepers of the Songhay Oral Tradition in Niger.* University Park: Pennsylvania State University. Videocassette.

Holender, Jacques. 1991. *Juju Music!* New York: Rhapsody Films.

Knight, Roderic. 1992a. *Jali Nyama Suso: Kora Player of the Gambia.* Tivoli, N. Y.: Original Music. Videocassette.

———. 1992b. *Music of the Mande.* Tivoli, N. Y.: Original Music. Videocassette.

Locke, David. 1990. *A Performance of Kpegisu by the Wodome-Akatsi Kpegisu Habobo.* Tempe, Ariz.: White Cliffs Media. Videocassette.

Marre, Jeremy. 1983. *Konkombe: Nigerian Pop Music Scene.* Newton, N. J.: Shanachie Records. Videocassette.

Rossellini, Jim. 1983. *Dance of the Bella.* Venice, Calif.: African Family Films. Videocassette.

NORTH AFRICA

Guindi, Fadwa El. 1990. *El Moulid: Egyptian Religious Festival.* Los Angeles: El Nil Research. Videocassette, 16mm.

Llewellyn-Davies, Melissa, and Elizabeth Fernea. 1978. *Saints and Spirits.* Chicago: Films Incorporated Video. Videocassette.

Marre, Jeremy. 1991 [1983]. *The Romany Trail: Part I, Gypsy Music into Africa.* Newton, N. J.: Shanachie Records.

Mendizza, Michael, and Philip D. Schuyler. 1983. *The Master Musicians of Jabjouka.* New York: Alegrías Productions.

Wickett, Elizabeth. 1990. *For Those Who Sail to Heaven.* New York: Icarus Films. Videocassette, 16mm.

EAST AFRICA

Hawkins, Richard, and Suzette Heald. 1988. *Imbalu: Ritual of Manhood of the Bagisu of Uganda.* London: Royal Anthropological Institute, University of Manchester, Media Support and Development Centre.

Woodhead, Leslie. 1991. *The Mursi: Nitha.* New York: Granada Television. Videocassette.

CENTRAL AFRICA

Villers, Violaine de. 1992. *Mizike Mama.* New York: Interama. 16mm.

SOUTHERN AFRICA

Gavshon, Harriet. 1992. *A Stranger in a Strange Land: Paul Simon in South Africa.* Johannesburg: Free Film-Makers. Videocassette.

Hallis, Ron, and Ophera Hallis. 1989. *Music of the Spirits.* El Cerrito, Calif.: Flower Films. Videocassette.

———. 1992. *Chopi Music of Mozambique and Banguza.* El Cerrito, Calif.: Flower Films. Videocassette, 16mm.

Marshall, John, Robert Gardner, and Lorna Marshall. 1989. *The Hunters.* Chicago: Films Incorporated Video. Videocassette.

Morell, Karen, and Steven Friedson. *Prophet Healers of Northern Malawi.* 1990. Seattle: African Encounters PC-45. Videocassette.

May, Deborah. 1991. *We Jive Like This.* New York: Filmakers Library. Videocassette.

Poschl, Rupert, and Ulrike Poschl. 1990. *Vimbuza-Chilopa: A Spirit Possession Cult among the Tumbuka of Malawi.* University Park: Pennsylvania State University, Audio-Visual Services. Videocassette.

Notes on the Audio Examples

1. Kpelle *Woi-mene-pele* epic excerpt (4:27)
   Performed by Kulung of Koloboi and a chorus from Yilataa
   Instruments: struck beer bottles

   Recorded by Ruth and Verlon Stone on 31 March 1976 in Totota, Liberia

2. Ethiopian *Lidet* (Christmas) celebration (3:08)
   Performed by priests and *debteras* of the Holy Trinity Church of Addis Ababa
   Instruments: *tsenatsel* (sistrum) and *kebaro* (liturgical drum)

   Recorded by Kay Kaufman Shelemay on 1 June 1974 in Addis Ababa, Ethiopia

3. *Inanga Chuchotée* (whispered *inanga*) (4:12)
   Performed by Joseph Torobeka, *inanga* (trough zither) and voice

   Performed on 19 August 1986 in Bujumbura, Burundi
   Collected by Cornelia Fales

4. Vai call to prayer (5:07)
   Performed by Muhammad Manobala, voice

   Recorded by Lester P. Monts in 1987–1988 in Bulumi, Liberia

5. Palm-wine highlife song (2:56)
   Performed by Koo Nimo and band; Koo Nimo, guitar and lead voice
   Additional instruments: one pair of struck wooden sticks, one goblet-shaped drum, and one *apremprensemma* (bass sanza)

   Recorded by David B. Coplan on 19 December 1970, in Kumasi, Ghana

6. Anlo-Ewe *kinka* drumming (2:16)
   Performed by the Avenor Youth Association
   Instruments: one *atsimevu* (master drum), one *bombal agboba* (submaster drum), one *sogo* (response drum), one *kidi* (response drum), one *kagaŋ* (ostinato drum), several *axatsɛ*(s) (shakers), and single- and double-slit bells

   Recorded by Trevor Wiggins on 29 January 1989 in Accra, Ghana

7. Anlo-Ewe *kinka* songs (2:13)
   Performed by the Avenor Youth Association
   Instruments: one *atsimevu* (master drum), one *bombal agboba* (submaster drum), one *sogo* (response

drum), one *kidi* (response drum), one *kagaŋ* (ostinato drum), several *axatsɛ*(s) (shakers), and single- and double-slit bells

Recorded by Trevor Wiggins on 29 January 1989 in Accra, Ghana

8. Maninka *Mansareh* praise song (*balabolo*) including "*Nyin min nyama, nyama*" (5:44)
Performed by Pa Sanasi Kuyateh, *bala* (frame xylophone with gourd resonators, played with rubber-tipped mallets; rattles are attached to the hands); Hawa Kuyateh, *karinyan* (cylindrical iron bell struck with iron beater) and solo voice; Nimeh Kaleh, Sayo Kaleh, Mariama Kaleh and others, chorus

Recorded by Laura Arntson on 20 January 1988 in Sukurala, Sierra Leone

9. *Bala* pattern of Maninka *Mansareh bolo* (0:51)
Performed by Pa Sanasi Kuyateh, *bala*

Recorded by Laura Arntson on 27 January 1988 in Sukurala, Sierra Leone

10. Maninka *Duwa* praise song (1:15)
Performed by Pa Sanasi Kuyateh, *bala;* Hawa Kuyateh and Nimeh Kaleh, voices

Recorded by Laura Arntson on 9 February 1988 in Sukurala, Sierra Leone

11. Tuareg *Tihadanaren* (1:57)
Performed by Bouchit bint Loki, *anzad* (bowed lute)

Recorded by Caroline Card Wendt on 16 December 1976 in Tamanrasset, Algeria

12. Tuareg *takəmba* song "*Khadisia*" (1:32)
Performed by Hattaye ag Muhammed, *tahardent* (plucked lute) and voice

Recorded by Caroline Card Wendt on 20 May 1977 in Agadez, Algeria

13. Basoga *lusoga* song "*Enyhonyhi kolojo*" 'Thieving birds' (4:00)
Performed by Silagi Kirimungo and his family group of semiprofessional farmer-musicians
Instruments: one *akadongo* (lamellophone), one *embaire* (xylophone), 4 *enkwanzi* (panpipes), one *akalere* (notched flute with four finger holes), one *ndingidi* (tube fiddle), one long drum, one "Uganda" drum, one rattle

In this song, Silagi sings about the hard work of turning swamps into productive rice paddies. He compares the many birds that steal his rice just as it is ripening with the many relatives and friends who come to scrounge some rice once it is harvested.

Recorded by Peter Cooke on 10 September 1990 in Bukoona village, Busoga, eastern Uganda

14. Baganda *akadinda* song "*Gganga aluwa*" 'Gganga escaped with his life' (2:26)
Performed by Sheikh Burukan Kiwuuwa and his group of royal *akadinda* musicians
Instrument: *akadinda* (large xylophone played by six musicians)

This *akadinda* song was known to many of the former palace ensembles of the *kabaka* of Buganda. It celebrates the rough justice meted out to Gganga, a young page of the palace who was caught sexually molesting the Princess Nassolo. The song was probably composed by the king's harpist.

Recorded by Peter Cooke on 25 September 1987 in Kidinda Village, Mpigi, Buganda, Uganda

15. Somali *caayar "dhaanto,"* excerpt 1 (2:45)
Performed by Cabdillaahi Xirsi "Baarleex," Xasan Maxamed Faarax, and mixed chorus, voices

Recorded by John William Johnson on 29 May 1987 in Muqdishow, Somalia

16. Somali *caayar "dhaanto,"* excerpt 2 (0:16)
Performed by Cabdillaahi Xirsi "Baarleex," Xasan Maxamed Faarax, and mixed chorus, voices.

Recorded by John William Johnson on 29 May 1987 in Muqdishow, Somalia

17. Popular song *"Motike"* 'Orphans' (2:02)
Composed and arranged by Kaida Mongana
Performed by Zokela Original
Kaida Mongana, lead voice; Maurice Kpamanda, bass

First recorded by the band in the early 1980s, but still circulated on homemade cassettes for sale in Bangui kiosks by small entrepreneurs; one of these cassettes, purchased by Michelle Kisliuk in 1992, is the source of this selection.

(The distortion on this selection was on the original tape and is a common characteristic of cassettes recorded on makeshift equipment in Africa and copied informally for sale by street vendors.)

18. *"Makala,"* a song performed during a BaAka (pygmy) hunting dance called *Mabo* (2:30)
Performed by approximately thirty-five singers, three of whom, young women named Kwanga, Mbouya, and Ndami, lean close to the mic; their voices stand out from the rest of the group.
Instruments: two *(ba)ndumou* (drums)

Recorded by Michelle Kisliuk in December 1988 in a temporary BaAka camp outside Bagandou village, Lobaye prefecture, Central African Republic

19. BaAka of Dzanga perform a song during the *eboka ya nzapa* 'god dance' in the style of neighboring Bolamba pygmies (2:12)
Instrument: one drum

Recorded by Michelle Kisliuk in 1992 in Dzanga, a forest settlement in the Bagandou region (within the borderlands of Central African Republic and the Republic of the Congo)

20. Shona *Munyonga mbira* song, *"Tongore"** (2:25)
Performed by James Masango, *mbira* (plucked lamellophone)

Recorded by John E. Kaemmer on 13 February 1972, in Bondiya, Zimbabwe (then Rhodesia).

21. Shona ancestral spirit song, *"Nyama musango"** (2:45)
Performed by Elias Kunaka and Kidwell Mudzimirema (Mharadzirwa), wide *mbiras* (plucked lamellophones)

Recorded by John E. Kaemmer on 10 July 1973, in Jirira, Zimbabwe (then Rhodesia)

*The buzzing sound on these recordings is intentional. *Mbira* musicians attach metal rattles to their instruments to create this desired effect

ACKNOWLEDGMENTS

This compact disc was edited and mastered at the Archives of Traditional Music at Indiana University in Bloomington, Indiana. All recordings are reproduced with the permission of the original collectors and copyright holders.

Daniel Reed, Producer
Peter Alyea, Engineer, Mastering and Restoration

Archives of Traditional Music Staff:
Gloria J. Gibson, Director
Peter Alyea, Sound Audio Technician
Mary Russell Bucknum, Associate Director
Marilyn Graf, Archivist
Suzanne Mudge, Librarian
Jonathan Cargill, Office Manager
Jude Wilkinson, Indiana University Advanced Research and Technology Institute

Index

Page numbers in *italic* type indicate pages on which illustrations appear.

ORTHOGRAPHY

ɛ or ẹ = "eh" as in **bet**
ɔ or ọ = "aw" as in **awful**
ŋ or ṇ = "ng" as in **sing**
ɣ or yg = "ch" as in German **ach**
ʃ or ṣ = "sh" as in **sh**out
ɓ = implosive "b"
ɗ = implosive "d"
! = click sound

´ = high tone
` = low tone
^ = high-low tone
~ = nasalized sound